Computer Graphics
C Version

SECOND EDITION ———————————

Computer Graphics
C Version

Donald Hearn
Department of Computer Science and
National Center for Supercomputing Applications
University of Illinois

M. Pauline Baker
National Center for Supercomputing Applications
University of Illinois

Pearson
Education

PRENTICE HALL
Upper Saddle River, New Jersey 07458

Library of Congress Cataloging-in-Publication Data

Hearn, Donald.
    Computer graphics, C version / Donald Hearn, M. Pauline Baker. —
2nd ed.
        p. cm.
    Includes bibliographical references and index.
    ISBN 0-13-530924-7
    1. Computer graphics.   2. C (Computer program language)
I. Baker, M. Pauline.   II. Title.
T385.H385 1997
006.6'7—dc20   96-14941
                                                    CIP

Acquisitions Editor: *Alan Apt*
Editor-in-Chief: *Marcia Horton*
Developmental Editor: *Sondra Chavez*
Production Editor: *Joe Scordato*
Managing Editor: *Bayani Mendoza de Leon*
Copy Editor: *Peter Zurita*
Editorial Director: *David Riccardi*
Marketing Manager: *Joe Hayton*
Design Director: *Anne Bonanno Nieglos*
Designers: *Jules Perlmutter/Amy Rosen*
Cover Designer: *Jayne Conte*
Cover Photo: *Eric Haines*
Buyer: *Donna Sullivan*
Editorial Assistant: *Shirley McGuire*

© 1997, 1994, 1986 by Donald Hearn and M. Pauline Ba
Published by Prentice Hall, Inc.
Simon & Schuster / A Viacom Company
Upper Saddle River, New Jersey 07458

Printed in the United States of America

10   9   8   7

ISBN 0-13-530924-7

Prentice-Hall International (UK) Limited, *London*
Prentice-Hall of Australia Pty. Limited, *Sydney*
Prentice-Hall Canada Inc., *Toronto*
Prentice-Hall Hispanoamericana, S.A., *Mexico*
Prentice-Hall of India Private Limited, *New Delhi*
Prentice-Hall of Japan, Inc., *Tokyo*
Simon & Schuster Asia Pte. Ltd., *Singapore*
Editora Prentice-Hall do Brasil, Ltda., *Rio de Janeiro*

TO OUR FOLKS

Rose, John, Millie, and Jay

Contents

3 Output Primitives 83

4 Attributes of Output Primitives 143

5 Two-Dimensional Geometric Transformations 183

6 Two-Dimensional Viewing 216

7 Structures and Hierarchical Modeling 250

8 Graphical User Interfaces and Interactive Input Methods 271

9   Three-Dimensional Concepts   296

10   Three-Dimensional Object Representations   304

11 Three-Dimensional Geometric and Modeling Transformations   407

12 Three-Dimensional Viewing   431

Contents

15 Color Models and Color Applications 564

16 Computer Animation 583

A Mathematics for Computer Graphics 599

Preface

Computer graphics remains one of the most exciting and rapidly growing computer fields. Since the appearance of the first edition of this book, computer graphics has now become a common element in user interfaces, data visualization, television commercials, motion pictures, and many, many other applications. Hardware devices and algorithms have been developed for improving the effectiveness, realism, and speed of picture generation, and the current trend in computer graphics is to incorporate more physics principles into three-dimensional graphics algorithms to better simulate the complex interactions between objects and the lighting environment.

Software Standards

Significant improvements in graphics software standards have been developed since the acceptance of the first graphics package, the Graphical Kernel System (GKS), by the International Standards Organization (ISO) and the American National Standards Institute (ANSI). The Programmer's Hierarchical Interactive Graphics Standard (PHIGS) is now both an ANSI and an ISO standard. Both PHIGS and the expanded PHIGS+ packages are widely available. In addition, a number of popular industry packages have emerged, including Silicon Graphics GL (Graphics Library), OpenGL, the Pixar RenderMan interface, PostScript interpreters for page descriptions, and a variety of painting, drawing, and design systems.

New Topics

Because of the tremendous number of changes that have occurred in the field of computer graphics, we decided to completely rewrite the book for the second edition, while maintaining the general organization of the first edition. All topics from the first edition were expanded to include discussions of current technology, and a great many new topics have been added. Topics that have been significantly expanded include antialiasing, fractal and other object-representation methods, ray tracing, spline curves and surfaces, illumination models, surface-rendering methods, and computer animation. New topics that have been added to this second edition include virtual reality, parallel implementations for graphics algorithms, superquadrics, BSP trees, shape grammars, particle systems, physically based modeling, scientific visualization, business visualization, quaternion methods in graphics algorithms, distribution ray tracing, fast-Phong shading, radiosity, bump mapping, morphing, and discussions of various mathematical methods useful in graphics applications.

This second edition can be used both as a text for students with no prior background in computer graphics and as a reference for graphics professionals. We emphasize basic principles needed to design, use, and understand computer graphics systems. Both hardware and software components of graphics systems are discussed, as well as various applications of computer graphics. We also include programming examples written in C to demonstrate the implementation and applications of the graphics algorithms. And we explore the features of PHIGS, PHIGS+, GKS, and other graphics libraries, while using PHIGS and PHIGS+ functions in the C programs to illustrate algorithm implementations and graphics applications.

Required Background

We assume no prior familiarity with computer graphics, but we do assume the reader has some knowledge of computer programming and basic data structures. A variety of mathematical methods are used in computer graphics algorithms, and these methods are discussed in some detail in the appendix. Mathematical topics covered in the appendix include techniques from analytic geometry, linear algebra, vector and tensor analysis, complex numbers, quaternions, and numerical analysis.

How to Use This Book as a Text

The material in this second edition evolved from notes used in a number of courses we have taught over the past several years, including introductory computer graphics, advanced graphics topics, scientific visualization, and graphics project courses. For a one-semester course, a subset of topics dealing with either two-dimensional methods or a combination of two-dimensional and three-dimensional topics can be chosen, depending on the requirements of a particular course. A two-semester course sequence can be used to cover the basic graphics concepts and methods in the first course and advanced three-dimensional methods and algorithms in the second course. For the self-study reader, early chapters can be used to provide an understanding of graphics concepts, with individual topics selected from the later chapters according to the interests of the reader.

At the undergraduate level, an introductory two-dimensional graphics course can be organized with a detailed treatment of fundamental topics from Chapters 2 through 8 plus the introduction to three-dimensional concepts and methods given in Chapter 9. Selected topics, such as color models, animation, spline curves, or two-dimensional fractal representations, from the later chapters could be used as supplemental material. For a graduate or upper-level undergraduate course, basic two-dimensional concepts and methods can be covered in the first half of the course, with selected topics from three-dimensional modeling, viewing, and rendering covered in the second half. A second, or advanced-topics, course can be used to cover selected topics from object representations, surface rendering, and computer animation.

Chapter 1 is a survey of computer graphics, illustrating the diversity of applications areas. Following an introduction to the hardware and software components of graphics systems in Chapter 2, fundamental algorithms for the representation and display of two-dimensional graphics objects are presented in Chapters 3 and 4. These two chapters examine methods for producing basic picture components and techniques for adjusting size, color, and other object attributes. This introduces students to the programming techniques necessary for implementing graphics routines. Chapters 5 and 6 discuss two-dimensional geometric transformations and viewing algorithms. Methods for modeling and organizing two-dimensional picture components into separate structures are given in Chapter 7. In Chapter 8, we present graphics methods for user interfaces and for interactive input in various applications, including virtual-reality systems.

Three-dimensional techniques are introduced in Chapter 9. We then discuss in Chapter 10 the different ways that three-dimensional objects can be graphically represented, depending on the characteristics of the objects. Chapter 11 presents methods for modeling and performing geometric transformations in three-dimensions. Methods for obtaining views of a three-dimensional scene are detailed in Chapter 12. The various algorithms for identifying visible surfaces in a scene are discussed in Chapter 13. Illumination models and surface-rendering methods, such as ray tracing and radiosity, are taken up in Chapter 14. Color models and methods are discussed in Chapter 15, and animation techniques are explored in Chapter 16.

Acknowledgments

Many people have contributed to this project in a variety of ways over the years. To the organizations and individuals who furnished photographs and other materials, we again express our appreciation. We also acknowledge the many helpful comments received form our students in various computer graphics and visualization courses and seminars. We are indebted to all those who provided reviews or suggestions for improving the material covered in this book, and we extend our apologies to anyone we may have failed to mention. Thank you: Ed Angel, Norman Badler, Phillip Barry, Brian Barsky, Hedley Bond, Bart Braden, Lara Burton, Robert Burton, Greg Chwelos, John Cross, Steve Cunningham, John DeCatrel, Victor Duvaneko, Gary Eerkes, Parris Egbert, Tony Faustini, Thomas Foley, Thomas Frank, Don Gillies, Jack Goldfeather, Georges Grinstein, Eric Haines, Robert Herbst, Larry Hodges, Eng-Kiat Koh, Mike Krogh, Michael Laszlo, Suzanne Lea, Michael May, Nelson Max, David McAllister, Jeffrey McConnell, Gary McDonald, C. L. Morgan, Gred Nielson, James Oliver, Lee-Hian Quek, Laurence Rainville, Paul Ross, David Salomon, Günther Schrack, Steven Shafer, Cliff Shaffer, Pete Shirley, Carol Smith, Stephanie Smullen, Jeff Spears, William Taffe, Wai Wan Tsang, Spencer Thomas, Sam Uselton, David Wen, Bill Wicker, Andrew Woo, Angelo Yfantis, Marek Zaremba, and Michael Zyda. Our thanks go also to Robert Burton's Fall 1995 Computer Graphics course at

Brigham Young University for running and testing the C code for this book. And we thank our editor Alan Apt, Sondra Chavez, and the Colorado staff for their help, suggestions, and encouragement during the preparation of this C version of the second edition. To our production editors, Bayani DeLeon and Joe Scordato, and the Prentice Hall staff, we offer our thanks for another outstanding production job. Finally, a special thanks goes to Carol Hubbard for her help in developing the C code.

Urbana-Champaign

Donald Hearn
M. Pauline Baker

Computer Graphics
C Version

1 A Survey of Computer Graphics

Computers have become a powerful tool for the rapid and economical production of pictures. There is virtually no area in which graphical displays cannot be used to some advantage, and so it is not surprising to find the use of computer graphics so widespread. Although early applications in engineering and science had to rely on expensive and cumbersome equipment, advances in computer technology have made interactive computer graphics a practical tool. Today, we find computer graphics used routinely in such diverse areas as science, engineering, medicine, business, industry, government, art, entertainment, advertising, education, and training. Figure 1-1 summarizes the many applications of graphics in simulations, education, and graph presentations. Before we get into the details of how to do computer graphics, we first take a short tour through a gallery of graphics applications.

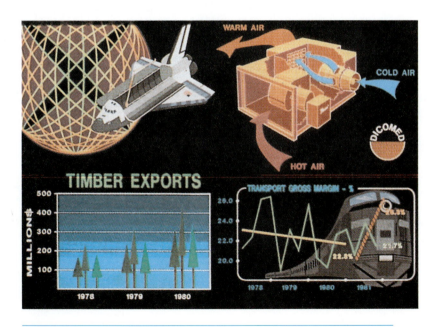

Figure 1-1
Examples of computer graphics applications. (*Courtesy of DICOMED Corporation.*)

1-1

COMPUTER-AIDED DESIGN

A major use of computer graphics is in design processes, particularly for engineering and architectural systems, but almost all products are now computer designed. Generally referred to as **CAD, computer-aided design** methods are now routinely used in the design of buildings, automobiles, aircraft, watercraft, spacecraft, computers, textiles, and many, many other products.

For some design applications, objects are first displayed in a wireframe outline form that shows the overall shape and internal features of objects. Wireframe displays also allow designers to quickly see the effects of interactive adjustments to design shapes. Figures 1-2 and 1-3 give examples of wireframe displays in design applications.

Software packages for CAD applications typically provide the designer with a multi-window environment, as in Figs. 1-4 and 1-5. The various displayed windows can show enlarged sections or different views of objects.

Circuits such as the one shown in Fig. 1-5 and networks for communications, water supply, or other utilities are constructed with repeated placement of a few graphical shapes. The shapes used in a design represent the different network or circuit components. Standard shapes for electrical, electronic, and logic circuits are often supplied by the design package. For other applications, a designer can create personalized symbols that are to be used to construct the network or circuit. The system is then designed by successively placing components into the layout, with the graphics package automatically providing the connections between components. This allows the designer to quickly try out alternate circuit schematics for minimizing the number of components or the space required for the system.

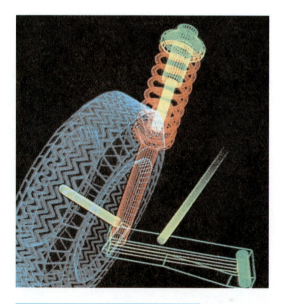

Figure 1-2
Color-coded wireframe display for an automobile wheel assembly.
(*Courtesy of Evans & Sutherland.*)

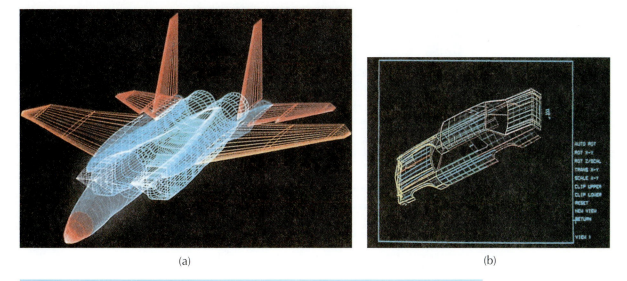

(a)   (b)

Figure 1-3
Color-coded wireframe displays of body designs for an aircraft and an automobile.
(*Courtesy of (a) Evans & Sutherland and (b) Megatek Corporation.*)

Animations are often used in CAD applications. Real-time animations using wireframe displays on a video monitor are useful for testing performance of a vehicle or system, as demonstrated in Fig. 1-6. When we do not display objects with rendered surfaces, the calculations for each segment of the animation can be performed quickly to produce a smooth real-time motion on the screen. Also, wireframe displays allow the designer to see into the interior of the vehicle and to watch the behavior of inner components during motion. Animations in *virtual-reality* environments are used to determine how vehicle operators are affected by

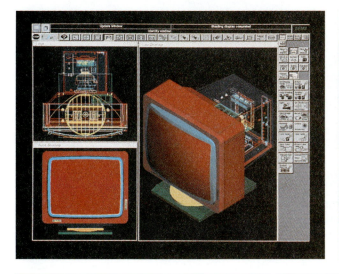 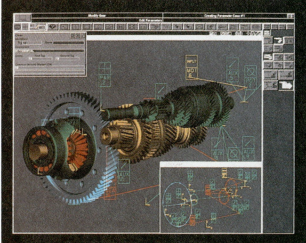

Figure 1-4
Multiple-window, color-coded CAD workstation displays. (*Courtesy of Intergraph Corporation.*)

A circuit-design application, using multiple windows and color-coded logic components, displayed on a Sun workstation with attached speaker and microphone. (*Courtesy of Sun Microsystems.*)

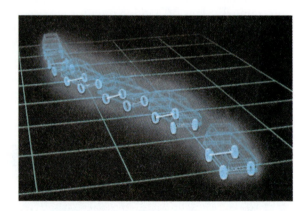

Figure 1-6
Simulation of vehicle performance during lane changes. (*Courtesy of Evans & Sutherland and Mechanical Dynamics, Inc.*)

certain motions. As the tractor operator in Fig. 1-7 manipulates the controls, the headset presents a stereoscopic view (Fig. 1-8) of the front-loader bucket or the backhoe, just as if the operator were in the tractor seat. This allows the designer to explore various positions of the bucket or backhoe that might obstruct the operator's view, which can then be taken into account in the overall tractor design. Figure 1-9 shows a composite, wide-angle view from the tractor seat, displayed on a standard video monitor instead of in a virtual three-dimensional scene. And Fig. 1-10 shows a view of the tractor that can be displayed in a separate window or on another monitor.

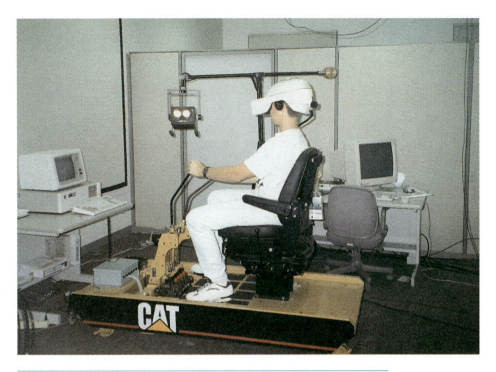

Figure 1-7
Operating a tractor in a virtual-reality environment. As the controls are moved, the operator views the front loader, backhoe, and surroundings through the headset. (*Courtesy of the National Center for Supercomputing Applications, University of Illinois at Urbana-Champaign, and Caterpillar, Inc.*)

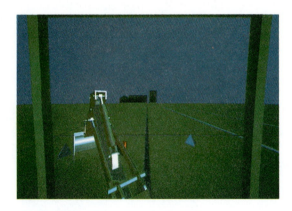

Figure 1-8
A headset view of the backhoe presented to the tractor operator. (*Courtesy of the National Center for Supercomputing Applications, University of Illinois at Urbana-Champaign, and Caterpillar, Inc.*)

Figure 1-9
Operator's view of the tractor bucket, composited in several sections to form a wide-angle view on a standard monitor. (*Courtesy of the National Center for Supercomputing Applications, University of Illinois at Urbana-Champaign, and Caterpillar, Inc.*)

Figure 1-10
View of the tractor displayed on a standard monitor. (*Courtesy of the National Center for Supercomputing Applications, University of Illinois at Urbana-Champaign, and Caterpillar, Inc.*)

When object designs are complete, or nearly complete, realistic lighting models and surface rendering are applied to produce displays that will show the appearance of the final product. Examples of this are given in Fig. 1-11. Realistic displays are also generated for advertising of automobiles and other vehicles using special lighting effects and background scenes (Fig. 1-12).

The manufacturing process is also tied in to the computer description of designed objects to automate the construction of the product. A circuit board layout, for example, can be transformed into a description of the individual processes needed to construct the layout. Some mechanical parts are manufactured by describing how the surfaces are to be formed with machine tools. Figure 1-13 shows the path to be taken by machine tools over the surfaces of an object during its construction. Numerically controlled machine tools are then set up to manufacture the part according to these construction layouts.

(a)

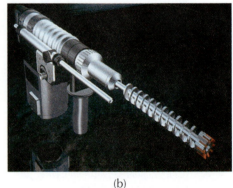

(b)

Figure 1-11
Realistic renderings of design products. (*Courtesy of (a) Intergraph Corporation and (b) Evans & Sutherland.*)

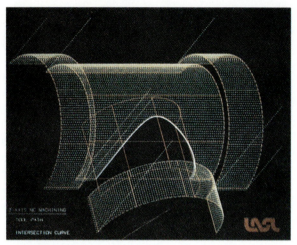

Figure 1-12
Studio lighting effects and realistic surface-rendering techniques are applied to produce advertising pieces for finished products. The data for this rendering of a Chrysler Laser was supplied by Chrysler Corporation. (*Courtesy of Eric Haines, 3D/EYE Inc.*)

Figure 1-13
A CAD layout for describing the numerically controlled machining of a part. The part surface is displayed in one color and the tool path in another color. (*Courtesy of Los Alamos National Laboratory.*)

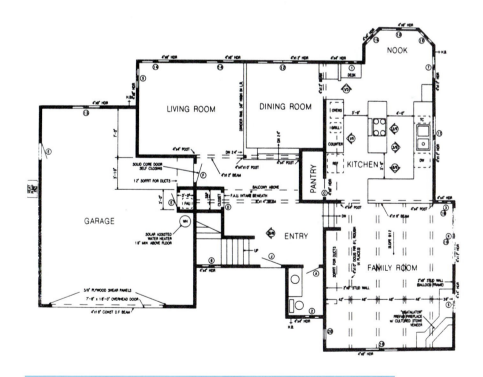

Figure 1-14
Architectural CAD layout for a building design. (*Courtesy of Precision Visuals, Inc., Boulder, Colorado.*)

Architects use interactive graphics methods to lay out floor plans, such as Fig. 1-14, that show the positioning of rooms, doors, windows, stairs, shelves, counters, and other building features. Working from the display of a building layout on a video monitor, an electrical designer can try out arrangements for wiring, electrical outlets, and fire warning systems. Also, facility-layout packages can be applied to the layout to determine space utilization in an office or on a manufacturing floor.

Realistic displays of architectural designs, as in Fig. 1-15, permit both architects and their clients to study the appearance of a single building or a group of buildings, such as a campus or industrial complex. With virtual-reality systems, designers can even go for a simulated "walk" through the rooms or around the outsides of buildings to better appreciate the overall effect of a particular design. In addition to realistic exterior building displays, architectural CAD packages also provide facilities for experimenting with three-dimensional interior layouts and lighting (Fig. 1-16).

Many other kinds of systems and products are designed using either general CAD packages or specially developed CAD software. Figure 1-17, for example, shows a rug pattern designed with a CAD system.

(a)

(b)

Figure 1-15
Realistic, three-dimensional renderings of building designs. (a) A street-level perspective for the World Trade Center project. (*Courtesy of Skidmore, Owings & Merrill.*)
(b) Architectural visualization of an atrium, created for a computer animation by Marialine Prieur, Lyon, France. (*Courtesy of Thomson Digital Image, Inc.*)

Figure 1-16
A hotel corridor providing a sense of movement by placing light fixtures along an undulating path and creating a sense of entry by using light towers at each hotel room. (*Courtesy of Skidmore, Owings & Merrill.*)

Figure 1-17
Oriental rug pattern created with computer graphics design methods. (*Courtesy of Lexidata Corporation.*)

1-2
PRESENTATION GRAPHICS

Another major application area is **presentation graphics**, used to produce illustrations for reports or to generate 35-mm slides or transparencies for use with projectors. Presentation graphics is commonly used to summarize financial, statistical, mathematical, scientific, and economic data for research reports, managerial reports, consumer information bulletins, and other types of reports. Workstation devices and service bureaus exist for converting screen displays into 35-mm slides or overhead transparencies for use in presentations. Typical examples of presentation graphics are bar charts, line graphs, surface graphs, pie charts, and other displays showing relationships between multiple parameters.

Figure 1-18 gives examples of two-dimensional graphics combined with geographical information. This illustration shows three color-coded bar charts combined onto one graph and a pie chart with three sections. Similar graphs and charts can be displayed in three dimensions to provide additional information. Three-dimensional graphs are sometimes used simply for effect; they can provide a more dramatic or more attractive presentation of data relationships. The charts in Fig. 1-19 include a three-dimensional bar graph and an exploded pie chart.

Additional examples of three-dimensional graphs are shown in Figs. 1-20 and 1-21. Figure 1-20 shows one kind of surface plot, and Fig. 1-21 shows a two-dimensional contour plot with a height surface.

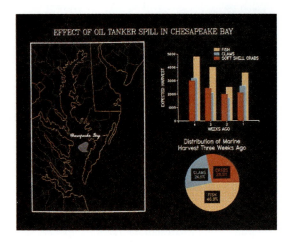

Figure 1-18
Two-dimensional bar chart and pie chart linked to a geographical chart. (*Courtesy of Computer Associates, copyright © 1992. All rights reserved.*)

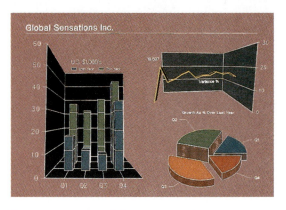

Figure 1-19
Three-dimensional bar chart, exploded pie chart, and line graph. (*Courtesy of Computer Associates, copyright © 1992. All rights reserved.*)

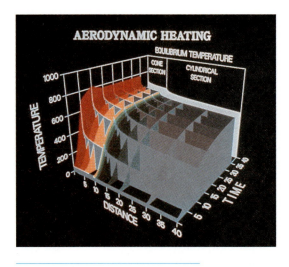

Figure 1-20
Showing relationships with a surface chart. (*Courtesy of Computer Associates, copyright © 1992. All rights reserved.*)

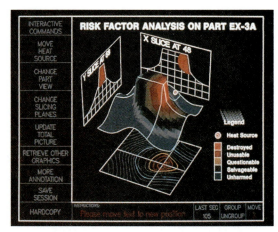

Figure 1-21
Plotting two-dimensional contours in the ground plane, with a height field plotted as a surface above the ground plane. (*Courtesy of Computer Associates, copyright © 1992. All rights reserved.*)

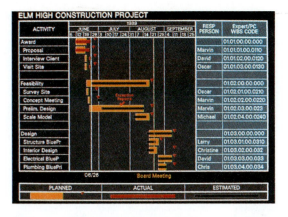

Figure 1-22 illustrates a time chart used in task planning. Time charts and task network layouts are used in project management to schedule and monitor the progress of projects.

1-3
COMPUTER ART

Computer graphics methods are widely used in both fine art and commercial art applications. Artists use a variety of computer methods, including special-purpose hardware, artist's paintbrush programs (such as Lumena), other paint packages (such as PixelPaint and SuperPaint), specially developed software, symbolic mathematics packages (such as Mathematica), CAD packages, desktop publishing software, and animation packages that provide facilities for designing object shapes and specifiying object motions.

Figure 1-23 illustrates the basic idea behind a *paintbrush* program that allows artists to "paint" pictures on the screen of a video monitor. Actually, the picture is usually painted electronically on a graphics tablet (digitizer) using a stylus, which can simulate different brush strokes, brush widths, and colors. A paintbrush program was used to create the characters in Fig. 1-24, who seem to be busy on a creation of their own.

A paintbrush system, with a Wacom cordless, pressure-sensitive stylus, was used to produce the electronic painting in Fig. 1-25 that simulates the brush strokes of Van Gogh. The stylus translates changing hand pressure into variable line widths, brush sizes, and color gradations. Figure 1-26 shows a watercolor painting produced with this stylus and with software that allows the artist to create watercolor, pastel, or oil brush effects that simulate different drying out times, wetness, and footprint. Figure 1-27 gives an example of paintbrush methods combined with scanned images.

Fine artists use a variety of other computer technologies to produce images. To create pictures such as the one shown in Fig. 1-28, the artist uses a combination of three-dimensional modeling packages, texture mapping, drawing programs, and CAD software. In Fig. 1-29, we have a painting produced on a pen

13

Figure 1-23
Cartoon drawing produced with a paintbrush program, symbolically illustrating an artist at work on a video monitor. (*Courtesy of Gould Inc., Imaging & Graphics Division and Aurora Imaging.*)

plotter with specially designed software that can create "automatic art" without intervention from the artist.

Figure 1-30 shows an example of "mathematical" art. This artist uses a combination of mathematical functions, fractal procedures, Mathematica software, ink-jet printers, and other systems to create a variety of three-dimensional and two-dimensional shapes and stereoscopic image pairs. Another example of elec-

(a)

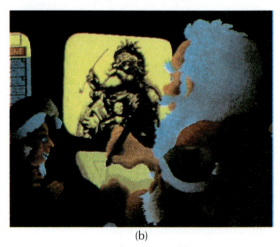

(b)

Figure 1-24
Cartoon demonstrations of an "artist" creating a picture with a paintbrush system. The picture, drawn on a graphics tablet, is displayed on the video monitor as the elves look on. In (b), the cartoon is superimposed on the famous Thomas Nast drawing of Saint Nicholas, which was input to the system with a video camera, then scaled and positioned. (*Courtesy Gould Inc., Imaging & Graphics Division and Aurora Imaging.*)

Figure 1-25
A Van Gogh look-alike created by graphics artist Elizabeth O'Rourke with a cordless, pressure-sensitive stylus. (*Courtesy of Wacom Technology Corporation.*)

Figure 1-26
An electronic watercolor, painted by John Derry of Time Arts, Inc. using a cordless, pressure-sensitive stylus and Lumena gouache-brush software. (*Courtesy of Wacom Technology Corporation.*)

Figure 1-27
The artist of this picture, called *Electronic Avalanche*, makes a statement about our entanglement with technology using a personal computer with a graphics tablet and Lumena software to combine renderings of leaves, flower petals, and electronics components with scanned images. (*Courtesy of the Williams Gallery. Copyright © 1991 by Joan Truckenbrod, The School of the Art Institute of Chicago.*)

15

Figure 1-28
From a series called *Spheres of Influence,* this electronic painting (entitled, *Whigmalaree*) was created with a combination of methods using a graphics tablet, three-dimensional modeling, texture mapping, and a series of transformations. (*Courtesy of the Williams Gallery. Copyright © 1992 by Wynne Ragland, Jr.*)

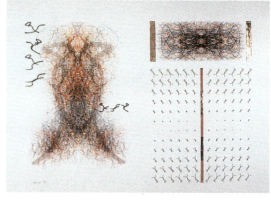

Figure 1-29
Electronic art output to a pen plotter from software specially designed by the artist to emulate his style. The pen plotter includes multiple pens and painting instruments, including Chinese brushes. (*Courtesy of the Williams Gallery. Copyright © by Roman Verostko, Minneapolis College of Art & Design.*)

Figure 1-30
This creation is based on a visualization of Fermat's Last Theorem, $x^n + y^n = z^n$, with $n = 5$, by Andrew Hanson, Department of Computer Science, Indiana University. The image was rendered using Mathematica and Wavefront software. (*Courtesy of the Williams Gallery. Copyright © 1991 by Stewart Dickson.*)

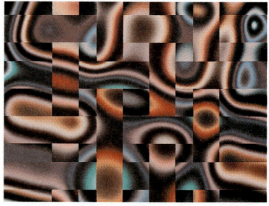

Figure 1-31
Using mathematical functions, fractal procedures, and supercomputers, this artist-composer experiments with various designs to synthesize form and color with musical composition. (*Courtesy of Brian Evans, Vanderbilt University.*)

tronic art created with the aid of mathematical relationships is shown in Fig. 1-31. The artwork of this composer is often designed in relation to frequency variations and other parameters in a musical composition to produce a video that integrates visual and aural patterns.

Although we have spent some time discussing current techniques for generating electronic images in the fine arts, these methods are also applied in commercial art for logos and other designs, page layouts combining text and graphics, TV advertising spots, and other areas. A workstation for producing page layouts that combine text and graphics is illustrated in Fig. 1-32.

For many applications of commercial art (and in motion pictures and other applications), photorealistic techniques are used to render images of a product. Figure 1-33 shows an example of logo design, and Fig. 1-34 gives three computer graphics images for product advertising. Animations are also used frequently in advertising, and television commercials are produced frame by frame, where

Figure 1-32
Page-layout workstation. (*Courtesy of Visual Technology.*)

Figure 1-33
Three-dimensional rendering for a logo. (*Courtesy of Vertigo Technology, Inc.*)

(a)

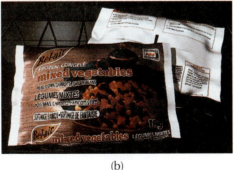

(b)

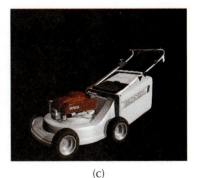

(c)

Figure 1-34
Product advertising. (*Courtesy of (a) Audrey Fleisher and (b) and (c) SOFTIMAGE, Inc.*)

each frame of the motion is rendered and saved as an image file. In each successive frame, the motion is simulated by moving object positions slightly from their positions in the previous frame. When all frames in the animation sequence have been rendered, the frames are transferred to film or stored in a video buffer for playback. Film animations require 24 frames for each second in the animation sequence. If the animation is to be played back on a video monitor, 30 frames per second are required.

A common graphics method employed in many commercials is *morphing*, where one object is transformed (metamorphosed) into another. This method has been used in TV commercials to turn an oil can into an automobile engine, an automobile into a tiger, a puddle of water into a tire, and one person's face into another face. An example of morphing is given in Fig. 1-40.

1-4
ENTERTAINMENT

Computer graphics methods are now commonly used in making motion pictures, music videos, and television shows. Sometimes the graphics scenes are displayed by themselves, and sometimes graphics objects are combined with the actors and live scenes.

A graphics scene generated for the movie *Star Trek—The Wrath of Khan* is shown in Fig. 1-35. The planet and spaceship are drawn in wireframe form and will be shaded with rendering methods to produce solid surfaces. Figure 1-36 shows scenes generated with advanced modeling and surface-rendering methods for two award-winning short films.

Many TV series regularly employ computer graphics methods. Figure 1-37 shows a scene produced for the series *Deep Space Nine*. And Fig. 1-38 shows a wireframe person combined with actors in a live scene for the series *Stay Tuned*.

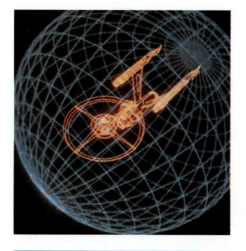

Figure 1-35
Graphics developed for the Paramount Pictures movie *Star Trek—The Wrath of Khan. (Courtesy of Evans & Sutherland.)*

In Fig. 1-39, we have a highly realistic image taken from a reconstruction of thirteenth-century Dadu (now Beijing) for a Japanese broadcast.

Music videos use graphics in several ways. Graphics objects can be combined with the live action, as in Fig.1-38, or graphics and image processing techniques can be used to produce a transformation of one person or object into another (morphing). An example of morphing is shown in the sequence of scenes in Fig. 1-40, produced for the David Byrne video *She's Mad*.

(a)

(b)

Figure 1-36

(a) A computer-generated scene from the film *Red's Dream*, copyright © Pixar 1987. (b) A computer-generated scene from the film *Knickknack*, copyright © Pixar 1989. (*Courtesy of Pixar.*)

Figure 1-37

A graphics scene in the TV series *Deep Space Nine*. (*Courtesy of Rhythm & Hues Studios.*)

19

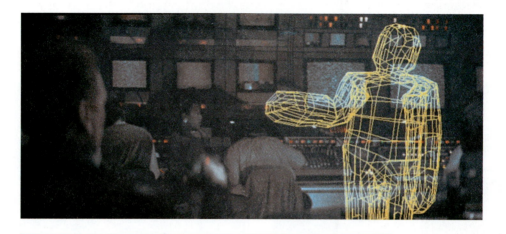

Figure 1-38
Graphics combined with a live scene in the TV series *Stay Tuned*.
(*Courtesy of Rhythm & Hues Studios.*)

Figure 1-39
An image from a reconstruction of thirteenth-century Dadu (Beijing today), created by Taisei Corporation (Tokyo) and rendered with TDI software. (*Courtesy of Thompson Digital Image, Inc.*)

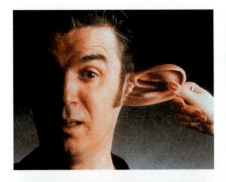

Figure 1-40
Examples of morphing from the David Byrne video *She's Mad*. (*Courtesy of David Byrne, Index Video, and Pacific Data Images.*)

1-5
EDUCATION AND TRAINING

Computer-generated models of physical, financial, and economic systems are often used as educational aids. Models of physical systems, physiological systems, population trends, or equipment, such as the color-coded diagram in Fig. 1-41, can help trainees to understand the operation of the system.

For some training applications, special systems are designed. Examples of such specialized systems are the simulators for practice sessions or training of ship captains, aircraft pilots, heavy-equipment operators, and air traffic-control personnel. Some simulators have no video screens; for example, a flight simulator with only a control panel for instrument flying. But most simulators provide graphics screens for visual operation. Two examples of large simulators with internal viewing systems are shown in Figs. 1-42 and 1-43. Another type of viewing system is shown in Fig. 1-44. Here a viewing screen with multiple panels is mounted in front of the simulator, and color projectors display the flight scene on the screen panels. Similar viewing systems are used in simulators for training aircraft control-tower personnel. Figure 1-45 gives an example of the instructor's area in a flight simulator. The keyboard is used to input parameters affecting the airplane performance or the environment, and the pen plotter is used to chart the path of the aircraft during a training session.

Scenes generated for various simulators are shown in Figs. 1-46 through 1-48. An output from an automobile-driving simulator is given in Fig. 1-49. This simulator is used to investigate the behavior of drivers in critical situations. The drivers' reactions are then used as a basis for optimizing vehicle design to maximize traffic safety.

21

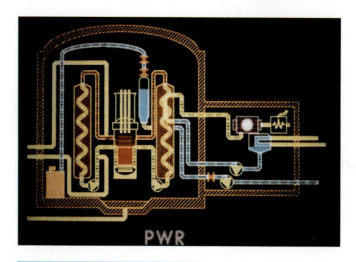

Figure 1-41
Color-coded diagram used to explain the operation of a nuclear reactor. (*Courtesy of Los Alamos National Laboratory.*)

Figure 1-42
A large, enclosed flight simulator with a full-color visual system and six degrees of freedom in its motion. (*Courtesy of Frasca International.*)

Figure 1-43
A military tank simulator with a visual imagery system. (*Courtesy of Mediatech and GE Aerospace.*)

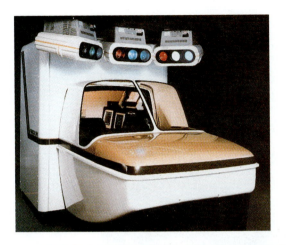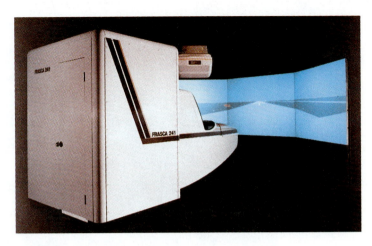

Figure 1-44
A flight simulator with an external full-color viewing system. (*Courtesy of Frasca International.*)

Figure 1-45
An instructor's area in a flight simulator. The equipment allows the instructor to monitor flight conditions and to set airplane and environment parameters. (*Courtesy of Frasca International.*)

23

Figure 1-46
Flight-simulator imagery. (*Courtesy of Evans & Sutherland.*)

Figure 1-47
Imagery generated for a naval simulator. (*Courtesy of Evans & Sutherland.*)

Figure 1-48
Space shuttle imagery. (*Courtesy of Mediatech and GE Aerospace.*)

Figure 1-49
Imagery from an automobile
simulator used to test driver
reaction. (*Courtesy of Evans &
Sutherland.*)

1-6
VISUALIZATION

Scientists, engineers, medical personnel, business analysts, and others often need
to analyze large amounts of information or to study the behavior of certain
processes. Numerical simulations carried out on supercomputers frequently produce data files containing thousands and even millions of data values. Similarly,
satellite cameras and other sources are amassing large data files faster than they
can be interpreted. Scanning these large sets of numbers to determine trends and
relationships is a tedious and ineffective process. But if the data are converted to
a visual form, the trends and patterns are often immediately apparent. Figure 1-
50 shows an example of a large data set that has been converted to a color-coded
display of relative heights above a ground plane. Once we have plotted the density values in this way, we can see easily the overall pattern of the data. Producing graphical representations for scientific, engineering, and medical data sets
and processes is generally referred to as *scientific visualization*. And the term *business visualization* is used in connection with data sets related to commerce, industry, and other nonscientific areas.

There are many different kinds of data sets, and effective visualization
schemes depend on the characteristics of the data. A collection of data can contain scalar values, vectors, higher-order tensors, or any combination of these data
types. And data sets can be two-dimensional or three-dimensional. Color coding
is just one way to visualize a data set. Additional techniques include contour
plots, graphs and charts, surface renderings, and visualizations of volume interiors. In addition, image processing techniques are combined with computer
graphics to produce many of the data visualizations.

Mathematicians, physical scientists, and others use visual techniques to analyze mathematical functions and processes or simply to produce interesting
graphical representations. A color plot of mathematical curve functions is shown
in Fig. 1-51, and a surface plot of a function is shown in Fig. 1-52. Fractal proce-

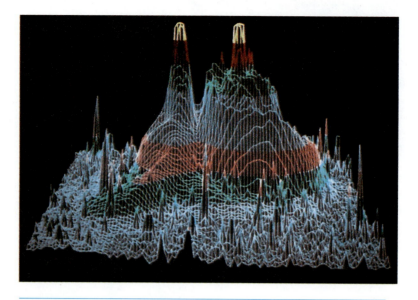

Figure 1-50
A color-coded plot with 16 million density points of relative brightness observed for the Whirlpool Nebula reveals two distinct galaxies. (*Courtesy of Los Alamos National Laboratory.*)

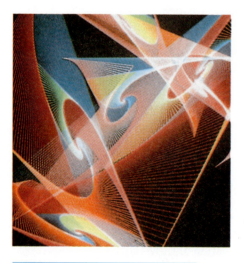

Figure 1-51
Mathematical curve functions plotted in various color combinations. (*Courtesy of Melvin L. Prueitt, Los Alamos National Laboratory.*)

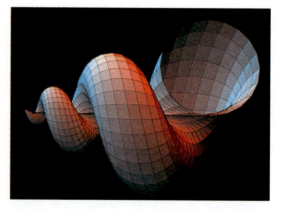

Figure 1-52
Lighting effects and surface-rendering techniques were applied to produce this surface representation for a three-dimensional function. (*Courtesy of Wolfram Research, Inc, The Maker of Mathematica.*)

dures using quaternions generated the object shown in Fig. 1-53, and a topological structure is displayed in Fig. 1-54. Scientists are also developing methods for visualizing general classes of data. Figure 1-55 shows a general technique for graphing and modeling data distributed over a spherical surface.

A few of the many other visualization applications are shown in Figs. 1-56 through 1-69. These figures show airflow over the surface of a space shuttle, numerical modeling of thunderstorms, study of crack propagation in metals, a color-coded plot of fluid density over an airfoil, a cross-sectional slicer for data sets, protein modeling, stereoscopic viewing of molecular structure, a model of the ocean floor, a Kuwaiti oil-fire simulation, an air-pollution study, a corn-growing study, reconstruction of Arizona's Chaco Canyon ruins, and a graph of automobile accident statistics.

Figure 1-53
A four-dimensional object projected into three-dimensional space, then projected to a video monitor, and color coded. The object was generated using quaternions and fractal squaring procedures, with an octant subtracted to show the complex Julia set. (*Courtesy of John C. Hart, School of Electrical Engineering and Computer Science, Washington State University.*)

Figure 1-54
Four views from a real-time, interactive computer-animation study of minimal surfaces ("snails") in the 3-sphere projected to three-dimensional Euclidean space. (*Courtesy of George Francis, Department of Mathematics and the National Center for Supercomputing Applications, University of Illinois at Urbana-Champaign. Copyright © 1993.*)

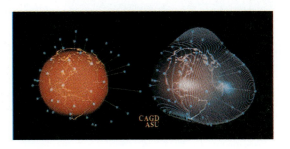

Figure 1-55
A method for graphing and modeling data distributed over a spherical surface. (*Courtesy of Greg Nielson, Computer Science Department, Arizona State University.*)

27

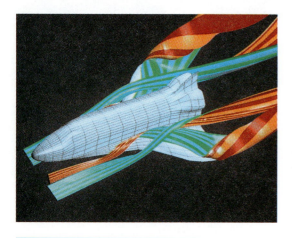

Figure 1-56
A visualization of stream surfaces flowing past a space shuttle by Jeff Hultquist and Eric Raible, NASA Ames. (*Courtesy of Sam Uselton, NASA Ames Research Center.*)

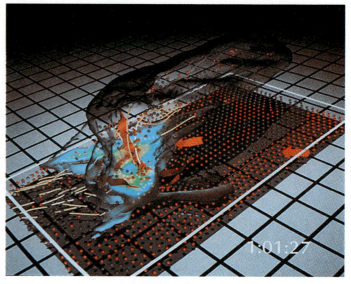

Figure 1-57
Numerical model of airflow inside a thunderstorm. (*Courtesy of Bob Wilhelmson, Department of Atmospheric Sciences and the National Center for Supercomputing Applications, University of Illinois at Urbana-Champaign.*)

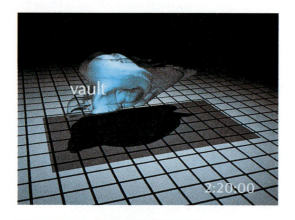

Figure 1-58
Numerical model of the surface of a thunderstorm. (*Courtesy of Bob Wilhelmson, Department of Atmospheric Sciences and the National Center for Supercomputing Applications, University of Illinois at Urbana-Champaign.*)

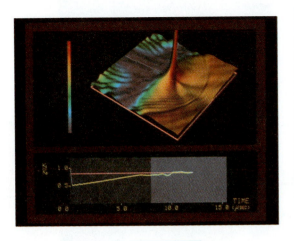

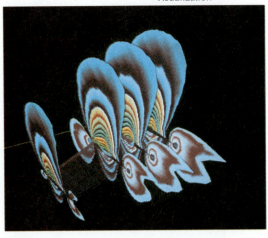

Figure 1-59
Color-coded visualization of stress energy density in a crack-propagation study for metal plates, modeled by Bob Haber. (*Courtesy of the National Center for Supercomputing Applications, University of Illinois at Urbana-Champaign.*)

Figure 1-60
A fluid dynamic simulation, showing a color-coded plot of fluid density over a span of grid planes around an aircraft wing, developed by Lee-Hian Quek, John Eickemeyer, and Jeffery Tan. (*Courtesy of the Information Technology Institute, Republic of Singapore.*)

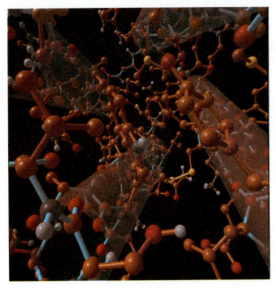

Figure 1-61
Commercial slicer-dicer software, showing color-coded data values over cross-sectional slices of a data set. (*Courtesy of Spyglass, Inc.*)

Figure 1-62
Visualization of a protein structure by Jay Siegel and Kim Baldridge, SDSC. (*Courtesy of Stephanie Sides, San Diego Supercomputer Center.*)

Stereoscopic viewing of a molecular structure using a "boom" device.
(Courtesy of the National Center for Supercomputing Applications, University of Illinois at Urbana-Champaign.)

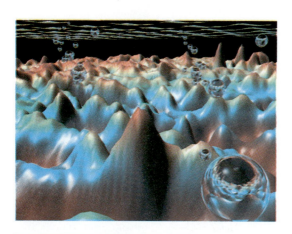

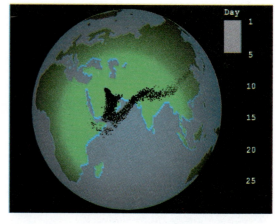

Figure 1-64
One image from a stereoscopic pair, showing a visualization of the ocean floor obtained from satellite data, by David Sandwell and Chris Small, Scripps Institution of Oceanography, and Jim Mcleod, SDSC. *(Courtesy of Stephanie Sides, San Diego Supercomputer Center.)*

Figure 1-65
A simulation of the effects of the Kuwaiti oil fire, by Gary Glatzmeier, Chuck Hanson, and Paul Hinker. *(Courtesy of Mike Krogh, Advanced Computing Laboratory at Los Alamos National Laboratory.)*

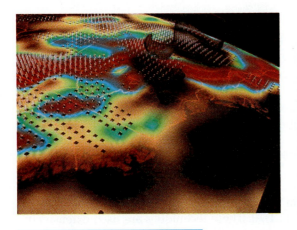

Figure 1-66
A visualization of pollution over the earth's surface by Tom Palmer, Cray Research Inc./NCSC; Chris Landreth, NCSC; and Dave Bock, NCSC. Pollutant SO_4 is plotted as a blue surface, acid-rain deposition is a color plane on the map surface, and rain concentration is shown as clear cylinders. (*Courtesy of the North Carolina Supercomputing Center/MCNC.*)

Figure 1-67
One frame of an animation sequence showing the development of a corn ear. (*Courtesy of the National Center for Supercomputing Applications, University of Illinois at Urbana-Champaign.*)

Figure 1-68
A visualization of the reconstruction of the ruins at Chaco Canyon, Arizona. (*Courtesy of Melvin L. Prueitt, Los Alamos National Laboratory. Data supplied by Stephen H. Lekson.*)

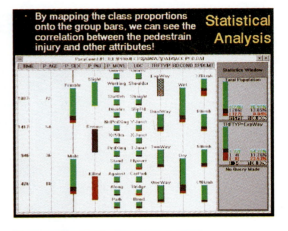

Figure 1-69
A prototype technique, called *WinViz*, for visualizing tabular multidimensional data is used here to correlate statistical information on pedestrians involved in automobile accidents, developed by a visualization team at ITT. (*Courtesy of Lee-Hian Quek, Information Technology Institute, Republic of Singapore.*)

31

IMAGE PROCESSING

Although methods used in computer graphics and image processing overlap, the two areas are concerned with fundamentally different operations. In computer graphics, a computer is used to create a picture. **Image processing**, on the other hand, applies techniques to modify or interpret existing pictures, such as photographs and TV scans. Two principal applications of image processing are (1) improving picture quality and (2) machine perception of visual information, as used in robotics.

To apply image-processing methods, we first digitize a photograph or other picture into an image file. Then digital methods can be applied to rearrange picture parts, to enhance color separations, or to improve the quality of shading. An example of the application of image-processing methods to enhance the quality of a picture is shown in Fig. 1-70. These techniques are used extensively in commercial art applications that involve the retouching and rearranging of sections of photographs and other artwork. Similar methods are used to analyze satellite photos of the earth and photos of galaxies.

Medical applications also make extensive use of image-processing techniques for picture enhancements, in tomography and in simulations of operations. Tomography is a technique of X-ray photography that allows cross-sectional views of physiological systems to be displayed. Both *computed X-ray tomography* (CT) and *position emission tomography* (PET) use projection methods to reconstruct cross sections from digital data. These techniques are also used to

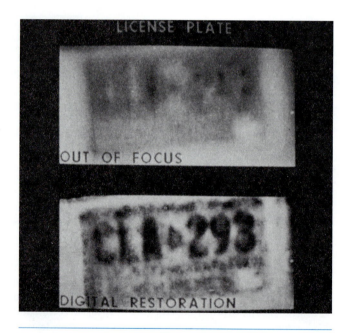

Figure 1-70

A blurred photograph of a license plate becomes legible after the application of image-processing techniques. (*Courtesy of Los Alamos National Laboratory.*)

monitor internal functions and show cross sections during surgery. Other medical imaging techniques include ultrasonics and nuclear medicine scanners. With ultrasonics, high-frequency sound waves, instead of X-rays, are used to generate digital data. Nuclear medicine scanners collect digital data from radiation emitted from ingested radionuclides and plot color-coded images.

Image processing and computer graphics are typically combined in many applications. Medicine, for example, uses these techniques to model and study physical functions, to design artificial limbs, and to plan and practice surgery. The last application is generally referred to as *computer-aided surgery*. Two-dimensional cross sections of the body are obtained using imaging techniques. Then the slices are viewed and manipulated using graphics methods to simulate actual surgical procedures and to try out different surgical cuts. Examples of these medical applications are shown in Figs. 1-71 and 1-72.

Figure 1-71
One frame from a computer animation visualizing cardiac activation levels within regions of a semitransparent volume-rendered dog heart. Medical data provided by William Smith, Ed Simpson, and G. Allan Johnson, Duke University. Image-rendering software by Tom Palmer, Cray Research, Inc./NCSC. (*Courtesy of Dave Bock, North Carolina Supercomputing Center/MCNC.*)

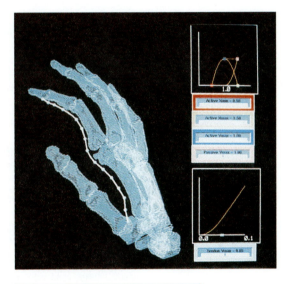

Figure 1-72
One image from a stereoscopic pair showing the bones of a human hand. The images were rendered by Inmo Yoon, D. E. Thompson, and W. N. Waggenspack, Jr., LSU, from a data set obtained with CT scans by Rehabilitation Research, GWLNHDC. These images show a possible tendon path for reconstructive surgery. (*Courtesy of IMRLAB, Mechanical Engineering, Louisiana State University.*)

1-8

GRAPHICAL USER INTERFACES

It is common now for software packages to provide a **graphical interface**. A major component of a graphical interface is a window manager that allows a user to display multiple-window areas. Each window can contain a different process that can contain graphical or nongraphical displays. To make a particular window active, we simply click in that window using an interactive pointing device.

Interfaces also display menus and icons for fast selection of processing options or parameter values. An **icon** is a graphical symbol that is designed to look like the processing option it represents. The advantages of icons are that they take up less screen space than corresponding textual descriptions and they can be understood more quickly if well designed. Menus contain lists of textual descriptions and icons.

Figure 1-73 illustrates a typical graphical interface, containing a window manager, menu displays, and icons. In this example, the menus allow selection of processing options, color values, and graphics parameters. The icons represent options for painting, drawing, zooming, typing text strings, and other operations connected with picture construction.

Figure 1-73
A graphical user interface, showing multiple window areas, menus, and icons. (*Courtesy of Image-In Corporation.*)

CHAPTER

2

Overview of Graphics Systems

D ue to the widespread recognition of the power and utility of computer graphics in virtually all fields, a broad range of graphics hardware and software systems is now available. Graphics capabilities for both two-dimensional and three-dimensional applications are now common on general-purpose computers, including many hand-held calculators. With personal computers, we can use a wide variety of interactive input devices and graphics software packages. For higher-quality applications, we can choose from a number of sophisticated special-purpose graphics hardware systems and technologies. In this chapter, we explore the basic features of graphics hardware components and graphics software packages.

2-1
VIDEO DISPLAY DEVICES

Typically, the primary output device in a graphics system is a video monitor (Fig. 2-1). The operation of most video monitors is based on the standard **cathode-ray tube** (**CRT**) design, but several other technologies exist and solid-state monitors may eventually predominate.

Figure 2-1
A computer graphics workstation. (*Courtesy of Tektronix, Inc.*)

36

Refresh Cathode-Ray Tubes

Figure 2-2 illustrates the basic operation of a CRT. A beam of electrons (*cathode rays*), emitted by an electron gun, passes through focusing and deflection systems that direct the beam toward specified positions on the phosphor-coated screen. The phosphor then emits a small spot of light at each position contacted by the electron beam. Because the light emitted by the phosphor fades very rapidly, some method is needed for maintaining the screen picture. One way to keep the phosphor glowing is to redraw the picture repeatedly by quickly directing the electron beam back over the same points. This type of display is called a **refresh CRT**.

The primary components of an electron gun in a CRT are the heated metal cathode and a control grid (Fig. 2-3). Heat is supplied to the cathode by directing a current through a coil of wire, called the filament, inside the cylindrical cathode structure. This causes electrons to be "boiled off" the hot cathode surface. In the vacuum inside the CRT envelope, the free, negatively charged electrons are then accelerated toward the phosphor coating by a high positive voltage. The acceler-

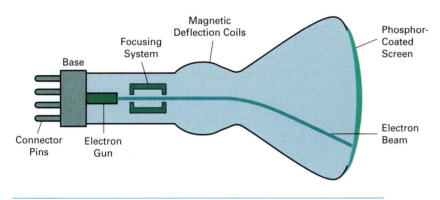

Figure 2-2
Basic design of a magnetic-deflection CRT.

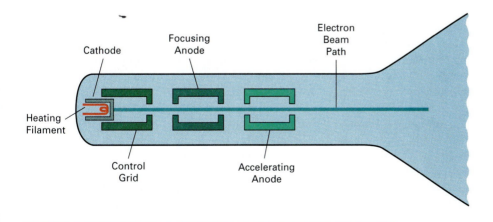

Figure 2-3
Operation of an electron gun with an accelerating anode.

37

ating voltage can be generated with a positively charged metal coating on the inside of the CRT envelope near the phosphor screen, or an accelerating anode can be used, as in Fig. 2-3. Sometimes the electron gun is built to contain the accelerating anode and focusing system within the same unit.

Intensity of the electron beam is controlled by setting voltage levels on the control grid, which is a metal cylinder that fits over the cathode. A high negative voltage applied to the control grid will shut off the beam by repelling electrons and stopping them from passing through the small hole at the end of the control grid structure. A smaller negative voltage on the control grid simply decreases the number of electrons passing through. Since the amount of light emitted by the phosphor coating depends on the number of electrons striking the screen, we control the brightness of a display by varying the voltage on the control grid. We specify the intensity level for individual screen positions with graphics software commands, as discussed in Chapter 3.

The focusing system in a CRT is needed to force the electron beam to converge into a small spot as it strikes the phosphor. Otherwise, the electrons would repel each other, and the beam would spread out as it approaches the screen. Focusing is accomplished with either electric or magnetic fields. Electrostatic focusing is commonly used in television and computer graphics monitors. With electrostatic focusing, the electron beam passes through a positively charged metal cylinder that forms an electrostatic lens, as shown in Fig. 2-3. The action of the electrostatic lens focuses the electron beam at the center of the screen, in exactly the same way that an optical lens focuses a beam of light at a particular focal distance. Similar lens focusing effects can be accomplished with a magnetic field set up by a coil mounted around the outside of the CRT envelope. Magnetic lens focusing produces the smallest spot size on the screen and is used in special-purpose devices.

Additional focusing hardware is used in high-precision systems to keep the beam in focus at all screen positions. The distance that the electron beam must travel to different points on the screen varies because the radius of curvature for most CRTs is greater than the distance from the focusing system to the screen center. Therefore, the electron beam will be focused properly only at the center of the screen. As the beam moves to the outer edges of the screen, displayed images become blurred. To compensate for this, the system can adjust the focusing according to the screen position of the beam.

As with focusing, deflection of the electron beam can be controlled either with electric fields or with magnetic fields. Cathode-ray tubes are now commonly constructed with magnetic deflection coils mounted on the outside of the CRT envelope, as illustrated in Fig. 2-2. Two pairs of coils are used, with the coils in each pair mounted on opposite sides of the neck of the CRT envelope. One pair is mounted on the top and bottom of the neck, and the other pair is mounted on opposite sides of the neck. The magnetic field produced by each pair of coils results in a transverse deflection force that is perpendicular both to the direction of the magnetic field and to the direction of travel of the electron beam. Horizontal deflection is accomplished with one pair of coils, and vertical deflection by the other pair. The proper deflection amounts are attained by adjusting the current through the coils. When electrostatic deflection is used, two pairs of parallel plates are mounted inside the CRT envelope. One pair of plates is mounted horizontally to control the vertical deflection, and the other pair is mounted vertically to control horizontal deflection (Fig. 2-4).

Spots of light are produced on the screen by the transfer of the CRT beam energy to the phosphor. When the electrons in the beam collide with the phos-

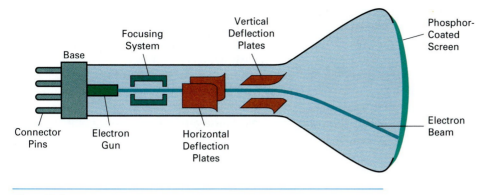

Figure 2-4

Electrostatic deflection of the electron beam in a CRT.

phor coating, they are stopped and their kinetic energy is absorbed by the phosphor. Part of the beam energy is converted by friction into heat energy, and the remainder causes electrons in the phosphor atoms to move up to higher quantum-energy levels. After a short time, the "excited" phosphor electrons begin dropping back to their stable ground state, giving up their extra energy as small quantums of light energy. What we see on the screen is the combined effect of all the electron light emissions: a glowing spot that quickly fades after all the excited phosphor electrons have returned to their ground energy level. The frequency (or color) of the light emitted by the phosphor is proportional to the energy difference between the excited quantum state and the ground state.

Different kinds of phosphors are available for use in a CRT. Besides color, a major difference between phosphors is their **persistence**: how long they continue to emit light (that is, have excited electrons returning to the ground state) after the CRT beam is removed. Persistence is defined as the time it takes the emitted light from the screen to decay to one-tenth of its original intensity. Lower-persistence phosphors require higher refresh rates to maintain a picture on the screen without flicker. A phosphor with low persistence is useful for animation; a high-persistence phosphor is useful for displaying highly complex, static pictures. Although some phosphors have a persistence greater than 1 second, graphics monitors are usually constructed with a persistence in the range from 10 to 60 microseconds.

Figure 2-5 shows the intensity distribution of a spot on the screen. The intensity is greatest at the center of the spot, and decreases with a Gaussian distribution out to the edges of the spot. This distribution corresponds to the cross-sectional electron density distribution of the CRT beam.

Figure 2-5

Intensity distribution of an illuminated phosphor spot on a CRT screen.

The maximum number of points that can be displayed without overlap on a CRT is referred to as the **resolution**. A more precise definition of resolution is the number of points per centimeter that can be plotted horizontally and vertically, although it is often simply stated as the total number of points in each direction. Spot intensity has a Gaussian distribution (Fig. 2-5), so two adjacent spots will appear distinct as long as their separation is greater than the diameter at which each spot has an intensity of about 60 percent of that at the center of the spot. This overlap position is illustrated in Fig. 2-6. Spot size also depends on intensity. As more electrons are accelerated toward the phospher per second, the CRT beam diameter and the illuminated spot increase. In addition, the increased excitation energy tends to spread to neighboring phosphor atoms not directly in the

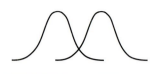

Figure 2-6

Two illuminated phosphor spots are distinguishable when their separation is greater than the diameter at which a spot intensity has fallen to 60 percent of maximum.

path of the beam, which further increases the spot diameter. Thus, resolution of a CRT is dependent on the type of phosphor, the intensity to be displayed, and the focusing and deflection systems. Typical resolution on high-quality systems is 1280 by 1024, with higher resolutions available on many systems. High-resolution systems are often referred to as *high-definition systems*. The physical size of a graphics monitor is given as the length of the screen diagonal, with sizes varying from about 12 inches to 27 inches or more. A CRT monitor can be attached to a variety of computer systems, so the number of screen points that can actually be plotted depends on the capabilities of the system to which it is attached.

Another property of video monitors is **aspect ratio**. This number gives the ratio of vertical points to horizontal points necessary to produce equal-length lines in both directions on the screen. (Sometimes aspect ratio is stated in terms of the ratio of horizontal to vertical points.) An aspect ratio of 3/4 means that a vertical line plotted with three points has the same length as a horizontal line plotted with four points.

Raster-Scan Displays

The most common type of graphics monitor employing a CRT is the **raster-scan** display, based on television technology. In a raster-scan system, the electron beam is swept across the screen, one row at a time from top to bottom. As the electron beam moves across each row, the beam intensity is turned on and off to create a pattern of illuminated spots. Picture definition is stored in a memory area called the **refresh buffer** or **frame buffer**. This memory area holds the set of intensity values for all the screen points. Stored intensity values are then retrieved from the refresh buffer and "painted" on the screen one row (**scan line**) at a time (Fig. 2-7). Each screen point is referred to as a **pixel** or **pel** (shortened forms of **picture element**). The capability of a raster-scan system to store intensity information for each screen point makes it well suited for the realistic display of scenes containing subtle shading and color patterns. Home television sets and printers are examples of other systems using raster-scan methods.

Intensity range for pixel positions depends on the capability of the raster system. In a simple black-and-white system, each screen point is either on or off, so only one bit per pixel is needed to control the intensity of screen positions. For a bilevel system, a bit value of 1 indicates that the electron beam is to be turned on at that position, and a value of 0 indicates that the beam intensity is to be off. Additional bits are needed when color and intensity variations can be displayed. Up to 24 bits per pixel are included in high-quality systems, which can require several megabytes of storage for the frame buffer, depending on the resolution of the system. A system with 24 bits per pixel and a screen resolution of 1024 by 1024 requires 3 megabytes of storage for the frame buffer. On a black-and-white system with one bit per pixel, the frame buffer is commonly called a **bitmap**. For systems with multiple bits per pixel, the frame buffer is often referred to as a **pixmap**.

Refreshing on raster-scan displays is carried out at the rate of 60 to 80 frames per second, although some systems are designed for higher refresh rates. Sometimes, refresh rates are described in units of cycles per second, or Hertz (Hz), where a cycle corresponds to one frame. Using these units, we would describe a refresh rate of 60 frames per second as simply 60 Hz. At the end of each scan line, the electron beam returns to the left side of the screen to begin displaying the next scan line. The return to the left of the screen, after refreshing each

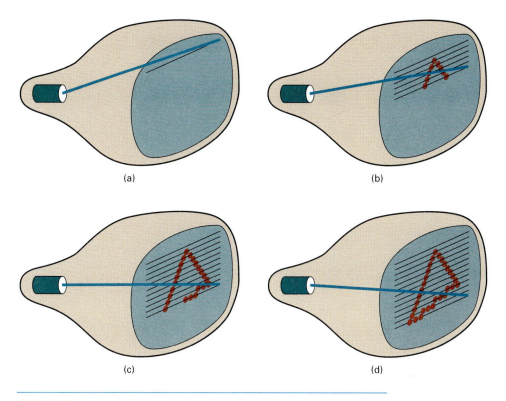

Figure 2-7
A raster-scan system displays an object as a set of discrete points across each scan line.

scan line, is called the **horizontal retrace** of the electron beam. And at the end of each frame (displayed in 1/80th to 1/60th of a second), the electron beam returns (**vertical retrace**) to the top left corner of the screen to begin the next frame.

On some raster-scan systems (and in TV sets), each frame is displayed in two passes using an *interlaced* refresh procedure. In the first pass, the beam sweeps across every other scan line from top to bottom. Then after the vertical retrace, the beam sweeps out the remaining scan lines (Fig. 2-8). Interlacing of the scan lines in this way allows us to see the entire screen displayed in one-half the time it would have taken to sweep across all the lines at once from top to bottom. Interlacing is primarily used with slower refreshing rates. On an older, 30 frame-per-second, noninterlaced display, for instance, some flicker is noticeable. But with interlacing, each of the two passes can be accomplished in 1/60th of a second, which brings the refresh rate nearer to 60 frames per second. This is an effective technique for avoiding flicker, providing that adjacent scan lines contain similar display information.

Random-Scan Displays

When operated as a **random-scan** display unit, a CRT has the electron beam directed only to the parts of the screen where a picture is to be drawn. Random-scan monitors draw a picture one line at a time and for this reason are also referred to as **vector** displays (or **stroke-writing** or **calligraphic** displays). The component lines of a picture can be drawn and refreshed by a random-scan sys-

41

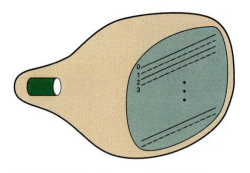

Figure 2-8
Interlacing scan lines on a raster-
scan display. First, all points on the
even-numbered (solid) scan lines
are displayed; then all points along
the odd-numbered (dashed) lines
are displayed.

tem in any specified order (Fig. 2-9). A pen plotter operates in a similar way and is an example of a random-scan, hard-copy device.

Refresh rate on a random-scan system depends on the number of lines to be displayed. Picture definition is now stored as a set of line-drawing commands in an area of memory referred to as the **refresh display file**. Sometimes the refresh display file is called the **display list**, **display program**, or simply the **refresh buffer**. To display a specified picture, the system cycles through the set of commands in the display file, drawing each component line in turn. After all line-drawing commands have been processed, the system cycles back to the first line command in the list. Random-scan displays are designed to draw all the component lines of a picture 30 to 60 times each second. High-quality vector systems are capable of handling approximately 100,000 "short" lines at this refresh rate. When a small set of lines is to be displayed, each refresh cycle is delayed to avoid refresh rates greater than 60 frames per second. Otherwise, faster refreshing of the set of lines could burn out the phosphor.

Random-scan systems are designed for line-drawing applications and cannot display realistic shaded scenes. Since picture definition is stored as a set of line-drawing instructions and not as a set of intensity values for all screen points, vector displays generally have higher resolution than raster systems. Also, vector displays produce smooth line drawings because the CRT beam directly follows the line path. A raster system, in contrast, produces jagged lines that are plotted as discrete point sets.

Color CRT Monitors

A CRT monitor displays color pictures by using a combination of phosphors that emit different-colored light. By combining the emitted light from the different phosphors, a range of colors can be generated. The two basic techniques for producing color displays with a CRT are the beam-penetration method and the shadow-mask method.

The **beam-penetration** method for displaying color pictures has been used with random-scan monitors. Two layers of phosphor, usually red and green, are

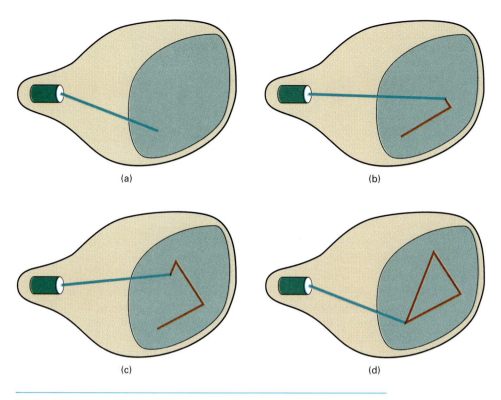

(a)　　　　　　　　　　　　　(b)

(c)　　　　　　　　　　　　　(d)

Figure 2-9
A random-scan system draws the component lines of an object in any
order specified.

coated onto the inside of the CRT screen, and the displayed color depends on
how far the electron beam penetrates into the phosphor layers. A beam of slow
electrons excites only the outer red layer. A beam of very fast electrons penetrates
through the red layer and excites the inner green layer. At intermediate beam
speeds, combinations of red and green light are emitted to show two additional
colors, orange and yellow. The speed of the electrons, and hence the screen color
at any point, is controlled by the beam-acceleration voltage. Beam penetration
has been an inexpensive way to produce color in random-scan monitors, but only
four colors are possible, and the quality of pictures is not as good as with other
methods.

　　Shadow-mask methods are commonly used in raster-scan systems (including color TV) because they produce a much wider range of colors than the beam-
penetration method. A shadow-mask CRT has three phosphor color dots at each
pixel position. One phosphor dot emits a red light, another emits a green light,
and the third emits a blue light. This type of CRT has three electron guns, one for
each color dot, and a shadow-mask grid just behind the phosphor-coated screen.
Figure 2-10 illustrates the *delta-delta* shadow-mask method, commonly used in
color CRT systems. The three electron beams are deflected and focused as a
group onto the shadow mask, which contains a series of holes aligned with the
phosphor-dot patterns. When the three beams pass through a hole in the shadow
mask, they activate a dot triangle, which appears as a small color spot on the
screen. The phosphor dots in the triangles are arranged so that each electron
beam can activate only its corresponding color dot when it passes through the

43

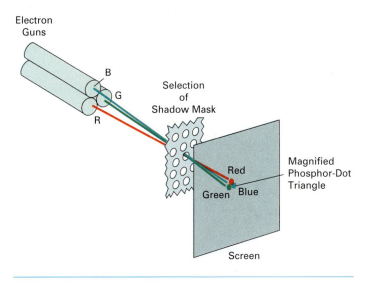

Electron Guns

B
G
R

Selection of Shadow Mask

Magnified Phosphor-Dot Triangle

Red
Green Blue

Screen

Figure 2-10
Operation of a delta-delta, shadow-mask CRT. Three electron guns, aligned with the triangular color-dot patterns on the screen, are directed to each dot triangle by a shadow mask.

shadow mask. Another configuration for the three electron guns is an *in-line* arrangement in which the three electron guns, and the corresponding red–green–blue color dots on the screen, are aligned along one scan line instead of in a triangular pattern. This in-line arrangement of electron guns is easier to keep in alignment and is commonly used in high-resolution color CRTs.

We obtain color variations in a shadow-mask CRT by varying the intensity levels of the three electron beams. By turning off the red and green guns, we get only the color coming from the blue phosphor. Other combinations of beam intensities produce a small light spot for each pixel position, since our eyes tend to merge the three colors into one composite. The color we see depends on the amount of excitation of the red, green, and blue phosphors. A white (or gray) area is the result of activating all three dots with equal intensity. Yellow is produced with the green and red dots only, magenta is produced with the blue and red dots, and cyan shows up when blue and green are activated equally. In some low-cost systems, the electron beam can only be set to on or off, limiting displays to eight colors. More sophisticated systems can set intermediate intensity levels for the electron beams, allowing several million different colors to be generated.

Color graphics systems can be designed to be used with several types of CRT display devices. Some inexpensive home-computer systems and video games are designed for use with a color TV set and an RF (radio-frequency) modulator. The purpose of the RF modulator is to simulate the signal from a broadcast TV station. This means that the color and intensity information of the picture must be combined and superimposed on the broadcast-frequency carrier signal that the TV needs to have as input. Then the circuitry in the TV takes this signal from the RF modulator, extracts the picture information, and paints it on the screen. As we might expect, this extra handling of the picture information by the RF modulator and TV circuitry decreases the quality of displayed images.

Composite monitors are adaptations of TV sets that allow bypass of the broadcast circuitry. These display devices still require that the picture information be combined, but no carrier signal is needed. Picture information is combined into a composite signal and then separated by the monitor, so the resulting picture quality is still not the best attainable.

Color CRTs in graphics systems are designed as **RGB monitors**. These monitors use shadow-mask methods and take the intensity level for each electron gun (red, green, and blue) directly from the computer system without any intermediate processing. High-quality raster-graphics systems have 24 bits per pixel in the frame buffer, allowing 256 voltage settings for each electron gun and nearly 17 million color choices for each pixel. An RGB color system with 24 bits of storage per pixel is generally referred to as a **full-color system** or a **true-color system**.

Direct-View Storage Tubes

An alternative method for maintaining a screen image is to store the picture information inside the CRT instead of refreshing the screen. A **direct-view storage tube** (**DVST**) stores the picture information as a charge distribution just behind the phosphor-coated screen. Two electron guns are used in a DVST. One, the primary gun, is used to store the picture pattern; the second, the flood gun, maintains the picture display.

A DVST monitor has both disadvantages and advantages compared to the refresh CRT. Because no refreshing is needed, very complex pictures can be displayed at very high resolutions without flicker. Disadvantages of DVST systems are that they ordinarily do not display color and that selected parts of a picture cannot be erased. To eliminate a picture section, the entire screen must be erased and the modified picture redrawn. The erasing and redrawing process can take several seconds for a complex picture. For these reasons, storage displays have been largely replaced by raster systems.

Flat-Panel Displays

Although most graphics monitors are still constructed with CRTs, other technologies are emerging that may soon replace CRT monitors. The term **flat-panel display** refers to a class of video devices that have reduced volume, weight, and power requirements compared to a CRT. A significant feature of flat-panel displays is that they are thinner than CRTs, and we can hang them on walls or wear them on our wrists. Since we can even write on some flat-panel displays, they will soon be available as pocket notepads. Current uses for flat-panel displays include small TV monitors, calculators, pocket video games, laptop computers, armrest viewing of movies on airlines, as advertisement boards in elevators, and as graphics displays in applications requiring rugged, portable monitors.

We can separate flat-panel displays into two categories: **emissive displays** and **nonemissive displays**. The emissive displays (or **emitters**) are devices that convert electrical energy into light. Plasma panels, thin-film electroluminescent displays, and light-emitting diodes are examples of emissive displays. Flat CRTs have also been devised, in which electron beams are accelerated parallel to the screen, then deflected 90° to the screen. But flat CRTs have not proved to be as successful as other emissive devices. Nonemissive displays (or **nonemitters**) use optical effects to convert sunlight or light from some other source into graphics patterns. The most important example of a nonemissive flat-panel display is a liquid-crystal device.

Plasma panels, also called **gas-discharge displays**, are constructed by filling the region between two glass plates with a mixture of gases that usually includes neon. A series of vertical conducting ribbons is placed on one glass panel, and a set of horizontal ribbons is built into the other glass panel (Fig. 2-11). Firing voltages applied to a pair of horizontal and vertical conductors cause the gas at the intersection of the two conductors to break down into a glowing plasma of electrons and ions. Picture definition is stored in a refresh buffer, and the firing voltages are applied to refresh the pixel positions (at the intersections of the conductors) 60 times per second. Alternating-current methods are used to provide faster application of the firing voltages, and thus brighter displays. Separation between pixels is provided by the electric field of the conductors. Figure 2-12 shows a high-definition plasma panel. One disadvantage of plasma panels has been that they were strictly monochromatic devices, but systems have been developed that are now capable of displaying color and grayscale.

Thin-film electroluminescent displays are similar in construction to a plasma panel. The difference is that the region between the glass plates is filled with a phosphor, such as zinc sulfide doped with manganese, instead of a gas (Fig. 2-13). When a sufficiently high voltage is applied to a pair of crossing electrodes, the phosphor becomes a conductor in the area of the intersection of the two electrodes. Electrical energy is then absorbed by the manganese atoms, which then release the energy as a spot of light similar to the glowing plasma effect in a plasma panel. Electroluminescent displays require more power than plasma panels, and good color and gray scale displays are hard to achieve.

A third type of emissive device is the **light-emitting diode** (**LED**). A matrix of diodes is arranged to form the pixel positions in the display, and picture definition is stored in a refresh buffer. As in scan-line refreshing of a CRT, information

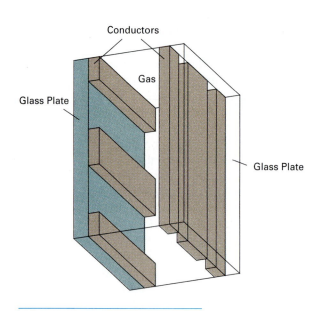

Conductors

Gas

Glass Plate

Glass Plate

Figure 2-11
Basic design of a plasma-panel
display device.

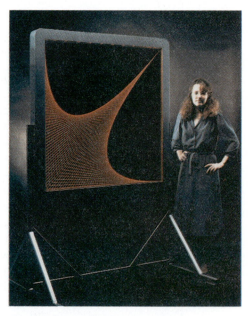

Figure 2-12
A plasma-panel display with a
resolution of 2048 by 2048 and a
screen diagonal of 1.5 meters.
(*Courtesy of Photonics Systems.*)

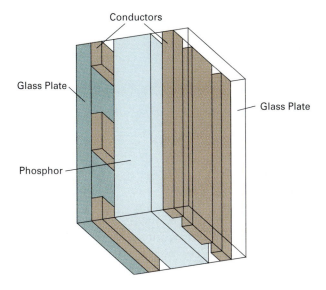

Figure 2-13
Basic design of a thin-film
electroluminescent display device.

is read from the refresh buffer and converted to voltage levels that are applied to
the diodes to produce the light patterns in the display.

Liquid-crystal displays (**LCD**s) are commonly used in small systems, such
as calculators (Fig. 2-14) and portable, laptop computers (Fig. 2-15). These nonemissive devices produce a picture by passing polarized light from the surroundings or from an internal light source through a liquid-crystal material that can be
aligned to either block or transmit the light.

The term *liquid crystal* refers to the fact that these compounds have a crys-
talline arrangement of molecules, yet they flow like a liquid. Flat-panel displays
commonly use nematic (threadlike) liquid-crystal compounds that tend to keep
the long axes of the rod-shaped molecules aligned. A flat-panel display can then
be constructed with a nematic liquid crystal, as demonstrated in Fig. 2-16. Two
glass plates, each containing a light polarizer at right angles to the other plate,
sandwich the liquid-crystal material. Rows of horizontal transparent conductors
are built into one glass plate, and columns of vertical conductors are put into the
other plate. The intersection of two conductors defines a pixel position. Normally, the molecules are aligned as shown in the "on state" of Fig. 2-16. Polarized
light passing through the material is twisted so that it will pass through the opposite polarizer. The light is then reflected back to the viewer. To turn off the
pixel, we apply a voltage to the two intersecting conductors to align the molecules so that the light is not twisted. This type of flat-panel device is referred to as
a **passive-matrix** LCD. Picture definitions are stored in a refresh buffer, and the
screen is refreshed at the rate of 60 frames per second, as in the emissive devices.
Back lighting is also commonly applied using solid-state electronic devices, so
that the system is not completely dependent on outside light sources. Colors can
be displayed by using different materials or dyes and by placing a triad of color
pixels at each screen location. Another method for constructing LCDs is to place
a transistor at each pixel location, using thin-film transistor technology. The tran-
sistors are used to control the voltage at pixel locations and to prevent charge
from gradually leaking out of the liquid-crystal cells. These devices are called
active-matrix displays.

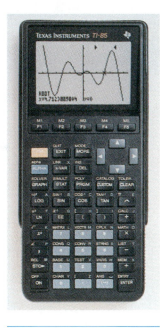

Figure 2-14
A hand calculator with an
LCD screen. (*Courtesy of Texas
Instruments.*)

47

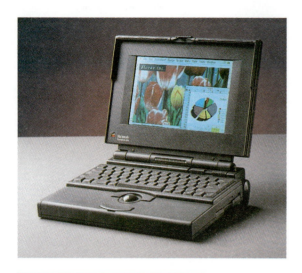

A backlit, passive-matrix, liquid-crystal display in a laptop computer, featuring 256 colors, a screen resolution of 640 by 400, and a screen diagonal of 9 inches.
(*Courtesy of Apple Computer, Inc.*)

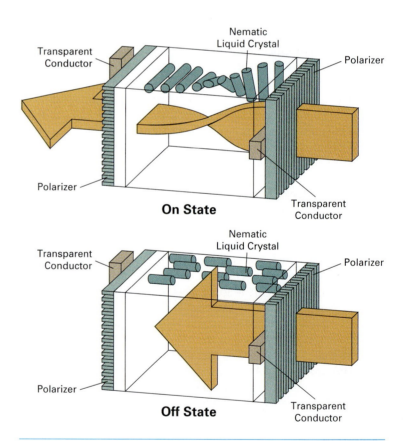

Figure 2-16
The light-twisting, shutter effect used in the design of most liquid-crystal display devices.

Three-Dimensional Viewing Devices

Graphics monitors for the display of three-dimensional scenes have been devised using a technique that reflects a CRT image from a vibrating, flexible mirror. The operation of such a system is demonstrated in Fig. 2-17. As the varifocal mirror vibrates, it changes focal length. These vibrations are synchronized with the display of an object on a CRT so that each point on the object is reflected from the mirror into a spatial position corresponding to the distance of that point from a specified viewing position. This allows us to walk around an object or scene and view it from different sides.

Figure 2-18 shows the Genisco SpaceGraph system, which uses a vibrating mirror to project three-dimensional objects into a 25-cm by 25-cm by 25-cm volume. This system is also capable of displaying two-dimensional cross-sectional "slices" of objects selected at different depths. Such systems have been used in medical applications to analyze data from ultrasonography and CAT scan devices, in geological applications to analyze topological and seismic data, in design applications involving solid objects, and in three-dimensional simulations of systems, such as molecules and terrain.

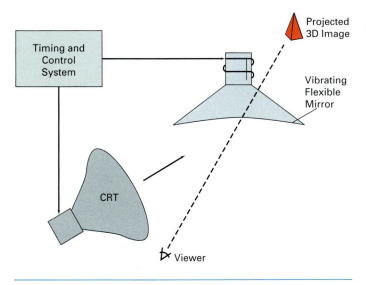

Figure 2-17
Operation of a three-dimensional display system using a vibrating mirror that changes focal length to match the depth of points in a scene.

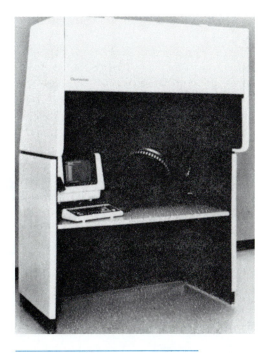

Figure 2-18
The SpaceGraph interactive graphics system displays objects in three dimensions using a vibrating, flexible mirror. (*Courtesy of Genisco Computers Corporation.*)

Stereoscopic and Virtual-Reality Systems

Another technique for representing three-dimensional objects is displaying stereoscopic views. This method does not produce true three-dimensional images, but it does provide a three-dimensional effect by presenting a different view to each eye of an observer so that scenes do appear to have depth (Fig. 2-19).

To obtain a stereoscopic projection, we first need to obtain two views of a scene generated from a viewing direction corresponding to each eye (left and right). We can construct the two views as computer-generated scenes with different viewing positions, or we can use a stereo camera pair to photograph some object or scene. When we simultaneous look at the left view with the left eye and the right view with the right eye, the two views merge into a single image and we perceive a scene with depth. Figure 2-20 shows two views of a computer-generated scene for stereographic projection. To increase viewing comfort, the areas at the left and right edges of this scene that are visible to only one eye have been eliminated.

Figure 2-19
Viewing a stereoscopic projection.
(*Courtesy of StereoGraphics Corporation.*)

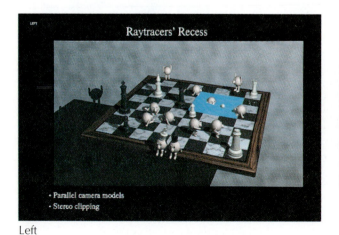

Left

Right

Figure 2-20
A stereoscopic viewing pair. (*Courtesy of Jerry Farm.*)

One way to produce a stereoscopic effect is to display each of the two views with a raster system on alternate refresh cycles. The screen is viewed through glasses, with each lens designed to act as a rapidly alternating shutter that is synchronized to block out one of the views. Figure 2-21 shows a pair of stereoscopic glasses constructed with liquid-crystal shutters and an infrared emitter that synchronizes the glasses with the views on the screen.

Stereoscopic viewing is also a component in **virtual-reality** systems, where users can step into a scene and interact with the environment. A headset (Fig. 2-22) containing an optical system to generate the stereoscopic views is commonly used in conjuction with interactive input devices to locate and manipulate objects in the scene. A sensing system in the headset keeps track of the viewer's position, so that the front and back of objects can be seen as the viewer

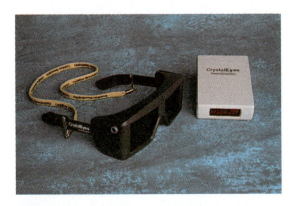

Figure 2-21
Glasses for viewing a
stereoscopic scene and an
 infrared synchronizing emitter.
(*Courtesy of StereoGraphics Corporation.*)

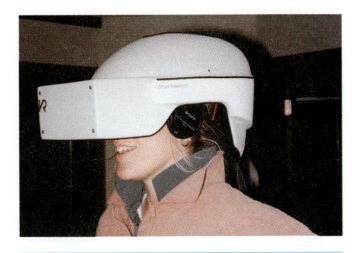

Figure 2-22
A headset used in virtual-reality systems. (*Courtesy of Virtual Research.*)

51

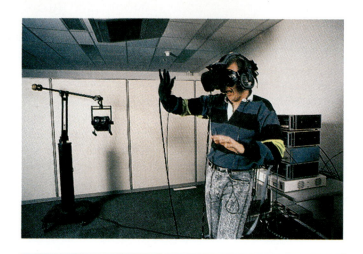

Figure 2-23
Interacting with a virtual-reality environment. (*Courtesy of the National Center for Supercomputing Applications, University of Illinois at Urbana-Champaign.*)

"walks through" and interacts with the display. Figure 2-23 illustrates interaction with a virtual scene, using a headset and a data glove worn on the right hand (Section 2-5).

An interactive virtual-reality environment can also be viewed with stereoscopic glasses and a video monitor, instead of a headset. This provides a means for obtaining a lower-cost virtual-reality system. As an example, Fig. 2-24 shows an ultrasound tracking device with six degrees of freedom. The tracking device is placed on top of the video display and is used to monitor head movements so that the viewing position for a scene can be changed as head position changes.

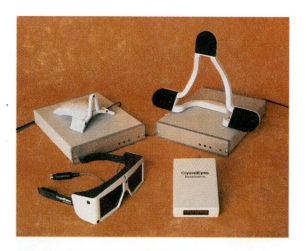

Figure 2-24
An ultrasound tracking device used with stereoscopic glasses to track head position. (*Courtesy of StereoGraphics Corporation.*)

RASTER-SCAN SYSTEMS

Interactive raster graphics systems typically employ several processing units. In addition to the central processing unit, or CPU, a special-purpose processor, called the **video controller** or **display controller**, is used to control the operation of the display device. Organization of a simple raster system is shown in Fig. 2-25. Here, the frame buffer can be anywhere in the system memory, and the video controller accesses the frame buffer to refresh the screen. In addition to the video controller, more sophisticated raster systems employ other processors as co-processors and accelerators to implement various graphics operations.

Video Controller

Figure 2-26 shows a commonly used organization for raster systems. A fixed area of the system memory is reserved for the frame buffer, and the video controller is given direct access to the frame-buffer memory.

Frame-buffer locations, and the corresponding screen positions, are referenced in Cartesian coordinates. For many graphics monitors, the coordinate ori-

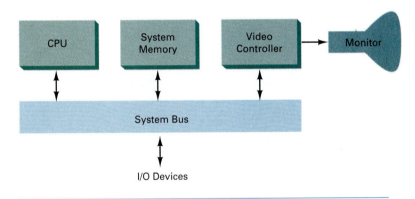

Figure 2-25
Architecture of a simple raster graphics system.

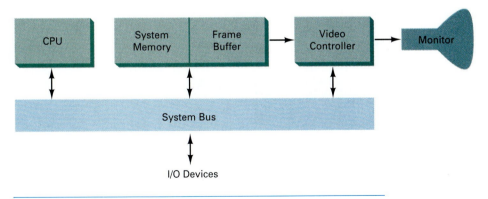

Figure 2-26
Architecture of a raster system with a fixed portion of the system memory reserved for the frame buffer.

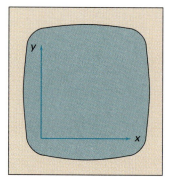

Figure 2-27

The origin of the coordinate system for identifying screen positions is usually specified in the lower-left corner.

gin is defined at the lower left screen corner (Fig. 2-27). The screen surface is then represented as the first quadrant of a two-dimensional system, with positive x values increasing to the right and positive y values increasing from bottom to top. (On some personal computers, the coordinate origin is referenced at the upper left corner of the screen, so the y values are inverted.) Scan lines are then labeled from y_{max} at the top of the screen to 0 at the bottom. Along each scan line, screen pixel positions are labeled from 0 to x_{max}.

In Fig. 2-28, the basic refresh operations of the video controller are diagrammed. Two registers are used to store the coordinates of the screen pixels. Initially, the x register is set to 0 and the y register is set to y_{max}. The value stored in the frame buffer for this pixel position is then retrieved and used to set the intensity of the CRT beam. Then the x register is incremented by 1, and the process repeated for the next pixel on the top scan line. This procedure is repeated for each pixel along the scan line. After the last pixel on the top scan line has been processed, the x register is reset to 0 and the y register is decremented by 1. Pixels along this scan line are then processed in turn, and the procedure is repeated for each successive scan line. After cycling through all pixels along the bottom scan line ($y = 0$), the video controller resets the registers to the first pixel position on the top scan line and the refresh process starts over.

Since the screen must be refreshed at the rate of 60 frames per second, the simple procedure illustrated in Fig. 2-28 cannot be accommodated by typical RAM chips. The cycle time is too slow. To speed up pixel processing, video controllers can retrieve multiple pixel values from the refresh buffer on each pass. The multiple pixel intensities are then stored in a separate register and used to control the CRT beam intensity for a group of adjacent pixels. When that group of pixels has been processed, the next block of pixel values is retrieved from the frame buffer.

A number of other operations can be performed by the video controller, besides the basic refreshing operations. For various applications, the video con-

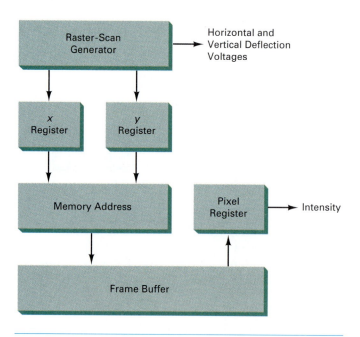

Figure 2-28

Basic video-controller refresh operations.

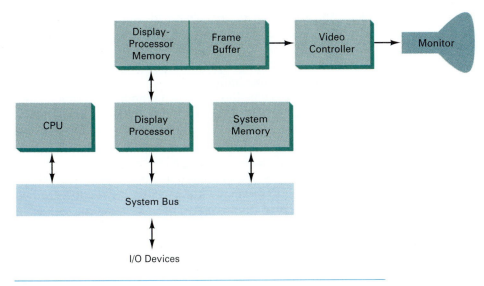

Figure 2-29
Architecture of a raster-graphics system with a display processor.

troller can retrieve pixel intensities from different memory areas on different refresh cycles. In high-quality systems, for example, two frame buffers are often
provided so that one buffer can be used for refreshing while the other is being
filled with intensity values. Then the two buffers can switch roles. This provides
a fast mechanism for generating real-time animations, since different views of
moving objects can be successively loaded into the refresh buffers. Also, some
transformations can be accomplished by the video controller. Areas of the screen
can be enlarged, reduced, or moved from one location to another during the refresh cycles. In addition, the video controller often contains a lookup table, so
that pixel values in the frame buffer are used to access the lookup table instead of
controlling the CRT beam intensity directly. This provides a fast method for
changing screen intensity values, and we discuss lookup tables in more detail in
Chapter 4. Finally, some systems are designed to allow the video controller to
mix the frame-buffer image with an input image from a television camera or
other input device.

Raster-Scan Display Processor

Figure 2-29 shows one way to set up the organization of a raster system containing a separate **display processor**, sometimes referred to as a **graphics controller**
or a **display coprocessor**. The purpose of the display processor is to free the CPU
from the graphics chores. In addition to the system memory, a separate display-
processor memory area can also be provided.

A major task of the display processor is digitizing a picture definition given
in an application program into a set of pixel-intensity values for storage in the
frame buffer. This digitization process is called **scan conversion**. Graphics commands specifying straight lines and other geometric objects are scan converted
into a set of discrete intensity points. Scan converting a straight-line segment, for
example, means that we have to locate the pixel positions closest to the line path
and store the intensity for each position in the frame buffer. Similar methods are
used for scan converting curved lines and polygon outlines. Characters can be
defined with rectangular grids, as in Fig. 2-30, or they can be defined with curved

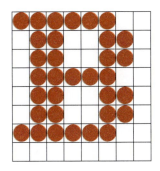

Figure 2-30
A character defined as a
rectangular grid of pixel
positions.

55

Figure 2-31
A character defined as a
curve outline.

outlines, as in Fig. 2-31. The array size for character grids can vary from about 5 by 7 to 9 by 12 or more for higher-quality displays. A character grid is displayed by superimposing the rectangular grid pattern into the frame buffer at a specified coordinate position. With characters that are defined as curve outlines, character shapes are scan converted into the frame buffer.

Display processors are also designed to perform a number of additional operations. These functions include generating various line styles (dashed, dotted, or solid), displaying color areas, and performing certain transformations and manipulations on displayed objects. Also, display processors are typically designed to interface with interactive input devices, such as a mouse.

In an effort to reduce memory requirements in raster systems, methods have been devised for organizing the frame buffer as a linked list and encoding the intensity information. One way to do this is to store each scan line as a set of integer pairs. One number of each pair indicates an intensity value, and the second number specifies the number of adjacent pixels on the scan line that are to have that intensity. This technique, called **run-length encoding,** can result in a considerable saving in storage space if a picture is to be constructed mostly with long runs of a single color each. A similar approach can be taken when pixel intensities change linearly. Another approach is to encode the raster as a set of rectangular areas (**cell encoding**). The disadvantages of encoding runs are that intensity changes are difficult to make and storage requirements actually increase as the length of the runs decreases. In addition, it is difficult for the display controller to process the raster when many short runs are involved.

2-3
RANDOM-SCAN SYSTEMS

The organization of a simple random-scan (vector) system is shown in Fig. 2-32. An application program is input and stored in the system memory along with a graphics package. Graphics commands in the application program are translated by the graphics package into a display file stored in the system memory. This display file is then accessed by the display processor to refresh the screen. The display processor cycles through each command in the display file program once during every refresh cycle. Sometimes the display processor in a random-scan system is referred to as a **display processing unit** or a **graphics controller**.

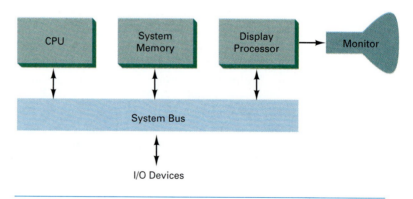

Figure 2-32
Architecture of a simple random-scan system.

Graphics patterns are drawn on a random-scan system by directing the electron beam along the component lines of the picture. Lines are defined by the values for their coordinate endpoints, and these input coordinate values are converted to x and y deflection voltages. A scene is then drawn one line at a time by positioning the beam to fill in the line between specified endpoints.

2-4
GRAPHICS MONITORS AND WORKSTATIONS

Most graphics monitors today operate as raster-scan displays, and here we survey a few of the many graphics hardware configurations available. Graphics systems range from small general-purpose computer systems with graphics capabilities (Fig. 2-33) to sophisticated full-color systems that are designed specifically for graphics applications (Fig. 2-34). A typical screen resolution for personal com-

Figure 2-33
A desktop general-purpose computer system that can be used for graphics applications. (*Courtesy of Apple Computer, Inc.*)

Figure 2-34
Computer graphics workstations with keyboard and mouse input devices. (a) The Iris Indigo. (*Courtesy of Silicon Graphics Corporation.*) (b) SPARCstation 10. (*Courtesy of Sun Microsystems.*)

57

puter systems, such as the Apple Quadra shown in Fig. 2-33, is 640 by 480, although screen resolution and other system capabilities vary depending on the size and cost of the system. Diagonal screen dimensions for general-purpose personal computer systems can range from 12 to 21 inches, and allowable color selections range from 16 to over 32,000. For workstations specifically designed for graphics applications, such as the systems shown in Fig. 2-34, typical screen resolution is 1280 by 1024, with a screen diagonal of 16 inches or more. Graphics workstations can be configured with from 8 to 24 bits per pixel (full-color systems), with higher screen resolutions, faster processors, and other options available in high-end systems.

Figure 2-35 shows a high-definition graphics monitor used in applications such as air traffic control, simulation, medical imaging, and CAD. This system has a diagonal screen size of 27 inches, resolutions ranging from 2048 by 1536 to 2560 by 2048, with refresh rates of 80 Hz or 60 Hz noninterlaced.

A multiscreen system called the MediaWall, shown in Fig. 2-36, provides a large "wall-sized" display area. This system is designed for applications that require large area displays in brightly lighted environments, such as at trade shows, conventions, retail stores, museums, or passenger terminals. MediaWall operates by splitting images into a number of sections and distributing the sections over an array of monitors or projectors using a graphics adapter and satellite control units. An array of up to 5 by 5 monitors, each with a resolution of 640 by 480, can be used in the MediaWall to provide an overall resolution of 3200 by 2400 for either static scenes or animations. Scenes can be displayed behind mullions, as in Fig. 2-36, or the mullions can be eliminated to display a continuous picture with no breaks between the various sections.

Many graphics workstations, such as some of those shown in Fig. 2-37, are configured with two monitors. One monitor can be used to show all features of an object or scene, while the second monitor displays the detail in some part of the picture. Another use for dual-monitor systems is to view a picture on one monitor and display graphics options (menus) for manipulating the picture components on the other monitor.

Figure 2-35
A very high-resolution (2560 by 2048) color monitor. (*Courtesy of BARCO Chromatics.*)

Figure 2-36
The MediaWall: A multiscreen display system. The image displayed on this 3-by-3 array of monitors was created by Deneba Software. (*Courtesy of RGB Spectrum.*)

Figure 2-37
Single- and dual-monitor graphics workstations. (*Courtesy of Intergraph Corporation.*)

Figures 2-38 and 2-39 illustrate examples of interactive graphics workstations containing multiple input and other devices. A typical setup for CAD applications is shown in Fig. 2-38. Various keyboards, button boxes, tablets, and mice are attached to the video monitors for use in the design process. Figure 2-39 shows features of some types of artist's workstations.

Figure 2-38
Multiple workstations for a CAD group. (*Courtesy of Hewlett-Packard Company.*)

Figure 2-39
An artist's workstation, featuring a color raster monitor, keyboard, graphics tablet with hand cursor, and a light table, in addition to data storage and telecommunications devices. (*Courtesy of DICOMED Corporation.*)

2-5
INPUT DEVICES

Various devices are available for data input on graphics workstations. Most systems have a keyboard and one or more additional devices specially designed for interactive input. These include a mouse, trackball, spaceball, joystick, digitizers, dials, and button boxes. Some other input devices used in particular applications are data gloves, touch panels, image scanners, and voice systems.

Keyboards

An alphanumeric keyboard on a graphics system is used primarily as a device for entering text strings. The keyboard is an efficient device for inputting such nongraphic data as picture labels associated with a graphics display. Keyboards can also be provided with features to facilitate entry of screen coordinates, menu selections, or graphics functions.

Cursor-control keys and function keys are common features on general-purpose keyboards. Function keys allow users to enter frequently used operations in a single keystroke, and cursor-control keys can be used to select displayed objects or coordinate positions by positioning the screen cursor. Other types of cursor-positioning devices, such as a trackball or joystick, are included on some keyboards. Additionally, a numeric keypad is often included on the keyboard for fast entry of numeric data. Typical examples of general-purpose keyboards are given in Figs. 2-1, 2-33, and 2-34. Fig. 2-40 shows an ergonomic keyboard design.

For specialized applications, input to a graphics application may come from a set of buttons, dials, or switches that select data values or customized graphics operations. Figure 2-41 gives an example of a button box and a set of input dials. Buttons and switches are often used to input predefined functions, and dials are common devices for entering scalar values. Real numbers within some defined range are selected for input with dial rotations. Potentiometers are used to measure dial rotations, which are then converted to deflection voltages for cursor movement.

Mouse

A **mouse** is small hand-held box used to position the screen cursor. Wheels or rollers on the bottom of the mouse can be used to record the amount and direc-

Figure 2-40
Ergonomically designed keyboard with removable palm rests. The slope of each half of the keyboard can be adjusted separately. (*Courtesy of Apple Computer, Inc.*)

61

tion of movement. Another method for detecting mouse motion is with an optical sensor. For these systems, the mouse is moved over a special mouse pad that has a grid of horizontal and vertical lines. The optical sensor detects movement across the lines in the grid.

Since a mouse can be picked up and put down at another position without change in cursor movement, it is used for making relative changes in the position of the screen cursor. One, two, or three buttons are usually included on the top of the mouse for signaling the execution of some operation, such as recording cursor position or invoking a function. Most general-purpose graphics systems now include a mouse and a keyboard as the major input devices, as in Figs. 2-1, 2-33, and 2-34.

Additional devices can be included in the basic mouse design to increase the number of allowable input parameters. The Z mouse in Fig. 2-42 includes

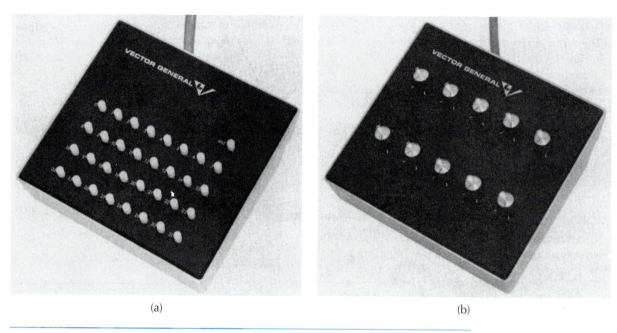

(a)   (b)

Figure 2-41
A button box (a) and a set of input dials (b). (*Courtesy of Vector General.*)

Figure 2-42
The Z mouse features three buttons, a mouse ball underneath, a thumbwheel on the side, and a trackball on top. (*Courtesy of Multipoint Technology Corporation.*)

three buttons, a thumbwheel on the side, a trackball on the top, and a standard mouse ball underneath. This design provides six degrees of freedom to select spatial positions, rotations, and other parameters. With the Z mouse, we can pick up an object, rotate it, and move it in any direction, or we can navigate our viewing position and orientation through a three-dimensional scene. Applications of the Z mouse include virtual reality, CAD, and animation.

Trackball and Spaceball

As the name implies, a **trackball** is a ball that can be rotated with the fingers or palm of the hand, as in Fig. 2-43, to produce screen-cursor movement. Potentiometers, attached to the ball, measure the amount and direction of rotation. Trackballs are often mounted on keyboards (Fig. 2-15) or other devices such as the Z mouse (Fig. 2-42).

While a trackball is a two-dimensional positioning device, a **spaceball** (Fig. 2-45) provides six degrees of freedom. Unlike the trackball, a spaceball does not actually move. Strain gauges measure the amount of pressure applied to the spaceball to provide input for spatial positioning and orientation as the ball is pushed or pulled in various directions. Spaceballs are used for three-dimensional positioning and selection operations in virtual-reality systems, modeling, animation, CAD, and other applications.

Joysticks

A **joystick** consists of a small, vertical lever (called the stick) mounted on a base that is used to steer the screen cursor around. Most joysticks select screen positions with actual stick movement; others respond to pressure on the stick. Figure 2-44 shows a movable joystick. Some joysticks are mounted on a keyboard; others function as stand-alone units.

The distance that the stick is moved in any direction from its center position corresponds to screen-cursor movement in that direction. Potentiometers mounted at the base of the joystick measure the amount of movement, and springs return the stick to the center position when it is released. One or more buttons can be programmed to act as input switches to signal certain actions once a screen position has been selected.

Figure 2-43
A three-button track ball. (*Courtesy of Measurement Systems Inc., Norwalk, Connecticut.*)

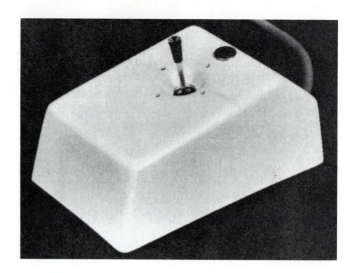

Figure 2-44
A moveable joystick. (*Courtesy of CalComp Group; Sanders Associates, Inc.*)

In another type of movable joystick, the stick is used to activate switches that cause the screen cursor to move at a constant rate in the direction selected. Eight switches, arranged in a circle, are sometimes provided, so that the stick can select any one of eight directions for cursor movement. Pressure-sensitive joysticks, also called isometric joysticks, have a nonmovable stick. Pressure on the stick is measured with strain gauges and converted to movement of the cursor in the direction specified.

Data Glove

Figure 2-45 shows a **data glove** that can be used to grasp a "virtual" object. The glove is constructed with a series of sensors that detect hand and finger motions. Electromagnetic coupling between transmitting antennas and receiving antennas is used to provide information about the position and orientation of the hand. The transmitting and receiving antennas can each be structured as a set of three mutually perpendicular coils, forming a three-dimensional Cartesian coordinate system. Input from the glove can be used to position or manipulate objects in a virtual scene. A two-dimensional projection of the scene can be viewed on a video monitor, or a three-dimensional projection can be viewed with a headset.

Digitizers

A common device for drawing, painting, or interactively selecting coordinate positions on an object is a **digitizer**. These devices can be used to input coordinate values in either a two-dimensional or a three-dimensional space. Typically, a digitizer is used to scan over a drawing or object and to input a set of discrete coordinate positions, which can be joined with straight-line segments to approximate the curve or surface shapes.

One type of digitizer is the **graphics tablet** (also referred to as a data tablet), which is used to input two-dimensional coordinates by activating a hand cursor or stylus at selected positions on a flat surface. A hand cursor contains cross hairs for sighting positions, while a stylus is a pencil-shaped device that is pointed at

Figure 2-45
A virtual-reality scene, displayed
on a two-dimensional video
monitor, with input from a data
glove and a spaceball. (*Courtesy of The
Computer Graphics Center, Darmstadt,
Germany.*)

positions on the tablet. Figures 2-46 and 2-47 show examples of desktop and
floor-model tablets, using hand cursors that are available with 2, 4, or 16 buttons.
Examples of stylus input with a tablet are shown in Figs. 2-48 and 2-49. The
artist's digitizing system in Fig. 2-49 uses electromagnetic resonance to detect the
three-dimensional position of the stylus. This allows an artist to produce different
brush strokes with different pressures on the tablet surface. Tablet size varies
from 12 by 12 inches for desktop models to 44 by 60 inches or larger for floor
models. Graphics tablets provide a highly accurate method for selecting coordinate positions, with an accuracy that varies from about 0.2 mm on desktop models to about 0.05 mm or less on larger models.

Many graphics tablets are constructed with a rectangular grid of wires em-
bedded in the tablet surface. Electromagnetic pulses are generated in sequence

Figure 2-46
The SummaSketch III desktop tablet with a 16-button
hand cursor. (*Courtesy of Summagraphics Corporation.*)

Figure 2-47
The Microgrid III tablet with a 16-
button hand cursor, designed for
digitizing larger drawings. (*Courtesy
of Summagraphics Corporation.*)

along the wires, and an electric signal is induced in a wire coil in an activated stylus or hand cursor to record a tablet position. Depending on the technology, either signal strength, coded pulses, or phase shifts can be used to determine the position on the tablet.

Acoustic (or sonic) tablets use sound waves to detect a stylus position. Either strip microphones or point microphones can be used to detect the sound emitted by an electrical spark from a stylus tip. The position of the stylus is calcu-

Figure 2-48
The NotePad desktop tablet
with stylus. (*Courtesy of
CalComp Digitizer Division,
a part of CalComp, Inc.*)

Figure 2-49
An artist's digitizer system, with a
pressure-sensitive, cordless stylus.
(*Courtesy of Wacom Technology
Corporation.*)

66

lated by timing the arrival of the generated sound at the different microphone positions. An advantage of two-dimensional accoustic tablets is that the microphones can be placed on any surface to form the "tablet" work area. This can be convenient for various applications, such as digitizing drawings in a book.

Three-dimensional digitizers use sonic or electromagnetic transmissions to record positions. One electromagnetic transmission method is similar to that used in the data glove: A coupling between the transmitter and receiver is used to compute the location of a stylus as it moves over the surface of an object. Figure 2-50 shows a three-dimensional digitizer designed for Apple Macintosh computers. As the points are selected on a nonmetallic object, a wireframe outline of the surface is displayed on the computer screen. Once the surface outline is constructed, it can be shaded with lighting effects to produce a realistic display of the object. Resolution of this system is from 0.8 mm to 0.08 mm, depending on the model.

Image Scanners

Drawings, graphs, color and black-and-white photos, or text can be stored for computer processing with an **image scanner** by passing an optical scanning mechanism over the information to be stored. The gradations of gray scale or color are then recorded and stored in an array. Once we have the internal representation of a picture, we can apply transformations to rotate, scale, or crop the picture to a particular screen area. We can also apply various image-processing methods to modify the array representation of the picture. For scanned text input, various editing operations can be performed on the stored documents. Some scanners are able to scan either graphical representations or text, and they come in a variety of sizes and capabilities. A small hand-model scanner is shown in Fig. 2-51, while Figs 2-52 and 2-53 show larger models.

Figure 2-50
A three-dimensional digitizing system for use with Apple Macintosh computers. (*Courtesy of Mira Imaging.*)

Figure 2-51
A hand-held scanner that can be used to input either text or graphics images. (*Courtesy of Thunderware, Inc.*)

Figure 2-52
Desktop full-color scanners: (a) Flatbed scanner with a resolution of 600 dots per inch. (*Courtesy of Sharp Electronics Corporation.*) (b) Drum scanner with a selectable resolution from 50 to 4000 dots per inch. (*Courtesy of Howtek, Inc.*)

Touch Panels

As the name implies, **touch panels** allow displayed objects or screen positions to be selected with the touch of a finger. A typical application of touch panels is for the selection of processing options that are represented with graphical icons. Some systems, such as the plasma panels shown in Fig. 2-54, are designed with touch screens. Other systems can be adapted for touch input by fitting a transparent device with a touch-sensing mechanism over the video monitor screen. Touch input can be recorded using optical, electrical, or acoustical methods.

Optical touch panels employ a line of infrared light-emitting diodes (LEDs) along one vertical edge and along one horizontal edge of the frame. The opposite vertical and horizontal edges contain light detectors. These detectors are used to record which beams are interrupted when the panel is touched. The two crossing

Figure 2-53
A large floor-model scanner used to
scan architectural and engineering
drawings up to 40 inches wide and
100 feet long. (*Courtesy of
Summagraphics Corporation.*)

beams that are interrupted identify the horizontal and vertical coordinates of the
screen position selected. Positions can be selected with an accuracy of about 1/4
inch. With closely spaced LEDs, it is possible to break two horizontal or two vertical beams simultaneously. In this case, an average position between the two interrupted beams is recorded. The LEDs operate at infrared frequencies, so that
the light is not visible to a user. Figure 2-55 illustrates the arrangement of LEDs in
an optical touch panel that is designed to match the color and contours of the
system to which it is to be fitted.

An electrical touch panel is constructed with two transparent plates separated by a small distance. One of the plates is coated with a conducting material,
and the other plate is coated with a resistive material. When the outer plate is
touched, it is forced into contact with the inner plate. This contact creates a voltage drop across the resistive plate that is converted to the coordinate values of
the selected screen position.

In acoustical touch panels, high-frequency sound waves are generated in
the horizontal and vertical directions across a glass plate. Touching the screen
causes part of each wave to be reflected from the finger to the emitters. The screen
position at the point of contact is calculated from a measurement of the time interval between the transmission of each wave and its reflection to the emitter.

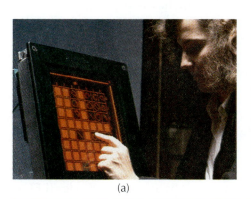
(a)

(b)

Figure 2-54
Plasma panels with touch screens. (*Courtesy of Photonics Systems.*)

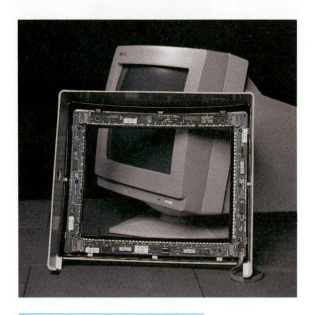

Figure 2-55
An optical touch panel, showing
the arrangement of infrared LED
units and detectors around the
edges of the frame. (*Courtesy of Carroll
Touch, Inc.*)

Light Pens

Figure 2-56 shows the design of one type of **light pen**. Such pencil-shaped devices are used to select screen positions by detecting the light coming from points on the CRT screen. They are sensitive to the short burst of light emitted from the phosphor coating at the instant the electron beam strikes a particular point. Other light sources, such as the background light in the room, are usually not detected by a light pen. An activated light pen, pointed at a spot on the screen as the electron beam lights up that spot, generates an electrical pulse that causes the coordinate position of the electron beam to be recorded. As with cursor-positioning devices, recorded light-pen coordinates can be used to position an object or to select a processing option.

Although light pens are still with us, they are not as popular as they once were since they have several disadvantages compared to other input devices that have been developed. For one, when a light pen is pointed at the screen, part of the screen image is obscured by the hand and pen. And prolonged use of the light pen can cause arm fatigue. Also, light pens require special implementations for some applications because they cannot detect positions within black areas. To be able to select positions in any screen area with a light pen, we must have some nonzero intensity assigned to each screen pixel. In addition, light pens sometimes give false readings due to background lighting in a room.

Voice Systems

Speech recognizers are used in some graphics workstations as input devices to accept voice commands. The **voice-system** input can be used to initiate graphics

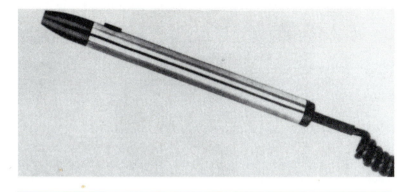

Figure 2-56
A light pen activated with a button switch. (*Courtesy of Interactive Computer Products.*)

operations or to enter data. These systems operate by matching an input against a predefined dictionary of words and phrases.

A dictionary is set up for a particular operator by having the operator speak the command words to be used into the system. Each word is spoken several times, and the system analyzes the word and establishes a frequency pattern for that word in the dictionary along with the corresponding function to be performed. Later, when a voice command is given, the system searches the dictionary for a frequency-pattern match. Voice input is typically spoken into a microphone mounted on a headset, as in Fig. 2-57. The microphone is designed to minimize input of other background sounds. If a different operator is to use the system, the dictionary must be reestablished with that operator's voice patterns. Voice systems have some advantage over other input devices, since the attention of the operator does not have to be switched from one device to another to enter a command.

Figure 2-57
A speech-recognition system. (*Courtesy of Threshold Technology, Inc.*)

2-6

HARD-COPY DEVICES

We can obtain hard-copy output for our images in several formats. For presentations or archiving, we can send image files to devices or service bureaus that will produce 35-mm slides or overhead transparencies. To put images on film, we can simply photograph a scene displayed on a video monitor. And we can put our pictures on paper by directing graphics output to a printer or plotter.

The quality of the pictures obtained from a device depends on dot size and the number of dots per inch, or lines per inch, that can be displayed. To produce smooth characters in printed text strings, higher-quality printers shift dot positions so that adjacent dots overlap.

Printers produce output by either impact or nonimpact methods. *Impact* printers press formed character faces against an inked ribbon onto the paper. A line printer is an example of an impact device, with the typefaces mounted on bands, chains, drums, or wheels. *Nonimpact* printers and plotters use laser techniques, ink-jet sprays, xerographic processes (as used in photocopying machines), electrostatic methods, and electrothermal methods to get images onto paper.

Character impact printers often have a *dot-matrix* print head containing a rectangular array of protruding wire pins, with the number of pins depending on the quality of the printer. Individual characters or graphics patterns are obtained by retracting certain pins so that the remaining pins form the pattern to be printed. Figure 2-58 shows a picture printed on a dot-matrix printer.

In a *laser* device, a laser beam creates a charge distribution on a rotating drum coated with a photoelectric material, such as selenium. Toner is applied to the drum and then transferred to paper. Figure 2-59 shows examples of desktop laser printers with a resolution of 360 dots per inch.

Ink-jet methods produce output by squirting ink in horizontal rows across a roll of paper wrapped on a drum. The electrically charged ink stream is deflected by an electric field to produce dot-matrix patterns. A desktop ink-jet plotter with

Figure 2-58
A picture generated on a dot-matrix printer showing how the density of the dot patterns can be varied to produce light and dark areas. (*Courtesy of Apple Computer, Inc.*)

Figure 2-59
Small-footprint laser printers.
(*Courtesy of Texas Instruments.*)

a resolution of 360 dots per inch is shown in Fig. 2-60, and examples of larger high-resolution ink-jet printer/plotters are shown in Fig. 2-61.

An *electrostatic* device places a negative charge on the paper, one complete row at a time along the length of the paper. Then the paper is exposed to a toner. The toner is positively charged and so is attracted to the negatively charged areas, where it adheres to produce the specified output. A color electrostatic printer/plotter is shown in Fig. 2-62. *Electrothermal* methods use heat in a dot-matrix print head to output patterns on heat-sensitive paper.

We can get limited color output on an impact printer by using different-colored ribbons. Nonimpact devices use various techniques to combine three color pigments (cyan, magenta, and yellow) to produce a range of color patterns. Laser and xerographic devices deposit the three pigments on separate passes; ink-jet methods shoot the three colors simultaneously on a single pass along each print line on the paper.

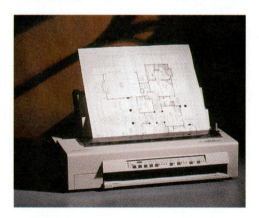

Figure 2-60
A 360-dot-per-inch desktop ink-jet plotter. (*Courtesy of Summagraphics Corporation.*)

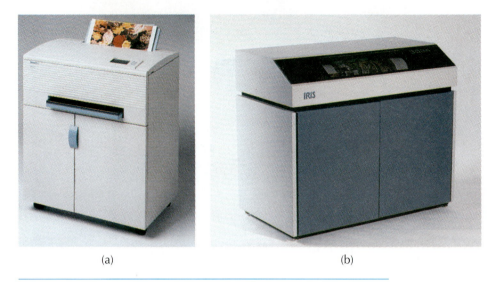

(a)   (b)

Figure 2-61
Floor-model, ink-jet color printers that use variable dot size to achieve
an equivalent resolution of 1500 to 1800 dots per inch. (*Courtesy of IRIS
Graphics Inc., Bedford, Massachusetts.*)

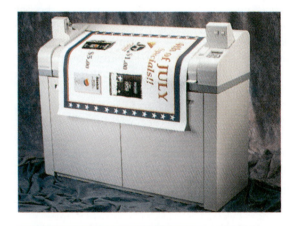

Figure 2-62
An electrostatic printer that can
display 400 dots per inch. (*Courtesy of
CalComp Digitizer Division, a part of
CalComp, Inc.*)

Drafting layouts and other drawings are typically generated with ink-jet or
pen plotters. A pen plotter has one or more pens mounted on a carriage, or cross-
bar, that spans a sheet of paper. Pens with varying colors and widths are used to
produce a variety of shadings and line styles. Wet-ink, ball-point, and felt-tip
pens are all possible choices for use with a pen plotter. Plotter paper can lie flat or
be rolled onto a drum or belt. Crossbars can be either moveable or stationary,
while the pen moves back and forth along the bar. Either clamps, a vacuum, or
an electrostatic charge hold the paper in position. An example of a table-top
flatbed pen plotter is given in Figure 2-63, and a larger, rollfeed pen plotter is
shown in Fig. 2-64.

Figure 2-63
A desktop pen plotter with a
resolution of 0.025 mm. (*Courtesy of
Summagraphics Corporation.*)

Figure 2-64
A large, rollfeed pen plotter with
automatic multicolor 8-pen changer
and a resolution of 0.0127 mm.
(*Courtesy of Summagraphics Corporation.*)

2-7

GRAPHICS SOFTWARE

There are two general classifications for graphics software: general programming
packages and special-purpose applications packages. A general graphics programming package provides an extensive set of graphics functions that can be

used in a high-level programming language, such as C or FORTRAN. An example of a general graphics programming package is the GL (Graphics Library) system on Silicon Graphics equipment. Basic functions in a general package include those for generating picture components (straight lines, polygons, circles, and other figures), setting color and intensity values, selecting views, and applying transformations. By contrast, application graphics packages are designed for nonprogrammers, so that users can generate displays without worrying about how graphics operations work. The interface to the graphics routines in such packages allows users to communicate with the programs in their own terms. Examples of such applications packages are the artist's painting programs and various business, medical, and CAD systems.

Coordinate Representations

With few exceptions, general graphics packages are designed to be used with Cartesian coordinate specifications. If coordinate values for a picture are specified in some other reference frame (spherical, hyberbolic, etc.), they must be converted to Cartesian coordinates before they can be input to the graphics package. Special-purpose packages may allow use of other coordinate frames that are appropriate to the application. In general, several different Cartesian reference frames are used to construct and display a scene. We can construct the shape of individual objects, such as trees or furniture, in a scene within separate coordinate reference frames called **modeling coordinates**, or sometimes **local coordinates** or **master coordinates**. Once individual object shapes have been specified, we can place the objects into appropriate positions within the scene using a reference frame called **world coordinates**. Finally, the world-coordinate description of the scene is transferred to one or more output-device reference frames for display. These display coordinate systems are referred to as **device coordinates**, or **screen coordinates** in the case of a video monitor. Modeling and world-coordinate definitions allow us to set any convenient floating-point or integer dimensions without being hampered by the constraints of a particular output device. For some scenes, we might want to specify object dimensions in fractions of a foot, while for other applications we might want to use millimeters, kilometers, or light-years.

Generally, a graphics system first converts world-coordinate positions to **normalized device coordinates**, in the range from 0 to 1, before final conversion to specific device coordinates. This makes the system independent of the various devices that might be used at a particular workstation. Figure 2-65 illustrates the sequence of coordinate transformations from modeling coordinates to device coordinates for a two-dimensional application. An initial modeling-coordinate position (x_{mc}, y_{mc}) in this illustration is transferred to a device coordinate position (x_{dc}, y_{dc}) with the sequence:

$$(x_{mc}, y_{mc}) \rightarrow (x_{wc}, y_{wc}) \rightarrow (x_{nc}, y_{nc}) \rightarrow (x_{dc}, y_{dc})$$

The modeling and world-coordinate positions in this transformation can be any floating-point values; normalized coordinates satisfy the inequalities: $0 \leq x_{nc} \leq 1$, $0 \leq y_{nc} \leq 1$; and the device coordinates x_{dc} and y_{dc} are integers within the range $(0, 0)$ to (x_{max}, y_{max}) for a particular output device. To accommodate differences in scales and aspect ratios, normalized coordinates are mapped into a square area of the output device so that proper proportions are maintained.

Graphics Functions

A general-purpose graphics package provides users with a variety of functions for creating and manipulating pictures. These routines can be categorized according to whether they deal with output, input, attributes, transformations, viewing, or general control.

The basic building blocks for pictures are referred to as **output primitives**. They include character strings and geometric entities, such as points, straight lines, curved lines, filled areas (polygons, circles, etc.), and shapes defined with arrays of color points. Routines for generating output primitives provide the basic tools for constructing pictures.

Attributes are the properties of the output primitives; that is, an attribute describes how a particular primitive is to be displayed. They include intensity and color specifications, line styles, text styles, and area-filling patterns. Functions within this category can be used to set attributes for an individual primitive class or for groups of output primitives.

We can change the size, position, or orientation of an object within a scene using **geometric transformations**. Similar **modeling transformations** are used to construct a scene using object descriptions given in modeling coordinates.

Given the primitive and attribute definition of a picture in world coordinates, a graphics package projects a selected view of the picture on an output device. **Viewing transformations** are used to specify the view that is to be presented and the portion of the output display area that is to be used.

Pictures can be subdivided into component parts, called **structures** or **segments** or **objects,** depending on the software package in use. Each structure defines one logical unit of the picture. A scene with several objects could reference each individual object in a separate named structure. Routines for processing

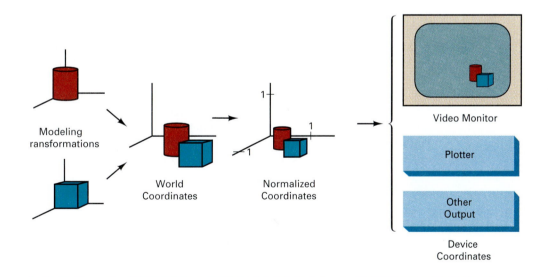

Figure 2-65

The transformation sequence from modeling coordinates to device coordinates for a two-dimensional scene. Object shapes are defined in local modeling-coordinate systems, then positioned within the overall world-coordinate scene. World-coordinate specifications are then transformed into normalized coordinates. At the final step, individual device drivers transfer the normalized-coordinate representation of the scene to the output devices for display.

structures carry out operations such as the creation, modification, and transformation of structures.

Interactive graphics applications use various kinds of input devices, such as a mouse, a tablet, or a joystick. **Input functions** are used to control and process the data flow from these interactive devices.

Finally, a graphics package contains a number of housekeeping tasks, such as clearing a display screen and initializing parameters. We can lump the functions for carrying out these chores under the heading **control operations**.

Software Standards

The primary goal of standardized graphics software is portability. When packages are designed with standard graphics functions, software can be moved easily from one hardware system to another and used in different implementations and applications. Without standards, programs designed for one hardware system often cannot be transferred to another system without extensive rewriting of the programs.

International and national standards planning organizations in many countries have cooperated in an effort to develop a generally accepted standard for computer graphics. After considerable effort, this work on standards led to the development of the **Graphical Kernel System (GKS)**. This system was adopted as the first graphics software standard by the International Standards Organization (ISO) and by various national standards organizations, including the American National Standards Institute (ANSI). Although GKS was originally designed as a two-dimensional graphics package, a three-dimensional GKS extension was subsequently developed. The second software standard to be developed and approved by the standards orgainzations was **PHIGS (Programmer's Hierarchical Interactive Graphics Standard)**, which is an extension of GKS. Increased capabilities for object modeling, color specifications, surface rendering, and picture manipulations are provided in PHIGS. Subsequently, an extension of PHIGS, called PHIGS+, was developed to provide three-dimensional surface-shading capabilities not available in PHIGS.

Standard graphics functions are defined as a set of specifications that is independent of any programming language. A **language binding** is then defined for a particular high-level programming language. This binding gives the syntax for accessing the various standard graphics functions from this language. For example, the general form of the PHIGS (and GKS) function for specifying a sequence of $n-1$ connected two-dimensional straight line segments is

```
polyline(n, x, y)
```

In FORTRAN, this procedure is implemented as a subroutine with the name *GPL*. A graphics programmer, using FORTRAN, would invoke this procedure with the subroutine call statement CALL GPL(N, X, Y), where X and Y are one-dimensional arrays of coordinate values for the line endpoints. In C, the procedure would be invoked with ppolyline(n, pts), where pts is the list of coordinate endpoint positions. Each language binding is defined to make best use of the corresponding language capabilities and to handle various syntax issues, such as data types, parameter passing, and errors.

In the following chapters, we use the standard functions defined in PHIGS as a framework for discussing basic graphics concepts and the design and application of graphics packages. Example programs are presented in Pascal to illustrate the algorithms for implementation of the graphics functions and to illustrate also some applications of the functions. Descriptive names for functions, based on the PHIGS definitions, are used whenever a graphics function is referenced in a program.

Although PHIGS presents a specification for basic graphics functions, it does not provide a standard methodology for a graphics interface to output devices. Nor does it specify methods for storing and transmitting pictures. Separate standards have been developed for these areas. Standardization for device interface methods is given in the **Computer Graphics Interface (CGI)** system. And the **Computer Graphics Metafile (CGM)** system specifies standards for archiving and transporting pictures.

PHIGS Workstations

Generally, the term *workstation* refers to a computer system with a combination of input and output devices that is designed for a single user. In PHIGS and GKS, however, the term **workstation** is used to identify various combinations of graphics hardware and software. A PHIGS workstation can be a single output device, a single input device, a combination of input and output devices, a file, or even a window displayed on a video monitor.

To define and use various "workstations" within an applications program, we need to specify a *workstation identifier* and the workstation type. The following statements give the general structure of a PHIGS program:

```
openPhigs (errorFile, memorySize)
openWorkstation (ws, connection, type)
    { create and display picture}
closeWorkstation (ws)
closePhigs
```

where parameter `errorFile` is to contain any error messages that are generated, and parameter `memorySize` specifies the size of an internal storage area. The workstation identifier (an integer) is given in parameter `ws`, and parameter `connection` states the access mechanism for the workstation. Parameter `type` specifies the particular category for the workstation, such as an *input* device, an *output* device, a combination *outin* device, or an input or output metafile.

Any number of workstations can be open in a particular application, with input coming from the various open input devices and output directed to all the open output devices. We discuss input and output methods in applications programs in Chapter 8, after we have explored the basic procedures for creating and manipulating pictures.

SUMMARY

In this chapter, we have surveyed the major hardware and software features of computer graphics systems. Hardware components include video monitors, hard-copy devices, keyboards, and other devices for graphics input or output. Graphics software includes special applications packages and general programming packages.

The predominant graphics display device is the raster refresh monitor, based on television technology. A raster system uses a frame buffer to store intensity information for each screen position (pixel). Pictures are then painted on the screen by retrieving this information from the frame buffer as the electron beam in the CRT sweeps across each scan line, from top to bottom. Older vector displays construct pictures by drawing lines between specified line endpoints. Picture information is then stored as a set of line-drawing instructions.

Many other video display devices are available. In particular, flat-panel display technology is developing at a rapid rate, and these devices may largely replace raster displays in the near future. At present, flat-panel displays are commonly used in small systems and in special-purpose systems. Flat-panel displays include plasma panels and liquid-crystal devices. Although vector monitors can be used to display high-quality line drawings, improvements in raster display technology have caused vector monitors to be largely replaced with raster systems.

Other display technologies include three-dimensional and stereoscopic viewing systems. Virtual-reality systems can include either a stereoscopic headset or a standard video monitor.

For graphical input, we have a range of devices to choose from. Keyboards, button boxes, and dials are used to input text, data values, or programming options. The most popular "pointing" device is the mouse, but trackballs, spaceballs, joysticks, cursor-control keys, and thumbwheels are also used to position the screen cursor. In virtual-reality environments, data gloves are commonly used. Other input devices include image scanners, digitizers, touch panels, light pens, and voice systems.

Hard-copy devices for graphics workstations include standard printers and plotters, in addition to devices for producing slides, transparencies, and film output. Printing methods include dot matrix, laser, ink jet, electrostatic, and electrothermal. Plotter methods include pen plotting and combination printer-plotter devices.

Graphics software can be roughly classified as applications packages or programming packages. Applications graphics software include CAD packages, drawing and painting programs, graphing packages, and visualization programs. Common graphics programming packages include PHIGS, PHIGS+, GKS, 3D GKS, and GL. Software standards, such as PHIGS, GKS, CGI, and CGM, are evolving and are becoming widely available on a variety of machines.

Normally, graphics packages require coordinate specifications to be given with respect to Cartesian reference frames. Each object for a scene can be defined in a separate modeling Cartesian coordinate system, which is then mapped to world coordinates to construct the scene. From world coordinates, objects are transferred to normalized device coordinates, then to the final display device coordinates. The transformations from modeling coordinates to normalized device coordinates are independent of particular devices that might be used in an application. Device drivers are then used to convert normalized coordinates to integer device coordinates.

Functions in graphics programming packages can be divided into the following categories: output primitives, attributes, geometric and modeling transformations, viewing transformations, structure operations, input functions, and control operations.

Some graphics systems, such as PHIGS and GKS, use the concept of a "workstation" to specify devices or software that are to be used for input or output in a particular application. A workstation identifier in these systems can refer to a file; a single device, such as a raster monitor; or a combination of devices, such as a monitor, keyboard, and a mouse. Multiple workstations can be open to provide input or to receive output in a graphics application.

REFERENCES

A general treatment of electronic displays, including flat-panel devices, is available in Sherr (1993). Flat-panel devices are discussed in Depp and Howard (1993). Tannas (1985) provides a reference for both flat-panel displays and CRTs. Additional information on raster-graphics architecture can be found in Foley, et al. (1990). Three-dimensional terminals are discussed in Fuchs et al. (1982), Johnson (1982), and Ikedo (1984). Head-mounted displays and virtual-reality environments are discussed in Chung et al. (1989).

For information on PHIGS and PHIGS+, see Hopgood and Duce (1991), Howard et al. (1991), Gaskins (1992), and Blake (1993). Information on the two-dimensional GKS standard and on the evolution of graphics standards is available in Hopgood et al. (1983). An additional reference for GKS is Enderle, Kansy, and Pfaff (1984).

EXERCISES

2-1. List the operating characteristics for the following display technologies: raster refresh systems, vector refresh systems, plasma panels, and LCDs.

2-2. List some applications appropriate for each of the display technologies in Exercise 2-1.

2-3. Determine the resolution (pixels per centimeter) in the x and y directions for the video monitor in use on your system. Determine the aspect ratio, and explain how relative proportions of objects can be maintained on your system.

2-4. Consider three different raster systems with resolutions of 640 by 480, 1280 by 1024, and 2560 by 2048. What size frame buffer (in bytes) is needed for each of these systems to store 12 bits per pixel? How much storage is required for each system if 24 bits per pixel are to be stored?

2-5. Suppose an RGB raster system is to be designed using an 8-inch by 10-inch screen with a resolution of 100 pixels per inch in each direction. If we want to store 6 bits per pixel in the frame buffer, how much storage (in bytes) do we need for the frame buffer?

2-6. How long would it take to load a 640 by 480 frame buffer with 12 bits per pixel, if 10^5 bits can be transferred per second? How long would it take to load a 24-bit per pixel frame buffer with a resolution of 1280 by 1024 using this same transfer rate?

2-7. Suppose we have a computer with 32 bits per word and a transfer rate of 1 mip (one million instructions per second). How long would it take to fill the frame buffer of a 300-dpi (dot per inch) laser printer with a page size of 8 1/2 inches by 11 inches?

2-8. Consider two raster systems with resolutions of 640 by 480 and 1280 by 1024. How many pixels could be accessed per second in each of these systems by a display controller that refreshes the screen at a rate of 60 frames per second? What is the access time per pixel in each system?

2-9. Suppose we have a video monitor with a display area that measures 12 inches across and 9.6 inches high. If the resolution is 1280 by 1024 and the aspect ratio is 1, what is the diameter of each screen point?

2-10. How much time is spent scanning across each row of pixels during screen refresh on a raster system with a resolution of 1280 by 1024 and a refresh rate of 60 frames per second?

2-11. Consider a noninterlaced raster monitor with a resolution of n by m (m scan lines and n pixels per scan line), a refresh rate of r frames per second, a horizontal retrace time of t_{horiz}, and a vertical retrace time of t_{vert}. What is the fraction of the total refresh time per frame spent in retrace of the electron beam?

2-12. What is the fraction of the total refresh time per frame spent in retrace of the electron beam for a noninterlaced raster system with a resolution of 1280 by 1024, a refresh rate of 60 Hz, a horizontal retrace time of 5 microseconds, and a vertical retrace time of 500 microseconds?

2-13. Assuming that a certain full-color (24-bit per pixel) RGB raster system has a 512-by-512 frame buffer, how many distinct color choices (intensity levels) would we have available? How many different colors could we display at any one time?

2-14. Compare the advantages and disadvantages of a three-dimensional monitor using a varifocal mirror with a stereoscopic system.

2-15. List the different input and output components that are typically used with virtual-reality systems. Also explain how users interact with a virtual scene displayed with different output devices, such as two-dimensional and stereoscopic monitors.

2-16. Explain how virtual-reality systems can be used in design applications. What are some other applications for virtual-reality systems?

2-17. List some applications for large-screen displays.

2-18. Explain the differences between a general graphics system designed for a programmer and one designed for a specific application, such as architectural design?

Output Primitives

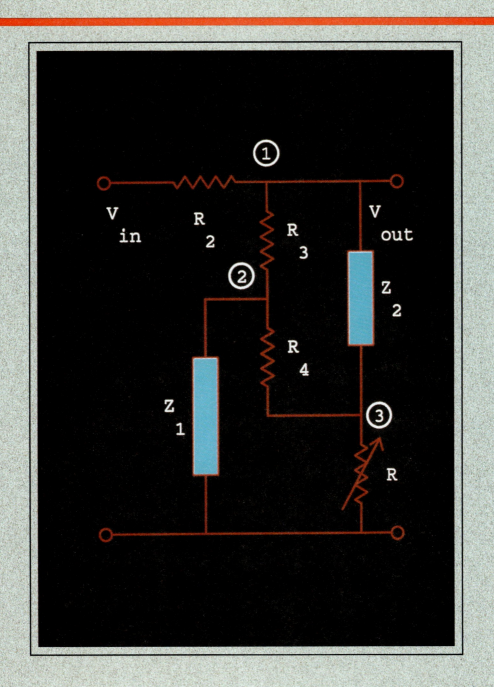

A picture can be described in several ways. Assuming we have a raster display, a picture is completely specified by the set of intensities for the pixel positions in the display. At the other extreme, we can describe a picture as a set of complex objects, such as trees and terrain or furniture and walls, positioned at specified coordinate locations within the scene. Shapes and colors of the objects can be described internally with pixel arrays or with sets of basic geometric structures, such as straight line segments and polygon color areas. The scene is then displayed either by loading the pixel arrays into the frame buffer or by scan converting the basic geometric-structure specifications into pixel patterns. Typically, graphics programming packages provide functions to describe a scene in terms of these basic geometric structures, referred to as **output primitives**, and to group sets of output primitives into more complex structures. Each output primitive is specified with input coordinate data and other information about the way that object is to be displayed. Points and straight line segments are the simplest geometric components of pictures. Additional output primitives that can be used to construct a picture include circles and other conic sections, quadric surfaces, spline curves and surfaces, polygon color areas, and character strings. We begin our discussion of picture-generation procedures by examining device-level algorithms for displaying two-dimensional output primitives, with particular emphasis on scan-conversion methods for raster graphics systems. In this chapter, we also consider how output functions can be provided in graphics packages, and we take a look at the output functions available in the PHIGS language.

3-1
POINTS AND LINES

Point plotting is accomplished by converting a single coordinate position furnished by an application program into appropriate operations for the output device in use. With a CRT monitor, for example, the electron beam is turned on to illuminate the screen phosphor at the selected location. How the electron beam is positioned depends on the display technology. A random-scan (vector) system stores point-plotting instructions in the display list, and coordinate values in these instructions are converted to deflection voltages that position the electron beam at the screen locations to be plotted during each refresh cycle. For a black-and-white raster system, on the other hand, a point is plotted by setting the bit value corresponding to a specified screen position within the frame buffer to 1. Then, as the electron beam sweeps across each horizontal scan line, it emits a burst of electrons (plots a point) whenever a value of 1 is encountered in the frame buffer. With an RGB system, the frame buffer is loaded with the color codes for the intensities that are to be displayed at the screen pixel positions.

Line drawing is accomplished by calculating intermediate positions along the line path between two specified endpoint positions. An output device is then directed to fill in these positions between the endpoints. For analog devices, such as a vector pen plotter or a random-scan display, a straight line can be drawn smoothly from one endpoint to the other. Linearly varying horizontal and vertical deflection voltages are generated that are proportional to the required changes in the x and y directions to produce the smooth line.

Digital devices display a straight line segment by plotting discrete points between the two endpoints. Discrete coordinate positions along the line path are calculated from the equation of the line. For a raster video display, the line color (intensity) is then loaded into the frame buffer at the corresponding pixel coordinates. Reading from the frame buffer, the video controller then "plots" the screen pixels. Screen locations are referenced with integer values, so plotted positions may only approximate actual line positions between two specified endpoints. A computed line position of (10.48, 20.51), for example, would be converted to pixel position (10, 21). This rounding of coordinate values to integers causes lines to be displayed with a stairstep appearance ("the jaggies"), as represented in Fig 3-1. The characteristic stairstep shape of raster lines is particularly noticeable on systems with low resolution, and we can improve their appearance somewhat by displaying them on high-resolution systems. More effective techniques for smoothing raster lines are based on adjusting pixel intensities along the line paths.

For the raster-graphics device-level algorithms discussed in this chapter, object positions are specified directly in integer device coordinates. For the time being, we will assume that pixel positions are referenced according to scan-line number and column number (pixel position across a scan line). This addressing scheme is illustrated in Fig. 3-2. Scan lines are numbered consecutively from 0, starting at the bottom of the screen; and pixel columns are numbered from 0, left to right across each scan line. In Section 3-10, we consider alternative pixel addressing schemes.

To load a specified color into the frame buffer at a position corresponding to column x along scan line y, we will assume we have available a low-level procedure of the form

```
setPixel (x, y)
```

Figure 3-1
Stairstep effect (jaggies) produced
when a line is generated as a series
of pixel positions.

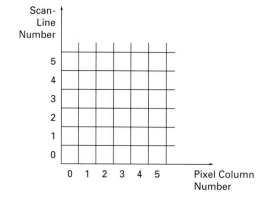

Figure 3-2
Pixel positions referenced by scan-line number and column number.

We sometimes will also want to be able to retrieve the current frame-buffer intensity setting for a specified location. We accomplish this with the low-level function

```
getPixel (x, y)
```

3-2

LINE-DRAWING ALGORITHMS

The Cartesian *slope-intercept equation* for a straight line is

$$y = m \cdot x + b \tag{3-1}$$

with m representing the slope of the line and b as the y intercept. Given that the two endpoints of a line segment are specified at positions (x_1, y_1) and (x_2, y_2), as shown in Fig. 3-3, we can determine values for the slope m and y intercept b with the following calculations:

$$m = \frac{y_2 - y_1}{x_2 - x_1} \tag{3-2}$$

$$b = y_1 - m \cdot x_1 \tag{3-3}$$

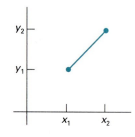

Figure 3-3
Line path between endpoint positions (x_1, y_1) and (x_2, y_2).

Algorithms for displaying straight lines are based on the line equation 3-1 and the calculations given in Eqs. 3-2 and 3-3.

For any given x interval Δx along a line, we can compute the corresponding y interval Δy from Eq. 3-2 as

$$\Delta y = m \, \Delta x \tag{3-4}$$

Similarly, we can obtain the x interval Δx corresponding to a specified Δy as

$$\Delta x = \frac{\Delta y}{m} \tag{3-5}$$

These equations form the basis for determining deflection voltages in analog devices. For lines with slope magnitudes $|m| < 1$, Δx can be set proportional to a small horizontal deflection voltage and the corresponding vertical deflection is then set proportional to Δy as calculated from Eq. 3-4. For lines whose slopes have magnitudes $|m| > 1$, Δy can be set proportional to a small vertical deflection voltage with the corresponding horizontal deflection voltage set proportional to Δx, calculated from Eq. 3-5. For lines with $m = 1$, $\Delta x = \Delta y$ and the horizontal and vertical deflections voltages are equal. In each case, a smooth line with slope m is generated between the specified endpoints.

On raster systems, lines are plotted with pixels, and step sizes in the horizontal and vertical directions are constrained by pixel separations. That is, we must "sample" a line at discrete positions and determine the nearest pixel to the line at each sampled position. This scan-conversion process for straight lines is illustrated in Fig. 3-4, for a near horizontal line with discrete sample positions along the x axis.

DDA Algorithm

The *digital differential analyzer* (DDA) is a scan-conversion line algorithm based on calculating either Δy or Δx, using Eq. 3-4 or Eq. 3-5. We sample the line at unit intervals in one coordinate and determine corresponding integer values nearest the line path for the other coordinate.

Consider first a line with positive slope, as shown in Fig. 3-3. If the slope is less than or equal to 1, we sample at unit x intervals ($\Delta x = 1$) and compute each successive y value as

$$y_{k+1} = y_k + m \tag{3-6}$$

Subscript k takes integer values starting from 1, for the first point, and increases by 1 until the final endpoint is reached. Since m can be any real number between 0 and 1, the calculated y values must be rounded to the nearest integer.

For lines with a positive slope greater than 1, we reverse the roles of x and y. That is, we sample at unit y intervals ($\Delta y = 1$) and calculate each succeeding x value as

$$x_{k+1} = x_k + \frac{1}{m} \tag{3-7}$$

Equations 3-6 and 3-7 are based on the assumption that lines are to be processed from the left endpoint to the right endpoint (Fig. 3-3). If this processing is reversed, so that the starting endpoint is at the right, then either we have $\Delta x = -1$ and

$$y_{k+1} = y_k - m \tag{3-8}$$

or (when the slope is greater than 1) we have $\Delta y = -1$ with

$$x_{k+1} = x_k - \frac{1}{m} \tag{3-9}$$

Equations 3-6 through 3-9 can also be used to calculate pixel positions along a line with negative slope. If the absolute value of the slope is less than 1 and the start endpoint is at the left, we set $\Delta x = 1$ and calculate y values with Eq. 3-6.

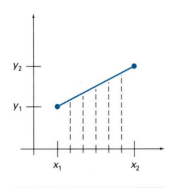

Figure 3-4
Straight line segment with five sampling positions along the x axis between x_1 and x_2.

87

When the start endpoint is at the right (for the same slope), we set $\Delta x = -1$ and obtain y positions from Eq. 3-8. Similarly, when the absolute value of a negative slope is greater than 1, we use $\Delta y = -1$ and Eq. 3-9 or we use $\Delta y = 1$ and Eq. 3-7.

This algorithm is summarized in the following procedure, which accepts as input the two endpoint pixel positions. Horizontal and vertical differences between the endpoint positions are assigned to parameters dx and dy. The difference with the greater magnitude determines the value of parameter steps. Starting with pixel position (x_a, y_a), we determine the offset needed at each step to generate the next pixel position along the line path. We loop through this process steps times. If the magnitude of dx is greater than the magnitude of dy and xa is less than xb, the values of the increments in the x and y directions are 1 and m, respectively. If the greater change is in the x direction, but xa is greater than xb, then the decrements -1 and $-m$ are used to generate each new point on the line. Otherwise, we use a unit increment (or decrement) in the y direction and an x increment (or decrement) of $1/m$.

```
#include "device.h"

#define ROUND(a) ((int)(a+0.5))

void lineDDA (int xa, int ya, int xb, int yb)
{
  int dx = xb - xa, dy = yb - ya, steps, k;
  float xIncrement, yIncrement, x = xa, y = ya;

  if (abs (dx) > abs (dy)) steps = abs (dx);
  else steps = abs (dy);
  xIncrement = dx / (float) steps;
  yIncrement = dy / (float) steps;

  setPixel (ROUND(x), ROUND(y));
  for (k=0; k<steps; k++) {
    x += xIncrement;
    y += yIncrement;
    setPixel (ROUND(x), ROUND(y));
  }
}
```

The DDA algorithm is a faster method for calculating pixel positions than the direct use of Eq. 3-1. It eliminates the multiplication in Eq. 3-1 by making use of raster characteristics, so that appropriate increments are applied in the x or y direction to step to pixel positions along the line path. The accumulation of roundoff error in successive additions of the floating-point increment, however, can cause the calculated pixel positions to drift away from the true line path for long line segments. Furthermore, the rounding operations and floating-point arithmetic in procedure lineDDA are still time-consuming. We can improve the performance of the DDA algorithm by separating the increments m and $1/m$ into integer and fractional parts so that all calculations are reduced to integer operations. A method for calculating $1/m$ increments in integer steps is discussed in Section 3-11. In the following sections, we consider more general scan-line procedures that can be applied to both lines and curves.

Bresenham's Line Algorithm

An accurate and efficient raster line-generating algorithm, developed by Bresenham, scan converts lines using only incremental integer calculations that can be adapted to display circles and other curves. Figures 3-5 and 3-6 illustrate sections of a display screen where straight line segments are to be drawn. The vertical axes show scan-line positions, and the horizontal axes identify pixel columns. Sampling at unit x intervals in these examples, we need to decide which of two possible pixel positions is closer to the line path at each sample step. Starting from the left endpoint shown in Fig. 3-5, we need to determine at the next sample position whether to plot the pixel at position (11, 11) or the one at (11, 12). Similarly, Fig. 3-6 shows a negative slope line path starting from the left endpoint at pixel position (50, 50). In this one, do we select the next pixel position as (51, 50) or as (51, 49)? These questions are answered with Bresenham's line algorithm by testing the sign of an integer parameter, whose value is proportional to the difference between the separations of the two pixel positions from the actual line path.

To illustrate Bresenham's approach, we first consider the scan-conversion process for lines with positive slope less than 1. Pixel positions along a line path are then determined by sampling at unit x intervals. Starting from the left endpoint (x_0, y_0) of a given line, we step to each successive column (x position) and plot the pixel whose scan-line y value is closest to the line path. Figure 3-7 demonstrates the kth step in this process. Assuming we have determined that the pixel at (x_k, y_k) is to be displayed, we next need to decide which pixel to plot in column x_{k+1}. Our choices are the pixels at positions (x_k+1, y_k) and (x_k+1, y_k+1).

At sampling position x_k+1, we label vertical pixel separations from the mathematical line path as d_1 and d_2 (Fig. 3-8). The y coordinate on the mathematical line at pixel column position x_k+1 is calculated as

$$y = m(x_k + 1) + b \tag{3-10}$$

Then

$$d_1 = y - y_k$$
$$= m(x_k + 1) + b - y_k$$

and

$$d_2 = (y_k + 1) - y$$
$$= y_k + 1 - m(x_k + 1) - b$$

The difference between these two separations is

$$d_1 - d_2 = 2m(x_k + 1) - 2y_k + 2b - 1 \tag{3-11}$$

A decision parameter p_k for the kth step in the line algorithm can be obtained by rearranging Eq. 3-11 so that it involves only integer calculations. We accomplish this by substituting $m = \Delta y / \Delta x$, where Δy and Δx are the vertical and horizontal separations of the endpoint positions, and defining:

$$p_k = \Delta x(d_1 - d_2)$$
$$= 2\Delta y \cdot x_k - 2\Delta x \cdot y_k + c \tag{3-12}$$

The sign of p_k is the same as the sign of $d_1 - d_2$, since $\Delta x > 0$ for our example. Parameter c is constant and has the value $2\Delta y + \Delta x(2b - 1)$, which is independent

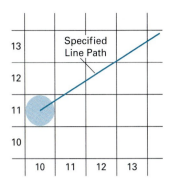

Figure 3-5
Section of a display screen where a straight line segment is to be plotted, starting from the pixel at column 10 on scan line 11.

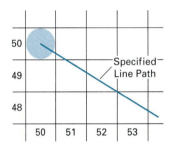

Figure 3-6
Section of a display screen where a negative slope line segment is to be plotted, starting from the pixel at column 50 on scan line 50.

89

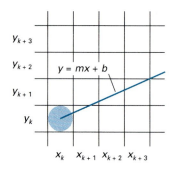

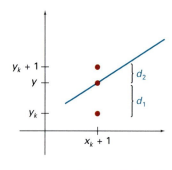

Figure 3-7
Section of the screen grid showing a pixel in column x_k on scan line y_k that is to be plotted along the path of a line segment with slope $0 < m < 1$.

Figure 3-8
Distances between pixel positions and the line y coordinate at sampling position x_k+1.

of pixel position and will be eliminated in the recursive calculations for p_k. If the pixel at y_k is closer to the line path than the pixel at y_k+1 (that is, $d_1 < d_2$), then decision parameter p_k is negative. In that case, we plot the lower pixel; otherwise, we plot the upper pixel.

Coordinate changes along the line occur in unit steps in either the x or y directions. Therefore, we can obtain the values of successive decision parameters using incremental integer calculations. At step $k + 1$, the decision parameter is evaluated from Eq. 3-12 as

$$p_{k+1} = 2\Delta y \cdot x_{k+1} - 2\Delta x \cdot y_{k+1} + c$$

Subtracting Eq. 3-12 from the preceding equation, we have

$$p_{k+1} - p_k = 2\Delta y(x_{k+1} - x_k) - 2\Delta x(y_{k+1} - y_k)$$

But $x_{k+1} = x_k + 1$, so that

$$p_{k+1} = p_k + 2\Delta y - 2\Delta x(y_{k+1} - y_k) \qquad (3\text{-}13)$$

where the term $y_{k+1} - y_k$ is either 0 or 1, depending on the sign of parameter p_k.

This recursive calculation of decision parameters is performed at each integer x position, starting at the left coordinate endpoint of the line. The first parameter, p_0, is evaluated from Eq. 3-12 at the starting pixel position (x_0, y_0) and with m evaluated as $\Delta y/\Delta x$:

$$p_0 = 2\Delta y - \Delta x \qquad (3\text{-}14)$$

We can summarize Bresenham line drawing for a line with a positive slope less than 1 in the following listed steps. The constants $2\Delta y$ and $2\Delta y - 2\Delta x$ are calculated once for each line to be scan converted, so the arithmetic involves only integer addition and subtraction of these two constants.

Bresenham's Line-Drawing Algorithm for $|m| < 1$

1. Input the two line endpoints and store the left endpoint in (x_0, y_0).
2. Load (x_0, y_0) into the frame buffer; that is, plot the first point.
3. Calculate constants Δx, Δy, $2\Delta y$, and $2\Delta y - 2\Delta x$, and obtain the starting value for the decision parameter as

$$p_0 = 2\Delta y - \Delta x$$

4. At each x_k along the line, starting at $k = 0$, perform the following test: If $p_k < 0$, the next point to plot is $(x_k + 1, y_k)$ and

$$p_{k+1} = p_k + 2\Delta y$$

Otherwise, the next point to plot is $(x_k + 1, y_k + 1)$ and

$$p_{k+1} = p_k + 2\Delta y - 2\Delta x$$

5. Repeat step 4 Δx times.

Example 3-1 Bresenham Line Drawing

To illustrate the algorithm, we digitize the line with endpoints (20, 10) and (30, 18). This line has a slope of 0.8, with

$$\Delta x = 10, \qquad \Delta y = 8$$

The initial decision parameter has the value

$$p_0 = 2\Delta y - \Delta x$$
$$= 6$$

and the increments for calculating successive decision parameters are

$$2\Delta y = 16, \qquad 2\Delta y - 2\Delta x = -4$$

We plot the initial point $(x_0, y_0) = (20, 10)$, and determine successive pixel positions along the line path from the decision parameter as

k	p_k	(x_{k+1}, y_{k+1})	k	p_k	(x_{k+1}, y_{k+1})
0	6	(21, 11)	5	6	(26, 15)
1	2	(22, 12)	6	2	(27, 16)
2	−2	(23, 12)	7	−2	(28, 16)
3	14	(24, 13)	8	14	(29, 17)
4	10	(25, 14)	9	10	(30, 18)

A plot of the pixels generated along this line path is shown in Fig. 3-9.

An implementation of Bresenham line drawing for slopes in the range $0 < m < 1$ is given in the following procedure. Endpoint pixel positions for the line are passed to this procedure, and pixels are plotted from the left endpoint to the right endpoint. The call to setPixel loads a preset color value into the frame buffer at the specified (x, y) pixel position.

```
#include "device.h"

void lineBres (int xa, int ya, int xb, int yb)
{
  int dx = abs (xa - xb), dy = abs (ya - yb);
  int p = 2 * dy - dx;
  int twoDy = 2 * dy, twoDyDx = 2 * (dy - dx);
  int x, y, xEnd;

  /* Determine which point to use as start, which as end */
  if (xa > xb) {
    x = xb;
    y = yb;
    xEnd = xa;
  }
  else {
```

```
      x = xa;
      y = ya;
      xEnd = xb;
  }
  setPixel (x, y);

  while (x < xEnd) {
    x++;
    if (p < 0)
      p += twoDy;
    else {
      y++;
      p += twoDyDx;
    }
    setPixel (x, y);
  }
}
```

Bresenham's algorithm is generalized to lines with arbitrary slope by considering the symmetry between the various octants and quadrants of the xy plane. For a line with positive slope greater than 1, we interchange the roles of the x and y directions. That is, we step along the y direction in unit steps and calculate successive x values nearest the line path. Also, we could revise the program to plot pixels starting from either endpoint. If the initial position for a line with positive slope is the right endpoint, both x and y decrease as we step from right to left. To ensure that the same pixels are plotted regardless of the starting endpoint, we always choose the upper (or the lower) of the two candidate pixels whenever the two vertical separations from the line path are equal ($d_1 = d_2$). For negative slopes, the procedures are similar, except that now one coordinate decreases as the other increases. Finally, special cases can be handled separately: Horizontal lines ($\Delta y = 0$), vertical lines ($\Delta x = 0$), and diagonal lines with $|\Delta x| = |\Delta y|$ each can be loaded directly into the frame buffer without processing them through the line-plotting algorithm.

Parallel Line Algorithms

The line-generating algorithms we have discussed so far determine pixel positions sequentially. With a parallel computer, we can calculate pixel positions

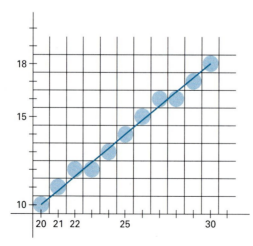

Figure 3-9
Pixel positions along the line path between endpoints (20, 10) and (30, 18), plotted with Bresenham's line algorithm.

along a line path simultaneously by partitioning the computations among the various processors available. One approach to the partitioning problem is to adapt an existing sequential algorithm to take advantage of multiple processors. Alternatively, we can look for other ways to set up the processing so that pixel positions can be calculated efficiently in parallel. An important consideration in devising a parallel algorithm is to balance the processing load among the available processors.

Given n_p processors, we can set up a parallel Bresenham line algorithm by subdividing the line path into n_p partitions and simultaneously generating line segments in each of the subintervals. For a line with slope $0 < m < 1$ and left endpoint coordinate position (x_0, y_0), we partition the line along the positive x direction. The distance between beginning x positions of adjacent partitions can be calculated as

$$\Delta x_p = \frac{\Delta x + n_p - 1}{n_p} \tag{3-15}$$

where Δx is the width of the line, and the value for partition width Δx_p is computed using integer division. Numbering the partitions, and the processors, as 0, 1, 2, up to $n_p - 1$, we calculate the starting x coordinate for the kth partition as

$$x_k = x_0 + k\Delta x_p \tag{3-16}$$

As an example, suppose $\Delta x = 15$ and we have $n_p = 4$ processors. Then the width of the partitions is 4 and the starting x values for the partitions are $x_0, x_0 + 4, x_0 + 8$, and $x_0 + 12$. With this partitioning scheme, the width of the last (rightmost) subinterval will be smaller than the others in some cases. In addition, if the line endpoints are not integers, truncation errors can result in variable width partitions along the length of the line.

To apply Bresenham's algorithm over the partitions, we need the initial value for the y coordinate and the initial value for the decision parameter in each partition. The change Δy_p in the y direction over each partition is calculated from the line slope m and partition width Δx_p:

$$\Delta y_p = m\Delta x_p \tag{3-17}$$

At the kth partition, the starting y coordinate is then

$$y_k = y_0 + \text{round}(k\Delta y_p) \tag{3-18}$$

The initial decision parameter for Bresenham's algorithm at the start of the kth subinterval is obtained from Eq. 3-12:

$$p_k = (k\Delta x_p)(2\Delta y) - \text{round}(k\Delta y_p)(2\Delta x) + 2\Delta y - \Delta x \tag{3-19}$$

Each processor then calculates pixel positions over its assigned subinterval using the starting decision parameter value for that subinterval and the starting coordinates (x_k, y_k). We can also reduce the floating-point calculations to integer arithmetic in the computations for starting values y_k and p_k by substituting $m = \Delta y/\Delta x$ and rearranging terms. The extension of the parallel Bresenham algorithm to a line with slope greater than 1 is achieved by partitioning the line in the y di-

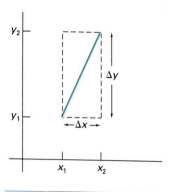

Figure 3-10

Bounding box for a line with
coordinate extents Δx and Δy.

rection and calculating beginning x values for the partitions. For negative slopes, we increment coordinate values in one direction and decrement in the other.

Another way to set up parallel algorithms on raster systems is to assign each processor to a particular group of screen pixels. With a sufficient number of processors (such as a Connection Machine CM-2 with over 65,000 processors), we can assign each processor to one pixel within some screen region. This approach can be adapted to line display by assigning one processor to each of the pixels within the limits of the line coordinate extents (*bounding rectangle*) and calculating pixel distances from the line path. The number of pixels within the bounding box of a line is $\Delta x \cdot \Delta y$ (Fig. 3-10). Perpendicular distance d from the line in Fig. 3-10 to a pixel with coordinates (x, y) is obtained with the calculation

$$d = Ax + By + C \tag{3-20}$$

where

$$A = \frac{-\Delta y}{\text{linelength}}$$

$$B = \frac{\Delta x}{\text{linelength}}$$

$$C = \frac{x_0 \Delta y - y_0 \Delta x}{\text{linelength}}$$

with

$$\text{linelength} = \sqrt{\Delta x^2 + \Delta y^2}$$

Once the constants A, B, and C have been evaluated for the line, each processor needs to perform two multiplications and two additions to compute the pixel distance d. A pixel is plotted if d is less than a specified line-thickness parameter.

Instead of partitioning the screen into single pixels, we can assign to each processor either a scan line or a column of pixels depending on the line slope. Each processor then calculates the intersection of the line with the horizontal row or vertical column of pixels assigned that processor. For a line with slope $|m| < 1$, each processor simply solves the line equation for y, given an x column value. For a line with slope magnitude greater than 1, the line equation is solved for x by each processor, given a scan-line y value. Such direct methods, although slow on sequential machines, can be performed very efficiently using multiple processors.

3-3

LOADING THE FRAME BUFFER

When straight line segments and other objects are scan converted for display with a raster system, frame-buffer positions must be calculated. We have assumed that this is accomplished with the `setPixel` procedure, which stores intensity values for the pixels at corresponding addresses within the frame-buffer array. Scan-conversion algorithms generate pixel positions at successive unit in-

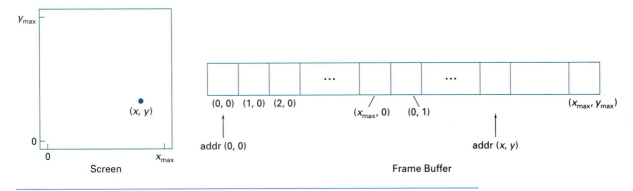

Figure 3-11
Pixel screen positions stored linearly in row-major order within the frame buffer.

tervals. This allows us to use incremental methods to calculate frame-buffer addresses.

As a specific example, suppose the frame-buffer array is addressed in row-major order and that pixel positions vary from $(0, 0)$ at the lower left screen corner to (x_{max}, y_{max}) at the top right corner (Fig. 3-11). For a bilevel system (1 bit per pixel), the frame-buffer bit address for pixel position (x, y) is calculated as

$$\text{addr}(x, y) = \text{addr}(0, 0) + y(x_{max} + 1) + x \qquad (3\text{-}21)$$

Moving across a scan line, we can calculate the frame-buffer address for the pixel at $(x + 1, y)$ as the following offset from the address for position (x, y):

$$\text{addr}(x + 1, y) = \text{addr}(x, y) + 1 \qquad (3\text{-}22)$$

Stepping diagonally up to the next scan line from (x, y), we get to the frame-buffer address of $(x + 1, y + 1)$ with the calculation

$$\text{addr}(x + 1, y + 1) = \text{addr}(x, y) + x_{max} + 2 \qquad (3\text{-}23)$$

where the constant $x_{max} + 2$ is precomputed once for all line segments. Similar incremental calculations can be obtained from Eq. 3-21 for unit steps in the negative x and y screen directions. Each of these address calculations involves only a single integer addition.

Methods for implementing the `setPixel` procedure to store pixel intensity values depend on the capabilities of a particular system and the design requirements of the software package. With systems that can display a range of intensity values for each pixel, frame-buffer address calculations would include pixel width (number of bits), as well as the pixel screen location.

3-4
LINE FUNCTION

A procedure for specifying straight-line segments can be set up in a number of different forms. In PHIGS, GKS, and some other packages, the two-dimensional line function is

```
polyline (n, wcPoints)
```

where parameter n is assigned an integer value equal to the number of coordinate positions to be input, and `wcPoints` is the array of input world-coordinate values for line segment endpoints. This function is used to define a set of $n - 1$ connected straight line segments. Because series of connected line segments occur more often than isolated line segments in graphics applications, `polyline` provides a more general line function. To display a single straight-line segment, we set $n = 2$ and list the x and y values of the two endpoint coordinates in `wcPoints`.

As an example of the use of `polyline`, the following statements generate two connected line segments, with endpoints at (50, 100), (150, 250), and (250, 100):

```
wcPoints[1].x = 50;
wcPoints[1].y = 100;
wcPoints[2].x = 150;
wcPoints[2].y = 250;
wcPoints[3].x = 250;
wcPoints[3].y = 100;
polyline (3, wcPoints);
```

Coordinate references in the `polyline` function are stated as **absolute coordinate** values. This means that the values specified are the actual point positions in the coordinate system in use.

Some graphics systems employ line (and point) functions with **relative coordinate** specifications. In this case, coordinate values are stated as offsets from the last position referenced (called the **current position**). For example, if location (3, 2) is the last position that has been referenced in an application program, a relative coordinate specification of (2, −1) corresponds to an absolute position of (5, 1). An additional function is also available for setting the current position before the line routine is summoned. With these packages, a user lists only the single pair of offsets in the line command. This signals the system to display a line starting from the current position to a final position determined by the offsets. The current position is then updated to this final line position. A series of connected lines is produced with such packages by a sequence of line commands, one for each line section to be drawn. Some graphics packages provide options allowing the user to specify line endpoints using either relative or absolute coordinates.

Implementation of the `polyline` procedure is accomplished by first performing a series of coordinate transformations, then making a sequence of calls to a device-level line-drawing routine. In PHIGS, the input line endpoints are actually specified in modeling coordinates, which are then converted to world coordinates. Next, world coordinates are converted to normalized coordinates, then to device coordinates. We discuss the details for carrying out these two-dimensional coordinate transformations in Chapter 6. Once in device coordinates, we display the polyline by invoking a line routine, such as Bresenham's algorithm, $n - 1$ times to connect the n coordinate points. Each successive call passes the coordinate pair needed to plot the next line section, where the first endpoint of each coordinate pair is the last endpoint of the previous section. To avoid setting the intensity of some endpoints twice, we could modify the line algorithm so that the last endpoint of each segment is not plotted. We discuss methods for avoiding overlap of displayed objects in more detail in Section 3-10.

3-5

CIRCLE-GENERATING ALGORITHMS

Since the circle is a frequently used component in pictures and graphs, a procedure for generating either full circles or circular arcs is included in most graphics packages. More generally, a single procedure can be provided to display either circular or elliptical curves.

Properties of Circles

A circle is defined as the set of points that are all at a given distance r from a center position (x_c, y_c) (Fig. 3-12). This distance relationship is expressed by the Pythagorean theorem in Cartesian coordinates as

$$(x - x_c)^2 + (y - y_c)^2 = r^2 \qquad (3\text{-}24)$$

We could use this equation to calculate the position of points on a circle circumference by stepping along the x axis in unit steps from $x_c - r$ to $x_c + r$ and calculating the corresponding y values at each position as

$$y = y_c \pm \sqrt{r^2 - (x_c - x)^2} \qquad (3\text{-}25)$$

But this is not the best method for generating a circle. One problem with this approach is that it involves considerable computation at each step. Moreover, the spacing between plotted pixel positions is not uniform, as demonstrated in Fig. 3-13. We could adjust the spacing by interchanging x and y (stepping through y values and calculating x values) whenever the absolute value of the slope of the circle is greater than 1. But this simply increases the computation and processing required by the algorithm.

Another way to eliminate the unequal spacing shown in Fig. 3-13 is to calculate points along the circular boundary using polar coordinates r and θ (Fig. 3-12). Expressing the circle equation in parametric polar form yields the pair of equations

$$\begin{aligned} x &= x_c + r\cos\theta \\ y &= y_c + r\sin\theta \end{aligned} \qquad (3\text{-}26)$$

When a display is generated with these equations using a fixed angular step size, a circle is plotted with equally spaced points along the circumference. The step size chosen for θ depends on the application and the display device. Larger angular separations along the circumference can be connected with straight line segments to approximate the circular path. For a more continuous boundary on a raster display, we can set the step size at $1/r$. This plots pixel positions that are approximately one unit apart.

Computation can be reduced by considering the symmetry of circles. The shape of the circle is similar in each quadrant. We can generate the circle section in the second quadrant of the xy plane by noting that the two circle sections are symmetric with respect to the y axis. And circle sections in the third and fourth quadrants can be obtained from sections in the first and second quadrants by

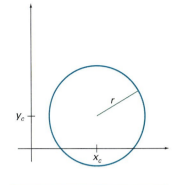

Figure 3-12
Circle with center coordinates (x_c, y_c) and radius r.

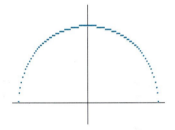

Figure 3-13
Positive half of a circle plotted with Eq. 3-25 and with $(x_c, y_c) = (0, 0)$.

97

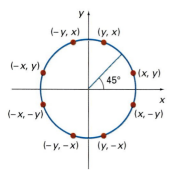

Figure 3-14

Symmetry of a circle. Calculation of a circle point (x, y) in one octant yields the circle points shown for the other seven octants.

considering symmetry about the x axis. We can take this one step further and note that there is also symmetry between octants. Circle sections in adjacent octants within one quadrant are symmetric with respect to the 45° line dividing the two octants. These symmetry conditions are illustrated in Fig.3-14, where a point at position (x, y) on a one-eighth circle sector is mapped into the seven circle points in the other octants of the xy plane. Taking advantage of the circle symmetry in this way, we can generate all pixel positions around a circle by calculating only the points within the sector from $x = 0$ to $x = y$.

Determining pixel positions along a circle circumference using either Eq. 3-24 or Eq. 3-26 still requires a good deal of computation time. The Cartesian equation 3-24 involves multiplications and square-root calculations, while the parametric equations contain multiplications and trigonometric calculations. More efficient circle algorithms are based on incremental calculation of decision parameters, as in the Bresenham line algorithm, which involves only simple integer operations.

Bresenham's line algorithm for raster displays is adapted to circle generation by setting up decision parameters for finding the closest pixel to the circumference at each sampling step. The circle equation 3-24, however, is nonlinear, so that square-root evaluations would be required to compute pixel distances from a circular path. Bresenham's circle algorithm avoids these square-root calculations by comparing the squares of the pixel separation distances.

A method for direct distance comparison is to test the halfway position between two pixels to determine if this midpoint is inside or outside the circle boundary. This method is more easily applied to other conics; and for an integer circle radius, the midpoint approach generates the same pixel positions as the Bresenham circle algorithm. Also, the error involved in locating pixel positions along any conic section using the midpoint test is limited to one-half the pixel separation.

Midpoint Circle Algorithm

As in the raster line algorithm, we sample at unit intervals and determine the closest pixel position to the specified circle path at each step. For a given radius r and screen center position (x_c, y_c), we can first set up our algorithm to calculate pixel positions around a circle path centered at the coordinate origin (0, 0). Then each calculated position (x, y) is moved to its proper screen position by adding x_c to x and y_c to y. Along the circle section from $x = 0$ to $x = y$ in the first quadrant, the slope of the curve varies from 0 to −1. Therefore, we can take unit steps in the positive x direction over this octant and use a decision parameter to determine which of the two possible y positions is closer to the circle path at each step. Positions in the other seven octants are then obtained by symmetry.

To apply the midpoint method, we define a circle function:

$$f_{\text{circle}}(x, y) = x^2 + y^2 - r^2 \qquad (3\text{-}27)$$

Any point (x, y) on the boundary of the circle with radius r satisfies the equation $f_{\text{circle}}(x, y) = 0$. If the point is in the interior of the circle, the circle function is negative. And if the point is outside the circle, the circle function is positive. To summarize, the relative position of any point (x, y) can be determined by checking the sign of the circle function:

$$f_{circle}(x, y) \begin{cases} < 0, & \text{if } (x, y) \text{ is inside the circle boundary} \\ = 0, & \text{if } (x, y) \text{ is on the circle boundary} \\ > 0, & \text{if } (x, y) \text{ is outside the circle boundary} \end{cases} \qquad (3\text{-}28)$$

The circle-function tests in 3-28 are performed for the midpositions between pixels near the circle path at each sampling step. Thus, the circle function is the decision parameter in the midpoint algorithm, and we can set up incremental calculations for this function as we did in the line algorithm.

Figure 3-15 shows the midpoint between the two candidate pixels at sampling position $x_k + 1$. Assuming we have just plotted the pixel at (x_k, y_k), we next need to determine whether the pixel at position $(x_k + 1, y_k)$ or the one at position $(x_k + 1, y_k - 1)$ is closer to the circle. Our decision parameter is the circle function 3-27 evaluated at the midpoint between these two pixels:

$$p_k = f_{circle}\left(x_k + 1, y_k - \frac{1}{2}\right)$$

$$= (x_k + 1)^2 + \left(y_k - \frac{1}{2}\right)^2 - r^2 \qquad (3\text{-}29)$$

If $p_k < 0$, this midpoint is inside the circle and the pixel on scan line y_k is closer to the circle boundary. Otherwise, the midposition is outside or on the circle boundary, and we select the pixel on scanline $y_k - 1$.

Successive decision parameters are obtained using incremental calculations. We obtain a recursive expression for the next decision parameter by evaluating the circle function at sampling position $x_{k+1} + 1 = x_k + 2$:

$$p_{k+1} = f_{circle}\left(x_{k+1} + 1, y_{k+1} - \frac{1}{2}\right)$$

$$= [(x_k + 1) + 1]^2 + \left(y_{k+1} - \frac{1}{2}\right)^2 - r^2$$

or

$$p_{k+1} = p_k + 2(x_k + 1) + (y_{k+1}^2 - y_k^2) - (y_{k+1} - y_k) + 1 \qquad (3\text{-}30)$$

.

where y_{k+1} is either y_k or y_{k-1}, depending on the sign of p_k.

Increments for obtaining p_{k+1} are either $2x_{k+1} + 1$ (if p_k is negative) or $2x_{k+1} + 1 - 2y_{k+1}$. Evaluation of the terms $2x_{k+1}$ and $2y_{k+1}$ can also be done incrementally as

$$2x_{k+1} = 2x_k + 2$$

$$2y_{k+1} = 2y_k - 2$$

At the start position $(0, r)$, these two terms have the values 0 and $2r$, respectively. Each successive value is obtained by adding 2 to the previous value of $2x$ and subtracting 2 from the previous value of $2y$.

The initial decision parameter is obtained by evaluating the circle function at the start position $(x_0, y_0) = (0, r)$:

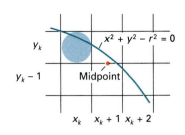

Figure 3-15
Midpoint between candidate pixels at sampling position x_k+1 along a circular path.

$$p_0 = f_{\text{circle}}\left(1, r - \frac{1}{2}\right)$$

$$= 1 + \left(r - \frac{1}{2}\right)^2 - r^2$$

or

$$p_0 = \frac{5}{4} - r \qquad\qquad (3\text{-}31)$$

If the radius r is specified as an integer, we can simply round p_0 to

$$p_0 = 1 - r \qquad \text{(for } r \text{ an integer)}$$

since all increments are integers.

As in Bresenham's line algorithm, the midpoint method calculates pixel positions along the circumference of a circle using integer additions and subtractions, assuming that the circle parameters are specified in integer screen coordinates. We can summarize the steps in the midpoint circle algorithm as follows.

Midpoint Circle Algorithm

1. Input radius r and circle center (x_c, y_c), and obtain the first point on the circumference of a circle centered on the origin as

$$(x_0, y_0) = (0, r)$$

2. Calculate the initial value of the decision parameter as

$$p_0 = \frac{5}{4} - r$$

3. At each x_k position, starting at $k = 0$, perform the following test: If $p_k < 0$, the next point along the circle centered on $(0, 0)$ is (x_{k+1}, y_k) and

$$p_{k+1} = p_k + 2x_{k+1} + 1$$

Otherwise, the next point along the circle is $(x_k + 1, y_k - 1)$ and

$$p_{k+1} = p_k + 2x_{k+1} + 1 - 2y_{k+1}$$

where $2x_{k+1} = 2x_k + 2$ and $2y_{k+1} = 2y_k - 2$.

4. Determine symmetry points in the other seven octants.

5. Move each calculated pixel position (x, y) onto the circular path centered on (x_c, y_c) and plot the coordinate values:

$$x = x + x_c, \qquad y = y + y_c$$

6. Repeat steps 3 through 5 until $x \geq y$.

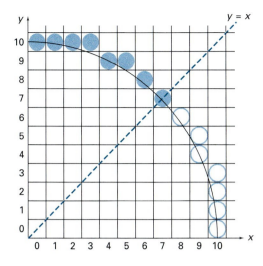

Figure 3-16
Selected pixel positions (solid
circles) along a circle path with
radius $r = 10$ centered on the origin,
using the midpoint circle algorithm.
Open circles show the symmetry
positions in the first quadrant.

Example 3-2 Midpoint Circle-Drawing

Given a circle radius $r = 10$, we demonstrate the midpoint circle algorithm by
determining positions along the circle octant in the first quadrant from $x = 0$ to
$x = y$. The initial value of the decision parameter is

$$p_0 = 1 - r = -9$$

For the circle centered on the coordinate origin, the initial point is $(x_0, y_0) =
(0, 10)$, and initial increment terms for calculating the decision parameters are

$$2x_0 = 0, \qquad 2y_0 = 20$$

Successive decision parameter values and positions along the circle path are calculated using the midpoint method as

k	p_k	(x_{k+1}, y_{k+1})	$2x_{k+1}$	$2y_{k+1}$
0	-9	(1, 10)	2	20
1	-6	(2, 10)	4	20
2	-1	(3, 10)	6	20
3	6	(4, 9)	8	18
4	-3	(5, 9)	10	18
5	8	(6, 8)	12	16
6	5	(7, 7)	14	14

A plot of the generated pixel positions in the first quadrant is shown in Fig. 3-16.

The following procedure displays a raster circle on a bilevel monitor using
the midpoint algorithm. Input to the procedure are the coordinates for the circle
center and the radius. Intensities for pixel positions along the circle circumference are loaded into the frame-buffer array with calls to the `setPixel` routine.

```
#include "device.h"

void circleMidpoint (int xCenter, int yCenter, int radius)
{
  int x = 0;
  int y = radius;
  int p = 1 - radius;
  void circlePlotPoints (int, int, int, int);

  /* Plot first set of points */
  circlePlotPoints (xCenter, yCenter, x, y);

  while (x < y) {
    x++;
    if (p < 0)
      p += 2 * x + 1;
    else {
      y--;
      p += 2 * (x - y) + 1;
    }
    circlePlotPoints (xCenter, yCenter, x, y);
  }
}

void circlePlotPoints (int xCenter, int yCenter, int x, int y)
{
  setPixel (xCenter + x, yCenter + y);
  setPixel (xCenter - x, yCenter + y);
  setPixel (xCenter + x, yCenter - y);
  setPixel (xCenter - x, yCenter - y);
  setPixel (xCenter + y, yCenter + x);
  setPixel (xCenter - y, yCenter + x);
  setPixel (xCenter + y, yCenter - x);
  setPixel (xCenter - y, yCenter - x);
}
```

3-6

ELLIPSE-GENERATING ALGORITHMS

Loosely stated, an ellipse is an elongated circle. Therefore, elliptical curves can be generated by modifying circle-drawing procedures to take into account the different dimensions of an ellipse along the major and minor axes.

Properties of Ellipses

An ellipse is defined as the set of points such that the sum of the distances from two fixed positions (foci) is the same for all points (Fig. 3-17). If the distances to the two foci from any point $P = (x, y)$ on the ellipse are labeled d_1 and d_2, then the general equation of an ellipse can be stated as

$$d_1 + d_2 = \text{constant} \tag{3-32}$$

Expressing distances d_1 and d_2 in terms of the focal coordinates $F_1 = (x_1, y_1)$ and $F_2 = (x_2, y_2)$, we have

$$\sqrt{(x - x_1)^2 + (y - y_1)^2} + \sqrt{(x - x_2)^2 + (y - y_2)^2} = \text{constant} \tag{3-33}$$

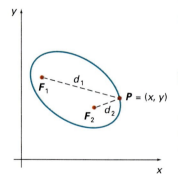

Figure 3-17

Ellipse generated about foci F_1 and F_2.

102

By squaring this equation, isolating the remaining radical, and then squaring again, we can rewrite the general ellipse equation in the form

$$Ax^2 + By^2 + Cxy + Dx + Ey + F = 0 \qquad (3\text{-}34)$$

where the coefficients A, B, C, D, E, and F are evaluated in terms of the focal coordinates and the dimensions of the major and minor axes of the ellipse. The major axis is the straight line segment extending from one side of the ellipse to the other through the foci. The minor axis spans the shorter dimension of the ellipse, bisecting the major axis at the halfway position (ellipse center) between the two foci.

An interactive method for specifying an ellipse in an arbitrary orientation is to input the two foci and a point on the ellipse boundary. With these three coordinate positions, we can evaluate the constant in Eq. 3-33. Then, the coefficients in Eq. 3-34 can be evaluated and used to generate pixels along the elliptical path.

Ellipse equations are greatly simplified if the major and minor axes are oriented to align with the coordinate axes. In Fig. 3-18, we show an ellipse in "standard position" with major and minor axes oriented parallel to the x and y axes. Parameter r_x for this example labels the semimajor axis, and parameter r_y labels the semiminor axis. The equation of the ellipse shown in Fig. 3-18 can be written in terms of the ellipse center coordinates and parameters r_x and r_y as

$$\left(\frac{x - x_c}{r_x}\right)^2 + \left(\frac{y - y_c}{r_y}\right)^2 = 1 \qquad (3\text{-}35)$$

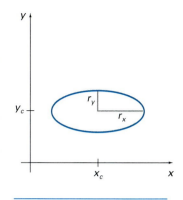

Figure 3-18
Ellipse centered at (x_c, y_c) with semimajor axis r_x and semiminor axis r_y.

Using polar coordinates r and θ, we can also describe the ellipse in standard position with the parametric equations:

$$x = x_c + r_x \cos\theta$$
$$y = y_c + r_y \sin\theta \qquad (3\text{-}36)$$

Symmetry considerations can be used to further reduce computations. An ellipse in standard position is symmetric between quadrants, but unlike a circle, it is not symmetric between the two octants of a quadrant. Thus, we must calculate pixel positions along the elliptical arc throughout one quadrant, then we obtain positions in the remaining three quadrants by symmetry (Fig 3-19).

Midpoint Ellipse Algorithm

Our approach here is similar to that used in displaying a raster circle. Given parameters r_x, r_y, and (x_c, y_c), we determine points (x, y) for an ellipse in standard position centered on the origin, and then we shift the points so the ellipse is centered at (x_c, y_c). If we wish also to display the ellipse in nonstandard position, we could then rotate the ellipse about its center coordinates to reorient the major and minor axes. For the present, we consider only the display of ellipses in standard position. We discuss general methods for transforming object orientations and positions in Chapter 5.

The midpoint ellipse method is applied throughout the first quadrant in two parts. Figure 3-20 shows the division of the first quadrant according to the slope of an ellipse with $r_x < r_y$. We process this quadrant by taking unit steps in the x direction where the slope of the curve has a magnitude less than 1, and taking unit steps in the y direction where the slope has a magnitude greater than 1.

Regions 1 and 2 (Fig. 3-20), can be processed in various ways. We can start at position $(0, r_y)$ and step clockwise along the elliptical path in the first quadrant,

103

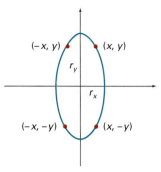

Figure 3-19
Symmetry of an ellipse. Calculation of a point (x, y) in one quadrant yields the ellipse points shown for the other three quadrants.

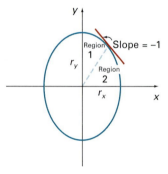

Figure 3-20
Ellipse processing regions. Over region 1, the magnitude of the ellipse slope is less than 1; over region 2, the magnitude of the slope is greater than 1.

shifting from unit steps in x to unit steps in y when the slope becomes less than -1. Alternatively, we could start at $(r_x, 0)$ and select points in a counterclockwise order, shifting from unit steps in y to unit steps in x when the slope becomes greater than -1. With parallel processors, we could calculate pixel positions in the two regions simultaneously. As an example of a sequential implementation of the midpoint algorithm, we take the start position at $(0, r_y)$ and step along the ellipse path in clockwise order throughout the first quadrant.

We define an ellipse function from Eq. 3-35 with $(x_c, y_c) = (0, 0)$ as

$$f_{\text{ellipse}}(x, y) = r_y^2 x^2 + r_x^2 y^2 - r_x^2 r_y^2 \qquad (3\text{-}37)$$

which has the following properties:

$$f_{\text{ellipse}}(x, y) \begin{cases} < 0, & \text{if } (x, y) \text{ is inside the ellipse boundary} \\ = 0, & \text{if } (x, y) \text{ is on the ellipse boundary} \\ > 0, & \text{if } (x, y) \text{ is outside the ellipse boundary} \end{cases} \qquad (3\text{-}38)$$

Thus, the ellipse function $f_{\text{ellipse}}(x, y)$ serves as the decision parameter in the midpoint algorithm. At each sampling position, we select the next pixel along the ellipse path according to the sign of the ellipse function evaluated at the midpoint between the two candidate pixels.

Starting at $(0, r_y)$, we take unit steps in the x direction until we reach the boundary between region 1 and region 2 (Fig. 3-20). Then we switch to unit steps in the y direction over the remainder of the curve in the first quadrant. At each step, we need to test the value of the slope of the curve. The ellipse slope is calculated from Eq. 3-37 as

$$\frac{dy}{dx} = -\frac{2r_y^2 x}{2r_x^2 y} \qquad (3\text{-}39)$$

At the boundary between region 1 and region 2, $dy/dx = -1$ and

$$2r_y^2 x = 2r_x^2 y$$

Therefore, we move out of region 1 whenever

$$2r_y^2 x \geq 2r_x^2 y \qquad (3\text{-}40)$$

Figure 3-21 shows the midpoint between the two candidate pixels at sampling position $x_k + 1$ in the first region. Assuming position (x_k, y_k) has been selected at the previous step, we determine the next position along the ellipse path by evaluating the decision parameter (that is, the ellipse function 3-37) at this midpoint:

$$p1_k = f_{\text{ellipse}}\left(x_k + 1, y_k - \frac{1}{2}\right)$$

$$= r_y^2(x_k + 1)^2 + r_x^2\left(y_k - \frac{1}{2}\right)^2 - r_x^2\, r_y^2 \qquad (3\text{-}41)$$

If $p1_k < 0$, the midpoint is inside the ellipse and the pixel on scan line y_k is closer to the ellipse boundary. Otherwise, the midposition is outside or on the ellipse boundary, and we select the pixel on scan line $y_k - 1$.

At the next sampling position $(x_{k+1} + 1 = x_k + 2)$, the decision parameter for region 1 is evaluated as

$$p1_{k+1} = f_{\text{ellipse}}\left(x_{k+1} + 1, y_{k+1} - \frac{1}{2}\right)$$

$$= r_y^2[(x_k + 1) + 1]^2 + r_x^2\left(y_{k+1} - \frac{1}{2}\right)^2 - r_x^2 r_y^2$$

or

$$p1_{k+1} = p1_k + 2r_y^2(x_k + 1) + r_y^2 + r_x^2\left[\left(y_{k+1} - \frac{1}{2}\right)^2 - \left(y_k - \frac{1}{2}\right)^2\right] \qquad (3\text{-}42)$$

where y_{k+1} is either y_k or $y_k - 1$, depending on the sign of $p1_k$.

Decision parameters are incremented by the following amounts:

$$\text{increment} = \begin{cases} 2r_y^2 x_{k+1} + r_y^2, & \text{if } p1_k < 0 \\ 2r_y^2 x_{k+1} + r_y^2 - 2r_x^2 y_{k+1}, & \text{if } p1_k \geq 0 \end{cases}$$

As in the circle algorithm, increments for the decision parameters can be calculated using only addition and subtraction, since values for the terms $2r_y^2 x$ and $2r_x^2 y$ can also be obtained incrementally. At the initial position $(0, r_y)$, the two terms evaluate to

$$2r_y^2 x = 0 \qquad (3\text{-}43)$$

$$2r_x^2 y = 2r_x^2 r_y \qquad (3\text{-}44)$$

As x and y are incremented, updated values are obtained by adding $2r_y^2$ to 3-43 and subtracting $2r_x^2$ from 3-44. The updated values are compared at each step, and we move from region 1 to region 2 when condition 3-40 is satisfied.

In region 1, the initial value of the decision parameter is obtained by evaluating the ellipse function at the start position $(x_0, y_0) = (0, r_y)$:

$$p1_0 = f_{\text{ellipse}}\left(1, r_y - \frac{1}{2}\right)$$

$$= r_y^2 + r_x^2\left(r_y - \frac{1}{2}\right)^2 - r_x^2 r_y^2$$

or

$$p1_0 = r_y^2 - r_x^2 r_y + \frac{1}{4}r_x^2 \qquad (3\text{-}45)$$

Over region 2, we sample at unit steps in the negative y direction, and the midpoint is now taken between horizontal pixels at each step (Fig. 3-22). For this region, the decision parameter is evaluated as

$$p2_k = f_{\text{ellipse}}\left(x_k + \frac{1}{2}, y_k - 1\right)$$

$$= r_y^2\left(x_k + \frac{1}{2}\right)^2 + r_x^2(y_k - 1)^2 - r_x^2 r_y^2 \qquad (3\text{-}46)$$

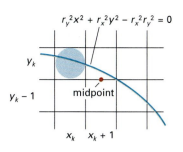

$r_y^2 x^2 + r_x^2 y^2 - r_x^2 r_y^2 = 0$

y_k

$y_k - 1$ midpoint

x_k $x_k + 1$

Figure 3-21
Midpoint between candidate pixels at sampling position x_k+1 along an elliptical path.

105

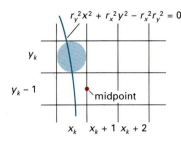

$$r_y^2 x^2 + r_x^2 y^2 - r_x^2 r_y^2 = 0$$

Figure 3-22

Midpoint between candidate pixels at sampling position $y_k - 1$ along an elliptical path.

If $p2_k > 0$, the midposition is outside the ellipse boundary, and we select the pixel at x_k. If $p2_k \le 0$, the midpoint is inside or on the ellipse boundary, and we select pixel position x_{k+1}.

To determine the relationship between successive decision parameters in region 2, we evaluate the ellipse function at the next sampling step $y_{k+1} - 1 = y_k - 2$:

$$p2_{k+1} = f_{\text{ellipse}}\left(x_{k+1} + \frac{1}{2}, y_{k+1} - 1\right)$$

(3-47)

$$= r_y^2\left(x_{k+1} + \frac{1}{2}\right)^2 + r_x^2[(y_k - 1) - 1]^2 - r_x^2 r_y^2$$

or

$$p2_{k+1} = p2_k - 2r_x^2(y_k - 1) + r_x^2 + r_y^2\left[\left(x_{k+1} + \frac{1}{2}\right)^2 - \left(x_k + \frac{1}{2}\right)^2\right] \quad (3\text{-}48)$$

with x_{k+1} set either to x_k or to $x_k + 1$, depending on the sign of $p2_k$.

When we enter region 2, the initial position (x_0, y_0) is taken as the last position selected in region 1 and the initial decision parameter in region 2 is then

$$p2_0 = f_{\text{ellipse}}\left(x_0 + \frac{1}{2}, y_0 - 1\right)$$

(3-49)

$$= r_y^2\left(x_0 + \frac{1}{2}\right)^2 + r_x^2(y_0 - 1)^2 - r_x^2 r_y^2$$

To simplify the calculation of $p2_0$, we could select pixel positions in counterclockwise order starting at $(r_x, 0)$. Unit steps would then be taken in the positive y direction up to the last position selected in region 1.

The midpoint algorithm can be adapted to generate an ellipse in nonstandard position using the ellipse function Eq. 3-34 and calculating pixel positions over the entire elliptical path. Alternatively, we could reorient the ellipse axes to standard position, using transformation methods discussed in Chapter 5, apply the midpoint algorithm to determine curve positions, then convert calculated pixel positions to path positions along the original ellipse orientation.

Assuming r_x, r_y, and the ellipse center are given in integer screen coordinates, we only need incremental integer calculations to determine values for the decision parameters in the midpoint ellipse algorithm. The increments r_x^2, r_y^2, $2r_x^2$, and $2r_y^2$ are evaluated once at the beginning of the procedure. A summary of the midpoint ellipse algorithm is listed in the following steps:

Midpoint Ellipse Algorithm

1. Input r_x, r_y, and ellipse center (x_c, y_c), and obtain the first point on an ellipse centered on the origin as

$$(x_0, y_0) = (0, r_y)$$

2. Calculate the initial value of the decision parameter in region 1 as

$$p1_0 = r_y^2 - r_x^2 r_y + \frac{1}{4} r_x^2$$

3. At each x_k position in region 1, starting at $k = 0$, perform the following test: If $p1_k < 0$, the next point along the ellipse centered on $(0, 0)$ is (x_{k+1}, y_k) and

$$p1_{k+1} = p1_k + 2r_y^2 x_{k+1} + r_y^2$$

Otherwise, the next point along the circle is $(x_k + 1, y_k - 1)$ and

$$p1_{k+1} = p1_k + 2r_y^2 x_{k+1} - 2r_x^2 y_{k+1} + r_y^2$$

with

$$2r_y^2 x_{k+1} = 2r_y^2 x_k + 2r_y^2, \qquad 2r_x^2 y_{k+1} = 2r_x^2 y_k - 2r_x^2$$

and continue until $2r_y^2 x \geq 2r_x^2 y$.

4. Calculate the initial value of the decision parameter in region 2 using the last point (x_0, y_0) calculated in region 1 as

$$p2_0 = r_y^2 \left(x_0 + \frac{1}{2} \right)^2 + r_x^2 (y_0 - 1)^2 - r_x^2 r_y^2$$

5. At each y_k position in region 2, starting at $k = 0$, perform the following test: If $p2_k > 0$, the next point along the ellipse centered on $(0, 0)$ is $(x_k, y_k - 1)$ and

$$p2_{k+1} = p2_k - 2r_x^2 y_{k+1} + r_x^2$$

Otherwise, the next point along the circle is $(x_k + 1, y_k - 1)$ and

$$p2_{k+1} = p2_k + 2r_y^2 x_{k+1} - 2r_x^2 y_{k+1} + r_x^2$$

using the same incremental calculations for x and y as in region 1.

6. Determine symmetry points in the other three quadrants.

7. Move each calculated pixel position (x, y) onto the elliptical path centered on (x_c, y_c) and plot the coordinate values:

$$x = x + x_c, \qquad y = y + y_c$$

8. Repeat the steps for region 1 until $2r_y^2 x \geq 2r_x^2 y$.

Example 3-3 Midpoint Ellipse Drawing

Given input ellipse parameters $r_x = 8$ and $r_y = 6$, we illustrate the steps in the midpoint ellipse algorithm by determining raster positions along the ellipse path in the first quadrant. Initial values and increments for the decision parameter calculations are

$$2r_y^2 x = 0 \qquad \text{(with increment } 2r_y^2 = 72)$$

$$2r_x^2 y = 2r_x^2 r_y \qquad \text{(with increment } -2r_x^2 = -128)$$

For region 1: The initial point for the ellipse centered on the origin is $(x_0, y_0) = (0, 6)$, and the initial decision parameter value is

$$p1_0 = r_y^2 - r_x^2 r_y + \frac{1}{4} r_x^2 = -332$$

Successive decision parameter values and positions along the ellipse path are calculated using the midpoint method as

k	$p1_k$	(x_{k+1}, y_{k+1})	$2r_y^2 x_{k+1}$	$2r_x^2 y_{k+1}$
0	−332	(1, 6)	72	768
1	−224	(2, 6)	144	768
2	−44	(3, 6)	216	768
3	208	(4, 5)	288	640
4	−108	(5, 5)	360	640
5	288	(6, 4)	432	512
6	244	(7, 3)	504	384

We now move out of region 1, since $2r_y^2 x > 2r_x^2 y$.

For region 2, the initial point is $(x_0, y_0) = (7, 3)$ and the initial decision parameter is

$$p2_0 = f\left(7 + \frac{1}{2}, 2\right) = -151$$

The remaining positions along the ellipse path in the first quadrant are then calculated as

k	$p2_k$	(x_{k+1}, y_{k+1})	$2r_y^2 x_{k+1}$	$2r_x^2 y_{k+1}$
0	−151	(8, 2)	576	256
1	233	(8, 1)	576	128
2	745	(8, 0)	—	—

A plot of the selected positions around the ellipse boundary within the first quadrant is shown in Fig. 3-23.

In the following procedure, the midpoint algorithm is used to display an ellipse with input parameters Rx, Ry, xCenter, and yCenter. Positions along the

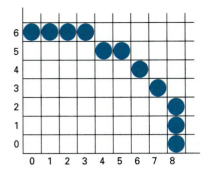

Figure 3-23
Positions along an elliptical path
centered on the origin with $r_x = 8$
and $r_y = 6$ using the midpoint
algorithm to calculate pixel
addresses in the first quadrant.

curve in the first quadrant are generated and then shifted to their proper screen
positions. Intensities for these positions and the symmetry positions in the other
three quadrants are loaded into the frame buffer using the setPixel routine.

```c
#include "device.h"

#define ROUND(a)  ((int)(a+0.5))

void ellipseMidpoint (int xCenter, int yCenter, int Rx, int Ry)
{
  int Rx2 = Rx*Rx;
  int Ry2 = Ry*Ry;
  int twoRx2 = 2*Rx2;
  int twoRy2 = 2*Ry2;
  int p;
  int x = 0;
  int y = Ry;
  int px = 0;
  int py = twoRx2 * y;
  void ellipsePlotPoints (int, int, int, int);

  /* Plot the first set of points */
  ellipsePlotPoints (xCenter, yCenter, x, y);

  /* Region 1 */
  p = ROUND (Ry2 - (Rx2 * Ry) + (0.25 * Rx2));
  while (px < py) {
    x++;
    px += twoRy2;
    if (p < 0)
      p += Ry2 + px;
    else {
      y--;
      py -= twoRx2;
      p += Ry2 + px - py;
    }
    ellipsePlotPoints (xCenter, yCenter, x, y);
  }

  /* Region 2 */
  p = ROUND (Ry2*(x+0.5)*(x+0.5) + Rx2*(y-1)*(y-1) - Rx2*Ry2);
  while (y > 0) {
    y--;
    py -= twoRx2;
    if (p > 0)
      p += Rx2 - py;
    else {
      x++;
      px += twoRy2;
      p += Rx2 - py + px;
```

```
    }
    ellipsePlotPoints (xCenter, yCenter, x, y);
  }
}

void ellipsePlotPoints (int xCenter, int yCenter, int x, int y)
{
  setPixel (xCenter + x, yCenter + y);
  setPixel (xCenter - x, yCenter + y);
  setPixel (xCenter + x, yCenter - y);
  setPixel (xCenter - x, yCenter - y);
}
```

3-7

OTHER CURVES

Various curve functions are useful in object modeling, animation path specifications, data and function graphing, and other graphics applications. Commonly encountered curves include conics, trigonometric and exponential functions, probability distributions, general polynomials, and spline functions. Displays of these curves can be generated with methods similar to those discussed for the circle and ellipse functions. We can obtain positions along curve paths directly from explicit representations $y = f(x)$ or from parametric forms. Alternatively, we could apply the incremental midpoint method to plot curves described with implicit functions $f(x, y) = 0$.

A straightforward method for displaying a specified curve function is to approximate it with straight line segments. Parametric representations are useful in this case for obtaining equally spaced line endpoint positions along the curve path. We can also generate equally spaced positions from an explicit representation by choosing the independent variable according to the slope of the curve. Where the slope of $y = f(x)$ has a magnitude less than 1, we choose x as the independent variable and calculate y values at equal x increments. To obtain equal spacing where the slope has a magnitude greater than 1, we use the inverse function, $x = f^{-1}(y)$, and calculate values of x at equal y steps.

Straight-line or curve approximations are used to graph a data set of discrete coordinate points. We could join the discrete points with straight line segments, or we could use linear regression (least squares) to approximate the data set with a single straight line. A nonlinear least-squares approach is used to display the data set with some approximating function, usually a polynomial.

As with circles and ellipses, many functions possess symmetries that can be exploited to reduce the computation of coordinate positions along curve paths. For example, the normal probability distribution function is symmetric about a center position (the mean), and all points along one cycle of a sine curve can be generated from the points in a 90° interval.

Conic Sections

In general, we can describe a **conic section** (or **conic**) with the second-degree equation:

$$Ax^2 + By^2 + Cxy + Dx + Ey + F = 0 \qquad (3\text{-}50)$$

where values for parameters $A, B, C, D, E,$ and F determine the kind of curve we are to display. Given this set of coefficients, we can determine the particular conic that will be generated by evaluating the discriminant $B^2 - 4AC$:

$$B^2 - 4AC \begin{cases} < 0, & \text{generates an ellipse (or circle)} \\ = 0, & \text{generates a parabola} \\ > 0, & \text{generates a hyperbola} \end{cases} \quad (3\text{-}51)$$

For example, we get the circle equation 3-24 when $A = B = 1$, $C = 0$, $D = -2x_c$, $E = -2y_c$, and $F = x_c^2 + y_c^2 - r^2$. Equation 3-50 also describes the "degenerate" conics: points and straight lines.

Ellipses, hyperbolas, and parabolas are particularly useful in certain animation applications. These curves describe orbital and other motions for objects subjected to gravitational, electromagnetic, or nuclear forces. Planetary orbits in the solar system, for example, are ellipses; and an object projected into a uniform gravitational field travels along a parabolic trajectory. Figure 3-24 shows a parabolic path in standard position for a gravitational field acting in the negative y direction. The explicit equation for the parabolic trajectory of the object shown can be written as

$$y = y_0 + a(x - x_0)^2 + b(x - x_0) \quad (3\text{-}52)$$

with constants a and b determined by the initial velocity v_0 of the object and the acceleration g due to the uniform gravitational force. We can also describe such parabolic motions with parametric equations using a time parameter t, measured in seconds from the initial projection point:

$$\begin{aligned} x &= x_0 + v_{x0}t \\ y &= y_0 + v_{y0}t - \frac{1}{2}gt^2 \end{aligned} \quad (3\text{-}53)$$

Here, v_{x0} and v_{y0} are the initial velocity components, and the value of g near the surface of the earth is approximately 980cm/sec^2. Object positions along the parabolic path are then calculated at selected time steps.

Hyperbolic motions (Fig. 3-25) occur in connection with the collision of charged particles and in certain gravitational problems. For example, comets or meteorites moving around the sun may travel along hyperbolic paths and escape to outer space, never to return. The particular branch (left or right, in Fig. 3-25) describing the motion of an object depends on the forces involved in the problem. We can write the standard equation for the hyperbola centered on the origin in Fig. 3-25 as

$$\left(\frac{x}{r_x}\right)^2 - \left(\frac{y}{r_y}\right)^2 = 1 \quad (3\text{-}54)$$

with $x \leq -r_x$ for the left branch and $x \geq r_x$ for the right branch. Since this equation differs from the standard ellipse equation 3-35 only in the sign between the x^2 and y^2 terms, we can generate points along a hyperbolic path with a slightly modified ellipse algorithm. We will return to the discussion of animation applications and methods in more detail in Chapter 16. And in Chapter 10, we discuss applications of computer graphics in scientific visualization.

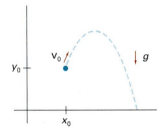

Figure 3-24
Parabolic path of an object tossed into a downward gravitational field at the initial position (x_0, y_0).

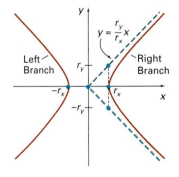

Figure 3-25
Left and right branches of a hyperbola in standard position with symmetry axis along the x axis.

111

Parabolas and hyperbolas possess a symmetry axis. For example, the parabola described by Eq. 3-53 is symmetric about the axis:

$$x = x_0 + v_{x0}v_{y0}/g$$

The methods used in the midpoint ellipse algorithm can be directly applied to obtain points along one side of the symmetry axis of hyperbolic and parabolic paths in the two regions: (1) where the magnitude of the curve slope is less than 1, and (2) where the magnitude of the slope is greater than 1. To do this, we first select the appropriate form of Eq. 3-50 and then use the selected function to set up expressions for the decision parameters in the two regions.

Polynomials and Spline Curves

A polynomial function of nth degree in x is defined as

$$y = \sum_{k=0}^{n} a_k x^k$$

$$= a_0 + a_1 x + \cdots + a_{n-1}x^{n-1} + a_n x^n$$

(3-55)

where n is a nonnegative integer and the a_k are constants, with $a_n \neq 0$. We get a quadratic when $n = 2$; a cubic polynomial when $n = 3$; a quartic when $n = 4$; and so forth. And we have a straight line when $n = 1$. Polynomials are useful in a number of graphics applications, including the design of object shapes, the specification of animation paths, and the graphing of data trends in a discrete set of data points.

Designing object shapes or motion paths is typically done by specifying a few points to define the general curve contour, then fitting the selected points with a polynomial. One way to accomplish the curve fitting is to construct a cubic polynomial curve section between each pair of specified points. Each curve section is then described in parametric form as

$$x = a_{x0} + a_{x1}u + a_{x2}u^2 + a_{x3}u^3$$

(3-56)

$$y = a_{y0} + a_{y1}u + a_{y2}u^2 + a_{y3}u^3$$

(3-57)

Figure 3-26

A spline curve formed with individual cubic polynomial sections between specified coordinate points.

where parameter u varies over the interval 0 to 1. Values for the coefficients of u in the parametric equations are determined from boundary conditions on the curve sections. One boundary condition is that two adjacent curve sections have the same coordinate position at the boundary, and a second condition is to match the two curve slopes at the boundary so that we obtain one continuous, smooth curve (Fig. 3-26). Continuous curves that are formed with polynomial pieces are called **spline curves**, or simply **splines**. There are other ways to set up spline curves, and the various spline-generating methods are explored in Chapter 10.

3-8

PARALLEL CURVE ALGORITHMS

Methods for exploiting parallelism in curve generation are similar to those used in displaying straight line segments. We can either adapt a sequential algorithm by allocating processors according to curve partitions, or we could devise other methods and assign processors to screen partitions.

A parallel midpoint method for displaying circles is to divide the circular arc from 90° to 45° into equal subarcs and assign a separate processor to each subarc. As in the parallel Bresenham line algorithm, we then need to set up computations to determine the beginning y value and decision parameter p_k value for each processor. Pixel positions are then calculated throughout each subarc, and positions in the other circle octants are then obtained by symmetry. Similarly, a parallel ellipse midpoint method divides the elliptical arc over the first quadrant into equal subarcs and parcels these out to separate processors. Pixel positions in the other quadrants are determined by symmetry. A screen-partitioning scheme for circles and ellipses is to assign each scan line crossing the curve to a separate processor. In this case, each processor uses the circle or ellipse equation to calculate curve-intersection coordinates.

For the display of elliptical arcs or other curves, we can simply use the scan-line partitioning method. Each processor uses the curve equation to locate the intersection positions along its assigned scan line. With processors assigned to individual pixels, each processor would calculate the distance (or distance squared) from the curve to its assigned pixel. If the calculated distance is less than a predefined value, the pixel is plotted.

3-9
CURVE FUNCTIONS

Routines for circles, splines, and other commonly used curves are included in many graphics packages. The PHIGS standard does not provide explicit functions for these curves, but it does include the following general curve function:

```
generalizedDrawingPrimitive (n, wcPoints, id, datalist)
```

where `wcPoints` is a list of `n` coordinate positions, `datalist` contains noncoordinate data values, and parameter `id` selects the desired function. At a particular installation, a circle might be referenced with `id = 1`, an ellipse with `id = 2`, and so on.

As an example of the definition of curves through this PHIGS function, a circle (`id = 1`, say) could be specified by assigning the two center coordinate values to `wcpoints` and assigning the radius value to `datalist`. The generalized drawing primitive would then reference the appropriate algorithm, such as the midpoint method, to generate the circle. With interactive input, a circle could be defined with two coordinate points: the center position and a point on the circumference. Similarly, interactive specification of an ellipse can be done with three points: the two foci and a point on the ellipse boundary, all stored in `wcpoints`. For an ellipse in standard position, *wcpoints* could be assigned only the center coordinates, with *datalist* assigned the values for r_x and r_y. Splines defined with control points would be generated by assigning the control point coordinates to `wcpoints`.

Functions to generate circles and ellipses often include the capability of drawing curve sections by specifying parameters for the line endpoints. Expanding the parameter list allows specification of the beginning and ending angular values for an arc, as illustrated in Fig. 3-27. Another method for designating a cir-

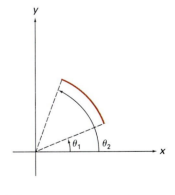

Figure 3-27
Circular arc specified by beginning and ending angles. Circle center is at the coordinate origin.

113

cular or elliptical arc is to input the beginning and ending coordinate positions of the arc.

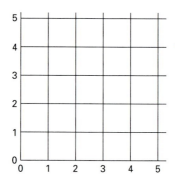

Figure 3-28
Lower-left section of the screen grid referencing integer coordinate positions.

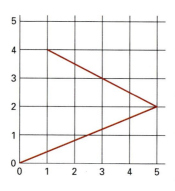

Figure 3-29
Line path for a series of connected line segments between screen grid coordinate positions.

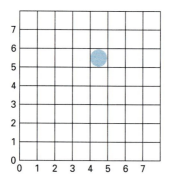

Figure 3-30
Illuminated pixel at raster position (4, 5).

3-10

PIXEL ADDRESSING AND OBJECT GEOMETRY

So far we have assumed that all input positions were given in terms of scan-line number and pixel-position number across the scan line. As we saw in Chapter 2, there are, in general, several coordinate references associated with the specification and generation of a picture. Object descriptions are given in a world-reference frame, chosen to suit a particular application, and input world coordinates are ultimately converted to screen display positions. World descriptions of objects are given in terms of precise coordinate positions, which are infinitesimally small mathematical points. Pixel coordinates, however, reference finite screen areas. If we want to preserve the specified geometry of world objects, we need to compensate for the mapping of mathematical input points to finite pixel areas. One way to do this is simply to adjust the dimensions of displayed objects to account for the amount of overlap of pixel areas with the object boundaries. Another approach is to map world coordinates onto screen positions between pixels, so that we align object boundaries with pixel boundaries instead of pixel centers.

Screen Grid Coordinates

An alternative to addressing display positions in terms of pixel centers is to reference screen coordinates with respect to the grid of horizontal and vertical pixel boundary lines spaced one unit apart (Fig. 3-28). A screen coordinate position is then the pair of integer values identifying a grid intersection position between two pixels. For example, the mathematical line path for a polyline with screen endpoints (0, 0), (5, 2), and (1, 4) is shown in Fig. 3-29.

With the coordinate origin at the lower left of the screen, each pixel area can be referenced by the integer grid coordinates of its lower left corner. Figure 3-30 illustrates this convention for an 8 by 8 section of a raster, with a single illuminated pixel at screen coordinate position (4, 5). In general, we identify the area occupied by a pixel with screen coordinates (x, y) as the unit square with diagonally opposite corners at (x, y) and $(x + 1, y + 1)$. This pixel-addressing scheme has several advantages: It avoids half-integer pixel boundaries, it facilitates precise object representations, and it simplifies the processing involved in many scan-conversion algorithms and in other raster procedures.

The algorithms for line drawing and curve generation discussed in the preceding sections are still valid when applied to input positions expressed as screen grid coordinates. Decision parameters in these algorithms are now simply a measure of screen grid separation differences, rather than separation differences from pixel centers.

Maintaining Geometric Properties of Displayed Objects

When we convert geometric descriptions of objects into pixel representations, we transform mathematical points and lines into finite screen areas. If we are to maintain the original geometric measurements specified by the input coordinates

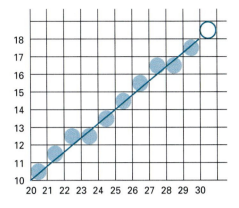

Figure 3-31
Line path and corresponding pixel display for input screen grid endpoint coordinates (20, 10) and (30, 18).

for an object, we need to account for the finite size of pixels when we transform the object definition to a screen display.

Figure 3-31 shows the line plotted in the Bresenham line-algorithm example of Section 3-2. Interpreting the line endpoints (20, 10) and (30, 18) as precise grid crossing positions, we see that the line should not extend past screen grid position (30, 18). If we were to plot the pixel with screen coordinates (30, 18), as in the example given in Section 3-2, we would display a line that spans 11 horizontal units and 9 vertical units. For the mathematical line, however, $\Delta x = 10$ and $\Delta y = 8$. If we are addressing pixels by their center positions, we can adjust the length of the displayed line by omitting one of the endpoint pixels. If we think of screen coordinates as addressing pixel boundaries, as shown in Fig. 3-31, we plot a line using only those pixels that are "interior" to the line path; that is, only those pixels that are between the line endpoints. For our example, we would plot the leftmost pixel at (20, 10) and the rightmost pixel at (29, 17). This displays a line that

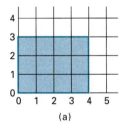

(a)

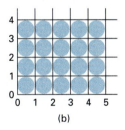

(b)

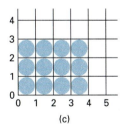

(c)

Figure 3-32
Conversion of rectangle (a) with vertices at screen coordinates (0, 0), (4, 0), (4, 3), and (0, 3) into display (b) that includes the right and top boundaries and into display (c) that maintains geometric magnitudes.

has the same geometric magnitudes as the mathematical line from (20, 10) to (30, 18).

For an enclosed area, input geometric properties are maintained by displaying the area only with those pixels that are interior to the object boundaries. The rectangle defined with the screen coordinate vertices shown in Fig. 3-32(a), for example, is larger when we display it filled with pixels up to and including the border pixel lines joining the specified vertices. As defined, the area of the rectangle is 12 units, but as displayed in Fig. 3-32(b), it has an area of 20 units. In Fig. 3-32(c), the original rectangle measurements are maintained by displaying

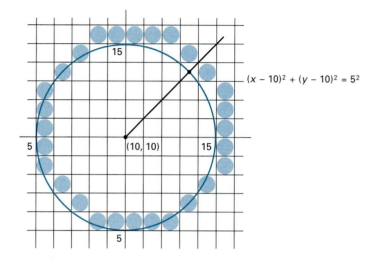

$$(x - 10)^2 + (y - 10)^2 = 5^2$$

Figure 3-33
Circle path and midpoint circle algorithm plot of a circle with radius 5 in screen coordinates.

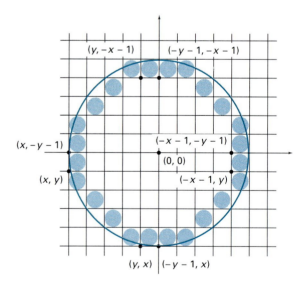

Figure 3-34
Modification of the circle plot in Fig. 3-33 to maintain the specified circle diameter of 10.

only the internal pixels. The right boundary of the input rectangle is at $x = 4$. To maintain this boundary in the display, we set the rightmost pixel grid coordinate at $x = 3$. The pixels in this vertical column then span the interval from $x = 3$ to $x = 4$. Similarly, the mathematical top boundary of the rectangle is at $y = 3$, so we set the top pixel row for the displayed rectangle at $y = 2$.

These compensations for finite pixel width along object boundaries can be applied to other polygons and to curved figures so that the raster display maintains the input object specifications. A circle of radius 5 and center position (10, 10), for instance, would be displayed as in Fig. 3-33 by the midpoint circle algorithm using screen grid coordinate positions. But the plotted circle has a diameter of 11. To plot the circle with the defined diameter of 10, we can modify the circle algorithm to shorten each pixel scan line and each pixel column, as in Fig. 3-34. One way to do this is to generate points clockwise along the circular arc in the third quadrant, starting at screen coordinates (10, 5). For each generated point, the other seven circle symmetry points are generated by decreasing the x coordinate values by 1 along scan lines and decreasing the y coordinate values by 1 along pixel columns. Similar methods are applied in ellipse algorithms to maintain the specified proportions in the display of an ellipse.

3-11
FILLED-AREA PRIMITIVES

A standard output primitive in general graphics packages is a solid-color or patterned polygon area. Other kinds of area primitives are sometimes available, but polygons are easier to process since they have linear boundaries.

There are two basic approaches to area filling on raster systems. One way to fill an area is to determine the overlap intervals for scan lines that cross the area. Another method for area filling is to start from a given interior position and paint outward from this point until we encounter the specified boundary conditions. The scan-line approach is typically used in general graphics packages to fill polygons, circles, ellipses, and other simple curves. Fill methods starting from an interior point are useful with more complex boundaries and in interactive painting systems. In the following sections, we consider methods for solid fill of specified areas. Other fill options are discussed in Chapter 4.

Scan-Line Polygon Fill Algorithm

Figure 3-35 illustrates the scan-line procedure for solid filling of polygon areas. For each scan line crossing a polygon, the area-fill algorithm locates the intersection points of the scan line with the polygon edges. These intersection points are then sorted from left to right, and the corresponding frame-buffer positions between each intersection pair are set to the specified fill color. In the example of Fig. 3-35, the four pixel intersection positions with the polygon boundaries define two stretches of interior pixels from $x = 10$ to $x = 14$ and from $x = 18$ to $x = 24$.

Some scan-line intersections at polygon vertices require special handling. A scan line passing through a vertex intersects two polygon edges at that position, adding two points to the list of intersections for the scan line. Figure 3-36 shows two scan lines at positions y and y' that intersect edge endpoints. Scan line y intersects five polygon edges. Scan line y', however, intersects an even number of edges although it also passes through a vertex. Intersection points along scan line

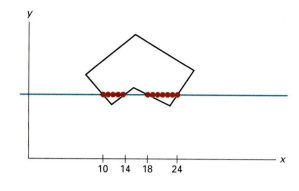

Figure 3-35
Interior pixels along a scan line
passing through a polygon area.

y' correctly identify the interior pixel spans. But with scan line y, we need to do some additional processing to determine the correct interior points.

The topological difference between scan line y and scan line y' in Fig. 3-36 is identified by noting the position of the intersecting edges relative to the scan line. For scan line y, the two intersecting edges sharing a vertex are on opposite sides of the scan line. But for scan line y', the two intersecting edges are both above the scan line. Thus, the vertices that require additional processing are those that have connecting edges on opposite sides of the scan line. We can identify these vertices by tracing around the polygon boundary either in clockwise or counterclockwise order and observing the relative changes in vertex y coordinates as we move from one edge to the next. If the endpoint y values of two consecutive edges mo-notonically increase or decrease, we need to count the middle vertex as a single intersection point for any scan line passing through that vertex. Otherwise, the shared vertex represents a local extremum (minimum or maximum) on the poly-gon boundary, and the two edge intersections with the scan line passing through that vertex can be added to the intersection list.

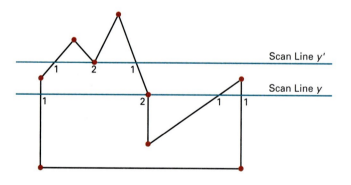

Figure 3-36
Intersection points along scan lines that intersect polygon vertices. Scan line y generates an odd number of intersections, but scan line y' generates an even number of intersections that can be paired to identify correctly the interior pixel spans.

One way to resolve the question as to whether we should count a vertex as one intersection or two is to shorten some polygon edges to split those vertices that should be counted as one intersection. We can process nonhorizontal edges around the polygon boundary in the order specified, either clockwise or counterclockwise. As we process each edge, we can check to determine whether that edge and the next nonhorizontal edge have either monotonically increasing or decreasing endpoint y values. If so, the lower edge can be shortened to ensure that only one intersection point is generated for the scan line going through the common vertex joining the two edges. Figure 3-37 illustrates shortening of an edge. When the endpoint y coordinates of the two edges are increasing, the y value of the upper endpoint for the current edge is decreased by 1, as in Fig. 3-37(a). When the endpoint y values are monotonically decreasing, as in Fig. 3-37(b), we decrease the y coordinate of the upper endpoint of the edge following the current edge.

Calculations performed in scan-conversion and other graphics algorithms typically take advantage of various **coherence** properties of a scene that is to be displayed. What we mean by coherence is simply that the properties of one part of a scene are related in some way to other parts of the scene so that the relationship can be used to reduce processing. Coherence methods often involve incremental calculations applied along a single scan line or between successive scan lines. In determining edge intersections, we can set up incremental coordinate calculations along any edge by exploiting the fact that the slope of the edge is constant from one scan line to the next. Figure 3-38 shows two successive scan lines crossing a left edge of a polygon. The slope of this polygon boundary line can be expressed in terms of the scan-line intersection coordinates:

$$m = \frac{y_{k+1} - y_k}{x_{k+1} - x_k} \qquad (3\text{-}58)$$

Since the change in y coordinates between the two scan lines is simply

$$y_{k+1} - y_k = 1 \qquad (3\text{-}59)$$

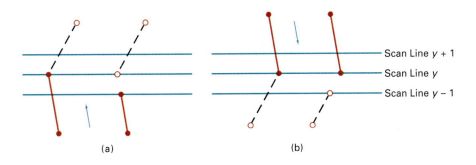

(a)   (b)

Scan Line $y + 1$

Scan Line y

Scan Line $y - 1$

Figure 3-37

Adjusting endpoint y values for a polygon, as we process edges in order around the polygon perimeter. The edge currently being processed is indicated as a solid line. In (a), the y coordinate of the upper endpoint of the current edge is decreased by 1. In (b), the y coordinate of the upper endpoint of the next edge is decreased by 1.

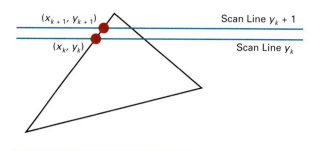

Figure 3-38
Two successive scan lines
intersecting a polygon boundary.

the x-intersection value x_{k+1} on the upper scan line can be determined from the x-intersection value x_k on the preceding scan line as

$$x_{k+1} = x_k + \frac{1}{m} \qquad (3\text{-}60)$$

Each successive x intercept can thus be calculated by adding the inverse of the slope and rounding to the nearest integer.

An obvious parallel implementation of the fill algorithm is to assign each scan line crossing the polygon area to a separate processor. Edge-intersection calculations are then performed independently. Along an edge with slope m, the intersection x_k value for scan line k above the initial scan line can be calculated as

$$x_k = x_0 + \frac{k}{m} \qquad (3\text{-}61)$$

In a sequential fill algorithm, the increment of x values by the amount $1/m$ along an edge can be accomplished with integer operations by recalling that the slope m is the ratio of two integers:

$$m = \frac{\Delta y}{\Delta x}$$

where Δx and Δy are the differences between the edge endpoint x and y coordinate values. Thus, incremental calculations of x intercepts along an edge for successive scan lines can be expressed as

$$x_{k+1} = x_k + \frac{\Delta x}{\Delta y} \qquad (3\text{-}62)$$

Using this equation, we can perform integer evaluation of the x intercepts by initializing a counter to 0, then incrementing the counter by the value of Δx each time we move up to a new scan line. Whenever the counter value becomes equal to or greater than Δy, we increment the current x intersection value by 1 and decrease the counter by the value Δy. This procedure is equivalent to maintaining integer and fractional parts for x intercepts and incrementing the fractional part until we reach the next integer value.

As an example of integer incrementing, suppose we have an edge with slope $m = 7/3$. At the initial scan line, we set the counter to 0 and the counter in-

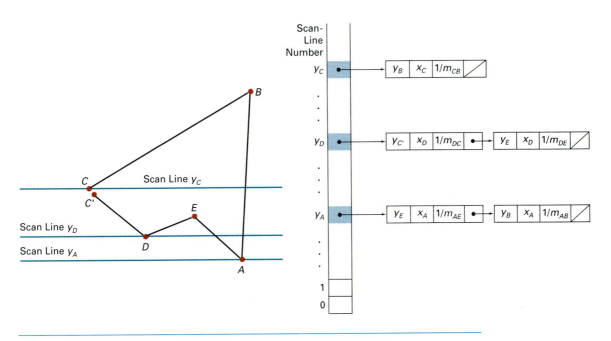

Figure 3-39
A polygon and its sorted edge table, with edge $\overline{DC}$ shortened by one unit in the y direction.

crement to 3. As we move up to the next three scan lines along this edge, the counter is successively assigned the values 3, 6, and 9. On the third scan line above the initial scan line, the counter now has a value greater than 7. So we increment the x-intersection coordinate by 1, and reset the counter to the value $9 - 7 = 2$. We continue determining the scan-line intersections in this way until we reach the upper endpoint of the edge. Similar calculations are carried out to obtain intersections for edges with negative slopes.

We can round to the nearest pixel x-intersection value, instead of truncating to obtain integer positions, by modifying the edge-intersection algorithm so that the increment is compared to $\Delta y/2$. This can be done with integer arithmetic by incrementing the counter with the value $2\Delta x$ at each step and comparing the increment to Δy. When the increment is greater than or equal to Δy, we increase the x value by 1 and decrement the counter by the value of $2\Delta y$. In our previous example with $m = 7/3$, the counter values for the first few scan lines above the initial scan line on this edge would now be 6, 12 (reduced to -2), 4, 10 (reduced to -4), 2, 8 (reduced to -6), 0, 6, and 12 (reduced to -2). Now x would be incremented on scan lines 2, 4, 6, 9, etc., above the initial scan line for this edge. The extra calculations required for each edge are $2\Delta x = \Delta x + \Delta x$ and $2\Delta y = \Delta y + \Delta y$.

To efficiently perform a polygon fill, we can first store the polygon boundary in a *sorted edge table* that contains all the information necessary to process the scan lines efficiently. Proceeding around the edges in either a clockwise or a counterclockwise order, we can use a bucket sort to store the edges, sorted on the smallest y value of each edge, in the correct scan-line positions. Only nonhorizontal edges are entered into the sorted edge table. As the edges are processed, we can also shorten certain edges to resolve the vertex-intersection question. Each entry in the table for a particular scan line contains the maximum y value for that edge, the x-intercept value (at the lower vertex) for the edge, and the inverse slope of the edge. For each scan line, the edges are in sorted order from left to right. Figure 3-39 shows a polygon and the associated sorted edge table.

121

Next, we process the scan lines from the bottom of the polygon to its top, producing an *active edge list* for each scan line crossing the polygon boundaries. The active edge list for a scan line contains all edges crossed by that scan line, with iterative coherence calculations used to obtain the edge intersections.

Implementation of edge-intersection calculations can also be facilitated by storing Δx and Δy values in the sorted edge table. Also, to ensure that we correctly fill the interior of specified polygons, we can apply the considerations discussed in Section 3-10. For each scan line, we fill in the pixel spans for each pair of x-intercepts starting from the leftmost x-intercept value and ending at one position before the rightmost x intercept. And each polygon edge can be shortened by one unit in the y direction at the top endpoint. These measures also guarantee that pixels in adjacent polygons will not overlap each other.

The following procedure performs a solid-fill scan conversion for an input set of polygon vertices. For each scan line within the vertical extents of the polygon, an active edge list is set up and edge intersections are calculated. Across each scan line, the interior fill is then applied between successive pairs of edge intersections, processed from left to right.

```
#include "device.h"

typedef struct tEdge {
  int yUpper;
  float xIntersect, dxPerScan;
  struct tEdge * next;
} Edge;

/* Inserts edge into list in order of increasing xIntersect field. */
void insertEdge (Edge * list, Edge * edge)
{
  Edge * p, * q = list;

  p = q->next;
  while (p != NULL) {
    if (edge->xIntersect < p->xIntersect)
      p = NULL;
    else {
      q = p;
      p = p->next;
    }
  }
  edge->next = q->next;
  q->next = edge;
}

/* For an index, return y-coordinate of next nonhorizontal line */
int yNext (int k, int cnt, dcPt * pts)
{
  int j;

  if ((k+1) > (cnt-1))
    j = 0;
  else
    j = k + 1;
  while (pts[k].y == pts[j].y)
    if ((j+1) > (cnt-1))
      j = 0;
    else
```

```
        j++;
  return (pts[j].y);
}

/* Store lower-y coordinate and inverse slope for each edge.  Adjust
   and store upper-y coordinate for edges that are the lower member
   of a monotonically increasing or decreasing pair of edges */
void makeEdgeRec
  (dcPt lower, dcPt upper, int yComp, Edge * edge, Edge * edges[])
{
  edge->dxPerScan =
    (float) (upper.x - lower.x) / (upper.y - lower.y);
  edge->xIntersect = lower.x;
  if (upper.y < yComp)
    edge->yUpper = upper.y - 1;
  else
    edge->yUpper = upper.y;
  insertEdge (edges[lower.y], edge);
}

void buildEdgeList (int cnt, dcPt * pts, Edge * edges[])
{
  Edge * edge;
  dcPt v1, v2;
  int i, yPrev = pts[cnt - 2].y;

  v1.x = pts[cnt-1].x; v1.y = pts[cnt-1].y;
  for (i=0; i<cnt; i++) {
    v2 = pts[i];
    if (v1.y != v2.y) {                    /* nonhorizontal line */
      edge = (Edge *) malloc (sizeof (Edge));
      if (v1.y < v2.y)                     /* up-going edge      */
        makeEdgeRec (v1, v2, yNext (i, cnt, pts), edge, edges);
      else                                 /* down-going edge    */
        makeEdgeRec (v2, v1, yPrev, edge, edges);
    }
    yPrev = v1.y;
    v1 = v2;
  }
}

void buildActiveList (int scan, Edge * active, Edge * edges[])
{
  Edge * p, * q;

  p = edges[scan]->next;
  while (p) {
    q = p->next;
    insertEdge (active, p);
    p = q;
  }
}

void fillScan (int scan, Edge * active)
{
  Edge * p1, * p2;
  int i;

  p1 = active->next;
  while (p1) {
    p2 = p1->next;
```

```c
      for (i=p1->xIntersect; i<p2->xIntersect; i++)
        setPixel ((int) i, scan);
      p1 = p2->next;
    }
}

void deleteAfter (Edge * q)
{
  Edge * p = q->next;

  q->next = p->next;
  free (p);
}

/* Delete completed edges. Update 'xIntersect' field for others */
void updateActiveList (int scan, Edge * active)
{
  Edge * q = active, * p = active->next;

  while (p)
    if (scan >= p->yUpper) {
      p = p->next;
      deleteAfter (q);
    }
    else {
      p->xIntersect = p->xIntersect + p->dxPerScan;
      q = p;
      p = p->next;
    }
}

void resortActiveList (Edge * active)
{
  Edge * q, * p = active->next;

  active->next = NULL;
  while (p) {
    q = p->next;
    insertEdge (active, p);
    p = q;
  }
}

void scanFill (int cnt, dcPt * pts)
{
  Edge * edges[WINDOW_HEIGHT], * active;
  int i, scan;

  for (i=0; i<WINDOW_HEIGHT; i++) {
    edges[i] = (Edge *) malloc (sizeof (Edge));
    edges[i]->next = NULL;
  }
  buildEdgeList (cnt, pts, edges);
  active = (Edge *) malloc (sizeof (Edge));
  active->next = NULL;

  for (scan=0; scan<WINDOW_HEIGHT; scan++) {
    buildActiveList (scan, active, edges);
    if (active->next) {
      fillScan (scan, active);
      updateActiveList (scan, active);
      resortActiveList (active);
    }
```

```
        }
        /* Free edge records that have been malloc'ed ... */
}
```

Inside-Outside Tests

Area-filling algorithms and other graphics processes often need to identify interior regions of objects. So far, we have discussed area filling only in terms of standard polygon shapes. In elementary geometry, a polygon is usually defined as having no self-intersections. Examples of standard polygons include triangles, rectangles, octagons, and decagons. The component edges of these objects are joined only at the vertices, and otherwise the edges have no common points in the plane. Identifying the interior regions of standard polygons is generally a straightforward process. But in most graphics applications, we can specify any sequence for the vertices of a fill area, including sequences that produce intersecting edges, as in Fig. 3-40. For such shapes, it is not always clear which regions of the xy plane we should call "interior" and which regions we should designate as "exterior" to the object. Graphics packages normally use either the odd-even rule or the nonzero winding number rule to identify interior regions of an object.

We apply the **odd-even rule**, also called the **odd parity rule** or the **even-odd rule**, by conceptually drawing a line from any position **P** to a distant point outside the coordinate extents of the object and counting the number of edge crossings along the line. If the number of polygon edges crossed by this line is odd, then **P** is an *interior* point. Otherwise, **P** is an *exterior* point. To obtain an accurate edge count, we must be sure that the line path we choose does not intersect any polygon vertices. Figure 3-40(a) shows the interior and exterior regions obtained from the odd-even rule for a self-intersecting set of edges. The scan-line polygon fill algorithm discussed in the previous section is an example of area filling using the odd-even rule.

Another method for defining interior regions is the **nonzero winding number rule**, which counts the number of times the polygon edges wind around a particular point in the counterclockwise direction. This count is called the **winding number**, and the interior points of a two-dimensional object are defined to be

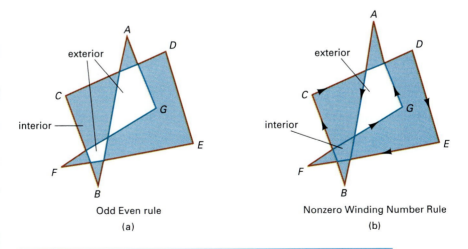

Odd Even rule

(a)

Nonzero Winding Number Rule

(b)

Figure 3-40
Identifying interior and exterior regions for a self-intersecting polygon.

those that have a nonzero value for the winding number. We apply the nonzero winding number rule to polygons by initializing the winding number to 0 and again imagining a line drawn from any position **P** to a distant point beyond the coordinate extents of the object. The line we choose must not pass through any vertices. As we move along the line from position **P** to the distant point, we count the number of edges that cross the line in each direction. We add 1 to the winding number every time we intersect a polygon edge that crosses the line from right to left, and we subtract 1 every time we intersect an edge that crosses from left to right. The final value of the winding number, after all edge crossings have been counted, determines the relative position of **P**. If the winding number is nonzero, **P** is defined to be an interior point. Otherwise, **P** is taken to be an exterior point. Figure 3-40(b) shows the interior and exterior regions defined by the nonzero winding number rule for a self-intersecting set of edges. For standard polygons and other simple shapes, the nonzero winding number rule and the odd-even rule give the same results. But for more complicated shapes, the two methods may yield different interior and exterior regions, as in the example of Fig. 3-40.

One way to determine directional edge crossings is to take the vector cross product of a vector **u** along the line from **P** to a distant point with the edge vector **E** for each edge that crosses the line. If the z component of the cross product **u** $\times$ **E** for a particular edge is positive, that edge crosses from right to left and we add 1 to the winding number. Otherwise, the edge crosses from left to right and we subtract 1 from the winding number. An edge vector is calculated by subtracting the starting vertex position for that edge from the ending vertex position. For example, the edge vector for the first edge in the example of Fig. 3-40 is

$$\mathbf{E}_{AB} = \mathbf{V}_B - \mathbf{V}_A$$

where $\mathbf{V}_A$ and $\mathbf{V}_B$ represent the point vectors for vertices A and B. A somewhat simpler way to compute directional edge crossings is to use vector dot products instead of cross products. To do this, we set up a vector that is perpendicular to **u** and that points from right to left as we look along the line from **P** in the direction of **u**. If the components of **u** are (u_x, u_y), then this perpendicular to **u** has components $(-u_y, u_x)$ (Appendix A). Now, if the dot product of the perpendicular and an edge vector is positive, that edge crosses the line from right to left and we add 1 to the winding number. Otherwise, the edge crosses the line from left to right, and we subtract 1 from the winding number.

Some graphics packages use the nonzero winding number rule to implement area filling, since it is more versatile than the odd-even rule. In general, objects can be defined with multiple, unconnected sets of vertices or disjoint sets of closed curves, and the direction specified for each set can be used to define the interior regions of objects. Examples include characters, such as letters of the alphabet and punctuation symbols, nested polygons, and concentric circles or ellipses. For curved lines, the odd-even rule is applied by determining intersections with the curve path, instead of finding edge intersections. Similarly, with the nonzero winding number rule, we need to calculate tangent vectors to the curves at the crossover intersection points with the line from position **P**.

Scan-Line Fill of Curved Boundary Areas

In general, scan-line fill of regions with curved boundaries requires more work than polygon filling, since intersection calculations now involve nonlinear boundaries. For simple curves such as circles or ellipses, performing a scan-line fill is a straightforward process. We only need to calculate the two scan-line intersections on opposite sides of the curve. This is the same as generating pixel positions along the curve boundary, and we can do that with the midpoint method. Then we simply fill in the horizontal pixel spans between the boundary points on opposite sides of the curve. Symmetries between quadrants (and between octants for circles) are used to reduce the boundary calculations.

Similar methods can be used to generate a fill area for a curve section. An elliptical arc, for example, can be filled as in Fig. 3-41. The interior region is bounded by the ellipse section and a straight-line segment that closes the curve by joining the beginning and ending positions of the arc. Symmetries and incremental calculations are exploited whenever possible to reduce computations.

Figure 3-41
Interior fill of an elliptical arc.

Boundary-Fill Algorithm

Another approach to area filling is to start at a point inside a region and paint the interior outward toward the boundary. If the boundary is specified in a single color, the fill algorithm proceeds outward pixel by pixel until the boundary color is encountered. This method, called the **boundary-fill algorithm**, is particularly useful in interactive painting packages, where interior points are easily selected. Using a graphics tablet or other interactive device, an artist or designer can sketch a figure outline, select a fill color or pattern from a color menu, and pick an interior point. The system then paints the figure interior. To display a solid color region (with no border), the designer can choose the fill color to be the same as the boundary color.

A boundary-fill procedure accepts as input the coordinates of an interior point (x, y), a fill color, and a boundary color. Starting from (x, y), the procedure tests neighboring positions to determine whether they are of the boundary color. If not, they are painted with the fill color, and their neighbors are tested. This process continues until all pixels up to the boundary color for the area have been tested. Both inner and outer boundaries can be set up to specify an area, and some examples of defining regions for boundary fill are shown in Fig. 3-42.

Figure 3-43 shows two methods for proceeding to neighboring pixels from the current test position. In Fig. 3-43(a), four neighboring points are tested. These are the pixel positions that are right, left, above, and below the current pixel. Areas filled by this method are called **4-connected**. The second method, shown in Fig. 3-43(b), is used to fill more complex figures. Here the set of neighboring positions to be tested includes the four diagonal pixels. Fill methods using this approach are called **8-connected**. An 8-connected boundary-fill algorithm would correctly fill the interior of the area defined in Fig. 3-44, but a 4-connected boundary-fill algorithm produces the partial fill shown.

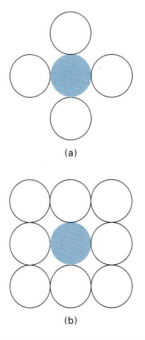

(a)

(b)

Figure 3-43
Fill methods applied to a 4-connected area (a) and to an 8-connected area (b). Open circles represent pixels to be tested from the current test position, shown as a solid color.

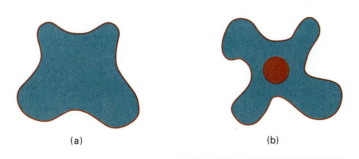

(a)   (b)

Figure 3-42
Example color boundaries for a boundary-fill procedure.

127

The following procedure illustrates a recursive method for filling a 4-connected area with an intensity specified in parameter `fill` up to a boundary color specified with parameter `boundary`. We can extend this procedure to fill an 8-connected region by including four additional statements to test diagonal positions, such as $(x + 1, y + 1)$.

```
void boundaryFill4 (int x, int y, int fill, int boundary)
{
  int current;

  current = getPixel (x, y);
  if ((current != boundary) && (current != fill)) {
    setColor (fill);
    setPixel (x, y);
    boundaryFill4 (x+1, y, fill, boundary);
    boundaryFill4 (x-1, y, fill, boundary);
    boundaryFill4 (x, y+1, fill, boundary);
    boundaryFill4 (x, y-1, fill, boundary);
  }
}
```

Recursive boundary-fill algorithms may not fill regions correctly if some interior pixels are already displayed in the fill color. This occurs because the algorithm checks next pixels both for boundary color and for fill color. Encountering a pixel with the fill color can cause a recursive branch to terminate, leaving other interior pixels unfilled. To avoid this, we can first change the color of any interior pixels that are initially set to the fill color before applying the boundary-fill procedure.

Also, since this procedure requires considerable stacking of neighboring points, more efficient methods are generally employed. These methods fill horizontal pixel spans across scan lines, instead of proceeding to 4-connected or 8-connected neighboring points. Then we need only stack a beginning position for each horizontal pixel span, instead of stacking all unprocessed neighboring positions around the current position. Starting from the initial interior point with this method, we first fill in the contiguous span of pixels on this starting scan line. Then we locate and stack starting positions for spans on the adjacent scan lines, where spans are defined as the contiguous horizontal string of positions

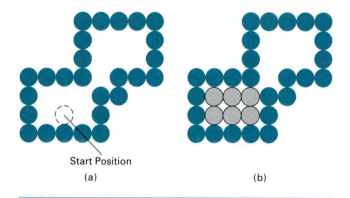

Start Position

(a)

(b)

Figure 3-44
The area defined within the color boundary (a) is only partially filled in (b) using a 4-connected boundary-fill algorithm.

Filled Pixel Spans   Stacked Positions

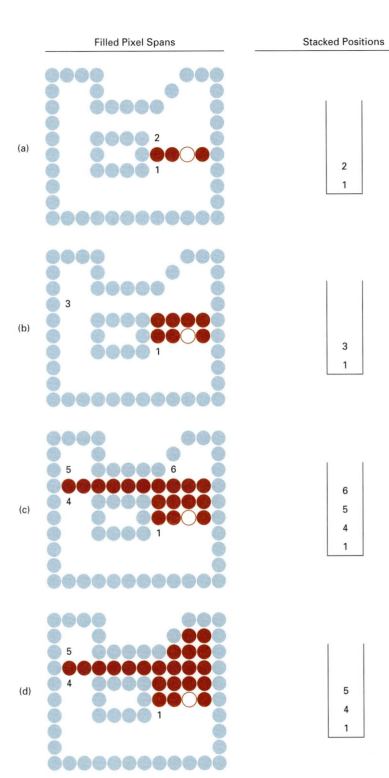

(a)

(b)

(c)

(d)

Figure 3-45
Boundary fill across pixel
spans for a 4-connected area.
(a) The filled initial pixel
span, showing the position of
the initial point (open circle)
and the stacked positions for
pixel spans on adjacent scan
lines. (b) Filled pixel span on
the first scan line above the
initial scan line and the
current contents of the stack.
(c) Filled pixel spans on the
first two scan lines above the
initial scan line and the
current contents of the stack.
(d) Completed pixel spans for
the upper-right portion of the
defined region and the
remaining stacked positions
to be processed.

bounded by pixels displayed in the area border color. At each subsequent step, we unstack the next start position and repeat the process.

An example of how pixel spans could be filled using this approach is illustrated for the 4-connected fill region in Fig. 3-45. In this example, we first process scan lines successively from the start line to the top boundary. After all upper scan lines are processed, we fill in the pixel spans on the remaining scan lines in order down to the bottom boundary. The leftmost pixel position for each horizontal span is located and stacked, in left to right order across successive scan lines, as shown in Fig. 3-45. In (a) of this figure, the initial span has been filled, and starting positions 1 and 2 for spans on the next scan lines (below and above) are stacked. In Fig. 3-45(b), position 2 has been unstacked and processed to produce the filled span shown, and the starting pixel (position 3) for the single span on the next scan line has been stacked. After position 3 is processed, the filled spans and stacked positions are as shown in Fig. 3-45(c). And Fig. 3-45(d) shows the filled pixels after processing all spans in the upper right of the specified area. Position 5 is next processed, and spans are filled in the upper left of the region; then position 4 is picked up to continue the processing for the lower scan lines.

Figure 3-46
An area defined within multiple color boundaries.

Flood-Fill Algorithm

Sometimes we want to fill in (or recolor) an area that is not defined within a single color boundary. Figure 3-46 shows an area bordered by several different color regions. We can paint such areas by replacing a specified interior color instead of searching for a boundary color value. This approach is called a **flood-fill algorithm**. We start from a specified interior point (x, y) and reassign all pixel values that are currently set to a given interior color with the desired fill color. If the area we want to paint has more than one interior color, we can first reassign pixel values so that all interior points have the same color. Using either a 4-connected or 8-connected approach, we then step through pixel positions until all interior points have been repainted. The following procedure flood fills a 4-connected region recursively, starting from the input position.

```
void floodFill4 (int x, int y, int fillColor, int oldColor)
{
  if (getPixel (x, y) == oldColor) {
    setColor (fillColor);
    setPixel (x, y);
    floodFill4 (x+1, y, fillColor, oldColor);
    floodFill4 (x-1, y, fillColor, oldColor);
    floodFill4 (x, y+1, fillColor, oldColor);
    floodFill4 (x, y-1, fillColor, oldColor);
  }
}
```

We can modify procedure `floodFill4` to reduce the storage requirements of the stack by filling horizontal pixel spans, as discussed for the boundary-fill algorithm. In this approach, we stack only the beginning positions for those pixel spans having the value `oldColor`. The steps in this modified flood-fill algorithm are similar to those illustrated in Fig. 3-45 for a boundary fill. Starting at the first position of each span, the pixel values are replaced until a value other than `oldColor` is encountered.

3-12
FILL-AREA FUNCTIONS

We display a filled polygon in PHIGS and GKS with the function

```
fillArea (n, wcVertices)
```

The displayed polygon area is bounded by a series of n straight line segments connecting the set of vertex positions specified in wcVertices. These packages do not provide fill functions for objects with curved boundaries.

Implementation of the fillArea function depends on the selected type of interior fill. We can display the polygon boundary surrounding a hollow interior, or we can choose a solid color or pattern fill with no border for the display of the polygon. For solid fill, the fillArea function is implemented with the scan-line fill algorithm to display a single color area. The various attribute options for displaying polygon fill areas in PHIGS are discussed in the next chapter.

Another polygon primitive available in PHIGS is fillAreaSet. This function allows a series of polygons to be displayed by specifying the list of vertices for each polygon. Also, in other graphics packages, functions are often provided for displaying a variety of commonly used fill areas besides general polygons. Some examples are fillRectangle, fillCircle, fillCircleArc, fill-Ellipse, and fillEllipseArc.

3-13
CELL ARRAY

The **cell array** is a primitive that allows users to display an arbitrary shape defined as a two-dimensional grid pattern. A predefined matrix of color values is mapped by this function onto a specified rectangular coordinate region. The PHIGS version of this function is

```
cellArray (wcPoints, n, m, colorArray)
```

where colorArray is the n by m matrix of integer color values and wcPoints lists the limits of the rectangular coordinate region: (x_{min}, y_{min}) and (x_{max}, y_{max}). Figure 3-47 shows the distribution of the elements of the color matrix over the coordinate rectangle.

Each coordinate cell in Fig. 3-47 has width $(x_{max} - x_{min})/n$ and height $(y_{max} - y_{min})/m$. Pixel color values are assigned according to the relative positions of the pixel center coordinates. If the center of a pixel lies within one of the n by m coordinate cells, that pixel is assigned the color of the corresponding element in the matrix colorArray.

3-14
CHARACTER GENERATION

Letters, numbers, and other characters can be displayed in a variety of sizes and styles. The overall design style for a set (or family) of characters is called a **type-**

131

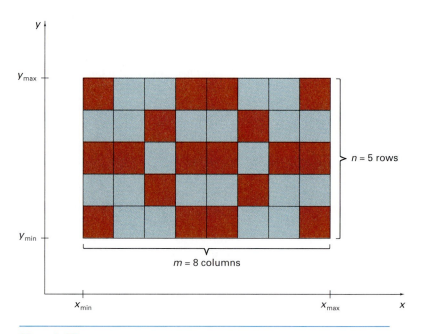

Figure 3-47
Mapping an *n* by *m* cell array into a rectangular coordinate region.

face. Today, there are hundreds of typefaces available for computer applications. Examples of a few common typefaces are Courier, Helvetica, New York, Palatino, and Zapf Chancery. Originally, the term **font** referred to a set of cast metal character forms in a particular size and format, such as 10-point Courier Italic or 12-point Palatino Bold. Now, the terms font and typeface are often used interchangeably, since printing is no longer done with cast metal forms.

Typefaces (or fonts) can be divided into two broad groups: *serif* and *sans serif*. Serif type has small lines or accents at the ends of the main character strokes, while sans-serif type does not have accents. For example, the text in this book is set in a serif font (Palatino). But this sentence is printed in a sans-serif font (Optima). Serif type is generally more *readable*; that is, it is easier to read in longer blocks of text. On the other hand, the individual characters in sans-serif type are easier to recognize. For this reason, sans-serif type is said to be more *legible*. Since sans-serif characters can be quickly recognized, this typeface is good for labeling and short headings.

Two different representations are used for storing computer fonts. A simple method for representing the character shapes in a particular typeface is to use rectangular grid patterns. The set of characters are then referred to as a **bitmap font** (or **bitmapped font**). Another, more flexible, scheme is to describe character shapes using straight-line and curve sections, as in PostScript, for example. In this case, the set of characters is called an **outline font**. Figure 3-48 illustrates the two methods for character representation. When the pattern in Fig. 3-48(a) is copied to an area of the frame buffer, the 1 bits designate which pixel positions are to be displayed on the monitor. To display the character shape in Fig. 3-48(b), the interior of the character outline must be filled using the scan-line fill procedure (Section 3-11).

Bitmap fonts are the simplest to define and display: The character grid only needs to be mapped to a frame-buffer position. In general, however, bitmap fonts

require more space, because each variation (size and format) must be stored in a
font cache. It is possible to generate different sizes and other variations, such as
bold and italic, from one set, but this usually does not produce good results.

In contrast to bitmap fonts, outline fonts require less storage since each variation does not require a distinct font cache. We can produce boldface, italic, or different sizes by manipulating the curve definitions for the character outlines. But it does take more time to process the outline fonts, because they must be scan converted into the frame buffer.

A character string is displayed in PHIGS with the following function:

```
text (wcPoint, string)
```

Parameter `string` is assigned a character sequence, which is then displayed at coordinate position `wcPoint` = (x, y). For example, the statement

```
text (wcPoint, ''Population Distribution'')
```

along with the coordinate specification for `wcPoint`, could be used as a label on a distribution graph.

Just how the string is positioned relative to coordinates (x, y) is a user option. The default is that (x, y) sets the coordinate location for the lower left corner of the first character of the horizontal string to be displayed. Other string orientations, such as vertical, horizontal, or slanting, are set as attribute options and will be discussed in the next chapter.

Another convenient character function in PHIGS is one that places a designated character, called a **marker symbol**, at one or more selected positions. This function is defined with the same parameter list as in the line function:

```
polymarker (n, wcPoints)
```

A predefined character is then centered at each of the n coordinate positions in the list `wcPoints`. The default symbol displayed by polymarker depends on the

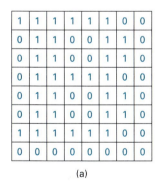
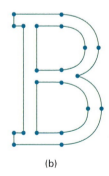

(a)   (b)

Figure 3-48
The letter B represented in (a) with an 8 by 8 bilevel bitmap pattern and in (b) with an outline shape defined with straight-line and curve segments.

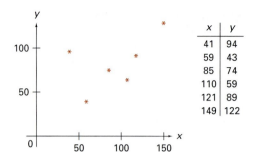

x	y
41	94
59	43
85	74
110	59
121	89
149	122

Figure 3-49
Sequence of data values plotted
with the `polymarker` function.

particular implementation, but we assume for now that an asterisk is to be used. Figure 3-49 illustrates plotting of a data set with the statement

```
polymarker (6, wcPoints)
```

SUMMARY

The output primitives discussed in this chapter provide the basic tools for constructing pictures with straight lines, curves, filled areas, cell-array patterns, and text. Examples of pictures generated with these primitives are given in Figs. 3-50 and 3-51.

Three methods that can be used to plot pixel positions along a straight-line path are the DDA algorithm, Bresenham's algorithm, and the midpoint method. For straight lines, Bresenham's algorithm and the midpoint method are identical and are the most efficient. Frame-buffer access in these methods can also be performed efficiently by incrementally calculating memory addresses. Any of the line-generating algorithms can be adapted to a parallel implementation by partitioning line segments.

Circles and ellipses can be efficiently and accurately scan converted using midpoint methods and taking curve symmetry into account. Other conic sections, parabolas and hyperbolas, can be plotted with similar methods. Spline curves, which are piecewise continuous polynomials, are widely used in design applications. Parallel implementation of curve generation can be accomplished by partitioning the curve paths.

To account for the fact that displayed lines and curves have finite widths, we must adjust the pixel dimensions of objects to coincide to the specified geometric dimensions. This can be done with an addressing scheme that references pixel positions at their lower left corner, or by adjusting line lengths.

Filled area primitives in many graphics packages refer to filled polygons. A common method for providing polygon fill on raster systems is the scan-line fill algorithm, which determines interior pixel spans across scan lines that intersect the polygon. The scan-line algorithm can also be used to fill the interior of objects with curved boundaries. Two other methods for filling the interior regions of objects are the boundary-fill algorithm and the flood-fill algorithm. These two fill procedures paint the interior, one pixel at a time, outward from a specified interior point.

The scan-line fill algorithm is an example of filling object interiors using the odd-even rule to locate the interior regions. Other methods for defining object interiors are also useful, particularly with unusual, self-intersecting objects. A common example is the nonzero winding number rule. This rule is more flexible than the odd-even rule for handling objects defined with multiple boundaries.

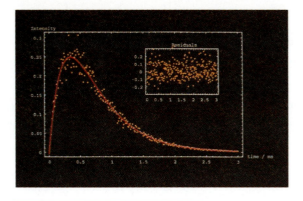

Figure 3-50
A data plot generated with straight line segments, a curve, circles (or markers), and text. *(Courtesy of Wolfram Research, Inc., The Maker of Mathematica.)*

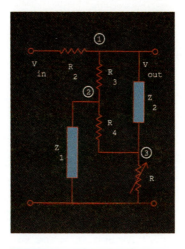

Figure 3-51
An electrical diagram drawn with straight line sections, circles, filled rectangles, and text. *(Courtesy of Wolfram Research, Inc., The Maker of Mathematica.)*

Additional primitives available in graphics packages include cell arrays, character strings, and marker symbols. Cell arrays are used to define and store color patterns. Character strings are used to provide picture and graph labeling. And marker symbols are useful for plotting the position of data points.

Table 3-1 lists implementations for some of the output primitives discussed in this chapter.

TABLE 3-1
OUTPUT PRIMITIVE IMPLEMENTATIONS

```
typedef struct { float x, y; } wcPt2;
```
 Defines a location in 2-dimensional world-coordinates.

```
pPolyline (int n, wcPt2 * pts)
```
 Draw a connected sequence of n-1 line segments, specified in pts.

```
pCircle (wcPt2 center, float r)
```
 Draw a circle of radius r at center.

```
pFillarea (int n, wcPt2 * pts)
```
 Draw a filled polygon with n vertices, specified in pts.

```
pCellArray (wcPt2 * pts, int n, int m, int colors)
```
 Map an n by m array of colors onto a rectangular area defined by pts.

```
pText (wcPt2 position, char * txt)
```
 Draw the character string txt at position.

```
pPolymarker (int n, wcPt2 * pts)
```
 Draw a collection of n marker symbols at pts.

135

Applications

Here, we present a few example programs illustrating applications of output primitives. Functions listed in Table 3-1 are defined in the header file graphics.h, along with the routines openGraphics, closeGraphics, setColor, and setBackground.

The first program produces a line graph for monthly data over a period of one year. Output of this procedure is drawn in Fig. 3-52. This data set is also used by the second program to produce the bar graph in Fig. 3-53 .

```c
#include <stdio.h>
#include "graphics.h"

#define WINDOW_WIDTH 600
#define WINDOW_HEIGHT 500
/* Amount of space to leave on each side of the chart */
#define MARGIN_WIDTH 0.05 * WINDOW_WIDTH
#define N_DATA 12

typedef enum
{ Jan, Feb, Mar, Apr, May, Jun, Jul, Aug, Sep, Oct, Nov, Dec } Months;

char * monthNames[N_DATA] = { "Jan", "Feb", "Mar", "Apr", "May", "Jun",
                              "Jul", "Aug", "Sep", "Oct", "Nov", "Dec" };

int readData (char * inFile, float * data)
{
  int fileError = FALSE;
  FILE * fp;
  Months month;

  if ((fp = fopen (inFile, "r")) == NULL)
    fileError = TRUE;
  else {
    for (month = Jan; month <= Dec; month++)
      fscanf (fp, "%f", &data[month]);
    fclose (fp);
  }
  return (fileError);
}

void lineChart (float * data)
{
  wcPt2 dataPos[N_DATA], labelPos;
  Months m;
  float mWidth = (WINDOW_WIDTH - 2 * MARGIN_WIDTH) / N_DATA;
  int chartBottom = 0.1 * WINDOW_HEIGHT;
  int offset = 0.05 * WINDOW_HEIGHT; /* Space between data and labels */
  int labelLength = 24;    /* Assuming fixed-width 8-pixel characters */

  labelPos.y = chartBottom;
  for (m = Jan; m <= Dec; m++) {
    /* Calculate x and y positions for data markers */
    dataPos[m].x = MARGIN_WIDTH + m * mWidth + 0.5 * mWidth;
    dataPos[m].y = chartBottom + offset + data[m];
    /* Shift the label to the left by one-half its length */
    labelPos.x = dataPos[m].x - 0.5 * labelLength;
    pText (labelPos, monthNames[m]);
  }
  pPolyline (N_DATA, dataPos);
  pPolymarker (N_DATA, dataPos);
```

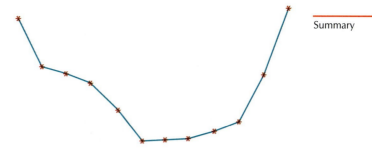

Jan Feb Mar Apr May Jun Jul Aug Sep Oct Nov Dec

Figure 3-52
A line plot of data points output by
the lineChart procedure.

```
}
void main (int argc, char ** argv)
{
  float data[N_DATA];
  int dataError = FALSE;
  long windowID;

  if (argc < 2) {
    fprintf (stderr, "Usage: %s dataFileName\n", argv[0]);
    exit ();
  }
  dataError = readData (argv[1], data);
  if (dataError) {
    fprintf (stderr, "%s error.  Can't read file %s\n", argv[1]);
    exit ();
  }
  windowID = openGraphics (*argv, WINDOW_WIDTH, WINDOW_HEIGHT);
  setBackground (WHITE);
  setColor (BLACK);
  lineChart (data);
  sleep (10);
  closeGraphics (windowID);
}
```

```
void barChart (float * data)
{
  wcPt2 dataPos[4], labelPos;
  Months m;
  float x, mWidth = (WINDOW_WIDTH - 2 * MARGIN_WIDTH) / N_DATA;
  int chartBottom = 0.1 * WINDOW_HEIGHT;
  int offset = 0.05 * WINDOW_HEIGHT; /* Space between data and labels */
  int labelLength = 24;     /* Assuming fixed-width 8-pixel characters */

  labelPos.y = chartBottom;
  for (m = Jan; m <= Dec; m++) {
    /* Find the center of this month's bar */
    x = MARGIN_WIDTH + m * mWidth + 0.5 * mWidth;

    /* Shift the label to the left by one-half its assumed length */
    labelPos.x = x - 0.5 * labelLength;
```

137

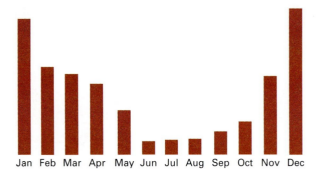

Figure 3-53
A bar-chart plot output by the
`barChart` procedure.

```
    pText (labelPos, monthNames[m]);

    /* Get the coordinates for this month's bar */
    dataPos[0].x = dataPos[3].x = x - 0.5 * labelLength;
    dataPos[1].x = dataPos[2].x = x + 0.5 * labelLength;
    dataPos[0].y = dataPos[1].y = chartBottom + offset;
    dataPos[2].y = dataPos[3].y = chartBottom + offset + data[m];
    pFillArea (4, dataPos);
  }
}
```

Pie charts are used to show the percentage contribution of individual parts to the whole. The next procedure constructs a pie chart, with the number and relative size of the slices determined by input. A sample output from this procedure appears in Fig. 3-54.

```
#define TWO_PI 6.28

void pieChart (float * data)
{
  wcPt2 pts[2], center;
  float radius = WINDOW_HEIGHT / 4.0;
  float newSlice, total = 0.0, lastSlice = 0.0;
  Months month;

  center.x = WINDOW_WIDTH / 2;
  center.y = WINDOW_HEIGHT / 2;
  pCircle (center, radius);
  for (month = Jan; month <= Dec; month++)
    total += data[month];
  pts[0].x = center.x; pts[0].y = center.y;
  for (month = Jan; month <= Dec; month++) {
    newSlice = TWO_PI * data[month] / total + lastSlice;
    pts[1].x = center.x + radius * cosf (newSlice);
    pts[1].y = center.y + radius * sinf (newSlice);
    pPolyline (2, pts);
    lastSlice = newSlice;
  }
}
```

138

Some variations on the circle equations are output by this next procedure. The shapes shown in Fig. 3-55 are generated by varying the radius *r* of a circle. Depending on how we vary *r*, we can produce a spiral, cardioid, limaçon, or other similar figure.

```c
#include <stdio.h>
#include <math.h>
#include "graphics.h"

#define TWO_PI 6.28

/* Limacon equation is r = a * cos(theta) + b.  Cardioid is the same,
   with a == b, so r = a * (1 + cos(theta)).
*/
typedef enum { spiral, cardioid, threeLeaf, fourLeaf, limacon } Fig;

void drawCurlyFig (Fig figure, wcPt2 pos, int * p)
{
  float r, theta = 0.0, dtheta = 1.0 / (float) p[0];
  int nPoints = (int) ceilf (TWO_PI * p[0]) + 1;
  wcPt2 * pt;

  if ((pt = (wcPt2 *) malloc (nPoints * sizeof (wcPt2))) == NULL) {
    fprintf (stderr, "Couldn't allocate points\n");
    return;
  }

  /* Set first point for figure */
  pt[0].y = pos.y;
  switch (figure) {
  case spiral:    pt[0].x = pos.x;                break;
  case limacon:   pt[0].x = pos.x + p[0] + p[1];  break;
  case cardioid:  pt[0].x = pos.x + p[0] * 2;     break;
  case threeLeaf: pt[0].x = pos.x + p[0];         break;
  case fourLeaf:  pt[0].x = pos.x + p[0];         break;
  }
  nPoints = 1;
  while (theta < TWO_PI) {
    switch (figure) {
    case spiral:    r = p[0] * theta;              break;
    case limacon:   r = p[0] * cosf (theta) + p[1]; break;
    case cardioid:  r = p[0] * (1 + cosf (theta));  break;
    case threeLeaf: r = p[0] * cosf (3 * theta);    break;
    case fourLeaf:  r = p[0] * cosf (2 * theta);    break;
    }
    pt[nPoints].x = pos.x + r * cosf (theta);
    pt[nPoints].y = pos.y + r * sinf (theta);
    nPoints++;
    theta += dtheta;
  }

  pPolyline (nPoints, pt);
  free (pt);
}

void main (int argc, char ** argv)
{
```

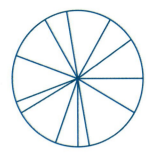

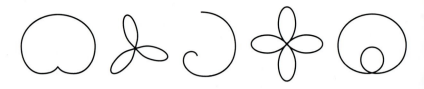

Figure 3-55
Curved figures produced with the drawShape procedure.

Figure 3-54
Output generated from the pieChart procedure.

```
  long windowID = openGraphics (*argv, 400, 100);
  Fig f;
  /* Center positions for each figure */
  wcPt2 center[] = { 50, 50, 100, 50, 175, 50, 250, 50, 300, 50 };

  /* Parameters to define each figure.  First four need one parameter.
     Fifth figure (limacon) needs two. */
  int p[5][2] = { 5, -1, 20, -1, 30, -1, 30, -1, 40, 10 };

  setBackground (WHITE);
  setColor (BLACK);
  for (f=spiral; f<=limacon; f++)
    drawCurlyFig (f, center[f], p[f]);
  sleep (10);
  closeGraphics (windowID);
}
```

REFERENCES

Information on Bresenham's algorithms can be found in Bresenham (1965, 1977). For midpoint methods, see Kappel (1985). Parallel methods for generating lines and circles are discussed in Pang (1990) and in Wright (1990).

Additional programming examples and information on PHIGS primitives can be found in Howard, et al. (1991), Hopgood and Duce (1991), Gaskins (1992), and Blake (1993). For information on GKS output primitive functions, see Hopgood et al. (1983) and Enderle, Kansy, and Pfaff (1984).

EXERCISES

3-1. Implement the polyline function using the DDA algorithm, given any number (n) of input points. A single point is to be plotted when $n = 1$.

3-2. Extend Bresenham's line algorithm to generate lines with any slope, taking symmetry between quadrants into account. Implement the polyline function using this algorithm as a routine that displays the set of straight lines connecting the n input points. For $n = 1$, the routine displays a single point.

3-3. Devise a consistent scheme for implementing the `polyline` function, for any set of input line endpoints, using a modified Bresenham line algorithm so that geometric magnitudes are maintained (Section 3-10).

3-4. Use the midpoint method to derive decision parameters for generating points along a straight-line path with slope in the range $0 < m < 1$. Show that the midpoint decision parameters are the same as those in the Bresenham line algorithm.

3-5. Use the midpoint method to derive decision parameters that can be used to generate straight line segments with any slope.

3-6. Set up a parallel version of Bresenham's line algorithm for slopes in the range $0 < m < 1$.

3-7. Set up a parallel version of Bresenham's algorithm for straight lines of any slope.

3-8. Suppose you have a system with an 8-inch by 10-inch video monitor that can display 100 pixels per inch. If memory is organized in one-byte words, the starting frame-buffer address is 0, and each pixel is assigned one byte of storage, what is the frame-buffer address of the pixel with screen coordinates (x, y)?

3-9. Suppose you have a system with an 8-inch by 10-inch video monitor that can display 100 pixels per inch. If memory is organized in one-byte words, the starting frame-buffer address is 0, and each pixel is assigned 6 bits of storage, what is the frame-buffer address (or addresses) of the pixel with screen coordinates (x, y)?

3-10. Implement the `setPixel` routine in Bresenham's line algorithm using iterative techniques for calculating frame-buffer addresses (Section 3-3).

3-11. Revise the midpoint circle algorithm to display so that geometric magnitudes are maintained (Section 3-10).

3-12. Set up a procedure for a parallel implementation of the midpoint circle algorithm.

3-13. Derive decision parameters for the midpoint ellipse algorithm assuming the start position is $(r_x, 0)$ and points are to be generated along the curve path in counterclockwise order.

3-14. Set up a procedure for a parallel implementation of the midpoint ellipse algorithm.

3-15. Devise an efficient algorithm that takes advantage of symmetry properties to display a sine function.

3-16. Devise an efficient algorithm, taking function symmetry into account, to display a plot of damped harmonic motion:

$$y = Ae^{-kx} \sin (\omega x + \theta)$$

where ω is the angular frequency and θ is the phase of the sine function. Plot y as a function of x for several cycles of the sine function or until the maximum amplitude is reduced to $A/10$.

3-17. Using the midpoint method, and taking symmetry into account, develop an efficient algorithm for scan conversion of the following curve over the interval $-10 \le x \le 10$:

$$y = \frac{1}{12} x^3$$

3-18. Use the midpoint method and symmetry considerations to scan convert the parabola

$$y = 100 - x^2$$

over the interval $-10 \le x \le 10$.

3-19. Use the midpoint method and symmetry considerations to scan convert the parabola

$$x = y^2$$

for the interval $-10 \le y \le 10$.

141

3-20. Set up a midpoint algorithm, taking symmetry considerations into account to scan convert any parabola of the form

$$y = ax^2 - b$$

with input values for parameters a, b, and the range of x.

3-21. Write a program to scan convert the interior of a specified ellipse into a solid color.

3-22. Devise an algorithm for determining interior regions for any input set of vertices using the nonzero winding number rule and cross-product calculations to identify the direction of edge crossings.

3-23. Devise an algorithm for determining interior regions for any input set of vertices using the nonzero winding number rule and dot-product calculations to identify the direction of edge crossings.

3-24. Write a procedure for filling the interior of any specified set of "polygon" vertices using the nonzero winding number rule to identify interior regions.

3-25. Modify the boundary-fill algorithm for a 4-connected region to avoid excessive stacking by incorporating scan-line methods.

3-26. Write a boundary-fill procedure to fill an 8-connected region.

3-27. Explain how an ellipse displayed with the midpoint method could be properly filled with a boundary-fill algorithm.

3-28. Develop and implement a flood-fill algorithm to fill the interior of any specified area.

3-29. Write a routine to implement the `text` function.

3-30. Write a routine to implement the `polymarker` function.

3-31. Write a program to display a bar graph using the `polyline` function. Input to the program is to include the data points and the labeling required for the x and y axes. The data points are to be scaled by the program so that the graph is displayed across the full screen area.

3-32. Write a program to display a bar graph in any selected screen area. Use the `polyline` function to draw the bars.

3-33. Write a procedure to display a line graph for any input set of data points in any selected area of the screen, with the input data set scaled to fit the selected screen area. Data points are to be displayed as asterisks joined with straight line segments, and the x and y axes are to be labeled according to input specifications. (Instead of asterisks, small circles or some other symbols could be used to plot the data points.)

3-34. Using a `circle` function, write a routine to display a pie chart with appropriate labeling. Input to the routine is to include a data set giving the distribution of the data over some set of intervals, the name of the pie chart, and the names of the intervals. Each section label is to be displayed outside the boundary of the pie chart near the corresponding pie section.

CHAPTER

Attributes of Output Primitives

In general, any parameter that affects the way a primitive is to be displayed is referred to as an **attribute parameter**. Some attribute parameters, such as color and size, determine the fundamental characteristics of a primitive. Others specify how the primitive is to be displayed under special conditions. Examples of attributes in this class include depth information for three-dimensional viewing and visibility or detectability options for interactive object-selection programs. These special-condition attributes will be considered in later chapters. Here, we consider only those attributes that control the basic display properties of primitives, without regard for special situations. For example, lines can be dotted or dashed, fat or thin, and blue or orange. Areas might be filled with one color or with a multicolor pattern. Text can appear reading from left to right, slanted diagonally across the screen, or in vertical columns. Individual characters can be displayed in different fonts, colors, and sizes. And we can apply intensity variations at the edges of objects to smooth out the raster stairstep effect.

One way to incorporate attribute options into a graphics package is to extend the parameter list associated with each output primitive function to include the appropriate attributes. A line-drawing function, for example, could contain parameters to set color, width, and other properties, in addition to endpoint coordinates. Another approach is to maintain a system list of current attribute values. Separate functions are then included in the graphics package for setting the current values in the attribute list. To generate an output primitive, the system checks the relevant attributes and invokes the display routine for that primitive using the current attribute settings. Some packages provide users with a combination of attribute functions and attribute parameters in the output primitive commands. With the GKS and PHIGS standards, attribute settings are accomplished with separate functions that update a system attribute list.

4-1

LINE ATTRIBUTES

Basic attributes of a straight line segment are its type, its width, and its color. In some graphics packages, lines can also be displayed using selected pen or brush options. In the following sections, we consider how line-drawing routines can be modified to accommodate various attribute specifications.

Line Type

Possible selections for the line-type attribute include solid lines, dashed lines, and dotted lines. We modify a line-drawing algorithm to generate such lines by setting the length and spacing of displayed solid sections along the line path. A dashed line could be displayed by generating an interdash spacing that is equal to the length of the solid sections. Both the length of the dashes and the interdash spacing are often specified as user options. A dotted line can be displayed by generating very short dashes with the spacing equal to or greater than the dash size. Similar methods are used to produce other line-type variations.

To set line type attributes in a PHIGS application program, a user invokes the function

```
        setLinetype (lt)
```

where parameter `lt` is assigned a positive integer value of 1, 2, 3, or 4 to generate lines that are, respectively, solid, dashed, dotted, or dash-dotted. Other values for the line-type parameter `lt` could be used to display variations in the dot-dash patterns. Once the line-type parameter has been set in a PHIGS application program, all subsequent line-drawing commands produce lines with this line type. The following program segment illustrates use of the `linetype` command to display the data plots in Fig. 4-1.

```c
#include <stdio.h>
#include "graphics.h"

#define MARGIN_WIDTH 0.05 * WINDOW_WIDTH

int readData (char * inFile, float * data)
{
  int fileError = FALSE;
  FILE * fp;
  int month;

  if ((fp = fopen (inFile, "r")) == NULL)
    fileError = TRUE;
  else {
    for (month=0; month<12; month++)
      fscanf (fp, "%f", &data[month]);
    fclose (fp);
  }
  return (fileError);
}

void chartData (float * data, pLineType lineType)
{
  wcPt2 pts[12];
  float monthWidth = (WINDOW_WIDTH - 2 * MARGIN_WIDTH) / 12;
  int i;

  for (i=0; i<12; i++) {
    pts[i].x = MARGIN_WIDTH + i * monthWidth + 0.5 * monthWidth;
    pts[i].y = data[i];
  }
  pSetLineType (lineType);
  pPolyline (12, pts);
}

int main (int argc, char ** argv)
{
  long windowID = openGraphics (*argv, WINDOW_WIDTH, WINDOW_HEIGHT);
  float data[12];

  setBackground (WHITE);
  setColor (BLUE);
  readData ("../data/data1960", data);
  chartData (data, SOLID);
  readData ("../data/data1970", data);
  chartData (data, DASHED);
  readData ("../data/data1980", data);
  chartData (data, DOTTED);
  sleep (10);
  closeGraphics (windowID);
}
```

145

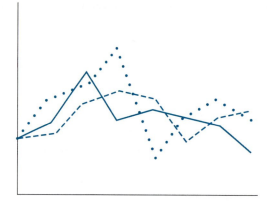

Figure 4-1
Plotting three data sets with three different line types, as output by the `chartData` procedure.

Raster line algorithms display line-type attributes by plotting pixel spans. For the various dashed, dotted, and dot-dashed patterns, the line-drawing procedure outputs sections of contiguous pixels along the line path, skipping over a number of intervening pixels between the solid spans. Pixel counts for the span length and interspan spacing can be specified in a pixel **mask**, which is a string containing the digits 1 and 0 to indicate which positions to plot along the line path. The mask 1111000, for instance, could be used to display a dashed line with a dash length of four pixels and an interdash spacing of three pixels. On a bilevel system, the mask gives the bit values that should be loaded into the frame buffer along the line path to display the selected line type.

Plotting dashes with a fixed number of pixels results in unequal-length dashes for different line orientations, as illustrated in Fig. 4-2. Both dashes shown are plotted with four pixels, but the diagonal dash is longer by a factor of $\sqrt{2}$. For precision drawings, dash lengths should remain approximately constant for any line orientation. To accomplish this, we can adjust the pixel counts for the solid spans and interspan spacing according to the line slope. In Fig. 4-2, we can display approximately equal-length dashes by reducing the diagonal dash to three pixels. Another method for maintaining dash length is to treat dashes as individual line segments. Endpoint coordinates for each dash are located and passed to the line routine, which then calculates pixel positions along the dash path.

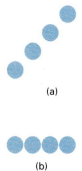

(a)

(b)

Figure 4-2
Unequal-length dashes displayed with the same number of pixels.

Line Width

Implementation of line-width options depends on the capabilities of the output device. A heavy line on a video monitor could be displayed as adjacent parallel lines, while a pen plotter might require pen changes. As with other PHIGS attributes, a line-width command is used to set the current line-width value in the attribute list. This value is then used by line-drawing algorithms to control the thickness of lines generated with subsequent output primitive commands.

We set the line-width attribute with the command:

```
setLinewidthScaleFactor (lw)
```

Line-width parameter `lw` is assigned a positive number to indicate the relative width of the line to be displayed. A value of 1 specifies a standard-width line. On a pen plotter, for instance, a user could set `lw` to a value of 0.5 to plot a line whose width is half that of the standard line. Values greater than 1 produce lines thicker than the standard.

For raster implementation, a standard-width line is generated with single pixels at each sample position, as in the Bresenham algorithm. Other-width lines are displayed as positive integer multiples of the standard line by plotting additional pixels along adjacent parallel line paths. For lines with slope magnitude less than 1, we can modify a line-drawing routine to display thick lines by plotting a vertical span of pixels at each x position along the line. The number of pixels in each span is set equal to the integer magnitude of parameter `lw`. In Fig. 4-3, we plot a double-width line by generating a parallel line above the original line path. At each x sampling position, we calculate the corresponding y coordinate and plot pixels with screen coordinates (x, y) and $(x, y+1)$. We display lines with $lw \geq 3$ by alternately plotting pixels above and below the single-width line path.

For lines with slope magnitude greater than 1, we can plot thick lines with horizontal spans, alternately picking up pixels to the right and left of the line path. This scheme is demonstrated in Fig. 4-4, where a line width of 4 is plotted with horizontal pixel spans.

Although thick lines are generated quickly by plotting horizontal or vertical pixel spans, the displayed width of a line (measured perpendicular to the line path) is dependent on its slope. A 45° line will be displayed thinner by a factor of $1/\sqrt{2}$ compared to a horizontal or vertical line plotted with the same-length pixel spans.

Another problem with implementing width options using horizontal or vertical pixel spans is that the method produces lines whose ends are horizontal or vertical regardless of the slope of the line. This effect is more noticeable with very thick lines. We can adjust the shape of the line ends to give them a better appearance by adding **line caps** (Fig. 4-5). One kind of line cap is the *butt cap* obtained by adjusting the end positions of the component parallel lines so that the thick line is displayed with square ends that are perpendicular to the line path. If the specified line has slope m, the square end of the thick line has slope $-1/m$. Another line cap is the *round cap* obtained by adding a filled semicircle to each butt cap. The circular arcs are centered on the line endpoints and have a diameter equal to the line thickness. A third type of line cap is the *projecting square cap*. Here, we simply extend the line and add butt caps that are positioned one-half of the line width beyond the specified endpoints.

Other methods for producing thick lines include displaying the line as a filled rectangle or generating the line with a selected pen or brush pattern, as discussed in the next section. To obtain a rectangle representation for the line

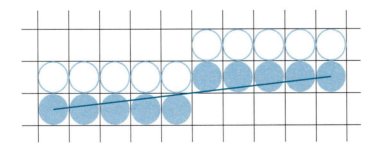

Figure 4-3
Double-wide raster line with slope $|m| < 1$ generated with vertical pixel spans.

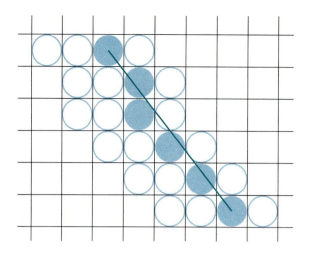

Figure 4-4
Raster line with slope $|m| > 1$
and line-width parameter $\mathtt{lw} = 4$
plotted with horizontal pixel spans.

boundary, we calculate the position of the rectangle vertices along perpendiculars to the line path so that vertex coordinates are displaced from the line endpoints by one-half the line width. The rectangular line then appears as in Fig. 4-5(a). We could then add round caps to the filled rectangle or extend its length to display projecting square caps.

Generating thick polylines requires some additional considerations. In general, the methods we have considered for displaying a single line segment will not produce a smoothly connected series of line segments. Displaying thick lines using horizontal and vertical pixel spans, for example, leaves pixel gaps at the boundaries between lines of different slopes where there is a shift from horizontal spans to vertical spans. We can generate thick polylines that are smoothly joined at the cost of additional processing at the segment endpoints. Figure 4-6 shows three possible methods for smoothly joining two line segments. A *miter join* is accomplished by extending the outer boundaries of each of the two lines until they meet. A *round join* is produced by capping the connection between the two segments with a circular boundary whose diameter is equal to the line

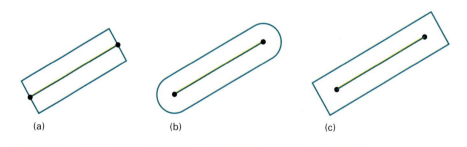

(a)   (b)   (c)

Figure 4-5
Thick lines drawn with (a) butt caps, (b) round caps, and (c) projecting square caps.

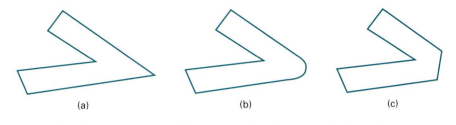

Figure 4-6
Thick line segments connected with (a) miter join, (b) round join, and (c) bevel join.

width. And a *bevel join* is generated by displaying the line segments with butt caps and filling in the triangular gap where the segments meet. If the angle between two connected line segments is very small, a miter join can generate a long spike that distorts the appearance of the polyline. A graphics package can avoid this effect by switching from a miter join to a bevel join, say, when any two consecutive segments meet at a small enough angle.

Pen and Brush Options

With some packages, lines can be displayed with pen or brush selections. Options in this category include shape, size, and pattern. Some possible pen or brush shapes are given in Fig. 4-7. These shapes can be stored in a pixel mask that identifies the array of pixel positions that are to be set along the line path. For example, a rectangular pen can be implemented with the mask shown in Fig. 4-8 by moving the center (or one corner) of the mask along the line path, as in Fig. 4-9. To avoid setting pixels more than once in the frame buffer, we can simply accumulate the horizontal spans generated at each position of the mask and keep track of the beginning and ending x positions for the spans across each scan line.

Lines generated with pen (or brush) shapes can be displayed in various widths by changing the size of the mask. For example, the rectangular pen line in Fig. 4-9 could be narrowed with a 2×2 rectangular mask or widened with a 4×4 mask. Also, lines can be displayed with selected patterns by superimposing the pattern values onto the pen or brush mask. Some examples of line patterns are shown in Fig. 4-10. An additional pattern option that can be provided in a paint package is the display of simulated brush strokes. Figure 4-11 illustrates some patterns that can be displayed by modeling different types of brush strokes.

Line Color

When a system provides color (or intensity) options, a parameter giving the current color index is included in the list of system-attribute values. A polyline routine displays a line in the current color by setting this color value in the frame buffer at pixel locations along the line path using the `setPixel` procedure. The number of color choices depends on the number of bits available per pixel in the frame buffer.

We set the line color value in PHIGS with the function

```
setPolylineColourIndex (lc)
```

149

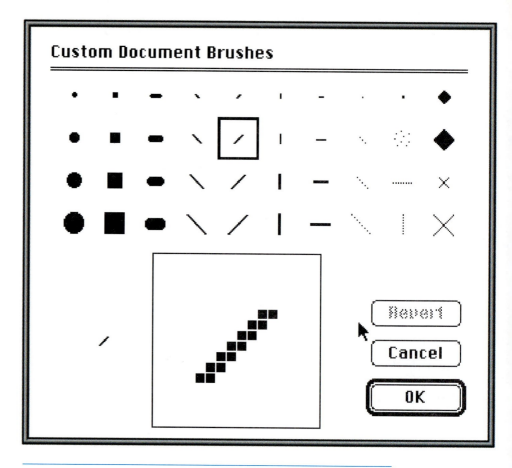

Figure 4-7
Pen and brush shapes for line display.

Nonnegative integer values, corresponding to allowed color choices, are assigned to the line color parameter lc. A line drawn in the background color is invisible, and a user can erase a previously displayed line by respecifying it in the background color (assuming the line does not overlap more than one background color area).

An example of the use of the various line attribute commands in an applications program is given by the following sequence of statements:

```
setLinetype (2);
setLinewidthScaleFactor (2);
setPolylineColourIndex (5);
polyline (n1, wcpoints1);

setPolylineColourIndex (6);
polyline (n2, wcpoints2);
```

This program segment would display two figures, drawn with double-wide dashed lines. The first is displayed in a color corresponding to code 5, and the second in color 6.

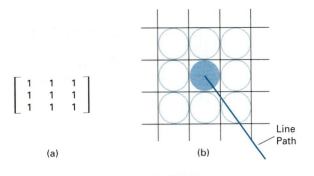

$$\begin{bmatrix} 1 & 1 & 1 \\ 1 & 1 & 1 \\ 1 & 1 & 1 \end{bmatrix}$$

(a)

(b)

Line
Path

Figure 4-8
(a) A pixel mask for a rectangular
pen, and (b) the associated array of
pixels displayed by centering the
mask over a specified pixel
position.

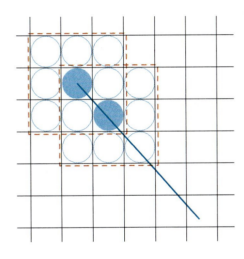

Figure 4-9
Generating a line with the pen
shape of Fig. 4-8.

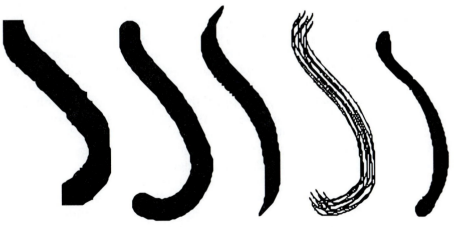

Figure 4-10
Curved lines drawn with a paint program using various shapes and
patterns. From left to right, the brush shapes are square, round,
diagonal line, dot pattern, and faded airbrush.

Figure 4-11

A daruma doll, a symbol of good
fortune in Japan, drawn by
computer artist Koichi Kozaki using
a paintbrush system. Daruma dolls
actually come without eyes. One
eye is painted in when a wish is
made, and the other is painted in
when the wish comes true.
(*Courtesy of Wacom Technology, Inc.*)

4-2
CURVE ATTRIBUTES

Parameters for curve attributes are the same as those for line segments. We can display curves with varying colors, widths, dot-dash patterns, and available pen or brush options. Methods for adapting curve-drawing algorithms to accommodate attribute selections are similar to those for line drawing.

The pixel masks discussed for implementing line-type options are also used in raster curve algorithms to generate dashed and dotted patterns. For example, the mask 11100 produces the dashed circle shown in Fig. 4-12. We can generate the dashes in the various octants using circle symmetry, but we must shift the pixel positions to maintain the correct sequence of dashes and spaces as we move from one octant to the next. Also, as in line algorithms, pixel masks display dashes and interdash spaces that vary in length according to the slope of the curve. If we want to display constant-length dashes, we need to adjust the number of pixels plotted in each dash as we move around the circle circumference. Instead of applying a pixel mask with constant spans, we plot pixels along equal angular arcs to produce equal length dashes.

Raster curves of various widths can be displayed using the method of horizontal or vertical pixel spans. Where the magnitude of the curve slope is less than 1, we plot vertical spans; where the slope magnitude is greater than 1, we plot horizontal spans. Figure 4-13 demonstrates this method for displaying a circular arc of width 4 in the first quadrant. Using circle symmetry, we generate the circle path with vertical spans in the octant from $x = 0$ to $x = y$, and then reflect pixel positions about the line $y = x$ to obtain the remainder of the curve shown. Circle sections in the other quadrants are obtained by reflecting pixel positions in the first quadrant about the coordinate axes. The thickness of curves displayed with this method is again a function of curve slope. Circles, ellipses, and other curves will appear thinnest where the slope has a magnitude of 1.

Another method for displaying thick curves is to fill in the area between two parallel curve paths, whose separation distance is equal to the desired width. We could do this using the specified curve path as one boundary and setting up the second boundary either inside or outside the original curve path. This approach, however, shifts the original curve path either inward or outward, depending on which direction we choose for the second boundary. We can maintain the original curve position by setting the two boundary curves at a distance of one-half the width on either side of the specified curve path. An example of this approach is shown in Fig. 4-14 for a circle segment with radius 16 and a specified width of 4. The boundary arcs are then set at a separation distance of 2 on either side of the radius of 16. To maintain the proper dimensions of the circular arc, as discussed in Section 3-10, we can set the radii for the concentric boundary arcs at $r = 14$ and $r = 17$. Although this method is accurate for generating thick circles, in general, it provides only an approximation to the true area of other thick

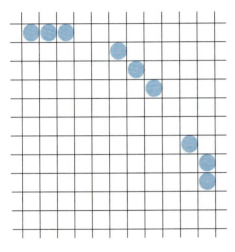

Figure 4-12
A dashed circular arc displayed with a dash span of 3 pixels and an interdash spacing of 2 pixels.

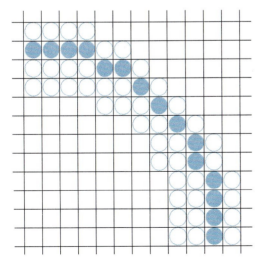

Figure 4-13
Circular arc of width 4 plotted with pixel spans.

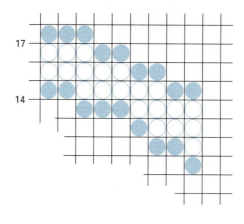

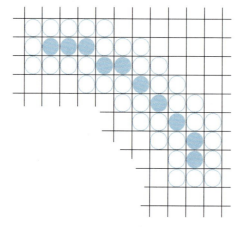

Figure 4-14
A circular arc of width 4 and radius 16 displayed by filling the region between two concentric arcs.

Figure 4-15
Circular arc displayed with a rectangular pen.

curves. For example, the inner and outer boundaries of a fat ellipse generated with this method do not have the same foci.

Pen (or brush) displays of curves are generated using the same techniques discussed for straight line segments. We replicate a pen shape along the line path, as illustrated in Fig. 4-15 for a circular arc in the first quadrant. Here, the center of the rectangular pen is moved to successive curve positions to produce the curve shape shown. Curves displayed with a rectangular pen in this manner will be thicker where the magnitude of the curve slope is 1. A uniform curve thickness can be displayed by rotating the rectangular pen to align it with the slope direction as we move around the curve or by using a circular pen shape. Curves drawn with pen and brush shapes can be displayed in different sizes and with superimposed patterns or simulated brush strokes.

4-3
COLOR AND GRAYSCALE LEVELS

Various color and intensity-level options can be made available to a user, depending on the capabilities and design objectives of a particular system. General-purpose raster-scan systems, for example, usually provide a wide range of colors, while random-scan monitors typically offer only a few color choices, if any. Color options are numerically coded with values ranging from 0 through the positive integers. For CRT monitors, these color codes are then converted to intensity-level settings for the electron beams. With color plotters, the codes could control ink-jet deposits or pen selections.

In a color raster system, the number of color choices available depends on the amount of storage provided per pixel in the frame buffer. Also, color information can be stored in the frame buffer in two ways: We can store color codes directly in the frame buffer, or we can put the color codes in a separate table and use pixel values as an index into this table. With the direct storage scheme, whenever a particular color code is specified in an application program, the corresponding binary value is placed in the frame buffer for each component pixel in the output primitives to be displayed in that color. A minimum number of colors can be provided in this scheme with 3 bits of storage per pixel, as shown in Table 4-1. Each of the three bit positions is used to control the intensity level (either on or off) of the corresponding electron gun in an RGB monitor. The leftmost bit controls the red gun, the middle bit controls the green gun, and the rightmost bit controls the blue gun. Adding more bits per pixel to the frame buffer increases the number of color choices. With 6 bits per pixel, 2 bits can be used for each gun. This allows four different intensity settings for each of the three color guns, and a total of 64 color values are available for each screen pixel. With a resolution of 1024 by 1024, a full-color (24-bit per pixel) RGB system needs 3 megabytes of storage for the frame buffer. Color tables are an alternate means for providing extended color capabilities to a user without requiring large frame buffers. Lower-cost personal computer systems, in particular, often use color tables to reduce frame-buffer storage requirements.

Color Tables

Figure 4-16 illustrates a possible scheme for storing color values in a **color lookup table** (or **video lookup table**), where frame-buffer values are now used as indices into the color table. In this example, each pixel can reference any one of the 256 table positions, and each entry in the table uses 24 bits to specify an RGB color. For the color code 2081, a combination green-blue color is displayed for pixel location (x, y). Systems employing this particular lookup table would allow

TABLE 4-1

THE EIGHT COLOR CODES FOR A THREE-BIT
PER PIXEL FRAME BUFFER

Color	Stored Color Values in Frame Buffer			Displayed Color
Code	RED	GREEN	BLUE	
0	0	0	0	Black
1	0	0	1	Blue
2	0	1	0	Green
3	0	1	1	Cyan
4	1	0	0	Red
5	1	0	1	Magenta
6	1	1	0	Yellow
7	1	1	1	White

a user to select any 256 colors for simultaneous display from a palette of nearly 17 million colors. Compared to a full-color system, this scheme reduces the number of simultaneous colors that can be displayed, but it also reduces the frame-buffer storage requirements to 1 megabyte. Some graphics systems provide 9 bits per pixel in the frame buffer, permitting a user to select 512 colors that could be used in each display.

A user can set color-table entries in a PHIGS applications program with the function

```
setColourRepresentation (ws, ci, colorptr)
```

Parameter `ws` identifies the workstation output device; parameter `ci` specifies the color index, which is the color-table position number (0 to 255 for the example in Fig. 4-16); and parameter `colorptr` points to a trio of RGB color values (r, g, b) each specified in the range from 0 to 1. An example of possible table entries for color monitors is given in Fig. 4-17.

There are several advantages in storing color codes in a lookup table. Use of a color table can provide a "reasonable" number of simultaneous colors without requiring large frame buffers. For most applications, 256 or 512 different colors are sufficient for a single picture. Also, table entries can be changed at any time, allowing a user to be able to experiment easily with different color combinations in a design, scene, or graph without changing the attribute settings for the graphics data structure. Similarly, visualization applications can store values for some physical quantity, such as energy, in the frame buffer and use a lookup table to try out various color encodings without changing the pixel values. And in visualization and image-processing applications, color tables are a convenient means for setting color thresholds so that all pixel values above or below a specified threshold can be set to the same color. For these reasons, some systems provide both capabilities for color-code storage, so that a user can elect either to use color tables or to store color codes directly in the frame buffer.

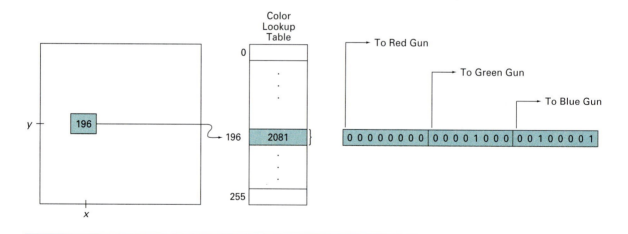

Figure 4-16

A color lookup table with 24 bits per entry accessed from a frame buffer with 8 bits per pixel. A value of 196 stored at pixel position (x, y) references the location in this table containing the value 2081. Each 8-bit segment of this entry controls the intensity level of one of the three electron guns in an RGB monitor.

WS = 1

Ci	Color
0	(0, 0, 0)
1	(0, 0, 0.2)
.	.
.	.
.	.
192	(0, 0.03, 0.13)
.	.
.	.
.	.

WS = 2

Ci	Color
0	(1, 1, 1)
1	(0.9, 1, 1)
2	(0.8, 1, 1)
.	
.	
.	

Figure 4-17
Workstation color tables.

Grayscale

With monitors that have no color capability, color functions can be used in an application program to set the shades of gray, or **grayscale,** for displayed primitives. Numeric values over the range from 0 to 1 can be used to specify grayscale levels, which are then converted to appropriate binary codes for storage in the raster. This allows the intensity settings to be easily adapted to systems with differing grayscale capabilities.

Table 4-2 lists the specifications for intensity codes for a four-level grayscale system. In this example, any intensity input value near 0.33 would be stored as the binary value 01 in the frame buffer, and pixels with this value would be displayed as dark gray. If additional bits per pixel are available in the frame buffer, the value of 0.33 would be mapped to the nearest level. With 3 bits per pixel, we can accommodate 8 gray levels; while 8 bits per pixel would give us 256 shades of gray. An alternative scheme for storing the intensity information is to convert each intensity code directly to the voltage value that produces this grayscale level on the output device in use.

When multiple output devices are available at an installation, the same color-table interface may be used for all monitors. In this case, a color table for a monochrome monitor can be set up using a range of RGB values as in Fig. 4-17, with the display intensity corresponding to a given color index c_i calculated as

$$intensity = 0.5[min(r, g, b) + max(r, g, b)]$$

TABLE 4-2

INTENSITY CODES FOR A FOUR-LEVEL GRAYSCALE SYSTEM

Intensity Codes	Stored Intensity Values In The Frame Buffer (Binary Code)		Displayed Grayscale
0.0	0	(00)	Black
0.33	1	(01)	Dark gray
0.67	2	(10)	Light gray
1.0	3	(11)	White

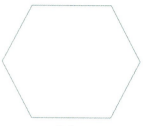

Hollow
(a)

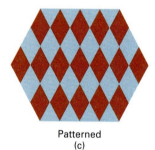

Solid
(b)

Patterned
(c)

Figure 4-18
Polygon fill styles.

AREA-FILL ATTRIBUTES

Options for filling a defined region include a choice between a solid color or a patterned fill and choices for the particular colors and patterns. These fill options can be applied to polygon regions or to areas defined with curved boundaries, depending on the capabilities of the available package. In addition, areas can be painted using various brush styles, colors, and transparency parameters.

Fill Styles

Areas are displayed with three basic fill styles: hollow with a color border, filled with a solid color, or filled with a specified pattern or design. A basic fill style is selected in a PHIGS program with the function

```
setInteriorStyle (fs)
```

Values for the fill-style parameter fs include *hollow*, *solid*, and *pattern* (Fig. 4-18). Another value for fill style is *hatch*, which is used to fill an area with selected hatching patterns—parallel lines or crossed lines—as in Fig. 4-19. As with line attributes, a selected fill-style value is recorded in the list of system attributes and applied to fill the interiors of subsequently specified areas. Fill selections for parameter fs are normally applied to polygon areas, but they can also be implemented to fill regions with curved boundaries.

Hollow areas are displayed using only the boundary outline, with the interior color the same as the background color. A solid fill is displayed in a single color up to and including the borders of the region. The color for a solid interior or for a hollow area outline is chosen with

```
setInteriorColourIndex (fc)
```

where fill-color parameter fc is set to the desired color code. A polygon hollow fill is generated with a line-drawing routine as a closed polyline. Solid fill of a region can be accomplished with the scan-line procedures discussed in Section 3-11.

Other fill options include specifications for the edge type, edge width, and edge color of a region. These attributes are set independently of the fill style or fill color, and they provide for the same options as the line-attribute parameters (line type, line width, and line color). That is, we can display area edges dotted or dashed, fat or thin, and in any available color regardless of how we have filled the interior.

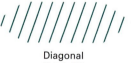

Diagonal
Hatch Fill

Diagonal
Cross-Hatch Fill

Figure 4-19
Polygon fill using hatch patterns.

Pattern Fill

We select fill patterns with

```
setInteriorStyleIndex (pi)
```

where pattern index parameter `pi` specifies a table position. For example, the following set of statements would fill the area defined in the `fillArea` command with the second pattern type stored in the pattern table:

```
setInteriorStyle (pattern);
setInteriorStyleIndex (2);
fillArea (n, points);
```

Separate tables are set up for hatch patterns. If we had selected *hatch* fill for the interior style in this program segment, then the value assigned to parameter `pi` is an index to the stored patterns in the hatch table.

For fill style *pattern*, table entries can be created on individual output devices with

```
setPatternRepresentation (ws, pi, nx, ny, cp)
```

Parameter `pi` sets the pattern index number for workstation code `ws`, and `cp` is a two-dimensional array of color codes with `nx` columns and `ny` rows. The following program segment illustrates how this function could be used to set the first entry in the pattern table for workstation 1.

```
cp[1,1] := 4;        cp[2,2] := 4;

cp[1,2] := 0;        cp[2,1] := 0;

setPatternRepresentation (1, 1, 2, 2, cp);
```

Table 4-3 shows the first two entries for this color table. Color array `cp` in this example specifies a pattern that produces alternate red and black diagonal pixel lines on an eight-color system.

When a color array `cp` is to be applied to fill a region, we need to specify the size of the area that is to be covered by each element of the array. We do this by setting the rectangular coordinate extents of the pattern:

```
setPatternSize (dx, dy)
```

where parameters `dx` and `dy` give the coordinate width and height of the array mapping. An example of the coordinate size associated with a pattern array is given in Fig. 4-20. If the values for `dx` and `dy` in this figure are given in screen coordinates, then each element of the color array would be applied to a 2 by 2 screen grid containing four pixels.

A reference position for starting a *pattern* fill is assigned with the statement

```
setPatternReferencePoint (position)
```

Parameter `position` is a pointer to coordinates *(xp, yp)* that fix the lower left corner of the rectangular pattern. From this starting position, the pattern is then replicated in the *x* and *y* directions until the defined area is covered by nonover-

TABLE 4-3
A WORKSTATION PATTERN TABLE WITH TWO ENTRIES, USING THE COLOR CODES OF TABLE 4-1

Index (pi)	Pattern (cp)
1	$\begin{bmatrix} 4 & 0 \\ 0 & 4 \end{bmatrix}$
2	$\begin{bmatrix} 2 & 1 & 2 \\ 1 & 2 & 1 \\ 2 & 1 & 2 \end{bmatrix}$

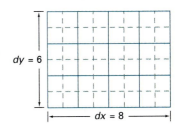

Figure 4-20
A pattern array with 4 columns and 3 rows mapped to an 8 by 6 coordinate rectangle.

lapping copies of the pattern array. The process of filling an area with a rectangular pattern is called **tiling** and rectangular fill patterns are sometimes referred to as **tiling patterns**. Figure 4-21 demonstrates tiling of a triangular fill area starting from a pattern reference point.

To illustrate the use of the pattern commands, the following program example displays a black-and-white pattern in the interior of a parallelogram fill area (Fig. 4-22). The pattern size in this program is set to map each array element to a single pixel.

```
#define WS 1

void patternFill ()
{
  wcPt2 pts[4];
  int bwPattern[3][3] = { 1, 0, 0, 0, 1, 1, 1, 0, 0 };

  pSetPatternRepresentation (WS, 8, 3, 3, bwPattern);

  pts[0].x = 10; pts[0].y = 10;
  pts[1].x = 20; pts[1].y = 10;
  pts[2].x = 28; pts[2].y = 18;
  pts[3].x = 18; pts[3].y = 18;

  pSetFillAreaInteriorStyle (PATTERN);
  pSetFillAreaPatternIndex (8);
  pSetPatternReferencePoint (14, 11);

  pFillArea (4, pts);
}
```

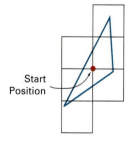

Start Position

Pattern fill can be implemented by modifying the scan-line procedures discussed in Chapter 3 so that a selected pattern is superimposed onto the scan lines. Beginning from a specified start position for a pattern fill, the rectangular patterns would be mapped vertically to scan lines between the top and bottom of the fill area and horizontally to interior pixel positions across these scan lines. Horizontally, the pattern array is repeated at intervals specified by the value of size parameter dx. Similarly, vertical repeats of the pattern are separated by intervals set with parameter dy. This scan-line pattern procedure applies both to polygons and to areas bounded by curves.

Figure 4-21
Tiling an area from a designated start position. Nonoverlapping adjacent patterns are laid out to cover all scan lines passing through the defined area.

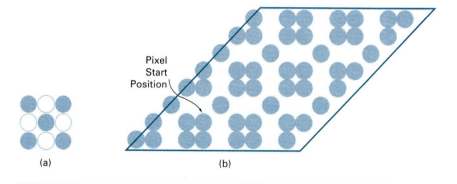

Pixel Start Position

(a)　　　　　(b)

Figure 4-22
A pattern array (a) superimposed on a parallelogram fill area to produce the display (b).

Hatch fill is applied to regions by displaying sets of parallel lines. The fill procedures are implemented to draw either single hatching or cross hatching. Spacing and slope for the hatch lines can be set as parameters in the hatch table. On raster systems, a hatch fill can be specified as a pattern array that sets color values for groups of diagonal pixels.

In many systems, the pattern reference point (xp, yp) is assigned by the system. For instance, the reference point could be set automatically at a polygon vertex. In general, for any fill region, the reference point can be chosen as the lower left corner of the *bounding rectangle* (or *bounding box*) determined by the coordinate extents of the region (Fig. 4-23). To simplify selection of the reference coordinates, some packages always use the screen coordinate origin as the pattern start position, and window systems often set the reference point at the coordinate origin of the window. Always setting (xp, yp) at the coordinate origin also simplifies the tiling operations when each color-array element of a pattern is to be mapped to a single pixel. For example, if the row positions in the pattern array are referenced in reverse (that is, from bottom to top starting at 1), a pattern value is then assigned to pixel position (x, y) in screen or window coordinates as

```
setPixel ( x, y, cp(y mod ny + 1, x mod nx + 1) )
```

where ny and nx specify the number of rows and number of columns in the pattern array. Setting the pattern start position at the coordinate origin, however, effectively attaches the pattern fill to the screen or window background, rather than to the fill regions. Adjacent or overlapping areas filled with the same pattern would show no apparent boundary between the areas. Also, repositioning and refilling an object with the same pattern can result in a shift in the assigned pixel values over the object interior. A moving object would appear to be transparent against a stationary pattern background, instead of moving with a fixed interior pattern.

It is also possible to combine a fill pattern with background colors (including grayscale) in various ways. With a bitmap pattern containing only the digits 1 and 0, the 0 values could be used as transparency indicators to let the background show through. Alternatively, the 1 and 0 digits can be used to fill an interior with two-color patterns. In general, color-fill patterns can be combined in several other ways with background colors. The pattern and background colors can be combined using Boolean operations, or the pattern colors can simply replace the background colors. Figure 4-24 demonstrates how the Boolean and replace operations for a 2 by 2 fill pattern would set pixel values on a binary (black-and-white) system against a particular background pattern.

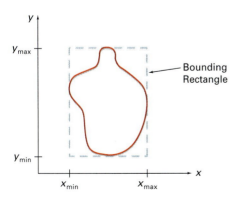

Bounding Rectangle

Figure 4-23
Bounding rectangle for a region with coordinate extents x_{min}, x_{max}, y_{min}, and y_{max} in the x and y directions.

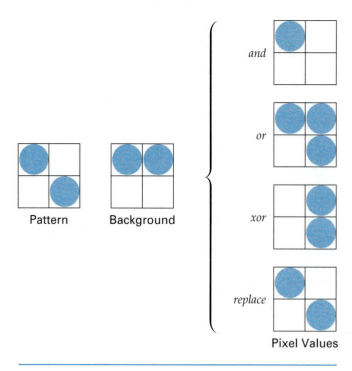

Figure 4-24
Combining a fill pattern with a background pattern using
Boolean operations, *and*, *or*, and *xor (exclusive or)*, and using
simple replacement.

Soft Fill

Modified boundary-fill and flood-fill procedures that are applied to repaint areas
so that the fill color is combined with the background colors are referred to as
soft-fill or **tint-fill** algorithms. One use for these fill methods is to soften the fill
colors at object borders that have been blurred to antialias the edges. Another is
to allow repainting of a color area that was originally filled with a semitransparent brush, where the current color is then a mixture of the brush color and the
background colors "behind" the area. In either case, we want the new fill color to
have the same variations over the area as the current fill color.

As an example of this type of fill, the **linear soft-fill** algorithm repaints an
area that was originally painted by merging a foreground color $\mathbf{F}$ with a single
background color $\mathbf{B}$, where $\mathbf{F} \neq \mathbf{B}$. Assuming we know the values for $\mathbf{F}$ and $\mathbf{B}$, we
can determine how these colors were originally combined by checking the cur-
rent color contents of the frame buffer. The current RGB color $\mathbf{P}$ of each pixel
within the area to be refilled is some linear combination of $\mathbf{F}$ and $\mathbf{B}$:

$$\mathbf{P} = t\mathbf{F} + (1 - t)\mathbf{B} \qquad (4\text{-}1)$$

where the "transparency" factor t has a value between 0 and 1 for each pixel. For
values of t less than 0.5, the background color contributes more to the interior
color of the region than does the fill color. Vector Equation 4-1 holds for each

162

RGB component of the colors, with

$$\mathbf{P} = (P_R, P_G, P_B), \qquad \mathbf{F} = (F_R, F_G, F_B), \qquad \mathbf{B} = (B_R, B_G, B_B) \qquad (4\text{-}2)$$

We can thus calculate the value of parameter t using one of the RGB color components as

$$t = \frac{P_k - B_k}{F_k - B_k} \qquad (4\text{-}3)$$

where $k = R$, G, or B; and $F_k \neq B_k$. Theoretically, parameter t has the same value for each RGB component, but roundoff to integer codes can result in different values of t for different components. We can minimize this roundoff error by selecting the component with the largest difference between $\mathbf{F}$ and $\mathbf{B}$. This value of t is then used to mix the new fill color $\mathbf{NF}$ with the background color, using either a modified flood-fill or boundary-fill procedure.

Similar soft-fill procedures can be applied to an area whose foreground color is to be merged with multiple background color areas, such as a checkerboard pattern. When two background colors B_1 and B_2 are mixed with foreground color $\mathbf{F}$, the resulting pixel color $\mathbf{P}$ is

$$\mathbf{P} = t_0 \mathbf{F} + t_1 \mathbf{B_1} + (1 - t_0 - t_1) \mathbf{B_2} \qquad (4\text{-}4)$$

where the sum of the coefficients t_0, t_1, and $(1 - t_0 - t_1)$ on the color terms must equal 1. We can set up two simultaneous equations using two of the three RGB color components to solve for the two proportionality parameters, t_0 and t_1. These parameters are then used to mix the new fill color with the two background colors to obtain the new pixel color. With three background colors and one foreground color, or with two background and two foreground colors, we need all three RGB equations to obtain the relative amounts of the four colors. For some foreground and background color combinations, however, the system of two or three RGB equations cannot be solved. This occurs when the color values are all very similar or when they are all proportional to each other.

4-5
CHARACTER ATTRIBUTES

The appearance of displayed characters is controlled by attributes such as font, size, color, and orientation. Attributes can be set both for entire character strings (text) and for individual characters defined as marker symbols.

Text Attributes

There are a great many text options that can be made available to graphics programmers. First of all, there is the choice of font (or typeface), which is a set of characters with a particular design style such as New York, Courier, Helvetica, London, Times Roman, and various special symbol groups. The characters in a selected font can also be displayed with assorted underlining styles (solid, dotted, double), in **boldface,** in *italics,* and in outline or shadow styles. A particular font and associated style is selected in a PHIGS program by setting an integer code for the text font parameter `tf` in the function

```
setTextFont (tf)
```

Font options can be made available as predefined sets of grid patterns or as character sets designed with polylines and spline curves.

Color settings for displayed text are stored in the system attribute list and used by the procedures that load character definitions into the frame buffer. When a character string is to be displayed, the current color is used to set pixel values in the frame buffer corresponding to the character shapes and positions. Control of text color (or intensity) is managed from an application program with

```
setTextColourIndex (tc)
```

where text color parameter `tc` specifies an allowable color code.

We can adjust text size by scaling the overall dimensions (height and width) of characters or by scaling only the character width. Character size is specified by printers and compositors in *points*, where 1 point is 0.013837 inch (or approximately 1/72 inch). For example, the text you are now reading is a 10-point font. Point measurements specify the size of the *body* of a character (Fig. 4-25), but different fonts with the same point specifications can have different character sizes, depending on the design of the typeface. The distance between the *bottomline* and the *topline* of the character body is the same for all characters in a particular size and typeface, but the body width may vary. *Proportionally spaced fonts* assign a smaller body width to narrow characters such as i, j, l, and f compared to broad characters such as W or M. *Character height* is defined as the distance between the *baseline* and the *capline* of characters. Kerned characters, such as f and j in Fig. 4-25, typically extend beyond the character-body limits, and letters with descenders (g, j, p, q, y) extend below the baseline. Each character is positioned within the character body by a font designer to allow suitable spacing along and between print lines when text is displayed with character bodies touching.

Text size can be adjusted without changing the width-to-height ratio of characters with

```
setCharacterHeight (ch)
```

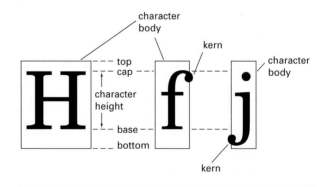

Figure 4-25
Character body.

Height 1

Height 2

Height 3

Figure 4-26
The effect of different character-height settings on displayed text.

Parameter ch is assigned a real value greater than 0 to set the coordinate height of capital letters: the distance between baseline and capline in user coordinates. This setting also affects character-body size, so that the width and spacing of characters is adjusted to maintain the same text proportions. For instance, doubling the height also doubles the character width and the spacing between characters. Figure 4-26 shows a character string displayed with three different character heights.

The width only of text can be set with the function

```
setCharacterExpansionFactor (cw)
```

where the character-width parameter cw is set to a positive real value that scales the body width of characters. Text height is unaffected by this attribute setting. Examples of text displayed with different character expansions is given in Fig. 4-27.

Spacing between characters is controlled separately with

```
setCharacterSpacing (cs)
```

where the character-spacing parameter cs can be assigned any real value. The value assigned to cs determines the spacing between character bodies along print lines. Negative values for cs overlap character bodies; positive values insert space to spread out the displayed characters. Assigning the value 0 to cs causes text to be displayed with no space between character bodies. The amount of spacing to be applied is determined by multiplying the value of cs by the character height (distance between baseline and capline). In Fig. 4-28, a character string is displayed with three different settings for the character-spacing parameter.

The orientation for a displayed character string is set according to the direction of the **character up vector:**

```
setCharacterUpVector (upvect)
```

Parameter upvect in this function is assigned two values that specify the *x* and *y* vector components. Text is then displayed so that the orientation of characters from baseline to capline is in the direction of the up vector. For example, with upvect = (1, 1), the direction of the up vector is 45° and text would be displayed as shown in Fig. 4-29. A procedure for orienting text rotates characters so that the sides of character bodies, from baseline to capline, are aligned with the up vector. The rotated character shapes are then scan converted into the frame buffer.

width 0.5

width 1.0

width 2.0

Figure 4-27
The effect of different character-width settings on displayed text.

Spacing 0.0

Spacing 0.5

Spacing 1.0

Figure 4-28
The effect of different character spacings on displayed text.

165

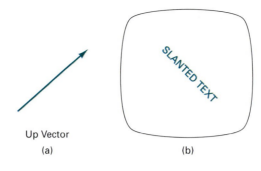

Figure 4-29
Direction of the up vector (a)
controls the orientation of
displayed text (b).

It is useful in many applications to be able to arrange character strings vertically or horizontally (Fig. 4-30). An attribute parameter for this option is set with the statement

```
setTextPath (tp)
```

Figure 4-30
Text path attributes can be set to produce horizontal or vertical arrangements of character strings.

where the text-path parameter `tp` can be assigned the value: *right, left, up,* or *down.* Examples of text displayed with these four options are shown in Fig. 4-31. A procedure for implementing this option must transform the character patterns into the specified orientation before transferring them to the frame buffer.

Character strings can also be oriented using a combination of up-vector and text-path specifications to produce slanted text. Figure 4-32 shows the directions of character strings generated by the various text-path settings for a 45° up vector. Examples of text generated for text-path values *down* and *right* with this up vector are illustrated in Fig. 4-33.

Another handy attribute for character strings is alignment. This attribute specifies how text is to be positioned with respect to the start coordinates. Alignment attributes are set with

```
setTextAlignment (h, v)
```

where parameters `h` and `v` control horizontal and vertical alignment, respectively. Horizontal alignment is set by assigning `h` a value of *left, centre,* or *right.* Vertical alignment is set by assigning `v` a value of *top, cap, half, base,* or *bottom.* The interpretation of these alignment values depends on the current setting for the text path. Figure 4-34 shows the position of the alignment settings when text is to be displayed horizontally to the right or vertically down. Similar interpretations apply to text path values of *left* and *up.* The "most natural" alignment for a particular text path is chosen by assigning the value *normal* to the `h` and `v` parameters. Figure 4-35 illustrates common alignment positions for horizontal and vertical text labels.

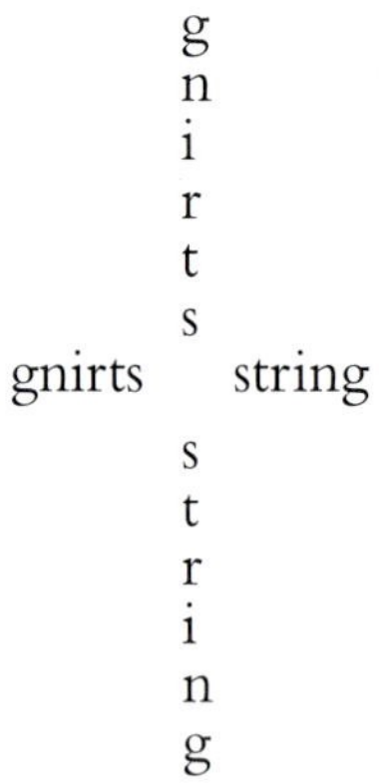

A precision specification for text display is given with

```
setTextPrecision (tpr)
```

Figure 4-31
Text displayed with the four text-path options.

where text precision parameter `tpr` is assigned one of the values: *string, char,* or *stroke.* The highest-quality text is displayed when the precision parameter is set to the value *stroke.* For this precision setting, greater detail would be used in defining the character shapes, and the processing of attribute selections and other string-manipulation procedures would be carried out to the highest possible accuracy. The lowest-quality precision setting, *string*, is used for faster display of character strings. At this precision, many attribute selections such as text path are ignored, and string-manipulation procedures are simplified to reduce processing time.

Marker Attributes

A marker symbol is a single character that can be displayed in different colors and in different sizes. Marker attributes are implemented by procedures that load the chosen character into the raster at the defined positions with the specified color and size.

We select a particular character to be the marker symbol with

```
setMarkerType (mt)
```

where marker type parameter `mt` is set to an integer code. Typical codes for marker type are the integers 1 through 5, specifying, respectively, a dot ($\cdot$), a vertical cross (+), an asterisk (*), a circle (o), and a diagonal cross ($\times$). Displayed marker types are centered on the marker coordinates.

We set the marker size with

```
setMarkerSizeScaleFactor (ms)
```

with parameter marker size `ms` assigned a positive number. This scaling parameter is applied to the nominal size for the particular marker symbol chosen. Values greater than 1 produce character enlargement; values less than 1 reduce the marker size.

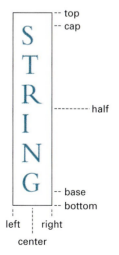

Direction of
Character up Vector
(a)

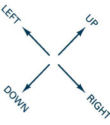

Text Path Direction
(b)

Figure 4-32
An up-vector specification (a) controls the direction of the text path (b).

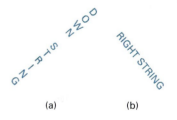

(a)   (b)

Figure 4-33
The 45° up vector in Fig. 4-32 produces the display (a) for a *down* path and the display (b) for a *right* path.

Figure 4-34
Alignment attribute values for horizontal and vertical strings.

167

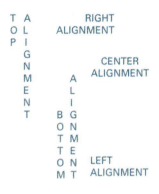

Figure 4-35
Character-string alignments.

Marker color is specified with

        setPolymarkerColourIndex (mc)

A selected color code for parameter `mc` is stored in the current attribute list and used to display subsequently specified marker primitives.

4-6
BUNDLED ATTRIBUTES

With the procedures we have considered so far, each function references a single attribute that specifies exactly how a primitive is to be displayed with that attribute setting. These specifications are called **individual** (or **unbundled**) attributes, and they are meant to be used with an output device that is capable of displaying primitives in the way specified. If an application program, employing individual attributes, is interfaced to several output devices, some of the devices may not have the capability to display the intended attributes. A program using individual color attributes, for example, may have to be modified to produce acceptable output on a monochromatic monitor.

Individual attribute commands provide a simple and direct method for specifying attributes when a single output device is used. When several kinds of output devices are available at a graphics installation, it is convenient for a user to be able to say how attributes are to be interpreted on each of the different devices. This is accomplished by setting up tables for each output device that lists sets of attribute values that are to be used on that device to display each primitive type. A particular set of attribute values for a primitive on each output device is then chosen by specifying the appropriate table index. Attributes specified in this manner are called **bundled** attributes. The table for each primitive that defines groups of attribute values to be used when displaying that primitive on a particular output device is called a **bundle table**.

Attributes that may be bundled into the workstation table entries are those that do not involve coordinate specifications, such as color and line type. The choice between a bundled or an unbundled specification is made by setting a switch called the **aspect source flag** for each of these attributes:

        setIndividualASF (attributeptr, flagptr)

where parameter `attributeptr` points to a list of attributes, and parameter `flagptr` points to the corresponding list of aspect source flags. Each aspect source flag can be assigned a value of *individual* or *bundled*. Attributes that may be bundled are listed in the following sections.

Bundled Line Attributes

Entries in the bundle table for line attributes on a specified workstation are set with the function

        setPolylineRepresentation (ws, li, lt, lw, lc)

168

Parameter ws is the workstation identifier, and line index parameter li defines the bundle table position. Parameters lt, lw, and lc are then bundled and assigned values to set the line type, line width, and line color specifications, respectively, for the designated table index. For example, the following statements define groups of line attributes that are to be referenced as index number 3 on two different workstations:

```
setPolylineRepresentation (1, 3, 2, 0.5, 1);

setPolylineRepresentation (4, 3, 1, 1, 7);
```

A polyline that is assigned a table index value of 3 would then be displayed using dashed lines at half thickness in a blue color on workstation 1; while on workstation 4, this same index generates solid, standard-sized white lines.

Once the bundle tables have been set up, a group of bundled line attributes is chosen for each workstation by specifying the table index value:

```
setPolylineIndex (li)
```

Subsequent polyline commands would then generate lines on each workstation according to the set of bundled attribute values defined at the table position specified by the value of the line index parameter li.

Bundled Area-Fill Attributes

Table entries for bundled area-fill attributes are set with

```
setInteriorRepresentation (ws, fi, fs, pi, fc)
```

which defines the attribute list corresponding to fill index fi on workstation ws. Parameters fs, pi, and fc are assigned values for the fill style, pattern index, and fill color, respectively, on the designated workstation. Similar bundle tables can also be set up for edge attributes of polygon fill areas.

A particular attribute bundle is then selected from the table with the function

```
setInteriorIndex (fi)
```

Subsequently defined fill areas are then displayed on each active workstation according to the table entry specified by the fill index parameter fi. Other fill-area attributes, such as pattern reference point and pattern size, are independent of the workstation designation and are set with the functions previously described.

Bundled Text Attributes

The function

```
setTextRepresentation (ws, ti, tf, tp, te, ts, tc)
```

bundles values for text font, precision, expansion factor, size, and color in a table position for workstation ws that is specified by the value assigned to text index

169

parameter `ti`. Other text attributes, including character up vector, text path, character height, and text alignment are set individually.

A particular text index value is then chosen with the function

```
setTextIndex (ti)
```

Each text function that is then invoked is displayed on each workstation with the set of attributes referenced by this table position.

Bundled Marker Attributes

Table entries for bundled marker attributes are set up with

```
setPolymarkerRepresentation (ws, mi, mt, ms, mc)
```

This defines the marker type, marker scale factor, and marker color for index `mi` on workstation `ws`. Bundle table selections are then made with the function

```
setPolymarkerIndex (mi)
```

4-7
INQUIRY FUNCTIONS

Current settings for attributes and other parameters, such as workstation types and status, in the system lists can be retrieved with inquiry functions. These functions allow current values to be copied into specified parameters, which can then be saved for later reuse or used to check the current state of the system if an error occurs.

We check current attribute values by stating the name of the attribute in the inquiry function. For example, the functions

```
inquirePolylineIndex (lastli)
```

and

```
inquireInteriorColourIndex (lastfc)
```

copy the current values for line index and fill color into parameters `lastli` and `lastfc`. The following program segment illustrates reusing the current line type value after a set of lines are drawn with a new line type.

```
inquireLinetype (oldlt);

setLinetype (newlt);
        .
        .
        .
setLinetype (oldlt);
```

ANTIALIASING

Displayed primitives generated by the raster algorithms discussed in Chapter 3 have a jagged, or stairstep, appearance because the sampling process digitizes coordinate points on an object to discrete integer pixel positions. This distortion of information due to low-frequency sampling (undersampling) is called **aliasing.** We can improve the appearance of displayed raster lines by applying **antialiasing** methods that compensate for the undersampling process.

An example of the effects of undersampling is shown in Fig. 4-36. To avoid losing information from such periodic objects, we need to set the sampling frequency to at least twice that of the highest frequency occurring in the object, referred to as the **Nyquist sampling frequency** (or Nyquist sampling rate) f_s:

$$f_s = 2f_{max} \qquad (4\text{-}5)$$

Another way to state this is that the sampling interval should be no larger than one-half the cycle interval (called the **Nyquist sampling interval**). For x-interval sampling, the Nyquist sampling interval Δx_s is

$$\Delta x_s = \frac{\Delta x_{cycle}}{2} \qquad (4\text{-}6)$$

where $\Delta x_{cycle} = 1/f_{max}$. In Fig. 4-36, our sampling interval is one and one-half times the cycle interval, so the sampling interval is at least three times too big. If we want to recover all the object information for this example, we need to cut the sampling interval down to one-third the size shown in the figure.

One way to increase sampling rate with raster systems is simply to display objects at higher resolution. But even at the highest resolution possible with current technology, the jaggies will be apparent to some extent. There is a limit to how big we can make the frame buffer and still maintain the refresh rate at 30 to 60 frames per second. And to represent objects accurately with continuous parameters, we need arbitrarily small sampling intervals. Therefore, unless hardware technology is developed to handle arbitrarily large frame buffers, increased screen resolution is not a complete solution to the aliasing problem.

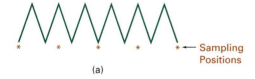

(a)

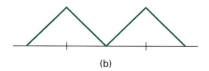

(b)

Figure 4-36
Sampling the periodic shape in (a) at the marked positions produces the aliased lower-frequency representation in (b).

171

With raster systems that are capable of displaying more than two intensity levels (color or gray scale), we can apply antialiasing methods to modify pixel intensities. By appropriately varying the intensities of pixels along the boundaries of primitives, we can smooth the edges to lessen the jagged appearance.

A straightforward antialiasing method is to increase sampling rate by treating the screen as if it were covered with a finer grid than is actually available. We can then use multiple sample points across this finer grid to determine an appropriate intensity level for each screen pixel. This technique of sampling object characteristics at a high resolution and displaying the results at a lower resolution is called **supersampling** (or **postfiltering**, since the general method involves computing intensities at subpixel grid positions, then combining the results to obtain the pixel intensities). Displayed pixel positions are spots of light covering a finite area of the screen, and not infinitesimal mathematical points. Yet in the line and fill-area algorithms we have discussed, the intensity of each pixel is determined by the location of a single point on the object boundary. By supersampling, we obtain intensity information from multiple points that contribute to the overall intensity of a pixel.

An alternative to supersampling is to determine pixel intensity by calculating the areas of overlap of each pixel with the objects to be displayed. Antialiasing by computing overlap areas is referred to as **area sampling** (or **prefiltering**, since the intensity of the pixel as a whole is determined without calculating subpixel intensities). Pixel overlap areas are obtained by determining where object boundaries intersect individual pixel boundaries.

Raster objects can also be antialiased by shifting the display location of pixel areas. This technique, called **pixel phasing**, is applied by "micropositioning" the electron beam in relation to object geometry.

Supersampling Straight Line Segments

Supersampling straight lines can be performed in several ways. For the gray-scale display of a straight-line segment, we can divide each pixel into a number of subpixels and count the number of subpixels that are along the line path. The intensity level for each pixel is then set to a value that is proportional to this subpixel count. An example of this method is given in Fig. 4-37. Each square pixel area is divided into nine equal-sized square subpixels, and the shaded regions show the subpixels that would be selected by Bresenham's algorithm. This scheme provides for three intensity settings above zero, since the maximum number of subpixels that can be selected within any pixel is three. For this example, the pixel at position (10, 20) is set to the maximum intensity (level 3); pixels at (11, 21) and (12, 21) are each set to the next highest intensity (level 2); and pixels at (11, 20) and (12, 22) are each set to the lowest intensity above zero (level 1). Thus the line intensity is spread out over a greater number of pixels, and the stairstep effect is smoothed by displaying a somewhat blurred line path in the vicinity of the stair steps (between horizontal runs). If we want to use more intensity levels to antialiase the line with this method, we increase the number of sampling positions across each pixel. Sixteen subpixels gives us four intensity levels above zero; twenty-five subpixels gives us five levels; and so on.

In the supersampling example of Fig. 4-37, we considered pixel areas of finite size, but we treated the line as a mathematical entity with zero width. Actually, displayed lines have a width approximately equal to that of a pixel. If we take the finite width of the line into account, we can perform supersampling by setting each pixel intensity proportional to the number of subpixels inside the

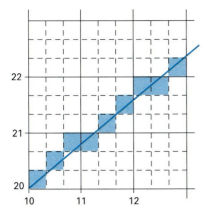

Figure 4-37
Supersampling subpixel positions
along a straight line segment whose
left endpoint is at screen
coordinates (10, 20).

polygon representing the line area. A subpixel can be considered to be inside the
line if its lower left corner is inside the polygon boundaries. An advantage of this
supersampling procedure is that the number of possible intensity levels for each
pixel is equal to the total number of subpixels within the pixel area. For the example in Fig. 4-37, we can represent this line with finite width by positioning the
polygon boundaries parallel to the line path as in Fig. 4-38. And each pixel can
now be set to one of nine possible brightness levels above zero.

Another advantage of supersampling with a finite-width line is that the
total line intensity is distributed over more pixels. In Fig. 4-38, we now have the
pixel at grid position (10, 21) turned on (at intensity level 2), and we also pick up
contributions from pixels immediately below and immediately to the left of position (10, 21). Also, if we have a color display, we can extend the method to take
background colors into account. A particular line might cross several different
color areas, and we can average subpixel intensities to obtain pixel color settings.
For instance, if five subpixels within a particular pixel area are determined to be
inside the boundaries for a red line and the remaining four pixels fall within a
blue background area, we can calculate the color for this pixel as

$$\text{pixel}_{\text{color}} = (5 \cdot \text{red} + 4 \cdot \text{blue})/9$$

The trade-off for these gains from supersampling a finite-width line is that
identifying interior subpixels requires more calculations than simply determining
which subpixels are along the line path. These calculations are also complicated
by the positioning of the line boundaries in relation to the line path. This posi-

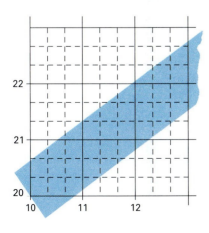

Figure 4-38
Supersampling subpixel positions
in relation to the interior of a line of
finite width.

tioning depends on the slope of the line. For a 45° line, the line path is centered on the polygon area; but for either a horizontal or a vertical line, we want the line path to be one of the polygon boundaries. For instance, a horizontal line passing through grid coordinates (10, 20) would be represented as the polygon bounded by horizontal grid lines $y = 20$ and $y = 21$. Similarly, the polygon representing a vertical line through (10, 20) would have vertical boundaries along grid lines $x = 10$ and $x = 11$. For lines with slope $|m| < 1$, the mathematical line path is positioned proportionately closer to the lower polygon boundary; and for lines with slope $|m| > 1$, this line path is placed closer to the upper polygon boundary.

Pixel-Weighting Masks

Supersampling algorithms are often implemented by giving more weight to subpixels near the center of a pixel area, since we would expect these subpixels to be more important in determining the overall intensity of a pixel. For the 3 by 3 pixel subdivisions we have considered so far, a weighting scheme as in Fig. 4-39 could be used. The center subpixel here is weighted four times that of the corner subpixels and twice that of the remaining subpixels. Intensities calculated for each grid of nine subpixels would then be averaged so that the center subpixel is weighted by a factor of 1/4; the top, bottom, and side subpixels are each weighted by a factor of 1/8; and the corner subpixels are each weighted by a factor of 1/16. An array of values specifying the relative importance of subpixels is sometimes referred to as a "mask" of subpixel weights. Similar masks can be set up for larger subpixel grids. Also, these masks are often extended to include contributions from subpixels belonging to neighboring pixels, so that intensities can be averaged over adjacent pixels.

Area Sampling Straight Line Segments

We perform area sampling for a straight line by setting each pixel intensity proportional to the area of overlap of the pixel with the finite-width line. The line can be treated as a rectangle, and the section of the line area between two adjacent vertical (or two adjacent horizontal) screen grid lines is then a trapezoid. Overlap areas for pixels are calculated by determining how much of the trapezoid overlaps each pixel in that vertical column (or horizontal row). In Fig. 4-38, the pixel with screen grid coordinates (10, 20) is about 90 percent covered by the line area, so its intensity would be set to 90 percent of the maximum intensity. Similarly, the pixel at (10, 21) would be set to an intensity of about 15 percent of maximum. A method for estimating pixel overlap areas is illustrated by the supersampling example in Fig. 4-38. The total number of subpixels within the line boundaries is approximately equal to the overlap area, and this estimation is improved by using finer subpixel grids. With color displays, the areas of pixel overlap with different color regions is calculated and the final pixel color is taken as the average color of the various overlap areas.

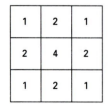

Filtering Techniques

Figure 4-39

Relative weights for a grid of 3 by 3 subpixels.

A more accurate method for antialiasing lines is to use **filtering** techniques. The method is similar to applying a weighted pixel mask, but now we imagine a continuous *weighting surface* (or *filter function*) covering the pixel. Figure 4-40 shows examples of rectangular, conical, and Gaussian filter functions. Methods for applying the filter function are similar to applying a weighting mask, but now we integrate over the pixel surface to obtain the weighted average intensity. To reduce computation, table lookups are commonly used to evaluate the integrals.

Pixel Phasing

On raster systems that can address subpixel positions within the screen grid, pixel phasing can be used to antialias objects. Stairsteps along a line path or object boundary are smoothed out by moving (micropositioning) the electron beam to more nearly approximate positions specified by the object geometry. Systems incorporating this technique are designed so that individual pixel positions can be shifted by a fraction of a pixel diameter. The electron beam is typically shifted by 1/4, 1/2, or 3/4 of a pixel diameter to plot points closer to the true path of a line or object edge. Some systems also allow the size of individual pixels to be adjusted as an additional means for distributing intensities. Figure 4-41 illustrates the antialiasing effects of pixel phasing on a variety of line paths.

Compensating for Line Intensity Differences

Antialiasing a line to soften the stairstep effect also compensates for another raster effect, illustrated in Fig. 4-42. Both lines are plotted with the same number of pixels, yet the diagonal line is longer than the horizontal line by a factor of $\sqrt{2}$. The visual effect of this is that the diagonal line appears less bright than the horizontal line, because the diagonal line is displayed with a lower intensity per unit length. A line-drawing algorithm could be adapted to compensate for this effect by adjusting the intensity of each line according to its slope. Horizontal and vertical lines would be displayed with the lowest intensity, while 45° lines would be given the highest intensity. But if antialiasing techniques are applied to a display,

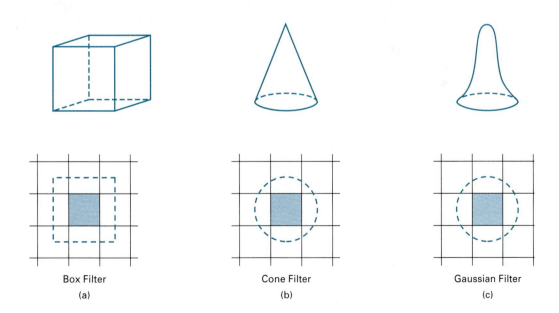

Box Filter
(a)

Cone Filter
(b)

Gaussian Filter
(c)

Figure 4-40
Common filter functions used to antialias line paths. The volume of each filter is normalized to 1, and the height gives the relative weight at any subpixel position.

175

intensities are automatically compensated. When the finite width of lines is taken into account, pixel intensities are adjusted so that lines display a total intensity proportional to their length.

Antialiasing Area Boundaries

The antialiasing concepts we have discussed for lines can also be applied to the boundaries of areas to remove their jagged appearance. We can incorporate these procedures into a scan-line algorithm to smooth the area outline as the area is generated.

If system capabilities permit the repositioning of pixels, area boundaries can be smoothed by adjusting boundary pixel positions so that they are along the line defining an area boundary. Other methods adjust each pixel intensity at a boundary position according to the percent of pixel area that is inside the boundary. In Fig. 4-43, the pixel at position (x, y) has about half its area inside the polygon boundary. Therefore, the intensity at that position would be adjusted to one-half its assigned value. At the next position $(x + 1, y + 1)$ along the boundary, the intensity is adjusted to about one-third the assigned value for that point. Similar adjustments, based on the percent of pixel area coverage, are applied to the other intensity values around the boundary.

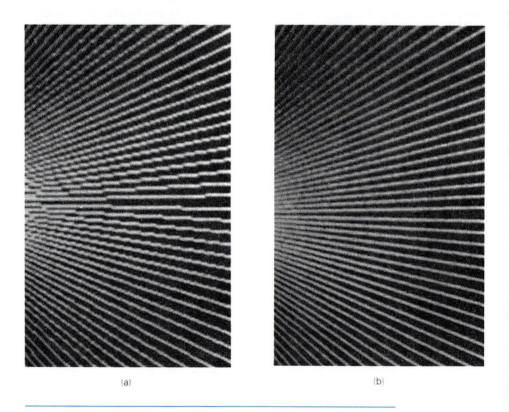

(a)

(b)

Figure 4-41

Jagged lines (a) , plotted on the Merlin 9200 system, are smoothed (b) with an antialiasing technique called pixel phasing. This technique increases the number of addressable points on the system from 768 × 576 to 3072 × 2304. (*Courtesy of Megatek Corp.*)

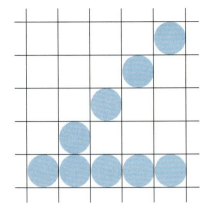

Section 4-8

Antialiasing

Figure 4-42
Unequal-length lines displayed
with the same number of pixels in
each line.

Supersampling methods can be applied by subdividing the total area and determining the number of subpixels inside the area boundary. A pixel partitioning into four subareas is shown in Fig. 4-44. The original 4 by 4 grid of pixels is turned into an 8 by 8 grid, and we now process eight scan lines across this grid instead of four. Figure 4-45 shows one of the pixel areas in this grid that overlaps an object boundary. Along the two scan lines we determine that three of the subpixel areas are inside the boundary. So we set the pixel intensity at 75 percent of its maximum value.

Another method for determining the percent of pixel area within a boundary, developed by Pitteway and Watkinson, is based on the midpoint line algorithm. This algorithm selects the next pixel along a line by determining which of two pixels is closer to the line by testing the location of the midposition between the two pixels. As in the Bresenham algorithm, we set up a decision parameter p whose sign tells us which of the next two candidate pixels is closer to the line. By slightly modifying the form of p, we obtain a quantity that also gives the percent of the current pixel area that is covered by an object.

We first consider the method for a line with slope m in the range from 0 to 1. In Fig. 4-46, a straight line path is shown on a pixel grid. Assuming that the pixel at position (x_k, y_k) has been plotted, the next pixel nearest the line at $x = x_k+1$ is either the pixel at y_k or the one at $y_k + 1$. We can determine which pixel is nearer with the calculation

$$y - y_{\text{mid}} = [m(x_k + 1) + b] - (y_k + 0.5) \qquad (4\text{-}7)$$

This gives the vertical distance from the actual y coordinate on the line to the halfway point between pixels at position y_k and $y_k + 1$. If this difference calculation is negative, the pixel at y_k is closer to the line. If the difference is positive, the

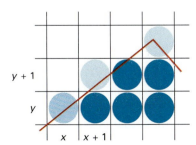

Figure 4-43
Adjusting pixel intensities along an
area boundary.

pixel at $y_k + 1$ is closer. We can adjust this calculation so that it produces a positive number in the range from 0 to 1 by adding the quantity $1 - m$:

$$p = [m(x_k + 1) + b] - (y_k + 0.5) + (1 - m) \qquad (4\text{-}8)$$

Now the pixel at y_k is nearer if $p < 1 - m$, and the pixel at $y_k + 1$ is nearer if $p > 1 - m$.

Parameter p also measures the amount of the current pixel that is overlapped by the area. For the pixel at (x_k, y_k) in Fig. 4-47, the interior part of the pixel has an area that can be calculated as

$$\text{area} = mx_k + b - y_k + 0.5 \qquad (4\text{-}9)$$

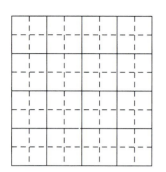

Figure 4-44

A 4 by 4 pixel section of a raster display subdivided into an 8 by 8 grid.

This expression for the overlap area of the pixel at (x_k, y_k) is the same as that for parameter p in Eq. 4-8. Therefore, by evaluating p to determine the next pixel position along the polygon boundary, we also determine the percent of area coverage for the current pixel.

We can generalize this algorithm to accommodate lines with negative slopes and lines with slopes greater than 1. This calculation for parameter p could then be incorporated into a midpoint line algorithm to locate pixel positions and an object edge and to concurrently adjust pixel intensities along the boundary lines. Also, we can adjust the calculations to reference pixel coordinates at their lower left coordinates and maintain area proportions as discussed in Section 3-10.

At polygon vertices and for very skinny polygons, as shown in Fig. 4-48, we have more than one boundary edge passing through a pixel area. For these cases, we need to modify the Pitteway–Watkinson algorithm by processing all edges passing through a pixel and determining the correct interior area.

Filtering techniques discussed for line antialiasing can also be applied to area edges. Also, the various antialiasing methods can be applied to polygon areas or to regions with curved boundaries. Boundary equations are used to estimate area overlap of pixel regions with the area to be displayed. And coherence techniques are used along and between scan lines to simplify the calculations.

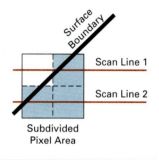

Figure 4-45

A subdivided pixel area with three subdivisions inside an object boundary line.

SUMMARY

In this chapter, we have explored the various attributes that control the appearance of displayed primitives. Procedures for displaying primitives use attribute settings to adjust the output of algorithms for line-generation, area-filling, and text-string displays.

The basic line attributes are line type, line color, and line width. Specifications for line type include solid, dashed, and dotted lines. Line-color specifications can be given in terms of RGB components, which control the intensity of the three electron guns in an RGB monitor. Specifications for line width are given in terms of multiples of a standard, one-pixel-wide line. These attributes can be applied to both straight lines and curves.

To reduce the size of the frame buffer, some raster systems use a separate color lookup table. This limits the number of colors that can be displayed to the size of the lookup table. Full-color systems are those that provide 24 bits per pixel and no separate color lookup table.

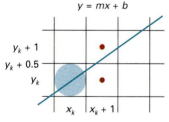

Figure 4-46

Boundary edge of an area passing through a pixel grid section.

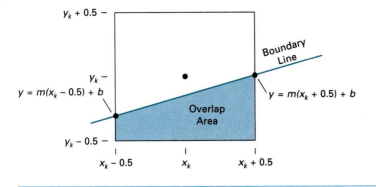

$y_k + 0.5$ —

y_k —

$y = m(x_k - 0.5) + b$

$y = m(x_k + 0.5) + b$

Boundary Line

Overlap Area

$y_k - 0.5$ —

$x_k - 0.5$

x_k

$x_k + 0.5$

Figure 4-47
Overlap area of a pixel rectangle, centered at position (x_k, y_k), with the interior of a polygon area.

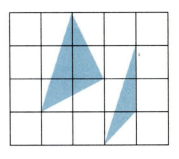

Figure 4-48
Polygons with more than one boundary line passing through individual pixel regions.

Fill-area attributes include the fill style and the fill color or the fill pattern. When the fill style is to be solid, the fill color specifies the color for the solid fill of the polygon interior. A hollow-fill style produces an interior in the background color and a border in the fill color. The third type of fill is patterned. In this case, a selected array pattern is used to fill the polygon interior.

An additional fill option provided in some packages is soft fill. This fill has applications in antialiasing and in painting packages. Soft-fill procedures provide a new fill color for a region that has the same variations as the previous fill color. One example of this approach is the linear soft-fill algorithm that assumes that the previous fill was a linear combination of foreground and background colors. This same linear relationship is then determined from the frame-buffer settings and used to repaint the area in a new color.

Characters, defined as pixel grid patterns or as outline fonts, can be displayed in different colors, sizes, and orientations. To set the orientation of a character string, we select a direction for the character up vector and a direction for the text path. In addition, we can set the alignment of a text string in relation to the start coordinate position. Marker symbols can be displayed using selected characters of various sizes and colors.

Graphics packages can be devised to handle both unbundled and bundled attribute specifications. Unbundled attributes are those that are defined for only one type of output device. Bundled attribute specifications allow different sets of attributes to be used on different devices, but accessed with the same index number in a bundle table. Bundle tables may be installation-defined, user-defined, or both. Functions to set the bundle table values specify workstation type and the attribute list for a given attribute index.

To determine current settings for attributes and other parameters, we can invoke inquiry functions. In addition to retrieving color and other attribute information, we can obtain workstation codes and status values with inquiry functions.

Because scan conversion is a digitizing process on raster systems, displayed primitives have a jagged appearance. This is due to the undersampling of information which rounds coordinate values to pixel positions. We can improve the appearance of raster primitives by applying antialiasing procedures that adjust pixel intensities. One method for doing this is to supersample. That is, we consider each pixel to be composed of subpixels and we calculate the intensity of the subpixels and average the values of all subpixels. Alternatively, we can perform area sampling and determine the percentage of area coverage for a screen pixel, then set the pixel intensity proportional to this percentage. We can also weight the subpixel contributions according to position, giving higher weights to the central subpixels. Another method for antialiasing is to build special hardware configurations that can shift pixel positions.

Table 4-4 lists the attributes discussed in this chapter for the output primitive classifications: line, fill area, text, and marker. The attribute functions that can be used in graphics packages are listed for each category.

TABLE 4-4
SUMMARY OF ATTRIBUTES

Output Primitive Type	Associated Attributes	Attribute-Setting Functions	Bundled-Attribute Functions
Line	Type	setLinetype	setPolylineIndex
	Width	setLineWidthScaleFactor	setPolylineRepresentation
	Color	setPolylineColourIndex	
Fill Area	Fill Style	setInteriorStyle	setInteriorIndex
	Fill Color	setInteriorColorIndex	setInteriorRepresentation
	Pattern	setInteriorStyleIndex	
		setPatternRepresentation	
		setPatternSize	
		setPatternReferencePoint	
Text	Font	setTextFont	setTextIndex
	Color	setTextColourIndex	setTextRepresentation
	Size	setCharacterHeight	
		setCharacterExpansionFactor	
	Orientation	setCharacterUpVector	
		setTextPath	
		setTextAlignment	
Marker	Type	setMarkerType	setPolymarkerIndex
	Size	setMarkerSizeScaleFactor	setPolymarkerRepresentation
	Color	setPolymarkerColourIndex	

REFERENCES

Color and grayscale considerations are discussed in Crow (1978) and in Heckbert (1982).

Soft-fill techniques are given in Fishkin and Barsky (1984).

Antialiasing techniques are discussed in Pitteway and Watkinson (1980), Crow (1981), Turkowski (1982), Korein and Badler (1983), and Kirk and Avro, Schilling, and Wu (1991).

Attribute functions in PHIGS are discussed in Howard et al. (1991), Hopgood and Duce (1991), Gaskins (1992), and Blake (1993). For information on GKS workstations and attributes, see Hopgood et al. (1983) and Enderle, Kansy, and Pfaff (1984).

EXERCISES

4-1. Implement the line-type function by modifying Bresenham's line-drawing algorithm to display either solid, dashed, or dotted lines.

4-2. Implement the line-type function with a midpoint line algorithm to display either solid, dashed, or dotted lines.

4-3. Devise a parallel method for implementing the line-type function.

4-4. Devise a parallel method for implementing the line-width function.

4-5. A line specified by two endpoints and a width can be converted to a rectangular polygon with four vertices and then displayed using a scan-line method. Develop an efficient algorithm for computing the four vertices needed to define such a rectangle using the line endpoints and line width.

4-6. Implement the line-width function in a line-drawing program so that any one of three line widths can be displayed.

4-7. Write a program to output a line graph of three data sets defined over the same x coordinate range. Input to the program is to include the three sets of data values, labeling for the axes, and the coordinates for the display area on the screen. The data sets are to be scaled to fit the specified area, each plotted line is to be displayed in a different line type (solid, dashed, dotted), and the axes are to be labeled. (Instead of changing the line type, the three data sets can be plotted in different colors.)

4-8. Set up an algorithm for displaying thick lines with either butt caps, round caps, or projecting square caps. These options can be provided in an option menu.

4-9. Devise an algorithm for displaying thick polylines with either a miter join, a round join, or a bevel join. These options can be provided in an option menu.

4-10. Implement pen and brush menu options for a line-drawing procedure, including at least two options: round and square shapes.

4-11. Modify a line-drawing algorithm so that the intensity of the output line is set according to its slope. That is, by adjusting pixel intensities according to the value of the slope, all lines are displayed with the same intensity per unit length.

4-12. Define and implement a function for controlling the line type (solid, dashed, dotted) of displayed ellipses.

4-13. Define and implement a function for setting the width of displayed ellipses.

4-14. Write a routine to display a bar graph in any specified screen area. Input is to include the data set, labeling for the coordinate axes, and the coordinates for the screen area. The data set is to be scaled to fit the designated screen area, and the bars are to be displayed in designated colors or patterns.

4-15. Write a procedure to display two data sets defined over the same x-coordinate range, with the data values scaled to fit a specified region of the display screen. The bars for one of the data sets are to be displaced horizontally to produce an overlapping bar pattern for easy comparison of the two sets of data. Use a different color or a different fill pattern for the two sets of bars.

4-16. Devise an algorithm for implementing a color lookup table and the `setColourRepresentation` operation.

4-17. Suppose you have a system with an 8-inch by 10-inch video screen that can display 100 pixels per inch. If a color lookup table with 64 positions is used with this system, what is the smallest possible size (in bytes) for the frame buffer?

4-18. Consider an RGB raster system that has a 512-by-512 frame buffer with a 20 bits per pixel and a color lookup table with 24 bits per pixel. (a) How many distinct gray levels can be displayed with this system? (b) How many distinct colors (including gray levels) can be displayed? (c) How many colors can be displayed at any one time? (d) What is the total memory size? (e) Explain two methods for reducing memory size while maintaining the same color capabilities.

4-19. Modify the scan-line algorithm to apply any specified rectangular fill pattern to a polygon interior, starting from a designated pattern position.

4-20. Write a procedure to fill the interior of a given ellipse with a specified pattern.

4-21. Write a procedure to implement the `setPatternRepresentation` function.

4-22. Define and implement a procedure for changing the size of an existing rectangular fill pattern.

4-23. Write a procedure to implement a soft-fill algorithm. Carefully define what the soft-fill algorithm is to accomplish and how colors are to be combined.

4-24. Devise an algorithm for adjusting the height and width of characters defined as rectangular grid patterns.

4-25. Implement routines for setting the character up vector and the text path for controlling the display of character strings.

4-26. Write a program to align text as specified by input values for the alignment parameters.

4-27. Develop procedures for implementing the marker attribute functions.

4-28. Compare attribute-implementation procedures needed by systems that employ bundled attributes to those needed by systems using unbundled attributes.

4-29. Develop procedures for storing and accessing attributes in unbundled system attribute tables. The procedures are to be designed to store designated attribute values in the system tables, to pass attributes to the appropriate output routines, and to pass attributes to memory locations specified in inquiry commands.

4-30. Set up the same procedures described in the previous exercise for bundled system attribute tables.

4-31. Implement an antialiasing procedure by extending Bresenham's line algorithm to adjust pixel intensities in the vicinity of a line path.

4-32. Implement an antialiasing procedure for the midpoint line algorithm.

4-33. Develop an algorithm for antialiasing elliptical boundaries.

4-34. Modify the scan-line algorithm for area fill to incorporate antialiasing. Use coherence techniques to reduce calculations on successive scan lines.

4-35. Write a program to implement the Pitteway–Watkinson antialiasing algorithm as a scan-line procedure to fill a polygon interior. Use the routine setPixel (x, y, intensity) to load the intensity value into the frame buffer at location (x, y).

CHAPTER

5

Two-Dimensional
Geometric Transformations

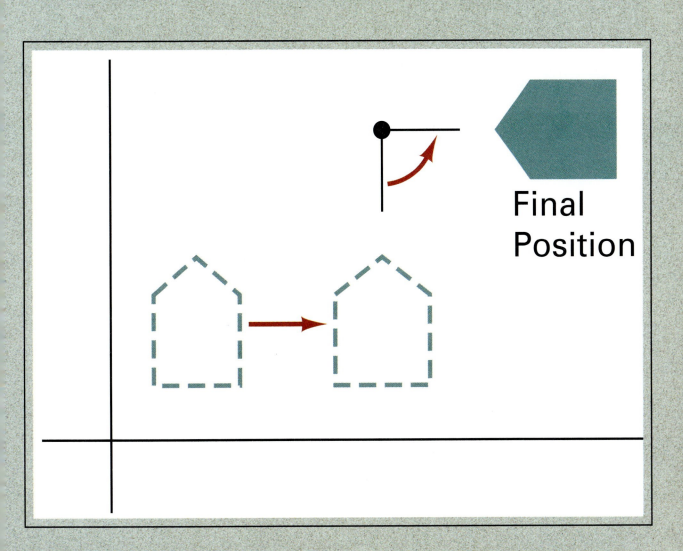

Final
Position

W ith the procedures for displaying output primitives and their attributes, we can create a variety of pictures and graphs. In many applications, there is also a need for altering or manipulating displays. Design applications and facility layouts are created by arranging the orientations and sizes of the component parts of the scene. And animations are produced by moving the "camera" or the objects in a scene along animation paths. Changes in orientation, size, and shape are accomplished with **geometric transformations** that alter the coordinate descriptions of objects. The basic geometric transformations are translation, rotation, and scaling. Other transformations that are often applied to objects include reflection and shear. We first discuss methods for performing geometric transformations and then consider how transformation functions can be incorporated into graphics packages.

5-1
BASIC TRANSFORMATIONS

Here, we first discuss general procedures for applying translation, rotation, and scaling parameters to reposition and resize two-dimensional objects. Then, in Section 5-2, we consider how transformation equations can be expressed in a more convenient matrix formulation that allows efficient combination of object transformations.

Translation

A **translation** is applied to an object by repositioning it along a straight-line path from one coordinate location to another. We translate a two-dimensional point by adding **translation distances**, t_x and t_y, to the original coordinate position (x, y) to move the point to a new position (x', y') (Fig. 5-1).

$$x' = x + t_x, \qquad y' = y + t_y \qquad (5\text{-}1)$$

The translation distance pair (t_x, t_y) is called a **translation vector** or **shift vector.**

We can express the translation equations 5-1 as a single matrix equation by using column vectors to represent coordinate positions and the translation vector:

$$\mathbf{P} = \begin{bmatrix} x_1 \\ x_2 \end{bmatrix}, \qquad \mathbf{P'} = \begin{bmatrix} x_1' \\ x_2' \end{bmatrix}, \qquad \mathbf{T} = \begin{bmatrix} t_x \\ t_y \end{bmatrix} \qquad (5\text{-}2)$$

This allows us to write the two-dimensional translation equations in the matrix form:

$$\mathbf{P'} = \mathbf{P} + \mathbf{T} \qquad (5\text{-}3)$$

Sometimes matrix-transformation equations are expressed in terms of coordinate row vectors instead of column vectors. In this case, we would write the matrix representations as $\mathbf{P} = [x \; y]$ and $\mathbf{T} = [t_x \; t_y]$. Since the column-vector representation for a point is standard mathematical notation, and since many graphics packages, for example, GKS and PHIGS, also use the column-vector representation, we will follow this convention.

Translation is a *rigid-body transformation* that moves objects without deformation. That is, every point on the object is translated by the same amount. A straight line segment is translated by applying the transformation equation 5-3 to each of the line endpoints and redrawing the line between the new endpoint positions. Polygons are translated by adding the translation vector to the coordinate position of each vertex and regenerating the polygon using the new set of vertex coordinates and the current attribute settings. Figure 5-2 illustrates the application of a specified translation vector to move an object from one position to another.

Similar methods are used to translate curved objects. To change the position of a circle or ellipse, we translate the center coordinates and redraw the figure in the new location. We translate other curves (for example, splines) by displacing the coordinate positions defining the objects, then we reconstruct the curve paths using the translated coordinate points.

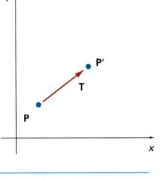

Figure 5-1
Translating a point from position **P** to position **P'** with translation vector **T**.

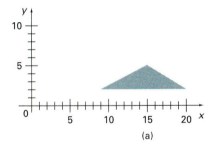

(a)

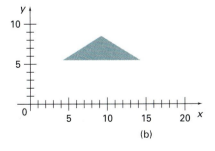

(b)

Figure 5-2
Moving a polygon from position (a) to position (b) with the translation vector (-5.50, 3.75).

185

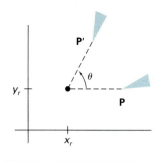

Figure 5-3
Rotation of an object through
angle θ about the pivot point
(x_r, y_r).

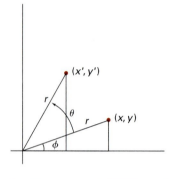

Figure 5-4
Rotation of a point from
position (x, y) to position
(x', y') through an angle θ
relative to the coordinate
origin. The original angular
displacement of the point
from the x axis is ϕ.

Rotation

A two-dimensional **rotation** is applied to an object by repositioning it along a circular path in the xy plane. To generate a rotation, we specify a **rotation angle** θ and the position (x_r, y_r) of the **rotation point** (or **pivot point**) about which the object is to be rotated (Fig. 5-3). Positive values for the rotation angle define counterclockwise rotations about the pivot point, as in Fig. 5-3, and negative values rotate objects in the clockwise direction. This transformation can also be described as a rotation about a **rotation axis** that is perpendicular to the xy plane and passes through the pivot point.

We first determine the transformation equations for rotation of a point position **P** when the pivot point is at the coordinate origin. The angular and coordinate relationships of the original and transformed point positions are shown in Fig. 5-4. In this figure, r is the constant distance of the point from the origin, angle ϕ is the original angular position of the point from the horizontal, and θ is the rotation angle. Using standard trigonometric identities, we can express the transformed coordinates in terms of angles θ and ϕ as

$$x' = r \cos (\phi + \theta) = r \cos \phi \cos \theta - r \sin \phi \sin \theta$$
$$y' = r \sin (\phi + \theta) = r \cos \phi \sin \theta + r \sin \phi \cos \theta \qquad (5\text{-}4)$$

The original coordinates of the point in polar coordinates are

$$x = r \cos \phi, \qquad y = r \sin \phi \qquad (5\text{-}5)$$

Substituting expressions 5-5 into 5-4, we obtain the transformation equations for rotating a point at position (x, y) through an angle θ about the origin:

$$x' = x \cos \theta - y \sin \theta$$
$$y' = x \sin \theta + y \cos \theta \qquad (5\text{-}6)$$

With the column-vector representations 5-2 for coordinate positions, we can write the rotation equations in the matrix form:

$$\mathbf{P}' = \mathbf{R} \cdot \mathbf{P} \qquad (5\text{-}7)$$

where the rotation matrix is

$$\mathbf{R} = \begin{bmatrix} \cos \theta & -\sin \theta \\ \sin \theta & \cos \theta \end{bmatrix} \qquad (5\text{-}8)$$

When coordinate positions are represented as row vectors instead of column vectors, the matrix product in rotation equation 5-7 is transposed so that the transformed row coordinate vector $[x'\ y']$ is calculated as

$$\mathbf{P}'^T = (\mathbf{R} \cdot \mathbf{P})^T$$
$$= \mathbf{P}^T \cdot \mathbf{R}^T$$

where $\mathbf{P}^T = [x\ y]$, and the transpose $\mathbf{R}^T$ of matrix $\mathbf{R}$ is obtained by interchanging rows and columns. For a rotation matrix, the transpose is obtained by simply changing the sign of the sine terms.

Rotation of a point about an arbitrary pivot position is illustrated in Fig. 5-5. Using the trigonometric relationships in this figure, we can generalize Eqs. 5-6 to obtain the transformation equations for rotation of a point about any specified rotation position (x_r, y_r):

$$x' = x_r + (x - x_r) \cos \theta - (y - y_r) \sin \theta$$

$$y' = y_r + (x - x_r) \sin \theta + (y - y_r) \cos \theta \qquad (5\text{-}9)$$

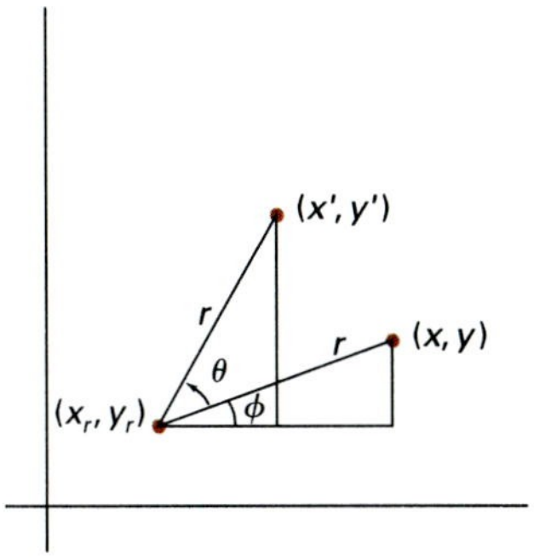

These general rotation equations differ from Eqs. 5-6 by the inclusion of additive terms, as well as the multiplicative factors on the coordinate values. Thus, the matrix expression 5-7 could be modified to include pivot coordinates by matrix addition of a column vector whose elements contain the additive (translational) terms in Eqs. 5-9. There are better ways, however, to formulate such matrix equations, and we discuss in Section 5-2 a more consistent scheme for representing the transformation equations.

As with translations, rotations are rigid-body transformations that move objects without deformation. Every point on an object is rotated through the same angle. A straight line segment is rotated by applying the rotation equations 5-9 to each of the line endpoints and redrawing the line between the new endpoint positions. Polygons are rotated by displacing each vertex through the specified rotation angle and regenerating the polygon using the new vertices. Curved lines are rotated by repositioning the defining points and redrawing the curves. A circle or an ellipse, for instance, can be rotated about a noncentral axis by moving the center position through the arc that subtends the specified rotation angle. An ellipse can be rotated about its center coordinates by rotating the major and minor axes.

Figure 5-5
Rotating a point from position (x, y) to position (x', y') through an angle θ about rotation point (x_r, y_r).

Scaling

A **scaling** transformation alters the size of an object. This operation can be carried out for polygons by multiplying the coordinate values (x, y) of each vertex by **scaling factors** s_x and s_y to produce the transformed coordinates (x', y'):

$$x' = x \cdot s_x, \qquad y' = y \cdot s_y \qquad (5\text{-}10)$$

Scaling factor s_x scales objects in the x direction, while s_y scales in the y direction. The transformation equations 5-10 can also be written in the matrix form:

$$\begin{bmatrix} x' \\ y' \end{bmatrix} = \begin{bmatrix} s_x & 0 \\ 0 & s_y \end{bmatrix} \cdot \begin{bmatrix} x \\ y \end{bmatrix} \qquad (5\text{-}11)$$

or

$$\mathbf{P}' = \mathbf{S} \cdot \mathbf{P} \qquad (5\text{-}12)$$

where **S** is the 2 by 2 scaling matrix in Eq. 5-11.

Any positive numeric values can be assigned to the scaling factors s_x and s_y. Values less than 1 reduce the size of objects; values greater than 1 produce an enlargement. Specifying a value of 1 for both s_x and s_y leaves the size of objects unchanged. When s_x and s_y are assigned the same value, a **uniform scaling** is pro-

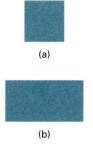

(a)

(b)

Figure 5-6
Turning a square (a) into a
rectangle (b) with scaling
factors $s_x = 2$ and $s_y = 1$.

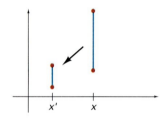

Figure 5-7
A line scaled with Eq. 5-12
using $s_x = s_y = 0.5$ is reduced
in size and moved closer to
the coordinate origin.

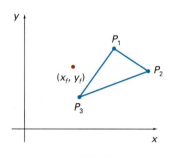

Figure 5-8
Scaling relative to a chosen
fixed point (x_f, y_f). Distances
from each polygon vertex to
the fixed point are scaled by
transformation equations
5-13.

duced that maintains relative object proportions. Unequal values for s_x and s_y result in a **differential scaling** that is often used in design applications, where pictures are constructed from a few basic shapes that can be adjusted by scaling and positioning transformations (Fig. 5-6).

Objects transformed with Eq. 5-11 are both scaled and repositioned. Scaling factors with values less than 1 move objects closer to the coordinate origin, while values greater than 1 move coordinate positions farther from the origin. Figure 5-7 illustrates scaling a line by assigning the value 0.5 to both s_x and s_y in Eq. 5-11. Both the line length and the distance from the origin are reduced by a factor of $1/2$.

We can control the location of a scaled object by choosing a position, called the **fixed point**, that is to remain unchanged after the scaling transformation. Coordinates for the fixed point (x_f, y_f) can be chosen as one of the vertices, the object centroid, or any other position (Fig. 5-8). A polygon is then scaled relative to the fixed point by scaling the distance from each vertex to the fixed point. For a vertex with coordinates (x, y), the scaled coordinates (x', y') are calculated as

$$x' = x_f + (x - x_f)s_x , \qquad y' = y_f + (y - y_f)s_y \qquad (5\text{-}13)$$

We can rewrite these scaling transformations to separate the multiplicative and additive terms:

$$
\begin{aligned}
x' &= x \cdot s_x + x_f(1 - s_x) \\
y' &= y \cdot s_y + y_f(1 - s_y)
\end{aligned}
\qquad (5\text{-}14)
$$

where the additive terms $x_f(1 - s_x)$ and $y_f(1 - s_y)$ are constant for all points in the object.

Including coordinates for a fixed point in the scaling equations is similar to including coordinates for a pivot point in the rotation equations. We can set up a column vector whose elements are the constant terms in Eqs. 5-14, then we add this column vector to the product $\mathbf{S} \cdot \mathbf{P}$ in Eq. 5-12. In the next section, we discuss a matrix formulation for the transformation equations that involves only matrix multiplication.

Polygons are scaled by applying transformations 5-14 to each vertex and then regenerating the polygon using the transformed vertices. Other objects are scaled by applying the scaling transformation equations to the parameters defining the objects. An ellipse in standard position is resized by scaling the semimajor and semiminor axes and redrawing the ellipse about the designated center coordinates. Uniform scaling of a circle is done by simply adjusting the radius. Then we redisplay the circle about the center coordinates using the transformed radius.

5-2

MATRIX REPRESENTATIONS AND HOMOGENEOUS COORDINATES

Many graphics applications involve sequences of geometric transformations. An animation, for example, might require an object to be translated and rotated at each increment of the motion. In design and picture construction applications, we perform translations, rotations, and scalings to fit the picture components into their proper positions. Here we consider how the matrix representations discussed in the previous sections can be reformulated so that such transformation sequences can be efficiently processed.

We have seen in Section 5-1 that each of the basic transformations can be expressed in the general matrix form

$$\mathbf{P}' = \mathbf{M}_1 \cdot \mathbf{P} + \mathbf{M}_2 \qquad (5\text{-}15)$$

with coordinate positions $\mathbf{P}$ and $\mathbf{P}'$ represented as column vectors. Matrix $\mathbf{M}_1$ is a 2 by 2 array containing multiplicative factors, and $\mathbf{M}_2$ is a two-element column matrix containing translational terms. For translation, $\mathbf{M}_1$ is the identity matrix. For rotation or scaling, $\mathbf{M}_2$ contains the translational terms associated with the pivot point or scaling fixed point. To produce a sequence of transformations with these equations, such as scaling followed by rotation then translation, we must calculate the transformed coordinates one step at a time. First, coordinate positions are scaled, then these scaled coordinates are rotated, and finally the rotated coordinates are translated. A more efficient approach would be to combine the transformations so that the final coordinate positions are obtained directly from the initial coordinates, thereby eliminating the calculation of intermediate coordinate values. To be able to do this, we need to reformulate Eq. 5-15 to eliminate the matrix addition associated with the translation terms in $\mathbf{M}_2$.

We can combine the multiplicative and translational terms for two-dimensional geometric transformations into a single matrix representation by expanding the 2 by 2 matrix representations to 3 by 3 matrices. This allows us to express all transformation equations as matrix multiplications, providing that we also expand the matrix representations for coordinate positions. To express any two-dimensional transformation as a matrix multiplication, we represent each Cartesian coordinate position (x, y) with the **homogeneous coordinate** triple (x_h, y_h, h), where

$$x = \frac{x_h}{h}, \qquad y = \frac{y_h}{h} \qquad (5\text{-}16)$$

Thus, a general homogeneous coordinate representation can also be written as $(h \cdot x, h \cdot y, h)$. For two-dimensional geometric transformations, we can choose the homogeneous parameter h to be any nonzero value. Thus, there is an infinite number of equivalent homogeneous representations for each coordinate point (x, y). A convenient choice is simply to set $h = 1$. Each two-dimensional position is then represented with homogeneous coordinates $(x, y, 1)$. Other values for parameter h are needed, for example, in matrix formulations of three-dimensional viewing transformations.

The term *homogeneous coordinates* is used in mathematics to refer to the effect of this representation on Cartesian equations. When a Cartesian point (x, y) is converted to a homogeneous representation (x_h, y_h, h), equations containing x and y, such as $f(x, y) = 0$, become homogeneous equations in the three parameters x_h, y_h, and h. This just means that if each of the three parameters is replaced by any value v times that parameter, the value v can be factored out of the equations.

Expressing positions in homogeneous coordinates allows us to represent all geometric transformation equations as matrix multiplications. Coordinates are represented with three-element column vectors, and transformation operations are written as 3 by 3 matrices. For translation, we have

$$\begin{bmatrix} x' \\ y' \\ 1 \end{bmatrix} = \begin{bmatrix} 1 & 0 & t_x \\ 0 & 1 & t_y \\ 0 & 0 & 1 \end{bmatrix} \cdot \begin{bmatrix} x \\ y \\ 1 \end{bmatrix} \qquad (5\text{-}17)$$

which we can write in the abbreviated form

$$\mathbf{P'} = \mathbf{T}(t_x, t_y) \cdot \mathbf{P} \qquad (5\text{-}18)$$

with $\mathbf{T}(t_x, t_y)$ as the 3 by 3 translation matrix in Eq. 5-17. The inverse of the translation matrix is obtained by replacing the translation parameters t_x and t_y with their negatives: $-t_x$ and $-t_y$.

Similarly, rotation transformation equations about the coordinate origin are now written as

$$\begin{bmatrix} x' \\ y' \\ 1 \end{bmatrix} = \begin{bmatrix} \cos\theta & -\sin\theta & 0 \\ \sin\theta & \cos\theta & 0 \\ 0 & 0 & 1 \end{bmatrix} \cdot \begin{bmatrix} x \\ y \\ 1 \end{bmatrix} \qquad (5\text{-}19)$$

or as

$$\mathbf{P'} = \mathbf{R}(\theta) \cdot \mathbf{P} \qquad (5\text{-}20)$$

The rotation transformation operator $\mathbf{R}(\theta)$ is the 3 by 3 matrix in Eq. 5-19 with rotation parameter θ. We get the inverse rotation matrix when θ is replaced with $-\theta$.

Finally, a scaling transformation relative to the coordinate origin is now expressed as the matrix multiplication

$$\begin{bmatrix} x' \\ y' \\ 1 \end{bmatrix} = \begin{bmatrix} s_x & 0 & 0 \\ 0 & s_y & 0 \\ 0 & 0 & 1 \end{bmatrix} \cdot \begin{bmatrix} x \\ y \\ 1 \end{bmatrix} \qquad (5\text{-}21)$$

or

$$\mathbf{P'} = \mathbf{S}(s_x, s_y) \cdot \mathbf{P} \qquad (5\text{-}22)$$

where $\mathbf{S}(s_x, s_y)$ is the 3 by 3 matrix in Eq. 5-21 with parameters s_x and s_y. Replacing these parameters with their multiplicative inverses ($1/s_x$ and $1/s_y$) yields the inverse scaling matrix.

Matrix representations are standard methods for implementing transformations in graphics systems. In many systems, rotation and scaling functions produce transformations with respect to the coordinate origin, as in Eqs. 5-19 and 5-21. Rotations and scalings relative to other reference positions are then handled as a succession of transformation operations. An alternate approach in a graphics package is to provide parameters in the transformation functions for the scaling fixed-point coordinates and the pivot-point coordinates. General rotation and scaling matrices that include the pivot or fixed point are then set up directly without the need to invoke a succession of transformation functions.

COMPOSITE TRANSFORMATIONS

With the matrix representations of the previous section, we can set up a matrix for any sequence of transformations as a **composite transformation matrix** by calculating the matrix product of the individual transformations. Forming products of transformation matrices is often referred to as a **concatenation**, or **composition**, of matrices. For column-matrix representation of coordinate positions, we form composite transformations by multiplying matrices in order from right to left. That is, each successive transformation matrix premultiplies the product of the preceding transformation matrices.

Translations

If two successive translation vectors (t_{x1}, t_{y1}) and (t_{x2}, t_{y2}) are applied to a coordinate position **P**, the final transformed location **P'** is calculated as

$$\mathbf{P'} = T(t_{x2}, t_{y2}) \cdot \{\mathbf{T}(t_{x1}, t_{y1}) \cdot \mathbf{P}\}$$
$$= \{\mathbf{T}(t_{x2}, t_{y2}) \cdot \mathbf{T}(t_{x1}, t_{y1})\} \cdot \mathbf{P} \tag{5-23}$$

where **P** and **P'** are represented as homogeneous-coordinate column vectors. We can verify this result by calculating the matrix product for the two associative groupings. Also, the composite transformation matrix for this sequence of translations is

$$\begin{bmatrix} 1 & 0 & t_{x2} \\ 0 & 1 & t_{y2} \\ 0 & 0 & 1 \end{bmatrix} \cdot \begin{bmatrix} 1 & 0 & t_{x1} \\ 0 & 1 & t_{y1} \\ 0 & 0 & 1 \end{bmatrix} = \begin{bmatrix} 1 & 0 & t_{x1} + t_{x2} \\ 0 & 1 & t_{y1} + t_{y2} \\ 0 & 0 & 1 \end{bmatrix} \tag{5-24}$$

or

$$\mathbf{T}(t_{x2}, t_{y2}) \cdot \mathbf{T}(t_{x1}, t_{y1}) = \mathbf{T}(t_{x1} + t_{x2}, t_{y1} + t_{y2}) \tag{5-25}$$

which demonstrates that two successive translations are additive.

Rotations

Two successive rotations applied to point **P** produce the transformed position

$$\mathbf{P'} = \mathbf{R}(\theta_2) \cdot \{\mathbf{R}(\theta_1) \cdot \mathbf{P}\}$$
$$= \{\mathbf{R}(\theta_2) \cdot \mathbf{R}(\theta_1)\} \cdot \mathbf{P} \tag{5-26}$$

By multiplying the two rotation matrices, we can verify that two successive rotations are additive:

$$\mathbf{R}(\theta_2) \cdot \mathbf{R}(\theta_1) = \mathbf{R}(\theta_1 + \theta_2) \tag{5-27}$$

so that the final rotated coordinates can be calculated with the composite rotation matrix as

$$\mathbf{P'} = \mathbf{R}(\theta_1 + \theta_2) \cdot \mathbf{P} \tag{5-28}$$

191

Scalings

Concatenating transformation matrices for two successive scaling operations produces the following composite scaling matrix:

$$\begin{bmatrix} s_{x2} & 0 & 0 \\ 0 & s_{y2} & 0 \\ 0 & 0 & 1 \end{bmatrix} \cdot \begin{bmatrix} s_{x1} & 0 & 0 \\ 0 & s_{y1} & 0 \\ 0 & 0 & 1 \end{bmatrix} = \begin{bmatrix} s_{x1} \cdot s_{x2} & 0 & 0 \\ 0 & s_{y1} \cdot s_{y2} & 0 \\ 0 & 0 & 1 \end{bmatrix} \quad (5\text{-}29)$$

or

$$\mathbf{S}(s_{x2}, s_{y2}) \cdot \mathbf{S}(s_{x1}, s_{y1}) = \mathbf{S}(s_{x1} \cdot s_{x2}, s_{y1} \cdot s_{y2}) \quad (5\text{-}30)$$

The resulting matrix in this case indicates that successive scaling operations are multiplicative. That is, if we were to triple the size of an object twice in succession, the final size would be nine times that of the original.

General Pivot-Point Rotation

With a graphics package that only provides a rotate function for revolving objects about the coordinate origin, we can generate rotations about any selected pivot point (x_r, y_r) by performing the following sequence of translate–rotate–translate operations:

1. Translate the object so that the pivot-point position is moved to the coordinate origin.
2. Rotate the object about the coordinate origin.
3. Translate the object so that the pivot point is returned to its original position.

This transformation sequence is illustrated in Fig. 5-9. The composite transforma-

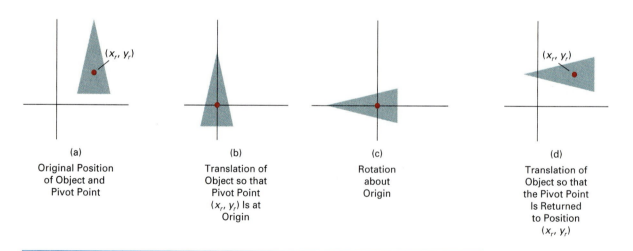

(a)	(b)	(c)	(d)
Original Position of Object and Pivot Point	Translation of Object so that Pivot Point (x_r, y_r) Is at Origin	Rotation about Origin	Translation of Object so that the Pivot Point Is Returned to Position (x_r, y_r)

Figure 5-9
A transformation sequence for rotating an object about a specified pivot point using the rotation matrix $\mathbf{R}(\theta)$ of transformation 5-19.

tion matrix for this sequence is obtained with the concatenation

$$
\begin{bmatrix} 1 & 0 & x_r \\ 0 & 1 & y_r \\ 0 & 0 & 1 \end{bmatrix} \cdot \begin{bmatrix} \cos \theta & -\sin \theta & 0 \\ \sin \theta & \cos \theta & 0 \\ 0 & 0 & 1 \end{bmatrix} \cdot \begin{bmatrix} 1 & 0 & -x_r \\ 0 & 1 & -y_r \\ 0 & 0 & 1 \end{bmatrix}
$$

$$
= \begin{bmatrix} \cos \theta & -\sin \theta & x_r(1 - \cos \theta) + y_r \sin \theta \\ \sin \theta & \cos \theta & y_r(1 - \cos \theta) - x_r \sin \theta \\ 0 & 0 & 1 \end{bmatrix} \tag{5-31}
$$

which can be expressed in the form

$$
\mathbf{T}(x_r, y_r) \cdot \mathbf{R}(\theta) \cdot \mathbf{T}(-x_r, -y_r) = \mathbf{R}(x_r, y_r, \theta) \tag{5-32}
$$

where $\mathbf{T}(-x_r, -y_r) = \mathbf{T}^{-1}(x_r, y_r)$. In general, a rotate function can be set up to accept parameters for pivot-point coordinates, as well as the rotation angle, and to generate automatically the rotation matrix of Eq. 5-31.

General Fixed-Point Scaling

Figure 5-10 illustrates a transformation sequence to produce scaling with respect to a selected fixed position (x_f, y_f) using a scaling function that can only scale relative to the coordinate origin.

1. Translate object so that the fixed point coincides with the coordinate origin.
2. Scale the object with respect to the coordinate origin.
3. Use the inverse translation of step 1 to return the object to its original position.

Concatenating the matrices for these three operations produces the required scaling matrix

$$
\begin{bmatrix} 1 & 0 & x_f \\ 0 & 1 & y_f \\ 0 & 0 & 1 \end{bmatrix} \cdot \begin{bmatrix} s_x & 0 & 0 \\ 0 & s_y & 0 \\ 0 & 0 & 1 \end{bmatrix} \cdot \begin{bmatrix} 1 & 0 & -x_f \\ 0 & 1 & -y_f \\ 0 & 0 & 1 \end{bmatrix} = \begin{bmatrix} s_x & 0 & x_f(1 - s_x) \\ 0 & s_y & y_f(1 - s_y) \\ 0 & 0 & 1 \end{bmatrix} \tag{5-33}
$$

or

$$
\mathbf{T}(x_f, y_f) \cdot \mathbf{S}(s_x, s_y) \cdot \mathbf{T}(-x_f, -y_f) = \mathbf{S}(x_f, y_f, s_x, s_y) \tag{5-34}
$$

This transformation is automatically generated on systems that provide a scale function that accepts coordinates for the fixed point.

General Scaling Directions

Parameters s_x and s_y scale objects along the x and y directions. We can scale an object in other directions by rotating the object to align the desired scaling directions with the coordinate axes before applying the scaling transformation.

Suppose we want to apply scaling factors with values specified by parameters s_1 and s_2 in the directions shown in Fig. 5-11. To accomplish the scaling with-

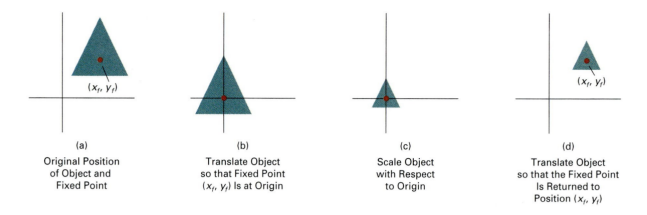

(a)
Original Position
of Object and
Fixed Point

(b)
Translate Object
so that Fixed Point
(x_f, y_f) Is at Origin

(c)
Scale Object
with Respect
to Origin

(d)
Translate Object
so that the Fixed Point
Is Returned to
Position (x_f, y_f)

Figure 5-10

A transformation sequence for scaling an object with respect to a specified fixed position
using the scaling matrix $\mathbf{S}(s_x, s_y)$ of transformation 5-21.

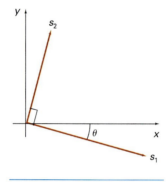

Figure 5-11

Scaling parameters s_1 and
s_2 are to be applied in
orthogonal directions
defined by the angular
displacement θ.

out changing the orientation of the object, we first perform a rotation so that the
directions for s_1 and s_2 coincide with the x and y axes, respectively. Then the scaling
transformation is applied, followed by an opposite rotation to return points
to their original orientations. The composite matrix resulting from the product of
these three transformations is

$$
\mathbf{R}^{-1}(\theta) \cdot \mathbf{S}(s_1, s_2) \cdot \mathbf{R}(\theta)
$$

$$
= \begin{bmatrix} s_1 \cos^2 \theta + s_2 \sin^2 \theta & (s_2 - s_1) \cos \theta \sin \theta & 0 \\ (s_2 - s_1) \cos \theta \sin \theta & s_1 \sin^2 \theta + s_2 \cos^2 \theta & 0 \\ 0 & 0 & 1 \end{bmatrix} \tag{5-35}
$$

As an example of this scaling transformation, we turn a unit square into a
parallelogram (Fig. 5-12) by stretching it along the diagonal from (0, 0) to (1, 1).
We rotate the diagonal onto the y axis and double its length with the transformation
parameters $\theta = 45°$, $s_1 = 1$, and $s_2 = 2$.

In Eq. 5-35, we assumed that scaling was to be performed relative to the origin.
We could take this scaling operation one step further and concatenate the
matrix with translation operators, so that the composite matrix would include
parameters for the specification of a scaling fixed position.

Concatenation Properties

Matrix multiplication is associative. For any three matrices, $\mathbf{A}$, $\mathbf{B}$, and $\mathbf{C}$, the matrix
product $\mathbf{A} \cdot \mathbf{B} \cdot \mathbf{C}$ can be performed by first multiplying $\mathbf{A}$ and $\mathbf{B}$ or by first
multiplying $\mathbf{B}$ and $\mathbf{C}$:

$$
\mathbf{A} \cdot \mathbf{B} \cdot \mathbf{C} = (\mathbf{A} \cdot \mathbf{B}) \cdot \mathbf{C} = \mathbf{A} \cdot (\mathbf{B} \cdot \mathbf{C}) \tag{5-36}
$$

Therefore, we can evaluate matrix products using either a left-to-right or a right-to-left
associative grouping.

On the other hand, transformation products may not be commutative: The
matrix product $\mathbf{A} \cdot \mathbf{B}$ is not equal to $\mathbf{B} \cdot \mathbf{A}$, in general. This means that if we want

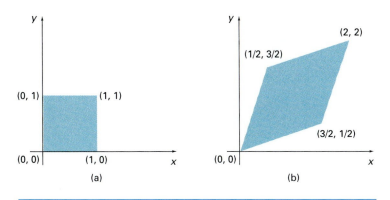

Figure 5-12
A square (a) is converted to a parallelogram (b) using the composite
transformation matrix 5-35, with $s_1 = 1$, $s_2 = 2$, and $\theta = 45°$.

to translate and rotate an object, we must be careful about the order in which the
composite matrix is evaluated (Fig. 5-13). For some special cases, such as a sequence of transformations all of the same kind, the multiplication of transformation matrices is commutative. As an example, two successive rotations could be
performed in either order and the final position would be the same. This commutative property holds also for two successive translations or two successive scalings. Another commutative pair of operations is rotation and uniform scaling
$(s_x = s_y)$.

General Composite Transformations and Computational Efficiency

A general two-dimensional transformation, representing a combination of translations, rotations, and scalings, can be expressed as

$$\begin{bmatrix} x' \\ y' \\ 1 \end{bmatrix} = \begin{bmatrix} rs_{xx} & rs_{xy} & trs_x \\ rs_{yx} & rs_{yy} & trs_y \\ 0 & 0 & 1 \end{bmatrix} \cdot \begin{bmatrix} x \\ y \\ 1 \end{bmatrix} \qquad (5\text{-}37)$$

The four elements rs_{ij} are the multiplicative rotation-scaling terms in the transformation that involve only rotation angles and scaling factors. Elements trs_x and
trs_y are the translational terms containing combinations of translation distances,
pivot-point and fixed-point coordinates, and rotation angles and scaling parameters. For example, if an object is to be scaled and rotated about its centroid coordinates (x_c, y_c) and then translated, the values for the elements of the composite
transformation matrix are

$$\mathbf{T}(t_x, t_y) \cdot \mathbf{R}(x_c, y_c, \theta) \cdot \mathbf{S}(x_c, y_c, s_x, s_y)$$
$$= \begin{bmatrix} s_x \cos\theta & -s_y \sin\theta & x_c(1 - s_x \cos\theta) + y_c s_y \sin\theta + t_x \\ s_x \sin\theta & s_y \cos\theta & y_c(1 - s_y \cos\theta) - x_c s_x \sin\theta + t_y \\ 0 & 0 & 1 \end{bmatrix} \qquad (5\text{-}38)$$

Although matrix equation 5-37 requires nine multiplications and six additions, the explicit calculations for the transformed coordinates are

195

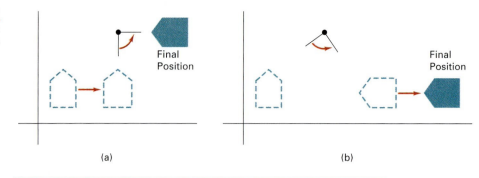

(a)   (b)

Figure 5-13

Reversing the order in which a sequence of transformations is
performed may affect the transformed position of an object. In (a), an
object is first translated, then rotated. In (b), the object is rotated first,
then translated.

$$x' = x \cdot rs_{xx} + y \cdot rs_{xy} + trs_x, \qquad y' = x \cdot rs_{yx} + y \cdot rs_{yy} + trs_y \qquad (5\text{-}39)$$

Thus, we actually only need to perform four multiplications and four additions
to transform coordinate positions. This is the maximum number of computations
required for any transformation sequence, once the individual matrices have
been concatenated and the elements of the composite matrix evaluated. Without
concatenation, the individual transformations would be applied one at a time
and the number of calculations could be significantly increased. An efficient implementation for the transformation operations, therefore, is to formulate transformation matrices, concatenate any transformation sequence, and calculate
transformed coordinates using Eq. 5-39. On parallel systems, direct matrix multiplications with the composite transformation matrix of Eq. 5-37 can be equally efficient.

A general **rigid-body transformation matrix**, involving only translations
and rotations, can be expressed in the form

$$\begin{bmatrix} r_{xx} & r_{xy} & tr_x \\ r_{yx} & r_{yy} & tr_y \\ 0 & 0 & 1 \end{bmatrix} \qquad (5\text{-}40)$$

where the four elements r_{ij} are the multiplicative rotation terms, and elements tr_x
and tr_y are the translational terms. A rigid-body change in coordinate position is
also sometimes referred to as a **rigid-motion** transformation. All angles and distances between coordinate positions are unchanged by the transformation. In addition, matrix 5-40 has the property that its upper-left 2-by-2 submatrix is an orthogonal matrix. This means that if we consider each row of the submatrix as a
vector, then the two vectors (r_{xx}, r_{xy}) and (r_{yx}, r_{yy}) form an orthogonal set of unit
vectors: Each vector has unit length

$$r_{xx}^2 + r_{xy}^2 = r_{yx}^2 + r_{yy}^2 = 1 \qquad (5\text{-}41)$$

and the vectors are perpendicular (their dot product is 0):

$$r_{xx}r_{yx} + r_{xy}r_{yy} = 0 \qquad (5\text{-}42)$$

Therefore, if these unit vectors are transformed by the rotation submatrix, (r_{xx}, r_{xy}) is converted to a unit vector along the x axis and (r_{yx}, r_{yy}) is transformed into a unit vector along the y axis of the coordinate system:

$$
\begin{bmatrix} r_{xx} & r_{xy} & 0 \\ r_{yx} & r_{yy} & 0 \\ 0 & 0 & 1 \end{bmatrix} \cdot \begin{bmatrix} r_{xx} \\ r_{xy} \\ 1 \end{bmatrix} = \begin{bmatrix} 1 \\ 0 \\ 1 \end{bmatrix}
\tag{5-43}
$$

$$
\begin{bmatrix} r_{xx} & r_{xy} & 0 \\ r_{yx} & r_{yy} & 0 \\ 0 & 0 & 1 \end{bmatrix} \cdot \begin{bmatrix} r_{yx} \\ r_{yy} \\ 1 \end{bmatrix} = \begin{bmatrix} 0 \\ 1 \\ 1 \end{bmatrix}
\tag{5-44}
$$

As an example, the following rigid-body transformation first rotates an object through an angle θ about a pivot point (x_r, y_r) and then translates:

$$
\mathbf{T}(t_x, t_y) \cdot \mathbf{R}(x_r, y_r, \theta)
$$
$$
= \begin{bmatrix} \cos\theta & -\sin\theta & x_r(1 - \cos\theta) + y_r\sin\theta + t_x \\ \sin\theta & \cos\theta & y_r(1 - \cos\theta) - x_r\sin\theta + t_y \\ 0 & 0 & 1 \end{bmatrix}
\tag{5-45}
$$

Here, orthogonal unit vectors in the upper-left 2-by-2 submatrix are $(\cos\theta, -\sin\theta)$ and $(\sin\theta, \cos\theta)$, and

$$
\begin{bmatrix} \cos\theta & -\sin\theta & 0 \\ \sin\theta & \cos\theta & 0 \\ 0 & 0 & 1 \end{bmatrix} \cdot \begin{bmatrix} \cos\theta \\ -\sin\theta \\ 1 \end{bmatrix} = \begin{bmatrix} 1 \\ 0 \\ 1 \end{bmatrix}
\tag{5-46}
$$

Similarly, unit vector $(\sin\theta, \cos\theta)$ is converted by the transformation matrix in Eq. 5-46 to the unit vector $(0, 1)$ in the y direction.

The orthogonal property of rotation matrices is useful for constructing a rotation matrix when we know the final orientation of an object rather than the amount of angular rotation necessary to put the object into that position. Directions for the desired orientation of an object could be determined by the alignment of certain objects in a scene or by selected positions in the scene. Figure 5-14 shows an object that is to be aligned with the unit direction vectors $\mathbf{u}'$ and $\mathbf{v}'$. Assuming that the original object orientation, as shown in Fig. 5-14(a), is aligned with the coordinate axes, we construct the desired transformation by assigning the elements of $\mathbf{u}'$ to the first row of the rotation matrix and the elements of $\mathbf{v}'$ to the second row. This can be a convenient method for obtaining the transformation matrix for rotation within a local (or "object") coordinate system when we know the final orientation vectors. A similar transformation is the conversion of object descriptions from one coordinate system to another, and in Section 5-5, we consider how to set up transformations to accomplish this coordinate conversion.

Since rotation calculations require trignometric evaluations and several multiplications for each transformed point, computational efficiency can become an important consideration in rotation transformations. In animations and other applications that involve many repeated transformations and small rotation angles, we can use approximations and iterative calculations to reduce computa-

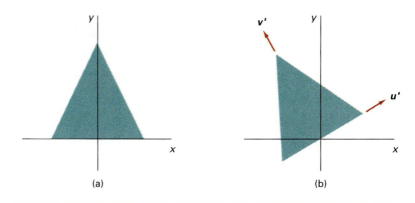

Figure 5-14

The rotation matrix for revolving an object from position (a) to position
(b) can be constructed with the values of the unit orientation vectors **u'**
and **v'** relative to the original orientation.

tions in the composite transformation equations. When the rotation angle is
small, the trigonometric functions can be replaced with approximation values
based on the first few terms of their power-series expansions. For small enough
angles (less than 10°), $\cos \theta$ is approximately 1 and $\sin \theta$ has a value very close to
the value of θ in radians. If we are rotating in small angular steps about the origin, for instance, we can set $\cos \theta$ to 1 and reduce transformation calculations at
each step to two multiplications and two additions for each set of coordinates to
be rotated:

$$x' = x - y \sin \theta, \qquad y' = x \sin \theta + y \qquad (5\text{-}47)$$

where $\sin \theta$ is evaluated once for all steps, assuming the rotation angle does not
change. The error introduced by this approximation at each step decreases as the
rotation angle decreases. But even with small rotation angles, the accumulated
error over many steps can become quite large. We can control the accumulated
error by estimating the error in x' and y' at each step and resetting object positions when the error accumulation becomes too great.

Composite transformations often involve inverse matrix calculations. Transformation sequences for general scaling directions and for reflections and shears
(Section 5-4), for example, can be described with inverse rotation components. As
we have noted, the inverse matrix representations for the basic geometric transformations can be generated with simple procedures. An inverse translation matrix is obtained by changing the signs of the translation distances, and an inverse
rotation matrix is obtained by performing a matrix transpose (or changing the
sign of the sine terms). These operations are much simpler than direct inverse
matrix calculations.

An implementation of composite transformations is given in the following
procedure. Matrix **M** is initialized to the identity matrix. As each individual
transformation is specified, it is concatenated with the total transformation matrix **M**. When all transformations have been specified, this composite transformation is applied to a given object. For this example, a polygon is scaled and rotated
about a given reference point. Then the object is translated. Figure 5-15 shows the
original and final positions of the polygon transformed by this sequence.

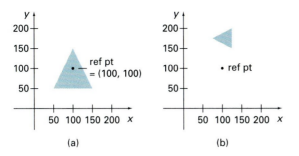

Figure 5-15
A polygon (a) is transformed into
(b) by the composite operations in
the following procedure.

```c
#include <math.h>
#include "graphics.h"

typedef float Matrix3x3[3][3];
Matrix3x3 theMatrix;

void matrix3x3SetIdentity (Matrix3x3 m)
{
  int i,j;

  for (i=0; i<3; i++) for (j=0; j<3; j++) m[i][j] = (i == j);
}

/* Multiplies matrix a times b, putting result in b */
void matrix3x3PreMultiply (Matrix3x3 a, Matrix3x3 b)
{
  int r,c;
  Matrix3x3 tmp;

  for (r = 0; r < 3; r++)
    for (c = 0; c < 3; c++)
      tmp[r][c] =
        a[r][0]*b[0][c] + a[r][1]*b[1][c] + a[r][2]*b[2][c];

  for (r = 0; r < 3; r++)
    for (c = 0; c < 3; c++)
      b[r][c] = tmp[r][c];
}

void translate2 (int tx, int ty)
{
  Matrix3x3 m;

  matrix3x3SetIdentity (m);
  m[0][2] = tx;
  m[1][2] = ty;
  matrix3x3PreMultiply (m, theMatrix);
```

199

```
}

void scale2 (float sx, float sy, wcPt2 refpt)
{
  Matrix3x3 m;

  matrix3x3SetIdentity (m);
  m[0][0] = sx;
  m[0][2] = (1 - sx) * refpt.x;
  m[1][1] = sy;
  m[1][2] = (1 - sy) * refpt.y;
  matrix3x3PreMultiply (m, theMatrix);
}

void rotate2 (float a, wcPt2 refPt)
{
  Matrix3x3 m;

  matrix3x3SetIdentity (m);
  a = pToRadians (a);
  m[0][0] = cosf (a);
  m[0][1] = -sinf (a);
  m[0][2] = refPt.x * (1 - cosf (a)) + refPt.y * sinf (a);
  m[1][0] = sinf (a);
  m[1][1] = cosf (a);
  m[1][2] = refPt.y * (1 - cosf (a)) - refPt.x * sinf (a);
  matrix3x3PreMultiply (m, theMatrix);
}

void transformPoints2 (int npts, wcPt2 *pts)
{
  int k;
  float tmp;

  for (k = 0; k < npts; k++) {
    tmp = theMatrix[0][0] * pts[k].x + theMatrix[0][1] *
      pts[k].y + theMatrix[0][2];
    pts[k].y = theMatrix[1][0] * pts[k].x + theMatrix[1][1] *
      pts[k].y + theMatrix[1][2];
    pts[k].x = tmp;
  }
}

void main (int argc, char ** argv)
{
  wcPt2 pts[3] = { 50.0, 50.0, 150.0, 50.0, 100.0, 150.0};
  wcPt2 refPt = {100.0, 100.0};
  long windowID = openGraphics (*argv, 200, 350);

  setBackground (WHITE);
  setColor (BLUE);
  pFillArea (3, pts);
  matrix3x3SetIdentity (theMatrix);
  scale2 (0.5, 0.5, refPt);
  rotate2 (90.0, refPt);
  translate2 (0, 150);
  transformPoints2 (3, pts);
  pFillArea (3,pts);
  sleep (10);
  closeGraphics (windowID);
}
```

OTHER TRANSFORMATIONS

Basic transformations such as translation, rotation, and scaling are included in most graphics packages. Some packages provide a few additional transformations that are useful in certain applications. Two such transformations are reflection and shear.

Reflection

A **reflection** is a transformation that produces a mirror image of an object. The mirror image for a two-dimensional reflection is generated relative to an **axis of reflection** by rotating the object 180° about the reflection axis. We can choose an axis of reflection in the xy plane or perpendicular to the xy plane. When the reflection axis is a line in the xy plane, the rotation path about this axis is in a plane perpendicular to the xy plane. For reflection axes that are perpendicular to the xy plane, the rotation path is in the xy plane. Following are examples of some common reflections.

Reflection about the line $y = 0$, the x axis, is accomplished with the transformation matrix

$$\begin{bmatrix} 1 & 0 & 0 \\ 0 & -1 & 0 \\ 0 & 0 & 1 \end{bmatrix} \tag{5-48}$$

This transformation keeps x values the same, but "flips" the y values of coordinate positions. The resulting orientation of an object after it has been reflected about the x axis is shown in Fig. 5-16. To envision the rotation transformation path for this reflection, we can think of the flat object moving out of the xy plane and rotating 180° through three-dimensional space about the x axis and back into the xy plane on the other side of the x axis.

A reflection about the y axis flips x coordinates while keeping y coordinates the same. The matrix for this transformation is

$$\begin{bmatrix} -1 & 0 & 0 \\ 0 & 1 & 0 \\ 0 & 0 & 1 \end{bmatrix} \tag{5-49}$$

Figure 5-17 illustrates the change in position of an object that has been reflected about the line $x = 0$. The equivalent rotation in this case is 180° through three-dimensional space about the y axis.

We flip both the x and y coordinates of a point by reflecting relative to an axis that is perpendicular to the xy plane and that passes through the coordinate origin. This transformation, referred to as a reflection relative to the coordinate origin, has the matrix representation:

$$\begin{bmatrix} -1 & 0 & 0 \\ 0 & -1 & 0 \\ 0 & 0 & 1 \end{bmatrix} \tag{5-50}$$

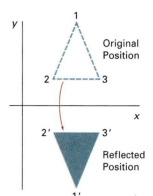

Figure 5-16
Reflection of an object about the x axis.

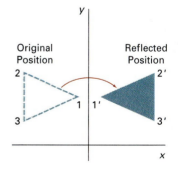

Figure 5-17
Reflection of an object about the y axis.

201

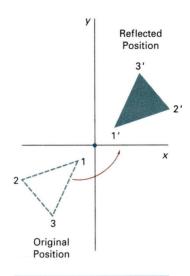

Figure 5-18

Reflection of an object relative to an axis perpendicular to the xy plane and passing through the coordinate origin.

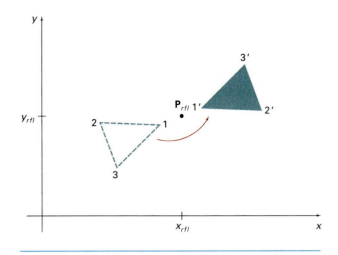

Figure 5-19

Reflection of an object relative to an axis perpendicular to the xy plane and passing through point $\mathbf{P}_{rfl}$.

An example of reflection about the origin is shown in Fig. 5-18. The reflection matrix 5-50 is the rotation matrix $\mathbf{R}(\theta)$ with $\theta = 180°$. We are simply rotating the object in the xy plane half a revolution about the origin.

Reflection 5-50 can be generalized to any reflection point in the xy plane (Fig. 5-19). This reflection is the same as a 180° rotation in the xy plane using the reflection point as the pivot point.

If we chose the reflection axis as the diagonal line $y = x$ (Fig. 5-20), the reflection matrix is

$$\begin{bmatrix} 0 & 1 & 0 \\ 1 & 0 & 0 \\ 0 & 0 & 1 \end{bmatrix} \qquad (5\text{-}51)$$

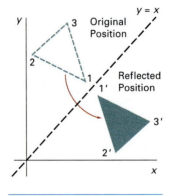

Figure 5-20

Reflection of an object with respect to the line $y = x$.

We can derive this matrix by concatenating a sequence of rotation and coordinate-axis reflection matrices. One possible sequence is shown in Fig. 5-21. Here, we first perform a clockwise rotation through a 45° angle, which rotates the line $y = x$ onto the x axis. Next, we perform a reflection with respect to the x axis. The final step is to rotate the line $y = x$ back to its original position with a counterclockwise rotation through 45°. An equivalent sequence of transformations is first to reflect the object about the x axis, and then to rotate counterclockwise 90°.

To obtain a transformation matrix for reflection about the diagonal $y = -x$, we could concatenate matrices for the transformation sequence: (1) clockwise rotation by 45°, (2) reflection about the y axis, and (3) counterclockwise rotation by 45°. The resulting transformation matrix is

$$\begin{bmatrix} 0 & -1 & 0 \\ -1 & 0 & 0 \\ 0 & 0 & 1 \end{bmatrix} \qquad (5\text{-}52)$$

202

Figure 5-22 shows the original and final positions for an object transformed with this reflection matrix.

Reflections about any line $y = mx + b$ in the xy plane can be accomplished with a combination of translate-rotate-reflect transformations. In general, we first translate the line so that it passes through the origin. Then we can rotate the line onto one of the coordinate axes and reflect about that axis. Finally, we restore the line to its original position with the inverse rotation and translation transformations.

We can implement reflections with respect to the coordinate axes or coordinate origin as scaling transformations with negative scaling factors. Also, elements of the reflection matrix can be set to values other than ± 1. Values whose magnitudes are greater than 1 shift the mirror image farther from the reflection axis, and values with magnitudes less than 1 bring the mirror image closer to the reflection axis.

Shear

A transformation that distorts the shape of an object such that the transformed shape appears as if the object were composed of internal layers that had been caused to slide over each other is called a **shear**. Two common shearing transformations are those that shift coordinate x values and those that shift y values.

An x-direction shear relative to the x axis is produced with the transformation matrix

$$\begin{bmatrix} 1 & sh_x & 0 \\ 0 & 1 & 0 \\ 0 & 0 & 1 \end{bmatrix} \qquad (5\text{-}53)$$

which transforms coordinate positions as

$$x' = x + sh_x \cdot y, \qquad y' = y \qquad (5\text{-}54)$$

Any real number can be assigned to the shear parameter sh_x. A coordinate position (x, y) is then shifted horizontally by an amount proportional to its distance (y value) from the x axis ($y = 0$). Setting sh_x to 2, for example, changes the square in Fig. 5-23 into a parallelogram. Negative values for sh_x shift coordinate positions to the left.

We can generate x-direction shears relative to other reference lines with

$$\begin{bmatrix} 1 & sh_x & -sh_x \cdot y_{\text{ref}} \\ 0 & 1 & 0 \\ 0 & 0 & 1 \end{bmatrix} \qquad (5\text{-}55)$$

with coordinate positions transformed as

$$x' = x + sh_x(y - y_{\text{ref}}), \qquad y' = y \qquad (5\text{-}56)$$

An example of this shearing transformation is given in Fig. 5-24 for a shear parameter value of $1/2$ relative to the line $y_{\text{ref}} = -1$.

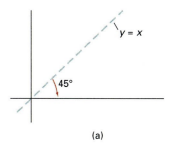

(a)

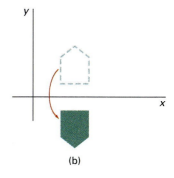

(b)

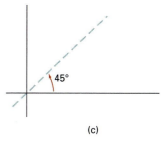

(c)

Figure 5-21
Sequence of transformations to produce reflection about the line $y = x$: (a) clockwise rotation of 45°, (b) reflection about the x axis, and (c) counterclockwise rotation by 45°.

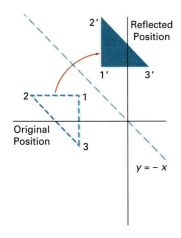

Figure 5-22
Reflection with respect to the
line $y = -x$.

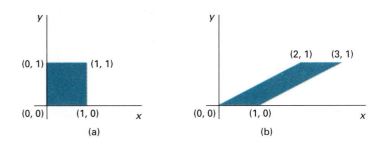

Figure 5-23
A unit square (a) is converted to a parallelogram (b) using the x-
direction shear matrix 5-53 with $sh_x = 2$.

A y-direction shear relative to the line $x = x_{\text{ref}}$ is generated with the transformation matrix

$$\begin{bmatrix} 1 & 0 & 0 \\ sh_y & 1 & -sh_y \cdot x_{\text{ref}} \\ 0 & 0 & 1 \end{bmatrix} \qquad (5\text{-}57)$$

which generates transformed coordinate positions

$$x' = x, \qquad y' = sh_y(x - x_{\text{ref}}) + y \qquad (5\text{-}58)$$

This transformation shifts a coordinate position vertically by an amount proportional to its distance from the reference line $x = x_{\text{ref}}$. Figure 5-25 illustrates the
conversion of a square into a parallelogram with $sh_y = 1/2$ and $x_{\text{ref}} = -1$.

Shearing operations can be expressed as sequences of basic transformations.
The x-direction shear matrix 5-53, for example, can be written as a composite
transformation involving a series of rotation and scaling matrices that would
scale the unit square of Fig. 5-23 along its diagonal, while maintaining the original lengths and orientations of edges parallel to the x axis. Shifts in the positions
of objects relative to shearing reference lines are equivalent to translations.

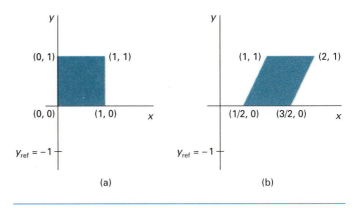

Figure 5-24
A unit square (a) is transformed to a shifted parallelogram (b)
with $sh_x = 1/2$ and $y_{\text{ref}} = -1$ in the shear matrix 5-55.

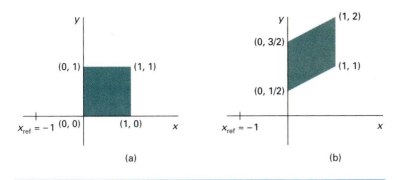

Figure 5-25
A unit square (a) is turned into a shifted parallelogram (b) with
parameter values $sh_y = 1/2$ and $x_{ref} = -1$ in the y-direction using
shearing transformation 5-57.

5-5

TRANSFORMATIONS BETWEEN COORDINATE SYSTEMS

Graphics applications often require the transformation of object descriptions
from one coordinate system to another. Sometimes objects are described in non-
Cartesian reference frames that take advantage of object symmetries. Coordinate
descriptions in these systems must then be converted to Cartesian device coordinates for display. Some examples of two-dimensional non-Cartesian systems are
polar coordinates, elliptical coordinates, and parabolic coordinates. In other
cases, we need to transform between two Cartesian systems. For modeling and
design applications, individual objects may be defined in their own local Cartesian references, and the local coordinates must then be transformed to position
the objects within the overall scene coordinate system. A facility management
program for office layouts, for instance, has individual coordinate reference descriptions for chairs and tables and other furniture that can be placed into a floor
plan, with multiple copies of the chairs and other items in different positions. In
other applications, we may simply want to reorient the coordinate reference for
displaying a scene. Relationships between Cartesian reference systems and some
common non-Cartesian systems are given in Appendix A. Here, we consider
transformations between two Cartesian frames of reference.

Figure 5-26 shows two Cartesian systems, with the coordinate origins at $(0,
0)$ and (x_0, y_0) and with an orientation angle θ between the x and x' axes. To trans-
form object descriptions from xy coordinates to $x'y'$ coordinates, we need to set
up a transformation that superimposes the $x'y'$ axes onto the xy axes. This is
done in two steps:

1. Translate so that the origin (x_0, y_0) of the $x'y'$ system is moved to the origin
   of the xy system.
2. Rotate the x' axis onto the x axis.

Translation of the coordinate origin is expressed with the matrix operation

$$T(-x_0, -y_0) = \begin{bmatrix} 1 & 0 & -x_0 \\ 0 & 1 & -y_0 \\ 0 & 0 & 1 \end{bmatrix} \qquad (5\text{-}59)$$

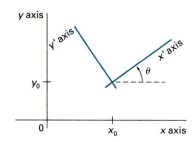

and the orientation of the two systems after the translation operation would appear as in Fig. 5-27. To get the axes of the two systems into coincidence, we then perform the clockwise rotation

$$R(-\theta) = \begin{bmatrix} \cos\theta & \sin\theta & 0 \\ -\sin\theta & \cos\theta & 0 \\ 0 & 0 & 1 \end{bmatrix} \tag{5-60}$$

Concatinating these two transformations matrices gives us the complete composite matrix for transforming object descriptions from the xy system to the $x'y'$ system:

$$\mathbf{M}_{xy,x'y'} = \mathbf{R}(-\theta) \cdot \mathbf{T}(-x_0, -y_0) \tag{5-61}$$

An alternate method for giving the orientation of the second coordinate system is to specify a vector $\mathbf{V}$ that indicates the direction for the positive y' axis, as shown in Fig. 5-28. Vector $\mathbf{V}$ is specified as a point in the xy reference frame relative to the origin of the xy system. A unit vector in the y' direction can then be obtained as

$$\mathbf{v} = \frac{\mathbf{V}}{|\mathbf{V}|} = (v_x, v_y) \tag{5-62}$$

And we obtain the unit vector $\mathbf{u}$ along the x' axis by rotating $\mathbf{v}$ 90° clockwise:

$$\mathbf{u} = (v_y, -v_x)$$
$$= (u_x, u_y) \tag{5-63}$$

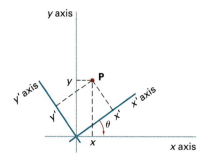

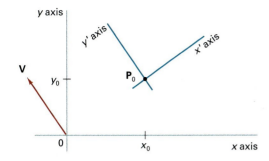

y axis

y' axis

x' axis

V

y_0

$\mathbf{P}_0$

0   x_0 x axis

Figure 5-28
Cartesian system $x'y'$ with origin at
$\mathbf{P}_0 = (x_0, y_0)$ and y' axis parallel to
vector **V**.

In Section 5-3, we noted that the elements of any rotation matrix could be expressed as elements of a set of orthogonal unit vectors. Therefore, the matrix to rotate the $x'y'$ system into coincidence with the xy system can be written as

$$R = \begin{bmatrix} u_x & u_y & 0 \\ v_x & v_y & 0 \\ 0 & 0 & 1 \end{bmatrix} \qquad (5\text{-}64)$$

As an example, suppose we choose the orientation for the y' axis as $\mathbf{V} = (-1, 0)$, then the x' axis is in the positive y direction and the rotation transformation matrix is

$$\begin{bmatrix} 0 & 1 & 0 \\ -1 & 0 & 0 \\ 0 & 0 & 1 \end{bmatrix}$$

Equivalently, we can obtain this rotation matrix from 5-60 by setting the orientation angle as $\theta = 90°$.

In an interactive application, it may be more convenient to choose the direction for **V** relative to position $\mathbf{P}_0$ than it is to specify it relative to the xy-coordinate origin. Unit vectors **u** and **v** would then be oriented as shown in Fig. 5-29. The components of **v** are now calculated as

$$\mathbf{v} = \frac{\mathbf{P}_1 - \mathbf{P}_0}{|\mathbf{P}_1 - \mathbf{P}_0|} \qquad (5\text{-}65)$$

and **u** is obtained as the perpendicular to **v** that forms a right-handed Cartesian system.

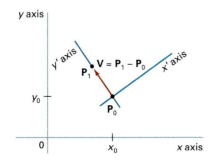

y axis

y' axis

$\mathbf{V} = \mathbf{P}_1 - \mathbf{P}_0$

x' axis

$\mathbf{P}_1$

y_0

$\mathbf{P}_0$

0   x_0 x axis

Figure 5-29
A Cartesian $x'y'$ system defined
with two coordinate positions, $\mathbf{P}_0$
and $\mathbf{P}_1$, within an xy reference
frame.

207

5-6

AFFINE TRANSFORMATIONS

A coordinate transformation of the form

$$x' = a_{xx}x + a_{xy}y + b_x, \qquad y' = a_{yx}x + a_{yy}y + b_y \qquad (5\text{-}66)$$

is called a two-dimensional **affine transformation**. Each of the transformed coordinates x' and y' is a linear function of the original coordinates x and y, and parameters a_{ij} and b_k are constants determined by the transformation type. Affine transformations have the general properties that parallel lines are transformed into parallel lines and finite points map to finite points.

Translation, rotation, scaling, reflection, and shear are examples of two-dimensional affine transformations. Any general two-dimensional affine transformation can always be expressed as a composition of these five transformations. Another affine transformation is the conversion of coordinate descriptions from one reference system to another, which can be described as a combination of translation and rotation. An affine transformation involving only rotation, translation, and reflection preserves angles and lengths, as well as parallel lines. For these three transformations, the lengths and angle between two lines remains the same after the transformation.

5-7

TRANSFORMATION FUNCTIONS

Graphics packages can be structured so that separate commands are provided to a user for each of the basic transformation operations, as in `procedure transformObject`. A composite transformation is then set up by referencing individual functions in the order required for the transformation sequence. An alternate formulation is to provide users with a single transformation function that includes parameters for each of the basic transformations. The output of this function is the composite transformation matrix for the specified parameter values. Both options are useful. Separate functions are convenient for simple transformation operations, and a composite function can provide an expedient method for specifying complex transformation sequences.

The PHIGS library provides users with both options. Individual commands for generating the basic transformation matrices are

```
translate (translateVector, matrixTranslate)
rotate (theta, matrixRotate)
scale (scaleVector, matrixScale)
```

Each of these functions produces a 3 by 3 transformation matrix that can then be used to transform coordinate positions expressed as homogeneous column vectors. Parameter `translateVector` is a pointer to the pair of translation distances t_x and t_y. Similarly, parameter `scaleVector` specifies the pair of scaling values s_x and s_y. Rotate and scale matrices (`matrixTranslate` and `matrixScale`) transform with respect to the coordinate origin.

We concatenate transformation matrices that have been previously set up with the function

```
composeMatrix (matrix2, matrix1, matrixOut)
```

where elements of the composite output matrix are calculated by postmultiplying `matrix2` by `matrix1`. A composite transformation matrix to perform a combination scaling, rotation, and translation is produced with the function

```
buildTransformationMatrix (referencePoint, translateVector,
                    theta, scaleVector, matrix)
```

Rotation and scaling are carried out with respect to the coordinate position specified by parameter `referencePoint`. The order for the transformation sequence is assumed to be (1) scale, (2) rotate, and (3) translate, with the elements for the composite transformation stored in parameter `matrix`. We can use this function to generate a single transformation matrix or a composite matrix for two or three transformations (in the order stated). We could generate a translation matrix by setting `scaleVector` = (1, 1), `theta` = 0, and assigning x and y shift values to parameter `translateVector`. Any coordinate values could be assigned to parameter `referencePoint`, since the transformation calculations are unaffected by this parameter when no scaling or rotation takes place. But if we only want to set up a translation matrix, we can use function `translate` and simply specify the translation vector. A rotation or scaling transformation matrix is specified by setting `translateVector` = (0, 0) and assigning appropriate values to parameters `referencePoint`, `theta`, and `scaleVector`. To obtain a rotation matrix, we set `scaleVector` = (1, 1); and for scaling only, we set `theta` = 0. If we want to rotate or scale with respect to the coordinate origin, it is simpler to set up the matrix using either the `rotate` or `scale` function.

Since the function `buildTransformationMatrix` always generates the transformation sequence in the order (1) scale, (2) rotate, and (3) translate, the following function is provided to allow specification of other sequences:

```
composeTransformationMatrix (matrixIn, referencePoint,
                translateVector, theta, scaleVector, matrixOut)
```

We can use this function in combination with the `buildTransformationMatrix` function or with any of the other matrix-construction functions to compose any transformation sequence. For example, we could set up a scale matrix about a fixed point with the `buildTransformationMatrix` function, then we could use the `composeTransformationMatrix` function to concatenate this scale matrix with a rotation about a specified pivot point. The composite rotate-scale sequence is then stored in `matrixOut`.

After we have set up a transformation matrix, we can apply the matrix to individual coordinate positions of an object with the function

```
transformPoint (inPoint, matrix, outPoint)
```

where parameter `inPoint` gives the initial xy-coordinate position of an object point, and parameter `outPoint` contains the corresponding transformed coordinates. Additional functions, discussed in Chapter 7, are available for performing two-dimensional modeling transformations.

5-8

RASTER METHODS FOR TRANSFORMATIONS

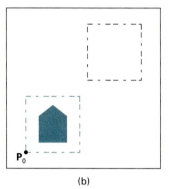

(a)

(b)

Figure 5-30
Translating an object from
screen position (a) to position
(b) by moving a rectangular
block of pixel values.
Coordinate positions P_{min}
and P_{max} specify the limits
of the rectangular block to
be moved, and P_0 is the
destination reference
position.

The particular capabilities of raster systems suggest an alternate method for transforming objects. Raster systems store picture information as pixel patterns in the frame buffer. Therefore, some simple transformations can be carried out rapidly by simply moving rectangular arrays of stored pixel values from one location to another within the frame buffer. Few arithmetic operations are needed, so the pixel transformations are particularly efficient.

Raster functions that manipulate rectangular pixel arrays are generally referred to as **raster ops**. Moving a block of pixels from one location to another is also called a **block transfer** of pixel values. On a bilevel system, this operation is called a **bitBlt (bit-block transfer),** particularly when the function is hardware implemented. The term **pixBlt** is sometimes used for block transfers on multi-level systems (multiple bits per pixel).

Figure 5-30 illustrates translation performed as a block transfer of a raster area. All bit settings in the rectangular area shown are copied as a block into another part of the raster. We accomplish this translation by first reading pixel intensities from a specified rectangular area of a raster into an array, then we copy the array back into the raster at the new location. The original object could be erased by filling its rectangular area with the background intensity (assuming the object does not overlap other objects in the scene).

Typical raster functions often provided in graphics packages are:

- *copy* - move a pixel block from one raster area to another.
- *read* - save a pixel block in a designated array.
- *write* - transfer a pixel array to a position in the frame buffer.

Some implementations provide options for combining pixel values. In *replace* mode, pixel values are simply transfered to the destination positions. Other options for combining pixel values include Boolean operations (*and*, *or*, and *exclusive or*) and binary arithmetic operations. With the *exclusive or* mode, two successive copies of a block to the same raster area restores the values that were originally present in that area. This technique can be used to move an object across a scene without destroying the background. Another option for adjusting pixel values is to combine the source pixels with a specified mask. This allows only selected positions within a block to be transferred or shaded by the patterns defined in the mask.

$$
\begin{bmatrix} 1 & 2 & 3 \\ 4 & 5 & 6 \\ 7 & 8 & 9 \\ 10 & 11 & 12 \end{bmatrix}
\qquad
\begin{bmatrix} 3 & 6 & 9 & 12 \\ 2 & 5 & 8 & 11 \\ 1 & 4 & 7 & 10 \end{bmatrix}
\qquad
\begin{bmatrix} 12 & 11 & 10 \\ 9 & 8 & 7 \\ 6 & 5 & 4 \\ 3 & 2 & 1 \end{bmatrix}
$$

(a) (b) (c)

Figure 5-31
Rotating an array of pixel values. The original array
orientation is shown in (a), the array orientation after a
90° counterclockwise rotation is shown in (b), and the
array orientation after a 180° rotation is shown in (c).

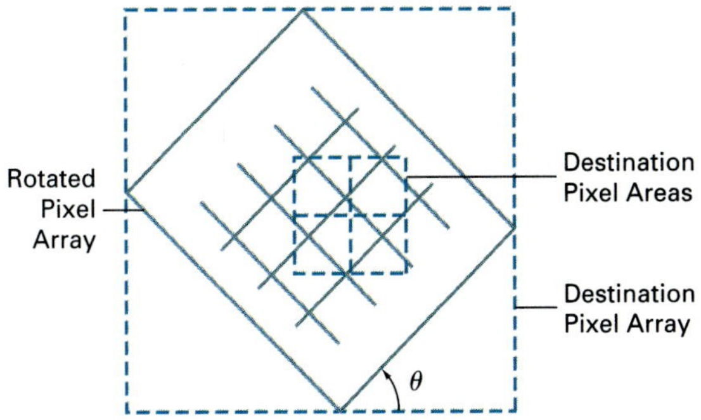

Figure 5-32
A raster rotation for a rectangular
block of pixels is accomplished by
mapping the destination pixel areas
onto the rotated block.

Rotations in 90-degree increments are easily accomplished with block transfers. We can rotate an object 90° counterclockwise by first reversing the pixel values in each row of the array, then we interchange rows and columns. A 180° rotation is obtained by reversing the order of the elements in each row of the array,
then reversing the order of the rows. Figure 5-31 demonstrates the array manipulations necessary to rotate a pixel block by 90° and by 180°.

For array rotations that are not multiples of 90°, we must perform more
computations. The general procedure is illustrated in Fig. 5-32. Each destination
pixel area is mapped onto the rotated array and the amount of overlap with the
rotated pixel areas is calculated. An intensity for the destination pixel is then
computed by averaging the intensities of the overlapped source pixels, weighted
by their percentage of area overlap.

Raster scaling of a block of pixels is analogous to the cell-array mapping
discussed in Section 3-13. We scale the pixel areas in the original block using
specified values for s_x and s_y and map the scaled rectangle onto a set of destination pixels. The intensity of each destination pixel is then assigned according to
its area of overlap with the scaled pixel areas (Fig. 5-33).

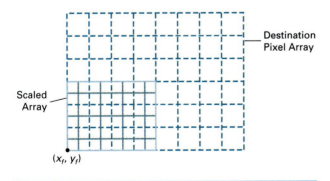

Figure 5-33
Mapping destination pixel areas onto a scaled array of
pixel values. Scaling factors $s_x = s_y = 0.5$ are applied
relative to fixed point (x_f, y_f).

SUMMARY

The basic geometric transformations are translation, rotation, and scaling. Translation moves an object in a straight-line path from one position to another. Rotation moves an object from one position to another in a circular path around a specified pivot point (rotation point). Scaling changes the dimensions of an object relative to a specified fixed point.

We can express two-dimensional geometric transformations as 3 by 3 matrix operators, so that sequences of transformations can be concatenated into a single composite matrix. This is an efficient formulation, since it allows us to reduce computations by applying the composite matrix to the initial coordinate positions of an object to obtain the final transformed positions. To do this, we also need to express two-dimensional coordinate positions as three-element column or row matrices. We choose a column-matrix representation for coordinate points because this is the standard mathematical convention and because many graphics packages also follow this convention. For two-dimensional transformations, coordinate positions are then represented with three-element homogeneous coordinates with the third (homogeneous) coordinate assigned the value 1.

Composite transformations are formed as multiplications of any combination of translation, rotation, and scaling matrices. We can use combinations of translation and rotation for animation applications, and we can use combinations of rotation and scaling to scale objects in any specified direction. In general, matrix multiplications are not commutative. We obtain different results, for example, if we change the order of a translate-rotate sequence. A transformation sequence involving only translations and rotations is a rigid-body transformation, since angles and distances are unchanged. Also, the upper-left submatrix of a rigid-body transformation is an orthogonal matrix. Thus, rotation matrices can be formed by setting the upper-left 2-by-2 submatrix equal to the elements of two orthogonal unit vectors. Computations in rotational transformations can be reduced by using approximations for the sine and cosine functions when the rotation angle is small. Over many rotational steps, however, the approximation error can accumulate to a significant value.

Other transformations include reflections and shears. Reflections are transformations that rotate an object 180° about a reflection axis. This produces a mirror image of the object with respect to that axis. When the reflection axis is perpendicular to the xy plane, the reflection is obtained as a rotation in the xy plane. When the reflection axis is in the xy plane, the reflection is obtained as a rotation in a plane that is perpendicular to the xy plane. Shear transformations distort the shape of an object by shifting x or y coordinate values by an amount proportional to the coordinate distance from a shear reference line.

Transformations between Cartesian coordinate systems are accomplished with a sequence of translate-rotate transformations. One way to specify a new coordinate reference frame is to give the position of the new coordinate origin and the direction of the new y axis. The direction of the new x axis is then obtained by rotating the y direction vector 90° clockwise. Coordinate descriptions of objects in the old reference frame are transferred to the new reference with the transformation matrix that superimposes the new coordinate axes onto the old coordinate axes. This transformation matrix can be calculated as the concatentation of a translation that moves the new origin to the old coordinate origin and a rotation to align the two sets of axes. The rotation matrix is obtained from unit vectors in the x and y directions for the new system.

Two-dimensional geometric transformations are affine transformations. That is, they can be expressed as a linear function of coordinates x and y. Affine transformations transform parallel lines to parallel lines and transform finite points to finite points. Geometric transformations that do not involve scaling or shear also preserve angles and lengths.

Transformation functions in graphics packages are usually provided only for translation, rotation, and scaling. These functions include individual procedures for creating a translate, rotate, or scale matrix, and functions for generating a composite matrix given the parameters for a transformation sequence.

Fast raster transformations can be performed by moving blocks of pixels. This avoids calculating transformed coordinates for an object and applying scan-conversion routines to display the object at the new position. Three common raster operations (bitBlts or pixBlts) are copy, read, and write. When a block of pixels is moved to a new position in the frame buffer, we can simply replace the old pixel values or we can combine the pixel values using Boolean or arithmetic operations. Raster translations are carried out by copying a pixel block to a new location in the frame buffer. Raster rotations in multiples of 90° are obtained by manipulating row and column positions of the pixel values in a block. Other rotations are performed by first mapping rotated pixel areas onto destination positions in the frame buffer, then calculating overlap areas. Scaling in raster transformations is also accomplished by mapping transformed pixel areas to the frame-buffer destination positions.

REFERENCES

For additional information on homogeneous coordinates in computer graphics, see Blinn (1977 and 1978).

Transformation functions in PHIGS are discussed in Hopgood and Duce (1991), Howard et al. (1991), Gaskins (1992), and Blake (1993). For information on GKS transformation functions, see Hopgood et al. (1983) and Enderle, Kansy, and Pfaff (1984).

EXERCISES

5-1 Write a program to continuously rotate an object about a pivot point. Small angles are to be used for each successive rotation, and approximations to the sine and cosine functions are to be used to speed up the calculations. The rotation angle for each step is to be chosen so that the object makes one complete revolution in less than 30 seconds. To avoid accumulation of coordinate errors, reset the original coordinate values for the object at the start of each new revolution.

5-2 Show that the composition of two rotations is additive by concatinating the matrix representations for $\mathbf{R}(\theta_1)$ and $\mathbf{R}(\theta_2)$ to obtain

$$\mathbf{R}(\theta_1) \cdot \mathbf{R}(\theta_2) = \mathbf{R}(\theta_1 + \theta_2)$$

5-3 Write a set of procedures to implement the `buildTransformationMatrix` and the `composeTransformationMatrix` functions to produce a composite transformation matrix for any set of input transformation parameters.

5-4 Write a program that applies any specified sequence of transformations to a displayed object. The program is to be designed so that a user selects the transformation sequence and associated parameters from displayed menus, and the composite transformation is then calculated and used to transform the object. Display the original object and the transformed object in different colors or different fill patterns.

5-5 Modify the transformation matrix (5-35), for scaling in an arbitrary direction, to include coordinates for any specified scaling fixed point (x_f, y_f).

5-6 Prove that the multiplication of transformation matrices for each of the following sequence of operations is commutative:
(a) Two successive rotations.
(b) Two successive translations.
(c) Two successive scalings.

5-7 Prove that a uniform scaling ($s_x = s_y$) and a rotation form a commutative pair of operations but that, in general, scaling and rotation are not commutative operations.

5-8 Multiply the individual scale, rotate, and translate matrices in Eq. 5-38 to verify the elements in the composite transformation matrix.

5-9 Show that transformation matrix (5-51), for a reflection about the line $y = x$, is equivalent to a reflection relative to the x axis followed by a counterclockwise rotation of 90°.

5-10 Show that transformation matrix (5-52), for a reflection about the line $y = -x$, is equivalent to a reflection relative to the y axis followed by a counterclockwise rotation of 90°.

5-11 Show that two successive reflections about either of the coordinate axes is equivalent to a single rotation about the coordinate origin.

5-12 Determine the form of the transformation matrix for a reflection about an arbitrary line with equation $y = mx + b$.

5-13 Show that two successive reflections about any line passing through the coordinate origin is equivalent to a single rotation about the origin.

5-14 Determine a sequence of basic transformations that are equivalent to the x-direction shearing matrix (5-53).

5-15 Determine a sequence of basic transformations that are equivalent to the y-direction shearing matrix (5-57).

5-10 Set up a shearing procedure to display italic characters, given a vector font definition. That is, all character shapes in this font are defined with straight-line segments, and italic characters are formed with shearing transformations. Determine an appropriate value for the shear parameter by comparing italics and plain text in some available font. Define a simple vector font for input to your routine.

5-17 Derive the following equations for transforming a coordinate point $\mathbf{P} = (x, y)$ in one Cartesian system to the coordinate values (x', y') in another Cartesian system that is rotated by an angle θ, as in Fig. 5-27. Project point $\mathbf{P}$ onto each of the four axes and analyse the resulting right triangles.

$$x' = x \cos \theta + y \sin \theta, \qquad y' = -x \sin \theta + y \cos \theta$$

5-18 Write a procedure to compute the elements of the matrix for transforming object descriptions from one Cartesian coordinate system to another. The second coordinate system is to be defined with an origin point $\mathbf{P}_0$ and a vector $\mathbf{V}$ that gives the direction for the positive y' axis of this system.

5-19 Set up procedures for implementing a block transfer of a rectangular area of a frame buffer, using one function to read the area into an array and another function to copy the array into the designated transfer area.

5-20 Determine the results of performing two successive block transfers into the same area of a frame buffer using the various Boolean operations.

5-21 What are the results of performing two successive block transfers into the same area of a frame buffer using the binary arithmetic operations?

5-22 Implement a routine to perform block transfers in a frame buffer using any specified Boolean operation or a replacement (copy) operation.

5-23 Write a routine to implement rotations in increments of 90° in frame-buffer block transfers.

5-24 Write a routine to implement rotations by any specified angle in a frame-buffer block transfer.

5-25 Write a routine to implement scaling as a raster transformation of a pixel block.

Two-Dimensional Viewing

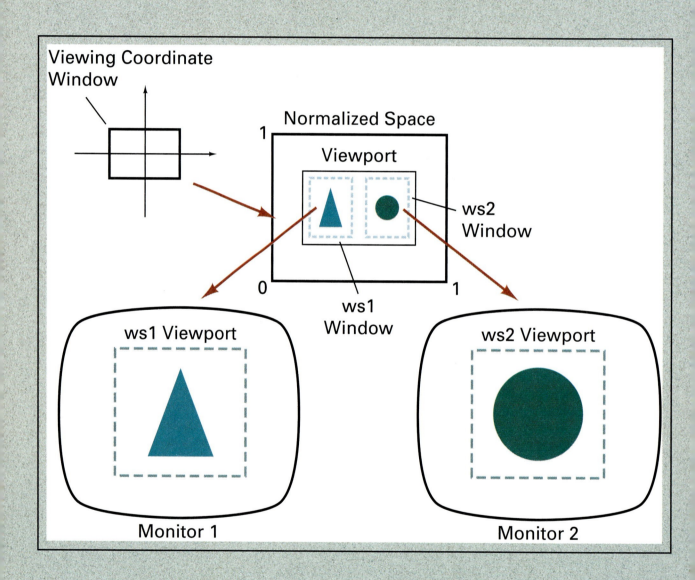

We now consider the formal mechanism for displaying views of a picture on an output device. Typically, a graphics package allows a user to specify which part of a defined picture is to be displayed and where that part is to be placed on the display device. Any convenient Cartesian coordinate system, referred to as the world-coordinate reference frame, can be used to define the picture. For a two-dimensional picture, a view is selected by specifying a subarea of the total picture area. A user can select a single area for display, or several areas could be selected for simultaneous display or for an animated panning sequence across a scene. The picture parts within the selected areas are then mapped onto specified areas of the device coordinates. When multiple view areas are selected, these areas can be placed in separate display locations, or some areas could be inserted into other, larger display areas. Transformations from world to device coordinates involve translation, rotation, and scaling operations, as well as procedures for deleting those parts of the picture that are outside the limits of a selected display area.

6-1
THE VIEWING PIPELINE

A world-coordinate area selected for display is called a **window**. An area on a display device to which a window is mapped is called a **viewport.** The window defines *what* is to be viewed; the viewport defines *where* it is to be displayed. Often, windows and viewports are rectangles in standard position, with the rectangle edges parallel to the coordinate axes. Other window or viewport geometries, such as general polygon shapes and circles, are used in some applications, but these shapes take longer to process. In general, the mapping of a part of a world-coordinate scene to device coordinates is referred to as a **viewing transformation**. Sometimes the two-dimensional viewing transformation is simply referred to as the *window-to-viewport transformation* or the *windowing transformation*. But, in general, viewing involves more than just the transformation from the window to the viewport. Figure 6-1 illustrates the mapping of a picture section that falls within a rectangular window onto a designated rectangular viewport.

In computer graphics terminology, the term *window* originally referred to an area of a picture that is selected for viewing, as defined at the beginning of this section. Unfortunately, the same term is now used in window-manager systems to refer to any rectangular screen area that can be moved about, resized, and made active or inactive. In this chapter, we will only use the term window to

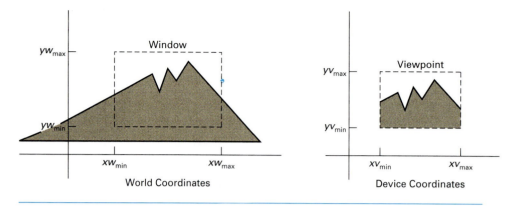

Figure 6-1

A viewing transformation using standard rectangles for the window and viewport.

refer to an area of a world-coordinate scene that has been selected for display. When we consider graphical user interfaces in Chapter 8, we will discuss screen windows and window-manager systems.

Some graphics packages that provide window and viewport operations allow only standard rectangles, but a more general approach is to allow the rectangular window to have any orientation. In this case, we carry out the viewing transformation in several steps, as indicated in Fig. 6-2. First, we construct the scene in world coordinates using the output primitives and attributes discussed in Chapters 3 and 4. Next, to obtain a particular orientation for the window, we can set up a two-dimensional **viewing-coordinate system** in the world-coordinate plane, and define a window in the viewing-coordinate system. The viewing-coordinate reference frame is used to provide a method for setting up arbitrary orientations for rectangular windows. Once the viewing reference frame is established, we can transform descriptions in world coordinates to viewing coordinates. We then define a viewport in normalized coordinates (in the range from 0 to 1) and map the viewing-coordinate description of the scene to normalized coordinates. At the final step, all parts of the picture that lie outside the viewport are clipped, and the contents of the viewport are transferred to device coordinates. Figure 6-3 illustrates a rotated viewing-coordinate reference frame and the mapping to normalized coordinates.

By changing the position of the viewport, we can view objects at different positions on the display area of an output device. Also, by varying the size of viewports, we can change the size and proportions of displayed objects. We achieve zooming effects by successively mapping different-sized windows on a

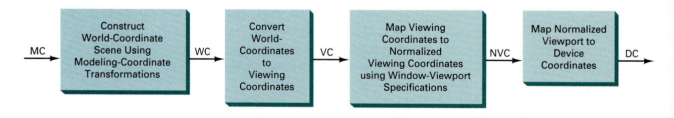

Figure 6-2

The two-dimensional viewing-transformation pipeline.

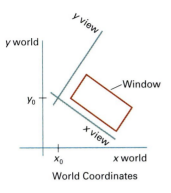

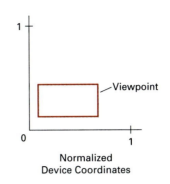

World Coordinates

Normalized
Device Coordinates

Figure 6-3
Setting up a rotated world window in viewing coordinates and the
corresponding normalized-coordinate viewport.

fixed-size viewport. As the windows are made smaller, we zoom in on some part
of a scene to view details that are not shown with larger windows. Similarly,
more overview is obtained by zooming out from a section of a scene with successively larger windows. Panning effects are produced by moving a fixed-size window across the various objects in a scene.

Viewports are typically defined within the unit square (normalized coordinates). This provides a means for separating the viewing and other transformations from specific output-device requirements, so that the graphics package is
largely device-independent. Once the scene has been transferred to normalized
coordinates, the unit square is simply mapped to the display area for the particular output device in use at that time. Different output devices can be used by providing the appropriate device drivers.

When all coordinate transformations are completed, viewport clipping can
be performed in normalized coordinates or in device coordinates. This allows us
to reduce computations by concatenating the various transformation matrices.
Clipping procedures are of fundamental importance in computer graphics. They
are used not only in viewing transformations, but also in window-manager systems, in painting and drawing packages to eliminate parts of a picture inside or
outside of a designated screen area, and in many other applications.

6-2

VIEWING COORDINATE REFERENCE FRAME

This coordinate system provides the reference frame for specifying the world-
coordinate window. We set up the viewing coordinate system using the procedures discussed in Section 5-5. First, a viewing-coordinate origin is selected at
some world position: $\mathbf{P}_0 = (x_0, y_0)$. Then we need to establish the orientation, or
rotation, of this reference frame. One way to do this is to specify a world vector $\mathbf{V}$
that defines the viewing y_v direction. Vector $\mathbf{V}$ is called the **view up vector**.

Given $\mathbf{V}$, we can calculate the components of unit vectors $\mathbf{v} = (v_x, v_y)$ and
$\mathbf{u} = (u_x, u_y)$ for the viewing y_v and x_v axes, respectively. These unit vectors are
used to form the first and second rows of the rotation matrix $\mathbf{R}$ that aligns the
viewing $x_v y_v$ axes with the world $x_w y_w$ axes.

219

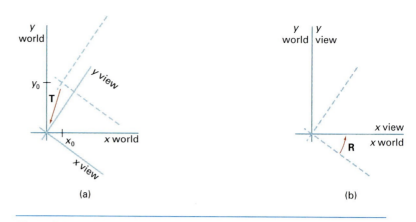

Figure 6-4
A viewing-coordinate frame is moved into coincidence with the world
frame in two steps: (a) translate the viewing origin to the world origin,
then (b) rotate to align the axes of the two systems.

We obtain the matrix for converting world-coordinate positions to viewing
coordinates as a two-step composite transformation: First, we translate the viewing origin to the world origin, then we rotate to align the two coordinate reference frames. The composite two-dimensional transformation to convert world
coordinates to viewing coordinates is

$$\mathbf{M}_{WC,VC} = \mathbf{R} \cdot \mathbf{T}$$

(6-1)

where $\mathbf{T}$ is the translation matrix that takes the viewing origin point $\mathbf{P}_0$ to the
world origin, and $\mathbf{R}$ is the rotation matrix that aligns the axes of the two reference
frames. Figure 6-4 illustrates the steps in this coordinate transformation.

6-3
WINDOW-TO-VIEWPORT COORDINATE TRANSFORMATION

Once object descriptions have been transferred to the viewing reference frame,
we choose the window extents in viewing coordinates and select the viewport
limits in normalized coordinates (Fig. 6-3). Object descriptions are then transferred to normalized device coordinates. We do this using a transformation that
maintains the same relative placement of objects in normalized space as they had
in viewing coordinates. If a coordinate position is at the center of the viewing
window, for instance, it will be displayed at the center of the viewport.

Figure 6-5 illustrates the window-to-viewport mapping. A point at position
(xw, yw) in the window is mapped into position (xv, yv) in the associated viewport. To maintain the same relative placement in the viewport as in the window,
we require that

$$\frac{xv - xv_{min}}{xv_{max} - xv_{min}} = \frac{xw - xw_{min}}{xw_{max} - xw_{min}}$$

$$\frac{yv - yv_{min}}{yv_{max} - yv_{min}} = \frac{yw - yw_{min}}{yw_{max} - yw_{min}}$$

(6-2)

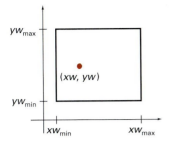
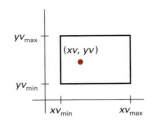

Figure 6-5

A point at position (xw, yw) in a designated window is mapped to
viewport coordinates (xv, yv) so that relative positions in the two areas
are the same.

Solving these expressions for the viewport position (xv, yv), we have

$$xv = xv_{min} + (xw - xw_{min})sx$$

$$yv = yv_{min} + (yw - yw_{min})sy$$

(6-3)

where the scaling factors are

$$sx = \frac{xv_{max} - xv_{min}}{xw_{max} - xw_{min}}$$

$$sy = \frac{yv_{max} - yv_{min}}{yw_{max} - yw_{min}}$$

(6-4)

Equations 6-3 can also be derived with a set of transformtions that converts the
window area into the viewport area. This conversion is performed with the following sequence of transformations:

1. Perform a scaling transformation using a fixed-point position of (xw_{min}, yw_{min}) that scales the window area to the size of the viewport.
2. Translate the scaled window area to the position of the viewport.

Relative proportions of objects are maintained if the scaling factors are the
same ($sx = sy$). Otherwise, world objects will be stretched or contracted in either
the x or y direction when displayed on the output device.

Character strings can be handled in two ways when they are mapped to a
viewport. The simplest mapping maintains a constant character size, even
though the viewport area may be enlarged or reduced relative to the window.
This method would be employed when text is formed with standard character
fonts that cannot be changed. In systems that allow for changes in character size,
string definitions can be windowed the same as other primitives. For characters
formed with line segments, the mapping to the viewport can be carried out as a
sequence of line transformations.

From normalized coordinates, object descriptions are mapped to the various display devices. Any number of output devices can be open in a particular
application, and another window-to-viewport transformation can be performed
for each open output device. This mapping, called the **workstation transforma-**

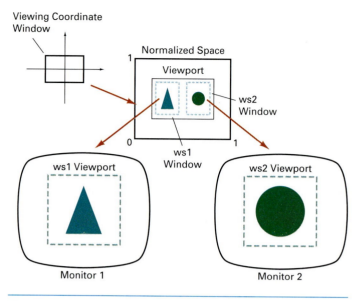

Figure 6-6
Mapping selected parts of a scene in normalized coordinates to
different video monitors with workstation transformations.

tion, is accomplished by selecting a window area in normalized space and a
viewport area in the coordinates of the display device. With the workstation
transformation, we gain some additional control over the positioning of parts of
a scene on individual output devices. As illustrated in Fig. 6-6, we can use workstation transformations to partition a view so that different parts of normalized
space can be displayed on different output devices.

6-4
TWO-DIMENSIONAL VIEWING FUNCTIONS

We define a viewing reference system in a PHIGS application program with the
following function:

```
evaluateViewOrientationMatrix (x0, y0, xV, yV,
                    error, viewMatrix)
```

where parameters `x0` and `y0` are the coordinates of the viewing origin, and parameters `xV` and `yV` are the world-coordinate positions for the view up vector. An
integer error code is generated if the input parameters are in error; otherwise, the
`viewMatrix` for the world-to-viewing transformation is calculated. Any number
of viewing transformation matrices can be defined in an application.

To set up the elements of a window-to-viewport mapping matrix, we invoke the function

```
evaluateViewMappingMatrix (xwmin, xwmax, ywmin, ywmax,
     xvmin, xvmax, yvmin, yvmax, error, viewMappingMatrix)
```

Here, the window limits in viewing coordinates are chosen with parameters
`xwmin`, `xwmax`, `ywmin`, and `ywmax`; and the viewport limits are set with the nor-

malized coordinate positions xvmin, xvmax, yvmin, yvmax. As with the viewing-transformation matrix, we can construct several window-viewport pairs and use them for projecting various parts of the scene to different areas of the unit square.

Next, we can store combinations of viewing and window–viewport mappings for various workstations in a *viewing table* with

```
setViewRepresentation (ws, viewIndex, viewMatrix,
    viewMappingMatrix, xclipmin, xclipmax, yclipmin,
        yclipmax, clipxy)
```

where parameter ws designates the output device (workstation), and parameter viewIndex sets an integer identifier for this particular window–viewport pair. The matrices viewMatrix and viewMappingMatrix can be concatenated and referenced by the viewIndex. Additional clipping limits can also be specified here, but they are usually set to coincide with the viewport boundaries. And parameter clipxy is assigned either the value *noclip* or the value *clip*. This allows us to turn off clipping if we want to view the parts of the scene outside the viewport. We can also select *noclip* to speed up processing when we know that all of the scene is included within the viewport limits.

The function

```
setViewIndex (viewIndex)
```

selects a particular set of options from the viewing table. This view-index selection is then applied to subsequently specified output primitives and associated attributes and generates a display on each of the active workstations.

At the final stage, we apply a workstation transformation by selecting a workstation window–viewport pair:

```
setWorkstationWindow (ws, xwsWindmin, xwsWindmax,
                    ywsWindmin, ywsWindmax)
setWorkstationViewport (ws, xwsVPortmin, xwsVPortmax,
                    ywsVPortmin, ywsVPortmax)
```

where parameter ws gives the workstation number. Window-coordinate extents are specified in the range from 0 to 1 (normalized space), and viewport limits are in integer device coordinates.

If a workstation viewport is not specified, the unit square of the normalized reference frame is mapped onto the largest square area possible on an output device. The coordinate origin of normalized space is mapped to the origin of device coordinates, and the aspect ratio is retained by transforming the unit square onto a square area on the output device.

Example 6-1 Two-Dimensional Viewing Example

As an example of the use of viewing functions, the following sequence of statements sets up a rotated window in world coordinates and maps its contents to the upper right corner of workstation 2. We keep the viewing coordinate origin at the world origin, and we choose the view up direction for the window as (1, 1). This gives us a viewing-coordinate system that is rotated 45° clockwise in the world-coordinate reference frame. The view index is set to the value 5.

223

```
evaluateViewOrientationMatrix (0, 0, 1, 1,
                                    viewError, viewMat);
evaluateViewMappingMatrix (-60.5, 41.24, -20.75, 82.5, 0.5,
         0.8, 0.7, 1.0, viewMapError, viewMapMat);
setViewRepresentation (2, 5, viewMat, viewMapMat, 0.5, 0.8,
                                   0.7, 1.0, clip);

setViewIndex (5);
```

Similarly, we could set up an additional transformation with view index 6 that would map a specified window into a viewport at the lower left of the screen. Two graphs, for example, could then be displayed at opposite screen corners with the following statements.

```
setViewIndex (5);
polyline (3, axes);
polyline (15, data1);
setViewIndex (6);
polyline (3, axes);
polyline (25, data2);
```

View index 5 selects a viewport in the upper right of the screen display, and view index 6 selects a viewport in the lower left corner. The function `polyline (3, axes)` produces the horizontal and vertical coordinate reference for the data plot in each graph.

6-5

CLIPPING OPERATIONS

Generally, any procedure that identifies those portions of a picture that are either inside or outside of a specified region of space is referred to as a **clipping algorithm,** or simply **clipping**. The region against which an object is to clipped is called a **clip window**.

Applications of clipping include extracting part of a defined scene for viewing; identifying visible surfaces in three-dimensional views; antialiasing line segments or object boundaries; creating objects using solid-modeling procedures; displaying a multiwindow environment; and drawing and painting operations that allow parts of a picture to be selected for copying, moving, erasing, or duplicating. Depending on the application, the clip window can be a general polygon or it can even have curved boundaries. We first consider clipping methods using rectangular clip regions, then we discuss methods for other clip-region shapes.

For the viewing transformation, we want to display only those picture parts that are within the window area (assuming that the clipping flags have not been set to *noclip*). Everything outside the window is discarded. Clipping algorithms can be applied in world coordinates, so that only the contents of the window interior are mapped to device coordinates. Alternatively, the complete world-coordinate picture can be mapped first to device coordinates, or normalized device coordinates, then clipped against the viewport boundaries. World-coordinate clipping removes those primitives outside the window from further consideration, thus eliminating the processing necessary to transform those primitives to device space. Viewport clipping, on the other hand, can reduce calculations by allowing concatenation of viewing and geometric transformation matrices. But viewport clipping does require that the transformation to device coordinates be performed for all objects, including those outside the window area. On raster systems, clipping algorithms are often combined with scan conversion.

In the following sections, we consider algorithms for clipping the following primitive types

- Point Clipping
- Line Clipping (straight-line segments)
- Area Clipping (polygons)
- Curve Clipping
- Text Clipping

Line and polygon clipping routines are standard components of graphics packages, but many packages accommodate curved objects, particularly spline curves and conics, such as circles and ellipses. Another way to handle curved objects is to approximate them with straight-line segments and apply the line- or polygon-clipping procedure.

6-6
POINT CLIPPING

Assuming that the clip window is a rectangle in standard position, we save a point $\mathbf{P} = (x, y)$ for display if the following inequalities are satisfied:

$$xw_{\min} \leq x \leq xw_{\max}$$
$$yw_{\min} \leq y \leq yw_{\max}$$

(6-5)

where the edges of the clip window $(xw_{\min}, xw_{\max}, yw_{\min}, yw_{\max})$ can be either the world-coordinate window boundaries or viewport boundaries. If any one of these four inequalities is not satisfied, the point is clipped (not saved for display).

Although point clipping is applied less often than line or polygon clipping, some applications may require a point-clipping procedure. For example, point clipping can be applied to scenes involving explosions or sea foam that are modeled with particles (points) distributed in some region of the scene.

6-7
LINE CLIPPING

Figure 6-7 illustrates possible relationships between line positions and a standard rectangular clipping region. A line-clipping procedure involves several parts. First, we can test a given line segment to determine whether it lies completely inside the clipping window. If it does not, we try to determine whether it lies completely outside the window. Finally, if we cannot identify a line as completely inside or completely outside, we must perform intersection calculations with one or more clipping boundaries. We process lines through the "inside-outside" tests by checking the line endpoints. A line with both endpoints inside all clipping boundaries, such as the line from $\mathbf{P}_1$ to $\mathbf{P}_2$, is saved. A line with both endpoints outside any one of the clip boundaries (line $\overline{\mathbf{P}_3\mathbf{P}_4}$ in Fig. 6-7) is outside the win-

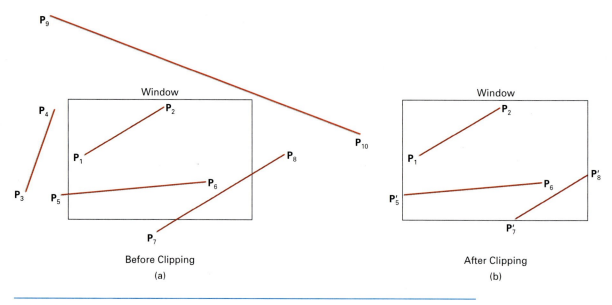

Window

P_9 P_2 P_4 P_1 P_{10} P_8 P_6 P_3 P_5 P_7

Before Clipping

(a)

Window

P_2 P_1 P_8' P_6 P_5' P_7'

After Clipping

(b)

Figure 6-7
Line clipping against a rectangular clip window.

dow. All other lines cross one or more clipping boundaries, and may require calculation of multiple intersection points. To minimize calculations, we try to devise clipping algorithms that can efficiently identify outside lines and reduce intersection calculations.

For a line segment with endpoints (x_1, y_1) and (x_2, y_2) and one or both endpoints outside the clipping rectangle, the parametric representation

$$x = x_1 + u(x_2 - x_1)$$
$$y = y_1 + u(y_2 - y_1), \qquad 0 \le u \le 1$$

(6-6)

could be used to determine values of parameter u for intersections with the clipping boundary coordinates. If the value of u for an intersection with a rectangle boundary edge is outside the range 0 to 1, the line does not enter the interior of the window at that boundary. If the value of u is within the range from 0 to 1, the line segment does indeed cross into the clipping area. This method can be applied to each clipping boundary edge in turn to determine whether any part of the line segment is to be displayed. Line segments that are parallel to window edges can be handled as special cases.

Clipping line segments with these parametric tests requires a good deal of computation, and faster approaches to clipping are possible. A number of efficient line clippers have been developed, and we survey the major algorithms in the next sections. Some algorithms are designed explicitly for two-dimensional pictures and some are easily adapted to three-dimensional applications.

Cohen–Sutherland Line Clipping

This is one of the oldest and most popular line-clipping procedures. Generally, the method speeds up the processing of line segments by performing initial tests that reduce the number of intersections that must be calculated. Every line end-

226

point in a picture is assigned a four-digit binary code, called a **region code**, that identifies the location of the point relative to the boundaries of the clipping rectangle. Regions are set up in reference to the boundaries as shown in Fig. 6-8. Each bit position in the region code is used to indicate one of the four relative coordinate positions of the point with respect to the clip window: to the left, right, top, or bottom. By numbering the bit positions in the region code as 1 through 4 from right to left, the coordinate regions can be correlated with the bit positions as

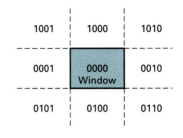

bit 1: left

bit 2: right

bit 3: below

bit 4: above

A value of 1 in any bit position indicates that the point is in that relative position; otherwise, the bit position is set to 0. If a point is within the clipping rectangle, the region code is 0000. A point that is below and to the left of the rectangle has a region code of 0101.

Bit values in the region code are determined by comparing endpoint coordinate values (x, y) to the clip boundaries. Bit 1 is set to 1 if $x < xw_{min}$. The other three bit values can be determined using similar comparisons. For languages in which bit manipulation is possible, region-code bit values can be determined with the following two steps: (1) Calculate differences between endpoint coordinates and clipping boundaries. (2) Use the resultant sign bit of each difference calculation to set the corresponding value in the region code. Bit 1 is the sign bit of $x - xw_{min}$; bit 2 is the sign bit of $xw_{max} - x$; bit 3 is the sign bit of $y - yw_{min}$; and bit 4 is the sign bit of $yw_{max} - y$.

Once we have established region codes for all line endpoints, we can quickly determine which lines are completely inside the clip window and which are clearly outside. Any lines that are completely contained within the window boundaries have a region code of 0000 for both endpoints, and we trivially accept these lines. Any lines that have a 1 in the same bit position in the region codes for each endpoint are completely outside the clipping rectangle, and we trivially reject these lines. We would discard the line that has a region code of 1001 for one endpoint and a code of 0101 for the other endpoint. Both endpoints of this line are left of the clipping rectangle, as indicated by the 1 in the first bit position of each region code. A method that can be used to test lines for total clipping is to perform the logical *and* operation with both region codes. If the result is not 0000, the line is completely outside the clipping region.

Lines that cannot be identified as completely inside or completely outside a clip window by these tests are checked for intersection with the window boundaries. As shown in Fig. 6-9, such lines may or may not cross into the window interior. We begin the clipping process for a line by comparing an outside endpoint to a clipping boundary to determine how much of the line can be discarded. Then the remaining part of the line is checked against the other boundaries, and we continue until either the line is totally discarded or a section is found inside the window. We set up our algorithm to check line endpoints against clipping boundaries in the order left, right, bottom, top.

To illustrate the specific steps in clipping lines against rectangular boundaries using the Cohen–Sutherland algorithm, we show how the lines in Fig. 6-9 could be processed. Starting with the bottom endpoint of the line from $\mathbf{P}_1$ to $\mathbf{P}_2$,

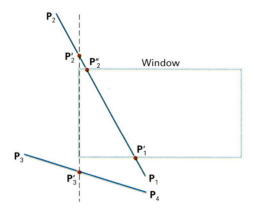

Figure 6-9
Lines extending from one coordinate region to another may pass through the clip window, or they may intersect clipping boundaries without entering the window.

we check $\mathbf{P}_1$ against the left, right, and bottom boundaries in turn and find that this point is below the clipping rectangle. We then find the intersection point $\mathbf{P}_1'$ with the bottom boundary and discard the line section from $\mathbf{P}_1$ to $\mathbf{P}_1'$. The line now has been reduced to the section from $\mathbf{P}_1'$ to $\mathbf{P}_2$. Since $\mathbf{P}_2$ is outside the clip window, we check this endpoint against the boundaries and find that it is to the left of the window. Intersection point $\mathbf{P}_2'$ is calculated, but this point is above the window. So the final intersection calculation yields $\mathbf{P}_2''$, and the line from $\mathbf{P}_1'$ to $\mathbf{P}_2''$ is saved. This completes processing for this line, so we save this part and go on to the next line. Point $\mathbf{P}_3$ in the next line is to the left of the clipping rectangle, so we determine the intersection $\mathbf{P}_3'$ and eliminate the line section from $\mathbf{P}_3$ to $\mathbf{P}_3'$. By checking region codes for the line section from $\mathbf{P}_3'$ to $\mathbf{P}_4$, we find that the remainder of the line is below the clip window and can be discarded also.

Intersection points with a clipping boundary can be calculated using the slope-intercept form of the line equation. For a line with endpoint coordinates (x_1, y_1) and (x_2, y_2), the y coordinate of the intersection point with a vertical boundary can be obtained with the calculation

$$y = y_1 + m(x - x_1) \tag{6-7}$$

where the x value is set either to xw_{min} or to xw_{max}, and the slope of the line is calculated as $m = (y_2 - y_1)/(x_2 - x_1)$. Similarly, if we are looking for the intersection with a horizontal boundary, the x coordinate can be calculated as

$$x = x_1 + \frac{y - y_1}{m} \tag{6-8}$$

with y set either to yw_{min} or to yw_{max}.

The following procedure demonstrates the Cohen-Sutherland line-clipping algorithm. Codes for each endpoint are stored as bytes and processed using bit manipulations.

```
#define ROUND(a)    ((int)(a+0.5))

/* Bit masks encode a point's position relative to the clip edges.  A
   point's status is encoded by OR'ing together appropriate bit masks.
*/
#define LEFT_EDGE   0x1
```

```
#define RIGHT_EDGE   0x2
#define BOTTOM_EDGE  0x4
#define TOP_EDGE     0x8

/* Points encoded as 0000 are completely Inside the clip rectangle;
   all others are outside at least one edge.  If OR'ing two codes is
   FALSE (no bits are set in either code), the line can be Accepted.  If
   the AND operation between two codes is TRUE, the line defined by those
   endpoints is completely outside the clip region and can be Rejected.
*/
#define INSIDE(a)     (!a)
#define REJECT(a,b)   (a&b)
#define ACCEPT(a,b)   (!(a|b))

unsigned char encode (wcPt2 pt, dcPt winMin, dcPt winMax)
{
  unsigned char code=0x00;

  if (pt.x < winMin.x)
    code = code | LEFT_EDGE;
  if (pt.x > winMax.x)
    code = code | RIGHT_EDGE;
  if (pt.y < winMin.y)
    code = code | BOTTOM_EDGE;
  if (pt.y > winMax.y)
    code = code | TOP_EDGE;
  return (code);
}

void swapPts (wcPt2 * p1, wcPt2 * p2)
{
  wcPt2 tmp;

  tmp = *p1; *p1 = *p2; *p2 = tmp;
}

void swapCodes (unsigned char * c1, unsigned char * c2)
{
  unsigned char tmp;

  tmp = *c1; *c1 = *c2; *c2 = tmp;
}

void clipLine (dcPt winMin, dcPt winMax, wcPt2 p1, wcPt2 p2)
{
  unsigned char code1, code2;
  int done = FALSE, draw = FALSE;
  float m;

  while (!done) {
    code1 = encode (p1, winMin, winMax);
    code2 = encode (p2, winMin, winMax);
    if (ACCEPT (code1, code2)) {
      done = TRUE;
      draw = TRUE;
    }
    else
      if (REJECT (code1, code2))
        done = TRUE;
      else {
        /* Ensure that p1 is outside window */
        if (INSIDE (code1)) {
```

```
          swapPts (&p1, &p2);
          swapCodes (&code1, &code2);
       }
     /* Use slope (m) to find line-clipEdge intersections */
     if (p2.x != p1.x)
       m = (p2.y - p1.y) / (p2.x - p1.x);
     if (code1 & LEFT_EDGE) {
       p1.y += (winMin.x - p1.x) * m;
       p1.x = winMin.x;
     }
     else
       if (code1 & RIGHT_EDGE) {
         p1.y += (winMax.x - p1.x) * m;
         p1.x = winMax.x;
       }
       else
         if (code1 & BOTTOM_EDGE) {
           /* Need to update p1.x for non-vertical lines only */
           if (p2.x != p1.x)
             p1.x += (winMin.y - p1.y) / m;
           p1.y = winMin.y;
         }
         else
           if (code1 & TOP_EDGE) {
             if (p2.x != p1.x)
               p1.x += (winMax.y - p1.y) / m;
             p1.y = winMax.y;
           }
    }
  }
  if (draw)
    lineDDA (ROUND(p1.x), ROUND(p1.y), ROUND(p2.x), ROUND(p2.y));
}
```

Liang–Barsky Line Clipping

Faster line clippers have been developed that are based on analysis of the parametric equation of a line segment, which we can write in the form

$$x = x_1 + u\Delta x$$
$$y = y_1 + u\Delta y, \qquad 0 \le u \le 1 \tag{6-9}$$

where $\Delta x = x_2 - x_1$ and $\Delta y = y_2 - y_1$. Using these parametric equations, Cyrus and Beck developed an algorithm that is generally more efficient than the Cohen–Sutherland algorithm. Later, Liang and Barsky independently devised an even faster parametric line-clipping algorithm. Following the Liang–Barsky approach, we first write the point-clipping conditions 6-5 in the parametric form:

$$xw_{min} \le x_1 + u\Delta x \le xw_{max}$$
$$yw_{min} \le y_1 + u\Delta y \le yw_{max} \tag{6-10}$$

Each of these four inequalities can be expressed as

$$up_k \le q_k, \qquad k = 1, 2, 3, 4 \tag{6-11}$$

230

where parameters p and q are defined as

$$
\begin{aligned}
p_1 &= -\Delta x, & q_1 &= x_1 - xw_{min} \\
p_2 &= \Delta x, & q_2 &= xw_{max} - x_1 \\
p_3 &= -\Delta y, & q_3 &= y_1 - yw_{min} \\
p_4 &= \Delta y, & q_4 &= yw_{max} - y_1
\end{aligned}
\qquad (6\text{-}12)
$$

Any line that is parallel to one of the clipping boundaries has $p_k = 0$ for the value of k corresponding to that boundary ($k = 1$, 2, 3, and 4 correspond to the left, right, bottom, and top boundaries, respectively). If, for that value of k, we also find $q_k < 0$, then the line is completely outside the boundary and can be eliminated from further consideration. If $q_k \geq 0$, the line is inside the parallel clipping boundary.

When $p_k < 0$, the infinite extension of the line proceeds from the outside to the inside of the infinite extension of this particular clipping boundary. If $p_k > 0$, the line proceeds from the inside to the outside. For a nonzero value of p_k, we can calculate the value of u that corresponds to the point where the infinitely extended line intersects the extension of boundary k as

$$
u = \frac{q_k}{p_k} \qquad (6\text{-}13)
$$

For each line, we can calculate values for parameters u_1 and u_2 that define that part of the line that lies within the clip rectangle. The value of u_1 is determined by looking at the rectangle edges for which the line proceeds from the outside to the inside ($p < 0$). For these edges, we calculate $r_k = q_k/p_k$. The value of u_1 is taken as the largest of the set consisting of 0 and the various values of r. Conversely, the value of u_2 is determined by examining the boundaries for which the line proceeds from inside to outside ($p > 0$). A value of r_k is calculated for each of these boundaries, and the value of u_2 is the minimum of the set consisting of 1 and the calculated r values. If $u_1 > u_2$, the line is completely outside the clip window and it can be rejected. Otherwise, the endpoints of the clipped line are calculated from the two values of parameter u.

This algorithm is presented in the following procedure. Line intersection parameters are initialized to the values $u_1 = 0$ and $u_2 = 1$. For each clipping boundary, the appropriate values for p and q are calculated and used by the function *clipTest* to determine whether the line can be rejected or whether the intersection parameters are to be adjusted. When $p < 0$, the parameter r is used to update u_1; when $p > 0$, parameter r is used to update u_2. If updating u_1 or u_2 results in $u_1 > u_2$, we reject the line. Otherwise, we update the appropriate u parameter only if the new value results in a shortening of the line. When $p = 0$ and $q < 0$, we can discard the line since it is parallel to and outside of this boundary. If the line has not been rejected after all four values of p and q have been tested, the endpoints of the clipped line are determined from values of u_1 and u_2.

```
#include "graphics.h"

#define ROUND(a)  ((int)(a+0.5))

int clipTest (float p, float q, float * u1, float * u2)
```

```
{
  float r;
  int retVal = TRUE;

  if (p < 0.0) {
    r = q / p;
    if (r > *u2)
      retVal = FALSE;
    else
      if (r > *u1)
        *u1 = r;
  }
  else
    if (p > 0.0) {
      r = q / p;
      if (r < *u1)
        retVal = FALSE;
      else if (r < *u2)
        *u2 = r;
    }
    else
      /* p = 0, so line is parallel to this clipping edge */
      if (q < 0.0)
        /* Line is outside clipping edge */
        retVal = FALSE;

  return (retVal);
}

void clipLine (dcPt winMin, dcPt winMax, wcPt2 p1, wcPt2 p2)
{
  float u1 = 0.0, u2 = 1.0, dx = p2.x - p1.x, dy;

  if (clipTest (-dx, p1.x - winMin.x, &u1, &u2))
    if (clipTest (dx, winMax.x - p1.x, &u1, &u2)) {
      dy = p2.y - p1.y;
      if (clipTest (-dy, p1.y - winMin.y, &u1, &u2))
        if (clipTest (dy, winMax.y - p1.y, &u1, &u2)) {
          if (u2 < 1.0) {
            p2.x = p1.x + u2 * dx;
            p2.y = p1.y + u2 * dy;
          }
          if (u1 > 0.0) {
            p1.x += u1 * dx;
            p1.y += u1 * dy;
          }
          lineDDA (ROUND(p1.x), ROUND(p1.y), ROUND(p2.x), ROUND(p2.y));
        }
    }
}
```

In general, the Liang–Barsky algorithm is more efficient than the Cohen–Sutherland algorithm, since intersection calculations are reduced. Each update of parameters u_1 and u_2 requires only one division; and window intersections of the line are computed only once, when the final values of u_1 and u_2 have been computed. In contrast, the Cohen–Sutherland algorithm can repeatedly calculate intersections along a line path, even though the line may be completely outside the clip window. And, each intersection calculation requires both a division and a multiplication. Both the Cohen–Sutherland and the Liang–Barsky algorithms can be extended to three-dimensional clipping (Chapter 12).

Nicholl–Lee–Nicholl Line Clipping

By creating more regions around the clip window, the Nicholl–Lee–Nicholl (or NLN) algorithm avoids multiple clipping of an individual line segment. In the Cohen–Sutherland method, for example, multiple intersections may be calculated along the path of a single line before an intersection on the clipping rectangle is located or the line is completely rejected. These extra intersection calculations are eliminated in the NLN algorithm by carrying out more region testing before intersection positions are calculated. Compared to both the Cohen–Sutherland and the Liang–Barsky algorithms, the Nicholl–Lee–Nicholl algorithm performs fewer comparisons and divisions. The trade-off is that the NLN algorithm can only be applied to two-dimensional clipping, whereas both the Liang–Barsky and the Cohen–Sutherland methods are easily extended to three-dimensional scenes.

For a line with endpoints P_1 and P_2, we first determine the position of point P_1 for the nine possible regions relative to the clipping rectangle. Only the three regions shown in Fig. 6-10 need be considered. If P_1 lies in any one of the other six regions, we can move it to one of the three regions in Fig. 6-10 using a symmetry transformation. For example, the region directly above the clip window can be transformed to the region left of the clip window using a reflection about the line $y = -x$, or we could use a 90° counterclockwise rotation.

Next, we determine the position of P_2 relative to P_1. To do this, we create some new regions in the plane, depending on the location of P_1. Boundaries of the new regions are half-infinite line segments that start at the position of P_1 and pass through the window corners. If P_1 is inside the clip window and P_2 is outside, we set up the four regions shown in Fig. 6-11. The intersection with the appropriate window boundary is then carried out, depending on which one of the four regions (L, T, R, or B) contains P_2. Of course, if both P_1 and P_2 are inside the clipping rectangle, we simply save the entire line.

If P_1 is in the region to the left of the window, we set up the four regions, L, LT, LR, and LB, shown in Fig. 6-12. These four regions determine a unique boundary for the line segment. For instance, if P_2 is in region L, we clip the line at the left boundary and save the line segment from this intersection point to P_2. But if P_2 is in region LT, we save the line segment from the left window boundary to the top boundary. If P_2 is not in any of the four regions, L, LT, LR, or LB, the entire line is clipped.

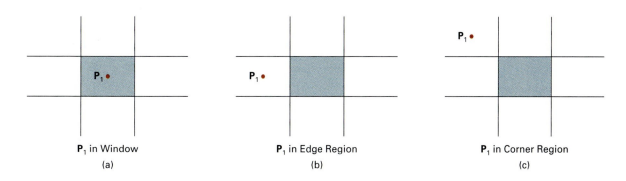

P_1 in Window	P_1 in Edge Region	P_1 in Corner Region
(a)	(b)	(c)

Figure 6-10
Three possible positions for a line endpoint P_1 in the NLN line-clipping algorithm.

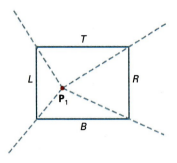

Figure 6-11
The four clipping regions used in the NLN algorithm when $\mathbf{P}_1$ is inside the clip window and $\mathbf{P}_2$ is outside.

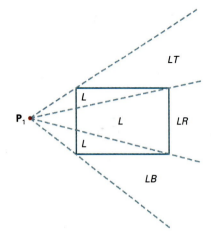

Figure 6-12
The four clipping regions used in the NLN algorithm when $\mathbf{P}_1$ is directly left of the clip window.

For the third case, when $\mathbf{P}_1$ is to the left and above the clip window, we use the clipping regions in Fig. 6-13. In this case, we have the two possibilites shown, depending on the position of $\mathbf{P}_1$ relative to the top left corner of the window. If $\mathbf{P}_2$ is in one of the regions T, L, TR, TB, LR, or LB, this determines a unique clip-window edge for the intersection calculations. Otherwise, the entire line is rejected.

To determine the region in which $\mathbf{P}_2$ is located, we compare the slope of the line to the slopes of the boundaries of the clip regions. For example, if $\mathbf{P}_1$ is left of the clipping rectangle (Fig. 6-12), then $\mathbf{P}_2$ is in region LT if

$$\text{slope } \overline{\mathbf{P}_1\mathbf{P}_{TR}} < \text{slope } \overline{\mathbf{P}_1\mathbf{P}_2} < \text{slope } \overline{\mathbf{P}_1\mathbf{P}_{TL}} \qquad (6\text{-}14)$$

or

$$\frac{y_T - y_1}{x_R - x_1} < \frac{y_2 - y_1}{x_2 - x_1} < \frac{y_T - y_1}{x_L - x_1} \qquad (6\text{-}15)$$

And we clip the entire line if

$$(y_T - y_1)(x_2 - x_1) < (x_L - x_1)(y_2 - y_1) \qquad (6\text{-}16)$$

The coordinate difference and product calculations used in the slope tests are saved and also used in the intersection calculations. From the parametric equations

$$x = x_1 + (x_2 - x_1)u$$
$$y = y_1 + (y_2 - y_1)u$$

an x-intersection position on the left window boundary is $x = x_L$, with $u = (x_L - x_1)/(x_2 - x_1)$, so that the y-intersection position is

$$y = y_1 + \frac{y_2 - y_1}{x_2 - x_1}(x_L - x_1) \qquad (6\text{-}17)$$

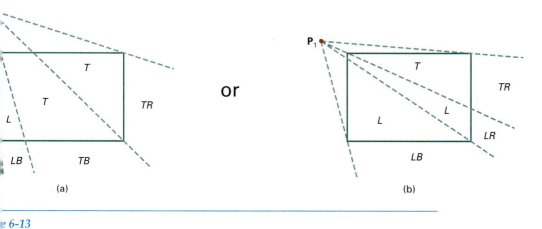

or

e 6-13
wo possible sets of clipping regions used in the NLN algorithm when $\mathbf{P}_1$ is above and
left of the clip window.

And an intersection position on the top boundary has $y = y_T$ and $u = (y_T - y_1)/(y_2 - y_1)$, with

$$x = x_1 + \frac{x_2 - x_1}{y_2 - y_1}(y_T - y_1) \qquad (6\text{-}18)$$

Line Clipping Using Nonrectangular Clip Windows

In some applications, it is often necessary to clip lines against arbitrarily shaped polygons. Algorithms based on parametric line equations, such as the Liang–Barsky method and the earlier Cyrus–Beck approach, can be extended easily to convex polygon windows. We do this by modifying the algorithm to include the parametric equations for the boundaries of the clip region. Preliminary screening of line segments can be accomplished by processing lines against the coordinate extents of the clipping polygon. For concave polygon-clipping regions, we can still apply these parametric clipping procedures if we first split the concave polygon into a set of convex polygons.

Circles or other curved-boundary clipping regions are also possible, but less commonly used. Clipping algorithms for these areas are slower because intersection calculations involve nonlinear curve equations. At the first step, lines can be clipped against the bounding rectangle (coordinate extents) of the curved clipping region. Lines that can be identified as completely outside the bounding rectangle are discarded. To identify inside lines, we can calculate the distance of line endpoints from the circle center. If the square of this distance for both endpoints of a line is less than or equal to the radius squared, we can save the entire line. The remaining lines are then processed through the intersection calculations, which must solve simultaneous circle-line equations.

Splitting Concave Polygons

We can identify a concave polygon by calculating the cross products of successive edge vectors in order around the polygon perimeter. If the z component of

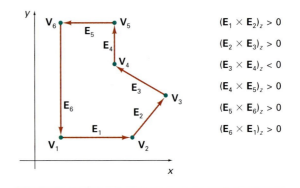

$$(\mathbf{E}_1 \times \mathbf{E}_2)_z > 0$$
$$(\mathbf{E}_2 \times \mathbf{E}_3)_z > 0$$
$$(\mathbf{E}_3 \times \mathbf{E}_4)_z < 0$$
$$(\mathbf{E}_4 \times \mathbf{E}_5)_z > 0$$
$$(\mathbf{E}_5 \times \mathbf{E}_6)_z > 0$$
$$(\mathbf{E}_6 \times \mathbf{E}_1)_z > 0$$

Figure 6-14

Identifying a concave polygon by calculating cross products of successive pairs of edge vectors.

some cross products is positive while others have a negative z component, we have a concave polygon. Otherwise, the polygon is convex. This is assuming that no series of three successive vertices are collinear, in which case the cross product of the two edge vectors for these vertices is zero. If all vertices are collinear, we have a degenerate polygon (a straight line). Figure 6-14 illustrates the edge-vector cross-product method for identifying concave polygons.

A *vector method* for splitting a concave polygon in the xy plane is to calculate the edge-vector cross products in a counterclockwise order and to note the sign of the z component of the cross products. If any z component turns out to be negative (as in Fig. 6-14), the polygon is concave and we can split it along the line of the first edge vector in the cross-product pair. The following example illustrates this method for splitting a concave polygon.

Example 6-2: Vector Method for Splitting Concave Polygons

Figure 6-15 shows a concave polygon with six edges. Edge vectors for this polygon can be expressed as

$$\mathbf{E}_1 = (1, 0, 0), \qquad \mathbf{E}_2 = (1, 1, 0)$$
$$\mathbf{E}_3 = (1, -1, 0), \qquad \mathbf{E}_4 = (0, 2, 0)$$
$$\mathbf{E}_5 = (-3, 0, 0), \qquad \mathbf{E}_6 = (0, -2, 0)$$

where the z component is 0, since all edges are in the xy plane. The cross product $\mathbf{E}_i \times \mathbf{E}_j$ for two successive edge vectors is a vector perpendicular to the xy plane with z component equal to $E_{ix}E_{jy} - E_{jx}E_{iy}$.

$$\mathbf{E}_1 \times \mathbf{E}_2 = (0, 0, 1), \qquad \mathbf{E}_2 \times \mathbf{E}_3 = (0, 0, -2)$$
$$\mathbf{E}_3 \times \mathbf{E}_4 = (0, 0, 2), \qquad \mathbf{E}_4 \times \mathbf{E}_5 = (0, 0, 6)$$
$$\mathbf{E}_5 \times \mathbf{E}_6 = (0, 0, 6), \qquad \mathbf{E}_6 \times \mathbf{E}_1 = (0, 0, 2)$$

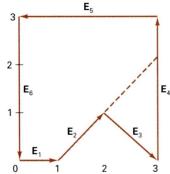

Figure 6-15

Splitting a concave polygon using the vector method.

236

Since the cross product $\mathbf{E}_2 \times \mathbf{E}_3$ has a negative z component, we split the polygon along the line of vector $\mathbf{E}_2$. The line equation for this edge has a slope of 1 and a y intercept of -1. We then determine the intersection of this line and the other

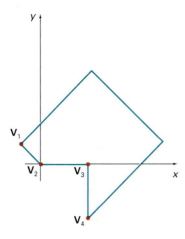

Figure 6-16
Splitting a concave polygon using the rotational method. After rotating V_3 onto the x axis, we find that V_4 is below the x axis. So we split the polygon along the line of $\overline{V_2V_3}$.

polygon edges to split the polygon into two pieces. No other edge cross products are negative, so the two new polygons are both convex.

We can also split a concave polygon using a *rotational method*. Proceeding counterclockwise around the polygon edges, we translate each polygon vertex V_k in turn to the coordinate origin. We then rotate in a clockwise direction so that the next vertex V_{k+1} is on the x axis. If the next vertex, V_{k+2}, is below the x axis, the polygon is concave. We then split the polygon into two new polygons along the x axis and repeat the concave test for each of the two new polygons. Otherwise, we continue to rotate vertices on the x axis and to test for negative y vertex values. Figure 6-16 illustrates the rotational method for splitting a concave polygon.

6-8
POLYGON CLIPPING

To clip polygons, we need to modify the line-clipping procedures discussed in the previous section. A polygon boundary processed with a line clipper may be displayed as a series of unconnected line segments (Fig. 6-17), depending on the orientation of the polygon to the clipping window. What we really want to display is a bounded area after clipping, as in Fig. 6-18. For polygon clipping, we require an algorithm that will generate one or more closed areas that are then scan converted for the appropriate area fill. The output of a polygon clipper should be a sequence of vertices that defines the clipped polygon boundaries.

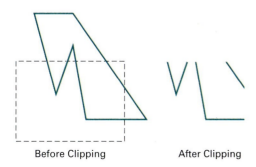

Before Clipping   After Clipping

Figure 6-17
Display of a polygon processed by a line-clipping algorithm.

237

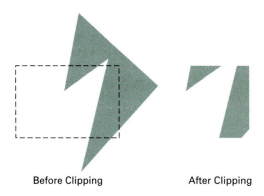

Before Clipping   After Clipping

Figure 6-18
Display of a correctly clipped polygon.

Sutherland–Hodgeman Polygon Clipping

We can correctly clip a polygon by processing the polygon boundary as a whole against each window edge. This could be accomplished by processing all polygon vertices against each clip rectangle boundary in turn. Beginning with the initial set of polygon vertices, we could first clip the polygon against the left rectangle boundary to produce a new sequence of vertices. The new set of vertices could then be successively passed to a right boundary clipper, a bottom boundary clipper, and a top boundary clipper, as in Fig. 6-19. At each step, a new sequence of output vertices is generated and passed to the next window boundary clipper.

There are four possible cases when processing vertices in sequence around the perimeter of a polygon. As each pair of adjacent polygon vertices is passed to a window boundary clipper, we make the following tests: (1) If the first vertex is outside the window boundary and the second vertex is inside, both the intersection point of the polygon edge with the window boundary and the second vertex are added to the output vertex list. (2) If both input vertices are inside the window boundary, only the second vertex is added to the output vertex list. (3) If the first vertex is inside the window boundary and the second vertex is outside, only the edge intersection with the window boundary is added to the output vertex list. (4) If both input vertices are outside the window boundary, nothing is added to the output list. These four cases are illustrated in Fig. 6-20 for successive pairs of polygon vertices. Once all vertices have been processed for one clip window boundary, the output list of vertices is clipped against the next window boundary.

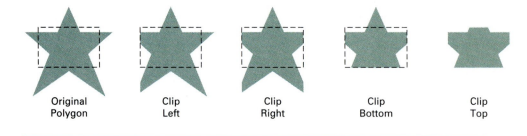

Original   Clip   Clip   Clip   Clip
Polygon   Left   Right   Bottom   Top

Figure 6-19
Clipping a polygon against successive window boundaries.

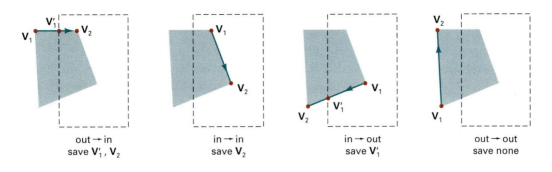

out → in
save V_1', V_2

in → in
save V_2

in → out
save V_1'

out → out
save none

Figure 6-20
Successive processing of pairs of polygon vertices against the left window boundary.

We illustrate this method by processing the area in Fig. 6-21 against the left window boundary. Vertices 1 and 2 are found to be on the outside of the boundary. Moving along to vertex 3, which is inside, we calculate the intersection and save both the intersection point and vertex 3. Vertices 4 and 5 are determined to be inside, and they also are saved. The sixth and final vertex is outside, so we find and save the intersection point. Using the five saved points, we would repeat the process for the next window boundary.

Implementing the algorithm as we have just described requires setting up storage for an output list of vertices as a polygon is clipped against each window boundary. We can eliminate the intermediate output vertex lists by simply clipping individual vertices at each step and passing the clipped vertices on to the next boundary clipper. This can be done with parallel processors or a single processor and a pipeline of clipping routines. A point (either an input vertex or a calculated intersection point) is added to the output vertex list only after it has been been determined to be inside or on a window boundary by all four boundary clippers. Otherwise, the point does not continue in the pipeline. Figure 6-22 shows a polygon and its intersection points with a clip window. In Fig. 6-23, we illustrate the progression of the polygon vertices in Fig. 6-22 through a pipeline of boundary clippers.

The following procedure demonstrates the pipeline clipping approach. An array, s, records the most recent point that was clipped for each clip-window boundary. The main routine passes each vertex p to the clipPoint routine for clipping against the first window boundary. If the line defined by endpoints p and s[boundary] crosses this window boundary, the intersection is calculated and passed to the next clipping stage. If p is inside the window, it is passed to the next clipping stage. Any point that survives clipping against all window boundaries is then entered into the output array of points. The array firstPoint stores for each window boundary the first point clipped against that boundary. After all polygon vertices have been processed, a closing routine clips lines defined by the first and last points clipped against each boundary.

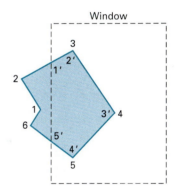

Figure 6-21
Clipping a polygon against the left boundary of a window, starting with vertex 1. Primed numbers are used to label the points in the output vertex list for this window boundary.

```
typedef enum { Left, Right, Bottom, Top } Edge;
#define N_EDGE 4

int inside (wcPt2 p, Edge b, dcPt wMin, dcPt wMax)
{
   switch (b) {
```

239

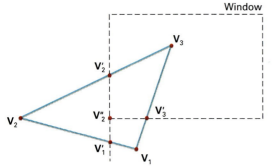

Window

V_3

V_2'

V_2'' V_3'

V_2

V_1' V_1

Figure 6-22

A polygon overlapping a rectangular clip window.

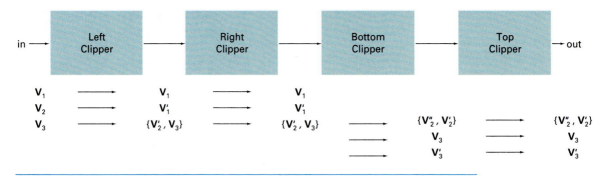

in →	Left Clipper	Right Clipper	Bottom Clipper	Top Clipper	→ out

$V_1 \longrightarrow V_1 \longrightarrow V_1$

$V_2 \longrightarrow V_1' \longrightarrow V_1'$

$V_3 \longrightarrow \{V_2', V_3\} \longrightarrow \{V_2', V_3\} \longrightarrow \{V_2'', V_2'\} \longrightarrow \{V_2'', V_2'\}$

$\longrightarrow V_3 \longrightarrow V_3$

$\longrightarrow V_3' \longrightarrow V_3'$

Figure 6-23

Processing the vertices of the polygon in Fig. 6-22 through a boundary-clipping pipeline. After all vertices are processed through the pipeline, the vertex list for the clipped polygon is $\{V_2'', V_2', V_3, V_3'\}$.

```
      case Left:   if (p.x < wMin.x) return (FALSE); break;
      case Right:  if (p.x > wMax.x) return (FALSE); break;
      case Bottom: if (p.y < wMin.y) return (FALSE); break;
      case Top:    if (p.y > wMax.y) return (FALSE); break;
      }
   return (TRUE);
}

int cross (wcPt2 p1, wcPt2 p2, Edge b, dcPt wMin, dcPt wMax)
{
   if (inside (p1, b, wMin, wMax) == inside (p2, b, wMin, wMax))
      return (FALSE);
   else return (TRUE);
}

wcPt2 intersect (wcPt2 p1, wcPt2 p2, Edge b, dcPt wMin, dcPt wMax)
{
   wcPt2 iPt;
   float m;

   if (p1.x != p2.x) m = (p1.y - p2.y) / (p1.x - p2.x);
   switch (b) {
   case Left:
      iPt.x = wMin.x;
      iPt.y = p2.y + (wMin.x - p2.x) * m;
      break;
   case Right:
      iPt.x = wMax.x;
```

```
      iPt.y = p2.y + (wMax.x - p2.x) * m;
      break;
    case Bottom:
      iPt.y = wMin.y;
      if (p1.x != p2.x) iPt.x = p2.x + (wMin.y - p2.y) / m;
      else iPt.x = p2.x;
      break;
    case Top:
      iPt.y = wMax.y;
      if (p1.x != p2.x) iPt.x = p2.x + (wMax.y - p2.y) / m;
      else iPt.x = p2.x;
      break;
  }
  return (iPt);
}

void clipPoint (wcPt2 p, Edge b, dcPt wMin, dcPt wMax,
                wcPt2 * pOut, int * cnt, wcPt2 * first[], wcPt2 * s)
{
  wcPt2 iPt;

  /* If no previous point exists for this edge, save this point. */
  if (!first[b])
    first[b] = &p;
  else
    /* Previous point exists.  If 'p' and previous point cross edge,
       find intersection.  Clip against next boundary, if any.  If
       no more edges, add intersection to output list. */
    if (cross (p, s[b], b, wMin, wMax)) {
      iPt = intersect (p, s[b], b, wMin, wMax);
      if (b < Top)
        clipPoint (iPt, b+1, wMin, wMax, pOut, cnt, first, s);
      else {
        pOut[*cnt] = iPt;  (*cnt)++;
      }
    }

  s[b] = p;              /* Save 'p' as most recent point for this edge */

  /* For all, if point is 'inside' proceed to next clip edge, if any */
  if (inside (p, b, wMin, wMax))
    if (b < Top)
      clipPoint (p, b+1, wMin, wMax, pOut, cnt, first, s);
    else {
      pOut[*cnt] = p;  (*cnt)++;
    }
}

void closeClip (dcPt wMin, dcPt wMax, wcPt2 * pOut,
                int * cnt, wcPt2 * first[], wcPt2 * s)
{
  wcPt2 i;
  Edge b;

  for (b = Left; b <= Top; b++) {
    if (cross (s[b], *first[b], b, wMin, wMax)) {
      i = intersect (s[b], *first[b], b, wMin, wMax);
      if (b < Top)
        clipPoint (i, b+1, wMin, wMax, pOut, cnt, first, s);
      else {
        pOut[*cnt] = i;  (*cnt)++;
      }
    }
```

```
    }
}

int clipPolygon (dcPt wMin, dcPt wMax, int n, wcPt2 * pIn, wcPt2 * pOut)
{
  /* 'first' holds pointer to first point processed against a clip
     edge.  's' holds most recent point processed against an edge */
  wcPt2 * first[N_EDGE] = { 0, 0, 0, 0 }, s[N_EDGE];
  int i, cnt = 0;

  for (i=0; i<n; i++)
    clipPoint (pIn[i], Left, wMin, wMax, pOut, &cnt, first, s);
  closeClip (wMin, wMax, pOut, &cnt, first, s);
  return (cnt);
}
```

Convex polygons are correctly clipped by the Sutherland–Hodgeman algorithm, but concave polygons may be displayed with extraneous lines, as demonstrated in Fig. 6-24. This occurs when the clipped polygon should have two or more separate sections. But since there is only one output vertex list, the last vertex in the list is always joined to the first vertex. There are several things we could do to correctly display concave polygons. For one, we could split the concave polygon into two or more convex polygons and process each convex polygon separately. Another possibility is to modify the Sutherland–Hodgeman approach to check the final vertex list for multiple vertex points along any clip window boundary and correctly join pairs of vertices. Finally, we could use a more general polygon clipper, such as either the Weiler–Atherton algorithm or the Weiler algorithm described in the next section.

Weiler–Atherton Polygon Clipping

Here, the vertex-processing procedures for window boundaries are modified so that concave polygons are displayed correctly. This clipping procedure was developed as a method for identifying visible surfaces, and so it can be applied with arbitrary polygon-clipping regions.

The basic idea in this algorithm is that instead of always proceeding around the polygon edges as vertices are processed, we sometimes want to follow the window boundaries. Which path we follow depends on the polygon-processing direction (clockwise or counterclockwise) and whether the pair of polygon vertices currently being processed represents an outside-to-inside pair or an inside-

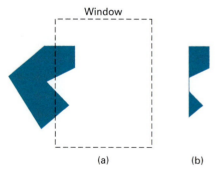

(a)   (b)

Figure 6-24
Clipping the concave polygon in (a) with the Sutherland–Hodgeman clipper produces the two connected areas in (b).

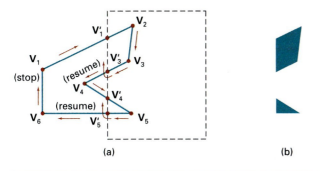

(a)   (b)

Figure 6-25
Clipping a concave polygon (a) with the Weiler–Atherton
algorithm generates the two separate polygon areas
in (b).

to-outside pair. For clockwise processing of polygon vertices, we use the following rules:

- For an outside-to-inside pair of vertices, follow the polygon boundary.
- For an inside-to-outside pair of vertices, follow the window boundary in a clockwise direction.

In Fig. 6-25, the processing direction in the Weiler–Atherton algorithm and the resulting clipped polygon is shown for a rectangular clipping window.

An improvement on the Weiler–Atherton algorithm is the Weiler algorithm, which applies constructive solid geometry ideas to clip an arbitrary polygon against any polygon-clipping region. Figure 6-26 illustrates the general idea in this approach. For the two polygons in this figure, the correctly clipped polygon is calculated as the intersection of the clipping polygon and the polygon object.

Other Polygon-Clipping Algorithms

Various parametric line-clipping methods have also been adapted to polygon clipping. And they are particularly well suited for clipping against convex polygon-clipping windows. The Liang–Barsky Line Clipper, for example, can be extended to polygon clipping with a general approach similar to that of the Sutherland–Hodgeman method. Parametric line representations are used to process polygon edges in order around the polygon perimeter using region-testing procedures similar to those used in line clipping.

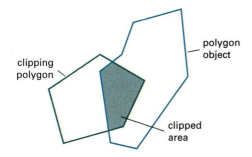

Figure 6-26
Clipping a polygon by determining
the intersection of two polygon
areas.

6-9

CURVE CLIPPING

Areas with curved boundaries can be clipped with methods similar to those discussed in the previous sections. Curve-clipping procedures will involve nonlinear equations, however, and this requires more processing than for objects with linear boundaries.

The bounding rectangle for a circle or other curved object can be used first to test for overlap with a rectangular clip window. If the bounding rectangle for the object is completely inside the window, we save the object. If the rectangle is determined to be completely outside the window, we discard the object. In either case, there is no further computation necessary. But if the bounding rectangle test fails, we can look for other computation-saving approaches. For a circle, we can use the coordinate extents of individual quadrants and then octants for preliminary testing before calculating curve-window intersections. For an ellipse, we can test the coordinate extents of individual quadrants. Figure 6-27 illustrates circle clipping against a rectangular window.

Similar procedures can be applied when clipping a curved object against a general polygon clip region. On the first pass, we can clip the bounding rectangle of the object against the bounding rectangle of the clip region. If the two regions overlap, we will need to solve the simultaneous line-curve equations to obtain the clipping intersection points.

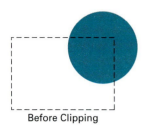

Before Clipping

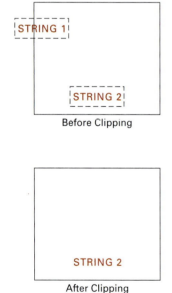

After Clipping

Figure 6-27
Clipping a filled circle.

6-10

TEXT CLIPPING

There are several techniques that can be used to provide text clipping in a graphics package. The clipping technique used will depend on the methods used to generate characters and the requirements of a particular application.

The simplest method for processing character strings relative to a window boundary is to use the *all-or-none string-clipping* strategy shown in Fig. 6-28. If all of the string is inside a clip window, we keep it. Otherwise, the string is discarded. This procedure is implemented by considering a bounding rectangle around the text pattern. The boundary positions of the rectangle are then compared to the window boundaries, and the string is rejected if there is any overlap. This method produces the fastest text clipping.

An alternative to rejecting an entire character string that overlaps a window boundary is to use the *all-or-none character-clipping* strategy. Here we discard only those characters that are not completely inside the window (Fig. 6-29). In this case, the boundary limits of individual characters are compared to the window. Any character that either overlaps or is outside a window boundary is clipped.

A final method for handling text clipping is to clip the components of individual characters. We now treat characters in much the same way that we treated lines. If an individual character overlaps a clip window boundary, we clip off the parts of the character that are outside the window (Fig. 6-30). Outline character fonts formed with line segments can be processed in this way using a line-clipping algorithm. Characters defined with bit maps would be clipped by comparing the relative position of the individual pixels in the character grid patterns to the clipping boundaries.

Before Clipping

After Clipping

Figure 6-28
Text clipping using a bounding rectangle about the entire string.

244

6-11

EXTERIOR CLIPPING

So far, we have considered only procedures for clipping a picture to the interior of a region by eliminating everything outside the clipping region. What is saved by these procedures is *inside* the region. In some cases, we want to do the reverse, that is, we want to clip a picture to the exterior of a specified region. The picture parts to be saved are those that are *outside* the region. This is referred to as **exterior clipping**.

A typical example of the application of exterior clipping is in multiple-window systems. To correctly display the screen windows, we often need to apply both internal and external clipping. Figure 6-31 illustrates a multiple-window display. Objects within a window are clipped to the interior of that window. When other higher-priority windows overlap these objects, the objects are also clipped to the exterior of the overlapping windows.

Exterior clipping is used also in other applications that require overlapping pictures. Examples here include the design of page layouts in advertising or publishing applications or for adding labels or design patterns to a picture. The technique can also be used for combining graphs, maps, or schematics. For these applications, we can use exterior clipping to provide a space for an insert into a larger picture.

Procedures for clipping objects to the interior of concave polygon windows can also make use of external clipping. Figure 6-32 shows a line $\overline{P_1P_2}$ that is to be clipped to the interior of a concave window with vertices $V_1V_2V_3V_4V_5$. Line $\overline{P_1P_2}$ can be clipped in two passes: (1) First, $\overline{P_1P_2}$ is clipped to the interior of the convex polygon $V_1V_2V_3V_4$ to yield the clipped segment $\overline{P_1'P_2'}$ (Fig. 6-32(b)). (2) Then an external clip of $\overline{P_1'P_2'}$ is performed against the convex polygon $V_1V_5V_4$ to yield the final clipped line segment $\overline{P_1''P_2'}$.

SUMMARY

In this chapter, we have seen how we can map a two-dimensional world-coordinate scene to a display device. The viewing-transformation pipeline in-

Figure 6-29
Text clipping using a bounding rectangle about individual characters.

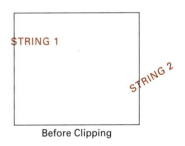
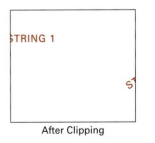

Figure 6-30
Text clipping performed on the components of individual characters.

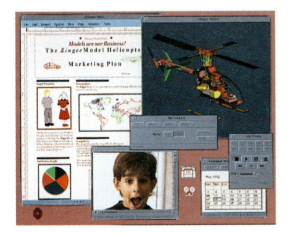

Figure 6-31
A multiple-window screen display showing examples of both interior and exterior clipping. (*Courtesy of Sun Microsystems*).

245

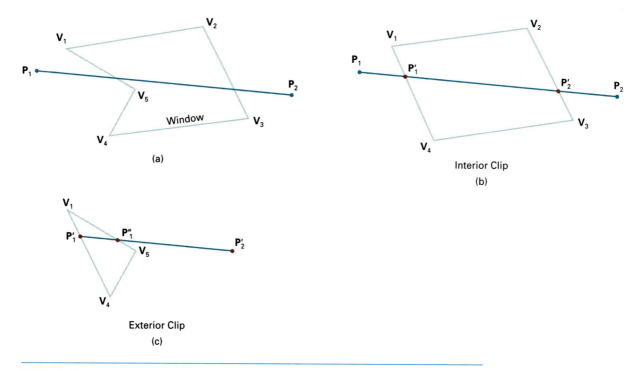

Figure 6-32
Clipping line $\overline{\mathbf{P_1P_2}}$ to the interior of a concave polygon with vertices $\mathbf{V_1V_2V_3V_4V_5}$ (a), using convex polygons $\mathbf{V_1V_2V_3V_4}$ (b) and $\mathbf{V_1V_5V_4}$ (c), to produce the clipped line $\overline{\mathbf{P_1''P_2'}}$.

cludes constructing the world-coordinate scene using modeling transformations, transferring world-coordinates to viewing coordinates, mapping the viewing-coordinate descriptions of objects to normalized device coordinates, and finally mapping to device coordinates. Normalized coordinates are specified in the range from 0 to 1, and they are used to make viewing packages independent of particular output devices.

Viewing coordinates are specified by giving the world-coordinate position of the viewing origin and the view up vector that defines the direction of the viewing *y* axis. These parameters are used to construct the viewing transformation matrix that maps world-coordinate object descriptions to viewing coordinates.

A window is then set up in viewing coordinates, and a viewport is specified in normalized device coordinates. Typically, the window and viewport are rectangles in standard position (rectangle boundaries are parallel to the coordinate axes). The mapping from viewing coordinates to normalized device coordinates is then carried out so that relative positions in the window are maintained in the viewport.

Viewing functions in a graphics programming package are used to create one or more sets of viewing parameters. One function is typically provided to calculate the elements of the matrix for transforming world coordinates to viewing coordinates. Another function is used to set up the window-to-viewport transformation matrix, and a third function can be used to specify combinations of viewing transformations and window mapping in a viewing table. We can then select different viewing combinations by specifying particular view indices listed in the viewing table.

When objects are displayed on the output device, all parts of a scene outside the window (and the viewport) are clipped off unless we set clip parameters to turn off clipping. In many packages, clipping is done in normalized device coordinates so that all transformations can be concatenated into a single transformation operation before applying the clipping algorithms. The clipping region is commonly referred to as the clipping window, or as the clipping rectangle when the window and viewport are standard rectangles. Several algorithms have been developed for clipping objects against the clip-window boundaries.

Line-clipping algorithms include the Cohen–Sutherland method, the Liang–Barsky method, and the Nicholl–Lee–Nicholl method. The Cohen–Sutherland method is widely used, since it was one of the first line-clipping algorithms to be developed. Region codes are used to identify the position of line endpoints relative to the rectangular, clipping window boundaries. Lines that cannot be immediately identified as completely inside the window or completely outside are then clipped against window boundaries. Liang and Barsky use a parametric line representation, similar to that of the earlier Cyrus–Beck algorithm, to set up a more efficient line-clipping procedure that reduces intersection calculations. The Nicholl–Lee–Nicholl algorithm uses more region testing in the xy plane to reduce intersection calculations even further. Parametric line clipping is easily extended to convex clipping windows and to three-dimensional clipping windows.

Line clipping can also be carried out for concave, polygon clipping windows and for clipping windows with curved boundaries. With concave polygons, we can use either the vector method or the rotational method to split a concave polygon into a number of convex polygons. With curved clipping windows, we calculate line intersections using the curve equations.

Polygon-clipping algorithms include the Sutherland–Hodgeman method, the Liang–Barsky method, and the Weiler–Atherton method. In the Sutherland–Hodgeman clipper, vertices of a convex polygon are processed in order against the four rectangular window boundaries to produce an output vertex list for the clipped polygon. Liang and Barsky use parametric line equations to represent the convex polygon edges, and they use similar testing to that performed in line clipping to produce an output vertex list for the clipped polygon. Both the Weiler–Atherland method and the Weiler method correctly clip both convex and concave polygons, and these polygon clippers also allow the clipping window to be a general polygon. The Weiler–Atherland algorithm processes polygon vertices in order to produce one or more lists of output polygon vertices. The Weiler method performs clipping by finding the intersection region of the two polygons.

Objects with curved boundaries are processed against rectangular clipping windows by calculating intersections using the curve equations. These clipping procedures are slower than line clippers or polygon clippers, because the curve equations are nonlinear.

The fastest text-clipping method is to completely clip a string if any part of the string is outside any window boundary. Another method for text clipping is to use the all-or-none approach with the individual characters in a string. A third method is to apply either point, line, polygon, or curve clipping to the individual characters in a string, depending on whether characters are defined as point grids or as outline fonts.

In some applications, such as creating picture insets and managing multiple-screen windows, exterior clipping is performed. In this case, all parts of a scene that are inside a window are clipped and the exterior parts are saved.

REFERENCES

Line-clipping algorithms are discussed in Sproull and Sutherland (1968), Cyrus and Beck (1978), and Liang and Barsky (1984). Methods for improving the speed of the Cohen–Sutherland line-clipping algorithm are given in Duvanenko (1990).

Polygon-clipping methods are presented in Sutherland and Hodgeman (1974) and in Liang and Barsky (1983). General techniques for clipping arbitrarily shaped polygons against each other are given in Weiler and Atherton (1977) and in Weiler (1980).

Two-dimensional viewing operations in PHIGS are discussed in Howard et al. (1991), Gaskins (1992), Hopgood and Duce (1991), and Blake (1993). For information on GKS viewing operations, see Hopgood et al. (1983) and Enderle et al. (1984).

EXERCISES

6-1. Write a procedure to to implement the `evaluateViewOrientationMatrix` function that calculates the elements of the matrix for transforming world coordinates to viewing coordinates, given the viewing coordinate origin P_0 and the view up vector V.

6-2. Derive the window-to-viewport transformation equations 6-3 by first scaling the window to the size of the viewport and then translating the scaled window to the viewport position.

6-3. Write a procedure to implement the `evaluateViewMappingMatrix` function that calculates the elements of a matrix for performing the window-to-viewport transformation.

6-4. Write a procedure to implement the `setViewRepresentation` function to concatenate `viewMatrix` and `viewMappingMatrix` and to store the result, referenced by a specified view index, in a viewing table.

6-5. Write a set of procedures to implement the viewing pipeline without clipping and without the workstation transformation. Your program should allow a scene to be constructed with modeling-coordinate transformations, a specified viewing system, and a specified window–viewport pair. As an option, a viewing table can be implemented to store different sets of viewing transformation parameters.

6-6. Derive the matrix representation for a workstation transformation.

6-7. Write a set of procedures to implement the viewing pipeline without clipping, but including the workstation transformation. Your program should allow a scene to be constructed with modeling-coordinate transformations, a specified viewing system, a specified window–viewport pair, and workstation transformation parameters. For a given world-coordinate scene, the composite viewing transformation matrix should transform the scene to an output device for display.

6-8. Implement the Cohen–Sutherland line-clipping algorithm.

6-9. Carefully discuss the rationale behind the various tests and methods for calculating the intersection parameters u_1 and u_2 in the Liang–Barsky line-clipping algorithm.

6-10. Compare the number of arithmetic operations performed in the Cohen–Sutherland and the Liang–Barsky line-clipping algorithms for several different line orientations relative to a clipping window.

6-11. Write a procedure to implement the Liang–Barsky line-clipping algorithm.

6-12. Devise symmetry transformations for mapping the intersection calculations for the three regions in Fig. 6-10 to the other six regions of the xy plane.

6-13. Set up a detailed algorithm for the Nicholl–Lee–Nicholl approach to line clipping for any input pair of line endpoints.

6-14. Compare the number of arithmetic operations performed in NLN algorithm to both the Cohen–Sutherland and the Liang–Barsky line-clipping algorithms for several different line orientations relative to a clipping window.

6-15. Write a routine to identify concave polygons by calculating cross products of pairs of edge vectors.

6-16. Write a routine to split a concave polygon using the vector method.

6-17. Write a routine to split a concave polygon using the rotational method.

6-18. Adapt the Liang–Barsky line-clipping algorithm to polygon clipping.

6-19. Set up a detailed algorithm for Weiler–Atherton polygon clipping assuming that the clipping window is a rectangle in standard position.

6-20. Devise an algorithm for Weiler–Atherton polygon clipping, where the clipping window can be any specified polygon.

6-21. Write a routine to clip an ellipse against a rectangular window.

6-22. Assuming that all characters in a text string have the same width, develop a text-clipping algorithm that clips a string according to the "all-or-none character-clipping" strategy.

6-23. Develop a text-clipping algorithm that clips individual characters assuming that the characters are defined in a pixel grid of a specified size.

6-24. Write a routine to implement exterior clipping on any part of a defined picture using any specified window.

6-25. Write a routine to perform both interior and exterior clipping, given a particular window-system display. Input to the routine is a set of window positions on the screen, the objects to be displayed in each window, and the window priorities. The individual objects are to be clipped to fit into their respective windows, then clipped to remove parts with overlapping windows of higher display priority.

7

Structures and Hierarchical Modeling

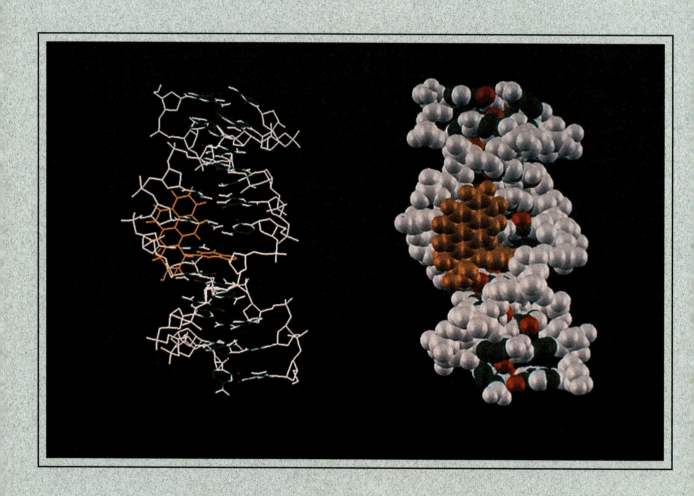

For a great many applications, it is convenient to be able to create and manipulate individual parts of a picture without affecting other picture parts. Most graphics packages provide this capability in one form or another. With the ability to define each object in a picture as a separate module, we can make modifications to the picture more easily. In design applications, we can try out different positions and orientations for a component of a picture without disturbing other parts of the picture. Or we can take out parts of the picture, then we can easily put the parts back into the display at a later time. Similarly, in modeling applications, we can separately create and position the subparts of a complex object or system into the overall hierarchy. And in animations, we can apply transformations to individual parts of the scene so that one object can be animated with one type of motion, while other objects in the scene move differently or remain stationary.

7-1
STRUCTURE CONCEPTS

A labeled set of output primitives (and associated attributes) in PHIGS is called a **structure**. Other commonly used names for a labeled collection of primitives are *segments* (GKS) and *objects* (Graphics Library on Silicon Graphics systems). In this section, we consider the basic structure-managing functions in PHIGS. Similar operations are available in other packages for handling labeled groups of primitives in a picture.

Basic Structure Functions

When we create a structure, the coordinate positions and attribute values specified for the structure are stored as a labeled group in a system structure list called the **central structure store**. We create a structure with the function

```
openStructure (id)
```

The label for the segment is the positive integer assigned to parameter id. In PHIGS+, we can use character strings to label the structures instead of using integer names. This makes it easier to remember the structure identifiers. After all primitives and attributes have been listed, the end of the structure is signaled with the closeStructure statement. For example, the following program statements define structure 6 as the line sequence specified in polyline with the designated line type and color:

```
openStructure (6);
    setLinetype (lt);
    setPolylineColourIndex (lc);
    polyline (n, pts);
closeStructure;
```

Any number of structures can be created for a picture, but only one structure can be open (in the creation process) at a time. Any open structure must be closed before a new structure can be created. This requirement eliminates the need for a structure identification number in the `closeStructure` statement.

Once a structure has been created, it can be displayed on a selected output device with the function

```
postStructure (ws, id, priority)
```

where parameter `ws` is the workstation identifier, `id` is the structure name, and `priority` is assigned a real value in the range from 0 to 1. Parameter `priority` sets the display priority relative to other structures. When two structures overlap on an output display device, the structure with the higher priority will be visible. For example, if structures 6 and 9 are posted to workstation 2 with the following priorities

```
postStructure (2, 6, 0.8)
postStructure (2, 9, 0.1)
```

then any parts of structure 9 that overlap structure 6 will be hidden, since structure 6 has higher priority. If two structures are assigned the same priority value, the last structure to be posted is given display precedence.

When a structure is posted to an active workstation, the primitives in the structure are scanned and interpreted for display on the selected output device (video monitor, laser printer, etc.). Scanning a structure list and sending the graphical output to a workstation is called **traversal**. A list of current attribute values for primitives is stored in a data structure called a **traversal state list**. As changes are made to posted structures, both the system structure list and the traversal state list are updated. This automatically modifies the display of the posted structures on the workstation.

To remove the display of a structure from a particular output device, we invoke the function

```
unpostStructure (ws, id)
```

This deletes the structure from the active list of structures for the designated output device, but the system structure list is not affected. On a raster system, a structure is removed from the display by redrawing the primitives in the background color. This process, however, may also affect the display of primitives from other structures that overlap the structure we want to erase. To remedy this, we can use the coordinate extents of the various structures in a scene to determine which ones overlap the structure we are erasing. Then we can simply re-draw these overlapping structures after we have erased the structure that is to be unposted. All structures can be removed from a selected output device with

```
unpostAllStructures (ws)
```

If we want to remove a particular structure from the system structure list, we accomplish that with the function

```
deleteStructure (id)
```

Of course, this also removes the display of the structure from all posted output devices. Once a structure has been deleted, its name can be reused for another set of primitives. The entire system structure list can be cleared with

```
deleteAllStructures
```

It is sometimes useful to be able to relabel a structure. This is accomplished with

```
changeStructureIdentifier (oldID, newID)
```

One reason for changing a structure label is to consolidate the numbering of the structures after several structures have been deleted. Another is to cycle through a set of structure labels while displaying a structure in multiple locations to test the structure positioning.

Setting Structure Attributes

We can set certain display characteristics for structures with **workstation filters**. The three properties we can set with filters are visibility, highlighting, and the capability of a structure to be selected with an interactive input device.

Visibility and invisibility settings for structures on a particular workstation for a selected device are specified with the function

```
setInvisibilityFilter (ws, devCode, invisSet, visSet)
```

where parameter `invisSet` contains the names of structures that will be invisible, and parameter `visSet` contains the names of those that will be visible. With the invisibility filter, we can turn the display of structures on and off at selected workstations without actually deleting them from the workstation lists. This allows us, for example, to view the outline of a building without all the interior details; and then to reset the visibility so that we can view the building with all internal features included. Additional parameters that we can specify are the number of structures for each of the two sets. Structures are made invisible on a raster monitor using the same procedures that we discussed for unposting and for deleting a structure. The difference, however, is that we do not remove the structure from the active structure list for a device when we are simply making it invisible.

Highlighting is another convenient structure characteristic. In a map display, we could highlight all cities with populations below a certain value; or for a

253

landscape layout, we could highlight certain varieties of shrubbery; or in a circuit diagram, we could highlight all components within a specific voltage range. This is done with the function

```
setHighlightingFilter (ws, devCode, highlightSet,
                       nohighlightSet)
```

Parameter `highlightSet` contains the names of the structures that are to be highlighted, and parameter `nohighlightSet` contains the names of those that are not to be highlighted. The kind of highlighting used to accent structures depends on the type and capabilities of the graphics system. For a color video monitor, highlighted structures could be displayed in a brighter intensity or in a color reserved for highlighting. Another common highlighting implementation is to turn the visibility on and off rapidly so that blinking structures are displayed. Blinking can also be accomplished by rapidly alternating the intensity of the highlighted structures between a low value and a high value.

The third display characteristic we can set for structures is *pickability*. This refers to the capability of the structure to be selected by pointing at it or positioning the screen cursor over it. If we want to be sure that certain structures in a display can never be selected, we can declare them to be nonpickable with the pickability filter. In the next chapter, we take up the topic of input methods in more detail.

7-2
EDITING STRUCTURES

Often, we would like to modify a structure after it has been created and closed. Structure modification is needed in design applications to try out different graphical arrangements, or to change the design configuration in response to new test data.

If additional primitives are to be added to a structure, this can be done by simply reopening the structure with the `openStructure` function and appending the required statements. As an example of simple appending, the following program segment first creates a structure with a single fill area and then adds a second fill area to the structure:

```
openStructure (shape);
    setInteriorStyle (solid);
    setInteriorColourIndex (4);
    fillArea (n1, verts1);
closeStructure;
            .
            .
            .
openStructure (shape);
    setInteriorStyle (hollow);
    fillArea (n2, verts2);
closeStructure;
```

This sequence of operations is equivalent to initially creating the structure with both fill areas:

```
openStructure (shape);
     setInteriorStyle (solid);
     setInteriorColourIndex (4);
     fillArea (n1, verts1);
     setInteriorStyle (hollow);
     fillArea (n2, verts2);
closeStructure;
```

In addition to appending, we may also want sometimes to delete certain items in a structure, to change primitives or attribute settings, or to insert items at selected positions within the structure. General editing operations are carried out by accessing the sequence numbers for the individual components of a structure and setting the edit mode.

Structure Lists and the Element Pointer

Individual items in a structure, such as output primitives and attribute values, are referred to as **structure elements**, or simply **elements**. Each element is assigned a reference position value as it is entered into the structure. Figure 7-1 shows the storage of structure elements and associated position numbers created by the following program segment.

```
openStructure (gizmo);
     setLinetype (lt1);
     setPolylineColourIndex (lc1);
     polyline (n1, pts1);
     setLinetype (lt2);
     setPolylineColourIndex (lc2);
     polyline (n2, pts2);
closeStructure;
```

Structure elements are numbered consecutively with integer values starting at 1, and the value 0 indicates the position just before the first element. When a structure is opened, an **element pointer** is set up and assigned a position value that can be used to edit the structure. If the opened structure is new (not already existing in the system structure list), the element pointer is set to 0. If the opened structure does already exist in the system list, the element pointer is set to the position value of the last element in the structure. As elements are added to a structure, the element pointer is incremented by 1.

We can set the value of the element pointer to any position within a structure with the function

```
setElementPointer (k)
```

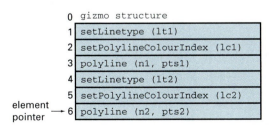

Figure 7-1
Element position values for structure gizmo.

255

where parameter k can be assigned any integer value from 0 to the maximum number of elements in the structure. It is also possible to position the element pointer using the following offset function that moves the pointer relative to the current position:

```
offsetElementPointer (dk)
```

with dk assigned a positive or negative integer offset from the present position of the pointer. Once we have positioned the element pointer, we can edit the structure at that position.

Setting the Edit Mode

Structures can be modified in one of two possible modes. This is referred to as the **edit mode** of the structure. We set the value of the edit mode with

```
setEditMode (mode)
```

where parameter mode is assigned either the value *insert*, or the value *replace*.

Inserting Structure Elements

When the edit mode is set to *insert*, the next item entered into a structure will be placed in the position immediately following the element pointer. Elements in the structure list following the inserted item are then automatically renumbered.

To illustrate the insertion operation, let's change the standard line width currently in structure gizmo (Fig. 7-2) to some other value. We can do this by inserting a line width statement anywhere before the first polyline command:

```
openStructure (gizmo);
    setEditMode (insert);
    setElementPointer (0);
    setLinewidth (lw);
            .
            .
            .
closeStructure;
```

Figure 7-2 shows the modified element list of gizmo, created by the previous insert operation. After this insert, the element pointer is assigned the value 1 (the position of the new line-width attribute). Also, all elements after the line-width statement have been renumbered, starting at the value 2.

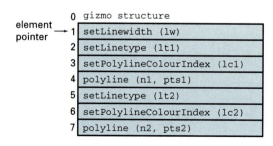

Figure 7-2
Modified element list and position of the element pointer after inserting a line-width attribute into structure gizmo.

When a new structure is created, the edit mode is automatically set to the value *insert*. Assuming the edit mode has not been changed from this default value before we reopen this structure, we can append items at the end of the element list without setting values for either the edit mode or element pointer, as demonstrated at the beginning of Section 7-2. This is because the edit mode remains at the value *insert* and the element pointer for the reopened structure points to the last element in the list.

Replacing Structure Elements

When the edit mode is set to the value *replace*, the next item entered into a structure is placed at the position of the element pointer. The element originally at that position is deleted, and the value of the element pointer remains unchanged.

As an example of the replace operation, suppose we want to change the color of the second polyline in structure gizmo (Fig. 7-1). We can do this with the sequence:

```
openStructure (gizmo);
    setEditMode (replace);
    setElementPointer (5);
    setPolylineColourIndex (lc2New);
        .
        .
        .
closeStructure;
```

Figure 7-3 shows the element list of gizmo with the new color for the second polyline. After the replace operation, the element pointer remains at position 5 (the position of the new line color attribute).

Deleting Structure Elements

We can delete the element at the current position of the element pointer with the function

```
deleteElement
```

This removes the element from the structure and sets the value of the element pointer to the immediately preceding element.

As an example of element deletion, suppose we decide to have both polylines in structure gizmo (Fig. 7-1) displayed in the same color. We can accomplish this by deleting the second color attribute:

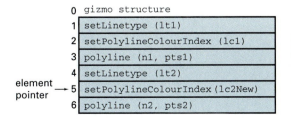

Figure 7-3

Modified element list and position of the element pointer after changing the color of the second polyline in structure gizmo.

```
openStructure (gizmo);
    setElementPointer (5);
    deleteElement;
            .
            .
            .
closeStructure;
```

The element pointer is then reset to the value 4 and all following elements are renumbered, as shown in Fig. 7-4.

A contiguous group of structure elements can be deleted with the function

```
deleteElementRange (k1, k2)
```

where integer parameter `k1` gives the beginning position number, and `k2` specifies the ending position number. For example, we can delete the second polyline and associated attributes in structure `gizmo` with

```
deleteElementRange (4, 6)
```

And all elements in a structure can be deleted with the function

```
emptyStructure (id)
```

Labeling Structure Elements

Once we have made a number of modifications to a structure, we could easily lose track of the element positions. Deleting and inserting elements shift the element position numbers. To avoid having to keep track of new position numbers as modifications are made, we can simply label the different elements in a structure with the function

```
label (k)
```

where parameter `k` is an integer position identifier. Labels can be inserted anywhere within the structure list as an aid to locating structure elements without referring to position number. The label function creates structure elements that have no effect on the structure traversal process. We simply use the labels stored in the structure as editing references rather than using the individual element positions. Also, the labeling of structure elements need not be unique. Sometimes it is convenient to give two or more elements the same label value, particularly if the same editing operations are likely to be applied to several positions in the structure.

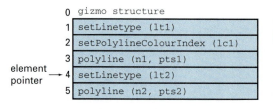

Figure 7-4
Modified element list and position of the element pointer after deleting the color-attribute statement for the second polyline in structure `gizmo`.

To illustrate the use of labeling, we create structure `labeledGizmo` in the following routine that has the elements and position numbers as shown in Fig. 7-5.

```
openStructure (labeledGizmo);
     label (object1Linetype);
     setLinetype (lt1);
     label (object1Color);
     setPolylineColourIndex (lc1);
     label (object1);
     polyline (n1, pts1);
     label (object2Linetype);
     setLinetype (lt2);
     label (object2Color);
     setPolylineColourIndex (lc2);
     label (object2);
     polyline (n2, pts2);
closeStructure;
```

Now if we want to change any of the primitives or attributes in this structure, we can do it by referencing the labels. Although we have labeled every item in this structure, other labeling schemes could be used depending on what type and how much editing is anticipated. For example, all attributes could be lumped under one label, or all color attributes could be given the same label identifier.

A label is referenced with the function

```
setElementPointerAtLabel (k)
```

which sets the element pointer to the value of parameter k. The search for the label begins at the current element-pointer position and proceeds forward through the element list. This means that we may have to reset the pointer when reopening a structure, since the pointer is always positioned at the last element in a reopened structure, and label searching is not done backward through the element list. If, for instance, we want to change the color of the second object in structure `labeledGizmo`, we could reposition the pointer at the start of the element list after reopening the structure to search for the appropriate color attribute statement label:

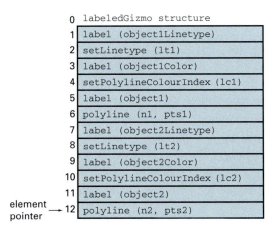

Figure 7-5

A set of labeled objects and associated position numbers stored in structure `labeledGizmo`.

```
openStructure (labeledGizmo);
    setElementPointer (0);
    setEditMode (replace);
    setElementPointerAtLabel (object2Color);
    offsetElementPointer (1);
    setPolylineColourIndex (lc2New);
        .
        .
        .
closeStructure;
```

Deleting an item referenced with a label is similar to the replacement operation illustrated in the last openStructure routine. We first locate the appropriate label and then offset the pointer. For example, the color attribute for the second polyline in structure labeledGizmo can be deleted with the sequence

```
openStructure (labeledGizmo);
    setElementPointer (0);
    setEditMode (replace);
    setElementPointerAtLabel (object2Color);
    offsetElementPointer (1);
    deleteElement;
        .
        .
        .
closeStructure;
```

We can also delete a group of structure elements between specified labels with the function

```
deleteElementsBetweenLabels (k1, k2)
```

After the set of elements is deleted, the element pointer is set to position k1.

Copying Elements from One Structure to Another

We can copy all the entries from a specified structure into an open structure with

```
copyAllElementsFromStructure (id)
```

The elements from structure id are inserted into the open structure starting at the position immediately following the element pointer, regardless of the setting of the edit mode. When the copy operation is complete, the element pointer is set to the position of the last item inserted into the open structure.

7-3
BASIC MODELING CONCEPTS

An important use of structures is in the design and representation of different types of systems. Architectural and engineering systems, such as building layouts and electronic circuit schematics, are commonly put together using computer-aided design methods. Graphical methods are used also for representing economic, financial, organizational, scientific, social, and environmental systems. Representations for these systems are often constructed to simulate the behavior of a system under various conditions. The outcome of the simulation can serve as an instructional tool or as a basis for making decisions about the system. To be effective in these various applications, a graphics package must possess efficient methods for constructing and manipulating the graphical system representations.

The creation and manipulation of a system representation is termed **modeling**. Any single representation is called a **model** of the system. Models for a system can be defined graphically, or they can be purely descriptive, such as a set of equations that defines the relationships between system parameters. Graphical models are often referred to as **geometric models**, because the component parts of a system are represented with geometric entities such as lines, polygons, or circles. We are concerned here only with graphics applications, so we will use the term model to mean a computer-generated geometric representation of a system.

Model Representations

Figure 7-6 shows a representation for a logic circuit, illustrating the features common to many system models. Component parts of the system are displayed as geometric structures, called **symbols**, and relationships between the symbols are represented in this example with a network of connecting lines. Three standard symbols are used to represent logic gates for the Boolean operations: *and*, *or*, and *not*. The connecting lines define relationships in terms of input and output flow (from left to right) through the system parts. One symbol, the *and* gate, is displayed at two different positions within the logic circuit. Repeated positioning of a few basic symbols is a common method for building complex models. Each such occurrence of a symbol within a model is called an **instance** of that symbol. We have one instance for the *or* and *not* symbols in Fig. 7-6 and two instances of the *and* symbol.

In many cases, the particular graphical symbols chosen to represent the parts of a system are dictated by the system description. For circuit models, standard electrical or logic symbols are used. With models representing abstract concepts, such as political, financial, or economic systems, symbols may be any convenient geometric pattern.

Information describing a model is usually provided as a combination of geometric and nongeometric data. Geometric information includes coordinate positions for locating the component parts, output primitives and attribute functions to define the structure of the parts, and data for constructing connections between the parts. Nongeometric information includes text labels, algorithms describing the operating characteristics of the model, and rules for determining the relationships or connections between component parts, if these are not specified as geometric data.

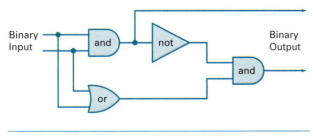

Figure 7-6
Model of a logic circuit.

261

There are two methods for specifying the information needed to construct and manipulate a model. One method is to store the infomation in a data structure, such as a table or linked list. The other method is to specify the information in procedures. In general, a model specification will contain both data structures and procedures, although some models are defined completely with data structures and others use only procedural specifications. An application to perform solid modeling of objects might use mostly information taken from some data structure to define coordinate positions, with very few procedures. A weather model, on the other hand, may need mostly procedures to calculate plots of temperature and pressure variations.

As an example of how combinations of data structures and procedures can be used, we consider some alternative model specifications for the logic circuit of Fig. 7-6. One method is to define the logic components in a data table (Table 7-1), with processing procedures used to specify how the network connections are to be made and how the circuit operates. Geometric data in this table include coordinates and parameters necessary for drawing and positioning the gates. These symbols could all be drawn as polygon shapes, or they could be formed as combinations of straight-line segments and elliptical arcs. Labels for each of the component parts also have been included in the table, although the labels could be omitted if the symbols are displayed as commonly recognized shapes. Procedures would then be used to display the gates and construct the connecting lines, based on the coordinate positions of the gates and a specified order for connecting them. An additional procedure is used to produce the circuit output (binary values) for any given input. This procedure could be set up to display only the final output, or it could be designed to display intermediate output values to illustrate the internal functioning of the circuit.

Alternatively, we might specify graphical information for the circuit model in data structures. The connecting lines, as well as the gates, could then be defined in a data table that explicitly lists endpoints for each of the lines in the circuit. A single procedure might then display the circuit and calculate the output. At the other extreme, we could completely define the model in procedures, using no external data structures.

Symbol Hierarchies

Many models can be organized as a hierarchy of symbols. The basic "building blocks" for the model are defined as simple geometric shapes appropriate to the type of model under consideration. These basic symbols can be used to form composite objects, called **modules**, which themselves can be grouped to form higher-level modules, and so on, for the various components of the model. In the

TABLE 7-1

A DATA TABLE DEFINING THE STRUCTURE AND
POSITION OF EACH GATE IN THE CIRCUIT OF FIG. 7-6

Symbol Code	Geometric Description	Identifying Label
Gate 1	(Coordinates and other parameters)	and
Gate 2	⋮	or
Gate 3	⋮	not
Gate 4	⋮	and

simplest case, we can describe a model by a one-level hierarchy of component parts, as in Fig. 7-7. For this circuit example, we assume that the gates are positioned and connected to each other with straight lines according to connection rules that are specified with each gate description. The basic symbols in this hierarchical description are the logic gates. Although the gates themselves could be described as hierarchies—formed from straight lines, elliptical arcs, and text— that sort of description would not be a convenient one for constructing logic circuits, in which the simplest building blocks are gates. For an application in which we were interested in designing different geometric shapes, the basic symbols could be defined as straight-line segments and arcs.

An example of a two-level symbol hierarchy appears in Fig. 7-8. Here a facility layout is planned as an arrangement of work areas. Each work area is outfitted with a collection of furniture. The basic symbols are the furniture items: worktable, chair, shelves, file cabinet, and so forth. Higher-order objects are the work areas, which are put together with different furniture organizations. An instance of a basic symbol is defined by specifying its size, position, and orientation within each work area. For a facility-layout package with fixed sizes for objects, only position and orientation need be specified by a user. Positions are given as coordinate locations in the work areas, and orientations are specified as rotations that determine which way the symbols are facing. At the second level up the hierarchy, each work area is defined by specifying its size, position, and orientation within the facility layout. The boundary for each work area might be fitted with a divider that encloses the work area and provides aisles within the facility.

More complex symbol hierarchies are formed by repeated grouping of symbol clusters at each higher level. The facility layout of Fig. 7-8 could be extended to include symbol clusters that form different rooms, different floors of a building, different buildings within a complex, and different complexes at widely separated physical locations.

Modeling Packages

Some general-purpose graphics systems, GKS, for example, are not designed to accommodate extensive modeling applications. Routines necessary to handle modeling procedures and data structures are often set up as separate modeling packages, and graphics packages then can be adapted to interface with the modeling package. The purpose of graphics routines is to provide methods for gener-

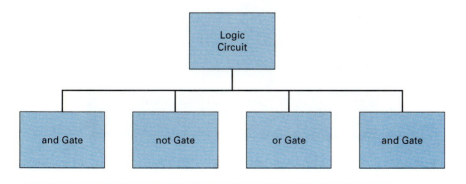

Figure 7-7
A one-level hierarchical description of a circuit formed with logic gates.

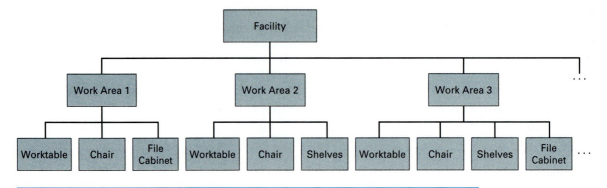

Figure 7-8

A two-level hierarchical description of a facility layout.

ating and manipulating final output displays. Modeling routines, by contrast, provide a means for defining and rearranging model representations in terms of symbol hierarchies, which are then processed by the graphics routines for display. Systems, such as PHIGS and Graphics Library (GL) on Silicon Graphics equipment, are designed so that modeling and graphics functions are integrated into one package.

Symbols available in an application modeling package are defined and structured according to the type of application the package has been designed to handle. Modeling packages can be designed for either two-dimensional or three-dimensional displays. Figure 7-9 illustrates a two-dimensional layout used in circuit design. An example of three-dimensional molecular modeling is shown in Fig. 7-10, and a three-dimensional facility layout is given in Fig. 7-11. Such three-dimensional displays give a designer a better appreciation of the appearance of a layout. In the following sections, we explore the characteristic features of modeling packages and the methods for interfacing or integrating modeling functions with graphics routines.

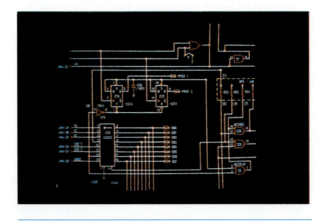

Figure 7-9
Two-dimensional modeling layout used in circuit design. *(Courtesy of Summagraphics)*

264

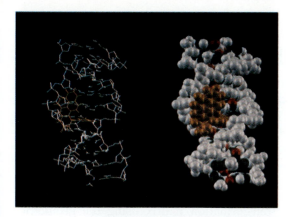

Figure 7-10
One-half of a stereoscopic image
pair showing a three-dimensional
molecular model of DNA. Data
supplied by Tamar Schlick, NYU,
and Wilma K. Olson, Rutgers
University; visualization by Jerry
Greenberg, SDSC. (*Courtesy of
Stephanie Sides, San Diego Supercomputer
Center.*)

Figure 7-11
A three-dimensional view of an office layout. *Courtesy of
Intergraph Corporation.*

7-4
HIERARCHICAL MODELING WITH STRUCTURES

A hierarchical model of a system can be created with structures by nesting the
structures into one another to form a tree organization. As each structure is
placed into the hierarchy, it is assigned an appropriate transformation so that it
will fit properly into the overall model. One can think of setting up an office facility in which furniture is placed into the various offices and work areas, which in
turn are placed into departments, and so forth on up the hierarchy.

Local Coordinates and Modeling Transformations

In many design applications, models are constructed with instances (transformed
copies) of the geometric shapes that are defined in a basic symbol set. Instances
are created by positioning the basic symbols within the world-coordinate reference of the model. The various graphical symbols to be used in an application are
each defined in an independent coordinate reference called the **modeling-coordinate system**. Modeling coordinates are also referred to as **local coordinates**, or
sometimes **master coordinates**. Figure 7-12 illustrates local coordinate definitions

for two symbols that could be used in a two-dimensional facility-layout application.

To construct the component parts of a graphical model, we apply transformations to the local-coordinate definitions of symbols to produce instances of the symbols in world coordinates. Transformations applied to the modeling-coordinate definitions of symbols are referred to as **modeling transformations**. Typically, modeling transformations involve translation, rotation, and scaling to position a symbol in world coordinates, but other transformations might also be used in some applications.

Modeling Transformations

We obtain a particular modeling-transformation matrix using the geometric-transformation functions discussed in Chapter 5. That is, we can set up the individual transformation matrices to accomplish the modeling transformation, or we can input the transformation parameters and allow the system to build the matrices. In either case, the modeling package concatenates the individual transformations to construct a homogeneous-coordinate modeling transformation matrix, **MT**. An instance of a symbol in world coordinates is then produced by applying **MT** to modeling-coordinate positions ($\mathbf{P}_{mc}$) to generate corresponding world-coordinate positions ($\mathbf{P}_{wc}$):

$$\mathbf{P}_{wc} = \mathbf{MT} \cdot \mathbf{P}_{mc} \qquad (7\text{-}1)$$

Structure Hierarchies

As we have seen, modeling applications typically require the composition of basic symbols into groups, called modules; these modules may be combined into

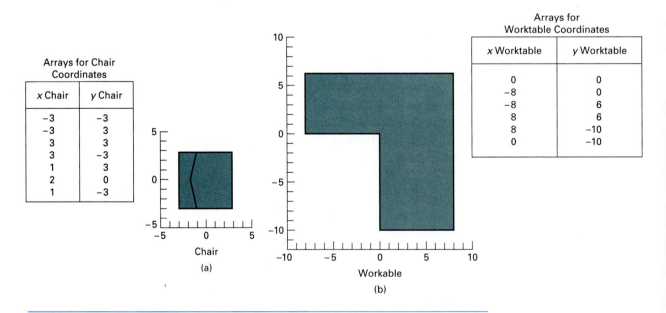

Arrays for Chair
Coordinates

x Chair	y Chair
-3	-3
-3	3
3	3
3	-3
1	3
2	0
1	-3

Chair

(a)

Arrays for
Worktable Coordinates

x Worktable	y Worktable
0	0
-8	0
-8	6
8	6
8	-10
0	-10

Workable

(b)

Figure 7-12
Objects defined in local coordinates.

higher-level modules; and so on. Such symbol hierarchies can be created by embedding structures within structures at each successive level in the tree. We can first define a module (structure) as a list of symbol instances and their transformation parameters. At the next level, we define each higher-level module as a list of the lower-module instances and their transformation parameters. This process is continued up to the root of the tree, which represents the total picture in world coordinates.

A structure is placed within another structure with the function

```
executeStructure (id)
```

To properly orient the structure, we first assign the appropriate local transformation to structure `id`. This is done with

```
setLocalTransformation (mlt, type)
```

where parameter `mlt` specifies the transformation matrix. Parameter `type` is assigned one of the following three values: *pre, post,* or *replace,* to indicate the type of matrix composition to be performed with the current modeling-transformation matrix. If we simply want to replace the current transformation matrix with `lmt`, we set parameter `type` to the value *replace.* If we want the current matrix to be premultipled with the local matrix we are specifying in this function, we choose *pre*; and similarly for the value *post.* The following code section illustrates a sequence of modeling statements to set the first instance of an object into the hierarchy below the root node.

```
createStructure (id0);
    setLocalTransformation (lmt, type);
    executeStructure (id1);
        .
        .
        .
closeStructure;
```

The same procedure is used to instance other objects within structure `id0` to set the other nodes into this level of the hierarchy. Then we can create the next level down the tree by instancing objects within structure `id1` and the other structures that are in `id0`. We repeat this process until the tree is complete. The entire tree is then displayed by posting the root node: structure `id0` in the previous example. In the following procedure, we illustrate how a hierarchical structure can be used to model an object.

```
void main ()
{
  enum { Frame, Wheel, Bicycle };
  int nPts;
  wcPt2 pts[256];
  pMatrix3 m;
  /* Routines to generate geometry */
  extern void getWheelVertices (int * nPts, wcPt2 pts);
  extern void getFrameVertices (int * nPts, wcPt2 pts);

  /* Make the wheel structure */
```

```
    getWheelVertices (nPts, pts);
    openStructure (Wheel);
    setLineWidth (2.0);
    polyline (nPts, pts);
    closeStructure;
    /* Make the frame structure */
    getFrameVertices (nPts, pts);
    openStructure (Frame);
    setLineWidth (2.0);
    polyline (nPts, pts);
    closeStructure;

    /* Make the bicycle */
    openStructure (Bicycle);
    /* Include the frame */
    executeStructure (Frame);
    /* Position and include rear wheel */
    matrixSetIdentity (m);
    m[0,2] := -1.0; m[1,2] := -0.5;
    setLocalTransformationMatrix (m, REPLACE);
    executeStructure (Wheel);
    /* Position and include front wheel */
    m[0,2] :=  1.0; m[1,2] := -0.5;
    setLocalTransformationmatrix (m, REPLACE);
    executeStructure (Wheel);
    closeStructure;
}
```

We delete a hierarchy with the function

```
deleteStructureNetwork (id)
```

where parameter `id` references the root structure of the tree. This deletes the root node of the hierarchy and all structures that have been placed below the root using the `executeStructure` function, assuming that the hierarchy is organized as a tree.

SUMMARY

A structure (also called a segment or an object in some systems) is a labeled group of output statements and associated attributes. By designing pictures as sets of structures, we can easily add, delete, or manipulate picture components independently of each another. As structures are created, they are entered into a central structure store. Structures are then displayed by posting them to various output devices with assigned priorities. When two structures overlap, the structure with the higher priority is displayed over the structure with the lower priority.

We can use workstation filters to set attributes, such as visibility and highlighting, for structures. With the visibility filter, we can turn off the display of a structure while retaining it in the structure list. The highlighting filter is used to emphasize a displayed structure with blinking, color, or high-intensity patterns.

Various editing operations can be applied to structures. We can reopen structures to carry out append, insert, or delete operations. Locations in a structure are referenced with the element pointer. In addition, we individually label the primitives or attributes in a structure.

The term model, in graphics applications, refers to a graphical representation for some system. Components of the system are represented as symbols, defined in local (modeling) coordinate reference frames. Many models, such as electrical circuits, are constructed by placing instances of the symbols at selected locations.

Many models are constructed as symbol hierarchies. A bicycle, for instance, can be constructed with a bicycle frame and the wheels. The frame can include such parts as the handlebars and the pedals. And the wheels contain spokes, rims, and tires. We can construct a hierarchial model by nesting structures. For example, we can set up a bike structure that contains a frame structure and a wheel structure. Both the frame and wheel structures can then contain primitives and additional structures. We continue this nesting down to structures that contain only output primitives (and attributes).

As each structure is nested within another structure, an associated modeling transformation can be set for the nested structure. This transformation describes the operations necessary to properly orient and scale the structure to fit into the hierarchy.

REFERENCES

Structure operations and hierarchical modeling in PHIGS are discussed in Hopgood and Duce (1991), Howard et al. (1991), Gaskins (1992), and Blake (1993).
For information on GKS segment operations see Hopgood (1983) and Enderle et al. (1984).

EXERCISES

7-1. Write a procedure for creating and manipulating the information in a central structure store. This procedure is to be invoked by functions such as `openStructure`, `deleteStructure`, and `changeStructureIdentifier`.

7-2. Write a routine for storing information in a traversal state list.

7-3. Write a routine for erasing a specified structure on a raster system, given the coordinate extents for all displayed structures in a scene.

7-4. Write a procedure to implement the `unpostStructure` function on a raster system.

7-5. Write a procedure to implement the `deleteStructure` function on a raster system.

7-6. Write a procedure to implement highlighting as a blinking operation.

7-7. Write a set of routines for editing structures. Your routines should provide for the following types of editing: appending, inserting, replacing, and deleting structure elements.

7-8. Discuss model representations that would be appropriate for several distinctly different kinds of systems. Also discuss how graphical representations might be implemented for each system.

7-9. For a logic-circuit modeling application, such as that in Fig. 7-6, give a detailed graphical description of the standard logic symbols to be used in constructing a display of a circuit.

7-10. Develop a modeling package for electrical design that will allow a user to position electrical symbols within a circuit network. Only translations need be applied to place an instance of one of the electrical menu shapes into the network. Once a component has been placed in the network, it is to be connected to other specified components with straight line segments.

7-11. Devise a two-dimensional facility-layout package. A menu of furniture shapes is to be provided to a designer, who can place the objects in any location within a single room (one-level hierarchy). Instance transformations can be limited to translations and rotations.

7-12. Devise a two-dimensional facility-layout package that presents a menu of furniture shapes. A two-level hierarchy is to be used so that furniture items can be placed into various work areas, and the work areas can be arranged within a larger area. Instance transformations may be limited to translations and rotations, but scaling could be used if furniture items of different sizes are to be available.

CHAPTER

8

Graphical User Interfaces and Interactive Input Methods

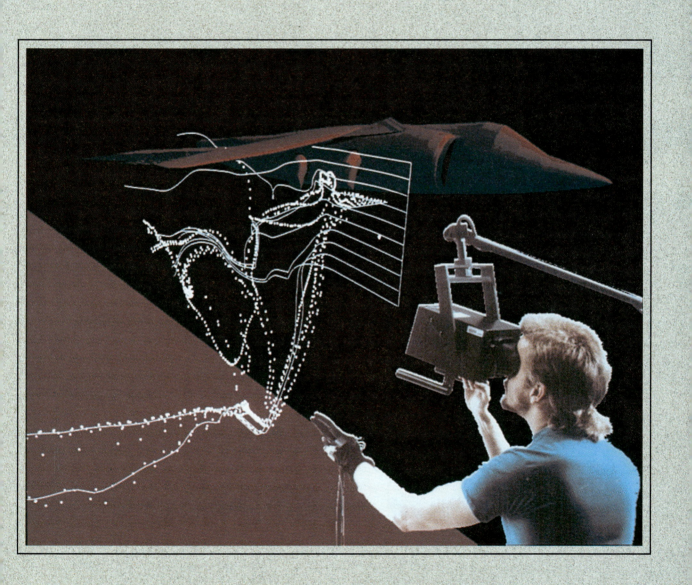

The human–computer interface for most systems involves extensive graphics, regardless of the application. Typically, general systems now consist of windows, pull-down and pop-up menus, icons, and pointing devices, such as a mouse or spaceball, for positioning the screen cursor. Popular graphical user interfaces include X Windows, Windows, Macintosh, OpenLook, and Motif. These interfaces are used in a variety of applications, including word processing, spreadsheets, databases and file-management systems, presentation systems, and page-layout systems. In graphics packages, specialized interactive dialogues are designed for individual applications, such as engineering design, architectural design, data visualization, drafting, business graphs, and artist's paintbrush programs. For general graphics packages, interfaces are usually provided through a standard system. An example is the X Window System interface with PHIGS. In this chapter, we take a look at the basic elements of graphical user interfaces and the techniques for interactive dialogues. We also consider how dialogues in graphics packages, in particular, can allow us to construct and manipulate picture components, select menu options, assign parameter values, and select and position text strings. A variety of input devices exists, and general graphics packages can be designed to interface with various devices and to provide extensive dialogue capabilities.

8-1

THE USER DIALOGUE

For a particular application, the *user's model* serves as the basis for the design of the dialogue. The user's model describes what the system is designed to accomplish and what graphics operations are available. It states the type of objects that can be displayed and how the objects can be manipulated. For example, if the graphics system is to be used as a tool for architectural design, the model describes how the package can be used to construct and display views of buildings by positioning walls, doors, windows, and other building components. Similarly, for a facility-layout system, objects could be defined as a set of furniture items (tables, chairs, etc.), and the available operations would include those for positioning and removing different pieces of furniture within the facility layout. And a circuit-design program might use electrical or logic elements for objects, with positioning operations available for adding or deleting elements within the overall circuit design.

All information in the user dialogue is then presented in the language of the application. In an architectural design package, this means that all interactions are described only in architectural terms, without reference to particular data structures or other concepts that may be unfamiliar to an architect. In the following sections, we discuss some of the general considerations in structuring a user dialogue.

Windows and Icons

Figure 8-1 shows examples of common window and icon graphical interfaces. Visual representations are used both for objects to be manipulated in an application and for the actions to be performed on the application objects.

A window system provides a window-manager interface for the user and functions for handling the display and manipulation of the windows. Common functions for the window system are opening and closing windows, repositioning windows, resizing windows, and display routines that provide interior and exterior clipping and other graphics functions. Typically, windows are displayed with sliders, buttons, and menu icons for selecting various window options. Some general systems, such as X Windows and NeWS, are capable of supporting multiple window managers so that different window styles can be accommodated, each with its own window manager. The window managers can then be designed for particular applications. In other cases, a window system is designed for one specific application and window style.

Icons representing objects such as furniture items and circuit elements are often referred to as **application icons**. The icons representing actions, such as rotate, magnify, scale, clip, and paste, are called **control icons**, or **command icons**.

Accommodating Multiple Skill Levels

Usually, interactive graphical interfaces provide several methods for selecting actions. For example, options could be selected by pointing at an icon and clicking different mouse buttons, or by accessing pull-down or pop-up menus, or by typing keyboard commands. This allows a package to accommodate users that have different skill levels.

For a less experienced user, an interface with a few easily understood operations and detailed prompting is more effective than one with a large, compre-

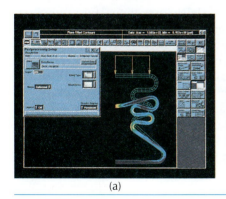 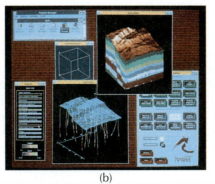 

| (a) | (b) | (c) |

Figure 8-1

Examples of screen layouts using window systems and icons. (*Courtesy of (a) Intergraph Corporation, (b) Visual Numerics, Inc., and (c) Sun Microsystems.*)

hensive operation set. A simplified set of menus and options is easy to learn and remember, and the user can concentrate on the application instead of on the details of the interface. Simple point-and-click operations are often easiest for an inexperienced user of an applications package. Therefore, interfaces typically provide a means for masking the complexity of a package, so that beginners can use the system without being overwhelmed with too much detail.

Experienced users, on the other hand, typically want speed. This means fewer prompts and more input from the keyboard or with multiple mouse-button clicks. Actions are selected with function keys or with simultaneous combinations of keyboard keys, since experienced users will remember these shortcuts for commonly used actions.

Similarly, help facilities can be designed on several levels so that beginners can carry on a detailed dialogue, while more experienced users can reduce or eliminate prompts and messages. Help facilities can also include one or more tutorial applications, which provide users with an introduction to the capabilities and use of the system.

Consistency

An important design consideration in an interface is consistency. For example, a particular icon shape should always have a single meaning, rather than serving to represent different actions or objects depending on the context. Some other examples of consistency are always placing menus in the same relative positions so that a user does not have to hunt for a particular option, always using a particular combination of keyboard keys for the same action, and always color coding so that the same color does not have different meanings in different situations.

Generally, a complicated, inconsistent model is difficult for a user to understand and to work with in an effective way. The objects and operations provided should be designed to form a minimum and consistent set so that the system is easy to learn, but not oversimplified to the point where it is difficult to apply.

Minimizing Memorization

Operations in an interface should also be structured so that they are easy to understand and to remember. Obscure, complicated, inconsistent, and abbreviated command formats lead to confusion and reduction in the effectiveness of the use of the package. One key or button used for all delete operations, for example, is easier to remember than a number of different keys for different types of delete operations.

Icons and window systems also aid in minimizing memorization. Different kinds of information can be separated into different windows, so that we do not have to rely on memorization when different information displays overlap. We can simply retain the multiple information on the screen in different windows, and switch back and forth between window areas. Icons are used to reduce memorizing by displaying easily recognizable shapes for various objects and actions. To select a particular action, we simply select the icon that resembles that action.

Backup and Error Handling

A mechanism for backing up, or aborting, during a sequence of operations is another common feature of an interface. Often an operation can be canceled before execution is completed, with the system restored to the state it was in before the operation was started. With the ability to back up at any point, we can confidently explore the capabilities of the system, knowing that the effects of a mistake can be erased.

Backup can be provided in many forms. A standard *undo* key or command is used to cancel a single operation. Sometimes a system can be backed up through several operations, allowing us to reset the system to some specified point. In a system with extensive backup capabilities, all inputs could be saved so that we can back up and "replay" any part of a session.

Sometimes operations cannot be undone. Once we have deleted the trash in the desktop wastebasket, for instance, we cannot recover the deleted files. In this case, the interface would ask us to verify the delete operation before proceeding.

Good diagnostics and error messages are designed to help determine the cause of an error. Additionally, interfaces attempt to minimize error possibilities by anticipating certain actions that could lead to an error. Examples of this are not allowing us to transform an object position or to delete an object when no object has been selected, not allowing us to select a line attribute if the selected object is not a line, and not allowing us to select the paste operation if nothing is in the clipboard.

Feedback

Interfaces are designed to carry on a continual interactive dialogue so that we are informed of actions in progress at each step. This is particularly important when the response time is high. Without feedback, we might begin to wonder what the system is doing and whether the input should be given again.

As each input is received, the system normally provides some type of response. An object is highlighted, an icon appears, or a message is displayed. This not only informs us that the input has been received, but it also tells us what the system is doing. If processing cannot be completed within a few seconds, several feedback messages might be displayed to keep us informed of the progress of the system. In some cases, this could be a flashing message indicating that the system is still working on the input request. It may also be possible for the system to display partial results as they are completed, so that the final display is built up a piece at a time. The system might also allow us to input other commands or data while one instruction is being processed.

Feedback messages are normally given clearly enough so that they have little chance of being overlooked, but not so overpowering that our concentration is interrupted. With function keys, feedback can be given as an audible click or by lighting up the key that has been pressed. Audio feedback has the advantage that it does not use up screen space, and we do not need to take attention from the work area to receive the message. When messages are displayed on the screen, a fixed message area can be used so that we always know where to look for messages. In some cases, it may be advantageous to place feedback messages in the work area near the cursor. Feedback can also be displayed in different colors to distinguish it from other displayed objects.

To speed system response, feedback techniques can be chosen to take advantage of the operating characteristics of the type of devices in use. A typical raster feedback technique is to invert pixel intensities, particularly when making menu selections. Other feedback methods include highlighting, blinking, and color changes.

Special symbols are designed for different types of feedback. For example, a cross, a frowning face, or a thumbs-down symbol is often used to indicate an error; and a blinking "at work" sign is used to indicate that processing is in progress. This type of feedback can be very effective with a more experienced user, but the beginner may need more detailed feedback that not only clearly indicates what the system is doing but also what the user should input next.

With some types of input, *echo* feedback is desirable. Typed characters can be displayed on the screen as they are input so that we can detect and correct errors immediately. Button and dial input can be echoed in the same way. Scalar values that are selected with dials or from displayed scales are usually echoed on the screen to let us check input values for accuracy. Selection of coordinate points can be echoed with a cursor or other symbol that appears at the selected position. For more precise echoing of selected positions, the coordinate values can be displayed on the screen.

8-2
INPUT OF GRAPHICAL DATA

Graphics programs use several kinds of input data. Picture specifications need values for coordinate positions, values for the character-string parameters, scalar values for the transformation parameters, values specifying menu options, and values for identification of picture parts. Any of the input devices discussed in Chapter 2 can be used to input the various graphical data types, but some devices are better suited for certain data types than others. To make graphics packages independent of the particular hardware devices used, input functions can be structured according to the data description to be handled by each function. This approach provides a **logical input-device classification** in terms of the kind of data to be input by the device.

Logical Classification of Input Devices

The various kinds of input data are summarized in the following six logical device classifications used by PHIGS and GKS:

> **LOCATOR**—a device for specifying a coordinate position (x, y)
>
> **STROKE**—a device for specifying a series of coordinate positions
>
> **STRING**—a device for specifying text input
>
> **VALUATOR**—a device for specifying scalar values
>
> **CHOICE**—a device for selecting menu options
>
> **PICK**—a device for selecting picture components

In some packages, a single logical device is used for both locator and stroke operations. Some other mechanism, such as a switch, can then be used to indicate whether one coordinate position or a "stream" of positions is to be input.

Each of the six logical input device classifications can be implemented with any of the hardware devices, but some hardware devices are more convenient for certain kinds of data than others. A device that can be pointed at a screen position is more convenient for entering coordinate data than a keyboard, for example. In the following sections, we discuss how the various physical devices are used to provide input within each of the logical classifications.

Locator Devices

A standard method for interactive selection of a coordinate point is by positioning the screen cursor. We can do this with a mouse, joystick, trackball, spaceball, thumbwheels, dials, a digitizer stylus or hand cursor, or some other cursor-positioning device. When the screen cursor is at the desired location, a button is activated to store the coordinates of that screen point.

Keyboards can be used for locator input in several ways. A general-purpose keyboard usually has four cursor-control keys that move the screen cursor up, down, left, and right. With an additional four keys, we can move the cursor diagonally as well. Rapid cursor movement is accomplished by holding down the selected cursor key. Alternatively, a joystick, joydisk, trackball, or thumbwheels can be mounted on the keyboard for relative cursor movement. As a last resort, we could actually type in coordinate values, but this is a slower process that also requires us to know exact coordinate values.

Light pens have also been used to input coordinate positions, but some special implementation considerations are necessary. Since light pens operate by detecting light emitted from the screen phosphors, some nonzero intensity level must be present at the coordinate position to be selected. With a raster system, we can paint a color background onto the screen. As long as no black areas are present, a light pen can be used to select any screen position. When it is not possible to eliminate all black areas in a display (such as on a vector system, for example), a light pen can be used as a locator by creating a small light pattern for the pen to detect. The pattern is moved around the screen until it finds the light pen.

Stroke Devices

This class of logical devices is used to input a sequence of coordinate positions. Stroke-device input is equivalent to multiple calls to a locator device. The set of input points is often used to display line sections.

Many of the physical devices used for generating locator input can be used as stroke devices. Continuous movement of a mouse, trackball, joystick, or tablet hand cursor is translated into a series of input coordinate values. The graphics tablet is one of the more common stroke devices. Button activation can be used to place the tablet into "continuous" mode. As the cursor is moved across the tablet surface, a stream of coordinate values is generated. This process is used in paint-brush systems that allow artists to draw scenes on the screen and in engineering systems where layouts can be traced and digitized for storage.

String Devices

The primary physical device used for string input is the keyboard. Input character strings are typically used for picture or graph labels.

Other physical devices can be used for generating character patterns in a "text-writing" mode. For this input, individual characters are drawn on the screen with a stroke or locator-type device. A pattern-recognition program then interprets the characters using a stored dictionary of predefined patterns.

Valuator Devices

This logical class of devices is employed in graphics systems to input scalar values. Valuators are used for setting various graphics parameters, such as rotation

277

angle and scale factors, and for setting physical parameters associated with a particular application (temperature settings, voltage levels, stress factors, etc.).

A typical physical device used to provide valuator input is a set of control dials. Floating-point numbers within any predefined range are input by rotating the dials. Dial rotations in one direction increase the numeric input value, and opposite rotations decrease the numeric value. Rotary potentiometers convert dial rotation into a corresponding voltage. This voltage is then translated into a real number within a defined scalar range, such as −10.5 to 25.5. Instead of dials, slide potentiometers are sometimes used to convert linear movements into scalar values.

Any keyboard with a set of numeric keys can be used as a valuator device. A user simply types the numbers directly in floating-point format, although this is a slower method than using dials or slide potentiometers.

Joysticks, trackballs, tablets, and other interactive devices can be adapted for valuator input by interpreting pressure or movement of the device relative to a scalar range. For one direction of movement, say, left to right, increasing scalar values can be input. Movement in the opposite direction decreases the scalar input value.

Another technique for providing valuator input is to display sliders, buttons, rotating scales, and menus on the video monitor. Figure 8-2 illustrates some possibilities for scale representations. Locator input from a mouse, joystick, spaceball, or other device is used to select a coordinate position on the display, and the screen coordinate position is then converted to a numeric input value. As a feedback mechanism for the user, the selected position on a scale can be marked with some symbol. Numeric values may also be echoed somewhere on the screen to confirm the selections.

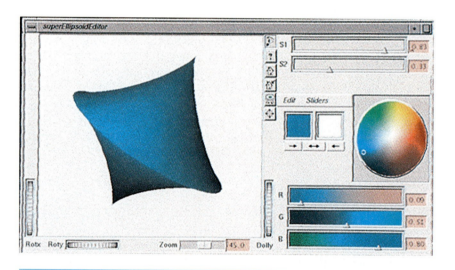

Figure 8-2

Scales displayed on a video monitor for interactive selection of parameter values. In this display, sliders are provided for selecting scalar values for superellipse parameters, s1 and s2, and for individual R, G, and B color values. In addition, a small circle can be positioned on the color wheel for selection of a combined RGB color, and buttons can be activated to make small changes in color values.

Choice Devices

Graphics packages use menus to select programming options, parameter values, and object shapes to be used in constructing a picture (Fig. 8-1). A choice device is defined as one that enters a selection from a list (menu) of alternatives. Commonly used choice devices are a set of buttons; a cursor positioning device, such as a mouse, trackball, or keyboard cursor keys; and a touch panel.

A function keyboard, or "button box", designed as a stand-alone unit, is often used to enter menu selections. Usually, each button is programmable, so that its function can be altered to suit different applications. Single-purpose buttons have fixed, predefined functions. Programmable function keys and fixed-function buttons are often included with other standard keys on a keyboard.

For screen selection of listed menu options, we can use cursor-control devices. When a coordinate position (x, y) is selected, it is compared to the coordinate extents of each listed menu item. A menu item with vertical and horizontal boundaries at the coordinate values x_{min}, x_{max}, y_{min}, and y_{max} is selected if the input coordinates (x, y) satisfy the inequalities

$$x_{min} \leq x \leq x_{max}, \qquad y_{min} \leq y \leq y_{max} \qquad (8\text{-}1)$$

For larger menus with a few options displayed at a time, a touch panel is commonly used. As with a cursor-control device, such as a mouse, a selected screen position is compared to the area occupied by each menu choice.

Alternate methods for choice input include keyboard and voice entry. A standard keyboard can be used to type in commands or menu options. For this method of choice input, some abbreviated format is useful. Menu listings can be numbered or given short identifying names. Similar codings can be used with voice-input systems. Voice input is particularly useful when the number of options is small (20 or less).

Pick Devices

Graphical object selection is the function of this logical class of devices. Pick devices are used to select parts of a scene that are to be transformed or edited in some way.

Typical devices used for object selection are the same as those for menu selection: the cursor-positioning devices. With a mouse or joystick, we can position the cursor over the primitives in a displayed structure and press the selection button. The position of the cursor is then recorded, and several levels of search may be necessary to locate the particular object (if any) that is to be selected. First, the cursor position is compared to the coordinate extents of the various structures in the scene. If the bounding rectangle of a structure contains the cursor coordinates, the picked structure has been identified. But if two or more structure areas contain the cursor coordinates, further checks are necessary. The coordinate extents of individual lines in each structure can be checked next. If the cursor coordinates are determined to be inside the coordinate extents of only one line, for example, we have identified the picked object. Otherwise, we need additional checks to determine the closest line to the cursor position.

One way to find the closest line to the cursor position is to calculate the distance squared from the cursor coordinates (x, y) to each line segment whose bounding rectangle contains the cursor position (Fig. 8-3). For a line with endpoints (x_1, y_1) and (x_2, y_2), distance squared from (x, y) to the line is calculated as

279

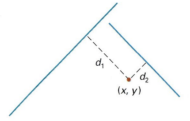

Figure 8-3
Distances to line segments from the
pick position.

$$d^2 = \frac{[\Delta x(y - y_1) - \Delta y(x - x_1)]^2}{\Delta x^2 + \Delta y^2} \qquad (8\text{-}2)$$

where $\Delta x = x_2 - x_1$, and $\Delta y = y_2 - y_1$. Various approximations can be used to speed up this distance calculation, or other identification schemes can be used.

Another method for finding the closest line to the cursor position is to specify the size of a **pick window**. The cursor coordinates are centered on this window and the candidate lines are clipped to the window, as shown in Fig. 8-4. By making the pick window small enough, we can ensure that a single line will cross the window. The method for selecting the size of a pick window is described in Section 8-4, where we consider the parameters associated with various input functions.

A method for avoiding the calculation of pick distances or window clipping intersections is to highlight the candidate structures and allow the user to resolve the pick ambiguity. One way to do this is to highlight the structures that overlap the cursor position one by one. The user then signals when the desired structure is highlighted.

An alternative to cursor positioning is to use button input to highlight successive structures. A second button is used to stop the process when the desired structure is highlighted. If very many structures are to be searched in this way, the process can be speeded up and an additional button is used to help identify the structure. The first button can initiate a rapid successive highlighting of structures. A second button can again be used to stop the process, and a third button can be used to back up more slowly if the desired structure passed before the operator pressed the stop button.

Finally, we could use a keyboard to type in structure names. This is a straightforward, but less interactive, pick-selection method. Descriptive names can be used to help the user in the pick process, but the method has several drawbacks. It is generally slower than interactive picking on the screen, and a user will probably need prompts to remember the various structure names. In addition, picking structure subparts from the keyboard can be more difficult than picking the subparts on the screen.

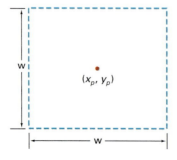

Figure 8-4
A pick window, centered on pick
coordinates (x_p, y_p), used to resolve
pick object overlaps.

INPUT FUNCTIONS

Graphical input functions can be set up to allow users to specify the following options:

- Which physical devices are to provide input within a particular logical classification (for example, a tablet used as a stroke device).
- How the graphics program and devices are to interact (input mode). Either the program or the devices can initiate data entry, or both can operate simultaneously.
- When the data are to be input and which device is to be used at that time to deliver a particular input type to the specified data variables.

Input Modes

Functions to provide input can be structured to operate in various **input modes**, which specify how the program and input devices interact. Input could be initiated by the program, or the program and input devices both could be operating simultaneously, or data input could be initiated by the devices. These three input modes are referred to as request mode, sample mode, and event mode.

In **request mode**, the application program initiates data entry. Input values are requested and processing is suspended until the required values are received. This input mode corresponds to typical input operation in a general programming language. The program and the input devices operate alternately. Devices are put into a wait state until an input request is made; then the program waits until the data are delivered.

In **sample mode**, the application program and input devices operate independently. Input devices may be operating at the same time that the program is processing other data. New input values from the input devices are stored, replacing previously input data values. When the program requires new data, it samples the *current* values from the input devices.

In **event mode**, the input devices initiate data input to the application program. The program and the input devices again operate concurrently, but now the input devices deliver data to an input queue. All input data are saved. When the program requires new data, it goes to the data queue.

Any number of devices can be operating at the same time in sample and event modes. Some can be operating in sample mode, while others are operating in event mode. But only one device at a time can be providing input in request mode.

An input mode within a logical class for a particular physical device operating on a specified workstation is declared with one of six input-class functions of the form

```
set ... Mode (ws, deviceCode, inputMode, echoFlag)
```

where `deviceCode` is a positive integer; `inputMode` is assigned one of the values: *request, sample,* or *event*; and parameter `echoFlag` is assigned either the value *echo* or the value *noecho*. How input data will be echoed on the display device is determined by parameters set in other input functions to be described later in this section.

TABLE 8-1

ASSIGNMENT OF INPUT-DEVICE
CODES

Device Code	Physical Device Type
1	Keyboard
2	Graphics Tablet
3	Mouse
4	Joystick
5	Trackball
6	Button

Device code assignment is installation-dependent. One possible assignment of device codes is shown in Table 8-1. Using the assignments in this table, we could make the following declarations:

```
setLocatorMode (1, 2, sample, noecho)
setTextMode (2, 1, request, echo)
setPickMode (4, 3, event, echo)
```

Thus, the graphics tablet is declared to be a locator device in sample mode on workstation 1 with no input data feedback echo; the keyboard is a text device in request mode on workstation 2 with input echo; and the mouse is declared to be a pick device in event mode on workstation 4 with input echo.

Request Mode

Input commands used in this mode correspond to standard input functions in a high-level programming language. When we ask for an input in request mode, other processing is suspended until the input is received. After a device has been assigned to request mode, as discussed in the preceding section, input requests can be made to that device using one of the six logical-class functions represented by the following:

```
request ... (ws, deviceCode, status, ... )
```

Values input with this function are the workstation code and the device code. Returned values are assigned to parameter `status` and to the data parameters corresponding to the requested logical class.

A value of *ok* or *none* is returned in parameter `status`, according to the validity of the input data. A value of *none* indicates that the input device was activated so as to produce invalid data. For locator input, this could mean that the coordinates were out of range. For pick input, the device could have been activated while not pointing at a structure. Or a "break" button on the input device could have been pressed. A returned value of *none* can be used as an end-of-data signal to terminate a programming sequence.

Locator and Stroke Input in Request Mode

The request functions for these two logical input classes are

```
requestLocator (ws, devCode, status, viewIndex, pt)
requestStroke (ws, devCode, nMax, status, viewIndex, n, pts)
```

For locator input, `pt` is the world-coordinate position selected. For stroke input, `pts` is a list of `n` coordinate positions, where parameter `nMax` gives the maximum number of points that can go in the input list. Parameter `viewIndex` is assigned the two-dimensional view index number.

Determination of a world-coordinate position is a two-step process: (1) The physical device selects a point in device coordinates (usually from the video-display screen) and the inverse of the workstation transformation is performed to obtain the corresponding point in normalized device coordinates. (2) Then, the inverse of the window-to-viewport mapping is carried out to get to viewing coordinates, then to world coordinates.

Since two or more views may overlap on a device, the correct viewing transformation is identified according to the **view-transformation input priority** number. By default, this is the same as the view index number, and the lower the number, the higher the priority. View index 0 has the highest priority. We can change the view priority relative to another (reference) viewing transformation with

```
setViewTransformationInputPriority (ws, viewIndex,
            refViewIndex, priority)
```

where `viewIndex` identifies the viewing transformation whose priority is to be changed, `refViewIndex` identifies the reference viewing transformation, and parameter `priority` is assigned either the value *lower* or the value *higher*. For example, we can alter the priority of the first four viewing transformations on workstation 1, as shown in Fig. 8-5, with the sequence of functions:

```
setViewTransformationInputPriority (1, 3, 1, higher)
setViewTransformationInputPriority (1, 0, 2, lower)
```

String Input in Request Mode

Here, the request input function is

```
requestString (ws, devCode, status, nChars, str)
```

Parameter `str` in this function is assigned an input string. The number of characters in the string is given in parameter `nChars`.

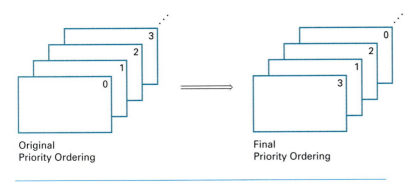

Original
Priority Ordering

Final
Priority Ordering

Figure 8-5
Rearranging viewing priorities.

Valuator Input in Request Mode

A numerical value is input in request mode with

```
requestValuator (ws, devCode, status, value)
```

Parameter `value` can be assigned any real-number value.

Choice Input in Request Mode

We make a menu selection with the following request function:

```
requestChoice (ws, devCode, status, itemNum)
```

Parameter `itemNum` is assigned a positive integer value corresponding to the menu item selected.

Pick Input in Request Mode

For this mode, we obtain a structure identifier number with the function

```
requestPick (ws, devCode, maxPathDepth, status, pathDepth,
                  pickPath)
```

Parameter `pickPath` is a list of information identifying the primitive selected. This list contains the structure name, pick identifier for the primitive, and the element sequence number. Parameter `pickDepth` is the number of levels returned in `pickPath`, and `maxPathDepth` is the specified maximum path depth that can be included in `pickPath`.

Subparts of a structure can be labeled for pick input with the following function:

```
setPickIdentifier (pickID)
```

An example of sublabeling during structure creation is given in the following programming sequence:

```
openStructure (id);
    for (k = 0; k < n; k++){
            setPickIdentifier (k);
                        .
                        .
                        .
    }
closeStructure;
```

Picking of structures and subparts of structures is also controlled by some workstation filters (Section 7-1). Objects cannot be picked if they are invisible. Also, we can set the ability to pick objects independently of their visibility. This is accomplished with the pick filter:

```
setPickFilter (ws, devCode, pickables, nonpickables)
```

where the set `pickables` contains the names of objects (structures and primitives) that we may want to select with the specified pick device. Similarly, the set `nonpickables` contains the names of objects that we do not want to be available for picking with this input device.

Sample Mode

Once sample mode has been set for one or more physical devices, data input begins without waiting for program direction. If a joystick has been designated as a locator device in sample mode, coordinate values for the current position of the activated joystick are immediately stored. As the activated stick position changes, the stored values are continually replaced with the coordinates of the current stick position.

Sampling of the current values from a physical device in this mode begins when a sample command is encountered in the application program. A locator device is sampled with one of the six logical-class functions represented by the following:

```
sample ... (ws, deviceCode, ... )
```

Some device classes have a status parameter in sample mode, and some do not. Other input parameters are the same as in request mode.

As an example of sample input, suppose we want to translate and rotate a selected object. A final translation position for the object can be obtained with a locator, and the rotation angle can be supplied by a valuator device, as demonstrated in the following statements.

```
sampleLocator (ws1, dev1, viewIndex, pt)
sampleValuator (ws2, dev2, angle)
```

Event Mode

When an input device is placed in event mode, the program and device operate simultaneously. Data input from the device is accumulated in an event queue, or input queue. All input devices active in event mode can enter data (referred to as "events") into this single-event queue, with each device entering data values as they are generated. At any one time, the event queue can contain a mixture of data types, in the order they were input. Data entered into the queue are identified according to logical class, workstation number, and physical-device code.

An application program can be directed to check the event queue for any input with the function

```
awaitEvent (time, ws, deviceClass, deviceCode)
```

Parameter `time` is used to set a maximum waiting time for the application program. If the queue happens to be empty, processing is suspended until either the number of seconds specified in `time` has elapsed or an input arrives. Should the waiting time run out before data values are input, the parameter `deviceClass` is assigned the value *none*. When `time` is given the value 0, the program checks the queue and immediately returns to other processing if the queue is empty.

If processing is directed to the event queue with the `awaitEvent` function and the queue is not empty, the first event in the queue is transferred to a *current event record*. The particular logical device class, such as locator or stroke, that made this input is stored in parameter `deviceClass`. Codes, identifying the particular workstation and physical device that made the input, are stored in parameters `ws` and `deviceCode`, respectively.

To retrieve a data input from the current event record, an event-mode input function is used. The functions in event mode are similar to those in request and sample modes. However, no workstation and device-code parameters are necessary in the commands, since the values for these parameters are stored in the data record. A user retrieves data with

```
get ... ( ... )
```

For example, to ask for locator input, we invoke the function

```
getLocator (viewIndex, pt)
```

In the following program section, we give an example of the use of the `awaitEvent` and `get` functions. A set of points from a tablet (device code 2) on workstation 1 is input to plot a series of straight-line segments connecting the input coordinates:

```
setStrokeMode (1, 2, event, noecho);

do {
  awaitEvent (0, ws, deviceClass, deviceCode)
} while (deviceClass != stroke);
getStroke (nMax, viewIndex, n, pts);
polyline (n, pts);
```

The `repeat-until` loop bypasses any data from other devices that might be in the queue. If the tablet is the only active input device in event mode, this loop is not necessary.

A number of devices can be used at the same time in event mode for rapid interactive processing of displays. The following statements plot input lines from a tablet with attributes specified by a button box:

```
setPolylineIndex (1);
/* set tablet to stroke device, event mode */
setStrokeMode (1, 2, event, noecho);

/* set buttons to choice device, event mode */
setChoiceMode (1, 6, event, noecho);

do {
  awaitEvent (60, ws, deviceClass, deviceCode);
  if (deviceClass == choice) {
    getChoice (status, option);
    setPolylineIndex (option);
  }
  else
    if (deviceClass == stroke) {
      getStroke (nMax, viewIndex, n, pts);
      polyline (n, pts);
    }
} while (deviceClass != none);
```

Some additional housekeeping functions can be used in event mode. Functions for clearing the event queue are useful when a process is terminated and a new application is to begin. These functions can be set to clear the entire queue or to clear only data associated with specified input devices and workstations.

Concurrent Use of Input Modes

An example of the simultaneous use of input devices in different modes is given in the following procedure. An object is dragged around the screen with a mouse. When a final position has been selected, a button is pressed to terminate any further movement of the object. The mouse positions are obtained in sample mode, and the button input is sent to the event queue.

```
/* drags object in response to mouse input */
/* terminate processing by button press */
setLocatorMode (1, 3, sample, echo);
setChoiceMode (1, 6, event, noecho);
do {
  sampleLocator (1, 3, viewIndex, pt);

  /* translate object centroid to position pt and draw */

  awaitEvent (0, ws, class, code);
} while (class != choice);
```

8-4

INITIAL VALUES FOR INPUT-DEVICE PARAMETERS

Quite a number of parameters can be set for input devices using the `initialize` function for each logical class:

```
initialize ... (ws, deviceCode, ... , pe, coordExt, dataRec)
```

Parameter `pe` is the prompt and echo type, parameter `coordExt` is assigned a set of four coordinate values, and parameter `dataRec` is a record of various control parameters.

For locator input, some values that can be assigned to the prompt and echo parameter are

pe = **1:** installation defined

pe = **2:** crosshair cursor centered at current position

pe = **3:** line from initial position to current position

pe = **4:** rectangle defined by current and initial points

Several other options are also available.

For structure picking, we have the following options:

pe = **1:** highlight picked primitives

pe = **2:** highlight all primitives with value of pick id

pe = **3:** highlight entire structure

as well as several others.

287

When an echo of the input data is requested, it is displayed within the bounding rectangle specified by the four coordinates in parameter `coordExt`. Additional options can also be set in parameter `dataRec`. For example, we can set any of the following:

- size of the pick window
- minimum pick distance
- type and size of cursor display
- type of structure highlighting during pick operations
- range (min and max) for valuator input
- resolution (scale) for valuator input

plus a number of other options.

8-5
INTERACTIVE PICTURE-CONSTRUCTION TECHNIQUES

There are several techniques that are incorporated into graphics packages to aid the interactive construction of pictures. Various input options can be provided, so that coordinate information entered with locator and stroke devices can be adjusted or interpreted according to a selected option. For example, we can restrict all lines to be either horizontal or vertical. Input coordinates can establish the position or boundaries for objects to be drawn, or they can be used to rearrange previously displayed objects.

Basic Positioning Methods

Coordinate values supplied by locator input are often used with positioning methods to specify a location for displaying an object or a character string. We interactively select coordinate positions with a pointing device, usually by positioning the screen cursor. Just how the object or text-string positioning is peformed depends on the selected options. With a text string, for example, the screen point could be taken as the center string position, or the start or end position of the string, or any of the other string-positioning options discussed in Chapter 4. For lines, straight line segments can be displayed between two selected screen positions.

As an aid in positioning objects, numeric values for selected positions can be echoed on the screen. Using the echoed coordinate values as a guide, we can make adjustments in the selected location to obtain accurate positioning.

Constraints

With some applications, certain types of prescribed orientations or object alignments are useful. A constraint is a rule for altering input-coordinate values to produce a specified orientation or alignment of the displayed coordinates. There are many kinds of constraint functions that can be specified, but the most common constraint is a horizontal or vertical alignment of straight lines. This type of constraint, shown in Figs. 8-6 and 8-7, is useful in forming network layouts. With this constraint, we can create horizontal and vertical lines without worrying about precise specification of endpoint coordinates.

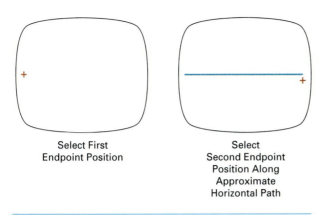

Select First Endpoint Position	Select Second Endpoint Position Along Approximate Horizontal Path

Figure 8-6
Horizontal line constraint.

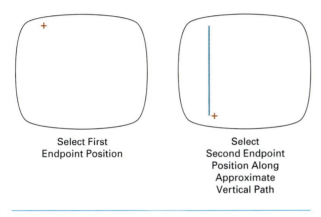

Select First Endpoint Position	Select Second Endpoint Position Along Approximate Vertical Path

Figure 8-7
Vertical line constraint.

A horizontal or vertical constraint is implemented by determining whether any two input coordinate endpoints are more nearly horizontal or more nearly vertical. If the difference in the y values of the two endpoints is smaller than the difference in x values, a horizontal line is displayed. Otherwise, a vertical line is drawn. Other kinds of constraints can be applied to input coordinates to produce a variety of alignments. Lines could be constrained to have a particular slant, such as 45°, and input coordinates could be constrained to lie along predefined paths, such as circular arcs.

Grids

Another kind of constraint is a grid of rectangular lines displayed in some part of the screen area. When a grid is used, any input coordinate position is rounded to the nearest intersecton of two grid lines. Figure 8-8 illustrates line drawing with a grid. Each of the two cursor positions is shifted to the nearest grid intersection point, and the line is drawn between these grid points. Grids facilitate object constructions, because a new line can be joined easily to a previously drawn line by selecting any position near the endpoint grid intersection of one end of the displayed line.

Select First Endpoint
Position Near a
Grid Intersection

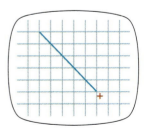

Select a Position
Near a Second
Grid Intersection

Figure 8-8
Line drawing using a grid.

289

Figure 8-9

Gravity field around a line.
Any selected point in the
shaded area is shifted to a
position on the line.

Spacing between grid lines is often an option that can be set by the user. Similarly, grids can be turned on and off, and it is sometimes possible to use partial grids and grids of different sizes in different screen areas.

Gravity Field

In the construction of figures, we sometimes need to connect lines at positions between endpoints. Since exact positioning of the screen cursor at the connecting point can be difficult, graphics packages can be designed to convert any input position near a line to a position on the line.

This conversion of input position is accomplished by creating a *gravity field* area around the line. Any selected position within the gravity field of a line is moved ("gravitated") to the nearest position on the line. A gravity field area around a line is illustrated with the shaded boundary shown in Fig. 8-9. Areas around the endpoints are enlarged to make it easier for us to connect lines at their endpoints. Selected positions in one of the circular areas of the gravity field are attracted to the endpoint in that area. The size of gravity fields is chosen large enough to aid positioning, but small enough to reduce chances of overlap with other lines. If many lines are displayed, gravity areas can overlap, and it may be difficult to specify points correctly. Normally, the boundary for the gravity field is not displayed.

Rubber-Band Methods

Straight lines can be constructed and positioned using *rubber-band* methods, which stretch out a line from a starting position as the screen cursor is moved. Figure 8-10 demonstrates the rubber-band method. We first select a screen position for one endpoint of the line. Then, as the cursor moves around, the line is displayed from the start position to the current position of the cursor. When we finally select a second screen position, the other line endpoint is set.

Rubber-band methods are used to construct and position other objects besides straight lines. Figure 8-11 demonstrates rubber-band construction of a rectangle, and Fig. 8-12 shows a rubber-band circle construction.

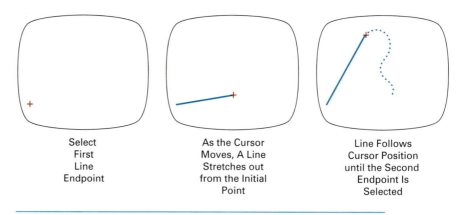

| Select First Line Endpoint | As the Cursor Moves, A Line Stretches out from the Initial Point | Line Follows Cursor Position until the Second Endpoint Is Selected |

Figure 8-10

Rubber-band method for drawing and positioning a straight line segment.

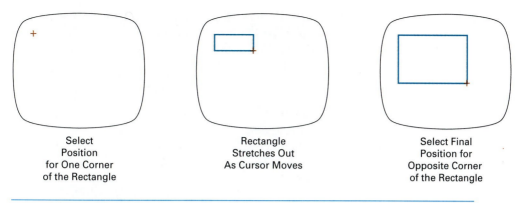

Select
Position
for One Corner
of the Rectangle

Rectangle
Stretches Out
As Cursor Moves

Select Final
Position for
Opposite Corner
of the Rectangle

Figure 8-11
Rubber-band method for constructing a rectangle.

Dragging

A technique that is often used in interactive picture construction is to move objects into position by dragging them with the screen cursor. We first select an object, then move the cursor in the direction we want the object to move, and the selected object follows the cursor path. Dragging objects to various positions in a scene is useful in applications where we might want to explore different possibilities before selecting a final location.

Painting and Drawing

Options for sketching, drawing, and painting come in a variety of forms. Straight lines, polygons, and circles can be generated with methods discussed in the previous sections. Curve-drawing options can be provided using standard curve shapes, such as circular arcs and splines, or with freehand sketching procedures. Splines are interactively constructed by specifying a set of discrete screen points that give the general shape of the curve. Then the system fits the set of points with a polynomial curve. In freehand drawing, curves are generated by following the path of a stylus on a graphics tablet or the path of the screen cursor on a video monitor. Once a curve is displayed, the designer can alter the curve shape by adjusting the positions of selected points along the curve path.

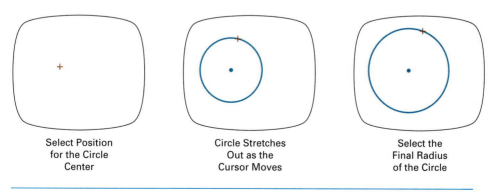

Select Position
for the Circle
Center

Circle Stretches
Out as the
Cursor Moves

Select the
Final Radius
of the Circle

Figure 8-12
Constructing a circle using a rubber-band method.

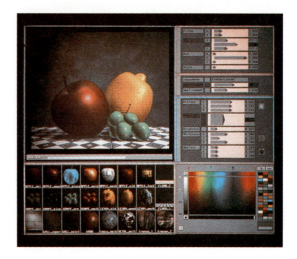

Figure 8-13
A screen layout showing one type
of interface to an artist's painting
package. (*Courtesy of Thomson Digital
Image.*)

Line widths, line styles, and other attribute options are also commonly found in painting and drawing packages. These options are implemented with the methods discussed in Chapter 4. Various brush styles, brush patterns, color combinations, object shapes, and surface-texture patterns are also available on many systems, particularly those designed as artist's workstations. Some paint systems vary the line width and brush strokes according to the pressure of the artist's hand on the stylus. Figure 8-13 shows a window and menu system used with a painting package that allows an artist to select variations of a specified object shape, different surface textures, and a variety of lighting conditions for a scene.

8-6
VIRTUAL-REALITY ENVIRONMENTS

A typical virtual-reality environment is illustrated in Fig. 8-14. Interactive input is accomplished in this environment with a data glove (Section 2-5), which is capable of grasping and moving objects displayed in a virtual scene. The computer-generated scene is displayed through a head-mounted viewing system (Section 2-1) as a stereoscopic projection. Tracking devices compute the position and orientation of the headset and data glove relative to the object positions in the scene. With this system, a user can move through the scene and rearrange object positions with the data glove.

Another method for generating virtual scenes is to display stereoscopic projections on a raster monitor, with the two stereoscopic views displayed on alternate refresh cycles. The scene is then viewed through stereoscopic glasses. Interactive object manipulations can again be accomplished with a data glove and a tracking device to monitor the glove position and orientation relative to the position of objects in the scene.

Figure 8-14
Using a head-tracking stereo display, called the BOOM (Fake Space Labs, Inc.), and a Dataglove (VPL, Inc.), a researcher interactively manipulates exploratory probes in the unsteady flow around a Harrier jet airplane. Software developed by Steve Bryson; data from Harrier. (*Courtesy of Sam Uselton, NASA Ames Research Center.*)

SUMMARY

A dialogue for an applications package can be designed from the user's model, which describes the functions of the applications package. All elements of the dialogue are presented in the language of the applications. Examples are electrical and architectural design packages.

Graphical interfaces are typically designed using windows and icons. A window system provides a window-manager interface with menus and icons that allows users to open, close, reposition, and resize windows. The window system then contains routines to carry out these operations, as well as the various graphics operations. General window systems are designed to support multiple window managers. Icons are graphical symbols that are designed for quick identification of application processes or control processes.

Considerations in user-dialogue design are ease of use, clarity, and flexibility. Specifically, graphical interfaces are designed to maintain consistency in user interaction and to provide for different user skill levels. In addition, interfaces are designed to minimize user memorization, to provide sufficient feedback, and to provide adequate backup and error-handling capabilities.

Input to graphics programs can come from many different hardware devices, with more than one device providing the same general class of input data. Graphics input functions can be designed to be independent of the particular input hardware in use, by adopting a logical classification for input devices. That is, devices are classified according to the type of graphics input, rather than a

293

hardware designation, such as mouse or tablet. The six logical devices in common use are locator, stroke, string, valuator, choice, and pick. Locator devices are any devices used by a program to input a single coordinate position. Stroke devices input a stream of coordinates. String devices are used to input text. Valuator devices are any input devices used to enter a scalar value. Choice devices enter menu selections. And pick devices input a structure name.

Input functions available in a graphics package can be defined in three input modes. Request mode places input under the control of the application program. Sample mode allows the input devices and program to operate concurrently. Event mode allows input devices to initiate data entry and control processing of data. Once a mode has been chosen for a logical device class and the particular physical device to be used to enter this class of data, input functions in the program are used to enter data values into the program. An application program can make simultaneous use of several physical input devices operating in different modes.

Interactive picture-construction methods are commonly used in a variety of applications, including design and painting packages. These methods provide users with the capability to position objects, to constrain figures to predefined orientations or alignments, to sketch figures, and to drag objects around the screen. Grids, gravity fields, and rubber-band methods are used to aid in positioning and other picture-construction operations.

REFERENCES

Guidelines for user-interface design are presented in Apple (1987), Bleser (1988), Digital (1989), and OSF/MOTIF (1989). For information on the X Window System, see Young (1990) and Cutler, Gilly, and Reilly (1992). Additional discussions of interface design can be found in Phillips (1977), Goodman and Spence (1978), Lodding (1983), Swezey and Davis (1983), Carroll and Carrithers (1984), Foley, Wallace, and Chan (1984), and Good et al. (1984).

The evolution of the concept of logical (or virtual) input devices is discussed in Wallace (1976) and in Rosenthal et al. (1982). An early discussion of input-device classifications is to be found in Newman (1968).

Input operations in PHIGS can be found in Hopgood and Duce (1991), Howard et al. (1991), Gaskins (1992), and Blake (1993). For information on GKS input functions, see Hopgood et al. (1983) and Enderle, Kansy, and Pfaff (1984).

EXERCISES

8-1. Select some graphics application with which you are familiar and set up a user model that will serve as the basis for the design of a user interface for graphics applications in that area.

8-2. List possible help facilities that can be provided in a user interface and discuss which types of help would be appropriate for different levels of users.

8-3. Summarize the possible ways of handling backup and errors. State which approaches are more suitable for the beginner and which are better suited to the experienced user.

8-4. List the possible formats for presenting menus to a user and explain under what circumstances each might be appropriate.

8-5. Discuss alternatives for feedback in terms of the various levels of users.

8-6. List the functions that must be performed by a window manager in handling screen layouts with multiple overlapping windows.

8-7. Set up a design for a window-manager package.

8-8. Design a user interface for a painting program.

8-9. Design a user interface for a two-level hierarchical modeling package.

8-10. For any area with which you are familiar, design a complete user interface to a graphics package providing capabilities to any users in that area.

8-11. Develop a program that allows objects to be positioned on the screen using a locator device. An object menu of geometric shapes is to be presented to a user who is to select an object and a placement position. The program should allow any number of objects to be positioned until a "terminate" signal is given.

8-12. Extend the program of the previous exercise so that selected objects can be scaled and rotated before positioning. The transformation choices and transformation parameters are to be presented to the user as menu options.

8-13. Write a program that allows a user to interactively sketch pictures using a stroke device.

8-14. Discuss the methods that could be employed in a pattern-recognition procedure to match input characters against a stored library of shapes.

8-15. Write a routine that displays a linear scale and a slider on the screen and allows numeric values to be selected by positioning the slider along the scale line. The number value selected is to be echoed in a box displayed near the linear scale.

8-16. Write a routine that displays a circular scale and a pointer or a slider that can be moved around the circle to select angles (in degrees). The angular value selected is to be echoed in a box displayed near the circular scale.

8-17. Write a drawing program that allows users to create a picture as a set of line segments drawn between specified endpoints. The coordinates of the individual line segments are to be selected with a locator device.

8-18. Write a drawing package that allows pictures to be created with straight line segments drawn between specified endpoints. Set up a gravity field around each line in a picture, as an aid in connecting new lines to existing lines.

8-19. Modify the drawing package in the previous exercise that allows lines to be constrained horizontally or vertically.

8-20. Develop a drawing package that can display an optional grid pattern so that selected screen positions are rounded to grid intersections. The package is to provide line-drawing capabilities, with line endpoints selected with a locator device.

8-21. Write a routine that allows a designer to create a picture by sketching straight lines with a rubber-band method.

8-22. Write a drawing package that allows straight lines, rectangles, and circles to be constructed with rubber-band methods.

8-23. Write a program that allows a user to design a picture from a menu of basic shapes by dragging each selected shape into position with a pick device.

8-24. Design an implementation of the input functions for request mode.

8-25. Design an implementation of the sample-mode input functions.

8-26. Design an implementation of the input functions for event mode.

8-27. Set up a general implementation of the input functions for request, sample, and event modes.

CHAPTER

9

Three-Dimensional Concepts

296

W   hen we model and display a three-dimensional scene, there are many
         more considerations we must take into account besides just including
coordinate values for the third dimension. Object boundaries can be constructed
with various combinations of plane and curved surfaces, and we sometimes need
to specify information about object interiors. Graphics packages often provide
routines for displaying internal components or cross-sectional views of solid objects. Also, some geometric transformations are more involved in three-dimensional space than in two dimensions. For example, we can rotate an object about
an axis with any spatial orientation in three-dimensional space. Two-dimensional
rotations, on the other hand, are always around an axis that is perpendicular to
the xy plane. Viewing transformations in three dimensions are much more complicated because we have many more parameters to select when specifying how
a three-dimensional scene is to be mapped to a display device. The scene description must be processed through viewing-coordinate transformations and projection routines that transform three-dimensional viewing coordinates onto two-dimensional device coordinates. Visible parts of a scene, for a selected view, must
be identified; and surface-rendering algorithms must be applied if a realistic rendering of the scene is required.

9-1

THREE-DIMENSIONAL DISPLAY METHODS

To obtain a display of a three-dimensional scene that has been modeled in world
coordinates, we must first set up a coordinate reference for the "camera". This coordinate reference defines the position and orientation for the plane of the camera film (Fig. 9-1), which is the plane we want to use to display a view of the objects in the scene. Object descriptions are then transferred to the camera reference
coordinates and projected onto the selected display plane. We can then display

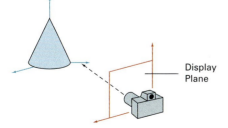

Display
Plane

Figure 9-1
Coordinate reference for obtaining
a particular view of a
three-dimensional scene.

297

the objects in wireframe (outline) form, as in Fig. 9-2, or we can apply lighting and surface-rendering techniques to shade the visible surfaces.

Parallel Projection

One method for generating a view of a solid object is to project points on the object surface along parallel lines onto the display plane. By selecting different viewing positions, we can project visible points on the object onto the display plane to obtain different two-dimensional views of the object, as in Fig. 9-3. In a *parallel projection*, parallel lines in the world-coordinate scene project into parallel lines on the two-dimensional display plane. This technique is used in engineering and architectural drawings to represent an object with a set of views that maintain relative proportions of the object. The appearance of the solid object can then be reconstructed from the major views.

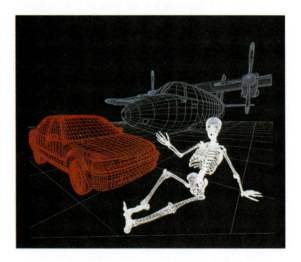

Figure 9-2
Wireframe display of three objects, with back lines removed, from a commercial database of object shapes. Each object in the database is defined as a grid of coordinate points, which can then be viewed in wireframe form or in a surface-rendered form. (*Courtesy of Viewpoint DataLabs.*)

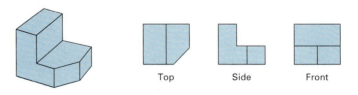

Figure 9-3
Three parallel-projection views of an object, showing relative proportions from different viewing positions.

Perspective Projection

Another method for generating a view of a three-dimensional scene is to project points to the display plane along converging paths. This causes objects farther from the viewing position to be displayed smaller than objects of the same size that are nearer to the viewing position. In a *perspective projection*, parallel lines in a scene that are not parallel to the display plane are projected into converging lines. Scenes displayed using perspective projections appear more realistic, since this is the way that our eyes and a camera lens form images. In the perspective-projection view shown in Fig. 9-4, parallel lines appear to converge to a distant point in the background, and distant objects appear smaller than objects closer to the viewing position.

Depth Cueing

With few exceptions, depth information is important so that we can easily identify, for a particular viewing direction, which is the front and which is the back of displayed objects. Figure 9-5 illustrates the ambiguity that can result when a wireframe object is displayed without depth information. There are several ways in which we can include depth information in the two-dimensional representation of solid objects.

A simple method for indicating depth with wireframe displays is to vary the intensity of objects according to their distance from the viewing position. Figure 9-6 shows a wireframe object displayed with *depth cueing*. The lines closest to

Figure 9-4
A perspective-projection view of an airport scene. (*Courtesy of Evans & Sutherland.*)

299

(a)

(b)

(c)

The wireframe
representation of the pyramid
in (a) contains no depth
information to indicate
whether the viewing
direction is (b) downward
from a position above the
apex or (c) upward from a
position below the base.

Figure 9-6
A wireframe object displayed
with depth cueing, so that the
intensity of lines decreases
from the front to the back of
the object.

300

the viewing position are displayed with the highest intensities, and lines farther away are displayed with decreasing intensities. Depth cueing is applied by choosing maximum and minimum intensity (or color) values and a range of distances over which the intensities are to vary.

Another application of depth cueing is modeling the effect of the atmosphere on the perceived intensity of objects. More distant objects appear dimmer to us than nearer objects due to light scattering by dust particles, haze, and smoke. Some atmospheric effects can change the perceived color of an object, and we can model these effects with depth cueing.

Visible Line and Surface Identification

We can also clarify depth relationships in a wireframe display by identifying visible lines in some way. The simplest method is to highlight the visible lines or to display them in a different color. Another technique, commonly used for engineering drawings, is to display the nonvisible lines as dashed lines. Another approach is to simply remove the nonvisible lines, as in Figs. 9-5(b) and 9-5(c). But removing the hidden lines also removes information about the shape of the back surfaces of an object. These visible-line methods also identify the visible surfaces of objects.

When objects are to be displayed with color or shaded surfaces, we apply surface-rendering procedures to the visible surfaces so that the hidden surfaces are obscured. Some visible-surface algorithms establish visibility pixel by pixel across the viewing plane; other algorithms determine visibility for object surfaces as a whole.

Surface Rendering

Added realism is attained in displays by setting the surface intensity of objects according to the lighting conditions in the scene and according to assigned surface characteristics. Lighting specifications include the intensity and positions of light sources and the general background illumination required for a scene. Surface properties of objects include degree of transparency and how rough or smooth the surfaces are to be. Procedures can then be applied to generate the correct illumination and shadow regions for the scene. In Fig. 9-7, surface-rendering methods are combined with perspective and visible-surface identification to generate a degree of realism in a displayed scene.

Exploded and Cutaway Views

Many graphics packages allow objects to be defined as hierarchical structures, so that internal details can be stored. Exploded and cutaway views of such objects can then be used to show the internal structure and relationship of the object parts. Figure 9-8 shows several kinds of exploded displays for a mechanical design. An alternative to exploding an object into its component parts is the cutaway view (Fig. 9-9), which removes part of the visible surfaces to show internal structure.

Three-Dimensional and Stereoscopic Views

Another method for adding a sense of realism to a computer-generated scene is to display objects using either three-dimensional or stereoscopic views. As we have seen in Chapter 2, three-dimensional views can be obtained by reflecting a

Figure 9-7

A realistic room display achieved
with stochastic ray-tracing
methods that apply a perspective
projection, surface-texture
mapping, and illumination models.
(*Courtesy of John Snyder, Jed Lengyel,
Devendra Kalra, and Al Barr, California
Institute of Technology.* Copyright © 1992
Caltech.)

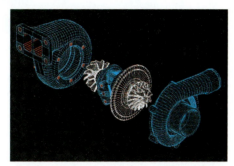

Figure 9-8

A fully rendered and assembled turbine display (a) can also be viewed
as (b) an exploded wireframe display, (c) a surface-rendered exploded
display, or (d) a surface-rendered, color-coded exploded display.
(*Courtesy of Autodesk, Inc.*)

raster image from a vibrating flexible mirror. The vibrations of the mirror are synchronized with the display of the scene on the CRT. As the mirror vibrates, the focal length varies so that each point in the scene is projected to a position corresponding to its depth.

Stereoscopic devices present two views of a scene: one for the left eye and the other for the right eye. The two views are generated by selecting viewing positions that correspond to the two eye positions of a single viewer. These two views then can be displayed on alternate refresh cycles of a raster monitor, and viewed through glasses that alternately darken first one lens then the other in synchronization with the monitor refresh cycles.

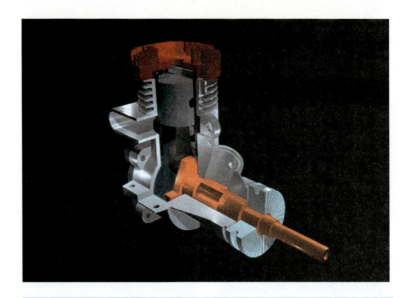

Figure 9-9
Color-coded cutaway view of a lawn mower engine showing the
structure and relationship of internal components. (*Courtesy of
Autodesk, Inc.*)

9-2

THREE-DIMENSIONAL GRAPHICS PACKAGES

Design of three-dimensional packages requires some considerations that are not
necessary with two-dimensional packages. A significant difference between the
two packages is that a three-dimensional package must include methods for
mapping scene descriptions onto a flat viewing surface. We need to consider implementation procedures for selecting different views and for using different projection techniques. We also need to consider how surfaces of solid objects are to
be modeled, how visible surfaces can be identified, how transformations of objects are performed in space, and how to describe the additional spatial properties introduced by three dimensions. Later chapters explore each of these considerations in detail.

Other considerations for three-dimensional packages are straightforward
extensions from two-dimensional methods. World-coordinate descriptions are
extended to three dimensions, and users are provided with output and input routines accessed with specifications such as

```
polyline3 (n, wcPoints)
fillarea3 (n, wcPoints)
text3 (wcPoint, string)
getLocator3 (wcPoint)
translate3(translateVector, matrixTranslate)
```

where points and vectors are specified with three components, and transformation matrices have four rows and four columns.

Two-dimensional attribute functions that are independent of geometric considerations can be applied in both two-dimensional and three-dimensional applications. No new attribute functions need be defined for colors, line styles, marker

Figure 9-10
Pipeline for transforming a view of a world-coordinate scene to device coordinates.

attributes, or text fonts. Attribute procedures for orienting character strings, however, need to be extended to accommodate arbitrary spatial orientations. Text-attribute routines associated with the up vector require expansion to include z-coordinate data so that strings can be given any spatial orientation. Area-filling routines, such as those for positioning the pattern reference point and for mapping patterns onto a fill area, need to be expanded to accommodate various orientations of the fill-area plane and the pattern plane. Also, most of the two-dimensional structure operations discussed in earlier chapters can be carried over to a three-dimensional package.

   Figure 9-10 shows the general stages in a three-dimensional transformation pipeline for displaying a world-coordinate scene. After object definitions have been converted to viewing coordinates and projected to the display plane, scan-conversion algorithms are applied to store the raster image.

10 Three-Dimensional Object Representations

G raphics scenes can contain many different kinds of objects: trees, flowers, clouds, rocks, water, bricks, wood paneling, rubber, paper, marble, steel, glass, plastic, and cloth, just to mention a few. So it is probably not too surprising that there is no one method that we can use to describe objects that will include all characteristics of these different materials. And to produce realistic displays of scenes, we need to use representations that accurately model object characteristics.

Polygon and quadric surfaces provide precise descriptions for simple Euclidean objects such as polyhedrons and ellipsoids; spline surfaces and construction techniques are useful for designing aircraft wings, gears, and other engineering structures with curved surfaces; procedural methods, such as fractal constructions and particle systems, allow us to give accurate representations for clouds, clumps of grass, and other natural objects; physically based modeling methods using systems of interacting forces can be used to describe the nonrigid behavior of a piece of cloth or a glob of jello; octree encodings are used to represent internal features of objects, such as those obtained from medical CT images; and isosurface displays, volume renderings, and other visualization techniques are applied to three-dimensional discrete data sets to obtain visual representations of the data.

Representation schemes for solid objects are often divided into two broad categories, although not all representations fall neatly into one or the other of these two categories. **Boundary representations (B-reps)** describe a three-dimensional object as a set of surfaces that separate the object interior from the environment. Typical examples of boundary representations are polygon facets and spline patches. **Space-partitioning representations** are used to describe interior properties, by partitioning the spatial region containing an object into a set of small, nonoverlapping, contiguous solids (usually cubes). A common space-partitioning description for a three-dimensional object is an octree representation. In this chapter, we consider the features of the various representation schemes and how they are used in applications.

10-1
POLYGON SURFACES

The most commonly used boundary representation for a three-dimensional graphics object is a set of surface polygons that enclose the object interior. Many graphics systems store all object descriptions as sets of surface polygons. This simplifies and speeds up the surface rendering and display of objects, since all surfaces are described with linear equations. For this reason, polygon descrip-

Figure 10-1
Wireframe representation of a
cylinder with back (hidden)
lines removed.

tions are often referred to as "standard graphics objects." In some cases, a polygonal representation is the only one available, but many packages allow objects to be described with other schemes, such as spline surfaces, that are then converted to polygonal representations for processing.

A polygon representation for a polyhedron precisely defines the surface features of the object. But for other objects, surfaces are *tesselated* (or *tiled*) to produce the polygon-mesh approximation. In Fig. 10-1, the surface of a cylinder is represented as a polygon mesh. Such representations are common in design and solid-modeling applications, since the wireframe outline can be displayed quickly to give a general indication of the surface structure. Realistic renderings are produced by interpolating shading patterns across the polygon surfaces to eliminate or reduce the presence of polygon edge boundaries. And the polygon-mesh approximation to a curved surface can be improved by dividing the surface into smaller polygon facets.

Polygon Tables

We specify a polygon surface with a set of vertex coordinates and associated attribute parameters. As information for each polygon is input, the data are placed into tables that are to be used in the subsequent processing, display, and manipulation of the objects in a scene. Polygon data tables can be organized into two groups: geometric tables and attribute tables. Geometric data tables contain vertex coordinates and parameters to identify the spatial orientation of the polygon surfaces. Attribute information for an object includes parameters specifying the degree of transparency of the object and its surface reflectivity and texture characteristics.

A convenient organization for storing geometric data is to create three lists: a vertex table, an edge table, and a polygon table. Coordinate values for each vertex in the object are stored in the vertex table. The edge table contains pointers back into the vertex table to identify the vertices for each polygon edge. And the polygon table contains pointers back into the edge table to identify the edges for each polygon. This scheme is illustrated in Fig. 10-2 for two adjacent polygons on an object surface. In addition, individual objects and their component polygon faces can be assigned object and facet identifiers for easy reference.

Listing the geometric data in three tables, as in Fig. 10-2, provides a convenient reference to the individual components (vertices, edges, and polygons) of each object. Also, the object can be displayed efficiently by using data from the edge table to draw the component lines. An alternative arrangement is to use just two tables: a vertex table and a polygon table. But this scheme is less convenient, and some edges could get drawn twice. Another possibility is to use only a polygon table, but this duplicates coordinate information, since explicit coordinate values are listed for each vertex in each polygon. Also edge information would have to be reconstructed from the vertex listings in the polygon table.

We can add extra information to the data tables of Fig. 10-2 for faster information extraction. For instance, we could expand the edge table to include forward pointers into the polygon table so that common edges between polygons could be identified more rapidly (Fig. 10-3). This is particularly useful for the rendering procedures that must vary surface shading smoothly across the edges from one polygon to the next. Similarly, the vertex table could be expanded so that vertices are cross-referenced to corresponding edges.

Additional geometric information that is usually stored in the data tables includes the slope for each edge and the coordinate extents for each polygon. As vertices are input, we can calculate edge slopes, and we can scan the coordinate

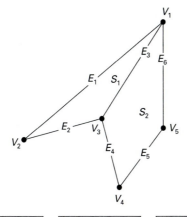

VERTEX TABLE

V_1: x_1, y_1, z_1
V_2: x_2, y_2, z_2
V_3: x_3, y_3, z_3
V_4: x_4, y_4, z_4
V_5: x_5, y_5, z_5

EDGE TABLE

E_1: V_1, V_2
E_2: V_2, V_3
E_3: V_3, V_1
E_4: V_3, V_4
E_5: V_4, V_5
E_6: V_5, V_1

POLYGON-SURFACE TABLE

S_1: E_1, E_2, E_3
S_2: E_3, E_4, E_5, E_6

Figure 10-2
Geometric data table representation for two adjacent polygon surfaces, formed with six edges and five vertices.

values to identify the minimum and maximum x, y, and z values for individual polygons. Edge slopes and bounding-box information for the polygons are needed in subsequent processing, for example, surface rendering. Coordinate extents are also used in some visible-surface determination algorithms.

Since the geometric data tables may contain extensive listings of vertices and edges for complex objects, it is important that the data be checked for consistency and completeness. When vertex, edge, and polygon definitions are specified, it is possible, particularly in interactive applications, that certain input errors could be made that would distort the display of the object. The more information included in the data tables, the easier it is to check for errors. Therefore, error checking is easier when three data tables (vertex, edge, and polygon) are used, since this scheme provides the most information. Some of the tests that could be performed by a graphics package are (1) that every vertex is listed as an endpoint for at least two edges, (2) that every edge is part of at least one polygon, (3) that every polygon is closed, (4) that each polygon has at least one shared edge, and (5) that if the edge table contains pointers to polygons, every edge referenced by a polygon pointer has a reciprocal pointer back to the polygon.

E_1: V_1, V_2, S_1
E_2: V_2, V_3, S_1
E_3: V_3, V_1, S_1, S_2
E_4: V_3, V_4, S_2
E_5: V_4, V_5, S_2
E_6: V_5, V_1, S_2

Figure 10-3
Edge table for the surfaces of Fig. 10-2 expanded to include pointers to the polygon table.

Plane Equations

To produce a display of a three-dimensional object, we must process the input data representation for the object through several procedures. These processing steps include transformation of the modeling and world-coordinate descriptions to viewing coordinates, then to device coordinates; identification of visible surfaces; and the application of surface-rendering procedures. For some of these processes, we need information about the spatial orientation of the individual

307

surface components of the object. This information is obtained from the vertex-coordinate values and the equations that describe the polygon planes.

The equation for a plane surface can be expressed in the form

$$Ax + By + Cz + D = 0 \tag{10-1}$$

where (x, y, z) is any point on the plane, and the coefficients A, B, C, and D are constants describing the spatial properties of the plane. We can obtain the values of A, B, C, and D by solving a set of three plane equations using the coordinate values for three noncollinear points in the plane. For this purpose, we can select three successive polygon vertices, (x_1, y_1, z_1), (x_2, y_2, z_2), and (x_3, y_3, z_3), and solve the following set of simultaneous linear plane equations for the ratios A/D, B/D, and C/D:

$$(A/D)x_k + (B/D)y_k + (C/D)z_k = -1, \qquad k = 1, 2, 3 \tag{10-2}$$

The solution for this set of equations can be obtained in determinant form, using Cramer's rule, as

$$A = \begin{vmatrix} 1 & y_1 & z_1 \\ 1 & y_2 & z_2 \\ 1 & y_3 & z_3 \end{vmatrix} \qquad B = \begin{vmatrix} x_1 & 1 & z_1 \\ x_2 & 1 & z_2 \\ x_3 & 1 & z_3 \end{vmatrix}$$

$$C = \begin{vmatrix} x_1 & y_1 & 1 \\ x_2 & y_2 & 1 \\ x_3 & y_3 & 1 \end{vmatrix} \qquad D = -\begin{vmatrix} x_1 & y_1 & z_1 \\ x_2 & y_2 & z_2 \\ x_3 & y_3 & z_3 \end{vmatrix} \tag{10-3}$$

Expanding the determinants, we can write the calculations for the plane coefficients in the form

$$A = y_1(z_2 - z_3) + y_2(z_3 - z_1) + y_3(z_1 - z_2)$$
$$B = z_1(x_2 - x_3) + z_2(x_3 - x_1) + z_3(x_1 - x_2)$$
$$C = x_1(y_2 - y_3) + x_2(y_3 - y_1) + x_3(y_1 - y_2) \tag{10-4}$$
$$D = -x_1(y_2 z_3 - y_3 z_2) - x_2(y_3 z_1 - y_1 z_3) - x_3(y_1 z_2 - y_2 z_1)$$

As vertex values and other information are entered into the polygon data structure, values for A, B, C, and D are computed for each polygon and stored with the other polygon data.

Orientation of a plane surface in space can be described with the normal vector to the plane, as shown in Fig. 10-4. This surface normal vector has Cartesian components (A, B, C), where parameters A, B, and C are the plane coefficients calculated in Eqs. 10-4.

Since we are usually dealing with polygon surfaces that enclose an object interior, we need to distinguish between the two sides of the surface. The side of the plane that faces the object interior is called the "inside" face, and the visible or outward side is the "outside" face. If polygon vertices are specified in a counterclockwise direction when viewing the outer side of the plane in a right-handed coordinate system, the direction of the normal vector will be from inside to outside. This is demonstrated for one plane of a unit cube in Fig. 10-5.

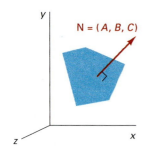

Figure 10-4

The vector **N**, normal to the surface of a plane described by the equation $Ax + By + Cz + D = 0$, has Cartesian components (A, B, C).

To determine the components of the normal vector for the shaded surface shown in Fig. 10-5, we select three of the four vertices along the boundary of the polygon. These points are selected in a counterclockwise direction as we view from outside the cube toward the origin. Coordinates for these vertices, in the order selected, can be used in Eqs. 10-4 to obtain the plane coefficients: $A = 1$, $B = 0$, $C = 0$, $D = -1$. Thus, the normal vector for this plane is in the direction of the positive x axis.

The elements of the plane normal can also be obtained using a vector cross-product calculation. We again select three vertex positions, $\mathbf{V}_1$, $\mathbf{V}_2$, and $\mathbf{V}_3$, taken in counterclockwise order when viewing the surface from outside to inside in a right-handed Cartesian system. Forming two vectors, one from $\mathbf{V}_1$ to $\mathbf{V}_2$ and the other from $\mathbf{V}_1$ to $\mathbf{V}_3$, we calculate $\mathbf{N}$ as the vector cross product:

$$\mathbf{N} = (\mathbf{V}_2 - \mathbf{V}_1) \times (\mathbf{V}_3 - \mathbf{V}_1) \qquad (10\text{-}5)$$

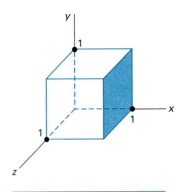

Figure 10-5
The shaded polygon surface of the unit cube has plane equation $x - 1 = 0$ and normal vector $\mathbf{N} = (1, 0, 0)$.

This generates values for the plane parameters A, B, and C. We can then obtain the value for parameter D by substituting these values and the coordinates for one of the polygon vertices in plane equation 10-1 and solving for D. The plane equation can be expressed in vector form using the normal $\mathbf{N}$ and the position $\mathbf{P}$ of any point in the plane as

$$\mathbf{N} \cdot \mathbf{P} = -D \qquad (10\text{-}6)$$

Plane equations are used also to identify the position of spatial points relative to the plane surfaces of an object. For any point (x, y, z) not on a plane with parameters A, B, C, D, we have

$$Ax + By + Cz + D \neq 0$$

We can identify the point as either inside or outside the plane surface according to the sign (negative or positive) of $Ax + By + Cz + D$:

if $Ax + By + Cz + D < 0$, the point (x, y, z) is inside the surface

if $Ax + By + Cz + D > 0$, the point (x, y, z) is outside the surface

These inequality tests are valid in a right-handed Cartesian system, provided the plane parameters A, B, C, and D were calculated using vertices selected in a counterclockwise order when viewing the surface in an outside-to-inside direction. For example, in Fig. 10-5, any point outside the shaded plane satisfies the inequality $x - 1 > 0$, while any point inside the plane has an x-coordinate value less than 1.

Polygon Meshes

Some graphics packages (for example, PHIGS) provide several polygon functions for modeling objects. A single plane surface can be specified with a function such as `fillArea`. But when object surfaces are to be tiled, it is more convenient to specify the surface facets with a mesh function. One type of polygon mesh is the *triangle strip*. This function produces $n - 2$ connected triangles, as shown in Fig. 10-6, given the coordinates for n vertices. Another similar function is the *quadrilateral mesh*, which generates a mesh of $(n - 1)$ by $(m - 1)$ quadrilaterals, given

Figure 10-6
A triangle strip formed with 11 triangles connecting 13 vertices.

309

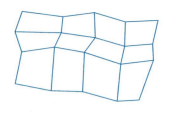

Figure 10-7
A quadrilateral mesh
containing 12 quadrilaterals
constructed from a 5 by 4
input vertex array.

the coordinates for an *n* by *m* array of vertices. Figure 10-7 shows 20 vertices forming a mesh of 12 quadrilaterals.

When polygons are specified with more than three vertices, it is possible that the vertices may not all lie in one plane. This can be due to numerical errors or errors in selecting coordinate positions for the vertices. One way to handle this situation is simply to divide the polygons into triangles. Another approach that is sometimes taken is to approximate the plane parameters A, B, and C. We can do this with averaging methods or we can project the polygon onto the coordinate planes. Using the projection method, we take A proportional to the area of the polygon projection on the yz plane, B proportional to the projection area on the xz plane, and C proportional to the projection area on the xy plane.

High-quality graphics systems typically model objects with polygon meshes and set up a database of geometric and attribute information to facilitate processing of the polygon facets. Fast hardware-implemented polygon renderers are incorporated into such systems with the capability for displaying hundreds of thousands to one million or more shaded polygons per second (usually triangles), including the application of surface texture and special lighting effects.

10-2
CURVED LINES AND SURFACES

Displays of three-dimensional curved lines and surfaces can be generated from an input set of mathematical functions defining the objects or from a set of user-specified data points. When functions are specified, a package can project the defining equations for a curve to the display plane and plot pixel positions along the path of the projected function. For surfaces, a functional description is often tesselated to produce a polygon-mesh approximation to the surface. Usually, this is done with triangular polygon patches to ensure that all vertices of any polygon are in one plane. Polygons specified with four or more vertices may not have all vertices in a single plane. Examples of display surfaces generated from functional descriptions include the quadrics and the superquadrics.

When a set of discrete coordinate points is used to specify an object shape, a functional description is obtained that best fits the designated points according to the constraints of the application. Spline representations are examples of this class of curves and surfaces. These methods are commonly used to design new object shapes, to digitize drawings, and to describe animation paths. Curve-fitting methods are also used to display graphs of data values by fitting specified curve functions to the discrete data set, using regression techniques such as the least-squares method.

Curve and surface equations can be expressed in either a parametric or a nonparametric form. Appendix A gives a summary and comparison of parametric and nonparametric equations. For computer graphics applications, parametric representations are generally more convenient.

10-3
QUADRIC SURFACES

A frequently used class of objects are the *quadric surfaces*, which are described with second-degree equations (quadratics). They include spheres, ellipsoids, tori, paraboloids, and hyperboloids. Quadric surfaces, particularly spheres and ellipsoids, are common elements of graphics scenes, and they are often available in graphics packages as primitives from which more complex objects can be constructed.

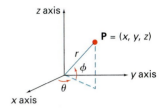

Sphere

In Cartesian coordinates, a spherical surface with radius r centered on the coordinate origin is defined as the set of points (x, y, z) that satisfy the equation

$$x^2 + y^2 + z^2 = r^2 \qquad (10\text{-}7)$$

We can also describe the spherical surface in parametric form, using latitude and longitude angles (Fig. 10-8):

$$x = r \cos \phi \cos \theta, \qquad -\pi/2 \leq \phi \leq \pi/2$$

$$y = r \cos \phi \sin \theta, \qquad -\pi \leq \theta \leq \pi \qquad (10\text{-}8)$$

$$z = r \sin \phi$$

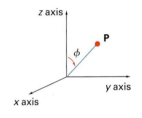

The parametric representation in Eqs. 10-8 provides a symmetric range for the angular parameters θ and ϕ. Alternatively, we could write the parametric equations using standard spherical coordinates, where angle ϕ is specified as the colatitude (Fig. 10-9). Then, ϕ is defined over the range $0 \leq \phi \leq \pi$, and θ is often taken in the range $0 \leq \theta \leq 2\pi$. We could also set up the representation using parameters u and v defined over the range from 0 to 1 by substituting $\phi = \pi u$ and $\theta = 2\pi v$.

Figure 10-9
Spherical coordinate parameters (r, θ, ϕ), using colatitude for angle ϕ.

Ellipsoid

An ellipsoidal surface can be described as an extension of a spherical surface, where the radii in three mutually perpendicular directions can have different values (Fig. 10-10). The Cartesian representation for points over the surface of an ellipsoid centered on the origin is

$$\left(\frac{x}{r_x}\right)^2 + \left(\frac{y}{r_y}\right)^2 + \left(\frac{z}{r_z}\right)^2 = 1 \qquad (10\text{-}9)$$

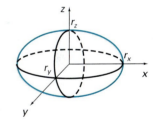

And a parametric representation for the ellipsoid in terms of the latitude angle ϕ and the longitude angle θ in Fig. 10-8 is

Figure 10-10
An ellipsoid with radii r_x, r_y, and r_z centered on the coordinate origin.

$$x = r_x \cos \phi \cos \theta, \qquad -\pi/2 \leq \phi \leq \pi/2$$

$$y = r_y \cos \phi \sin \theta, \qquad -\pi \leq \theta \leq \pi \qquad (10\text{-}10)$$

$$z = r_z \sin \phi$$

Torus

A torus is a doughnut-shaped object, as shown in Fig. 10-11. It can be generated by rotating a circle or other conic about a specified axis. The Cartesian represen-

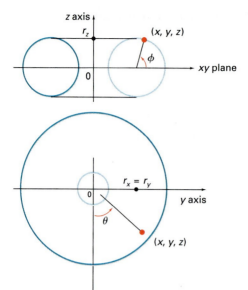

Figure 10-11
A torus with a circular cross section centered on the coordinate origin.

tation for points over the surface of a torus can be written in the form

$$\left[r - \sqrt{\left(\frac{x}{r_x}\right)^2 + \left(\frac{y}{r_y}\right)^2} \right]^2 + \left(\frac{z}{r_z}\right)^2 = 1 \qquad (10\text{-}11)$$

where r is any given offset value. Parametric representations for a torus are similar to those for an ellipse, except that angle ϕ extends over 360°. Using latitude and longitude angles ϕ and θ, we can describe the torus surface as the set of points that satisfy

$$
\begin{aligned}
x &= r_x(r + \cos\phi)\cos\theta, & -\pi \le \phi \le \pi \\
y &= r_y(r + \cos\phi)\sin\theta, & -\pi \le \theta \le \pi \\
z &= r_z \sin\phi
\end{aligned}
\qquad (10\text{-}12)
$$

10-4

SUPERQUADRICS

This class of objects is a generalization of the quadric representations. **Superquadrics** are formed by incorporating additional parameters into the quadric equations to provide increased flexibility for adjusting object shapes. The number of additional parameters used is equal to the dimension of the object: one parameter for curves and two parameters for surfaces.

Superellipse

We obtain a Cartesian representation for a superellipse from the corresponding equation for an ellipse by allowing the exponent on the x and y terms to be variable. One way to do this is to write the Cartesian superellipse equation in the form

$$\left(\frac{x}{r_x}\right)^{2/s} + \left(\frac{y}{r_y}\right)^{2/s} = 1 \qquad (10\text{-}13)$$

where parameter s can be assigned any real value. When $s = 1$, we get an ordinary ellipse.

Corresponding parametric equations for the superellipse of Eq. 10-13 can be expressed as

$$x = r_x \cos^s \theta, \qquad -\pi \le \theta \le \pi$$
$$y = r_y \sin^s \theta \qquad\qquad\qquad (10\text{-}14)$$

Figure 10-12 illustrates supercircle shapes that can be generated using various values for parameter s.

Superellipsoid

A Cartesian representation for a superellipsoid is obtained from the equation for an ellipsoid by incorporating two exponent parameters:

$$\left[\left(\frac{x}{r_x}\right)^{2/s_2} + \left(\frac{y}{r_y}\right)^{2/s_2}\right]^{s_2/s_1} + \left(\frac{z}{r_z}\right)^{2/s_1} = 1 \qquad (10\text{-}15)$$

For $s_1 = s_2 = 1$, we have an ordinary ellipsoid.

We can then write the corresponding parametric representation for the superellipsoid of Eq. 10-15 as

$$x = r_x \cos^{s_1} \phi \cos^{s_2} \theta, \qquad -\pi/2 \le \phi \le \pi/2$$
$$y = r_y \cos^{s_1} \phi \sin^{s_2} \theta, \qquad -\pi \le \theta \le \pi \qquad (10\text{-}16)$$
$$z = r_z \sin^{s_1} \phi$$

Figure 10-13 illustrates supersphere shapes that can be generated using various values for parameters s_1 and s_2. These and other superquadric shapes can be combined to create more complex structures, such as furniture, threaded bolts, and other hardware.

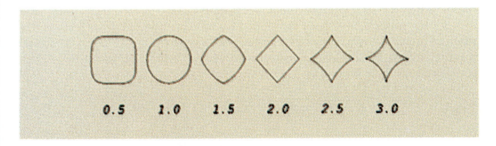

0.5   1.0   1.5   2.0   2.5   3.0

Figure 10-12
Superellipses plotted with different values for parameter s and with $r_x = r_y$.

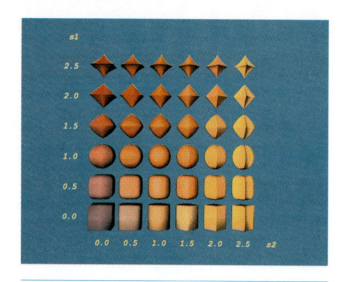

Figure 10-13
Superellipsoids plotted with different values for parameters
s_1 and s_2, and with $r_x = r_y = r_z$.

Figure 10-14
Molecular bonding. As two
molecules move away from
each other, the surface shapes
stretch, snap, and finally
contract into spheres.

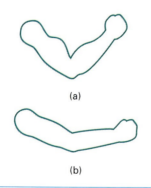

(a)

(b)

Figure 10-15
Blobby muscle shapes in a
human arm.

314

10-5

BLOBBY OBJECTS

Some objects do not maintain a fixed shape, but change their surface characteristics in certain motions or when in proximity to other objects. Examples in this class of objects include molecular structures, water droplets and other liquid effects, melting objects, and muscle shapes in the human body. These objects can be described as exhibiting "blobbiness" and are often simply referred to as **blobby objects**, since their shapes show a certain degree of fluidity.

A molecular shape, for example, can be described as spherical in isolation, but this shape changes when the molecule approaches another molecule. This distortion of the shape of the electron density cloud is due to the "bonding" that occurs between the two molecules. Figure 10-14 illustrates the stretching, snapping, and contracting effects on molecular shapes when two molecules move apart. These characteristics cannot be adequately described simply with spherical or elliptical shapes. Similarly, Fig. 10-15 shows muscle shapes in a human arm, which exhibit similar characteristics. In this case, we want to model surface shapes so that the total volume remains constant.

Several models have been developed for representing blobby objects as distribution functions over a region of space. One way to do this is to model objects as combinations of Gaussian density functions, or "bumps" (Fig. 10-16). A surface function is then defined as

$$f(x, y, z) = \sum_k b_k e^{-a_k r_k^2} - T = 0 \qquad (10\text{-}17)$$

where $r_k^2 = \sqrt{x_k^2 + y_k^2 + z_k^2}$, parameter T is some specified threshold, and parameters a and b are used to adjust the amount of blobbiness of the individual objects. Negative values for parameter b can be used to produce dents instead of bumps. Figure 10-17 illustrates the surface structure of a composite object modeled with four Gaussian density functions. At the threshold level, numerical root-finding techniques are used to locate the coordinate intersection values. The cross sections of the individual objects are then modeled as circles or ellipses. If two cross sections are near to each other, they are merged to form one blobby shape, as in Figure 10-14, whose structure depends on the separation of the two objects.

Other methods for generating blobby objects use density functions that fall off to 0 in a finite interval, rather than exponentially. The "metaball" model describes composite objects as combinations of quadratic density functions of the form

$$
f(r) = \begin{cases} b(1 - 3r^2/d^2), & \text{if } 0 < r \le d/3 \\ \dfrac{3}{2}b(1 - r/d)^2, & \text{if } d/3 < r \le d \\ 0, & \text{if } r > d \end{cases} \quad (10\text{-}18)
$$

And the "soft object" model uses the function

$$
f(r) = \begin{cases} 1 - \dfrac{22r^2}{9d^2} + \dfrac{17r^4}{9d^4} - \dfrac{4r^6}{9d^6}, & \text{if } 0 < r \le d \\ 0, & \text{if } r > d \end{cases} \quad (10\text{-}19)
$$

Some design and painting packages now provide blobby function modeling for handling applications that cannot be adequately modeled with polygon or spline functions alone. Figure 10-18 shows a user interface for a blobby object modeler using metaballs.

10-6
SPLINE REPRESENTATIONS

In drafting terminology, a spline is a flexible strip used to produce a smooth curve through a designated set of points. Several small weights are distributed along the length of the strip to hold it in position on the drafting table as the curve is drawn. The term *spline curve* originally referred to a curve drawn in this manner. We can mathematically describe such a curve with a piecewise cubic

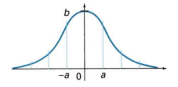

Figure 10-16
A three-dimensional Gaussian bump centered at position 0, with height b and standard deviation a.

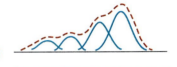

Figure 10-17
A composite blobby object formed with four Gaussian bumps.

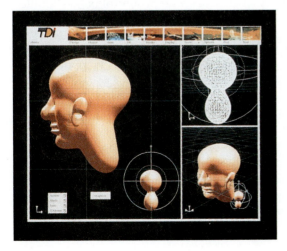

Figure 10-18
A screen layout, used in the Blob Modeler and the Blob Animator packages, for modeling objects with metaballs. (*Courtesy of Thomson Digital Image.*)

315

polynomial function whose first and second derivatives are continuous across the various curve sections. In computer graphics, the term **spline curve** now refers to any composite curve formed with polynomial sections satisfying specified continuity conditions at the boundary of the pieces. A **spline surface** can be described with two sets of orthogonal spline curves. There are several different kinds of spline specifications that are used in graphics applications. Each individual specification simply refers to a particular type of polynomial with certain specified boundary conditions.

Splines are used in graphics applications to design curve and surface shapes, to digitize drawings for computer storage, and to specify animation paths for the objects or the camera in a scene. Typical CAD applications for splines include the design of automobile bodies, aircraft and spacecraft surfaces, and ship hulls.

Interpolation and Approximation Splines

We specify a spline curve by giving a set of coordinate positions, called **control points**, which indicates the general shape of the curve. These control points are then fitted with piecewise continuous parametric polynomial functions in one of two ways. When polynomial sections are fitted so that the curve passes through each control point, as in Fig. 10-19, the resulting curve is said to **interpolate** the set of control points. On the other hand, when the polynomials are fitted to the general control-point path without necessarily passing through any control point, the resulting curve is said to **approximate** the set of control points (Fig. 10-20).

Interpolation curves are commonly used to digitize drawings or to specify animation paths. Approximation curves are primarily used as design tools to structure object surfaces. Figure 10-21 shows an approximation spline surface created for a design application. Straight lines connect the control-point positions above the surface.

A spline curve is defined, modified, and manipulated with operations on the control points. By interactively selecting spatial positions for the control points, a designer can set up an initial curve. After the polynomial fit is displayed for a given set of control points, the designer can then reposition some or all of the control points to restructure the shape of the curve. In addition, the curve can be translated, rotated, or scaled with transformations applied to the control points. CAD packages can also insert extra control points to aid a designer in adjusting the curve shapes.

The convex polygon boundary that encloses a set of control points is called the **convex hull**. One way to envision the shape of a convex hull is to imagine a rubber band stretched around the positions of the control points so that each control point is either on the perimeter of the hull or inside it (Fig. 10-22). Convex hulls provide a measure for the deviation of a curve or surface from the region bounding the control points. Some splines are bounded by the convex hull, thus ensuring that the polynomials smoothly follow the control points without erratic oscillations. Also, the polygon region inside the convex hull is useful in some algorithms as a clipping region.

A polyline connecting the sequence of control points for an approximation spline is usually displayed to remind a designer of the control-point ordering. This set of connected line segments is often referred to as the **control graph** of the curve. Other names for the series of straight-line sections connecting the control points in the order specified are **control polygon** and **characteristic polygon**. Figure 10-23 shows the shape of the control graph for the control-point sequences in Fig. 10-22.

Figure 10-19

A set of six control points interpolated with piecewise continuous polynomial sections.

Figure 10-20

A set of six control points approximated with piecewise continuous polynomial sections.

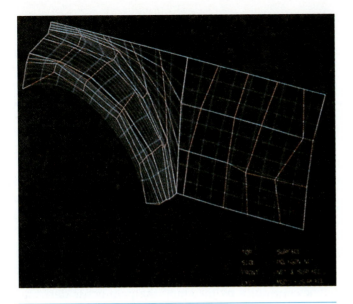

Figure 10-21
An approximation spline surface for a CAD application
in automotive design. Surface contours are plotted with
polynomial curve sections, and the surface control points are
connected with straight-line segments. (*Courtesy of Evans &
Sutherland.*)

Parametric Continuity Conditions

To ensure a smooth transition from one section of a piecewise parametric curve
to the next, we can impose various **continuity conditions** at the connection
points. If each section of a spline is described with a set of parametric coordinate
functions of the form

$$x = x(u), \qquad y = y(u), \qquad z = z(u), \qquad u_1 \leq u \leq u_2 \qquad (10\text{-}20)$$

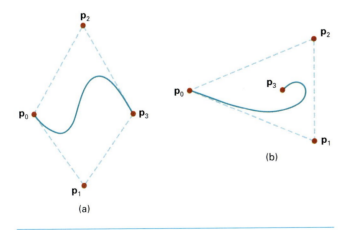

Figure 10-22
Convex-hull shapes (dashed lines) for two sets of control
points.

317

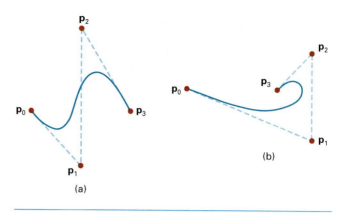

Figure 10-23
Control-graph shapes (dashed lines) for two different sets of
control points.

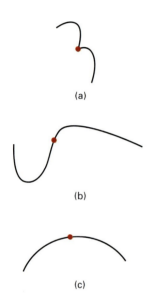

Figure 10-24
Piecewise construction of a
curve by joining two curve
segments using different
orders of continuity: (a) zero-
order continuity only,
(b) first-order continuity,
and (c) second-order
continuity.

we set **parametric continuity** by matching the parametric derivatives of adjoining curve sections at their common boundary.

Zero-order parametric continuity, described as C^0 continuity, means simply that the curves meet. That is, the values of x, y, and z evaluated at u_2 for the first curve section are equal, respectively, to the values of x, y, and z evaluated at u_1 for the next curve section. **First-order parametric continuity**, referred to as C^1 continuity, means that the first parametric derivatives (tangent lines) of the coordinate functions in Eq. 10-20 for two successive curve sections are equal at their joining point. **Second-order parametric continuity**, or C^2 continuity, means that both the first and second parametric derivatives of the two curve sections are the same at the intersection. Higher-order parametric continuity conditions are defined similarly. Figure 10-24 shows examples of C^0, C^1, and C^2 continuity.

With second-order continuity, the rates of change of the tangent vectors for connecting sections are equal at their intersection. Thus, the tangent line transitions smoothly from one section of the curve to the next (Fig. 10-24(c)). But with first-order continuity, the rates of change of the tangent vectors for the two sections can be quite different (Fig. 10-24(b)), so that the general shapes of the two adjacent sections can change abruptly. First-order continuity is often sufficient for digitizing drawings and some design applications, while second-order continuity is useful for setting up animation paths for camera motion and for many precision CAD requirements. A camera traveling along the curve path in Fig. 10-24(b) with equal steps in parameter u would experience an abrupt change in acceleration at the boundary of the two sections, producing a discontinuity in the motion sequence. But if the camera were traveling along the path in Fig. 10-24(c), the frame sequence for the motion would smoothly transition across the boundary.

Geometric Continuity Conditions

An alternate method for joining two successive curve sections is to specify conditions for **geometric continuity**. In this case, we only require parametric derivatives of the two sections to be proportional to each other at their common boundary instead of equal to each other.

Zero-order geometric continuity, described as G^0 continuity, is the same as zero-order parametric continuity. That is, the two curves sections must have the same coordinate position at the boundary point. **First-order geometric continuity**, or G^1 continuity, means that the parametric first derivatives are proportional at the intersection of two successive sections. If we denote the parametric position on the curve as $\mathbf{P}(u)$, the direction of the tangent vector $\mathbf{P}'(u)$, but not necessarily its magnitude, will be the same for two successive curve sections at their joining point under G^1 continuity. **Second-order geometric continuity**, or G^2 continuity, means that both the first and second parametric derivatives of the two curve sections are proportional at their boundary. Under G^2 continuity, curvatures of two curve sections will match at the joining position.

A curve generated with geometric continuity conditions is similar to one generated with parametric continuity, but with slight differences in curve shape. Figure 10-25 provides a comparison of geometric and parametric continuity. With geometric continuity, the curve is pulled toward the section with the greater tangent vector.

Spline Specifications

There are three equivalent methods for specifying a particular spline representation: (1) We can state the set of boundary conditions that are imposed on the spline; or (2) we can state the matrix that characterizes the spline; or (3) we can state the set of **blending functions** (or **basis functions**) that determine how specified geometric constraints on the curve are combined to calculate positions along the curve path.

To illustrate these three equivalent specifications, suppose we have the following parametric cubic polynomial representation for the x coordinate along the path of a spline section:

$$x(u) = a_x u^3 + b_x u^2 + c_x u + d_x, \qquad 0 \le u \le 1 \qquad (10\text{-}21)$$

Boundary conditions for this curve might be set, for example, on the endpoint coordinates $x(0)$ and $x(1)$ and on the parametric first derivatives at the endpoints $x'(0)$ and $x'(1)$. These four boundary conditions are sufficient to determine the values of the four coefficients a_x, b_x, c_x, and d_x.

From the boundary conditions, we can obtain the matrix that characterizes this spline curve by first rewriting Eq. 10-21 as the matrix product

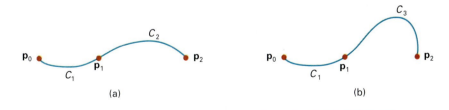

(a)   (b)

Figure 10-25
Three control points fitted with two curve sections joined with (a) parametric continuity and (b) geometric continuity, where the tangent vector of curve C_3 at point $\mathbf{p}_1$ has a greater magnitude than the tangent vector of curve C_1 at $\mathbf{p}_1$.

$$x(u) = [u^3 \; u^2 \; u \; 1] \begin{bmatrix} a_x \\ b_x \\ c_x \\ d_x \end{bmatrix}$$

(10-22)

$$= \mathbf{U} \cdot \mathbf{C}$$

where $\mathbf{U}$ is the row matrix of powers of parameter u, and $\mathbf{C}$ is the coefficient column matrix. Using Eq. 10-22, we can write the boundary conditions in matrix form and solve for the coefficient matrix $\mathbf{C}$ as

$$\mathbf{C} = \mathbf{M}_{\text{spline}} \cdot \mathbf{M}_{\text{geom}}$$

(10-23)

where $\mathbf{M}_{\text{geom}}$ is a four-element column matrix containing the geometric constraint values (boundary conditions) on the spline, and $\mathbf{M}_{\text{spline}}$ is the 4-by-4 matrix that transforms the geometric constraint values to the polynomial coefficients and provides a characterization for the spline curve. Matrix $\mathbf{M}_{\text{geom}}$ contains control-point coordinate values and other geometric constraints that have been specified. Thus, we can substitute the matrix representation for $\mathbf{C}$ into Eq. 10-22 to obtain

$$x(u) = \mathbf{U} \cdot \mathbf{M}_{\text{spline}} \cdot \mathbf{M}_{\text{geom}}$$

(10-24)

The matrix, $\mathbf{M}_{\text{spline}}$, characterizing a spline representation, sometimes called the *basis matrix*, is particularly useful for transforming from one spline representation to another.

Finally, we can expand Eq. 10-24 to obtain a polynomial representation for coordinate x in terms of the geometric constraint parameters

$$x(u) = \sum_{k=0}^{3} g_k \cdot BF_k(u)$$

(10-25)

where g_k are the constraint parameters, such as the control-point coordinates and slope of the curve at the control points, and $BF_k(u)$ are the polynomial blending functions. In the following sections, we discuss some commonly used splines and their matrix and blending-function specifications.

10-7
CUBIC SPLINE INTERPOLATION METHODS

This class of splines is most often used to set up paths for object motions or to provide a representation for an existing object or drawing, but interpolation splines are also used sometimes to design object shapes. Cubic polynomials offer a reasonable compromise between flexibility and speed of computation. Compared to higher-order polynomials, cubic splines require less calculations and memory and they are more stable. Compared to lower-order polynomials, cubic splines are more flexible for modeling arbitrary curve shapes.

Given a set of control points, cubic interpolation splines are obtained by fitting the input points with a piecewise cubic polynomial curve that passes through every control point. Suppose we have $n + 1$ control points specified with coordinates

$$\mathbf{p}_k = (x_k, y_k, z_k), \qquad k = 0, 1, 2, \ldots, n$$

A cubic interpolation fit of these points is illustrated in Fig. 10-26. We can describe the parametric cubic polynomial that is to be fitted between each pair of control points with the following set of equations:

$$x(u) = a_x u^3 + b_x u^2 + c_x u + d_x$$
$$y(u) = a_y u^3 + b_y u^2 + c_y u + d_y, \qquad (0 \leq u \leq 1) \qquad (10\text{-}26)$$
$$z(u) = a_z u^3 + b_z u^2 + c_z u + d_z$$

For each of these three equations, we need to determine the values of the four coefficients a, b, c, and d in the polynomial representation for each of the n curve sections between the $n + 1$ control points. We do this by setting enough boundary conditions at the "joints" between curve sections so that we can obtain numerical values for all the coefficients. In the following sections, we discuss common methods for setting the boundary conditions for cubic interpolation splines.

Natural Cubic Splines

One of the first spline curves to be developed for graphics applications is the **natural cubic spline**. This interpolation curve is a mathematical representation of the original drafting spline. We formulate a natural cubic spline by requiring that two adjacent curve sections have the same first and second parametric derivatives at their common boundary. Thus, natural cubic splines have C^2 continuity.

If we have $n + 1$ control points to fit, as in Fig. 10-26, then we have n curve sections with a total of $4n$ polynomial coefficients to be determined. At each of the $n - 1$ interior control points, we have four boundary conditions: The two curve sections on either side of a control point must have the same first and second parametric derivatives at that control point, and each curve must pass through that control point. This gives us $4n - 4$ equations to be satisfied by the $4n$ polynomial coefficients. We get an additional equation from the first control point $\mathbf{p}_0$, the position of the beginning of the curve, and another condition from control point $\mathbf{p}_n$, which must be the last point on the curve. We still need two more conditions to be able to determine values for all coefficients. One method for obtaining the two additional conditions is to set the second derivatives at $\mathbf{p}_0$ and $\mathbf{p}_n$ to 0. Another approach is to add two extra "dummy" control points, one at each end of the original control-point sequence. That is, we add a control point $\mathbf{p}_{-1}$ and a control point $\mathbf{p}_{n+1}$. Then all of the original control points are interior points, and we have the necessary $4n$ boundary conditions.

Although natural cubic splines are a mathematical model for the drafting spline, they have a major disadvantage. If the position of any one control point is altered, the entire curve is affected. Thus, natural cubic splines allow for no "local control", so that we cannot restructure part of the curve without specifying an entirely new set of control points.

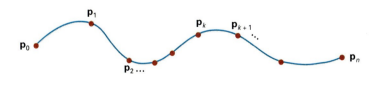

Figure 10-26
A piecewise continuous cubic-spline interpolation of $n + 1$ control points.

Hermite Interpolation

A **Hermite spline** (named after the French mathematician Charles Hermite) is an interpolating piecewise cubic polynomial with a specified tangent at each control point. Unlike the natural cubic splines, Hermite splines can be adjusted locally because each curve section is only dependent on its endpoint constraints.

If $\mathbf{P}(u)$ represents a parametric cubic point function for the curve section between control points $\mathbf{p}_k$ and $\mathbf{p}_{k+1}$, as shown in Fig. 10-27, then the boundary conditions that define this Hermite curve section are

$$\mathbf{P}(0) = \mathbf{p}_k$$
$$\mathbf{P}(1) = \mathbf{p}_{k+1}$$
$$\mathbf{P}'(0) = \mathbf{Dp}_k \qquad (10\text{-}27)$$
$$\mathbf{P}'(1) = \mathbf{Dp}_{k+1}$$

with $\mathbf{Dp}_k$ and $\mathbf{Dp}_{k+1}$ specifying the values for the parametric derivatives (slope of the curve) at control points $\mathbf{p}_k$ and $\mathbf{p}_{k+1}$, respectively.

We can write the vector equivalent of Eqs. 10-26 for this Hermite-curve section as

$$\mathbf{P}(u) = \mathbf{a}u^3 + \mathbf{b}u^2 + \mathbf{c}u + \mathbf{d}, \qquad 0 \le u \le 1 \qquad (10\text{-}28)$$

where the x component of $\mathbf{P}$ is $x(u) = a_x u^3 + b_x u^2 + c_x u + d_x$, and similarly for the y and z components. The matrix equivalent of Eq. 10-28 is

$$\mathbf{P}(u) = [u^3 \; u^2 \; u \; 1] \cdot \begin{bmatrix} \mathbf{a} \\ \mathbf{b} \\ \mathbf{c} \\ \mathbf{d} \end{bmatrix} \qquad (10\text{-}29)$$

and the derivative of the point function can be expressed as

$$\mathbf{P}'(u) = [3u^2 \; 2u \; 1 \; 0] \cdot \begin{bmatrix} \mathbf{a} \\ \mathbf{b} \\ \mathbf{c} \\ \mathbf{d} \end{bmatrix} \qquad (10\text{-}30)$$

Substituting endpoint values 0 and 1 for parameter u into the previous two equations, we can express the Hermite boundary conditions 10-27 in the matrix form:

$$\begin{bmatrix} \mathbf{p}_k \\ \mathbf{p}_{k+1} \\ \mathbf{Dp}_k \\ \mathbf{Dp}_{k+1} \end{bmatrix} = \begin{bmatrix} 0 & 0 & 0 & 1 \\ 1 & 1 & 1 & 1 \\ 0 & 0 & 1 & 0 \\ 3 & 2 & 1 & 0 \end{bmatrix} \cdot \begin{bmatrix} \mathbf{a} \\ \mathbf{b} \\ \mathbf{c} \\ \mathbf{d} \end{bmatrix} \qquad (10\text{-}31)$$

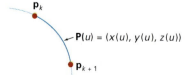

Figure 10-27

Parametric point function $\mathbf{P}(u)$ for a Hermite curve section between control points $\mathbf{p}_k$ and $\mathbf{p}_{k+1}$.

Solving this equation for the polynomial coefficients, we have

$$\begin{bmatrix} \mathbf{a} \\ \mathbf{b} \\ \mathbf{c} \\ \mathbf{d} \end{bmatrix} = \begin{bmatrix} 0 & 0 & 0 & 1 \\ 1 & 1 & 1 & 1 \\ 0 & 0 & 1 & 0 \\ 3 & 2 & 1 & 0 \end{bmatrix}^{-1} \cdot \begin{bmatrix} \mathbf{p}_k \\ \mathbf{p}_{k+1} \\ \mathbf{Dp}_k \\ \mathbf{Dp}_{k+1} \end{bmatrix}$$

$$= \begin{bmatrix} 2 & -2 & 1 & 1 \\ -3 & 3 & -2 & -1 \\ 0 & 0 & 1 & 0 \\ 1 & 0 & 0 & 0 \end{bmatrix} \cdot \begin{bmatrix} \mathbf{p}_k \\ \mathbf{p}_{k+1} \\ \mathbf{Dp}_k \\ \mathbf{Dp}_{k+1} \end{bmatrix} \qquad (10\text{-}32)$$

$$= \mathbf{M}_H \cdot \begin{bmatrix} \mathbf{p}_k \\ \mathbf{p}_{k+1} \\ \mathbf{Dp}_k \\ \mathbf{Dp}_{k+1} \end{bmatrix}$$

Do not memorize this

where $\mathbf{M}_H$, the Hermite matrix, is the inverse of the boundary constraint matrix. Equation 10-29 can thus be written in terms of the boundary conditions as

$$\mathbf{P}(u) = [u^3 \; u^2 \; u \; 1] \cdot \mathbf{M}_H \cdot \begin{bmatrix} \mathbf{p}_k \\ \mathbf{p}_{k+1} \\ \mathbf{Dp}_k \\ \mathbf{Dp}_{k+1} \end{bmatrix} \qquad (10\text{-}33)$$

Finally, we can determine expressions for the Hermite blending functions by carrying out the matrix multiplications in Eq. 10-33 and collecting coefficients for the boundary constraints to obtain the polynomial form:

$$\mathbf{P}(u) = \mathbf{p}_k(2u^3 - 3u^2 + 1) + \mathbf{p}_{k+1}(-2u^3 + 3u^2) + \mathbf{Dp}_k(u^3 - 2u^2 + u)$$
$$+ \mathbf{Dp}_{k+1}(u^3 - u^2) \qquad (10\text{-}34)$$
$$= \mathbf{p}_k H_0(u) + \mathbf{p}_{k+1} H_1(u) + \mathbf{Dp}_k H_2(u) + \mathbf{Dp}_{k+1} H_3(u)$$

The polynomials $H_k(u)$ for $k = 0, 1, 2, 3$ are referred to as blending functions because they blend the boundary constraint values (endpoint coordinates and slopes) to obtain each coordinate position along the curve. Figure 10-28 shows the shape of the four Hermite blending functions.

Hermite polynomials can be useful for some digitizing applications where it may not be too difficult to specify or approximate the curve slopes. But for most problems in computer graphics, it is more useful to generate spline curves without requiring input values for curve slopes or other geometric information, in addition to control-point coordinates. Cardinal splines and Kochanek–Bartels splines, discussed in the following two sections, are variations on the Hermite splines that do not require input values for the curve derivatives at the control points. Procedures for these splines compute parametric derivatives from the coordinate positions of the control points.

Cardinal Splines

As with Hermite splines, **cardinal splines** are interpolating piecewise cubics with specified endpoint tangents at the boundary of each curve section. The difference

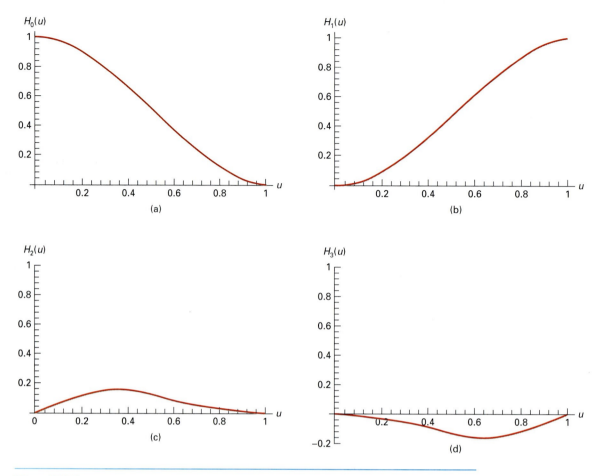

Figure 10-28
The Hermite blending functions.

is that we do not have to give the values for the endpoint tangents. For a cardinal spline, the value for the slope at a control point is calculated from the coordinates of the two adjacent control points.

A cardinal spline section is completely specified with four consecutive control points. The middle two control points are the section endpoints, and the other two points are used in the calculation of the endpoint slopes. If we take $\mathbf{P}(u)$ as the representation for the parametric cubic point function for the curve section between control points $\mathbf{p}_k$ and $\mathbf{p}_{k+1}$, as in Fig. 10-29, then the four control points from $\mathbf{p}_{k-1}$ to $\mathbf{p}_{k+1}$ are used to set the boundary conditions for the cardinal-spline section as

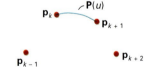

Figure 10-29
Parametric point function $\mathbf{P}(u)$ for a cardinal-spline section between control points $\mathbf{p}_k$ and $\mathbf{p}_{k+1}$.

$$\mathbf{P}(0) = \mathbf{p}_k$$
$$\mathbf{P}(1) = \mathbf{p}_{k+1}$$
$$\mathbf{P}'(0) = \tfrac{1}{2}(1 - t)(\mathbf{p}_{k+1} - \mathbf{p}_{k-1})$$
$$\mathbf{P}'(1) = \tfrac{1}{2}(1 - t)(\mathbf{p}_{k+2} - \mathbf{p}_k)$$

(10-35)

Thus, the slopes at control points $\mathbf{p}_k$ and $\mathbf{p}_{k+1}$ are taken to be proportional, respectively, to the chords $\overline{\mathbf{p}_{k-1}\mathbf{p}_{k+1}}$ and $\overline{\mathbf{p}_k\ \mathbf{p}_{k+2}}$ (Fig. 10-30). Parameter t is called the **tension** parameter since it controls how loosely or tightly the cardinal spline fits

324

the input control points. Figure 10-31 illustrates the shape of a cardinal curve for very small and very large values of tension t. When $t = 0$, this class of curves is referred to as **Catmull–Rom splines**, or **Overhauser splines**.

Using methods similar to those for Hermite splines, we can convert the boundary conditions 10-35 into the matrix form

$$\mathbf{P}(u) = [u^3 \; u^2 \; u \; 1] \cdot \mathbf{M}_C \cdot \begin{bmatrix} \mathbf{p}_{k-1} \\ \mathbf{p}_k \\ \mathbf{p}_{k+1} \\ \mathbf{p}_{k+2} \end{bmatrix} \qquad (10\text{-}36)$$

where the cardinal matrix is

$$\mathbf{M}_C = \begin{bmatrix} -s & 2-s & s-2 & s \\ 2s & s-3 & 3-2s & -s \\ -s & 0 & s & 0 \\ 0 & 1 & 0 & 0 \end{bmatrix} \qquad (10\text{-}37)$$

with $s = (1 - t)/2$.

Expanding matrix equation 10-36 into polynomial form, we have

$$\mathbf{P}(u) = \mathbf{p}_{k-1}(-su^3 + 2su^2 - su) + \mathbf{p}_k[(2 - s)u^3 + (s - 3)u^2 + 1]$$

$$+ \; \mathbf{p}_{k+1}[(s - 2)u^3 + (3 - 2s)u^2 + su] + \mathbf{p}_{k+2}(su^3 - su^2) \quad (10\text{-}38)$$

$$= \mathbf{p}_{k-1}CAR_0(u) + \mathbf{p}_k CAR_1(u) + \mathbf{p}_{k+1}CAR_2(u) + \mathbf{p}_{k+2}CAR_3(u)$$

where the polynomials $CAR_k(u)$ for $k = 0, 1, 2, 3$ are the cardinal blending functions. Figure 10-32 gives a plot of the basis functions for cardinal splines with $t = 0$.

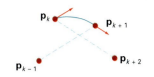

Figure 10-30
Tangent vectors at the endpoints of a cardinal-spline section are proportional to the chords formed with neighboring control points (dashed lines).

Kochanek–Bartels Splines

These interpolating cubic polynomials are extensions of the cardinal splines. Two additional parameters are introduced into the constraint equations defining **Kochanek–Bartels splines** to provide for further flexibility in adjusting the shape of curve sections.

Given four consecutive control points, labeled $\mathbf{p}_{k-1}$, $\mathbf{p}_k$, $\mathbf{p}_{k+1}$, and $\mathbf{p}_{k+2}$, we define the boundary conditions for a Kochanek–Bartels curve section between $\mathbf{p}_k$ and $\mathbf{p}_{k+1}$ as

$$\mathbf{P}(0) = \mathbf{p}_k$$

$$\mathbf{P}(1) = \mathbf{p}_{k+1}$$

$$\mathbf{P}'(0)_{\text{in}} = \tfrac{1}{2}(1 - t)[(1 + b)(1 - c)(\mathbf{p}_k - \mathbf{p}_{k-1})$$

$$+ (1 - b)(1 + c)(\mathbf{p}_{k+1} - \mathbf{p}_k)] \qquad (10\text{-}39)$$

$$\mathbf{P}'(1)_{\text{out}} = \tfrac{1}{2}(1 - t)[(1 + b)(1 + c)(\mathbf{p}_{k+1} - \mathbf{p}_k)$$

$$+ (1 - b)(1 - c)(\mathbf{p}_{k+2} - \mathbf{p}_{k+1})]$$

where t is the **tension** parameter, b is the **bias** parameter, and c is the **continuity** parameter. In the Kochanek-Bartels formulation, parametric derivatives may not be continuous across section boundaries.

$t < 0$
(Looser Curve)

$t > 0$
(Tighter Curve)

Figure 10-31
Effect of the tension parameter on the shape of a cardinal spline section.

Tension parameter t has the same interpretation as in the cardinal-spline formulation; that is, it controls the looseness or tightness of the curve sections. Bias (b) is used to adjust the amount that the curve bends at each end of a section, so that curve sections can be skewed toward one end or the other (Fig. 10-33). Parameter c controls the continuity of the tangent vector across the boundaries of sections. If c is assigned a nonzero value, there is a discontinuity in the slope of the curve across section boundaries.

Kochanek–Bartel splines were designed to model animation paths. In particular, abrupt changes in motion of a object can be simulated with nonzero values for parameter c.

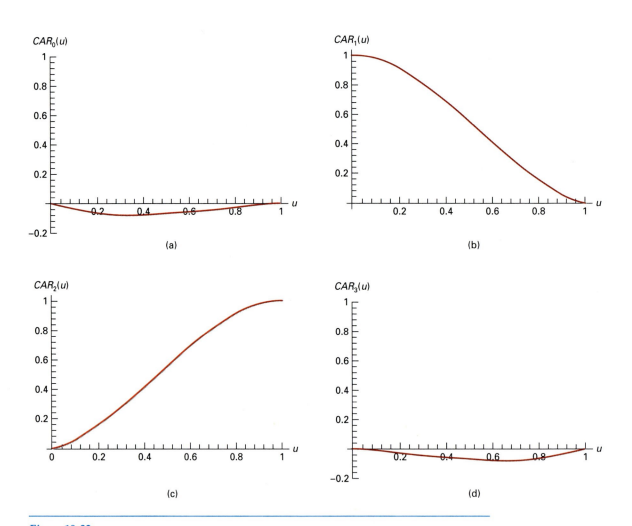

Figure 10-32
The cardinal blending functions for $t = 0$ and $s = 0.5$.

326

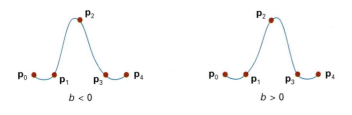

$b < 0$　　　　　　　　$b > 0$

Figure 10-33
Effect of the bias parameter on the shape of a
Kochanek–Bartels spline section.

10-8
BÉZIER CURVES AND SURFACES

This spline approximation method was developed by the French engineer Pierre
Bézier for use in the design of Renault automobile bodies. **Bézier splines** have a
number of properties that make them highly useful and convenient for curve and
surface design. They are also easy to implement. For these reasons, Bézier splines
are widely available in various CAD systems, in general graphics packages (such
as GL on Silicon Graphics systems), and in assorted drawing and painting packages (such as Aldus SuperPaint and Cricket Draw).

Bézier Curves

In general, a Bézier curve section can be fitted to any number of control points.
The number of control points to be approximated and their relative position determine the degree of the Bézier polynomial. As with the interpolation splines, a
Bézier curve can be specified with boundary conditions, with a characterizing
matrix, or with blending functions. For general Bézier curves, the blending-function specification is the most convenient.

Suppose we are given $n + 1$ control-point positions: $\mathbf{p}_k = (x_k, y_k, z_k)$, with k
varying from 0 to n. These coordinate points can be blended to produce the following position vector $\mathbf{P}(u)$, which describes the path of an approximating Bézier
polynomial function between $\mathbf{p}_0$ and $\mathbf{p}_n$.

$$\mathbf{P}(u) = \sum_{k=0}^{n} \mathbf{p}_k \, BEZ_{k,n}(u), \qquad 0 \le u \le 1 \qquad (10\text{-}40)$$

The Bézier blending functions $BEZ_{k,n}(u)$ are the *Bernstein polynomials*:

$$BEZ_{k,n}(u) = C(n, k) u^k (1 - u)^{n-k} \qquad (10\text{-}41)$$

where the $C(n, k)$ are the binomial coefficients:

$$C(n, k) = \frac{n!}{k!(n - k)!} \qquad (10\text{-}42)$$

Equivalently, we can define Bézier blending functions with the recursive calculation

$$BEZ_{k,n}(u) = (1 - u)\, BEZ_{k,n-1}(u) + u BEZ_{k-1,n-1}(u), \qquad n > k \ge 1 \quad (10\text{-}43)$$

with $BEZ_{k,k} = u^k$, and $BEZ_{0,k} = (1 - u)^k$. Vector equation 10-40 represents a set of three parametric equations for the individual curve coordinates:

$$x(u) = \sum_{k=0}^{n} x_k \, BEZ_{k,n}(u)$$

$$y(u) = \sum_{k=0}^{n} y_k \, BEZ_{k,n}(u) \qquad (10\text{-}44)$$

$$z(u) = \sum_{k=0}^{n} z_k \, BEZ_{k,n}(u)$$

As a rule, a Bézier curve is a polynomial of degree one less than the number of control points used: Three points generate a parabola, four points a cubic curve, and so forth. Figure 10-34 demonstrates the appearance of some Bezier curves for various selections of control points in the xy plane ($z = 0$). With certain control-point placements, however, we obtain degenerate Bézier polynomials. For example, a Bézier curve generated with three collinear control points is a straight-line segment. And a set of control points that are all at the same coordinate position produces a Bézier "curve" that is a single point.

Bézier curves are commonly found in painting and drawing packages, as well as CAD systems, since they are easy to implement and they are reasonably powerful in curve design. Efficient methods for determining coordinate positions along a Bézier curve can be set up using recursive calculations. For example, successive binomial coefficients can be calculated as

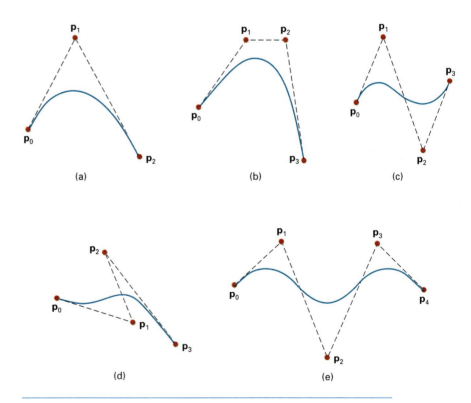

Figure 10-34
Examples of two-dimensional Bézier curves generated from three, four, and five control points. Dashed lines connect the control-point positions.

$$C(n, k) = \frac{n-k+1}{k} C(n, k-1) \qquad (10\text{-}45)$$

for $n \geq k$. The following example program illustrates a method for generating Bézier curves.

```
#include <math.h>
#include "graphics.h"

void computeCoefficients (int n, int * c)
{
  int k, i;

  for (k=0; k<=n; k++) {
    /* Compute n!/(k!(n-k)!) */
    c[k] = 1;
    for (i=n; i>=k+1; i--)
      c[k] *= i;
    for (i=n-k; i>=2; i--)
      c[k] /= i;
  }
}

void computePoint
  (float u, wcPt3 * pt, int nControls, wcPt3 * controls, int * c)
{
  int k, n = nControls - 1;
  float blend;

  pt->x = 0.0; pt->y = 0.0; pt->z = 0.0;

  /* Add in influence of each control point */
  for (k=0; k<nControls; k++) {
    blend = c[k] * powf (u,k) * powf (1-u,n-k);
    pt->x += controls[k].x * blend;
    pt->y += controls[k].y * blend;
    pt->z += controls[k].z * blend;
  }
}

void bezier (wcPt3 * controls, int nControls, int m, wcPt3 * curve)
{
  /* Allocate space for the coefficients */
  int * c = (int *) malloc (nControls * sizeof (int));
  int i;

  computeCoefficients (nControls-1, c);
  for (i=0; i<=m; i++)
    computePoint (i / (float) m, &curve[i], nControls, controls, c);
  free (c);
}
```

Properties of Bézier Curves

A very useful property of a Bézier curve is that it always passes through the first and last control points. That is, the boundary conditions at the two ends of the curve are

$$\mathbf{P}(0) = \mathbf{p}_0$$
$$\mathbf{P}(1) = \mathbf{p}_n \qquad (10\text{-}46)$$

329

Values of the parametric first derivatives of a Bézier curve at the endpoints can be calculated from control-point coordinates as

$$\mathbf{P}'(0) = -n\mathbf{p}_0 + n\mathbf{p}_1$$
$$\mathbf{P}'(1) = -n\mathbf{p}_{n-1} + n\mathbf{p}_n$$

(10-47)

Thus, the slope at the beginning of the curve is along the line joining the first two control points, and the slope at the end of the curve is along the line joining the last two endpoints. Similarly, the parametric second derivatives of a Bézier curve at the endpoints are calculated as

$$\mathbf{P}''(0) = n(n-1)[(\mathbf{p}_2 - \mathbf{p}_1) - (\mathbf{p}_1 - \mathbf{p}_0)]$$
$$\mathbf{P}''(1) = n(n-1)[(\mathbf{p}_{n-2} - \mathbf{p}_{n-1}) - (\mathbf{p}_{n-1} - \mathbf{p}_n)]$$

(10-48)

Another important property of any Bézier curve is that it lies within the convex hull (convex polygon boundary) of the control points. This follows from the properties of Bézier blending functions: They are all positive and their sum is always 1,

$$\sum_{k=0}^{n} BEZ_{k,n}(u) = 1$$

(10-49)

so that any curve position is simply the weighted sum of the control-point positions. The convex-hull property for a Bézier curve ensures that the polynomial smoothly follows the control points without erratic oscillations.

Design Techniques Using Bézier Curves

Closed Bézier curves are generated by specifying the first and last control points at the same position, as in the example shown in Fig. 10-35. Also, specifying multiple control points at a single coordinate position gives more weight to that position. In Fig. 10-36, a single coordinate position is input as two control points, and the resulting curve is pulled nearer to this position.

We can fit a Bézier curve to any number of control points, but this requires the calculation of polynomial functions of higher degree. When complicated curves are to be generated, they can be formed by piecing several Bézier sections of lower degree together. Piecing together smaller sections also gives us better control over the shape of the curve in small regions. Since Bézier curves pass through endpoints, it is easy to match curve sections (zero-order continuity). Also, Bézier curves have the important property that the tangent to the curve at an endpoint is along the line joining that endpoint to the adjacent control point. Therefore, to obtain first-order continuity between curve sections, we can pick control points $\mathbf{p}'_0$ and $\mathbf{p}'_1$ of a new section to be along the same straight line as control points $\mathbf{p}_{n-1}$ and $\mathbf{p}_n$ of the previous section (Fig. 10-37). When the two curve sections have the same number of control points, we obtain C^1 continuity by choosing the first control point of the new section as the last control point of the previous section and by positioning the second control point of the new section at position

$$\mathbf{p}_n + (\mathbf{p}_n - \mathbf{p}_{n-1})$$

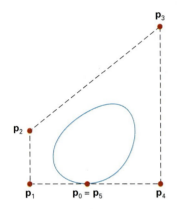

Figure 10-35
A closed Bézier curve generated by specifying the first and last control points at the same location.

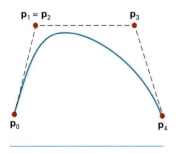

Figure 10-36
A Bézier curve can be made to pass closer to a given coordinate position by assigning multiple control points to that position.

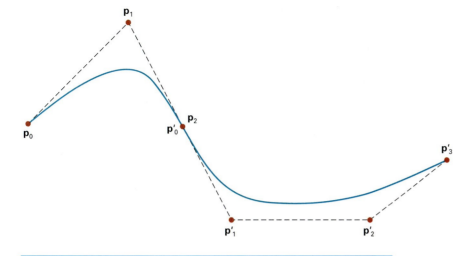

Figure 10-37
Piecewise approximation curve formed with two Bézier sections. Zero-order and first-order continuity are attained between curve sections by setting $\mathbf{p}'_0 = \mathbf{p}_2$ and by making points $\mathbf{p}_1$, $\mathbf{p}_2$, and $\mathbf{p}'_1$ collinear.

Thus, the three control points are collinear and equally spaced.

We obtain C^2 continuity between two Bézier sections by calculating the position of the third control point of a new section in terms of the positions of the last three control points of the previous section as

$$\mathbf{p}_{n-2} + 4(\mathbf{p}_n - \mathbf{p}_{n-1})$$

Requiring second-order continuity of Bézier curve sections can be unnecessarily restrictive. This is especially true with cubic curves, which have only four control points per section. In this case, second-order continuity fixes the position of the first three control points and leaves us only one point that we can use to adjust the shape of the curve segment.

Cubic Bézier Curves

Many graphics packages provide only cubic spline functions. This gives reasonable design flexibility while avoiding the increased calculations needed with higher-order polynomials. Cubic Bézier curves are generated with four control points. The four blending functions for cubic Bézier curves, obtained by substituting $n = 3$ into Eq. 10-41 are

$$BEZ_{0,3}(u) = (1 - u)^3$$
$$BEZ_{1,3}(u) = 3u(1 - u)^2$$
$$BEZ_{2,3}(u) = 3u^2(1 - u) \qquad (10\text{-}50)$$
$$BEZ_{3,3}(u) = u^3$$

Plots of the four cubic Bézier blending functions are given in Fig. 10-38. The form of the blending functions determine how the control points influence the shape of the curve for values of parameter u over the range from 0 to 1. At $u = 0$,

331

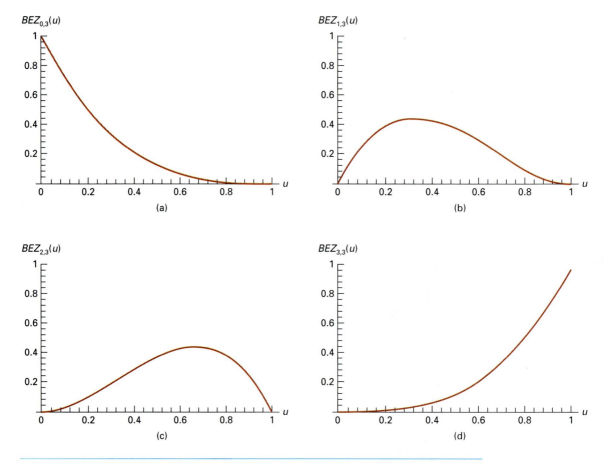

Figure 10-38
The four Bézier blending functions for cubic curves ($n = 3$).

the only nonzero blending function is $BEZ_{0,3}$, which has the value 1. At $u = 1$, the only nonzero function is $BEZ_{3,3}$, with a value of 1 at that point. Thus, the cubic Bézier curve will always pass through control points $\mathbf{p}_0$ and $\mathbf{p}_3$. The other functions, $BEZ_{1,3}$ and $BEZ_{2,3}$, influence the shape of the curve at intermediate values of parameter u, so that the resulting curve tends toward points $\mathbf{p}_1$ and $\mathbf{p}_2$. Blending function $BEZ_{1,3}$ is maximum at $u = 1/3$, and $BEZ_{2,3}$ is maximum at $u = 2/3$.

We note in Fig. 10-38 that each of the four blending functions is nonzero over the entire range of parameter u. Thus, Bézier curves do not allow for *local control* of the curve shape. If we decide to reposition any one of the control points, the entire curve will be affected.

At the end positions of the cubic Bézier curve, the parametric first derivatives (slopes) are

$$\mathbf{P}'(0) = 3(\mathbf{p}_1 - \mathbf{p}_0), \qquad \mathbf{P}'(1) = 3(\mathbf{p}_3 - \mathbf{p}_2)$$

And the parametric second derivatives are

$$\mathbf{P}''(0) = 6(\mathbf{p}_0 - 2\mathbf{p}_1 + \mathbf{p}_2), \qquad \mathbf{P}''(1) = 6(\mathbf{p}_1 - 2\mathbf{p}_2 + \mathbf{p}_3)$$

We can use these expressions for the parametric derivatives to construct piecewise curves with C^1 or C^2 continuity between sections.

By expanding the polynomial expressions for the blending functions, we can write the cubic Bézier point function in the matrix form

$$\mathbf{P}(u) = [u^3 \ u^2 \ u \ 1] \cdot \mathbf{M}_{\text{Bez}} \cdot \begin{bmatrix} \mathbf{p}_0 \\ \mathbf{p}_1 \\ \mathbf{p}_2 \\ \mathbf{p}_3 \end{bmatrix} \qquad (10\text{-}51)$$

where the **Bézier matrix** is

$$\mathbf{M}_{\text{Bez}} = \begin{bmatrix} -1 & 3 & -3 & 1 \\ 3 & -6 & 3 & 0 \\ -3 & 3 & 0 & 0 \\ 1 & 0 & 0 & 0 \end{bmatrix} \qquad (10\text{-}52)$$

We could also introduce additional parameters to allow adjustment of curve "tension" and "bias", as we did with the interpolating splines. But the more useful B-splines, as well as β-splines, provide this capability.

Bézier Surfaces

Two sets of orthogonal Bézier curves can be used to design an object surface by specifying by an input mesh of control points. The parametric vector function for the Bézier surface is formed as the Cartesian product of Bézier blending functions:

$$\mathbf{P}(u, v) = \sum_{j=0}^{m} \sum_{k=0}^{n} \mathbf{p}_{j,k} BEZ_{j,m}(v) BEZ_{k,n}(u) \qquad (10\text{-}53)$$

with $\mathbf{p}_{j,k}$ specifying the location of the $(m + 1)$ by $(n + 1)$ control points.

Figure 10-39 illustrates two Bézier surface plots. The control points are connected by dashed lines, and the solid lines show curves of constant u and constant v. Each curve of constant u is plotted by varying v over the interval from 0 to 1, with u fixed at one of the values in this unit interval. Curves of constant v are plotted similarly.

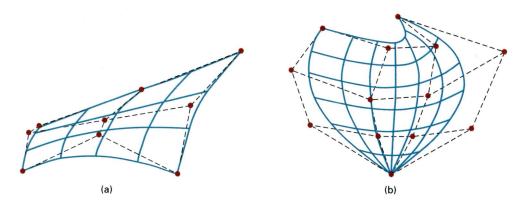

(a) (b)

Figure 10-39
Bézier surfaces constructed for (a) $m = 3$, $n = 3$, and (b) $m = 4$, $n = 4$. Dashed lines connect the control points.

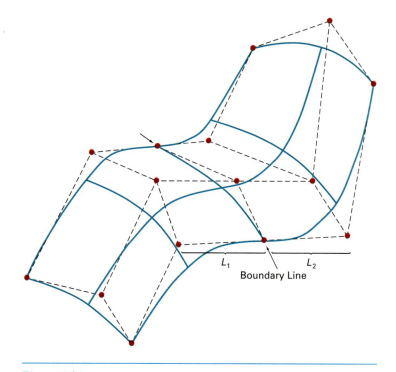

Figure 10-40
A composite Bézier surface constructed with two Bézier sections,
joined at the indicated boundary line. The dashed lines connect
specified control points. First-order continuity is established by
making the ratio of length L_1 to length L_2 constant for each collinear
line of control points across the boundary between the surface
sections.

Bézier surfaces have the same properties as Bézier curves, and they provide
a convenient method for interactive design applications. For each surface patch,
we can select a mesh of control points in the xy "ground" plane, then we choose
elevations above the ground plane for the z-coordinate values of the control
points. Patches can then be pieced together using the boundary constraints.

Figure 10-40 illustrates a surface formed with two Bézier sections. As with
curves, a smooth transition from one section to the other is assured by establishing both zero-order and first-order continuity at the boundary line. Zero-order
continuity is obtained by matching control points at the boundary. First-order
continuity is obtained by choosing control points along a straight line across the
boundary and by maintaining a constant ratio of collinear line segments for each
set of specified control points across section boundaries.

10-9
B-SPLINE CURVES AND SURFACES

These are the most widely used class of approximating splines. **B-splines** have
two advantages over Bézier splines: (1) the degree of a B-spline polynomial can
be set independently of the number of control points (with certain limitations),
and (2) B-splines allow local control over the shape of a spline curve or surface.
The trade-off is that B-splines are more complex than Bézier splines.

B-Spline Curves

We can write a general expression for the calculation of coordinate positions along a B-spline curve in a blending-function formulation as

$$\mathbf{P}(u) = \sum_{k=0}^{n} \mathbf{p}_k B_{k,d}(u), \qquad u_{\min} \leq u \leq u_{\max}, \qquad 2 \leq d \leq n + 1 \qquad (10\text{-}54)$$

where the $\mathbf{p}_k$ are an input set of $n + 1$ control points. There are several differences between this B-spline formulation and that for Bézier splines. The range of parameter u now depends on how we choose the B-spline parameters. And the B-spline blending functions $B_{k,d}$ are polynomials of degree $d - 1$, where parameter d can be chosen to be any integer value in the range from 2 up to the number of control points, $n + 1$. (Actually, we can also set the value of d at 1, but then our "curve" is just a point plot of the control points.) Local control for B-splines is achieved by defining the blending functions over subintervals of the total range of u.

Blending functions for B-spline curves are defined by the Cox–deBoor recursion formulas:

$$B_{k,1}(u) = \begin{cases} 1, & \text{if } u_k \leq u < u_{k+1} \\ 0, & \text{otherwise} \end{cases}$$

$$(10\text{-}55)$$

$$B_{k,d}(u) = \frac{u - u_k}{u_{k+d-1} - u_k} B_{k,d-1}(u) + \frac{u_{k+d} - u}{u_{k+d} - u_{k+1}} B_{k+1,d-1}(u)$$

where each blending function is defined over d subintervals of the total range of u. The selected set of subinterval endpoints u_j is referred to as a **knot vector**. We can choose any values for the subinterval endpoints satisfying the relation $u_j \leq u_{j+1}$. Values for $u_{\min}$ and $u_{\max}$ then depend on the number of control points we select, the value we choose for parameter d, and how we set up the subintervals (knot vector). Since it is possible to choose the elements of the knot vector so that the denominators in the previous calculations can have a value of 0, this formulation assumes that any terms evaluated as $0/0$ are to be assigned the value 0.

Figure 10-41 demonstrates the local-control characteristics of B-splines. In addition to local control, B-splines allow us to vary the number of control points used to design a curve without changing the degree of the polynomial. Also, any number of control points can be added or modified to manipulate curve shapes. Similarly, we can increase the number of values in the knot vector to aid in curve design. When we do this, however, we also need to add control points since the size of the knot vector depends on parameter n.

B-spline curves have the following properties:

- The polynomial curve has degree $d - 1$ and C^{d-2} continuity over the range of u.
- For $n + 1$ control points, the curve is described with $n + 1$ blending functions.
- Each blending function $B_{k,d}$ is defined over d subintervals of the total range of u, starting at knot value u_k.
- The range of parameter u is divided into $n + d$ subintervals by the $n + d + 1$ values specified in the knot vector.

Chapter 10

Three-Dimensional Object
Representations

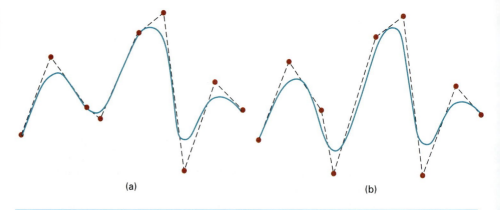

(a)   (b)

Figure 10-41
Local modification of a B-spline curve. Changing one of the control points in (a) produces curve (b), which is modified only in the neighborhood of the altered control point.

- With knot values labeled as $\{u_0, u_1, \ldots, u_{n+d}\}$, the resulting B-spline curve is defined only in the interval from knot value u_{d-1} up to knot value u_{n+1}.
- Each section of the spline curve (between two successive knot values) is influenced by d control points.
- Any one control point can affect the shape of at most d curve sections.

In addition, a B-spline curve lies within the convex hull of at most $d + 1$ control points, so that B-splines are tightly bound to the input positions. For any value of u in the interval from knot value u_{d-1} to u_{n+1}, the sum over all basis functions is 1:

$$\sum_{k=0}^{n} B_{k,d}(u) = 1 \qquad (10\text{-}56)$$

Given the control-point positions and the value of parameter d, we then need to specify the knot values to obtain the blending functions using the recurrence relations 10-55. There are three general classifications for knot vectors: uniform, open uniform, and nonuniform. B-splines are commonly described according to the selected knot-vector class.

Uniform, Periodic B-Splines

When the spacing between knot values is constant, the resulting curve is called a **uniform** B-spline. For example, we can set up a uniform knot vector as

$$\{-1.5, -1.0, -0.5, 0.0, 0.5, 1.0, 1.5, 2.0\}$$

Often knot values are normalized to the range between 0 and 1, as in

$$\{0.0, 0.2, 0.4, 0.6, 0.8, 1.0\}$$

It is convenient in many applications to set up uniform knot values with a separation of 1 and a starting value of 0. The following knot vector is an example of this specification scheme.

$$\{0, 1, 2, 3, 4, 5, 6, 7\}$$

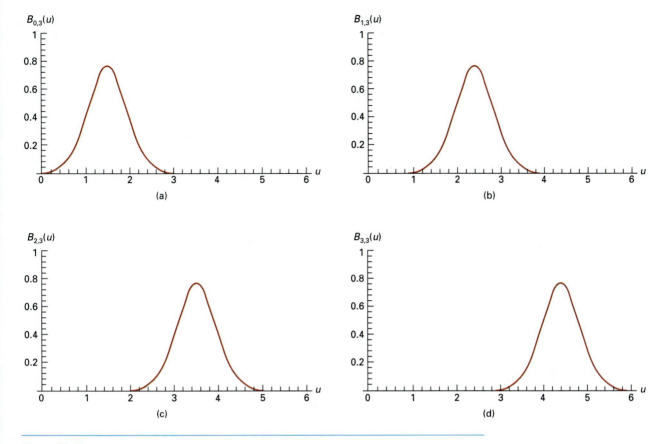

Figure 10-42

Periodic B-spline blending functions for $n = d = 3$ and a uniform, integer knot vector.

Uniform B-splines have **periodic** blending functions. That is, for given values of n and d, all blending functions have the same shape. Each successive blending function is simply a shifted version of the previous function:

$$B_{k,d}(u) = B_{k+1,d}(u + \Delta u) = B_{k+2,d}(u + 2\, \Delta u) \qquad (10\text{-}57)$$

where Δu is the interval between adjacent knot values. Figure 10-42 shows the quadratic, uniform B-spline blending functions generated in the following example for a curve with four control points.

Example 10-1 Uniform, Quadratic B-Splines

To illustrate the calculation of B-spline blending functions for a uniform, integer knot vector, we select parameter values $d = n = 3$. The knot vector must then contain $n + d + 1 = 7$ knot values:

$$\{0, 1, 2, 3, 4, 5, 6\}$$

and the range of parameter u is from 0 to 6, with $n + d = 6$ subintervals.

Each of the four blending functions spans $d = 3$ subintervals of the total range of u. Using the recurrence relations 10-55, we obtain the first blending function as

$$B_{0,3}(u) = \begin{cases} \frac{1}{2}u^2, & \text{for } 0 \leq u < 1 \\[2mm] \frac{1}{2}u(2-u) + \frac{1}{2}(u-1)(3-u), & \text{for } 1 \leq u < 2 \\[2mm] \frac{1}{2}(3-u)^2, & \text{for } 2 \leq u < 3 \end{cases}$$

We obtain the next periodic blending function using relationship 10-57, substituting $u - 1$ for u in $B_{0,3}$, and shifting the starting positions up by 1:

$$B_{1,3}(u) = \begin{cases} \frac{1}{2}(u-1)^2, & \text{for } 1 \leq u < 2 \\[2mm] \frac{1}{2}(u-1)(3-u) + \frac{1}{2}(u-2)(4-u), & \text{for } 2 \leq u < 3 \\[2mm] \frac{1}{2}(4-u)^2, & \text{for } 3 \leq u < 4 \end{cases}$$

Similarly, the remaining two periodic functions are obtained by successively shifting $B_{1,3}$ to the right:

$$B_{2,3}(u) = \begin{cases} \frac{1}{2}(u-2)^2, & \text{for } 2 \leq u < 3 \\[2mm] \frac{1}{2}(u-2)(4-u) + \frac{1}{2}(u-3)(5-u), & \text{for } 3 \leq u < 4 \\[2mm] \frac{1}{2}(5-u)^2, & \text{for } 4 \leq u < 5 \end{cases}$$

$$B_{3,3}(u) = \begin{cases} \frac{1}{2}(u-3)^2, & \text{for } 3 \leq u < 4 \\[2mm] \frac{1}{2}(u-3)(5-u) + \frac{1}{2}(u-4)(6-u), & \text{for } 4 \leq u < 5 \\[2mm] \frac{1}{2}(6-u)^2, & \text{for } 5 \leq u < 6 \end{cases}$$

A plot of the four periodic, quadratic blending functions is given in Fig. 10-42, which demonstrates the local feature of B-splines. The first control point is multiplied by blending function $B_{0,3}(u)$. Therefore, changing the position of the first control point only affects the shape of the curve up to $u = 3$. Similarly, the last control point influences the shape of the spline curve in the interval where $B_{3,3}$ is defined.

Figure 10-42 also illustrates the limits of the B-spline curve for this example. All blending functions are present in the interval from $u_{d-1} = 2$ to $u_{n+1} = 4$. Below 2 and above 4, not all blending functions are present. This is the range of the poly-

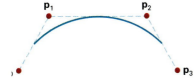

Figure 10-43
Quadratic, periodic B-spline fitted
to four control points in the xy
plane.

nomial curve, and the interval in which Eq. 10-56 is valid. Thus, the sum of all blending functions is 1 within this interval. Outside this interval, we cannot sum all blending functions, since they are not all defined below 2 and above 4.

Since the range of the resulting polynomial curve is from 2 to 4, we can determine the starting and ending positions of the curve by evaluating the blending functions at these points to obtain

$$\mathbf{P}_{\text{start}} = \tfrac{1}{2}(\mathbf{p}_0 + \mathbf{p}_1), \qquad \mathbf{P}_{\text{end}} = \tfrac{1}{2}(\mathbf{p}_2 + \mathbf{p}_3)$$

Thus, the curve starts at the midposition between the first two control points and ends at the midposition between the last two control points.

We can also determine the parametric derivatives at the starting and ending positions of the curve. Taking the derivatives of the blending functions and substituting the endpoint values for parameter u, we find that

$$\mathbf{P}'_{\text{start}} = \mathbf{p}_1 - \mathbf{p}_0, \qquad \mathbf{P}'_{\text{end}} = \mathbf{p}_3 - \mathbf{p}_2$$

The parametric slope of the curve at the start position is parallel to the line joining the first two control points, and the parametric slope at the end of the curve is parallel to the line joining the last two control points.

An example plot of the quadratic periodic B-spline curve is given in Figure 10-43 for four control points selected in the xy plane.

In the preceding example, we noted that the quadratic curve starts between the first two control points and ends at a position between the last two control points. This result is valid for a quadratic, periodic B-spline fitted to any number of distinct control points. In general, for higher-order polynomials, the start and end positions are each weighted averages of $d - 1$ control points. We can pull a spline curve closer to any control-point position by specifying that position multiple times.

General expressions for the boundary conditions for periodic B-splines can be obtained by reparameterizing the blending functions so that parameter u is mapped onto the unit interval from 0 to 1. Beginning and ending conditions are then obtained at $u = 0$ and $u = 1$.

Cubic, Periodic B-Splines

Since cubic, periodic B-splines are commonly used in graphics packages, we consider the formulation for this class of splines. Periodic splines are particularly useful for generating certain closed curves. For example, the closed curve in Fig. 10-44 can be generated in sections by cyclically specifying four of the six control

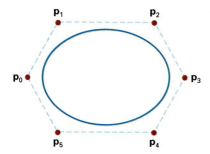

points shown at each step. If any three consecutive control points are identical, the curve passes through that coordinate position.

For cubics, $d = 4$ and each blending function spans four subintervals of the total range of u. If we are to fit the cubic to four control points, then we could use the integer knot vector

$$\{0, 1, 2, 3, 4, 5, 6, 7\}$$

and recurrence relations 10-55 to obtain the periodic blending functions, as we did in the last section for quadratic periodic B-splines.

In this section, we consider an alternate formulation for periodic cubic B-splines. We start with the boundary conditions and obtain the blending functions normalized to the interval $0 \le u \le 1$. Using this formulation, we can also easily obtain the characteristic matrix. The boundary conditions for periodic cubic B-splines with four consecutive control points, labeled $\mathbf{p}_0$, $\mathbf{p}_1$, $\mathbf{p}_2$, and $\mathbf{p}_3$, are

$$\mathbf{P}(0) = \tfrac{1}{6}(\mathbf{p}_0 + 4\mathbf{p}_1 + \mathbf{p}_2)$$

$$\mathbf{P}(1) = \tfrac{1}{6}(\mathbf{p}_1 + 4\mathbf{p}_2 + \mathbf{p}_3)$$

$$\mathbf{P}'(0) = \tfrac{1}{2}(\mathbf{p}_2 - \mathbf{p}_0)$$

$$\mathbf{P}'(1) = \tfrac{1}{2}(\mathbf{p}_3 - \mathbf{p}_1)$$

(10-58)

These boundary conditions are similar to those for cardinal splines: Curve sections are defined with four control points, and parametric derivatives (slopes) at the beginning and end of each curve section are parallel to the chords joining adjacent control points. The B-spline curve section starts at a position near $\mathbf{p}_1$ and ends at a position near $\mathbf{p}_2$.

A matrix formulation for a cubic periodic B-splines with four control points can then be written as

$$\mathbf{P}(u) = [u^3 \ u^2 \ u \ 1] \cdot \mathbf{M}_B \cdot \begin{bmatrix} \mathbf{p}_0 \\ \mathbf{p}_1 \\ \mathbf{p}_2 \\ \mathbf{p}_3 \end{bmatrix}$$

(10-59)

where the B-spline matrix for periodic cubic polynomials is

$$\mathbf{M}_B = \frac{1}{6} \begin{bmatrix} -1 & 3 & -3 & 1 \\ 3 & -6 & 3 & 0 \\ -3 & 0 & 3 & 0 \\ 1 & 4 & 1 & 0 \end{bmatrix} \qquad (10\text{-}60)$$

This matrix can be obtained by solving for the coefficients in a general cubic polynomial expression using the specified four boundary conditions.

We can also modify the B-spline equations to include a tension parameter t (as in cardinal splines). The periodic, cubic B-spline with tension matrix then has the form

$$\mathbf{M}_{Bt} = \frac{1}{6} \begin{bmatrix} -t & 12-9t & 9t-12 & t \\ 3t & 12t-18 & 18-15t & 0 \\ -3t & 0 & 3t & 0 \\ t & 6-2t & t & 0 \end{bmatrix} \qquad (10\text{-}61)$$

which reduces to M_B when $t = 1$.

We obtain the periodic, cubic B-spline blending functions over the parameter range from 0 to 1 by expanding the matrix representation into polynomial form. For example, for the tension value $t = 1$, we have

$$B_{0,3}(u) = \tfrac{1}{6}(1-u)^3, \qquad 0 \le u \le 1$$

$$B_{1,3}(u) = \tfrac{1}{6}(3u^3 - 6u^2 + 4)$$

$$\qquad (10\text{-}62)$$

$$B_{2,3}(u) = \tfrac{1}{6}(-3u^3 + 3u^2 + 3u + 1)$$

$$B_{3,3}(u) = \tfrac{1}{6}u^3$$

Open Uniform B-Splines

This class of B-splines is a cross between uniform B-splines and nonuniform B-splines. Sometimes it is treated as a special type of uniform B-spline, and sometimes it is considered to be in the nonuniform B-spline classification. For the **open uniform** B-splines, or simply **open** B-splines, the knot spacing is uniform except at the ends where knot values are repeated d times.

Following are two examples of open uniform, integer knot vectors, each with a starting value of 0:

$$\{0, 0, 1, 2, 3, 3,\}, \qquad \text{for } d = 2 \text{ and } n = 3$$

$$\{0, 0, 0, 0, 1, 2, 2, 2, 2,\}, \qquad \text{for } d = 4 \text{ and } n = 4$$

We can normalize these knot vectors to the unit interval from 0 to 1:

$$\{0, 0, 0.33, 0.67, 1, 1,\}, \qquad \text{for } d = 2 \text{ and } n = 3$$

$$\{0, 0, 0, 0, 0.5, 1, 1, 1, 1\}, \qquad \text{for } d = 4 \text{ and } n = 4$$

341

For any values of parameters d and n, we can generate an open uniform knot vector with integer values using the calculations

$$u_j = \begin{cases} 0, & \text{for } 0 \le j < d \\ j - d + 1, & \text{for } d \le j \le n \\ n - d + 2, & \text{for } j > n \end{cases} \qquad (10\text{-}63)$$

for values of j ranging from 0 to $n + d$. With this assignment, the first d knots are assigned the value 0, and the last d knots have the value $n - d + 2$.

Open uniform B-splines have characteristics that are very similar to Bézier splines. In fact, when $d = n + 1$ (degree of the polynomial is n) open B-splines reduce to Bézier splines, and all knot values are either 0 or 1. For example, with a cubic, open B-spline ($d = 4$) and four control points, the knot vector is

$$\{0, 0, 0, 0, 1, 1, 1, 1\}$$

The polynomial curve for an open B-spline passes through the first and last control points. Also, the slope of the parametric curves at the first control point is parallel to the line connecting the first two control points. And the parametric slope at the last control point is parallel to the line connecting the last two control points. So geometric constraints for matching curve sections are the same as for Bézier curves.

As with Bézier curves, specifying multiple control points at the same coordinate position pulls any B-spline curve closer to that position. Since open B-splines start at the first control point and end at the last specified control point, closed curves are generated by specifying the first and last control points at the same position.

Example 10-2 Open Uniform, Quadratic B-Splines

From conditions 10-63 with $d = 3$ and $n = 4$ (five control points), we obtain the following eight values for the knot vector:

$$\{u_0, u_1, u_2, u_3, u_4, u_5, u_6, u_7\} = \{0, 0, 0, 1, 2, 3, 3, 3\}$$

The total range of u is divided into seven subintervals, and each of the five blending functions $B_{k,3}$ is defined over three subintervals, starting at knot position u_k. Thus, $B_{0,3}$ is defined from $u_0 = 0$ to $u_3 = 1$, $B_{1,3}$ is defined from $u_1 = 0$ to $u_4 = 2$, and $B_{4,3}$ is defined from $u_4 = 2$ to $u_7 = 3$. Explicit polynomial expressions are obtained for the blending functions from recurrence relations 10-55 as

$$B_{0,3}(u) = (1 - u)^2, \qquad\qquad\qquad 0 \le u < 1$$

$$B_{1,3}(u) = \begin{cases} \frac{1}{2}u(4 - 3u), & 0 \le u < 1 \\[2mm] \frac{1}{2}(2 - u)^2, & 1 \le u < 2 \end{cases}$$

$$B_{2,3}(u) = \begin{cases} \frac{1}{2}u^2, & 0 \le u < 1 \\ \frac{1}{2}u(2-u) + \frac{1}{2}(u-1)(3-u), & 1 \le u < 2 \\ \frac{1}{2}(3-u)^2, & 2 \le u < 3 \end{cases}$$

$$B_{3,3}(u) = \begin{cases} \frac{1}{2}(u-1)^2, & 1 \le u < 2 \\ \frac{1}{2}(3-u)(3u-5), & 2 \le u < 3 \end{cases}$$

$$B_{4,3}(u) = (u-2)^2, \qquad\qquad 2 \le u < 3$$

Figure 10-45 shows the shape of the these five blending functions. The local features of B-splines are again demonstrated. Blending function $B_{0,3}$ is nonzero only in the subinterval from 0 to 1, so the first control point influences the curve only in this interval. Similarly, function $B_{4,3}$ is zero outside the interval from 2 to 3, and the position of the last control point does not affect the shape of the beginning and middle parts of the curve.

Matrix formulations for open B-splines are not as conveniently generated as they are for periodic, uniform B-splines. This is due to the multiplicity of knot values at the beginning and end of the knot vector.

Nonuniform B-Splines

For this class of splines, we can specify any values and intervals for the knot vector. With **nonuniform** B-splines, we can choose multiple internal knot values and unequal spacing between the knot values. Some examples are

$$\{0, 1, 2, 3, 3, 4\}$$

$$\{0, 2, 2, 3, 3, 6\}$$

$$\{0, 0, 0, 1, 1, 3, 3, 3\}$$

$$\{0, 0.2, 0.6, 0.9, 1.0\}$$

Nonuniform B-splines provide increased flexibility in controlling a curve shape. With unequally spaced intervals in the knot vector, we obtain different shapes for the blending functions in different intervals, which can be used to adjust spline shapes. By increasing knot multiplicity, we produce subtle variations in curve shape and even introduce discontinuities. Multiple knot values also reduce the continuity by 1 for each repeat of a particular value.

We obtain the blending functions for a nonuniform B-spline using methods similar to those discussed for uniform and open B-splines. Given a set of $n + 1$ control points, we set the degree of the polynomial and select the knot values. Then, using the recurrence relations, we could either obtain the set of blending functions or evaluate curve positions directly for the display of the curve. Graphics packages often restrict the knot intervals to be either 0 or 1 to reduce computations. A set of characteristic matrices then can be stored and used to compute

343

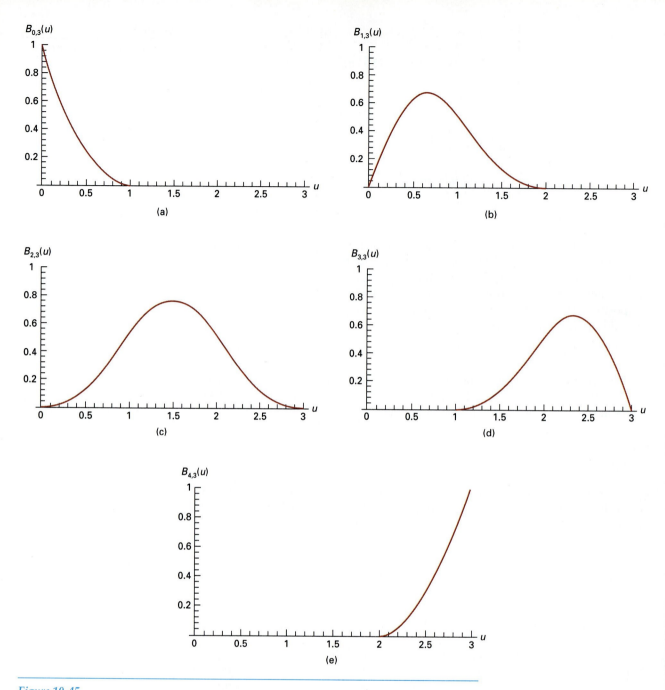

Figure 10-45

Open, uniform B-spline blending functions for $n = 4$ and $d = 3$.

values along the spline curve without evaluating the recurrence relations for each curve point to be plotted.

B-Spline Surfaces

Formulation of a B-spline surface is similar to that for Bézier splines. We can obtain a vector point function over a B-spline surface using the Cartesian product of B-spline blending functions in the form

Figure 10-46
A prototype helicopter, designed and modeled by
Daniel Langlois of SOFTIMAGE, Inc., Montreal,
using 180,000 B-spline surface patches. The scene
was then rendered using ray tracing, bump
mapping, and reflection mapping. (*Courtesy of Silicon
Graphics, Inc.*)

$$\mathbf{P}(u, v) = \sum_{k_1=0}^{n1} \sum_{k_2=0}^{n2} \mathbf{p}_{k_1,k_2} B_{k_1,d_1}(u) B_{k_2,d_2}(v) \tag{10-64}$$

where the vector values for $\mathbf{p}_{k_1,k_2}$ specify positions of the $(n_1 + 1)$ by $(n_2 + 1)$ control points.

B-spline surfaces exhibit the same properties as those of their component B-spline curves. A surface can be constructed from selected values for parameters d_1 and d_2 (which determine the polynomial degrees to be used) and from the specified knot vector. Figure 10-46 shows an object modeled with B-spline surfaces.

10-10
BETA-SPLINES

A generalization of B-splines are the **beta-splines**, also referred to as *β*-**splines**, that are formulated by imposing geometric continuity conditions on the first and second parametric derivatives. The continuity parameters for beta-splines are called *β parameters*.

Beta-Spline Continuity Conditions

For a specified knot vector, we can designate the spline sections to the left and right of a particular knot u_j with the position vectors $\mathbf{P}_{j-1}(u)$ and $\mathbf{P}_j(u)$ (Fig. 10-47). Zero-order continuity (*positional continuity*), G^0, at u_j is obtained by requiring

$$\mathbf{P}_{j-1}(u_j) = \mathbf{P}_j(u_j) \tag{10-65}$$

First-order continuity (*unit tangent continuity*), G^1, is obtained by requiring tangent vectors to be proportional:

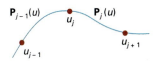

Figure 10-47
Position vectors along curve sections to the left and right of knot u_j.

345

$$\beta_1 \mathbf{P}'_{j-1}(u_j) = \mathbf{P}'_j(u_j), \qquad \beta_1 > 0 \qquad (10\text{-}66)$$

Here, parametric first derivatives are proportional, and the unit tangent vectors are continuous across the knot.

Second-order continuity (*curvature vector continuity*), G^2, is imposed with the condition

$$\beta_1^2 \mathbf{P}''_{j-1}(u_j) + \beta_2 \mathbf{P}'_{j-1}(u_j) = \mathbf{P}''_j(u_j) \qquad (10\text{-}67)$$

where β_2 can be assigned any real number, and $\beta_1 > 0$. The curvature vector provides a measure of the amount of bending of the curve at position u_j. When $\beta_1 = 1$ and $\beta_2 = 0$, beta-splines reduce to B-splines.

Parameter β_1 is called the *bias parameter* since it controls the skewness of the curve. For $\beta_1 > 1$, the curve tends to flatten to the right in the direction of the unit tangent vector at the knots. For $0 < \beta_1 < 1$, the curve tends to flatten to the left. The effect of β_1 on the shape of the spline curve is shown in Fig. 10-48.

Parameter β_2 is called the *tension parameter* since it controls how tightly or loosely the spline fits the control graph. As β_2 increases, the curve approaches the shape of the control graph, as shown in Fig. 10-49.

Cubic, Periodic Beta-Spline Matrix Representation

Applying the beta-spline boundary conditions to a cubic polynomial with a uniform knot vector, we obtain the following matrix representation for a periodic beta-spline:

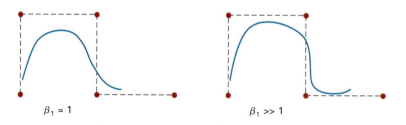

$\beta_1 = 1$ $\beta_1 \gg 1$

Figure 10-48
Effect of parameter β_1 on the shape of a beta-spline curve.

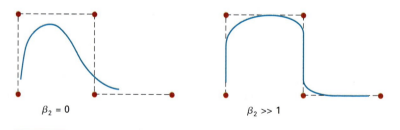

$\beta_2 = 0$ $\beta_2 \gg 1$

Figure 10-49
Effect of parameter β_2 on the shape of a beta-spline curve.

$$\mathbf{M}_\beta = \frac{1}{\delta} \begin{bmatrix} -2\beta_1^3 & 2(\beta_2 + \beta_1^3 + \beta_1^2 + \beta_1) & -2(\beta_2 + \beta_1^2 + \beta_1 + 1) & 2 \\ 6\beta_1^3 & -3(\beta_2 + 2\beta_1^3 + 2\beta_1^2) & 3(\beta_2 + 2\beta_1^2) & 0 \\ -6\beta_1^3 & 6(\beta_1^3 - \beta_1) & 6\beta_1 & 0 \\ 2\beta_1^3 & \beta_2 + 4(\beta_1^2 + \beta_1) & 2 & 0 \end{bmatrix} \qquad (10\text{-}68)$$

where $\delta = \beta_2 + 2\beta_1^3 + 4\beta_1^2 + 4\beta_1 + 2$.

We obtain the B-spline matrix $\mathbf{M}_B$ when $\beta_1 = 1$ and $\beta_2 = 0$. And we get the B-spline with tension matrix $\mathbf{M}_{Bt}$ when

$$\beta_1 = 1, \qquad \beta_2 = \frac{12}{t}(1 - t)$$

10-11

RATIONAL SPLINES

A rational function is simply the ratio of two polynomials. Thus, a **rational spline** is the ratio of two spline functions. For example, a rational B-spline curve can be described with the position vector:

$$\mathbf{P}(u) = \frac{\sum\limits_{k=0}^{n} \omega_k \mathbf{p}_k B_{k,d}(u)}{\sum\limits_{k=0}^{n} \omega_k B_{k,d}(u)} \qquad (10\text{-}69)$$

where the $\mathbf{p}_k$ are a set of $n + 1$ control-point positions. Parameters ω_k are weight factors for the control points. The greater the value of a particular ω_k, the closer the curve is pulled toward the control point $\mathbf{p}_k$ weighted by that parameter. When all weight factors are set to the value 1, we have the standard B-spline curve since the denominator in Eq. 10-69 is 1 (the sum of the blending functions).

Rational splines have two important advantages compared to nonrational splines. First, they provide an exact representation for quadric curves (conics), such as circles and ellipses. Nonrational splines, which are polynomials, can only approximate conics. This allows graphics packages to model all curve shapes with one representation—rational splines—without needing a library of curve functions to handle different design shapes. Another advantage of rational splines is that they are invariant with respect to a perspective viewing transformation (Section 12-3). This means that we can apply a perspective viewing transformation to the control points of the rational curve, and we will obtain the correct view of the curve. Nonrational splines, on the other hand, are not invariant with respect to a perspective viewing transformation. Typically, graphics design packages use nonuniform knot-vector representations for constructing rational B-splines. These splines are referred to as NURBs (*nonuniform rational B-splines*).

Homogeneous coordinate representations are used for rational splines, since the denominator can be treated as the homogeneous factor in a four-dimensional representation of the control points. Thus, a rational spline can be thought of as the projection of a four-dimensional nonrational spline into three-dimensional space.

Constructing a rational B-spline representation is carried out with the same procedures for constructing a nonrational representation. Given the set of control points, the degree of the polynomial, the weighting factors, and the knot vector, we apply the recurrence relations to obtain the blending functions.

To plot conic sections with NURBs, we use a quadratic spline function ($d = 3$) and three control points. We can do this with a B-spline function defined with the open knot vector:

$$\{0, 0, 0, 1, 1, 1\}$$

which is the same as a quadratic Bézier spline. We then set the weighting functions to the following values:

$$\omega_0 = \omega_2 = 1$$

$$\omega_1 = \frac{r}{1 - r}, \qquad 0 \le r < 1 \tag{10-70}$$

and the rational B-spline representation is

$$\mathbf{P}(u) = \frac{\mathbf{p}_0 B_{0,3}(u) + [r/(1 - r)]\mathbf{p}_1 B_{1,3}(u) + \mathbf{p}_2 B_{2,3}(u)}{B_{0,3}(u) + [r/(1 - r)]B_{1,3}(u) + B_{2,3}(u)} \tag{10-71}$$

We then obtain the various conics (Fig. 10-50) with the following values for parameter r:

$r > 1/2, \quad \omega_1 > 1$ (hyperbola section)
$r = 1/2, \quad \omega_1 = 1$ (parabola section)
$r < 1/2, \quad \omega_1 < 1$ (ellipse section)
$r = 0, \quad \omega_1 = 0 \quad$ (straight-line segment)

We can generate a one-quarter arc of a unit circle in the first quadrant of the xy plane (Fig. 10-51) by setting $\omega_1 = \cos\phi$ and by choosing the control points as

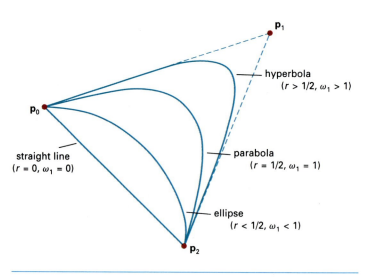

Figure 10-50
Conic sections generated with various values of the rational-spline weighting factor ω_1.

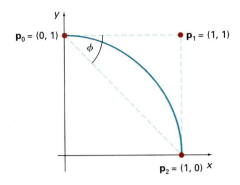

Figure 10-51
A circular arc in the first quadrant
of the xy plane.

$$\mathbf{p}_0 = (0, 1), \qquad \mathbf{p}_1 = (1, 1), \qquad \mathbf{p}_2 = (1, 0)$$

Other sections of a unit circle can be obtained with different control-point positions. A complete circle can be generated using geometric transformation in the xy plane. For example, we can reflect the one-quarter circular arc about the x and y axes to produce the circular arcs in the other three quadrants.

In some CAD systems, we construct a conic section by specifying three points on an arc. A rational homogeneous-coordinate spline representation is then determined by computing control-point positions that would generate the selected conic type. As an example, a homogeneous representation for a unit circular arc in the first quadrant of the xy plane is

$$\begin{bmatrix} x_h(u) \\ y_h(u) \\ z_h(u) \\ h \end{bmatrix} = \begin{bmatrix} 1 - u^2 \\ 2u \\ 0 \\ 1 + u^2 \end{bmatrix}$$

10-12
CONVERSION BETWEEN SPLINE REPRESENTATIONS

Sometimes it is desirable to be able to switch from one spline representation to another. For instance, a Bézier representation is the most convenient one for subdividing a spline curve, while a B-spline representation offers greater design flexibility. So we might design a curve using B-spline sections, then we can convert to an equivalent Bézier representation to display the object using a recursive subdivision procedure to locate coordinate positions along the curve.

Suppose we have a spline description of an object that can be expressed with the following matrix product:

$$\mathbf{P}(u) = \mathbf{U} \cdot \mathbf{M}_{\text{spline1}} \cdot \mathbf{M}_{\text{geom1}} \qquad (10\text{-}72)$$

where $\mathbf{M}_{\text{spline1}}$ is the matrix characterizing the spline representation, and $\mathbf{M}_{\text{geom1}}$ is the column matrix of geometric constraints (for example, control-point coordinates). To transform to a second representation with spline matrix $\mathbf{M}_{\text{spline2}}$, we need to determine the geometric constraint matrix $\mathbf{M}_{\text{geom2}}$ that produces the same vector point function for the object. That is,

$$\mathbf{P}(u) = \mathbf{U} \cdot \mathbf{M}_{\text{spline2}} \cdot \mathbf{M}_{\text{geom2}} \qquad (10\text{-}73)$$

or

$$\mathbf{U} \cdot \mathbf{M}_{\text{spline2}} \cdot \mathbf{M}_{\text{geom2}} = \mathbf{U} \cdot \mathbf{M}_{\text{spline1}} \cdot \mathbf{M}_{\text{geom1}}$$

Solving for $\mathbf{M}_{\text{geom2}}$, we have

$$\mathbf{M}_{\text{geom2}} = \mathbf{M}_{\text{spline2}}^{-1} \cdot \mathbf{M}_{\text{spline1}} \cdot \mathbf{M}_{\text{geom1}}$$
$$= \mathbf{M}_{s1,s2} \cdot \mathbf{M}_{\text{geom1}} \qquad (10\text{-}74)$$

and the required transformation matrix that converts from the first spline representation to the second is then calculated as

$$\mathbf{M}_{s1,s2} = \mathbf{M}_{\text{spline2}}^{-1} \cdot \mathbf{M}_{\text{spline1}} \qquad (10\text{-}75)$$

A nonuniform B-spline cannot be characterized with a general spline matrix. But we can rearrange the knot sequence to change the nonuniform B-spline to a Bézier representation. Then the Bézier matrix could be converted to any other form.

The following example calculates the transformation matrix for conversion from a periodic, cubic B-spline representation to a cubic, Bézier spline representation.

$$\mathbf{M}_{B,\text{Bez}} = \begin{bmatrix} -1 & 3 & -3 & 1 \\ 3 & -6 & 3 & 0 \\ -3 & 3 & 0 & 0 \\ 1 & 0 & 0 & 0 \end{bmatrix}^{-1} \cdot \frac{1}{6} \begin{bmatrix} -1 & 3 & -3 & 1 \\ 3 & -6 & 3 & 0 \\ -3 & 0 & 3 & 0 \\ 1 & 4 & 1 & 0 \end{bmatrix}$$

$$= 1/6 \begin{bmatrix} 1 & 4 & 1 & 0 \\ 0 & 4 & 2 & 0 \\ 0 & 2 & 4 & 0 \\ 0 & 1 & 4 & 1 \end{bmatrix} \qquad (10\text{-}76)$$

And the the transformation matrix for converting from a cubic Bézier representation to a periodic, cubic B-spline representation is

$$\mathbf{M}_{\text{Bez},B} = \begin{bmatrix} -1/6 & 1/2 & -1/2 & 1/6 \\ 1/2 & -1 & 1/2 & 0 \\ -1/2 & 0 & 1/2 & 0 \\ 1/6 & 2/3 & 1/6 & 0 \end{bmatrix}^{-1} \cdot \begin{bmatrix} -1 & 3 & -3 & 1 \\ 3 & -6 & 3 & 0 \\ -3 & 3 & 0 & 0 \\ 1 & 0 & 0 & 0 \end{bmatrix}$$

$$= \begin{bmatrix} 6 & -7 & 2 & 0 \\ 0 & 2 & -1 & 0 \\ 0 & -1 & 2 & 0 \\ 0 & 2 & -7 & 6 \end{bmatrix} \qquad (10\text{-}77)$$

DISPLAYING SPLINE CURVES AND SURFACES

To display a spline curve or surface, we must determine coordinate positions on the curve or surface that project to pixel positions on the display device. This means that we must evaluate the parametric polynomial spline functions in certain increments over the range of the functions. There are several methods we can use to calculate positions over the range of a spline curve or surface.

Horner's Rule

The simplest method for evaluating a polynomial, other than a brute-force calculation of each term in succession, is *Horner's rule*, which performs the calculations by successive factoring. This requires one multiplication and one addition at each step. For a polynomial of degree n, there are n steps.

As an example, suppose we have a cubic spline representation where coordinate positions are expressed as

$$x(u) = a_x u^3 + b_x u^2 + c_x u + d_x \qquad (10\text{-}78)$$

with similar expressions for the y and z coordinates. For a particular value of parameter u, we evaluate this polynomial in the following factored order:

$$x(u) = [(a_x u + b_x)u + c_x]u + d_x \qquad (10\text{-}79)$$

The calculation of each x value requires three multiplications and three additions, so that the determination of each coordinate position (x, y, z) along a cubic spline curve requires nine multiplications and nine additions.

Additional factoring tricks can be applied to reduce the number of computations required by Horner's method, especially for higher-order polynomials (degree greater than 3). But repeated determination of coordinate positions over the range of a spline function can be computed much faster using forward-difference calculations or spline-subdivision methods.

Forward-Difference Calculations

A fast method for evaluating polynomial functions is to generate successive values recursively by incrementing previously calculated values as, for example,

$$x_{k+1} = x_k + \Delta x_k \qquad (10\text{-}80)$$

Thus, once we know the increment and the value of x_k at any step, we get the next value by adding the increment to the value at that step. The increment Δx_k at each step is called the *forward difference*. If we divide the total range of u into subintervals of fixed size δ, then two successive x positions occur at $x_k = x(u_k)$ and $x_{k+1} = x(u_{k+1})$, where

$$u_{k+1} = u_k + \delta, \qquad k = 0, 1, 2, \ldots \qquad (10\text{-}81)$$

and $u_0 = 0$.

To illustrate the method, suppose we have the linear spline representation $x(u) = a_x u + b_x$. Two successive x-coordinate positions are represented as

$$x_k = a_x u_k + b_x$$
$$x_{k+1} = a_x(u_k + \delta) + b_x \qquad (10\text{-}82)$$

Subtracting the two equations, we obtain the forward difference: $\Delta x_k = a_x \delta$. In this case, the forward difference is a constant. With higher-order polynomials, the forward difference is itself a polynomial function of parameter u with degree one less than the original polynomial.

For the cubic spline representation in Eq. 10-78, two successive x-coordinate positions have the polynomial representations

$$x_k = a_x u_k^3 + b_x u_k^2 + c_x u_k + d_x$$
$$x_{k+1} = a_x(u_k + \delta)^3 + b_x(u_k + \delta)^2 + c_x(u_k + \delta) + d_x \qquad (10\text{-}83)$$

The forward difference now evaluates to

$$\Delta x_k = 3a_x \delta u_k^2 + (3a_x \delta^2 + 2b_x \delta)u_k + (a_x \delta^3 + b_x \delta^2 + c_x \delta) \qquad (10\text{-}84)$$

which is a quadratic function of parameter u_k. Since Δx_k is a polynomial function of u, we can use the same incremental procedure to obtain successive values of Δx_k. That is,

$$\Delta x_{k+1} = \Delta x_k + \Delta^2 x_k \qquad (10\text{-}85)$$

where the second forward difference is the linear function

$$\Delta^2 x_k = 6a_x \delta^2 u_k + 6a_x \delta^3 + 2b_x \delta^2 \qquad (10\text{-}86)$$

Repeating this process once more, we can write

$$\Delta^2 x_{k+1} = \Delta^2 x_k + \Delta^3 x_k \qquad (10\text{-}87)$$

with the third forward difference as the constant

$$\Delta^3 x_k = 6a_x \delta^3 \qquad (10\text{-}88)$$

Equations 10-80, 10-85, 10-87, and 10-88 provide an incremental forward-difference calculation of points along the cubic curve. Starting at $u_0 = 0$ with a step size δ, we obtain the initial values for the x coordinate and its first two forward differences as

$$x_0 = d_x$$
$$\Delta x_0 = a_x \delta^3 + b_x \delta^2 + c_x \delta \qquad (10\text{-}89)$$
$$\Delta^2 x_0 = 6a_x \delta^3 + 2b_x \delta^2$$

Once these initial values have been computed, the calculation for each successive x-coordinate position requires only three additions.

We can apply forward-difference methods to determine positions along spline curves of any degree n. Each successive coordinate position (x, y, z) is evaluated with a series of $3n$ additions. For surfaces, the incremental calculations are applied to both parameter u and parameter v.

Subdivision Methods

Recursive spline-subdivision procedures are used to repeatedly divide a given curve section in half, increasing the number of control points at each step. Subdivision methods are useful for displaying approximation spline curves since we can continue the subdivision process until the control graph approximates the curve path. Control-point coordinates then can be plotted as curve positions. Another application of subdivision is to generate more control points for shaping the curve. Thus, we could design a general curve shape with a few control points, then we could apply a subdivision procedure to obtain additional control points. With the added control points, we can make fine adjustments to small sections of the curve.

Spline subdivision is most easily applied to a Bézier curve section because the curve passes through the first and last control points, the range of parameter u is always between 0 and 1, and it is easy to determine when the control points are "near enough" to the curve path. Bézier subdivision can be applied to other spline representations with the following sequence of operations:

1. Convert the spline representation in use to a Bézier representation.
2. Apply the Bézier subdivision algorithm.
3. Convert the Bézier representation back to the original spline representation.

Figure 10-52 shows the first step in a recursive subdivision of a cubic Bézier curve section. Positions along the Bézier curve are described with the parametric point function $\mathbf{P}(u)$ for $0 \leq u \leq 1$. At the first subdivision step, we use the halfway point $\mathbf{P}(0.5)$ to divide the original curve into two sections. The first section is then described with the point function $\mathbf{P}_1(s)$, and the section is described with $\mathbf{P}_2(t)$, where

$$s = 2u, \qquad \text{for } 0 \leq u \leq 0.5$$
$$t = 2u - 1, \qquad \text{for } 0.5 \leq u \leq 1$$

$(10\text{-}90)$

Each of the two new curve sections has the same number of control points as the original curve section. Also, the boundary conditions (position and parametric

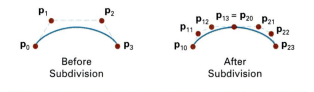

Before Subdivision

After Subdivision

Figure 10-52
Subdividing a cubic Bézier curve section into two sections, each with four control points.

slope) at the two ends of each new curve section must match the position and slope values for the original curve $\mathbf{P}(u)$. This gives us four conditions for each curve section that we can use to determine the control-point positions. For the first half of the curve, the four new control points are

$$\mathbf{P}_{1,0} = \mathbf{P}_0$$

$$\mathbf{P}_{1,1} = \tfrac{1}{2}(\mathbf{P}_0 + \mathbf{P}_1)$$

$$\mathbf{P}_{1,2} = \tfrac{1}{4}(\mathbf{P}_0 + 2\mathbf{P}_1 + \mathbf{P}_2)$$

$$\mathbf{P}_{1,3} = \tfrac{1}{8}(\mathbf{P}_0 + 3\mathbf{P}_1 + 3\mathbf{P}_2 + \mathbf{P}_3)$$

(10-91)

And for the second half of the curve, we obtain the four control points

$$\mathbf{P}_{2,0} = \tfrac{1}{8}(\mathbf{P}_0 + 3\mathbf{P}_1 + 3\mathbf{P}_2 + \mathbf{P}_3)$$

$$\mathbf{P}_{2,1} = \tfrac{1}{4}(\mathbf{P}_1 + 2\mathbf{P}_2 + \mathbf{P}_3)$$

$$\mathbf{P}_{2,2} = \tfrac{1}{2}(\mathbf{P}_2 + \mathbf{P}_3)$$

$$\mathbf{P}_{2,3} = \mathbf{P}_3$$

(10-92)

An efficient order for computing the new control points can be set up with only add and shift (division by 2) operations as

$$\mathbf{P}_{1,0} = \mathbf{P}_0$$

$$\mathbf{P}_{1,1} = \tfrac{1}{2}(\mathbf{P}_0 + \mathbf{P}_1)$$

$$\mathbf{T} = \tfrac{1}{2}(\mathbf{P}_1 + \mathbf{P}_2)$$

$$\mathbf{P}_{1,2} = \tfrac{1}{2}(\mathbf{P}_{1,1} + \mathbf{T})$$

$$\mathbf{P}_{2,3} = \mathbf{P}_3$$

(10-93)

$$\mathbf{P}_{2,2} = \tfrac{1}{2}(\mathbf{P}_2 + \mathbf{P}_3)$$

$$\mathbf{P}_{2,1} = \tfrac{1}{2}(\mathbf{T} + \mathbf{P}_{2,2})$$

$$\mathbf{P}_{2,0} = \tfrac{1}{2}(\mathbf{P}_{1,2} + \mathbf{P}_{2,1})$$

$$\mathbf{P}_{1,3} = \mathbf{P}_{2,0}$$

These steps can be repeated any number of times, depending on whether we are subdividing the curve to gain more control points or whether we are trying to locate approximate curve positions. When we are subdividing to obtain a set of display points, we can terminate the subdivision procedure when the curve sections are small enough. One way to determine this is to check the distances between adjacent pairs of control points for each section. If these distances are "sufficiently" small, we can stop subdividing. Or we could stop subdividing when the set of control points for each section is nearly along a straight-line path.

Subdivision methods can be applied to Bézier curves of any degree. For a Bézier polynomial of degree $n - 1$, the $2n$ control points for each half of the curve at the first subdivision step are

$$\mathbf{p}_{1,k} = \frac{1}{2^k} \sum_{i=0}^{k} C(k, i)\mathbf{p}_i, \qquad k = 0, 1, 2, \ldots, n$$

$$\mathbf{p}_{2,k} = \frac{1}{2^{n-k}} \sum_{i=k}^{n} C(n - k, n - i)\,\mathbf{p}_i \qquad (10\text{-}94)$$

where $C(k, i)$ and $C(n - k, n - i)$ are the binomial coefficients.

We can apply subdivision methods directly to nonuniform B-splines by adding values to the knot vector. But, in general, these methods are not as efficient as Bézier subdivision.

10-14

SWEEP REPRESENTATIONS

Solid-modeling packages often provide a number of construction techniques. **Sweep representations** are useful for constructing three-dimensional objects that possess translational, rotational, or other symmetries. We can represent such objects by specifying a two-dimensional shape and a sweep that moves the shape through a region of space. A set of two-dimensional primitives, such as circles and rectangles, can be provided for sweep representations as menu options. Other methods for obtaining two-dimensional figures include closed spline-curve constructions and cross-sectional slices of solid objects.

Figure 10-53 illustrates a translational sweep. The periodic spline curve in Fig. 10-53(a) defines the object cross section. We then perform a translational

(a) (b)

Figure 10-53

Constructing a solid with a translational sweep. Translating the control points of the periodic spline curve in (a) generates the solid shown in (b), whose surface can be described with point function $\mathbf{P}(u,v)$.

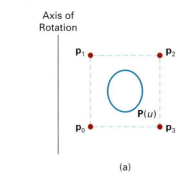

Axis of
Rotation

$\mathbf{p}_1$ $\mathbf{p}_2$

$P(u)$

$\mathbf{p}_0$ $\mathbf{p}_3$

(a)

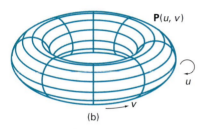

$\mathbf{P}(u, v)$

u

v

(b)

Figure 10-54
Constructing a solid with a
rotational sweep. Rotating the
control points of the periodic spline
curve in (a) about the given rotation
axis generates the solid shown in
(b), whose surface can be described
with point function $\mathbf{P}(u,v)$.

sweep by moving the control points $\mathbf{p}_0$ through $\mathbf{p}_3$ a set distance along a straight-line path perpendicular to the plane of the cross section. At intervals along this path, we replicate the cross-sectional shape and draw a set of connecting lines in the direction of the sweep to obtain the wireframe representation shown in Fig. 10-53(b).

An example of object design using a rotational sweep is given in Fig. 10-54. This time, the periodic spline cross section is rotated about an axis of rotation specified in the plane of the cross section to produce the wireframe representation shown in Fig. 10-54(b). Any axis can be chosen for a rotational sweep. If we use a rotation axis perpendicular to the plane of the spline cross section in Fig. 10-54(a), we generate a two-dimensional shape. But if the cross section shown in this figure has depth, then we are using one three-dimensional object to generate another.

In general, we can specify sweep constructions using any path. For rotational sweeps, we can move along a circular path through any angular distance from 0 to 360°. For noncircular paths, we can specify the curve function describing the path and the distance of travel along the path. In addition, we can vary the shape or size of the cross section along the sweep path. Or we could vary the orientation of the cross section relative to the sweep path as we move the shape through a region of space.

10-15
CONSTRUCTIVE SOLID-GEOMETRY METHODS

Another technique for solid modeling is to combine the volumes occupied by overlapping three-dimensional objects using set operations. This modeling method, called **constructive solid geometry** (**CSG**), creates a new volume by applying the union, intersection, or difference operation to two specified volumes.

Figures 10-55 and 10-56 show examples for forming new shapes using the set operations. In Fig. 10-55(a), a block and pyramid are placed adjacent to each other. Specifying the union operation, we obtain the combined object shown in Fig. 10-55(b). Figure 10-56(a) shows a block and a cylinder with overlapping volumes. Using the intersection operation, we obtain the resulting solid in Fig. 10-56(b). With a difference operation, we can get the solid shown in Fig. 10-56(c).

A CSG application starts with an initial set of three-dimensional objects (primitives), such as blocks, pyramids, cylinders, cones, spheres, and closed spline surfaces. The primitives can be provided by the CSG package as menu selections, or the primitives themselves could be formed using sweep methods, spline constructions, or other modeling procedures. To create a new three-dimensional shape using CSG methods, we first select two primitives and drag them into position in some region of space. Then we select an operation (union, intersection, or difference) for combining the volumes of the two primitives. Now we have a new object, in addition to the primitives, that we can use to form other objects. We continue to construct new shapes, using combinations of primitives and the objects created at each step, until we have the final shape. An object designed with this procedure is represented with a binary tree. An example tree representation for a CSG object is given in Fig. 10-57.

Ray-casting methods are commonly used to implement constructive solid-geometry operations when objects are described with boundary representations. We apply ray casting by constructing composite objects in world coordinates with the xy plane corresponding to the pixel plane of a video monitor. This plane is then referred to as the "firing plane" since we fire a ray from each pixel position through the objects that are to be combined (Fig. 10-58). We then determine surface intersections along each ray path, and sort the intersection points according to the distance from the firing plane. The surface limits for the composite object are then determined by the specified set operation. An example of the ray-casting determination of surface limits for a CSG object is given in Fig. 10-59, which shows yz cross sections of two primitives and the path of a pixel ray perpendicular to the firing plane. For the union operation, the new volume is the combined interior regions occupied by either or both primitives. For the intersection operation, the new volume is the interior region common to both primitives.

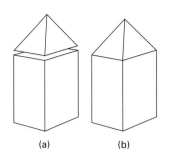

(a)   (b)

Figure 10-55
Combining two objects (a) with a union operation produces a single, composite solid object (b).

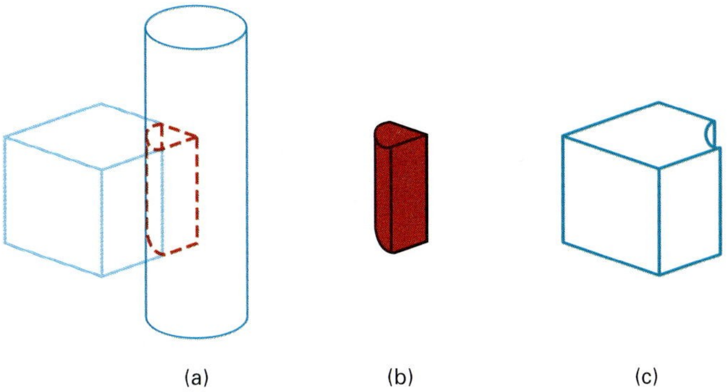

(a)   (b)   (c)

Figure 10-56
(a) Two overlapping objects. (b) A wedge-shaped CSG object formed with the intersection operation. (c) A CSG object formed with a difference operation by subtracting the overlapping volume of the cylinder from the block volume.

357

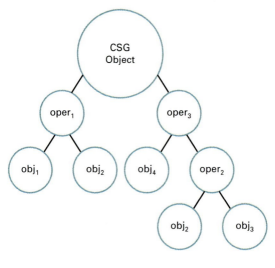

Figure 10-57
A CSG tree representation for an object.

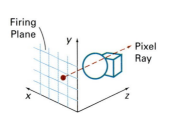

Firing Plane

Pixel Ray

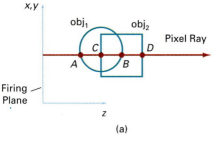

Firing Plane

(a)

Operation	Surface Limits
Union	A, D
Intersection	C, B
Difference	B, D
$(obj_2 - obj_1)$	

(b)

Figure 10-58
Implementing CSG operations using ray casting.

Figure 10-59
Determining surface limits along a pixel ray.

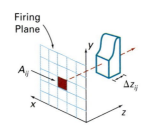

Figure 10-60
Determining object volume along a ray path for a small area A_{ij} on the firing plane.

358

And a difference operation subtracts the volume of one primitive from the other.

Each primitive can be defined in its own local (modeling) coordinates. Then, a composite shape can be formed by specifying the modeling-transformation matrices that would place two primitives in an overlapping position in world coordinates. The inverse of these modeling matrices can then be used to transform the pixel rays to modeling coordinates, where the surface-intersection calculations are carried out for the individual primitives. Then surface intersections for the two objects are sorted and used to determine the composite object limits according to the specified set operation. This procedure is repeated for each pair of objects that are to be combined in the CSG tree for a particular object.

Once a CSG object has been designed, ray casting is used to determine physical properties, such as volume and mass. To determine the volume of the object, we can divide the firing plane into any number of small squares, as shown in Fig. 10-60. We can then approximate the volume V_{ij} of the object for a cross-sectional slice with area A_{ij} along the path of a ray from the square at position (i, j) as

$$V_{ij} \approx A_{ij}\,\Delta z_{ij} \tag{10-95}$$

where Δz_{ij} is the depth of the object along the ray from position (i, j). If the object has internal holes, Δz_{ij} is the sum of the distances between pairs of intersection points along the ray. The total volume of the CSG object is then calculated as

Given the density function, $\rho(x, y, z)$, for the object, we can approximate the mass along the ray from position (i, j) as

$$m_{ij} \approx A_{ij} \int \rho(x_{ij}, y_{ij}, z) dz \qquad (10\text{-}97)$$

where the one-dimensional integral can often be approximated without actually carrying out the integration, depending on the form of the density function. The total mass of the CSG object is then approximated as

$$m \approx \sum_{m,i,j} M_{ij} \qquad (10\text{-}98)$$

Other physical properties, such as center of mass and moment of inertia, can be obtained with similar calculations. We can improve the approximate calculations for the values of the physical properties by taking finer subdivisions in the firing plane.

If object shapes are represented with octrees, we can implement the set operations in CSG procedures by scanning the tree structure describing the contents of spatial octants. This procedure, described in the following section, searches the octants and suboctants of a unit cube to locate the regions occupied by the two objects that are to be combined.

10-16
OCTREES

Hierarchical tree structures, called **octrees**, are used to represent solid objects in some graphics systems. Medical imaging and other applications that require displays of object cross sections commonly use octree representations. The tree structure is organized so that each node corresponds to a region of three-dimensional space. This representation for solids takes advantage of spatial coherence to reduce storage requirements for three-dimensional objects. It also provides a convenient representation for storing information about object interiors.

The octree encoding procedure for a three-dimensional space is an extension of an encoding scheme for two-dimensional space, called **quadtree** encoding. Quadtrees are generated by successively dividing a two-dimensional region (usually a square) into quadrants. Each node in the quadtree has four data elements, one for each of the quadrants in the region (Fig. 10-61). If all pixels within a quadrant have the same color (a homogeneous quadrant), the corresponding data element in the node stores that color. In addition, a flag is set in the data element to indicate that the quadrant is homogeneous. Suppose all pixels in quadrant 2 of Fig. 10-61 are found to be red. The color code for red is then placed in data element 2 of the node. Otherwise, the quadrant is said to be heterogeneous, and that quadrant is itself divided into quadrants (Fig. 10-62). The corresponding data element in the node now flags the quadrant as heterogeneous and stores the pointer to the next node in the quadtree.

An algorithm for generating a quadtree tests pixel-intensity values and sets up the quadtree nodes accordingly. If each quadrant in the original space has a

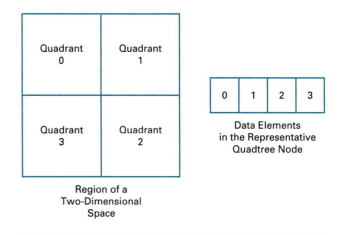

Figure 10-61
Region of a two-dimensional space divided into numbered quadrants and the associated quadtree node with four data elements.

single color specification, the quadtree has only one node. For a heterogeneous region of space, the successive subdivisions into quadrants continues until all quadrants are homogeneous. Figure 10-63 shows a quadtree representation for a region containing one area with a solid color that is different from the uniform color specified for all other areas in the region.

Quadtree encodings provide considerable savings in storage when large color areas exist in a region of space, since each single-color area can be represented with one node. For an area containing 2^n by 2^n pixels, a quadtree representation contains at most n levels. Each node in the quadtree has at most four immediate descendants.

An octree encoding scheme divides regions of three-dimensional space (usually cubes) into octants and stores eight data elements in each node of the tree (Fig. 10-64). Individual elements of a three-dimensional space are called **volume elements**, or **voxels**. When all voxels in an octant are of the same type, this

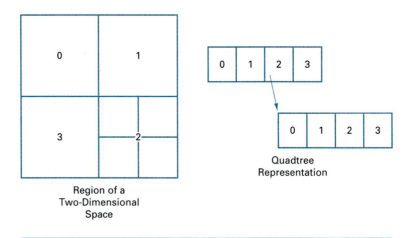

Figure 10-62
Region of a two-dimensional space with two levels of quadrant divisions and the associated quadtree representation.

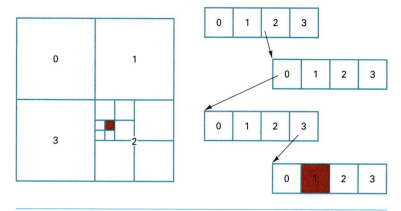

Figure 10-63
Quadtree representation for a region containing one foreground-color
pixel on a solid background.

type value is stored in the corresponding data element of the node. Empty regions of space are represented by voxel type "void." Any heterogeneous octant is subdivided into octants, and the corresponding data element in the node points to the next node in the octree. Procedures for generating octrees are similar to those for quadtrees: Voxels in each octant are tested, and octant subdivisions continue until the region of space contains only homogeneous octants. Each node in the octree can now have from zero to eight immediate descendants.

Algorithms for generating octrees can be structured to accept definitions of objects in any form, such as a polygon mesh, curved surface patches, or solid-geometry constructions. Using the minimum and maximum coordinate values of the object, we can define a box (parallelepiped) around the object. This region of three-dimensional space containing the object is then tested, octant by octant, to generate the octree representation.

Once an octree representation has been established for a solid object, various manipulation routines can be applied to the solid. An algorithm for performing set operations can be applied to two octree representations for the same region of space. For a union operation, a new octree is constructed with the combined regions for each of the input objects. Similarly, intersection or differ-

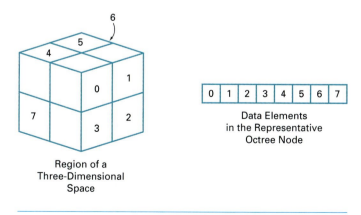

Region of a
Three-Dimensional
Space

Data Elements
in the Representative
Octree Node

Figure 10-64
Region of a three-dimensional space divided into numbered
octants and the associated octree node with eight data elements.

ence operations are performed by looking for regions of overlap in the two oc-trees. The new octree is then formed by either storing the octants where the two objects overlap or the region occupied by one object but not the other.

Three-dimensonal octree rotations are accomplished by applying the trans-formations to the occupied octants. Visible-surface identification is carried out by searching the octants from front to back. The first object detected is visible, so that information can be transferred to a quadtree representation for display.

10-17
BSP TREES

This representation scheme is similar to octree encoding, except we now divide space into two partitions instead of eight at each step. With a **binary space-partitioning (BSP)** tree, we subdivide a scene into two sections at each step with a plane that can be at any position and orientation. In an octree encoding, the scene is subdivided at each step with three mutually perpendicular planes aligned with the Cartesian coordinate planes.

For adaptive subdivision of space, BSP trees can provide a more efficient partitioning since we can position and orient the cutting planes to suit the spatial distribution of the objects. This can reduce the depth of the tree representation for a scene, compared to an octree, and thus reduce the time to search the tree. In ad-dition, BSP trees are useful for identifying visible surfaces and for space parti-tioning in ray-tracing algorithms.

10-18
FRACTAL-GEOMETRY METHODS

All the object representations we have considered in the previous sections used Euclidean-geometry methods; that is, object shapes were described with equa-tions. These methods are adequate for describing manufactured objects: those that have smooth surfaces and regular shapes. But natural objects, such as moun-tains and clouds, have irregular or fragmented features, and Euclidean methods do not realistically model these objects. Natural objects can be realistically de-scribed with **fractal-geometry methods,** where procedures rather than equations are used to model objects. As we might expect, procedurally defined objects have characteristics quite different from objects described with equations. Fractal-geometry representations for objects are commonly applied in many fields to de-scribe and explain the features of natural phenomena. In computer graphics, we use fractal methods to generate displays of natural objects and visualizations of various mathematical and physical systems.

A fractal object has two basic characteristics: infinite detail at every point and a certain *self-similarity* between the object parts and the overall features of the object. The self-similarity properties of an object can take different forms, de-pending on the choice of fractal representation. We describe a fractal object with a procedure that specifies a repeated operation for producing the detail in the ob-ject subparts. Natural objects are represented with procedures that theoretically repeat an infinite number of times. Graphics displays of natural objects are, of course, generated with a finite number of steps.

If we zoom in on a continuous Euclidean shape, no matter how compli-cated, we can eventually get the zoomed-in view to smooth out. But if we zoom

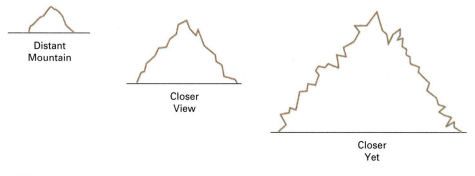

Figure 10-65
The ragged appearance of a mountain outline at different levels of magnification.

in on a fractal object, we continue to see as much detail in the magnification as we did in the original view. A mountain outlined against the sky continues to have the same jagged shape as we view it from a closer and closer position (Fig. 10-65). As we near the mountain, the smaller detail in the individual ledges and boulders becomes apparent. Moving even closer, we see the outlines of rocks, then stones, and then grains of sand. At each step, the outline reveals more twists and turns. If we took the grains of sand and put them under a microscope, we would again see the same detail repeated down through the molecular level. Similar shapes describe coastlines and the edges of plants and clouds.

Zooming in on a graphics display of a fractal object is obtained by selecting a smaller window and repeating the fractal procedures to generate the detail in the new window. A consequence of the infinite detail of a fractal object is that it has no definite size. As we consider more and more detail, the size of an object tends to infinity, but the coordinate extents of the object remain bound within a finite region of space.

We can describe the amount of variation in the object detail with a number called the *fractal dimension*. Unlike the Euclidean dimension, this number is not necessarily an integer. The fractal dimension of an object is sometimes referred to as the *fractional dimension*, which is the basis for the name "fractal".

Fractal methods have proven useful for modeling a very wide variety of natural phenomena. In graphics applications, fractal representations are used to model terrain, clouds, water, trees and other plants, feathers, fur, and various surface textures, and just to make pretty patterns. In other disciplines, fractal patterns have been found in the distribution of stars, river islands, and moon craters; in rain fields; in stock market variations; in music; in traffic flow; in urban property utilization; and in the boundaries of convergence regions for numerical-analysis techniques.

Fractal-Generation Procedures

A fractal object is generated by repeatedly applying a specified transformation function to points within a region of space. If $\mathbf{P}_0 = (x_0, y_0, z_0)$ is a selected initial point, each iteration of a transformation function F generates successive levels of detail with the calculations

$$\mathbf{P}_1 = F(\mathbf{P}_0), \qquad \mathbf{P}_2 = F(\mathbf{P}_1), \qquad \mathbf{P}_3 = F(\mathbf{P}_2), \quad \ldots \qquad (10\text{-}99)$$

363

In general, the transformation function can be applied to a specified point set, or we could apply the transformation function to an initial set of primitives, such as straight lines, curves, color areas, surfaces, and solid objects. Also, we can use either deterministic or random generation procedures at each iteration. The transformation function may be defined in terms of geometric transformations (scaling, translation, rotation), or it can be set up with nonlinear coordinate transformations and decision parameters.

Although fractal objects, by definition, contain infinite detail, we apply the transformation function a finite number of times. Therefore, the objects we display actually have finite dimensions. A procedural representation approaches a "true" fractal as the number of transformations is increased to produce more and more detail. The amount of detail included in the final graphical display of an object depends on the number of iterations performed and the resolution of the display system. We cannot display detail variations that are smaller than the size of a pixel. To see more of the object detail, we zoom in on selected sections and repeat the transformation function iterations.

Classification of Fractals

Self-similar fractals have parts that are scaled-down versions of the entire object. Starting with an initial shape, we construct the object subparts by apply a scaling parameter s to the overall shape. We can use the same scaling factor s for all subparts, or we can use different scaling factors for different scaled-down parts of the object. If we also apply random variations to the scaled-down subparts, the fractal is said to be *statistically self-similar*. The parts then have the same statistical properties. Statistically self-similar fractals are commonly used to model trees, shrubs, and other plants.

Self-affine fractals have parts that are formed with different scaling parameters, s_x, s_y, s_z, in different coordinate directions. And we can also include random variations to obtain *statistically self-affine* fractals. Terrain, water, and clouds are typically modeled with statistically self-affine fractal construction methods.

Invariant fractal sets are formed with nonlinear transformations. This class of fractals includes *self-squaring* fractals, such as the Mandelbrot set, which are formed with squaring functions in complex space; and *self-inverse* fractals, formed with inversion procedures.

Fractal Dimension

The detail variation in a fractal object can be described with a number D, called the **fractal dimension**, which is a measure of the roughness, or fragmentation, of the object. More jagged-looking objects have larger fractal dimensions. We can set up some iterative procedures to generate fractal objects using a given value for the fractal dimension D. With other procedures, we may be able to determine the fractal dimension from the properties of the constructed object, although, in general, the fractal dimension is difficult to calculate.

An expression for the fractal dimension of a self-similar fractal, constructed with a single scalar factor s, is obtained by analogy with the subdivision of a Euclidean object. Figure 10-66 shows the relationships between the scaling factor s and the number of subparts n for subdivision of a unit straight-line segment, a square, and a cube. With $s = 1/2$, the unit line segment (Fig. 10-66(a)) is divided into two equal-length subparts. Similarly, the square in Fig. 10-66(b) is divided into four equal-area subparts, and the cube (Fig. 10-66(c)) is divided into eight equal-volume subparts. For each of these objects, the relationship between the

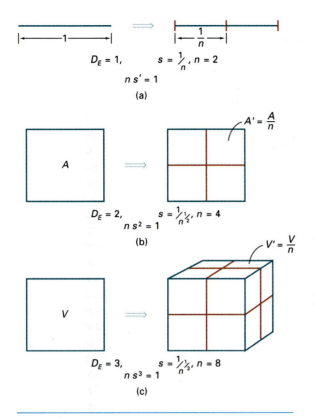

Figure 10-66
Subdividing objects with Euclidean dimensions
(a) $D_E = 1$, (b) $D_E = 2$, and (c) $D_E = 3$ using scaling
factor $s = 1/2$.

number of subparts and the scaling factor is $n \cdot s^{D_E} = 1$. In analogy with Euclidean objects, the fractal dimension D for self-similar objects can be obtained from

$$ns^D = 1 \qquad (10\text{-}100)$$

Solving this expression for D, the **fractal similarity dimension**, we have

$$D = \frac{\ln n}{\ln (1/s)} \qquad (10\text{-}101)$$

For a self-similar fractal constructed with different scaling factors for the different parts, the fractal similarity dimension is obtained from the implicit relationship

$$\sum_{k=1}^{n} s_k^D = 1 \qquad (10\text{-}102)$$

where s_k is the scaling factor for subpart number k.

In Fig. 10-66, we considered subdivision of simple shapes (straight line, rectangle, box). If we have more complicated shapes, including curved lines and objects with nonplanar surfaces, determining the structure and properties of the subparts is more difficult. For general object shapes, we can use *topological cover-*

365

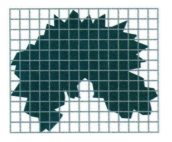

Figure 10-67
Box covering of an irregularly
shaped object.

ing methods that approximate object subparts with simple shapes. A subdivided curve, for example, can be approximated with straight-line sections, and a subdivided polygon could be approximated with small squares or rectangles. Other covering shapes, such as circles, spheres, and cylinders, can also be used to approximate the features of an object divided into a number of smaller parts. Covering methods are commonly used in mathematics to determine geometric properties, such as length, area, or volume, of an object by summing the properties of a set of smaller covering objects. We can also use covering methods to determine the fractal dimension D of some objects.

Topological covering concepts were originally used to extend the meaning of geometric properties to nonstandard shapes. An extension of covering methods using circles or spheres led to the notion of a *Hausdorff–Besicovitch dimension*, or *fractional dimension*. The Hausdorff–Besicovitch dimension can be used as the fractal dimension of some objects, but, in general, it is difficult to evaluate. More commonly, the fractal dimension of an object is estimated with *box-covering methods* using rectangles or parallelepipeds. Figure 10-67 illustrates the notion of a box covering. Here, the area inside the large irregular boundary can be approximated by the sum of the areas of the small covering rectangles.

We apply box-covering methods by first determining the coordinate extents of an object, then we subdivide the object into a number of small boxes using the given scaling factors. The number of boxes n that it takes to cover an object is called the *box dimension*, and n is related to the fractal dimension D of the object. For statistically self-similar objects with a single scaling factor s, we can cover the object with squares or cubes. We then count the number n of covering boxes and use Eq. 10-101 to estimate the fractal dimension. For self-affine objects, we cover the object with rectangular boxes, since different directions are scaled differently. In this case, the number of boxes n is used with the affine-transformation parameters to estimate the fractal dimension.

The fractal dimension of an object is always greater than the corresponding Euclidean dimension (or topological dimension), which is simply the least number of parameters needed to specify the object. A Euclidean curve is one-dimensional, a Euclidean surface is two-dimensional, and a Euclidean solid is three-dimensional.

For a fractal curve that lies completely within a two-dimensional plane, the fractal dimension D is greater than 1 (the Euclidean dimension of a curve). The closer D is to 1, the smoother the fractal curve. If $D = 2$, we have a *Peano curve*; that is, the "curve" completely fills a finite region of two-dimensional space. For $2 < D < 3$, the curve self-intersects and the area could be covered an infinite number of times. Fractal curves can be used to model natural-object boundaries, such as shorelines.

Spatial fractal curves (those that do not lie completely within a single plane) also have fractal dimension D greater than 1, but D can be greater than 2 without self-intersecting. A curve that fills a volume of space has dimension $D = 3$, and a self-intersecting space curve has fractal dimension $D > 3$.

Fractal surfaces typically have a dimension within the range $2 < D \leq 3$. If $D = 3$, the "surface" fills a volume of space. And if $D > 3$, there is an overlapping coverage of the volume. Terrain, clouds, and water are typically modeled with fractal surfaces.

The dimension of a fractal solid is usually in the range $3 < D \leq 4$. Again, if $D > 4$, we have a self-overlapping object. Fractal solids can be used, for example, to model cloud properties such as water-vapor density or temperature within a region of space.

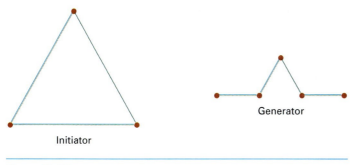

Figure 10-68
Initiator and generator for the Koch curve.

Geometric Construction of Deterministic Self-Similar Fractals

To geometrically construct a deterministic (nonrandom) self-similar fractal, we start with a given geometric shape, called the *initiator*. Subparts of the initiator are then replaced with a pattern, called the *generator*.

As an example, if we use the initiator and generator shown in Fig. 10-68, we can construct the snowflake pattern, or Koch curve, shown in Fig. 10-69. Each straight-line segment in the initiator is replaced with four equal-length line segments at each step. The scaling factor is $1/3$, so the fractal dimension is $D = \ln 4/\ln 3 \approx 1.2619$. Also, the length of each line segment in the initiator increases by

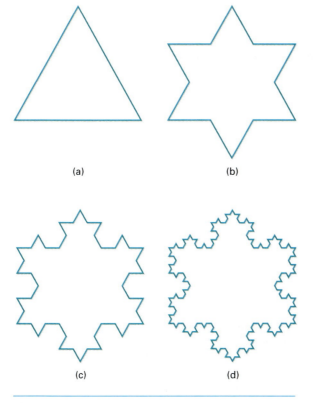

(a)   (b)

(c)   (d)

Figure 10-69
First three iterations in the generation of the Koch curve.

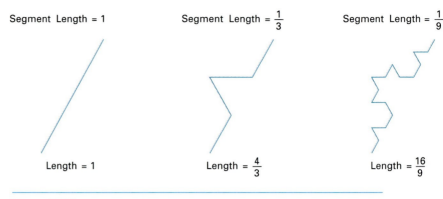

Segment Length = 1

Segment Length = $\frac{1}{3}$

Segment Length = $\frac{1}{9}$

Length = 1

Length = $\frac{4}{3}$

Length = $\frac{16}{9}$

Figure 10-70
Length of each side of the Koch curve increases by a factor of 4/3 at each step, while the line-segment lengths are reduced by a factor of 1/3.

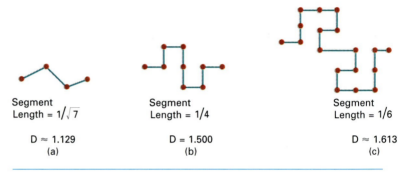

Segment Length = $1/\sqrt{7}$

$D \approx 1.129$
(a)

Segment Length = 1/4

$D = 1.500$
(b)

Segment Length = 1/6

$D \approx 1.613$
(c)

Figure 10-71
Self-similar curve constructions and associated fractal dimensions.

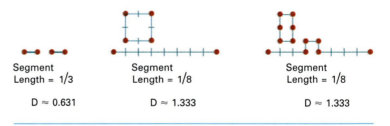

Segment Length = 1/3

$D \approx 0.631$

Segment Length = 1/8

$D \approx 1.333$

Segment Length = 1/8

$D \approx 1.333$

Figure 10-72
Generators with multiple, disjoint parts.

Figure 10-73
A snowflake-filling Peano curve.

a factor of 4/3 at each step, so that the length of the fractal curve tends to infinity as more detail is added to the curve (Fig. 10-70). Examples of other self-similar, fractal-curve constructions are shown in Fig. 10-71. These examples illustrate the more jagged appearance of objects with higher fractal dimensions.

We can also use generators with multiple disjoint components. Some examples of compound generators are shown in Fig. 10-72. Using random variations with compound generators, we can model various natural objects that have compound parts, such as island distributions along coastlines.

Figure 10-73 shows an example of a self-similar construction using multiple scaling factors. The fractal dimension of this object is determined from Eq. 10-102.

As an example of self-similar fractal construction for a surface, we scale the regular tetrahedron shown in Fig. 10-74 by a factor of 1/2, then place the scaled

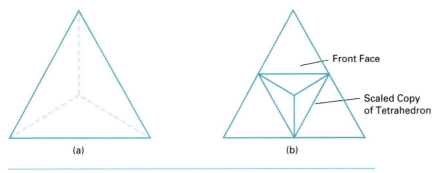

(a)   (b)

Front Face

Scaled Copy
of Tetrahedron

Figure 10-74
Scaling the tetrahedron in (a) by a factor of 1/2 and positioning the
scaled version on one face of the original tetrahedron produces the
fractal surface (b).

object on each of the original four surfaces of the tetrahedron. Each face of the
original tetrahedron is converted to 6 smaller faces and the original face area is
increased by a factor of 3/2. The fractal dimension of this surface is

$$D = \frac{\ln 6}{\ln 2} \approx 2.58496$$

which indicates a fairly fragmented surface.

Another way to create self-similar fractal objects is to punch holes in a given
initiator, instead of adding more surface area. Fig. 10-75 shows some examples of
fractal objects created in this way.

Geometric Construction of Statistically Self-Similar Fractals

One way we can introduce some randomness into the geometric construction of a
self-similar fractal is to choose a generator randomly at each step from a set of
predefined shapes. Another way to generate random self-similar objects is to
compute coordinate displacements randomly. For example, in Fig. 10-76 we create a random snowflake pattern by selecting a random, midpoint-displacement
distance at each step.

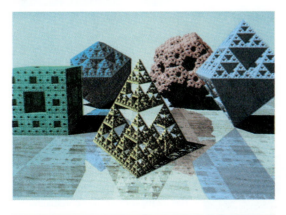

Figure 10-75
Self-similar, three-dimensional fractals formed with
generators that subtract subparts from an initiator.
(Courtesy of John C. Hart, Washington State University.)

369

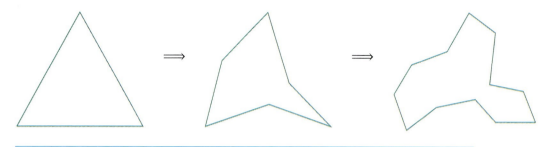

Figure 10-76
A modified "snowflake" pattern using random midpoint displacement.

Displays of trees and other plants can be constructed with similar geometric methods. Figure 10-77 shows a self-similar construction for a fern. In (a) of this figure, each branch is a scaled version of the total object, and (b) shows a fully rendered fern with a twist applied to each branch. Another example of this method is shown in Fig. 10-78. Here, random scaling parameters and branching directions are used to model the vein patterns in a leaf.

Once a set of fractal objects has been created, we can model a scene by placing several transformed instances of the fractal objects together. Figure 10-79 illustrates instancing with a simple fractal tree. In Fig. 10-80, a fractal forest is displayed.

To model the gnarled and contorted shapes of some trees, we can apply twisting functions as well as scaling to create the random, self-similar branches.

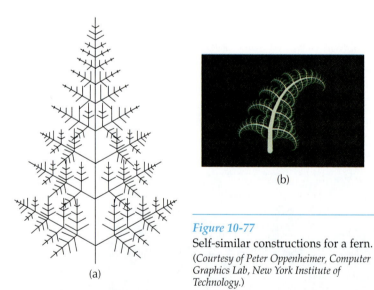

(a)

(b)

Figure 10-77
Self-similar constructions for a fern.
(*Courtesy of Peter Oppenheimer, Computer Graphics Lab, New York Institute of Technology.*)

Figure 10-78
Random, self-similar construction of vein branching in a fall leaf. Boundary of the leaf is the limit of the vein growth. (*Courtesy of Peter Oppenheimer, Computer Graphics Lab, New York Institute of Technology.*)

Figure 10-79
Modeling a scene using multiple object instancing. Fractal leaves are attached to a tree, and several instances of the tree are used to form a grove. The grass is modeled with multiple instances of green cones. (*Courtesy of John C. Hart, Washington State University.*)

This technique is illustrated in Fig. 10-81. Starting with the tapered cylinder on the left of this figure, we can apply transformations to produce (in succession from left to right) a spiral, a helix, and a random twisting pattern. A tree modeled with random twists is shown in Fig. 10-82. The tree bark in this display is modeled using bump mapping and fractal Brownian variations on the bump patterns, as discussed in the following section.

Figure 10-80
A fractal forest created with multiple instances of leaves, pine needles, grass, and tree bark. (*Courtesy of John C. Hart, Washington State University.*)

Figure 10-81
Modeling tree branches with spiral, helical, and random twists. (*Courtesy of Peter Oppenheimer, Computer Graphics Lab, New York Institute of Technology.*)

371

Figure 10-82
Tree branches modeled with random squiggles. (*Courtesy of Peter Oppenheimer, Computer Graphics Lab, New York Institute of Technology.*)

Affine Fractal-Construction Methods

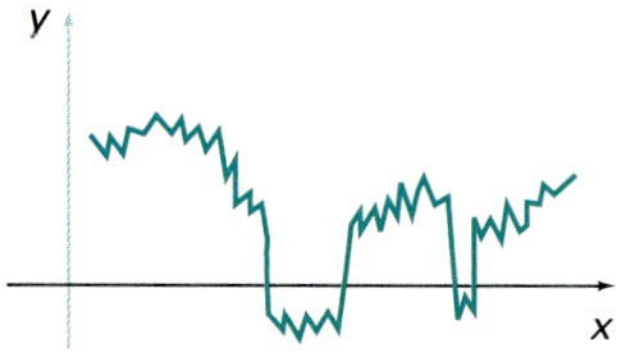

We can obtain highly realistic representations for terrain and other natural objects using affine fractal methods that model object features as *fractional Brownian motion*. This is an extension of standard Brownian motion, a form of "random walk", that describes the erratic, zigzag movement of particles in a gas or other fluid. Figure 10-83 illustrates a random-walk path in the xy plane. Starting from a given position, we generate a straight-line segment in a random direction and with a random length. We then move to the endpoint of the first line segment and repeat the process. This procedure is repeated for any number of line segments, and we can calculate the statistical properties of the line path over any time interval t. Fractional Brownian motion is obtained by adding an additional parameter to the statistical distribution describing Brownian motion. This additional parameter sets the fractal dimension for the "motion" path.

A single fractional Brownian path can be used to model a fractal curve. With a two-dimensional array of random fractional Brownian elevations over a

Figure 10-83
An example of Brownian motion (random walk) in the xy plane.

Figure 10-84
A Brownian-motion planet observed from the surface of a fractional Brownian-motion planet, with added craters, in the foreground. (*Courtesy of R. V. Voss and B. B. Mandelbrot, adapted from* The Fractal Geometry of Nature *by Benoit B. Mandelbrot (New York: W. H. Freeman and Co., 1983).*)

ground plane grid, we can model the surface of a mountain by connecting the elevations to form a set of polygon patches. If random elevations are generated on the surface of a sphere, we can model the mountains, valleys, and oceans of a planet. In Fig. 10-84, Brownian motion was used to create the elevation variations on the planet surface. The elevations were then color coded so that lowest elevations were painted blue (the oceans) and the highest elevations white (snow on the mountains). Fractional Brownian motion was used to create the terrain features in the foreground. Craters were created with random diameters and random positions, using affine fractal procedures that closely describe the distribution of observed craters, river islands, rain patterns, and other similar systems of objects.

By adjusting the fractal dimension in the fractional Brownian-motion calculations, we can vary the ruggedness of terrain features. Values for the fractal dimension in the neighborhood of $D \approx 2.15$ produce realistic mountain features, while higher values close to 3.0 can be used to create unusual-looking extraterrestrial landscapes. We can also scale the calculated elevations to deepen the valleys and to increase the height of mountain peaks. Some examples of terrain features that can be modeled with fractal procedures are given in Fig. 10-85. A scene modeled with fractal clouds over a fractal mountain is shown in Fig. 10-86.

Random Midpoint-Displacement Methods

Fractional Brownian-motion calculations are time-consuming, because the elevation coordinates of the terrain above a ground plane are calculated with Fourier series, which are sums of cosine and sine terms. Fast Fourier transform (FFT) methods are typically used, but it is still a slow process to generate fractal-mountain scenes. Therefore, faster **random midpoint-displacement methods**, similar to the random displacement methods used in geometric constructions, have been developed to approximate fractional Brownian-motion representations for terrain and other natural phenomena. These methods were originally used to generate animation frames for science-fiction films involving unusual terrain and planet features. Midpoint-displacement methods are now commonly used in many applications, including television advertising animations.

Although random midpoint-displacement methods are faster than fractional Brownian-motion calculations, they produce less realistic-looking terrain features. Figure 10-87 illustrates the midpoint-displacement method for generating a random-walk path in the xy plane. Starting with a straight-line segment, we calculate a displaced y value for the midposition of the line as the average of the endpoint y values plus a random offset:

$$y_{\text{mid}} = \frac{1}{2}[y(a) + y(b)] + r \qquad (10\text{-}103)$$

To approximate fractional Brownian motion, we choose a value for r from a Gaussian distribution with a mean of 0 and a variance proportional to $|b - a|^{2H}$, where $H = 2 - D$ and $D > 1$ is the fractal dimension. Another way to obtain a random offset is to take $r = sr_g|b - a|$, with parameter s as a selected "surface-roughness" factor, and r_g as a Gaussian random value with mean 0 and variance 1. Table lookups can be used to obtain the Gaussian values. The process is then repeated by calculating a displaced y value for the midposition of each half of the subdivided line. And we continue the subdivision until the subdivided line sections are less than some preset value. At each step, the value of the random vari-

373

(a)

(b)

(c)

Figure 10-85
Variations in terrain features modeled with fractional
Brownian motion. *(Courtesy of (a) R. V. Voss and B. B. Mandelbrot,
adapted from* The Fractal Geometry of Nature *by Benoit B. Mandelbrot
(New York: W. H. Freeman and Co., 1983); and (b) and (c) Ken
Musgrave and Benoit B. Mandelbrot, Mathematics and Computer
Science, Yale University.)*

Figure 10-86
A scene modeled with fractal clouds and mountains.
(*Courtesy of Ken Musgrave and Benoit B. Mandelbrot,
Mathematics and Computer Science, Yale University.*)

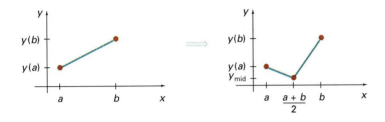

Figure 10-87
Random midpoint-displacement of a straight-line segment.

able r decreases, since it is proportional to the width $|b - a|$ of the line section to be subdivided. Figure 10-88 shows a fractal curve obtained with this method.

Terrain features are generated by applying the random midpoint-displacement procedures to a rectangular ground plane (Fig. 10-89). We begin by assigning an elevation z value to each of the four corners (**a**, **b**, **c**, and **d** in Fig. 10-89) of the ground plane. Then we divide the ground plane at the midpoint of each edge to obtain the five new grid positions: **e, f, g, h,** and **m**. Elevations at midpositions

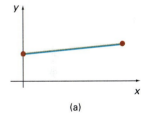

(a)

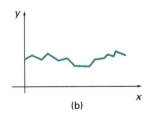

(b)

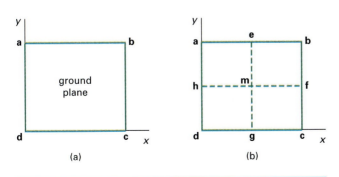

(a) (b)

Figure 10-89
A rectangular ground plane (a) is subdivided into four equal grid sections (b) for the first step in a random midpoint-displacement procedure to calculate terrain elevations.

Figure 10-88
A random-walk path generated from a straight-line segment with four iterations of the random midpoint-displacement procedure.

375

e, f, g, and **h** of the ground-plane edges can be calculated as the average elevation as the average elevation z_e at midposition **e** is calculated using vertices **a** and **b,** and the elevation at midposition **f** is calculated using vertices **b** and **c:**

$$z_e = (z_a + z_b)/2 + r_e, \qquad z_f = (z_b + z_c)/2 + r_f$$

Random values r_e and r_f can be obtained from a Gaussian distribution with mean 0 and variance proportional to the grid separation raised to the $2H$ power, with $H = 3 - D$, and where $D > 2$ is the fractal dimension for the surface. We could also calculate random offsets as the product of a surface-roughness factor times the grid separation times a table lookup value for a Gaussian value with mean 0 and variance 1. The elevation z_m of the ground-plane midposition **m** can be calculated using positions **e** and **g,** or positions **f** and **h.** Alternatively, we could calculate z_m using the assigned elevations of the four ground-plane corners:

$$z_m = (z_a + z_b + z_c + z_d)/4 + r_m$$

This process is repeated for each of the four new grid sections at each step until the grid separation becomes smaller than a selected value.

Triangular surface patches can be formed as the elevations are generated. Figure 10-90 shows the eight surface patches formed at the first subdivision step. At each level of recursion, the triangles are successively subdivided into smaller planar patches. When the subdivision process is completed, the patches are rendered according to the position of the light sources, the values for other illumination parameters, and the selected color and surface texture for the terrain.

The random midpoint-displacement method can be applied to generate other components of a scene besides the terrain. For instance, we could use the same methods to obtain surface features for water waves or cloud patterns above a ground plane.

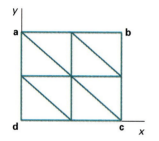

Figure 10-90
Eight surface patches formed over a ground plane at the first step of a random midpoint-displacement procedure for generating terrain features.

Controlling Terrain Topography

One way to control the placement of peaks and valleys in a fractal terrain scene modeled with a midpoint-displacement method is to constrain the calculated elevations to certain intervals over different regions of the ground plane. We can accomplish this by setting up a set of *control surfaces* over the ground plane, as illustrated in Fig. 10-91. Then we calculate a random elevation at each midpoint grid position on the ground plane that depends on the difference between the control elevation and the average elevation calculated for that position. This procedure constrains elevations to be within a preset interval about the control-surface elevations.

Figure 10-91
Control surfaces over a ground plane.

Control surfaces can be used to model existing terrain features in the Rocky Mountains, or some other region, by constructing the plane facets using the elevations in a contour plot for a particular region. Or we could set the elevations for the vertices of the control polygons to design our own terrain features. Also, control surfaces can have any shape. Planes are easiest to deal with, but we could use spherical surfaces or other curve shapes.

We use the random midpoint-displacement method to calculate grid elevations, but now we select random values from a Gaussian distribution where the mean μ and standard deviation σ are functions of the control elevations. One way to set the values for μ and σ is to make them both proportional to the difference between the calculated average elevation and the predefined control elevation at each grid position. For example, for grid position $\mathbf{e}$ in Fig. 10-89, we set the mean and standard deviation as

$$\mu_e = zc_e - (z_a + z_b)/2, \qquad \sigma_e = s\,|\mu_e|$$

where zc_e is the control elevation for ground-plane position $\mathbf{e}$, and $0 < s < 1$ is a preset scaling factor. Small values for s (say, $s < 0.1$) produce tighter conformity to the terrain envelope, and larger values of s allow greater fluctuations in terrain height.

To determine the values of the control elevations over a plane control surface, we first calculate the plane parameters A, B, C, and D. For any ground-plane position (x, y), the elevation in the plane containing that control polygon is then calculated as

$$zc = (-Ax - By - D)/C$$

Incremental methods can then be used to calculate control elevations over positions in the ground-plane grid. To efficiently carry out these calculations, we first subdivide the ground plane into a mesh of xy positions, as shown in Fig. 10-92. Then each polygon control surface is projected onto the ground plane. We can then determine which grid positions are within the projection of the control polygon using procedures similar to those in scan-line area filling. That is, for each y "scan line" in the ground-plane mesh that crosses the polygon edges, we calculate scan-line intersections and determine which grid positions are in the interior of the projection of the control polygon. Calculations for the control elevations at those grid positions can then be performed incrementally as

$$zc_{i+1,j} = zc_{i,j} - \Delta x(A/C), \qquad zc_{i,j+1} = zc_{i,j} - \Delta y(B/C) \qquad (10\text{-}104)$$

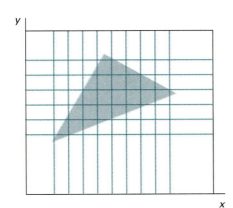

Figure 10-92
Projection of a triangular control surface onto the ground-plane grid.

Figure 10-93
A composite scene modeled with a random
midpoint-displacement method and planar control
surfaces over a ground plane. Surface features for
the terrain, water, and clouds were modeled and
rendered separately, then combined to form the
composite picture. (*Courtesy of Eng-Kiat Koh, Information
Technology Institute, Republic of Singapore.*)

with Δx and Δy as the grid spacing in the x and y directions. This procedure is
particularly fast when parallel vector methods are applied to process the control-
plane grid positions.

Figure 10-93 shows a scene constructed using control planes to structure the
surfaces for the terrain, water, and clouds above a ground plane. Surface-rendering algorithms were then applied to smooth out the polygon edges and to provide the appropriate surface colors.

Self-Squaring Fractals

Another method for generating fractal objects is to repeatedly apply a transformation function to points in complex space. In two dimensions, a complex number can be represented as $z = x + iy$, where x and y are real numbers, and $i^2 =
-1$. In three-dimensional and four-dimensional space, points are represented
with quaternions. A complex squaring function $f(z)$ is one that involves the calculation of z^2, and we can use some self-squaring functions to generate fractal
shapes.

Depending on the initial position selected for the iteration, repeated application of a self-squaring function will produce one of three possible results (Fig.
10-94):

- The transformed position can diverge to infinity.
- The transformed position can converge to a finite limit point, called an *at-
tractor*.
- The transformed position remains on the boundary of some object.

As an example, the nonfractal squaring operation $f(z) = z^2$ in the complex plane
transforms points according to their relation to the unit circle (Fig. 10-95). Any

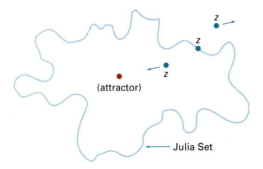

(attractor)

Julia Set

Figure 10-94
Possible outcomes of a self-squaring transformation $f(z)$ in the complex plane, depending on the position of the selected initial position.

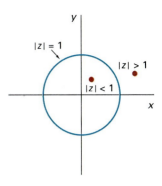

Figure 10-95
A unit circle in the complex plane. The nonfractal, complex squaring function $f(z) = z^2$ moves points that are inside the circle toward the origin, while points outside the circle are moved farther away from the circle. Any initial point on the circle remains on the circle.

point z whose magnitude $|z|$ is greater than 1 is transformed through a sequence of positions that tend to infinity. A point with $|z| < 1$ is transformed toward the coordinate origin. Points on the circle, $|z| = 1$, remain on the circle. For some functions, the boundary between those points that move toward infinity and those that tend toward a finite limit is a fractal. The boundary of the fractal object is called the *Julia set*.

In general, we can locate the fractal boundaries by testing the behavior of selected positions. If a selected position either diverges to infinity or converges to an attractor point, we can try another nearby position. We repeat this process until we eventually locate a position on the fractal boundary. Then, iteration of the squaring transformation generates the fractal shape. For simple transformations in the complex plane, a quicker method for locating positions on the fractal curve is to use the inverse of the transformation function. An initial point chosen on the inside or outside of the curve will then converge to a position on the fractal curve (Fig. 10-96).

A function that is rich in fractals is the squaring transformation

$$z' = f(z) = \lambda z(1 - z) \qquad (10\text{-}105)$$

where λ is assigned any constant complex value. For this function, we can use the inverse method to locate the fractal curve. We first rearrange terms to obtain the quadratic equation:

$$z^2 - z + z'/\lambda = 0 \qquad (10\text{-}106)$$

The inverse transformation is then the quadratic formula:

$$z = f^{-1}(z') = \frac{1}{2}\left(1 \pm \sqrt{1 - 4z'/\lambda}\right) \qquad (10\text{-}107)$$

Using complex arithmetic operations, we solve this equation for the real and imaginary parts of z as

Figure 10-96
Locating the fractal boundary with the inverse, self-squaring function $z' = f^{-1}(z)$.

379

$$x = \text{Re}(z) = \frac{1}{2}\left(1 \pm \sqrt{\frac{|\text{discr}| + \text{Re(discr)}}{2}}\right)$$

(10-108)

$$y = \text{Im}(z) = \pm\frac{1}{2}\sqrt{\frac{|\text{discr}| - \text{Re(discr)}}{2}}$$

with the discriminant of the quadratic formula as discr $= 1 - 4z'/\lambda$. A few initial values for x and y (say, 10) can be calculated and discarded before we begin to plot the fractal curve. Also, since this function yields two possible transformed (x, y) positions, we can randomly choose either the plus or the minus sign at each step of the iteration as long as $\text{Im(discr)} \geq 0$. Whenever $\text{Im(discr)} < 0$, the two possible positions are in the second and fourth quadrants. In this case, x and y must have opposite signs. The following procedure gives an implementation of this self-squaring function, and two example curves are plotted in Fig. 10-97.

```
#include <math.h>
#include <values.h>
#include "graphics.h"

typedef struct {
  float x, y;
} Complex;

void calculatePoint (Complex lambda, Complex * z)
{
  float lambdaMagSq, discrMag;
  Complex discr;
  static Complex fourOverLambda = { 0, 0 };
  static firstPoint = TRUE;

  if (firstPoint) {
    /* Compute 4 divided by lambda */
    lambdaMagSq = lambda.x * lambda.x + lambda.y * lambda.y;
    fourOverLambda.x =  4 * lambda.x / lambdaMagSq;
```

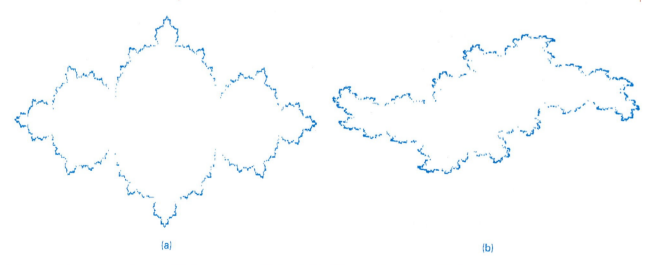

(a)   (b)

Figure 10-97

Two fractal curves generated with the inverse of the function $f(z) = \lambda z(1-z)$ by procedure selfSquare: (a) $\lambda = 3$ and (b) $\lambda = 2 + i$. Each curve is plotted with 10,000 points.

```
      fourOverLambda.y = -4 * lambda.y / lambdaMagSq;
      firstPoint = FALSE;
   }
   discr.x = 1.0 - (z->x * fourOverLambda.x - z->y * fourOver-
Lambda.y);
   discr.y = z->x * fourOverLambda.y + z->y * fourOverLambda.x;
   discrMag = sqrt (discr.x * discr.x + discr.y * discr.y);

   /* Update z, checking to avoid the sqrt of a negative number */
   if (discrMag + discr.x < 0)
      z->x = 0;
   else
      z->x = sqrt ((discrMag + discr.x) / 2.0);
   if (discrMag - discr.x < 0)
      z->y = 0;
   else
      z->y = 0.5 * sqrt ((discrMag - discr.x) / 2.0);

   /* For half the points, use negative root, placing point in quad-
rant 3 */
   if (random() < MAXINT/2) {
      z->x = -z->x;
      z->y = -z->y;
   }

   /* When imaginary part of discriminant is negative, point
      should lie in quadrant 2 or 4, so reverse sign of x */
   if (discr.y < 0) z->x = -z->x;

   /* Finish up calculation for the real part of z */
   z->x = 0.5 * (1 - z->x);
}

void selfSquare (Complex lambda, Complex z, int count)
{
   int k;

   /* Skip the first few points */
   for (k=0; k<10; k++)
      calculatePoint (lambda, &z);
   for (k=0; k<count; k++) {
      calculatePoint (lambda, &z);
      /* Scale point to fit window and draw */
      pPoint (z.x*WINDOW_WIDTH, 0.5*WINDOW_HEIGHT+z.y*WINDOW_HEIGHT);
   }
}
```

A three-dimensional plot in variables x, y, and λ of the self-squaring function $f(z) = \lambda z(1-z)$, with $|\lambda| = 1$, is given in Fig. 10-98. Each cross-sectional slice of this plot is a fractal curve in the complex plane.

A very famous fractal shape is obtained from the **Mandelbrot set**, which is the set of complex values z that do not diverge under the squaring transformation:

$$z_0 = z$$
$$z_k = z_{k-1}^2 + z_0, \qquad k = 1, 2, 3, \ldots$$

(10-109)

That is, we first select a point z in the complex plane, then we compute the transformed position $z^2 + z$. At the next step, we square this transformed position and add the original z value. We repeat this procedure until we can determine

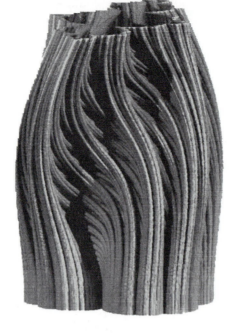

Figure 10-98
The function $f(z) = \lambda z(1-z)$
plotted in three dimensions
with normalized λ values
plotted as the vertical axis.
(*Courtesy of Alan Norton, IBM Research.*)

whether or not the transformation is diverging. The boundary of the convergence region in the complex plane is a fractal.

To implement transformation 10-109, we first choose a window in the complex plane. Positions in this window are then mapped to color-coded pixel positions in a selected screen viewport (Fig. 10-99). The pixel colors are chosen according to the rate of divergence of the corresponding point in the complex plane under transformation 10-109. If the magnitude of a complex number is greater than 2, then it will quickly diverge under this self-squaring operation. Therefore, we can set up a loop to repeat the squaring operations until either the magnitude of the complex number exceeds 2 or we have reached a preset number of iterations. The maximum number of iterations is usually set to some value between 100 and 1000, although lower values can be used to speed up the calculations. With lower settings for the iteration limit, however, we do tend to lose some detail along the boundary (Julia set) of the convergence region. At the end of the loop, we select a color value according to the number of iterations executed by the loop. For example, we can color the pixel black if the iteration count is at the

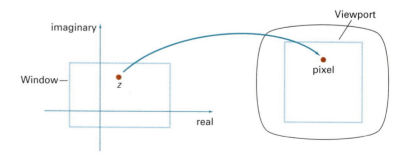

Figure 10-99
Mapping positions in the complex plane to color-coded pixel positions on a video monitor.

maximum value, and we can color the pixel red if the iteration count is near 0. Other color values can then be chosen according to the value of the iteration count within the interval from 0 to the maximum value. By choosing different color mappings, we can generate a variety of dramatic displays for the Mandelbrot set. One choice of color coding for the set is shown in Fig. 10-100(a).

An algorithm for displaying the Mandelbrot set is given in the following procedure. The major part of the set is contained within the following region of the complex plane:

$$-2.25 \leq \text{Re}(z) \leq 0.75$$

$$-1.25 \leq \text{Im}(z) \leq 1.25$$

We can explore the details along the boundary of the set by choosing successively smaller window regions so that we can zoom in on selected areas of the display. Figure 10-100 shows a color-coded display of the Mandelbrot set and a series of zooms that illustrate some of the features of this remarkable set.

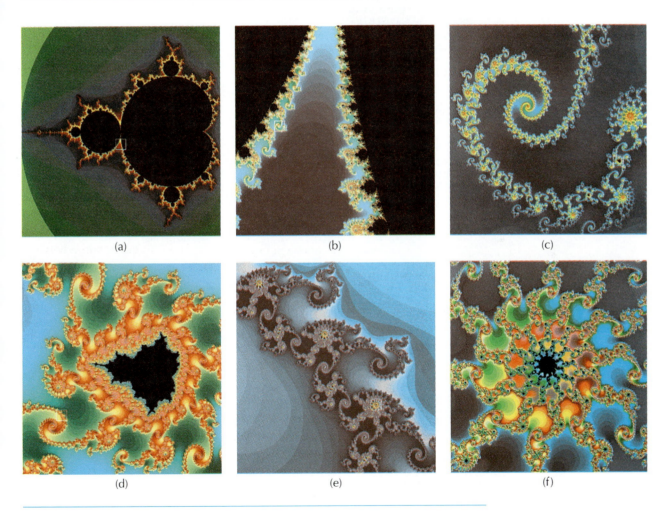

(a)　　　　　(b)　　　　　(c)

(d)　　　　　(e)　　　　　(f)

Figure 10-100
Zooming in on the Mandelbrot set. Starting with a display of the Mandelbrot set (a), we zoom in on selected regions (b) through (f). The white box outline shows the window area selected for each successive zoom. (*Courtesy of Brian Evans, Vanderbilt University.*)

```
#include "graphics.h"

typedef struct { float x, y; } Complex;

Complex complexSquare (Complex c)
{
  Complex cSq;

  cSq.x = c.x * c.x - c.y * c.y;
  cSq.y = 2 * c.x * c.y;
  return (cSq);
}

int iterate (Complex zInit, int maxIter)
{
  Complex z = zInit;
  int cnt = 0;

  /*  Quit when z * z > 4  */
  while ((z.x * z.x + z.y * z.y <- 4.0) && (cnt < maxIter)) {
    z = complexSquare (z);
    z.x += zInit.x;
    z.y += zInit.y;
    cnt++;
  }
  return (cnt);
}

void mandelbrot (int nx, int ny, int maxIter, float realMin,
                 float realMax, float imagMin, float imagMax)
{
  float realInc = (realMax - realMin) / nx;
  float imagInc = (imagMax - imagMin) / ny;
  Complex z;
  int x, y;
  int cnt;

  for (x=0, z.x=realMin; x<nx; x++, z.x+=realInc)
    for (y=0, z.y=imagMin; y<ny; y++, z.y+=imagInc) {
      cnt = iterate (z, maxIter);
      if (cnt == maxIter)
        setColor (BLACK);
      else
        setColor (cnt);
      pPoint (x, y);
    }
}
```

Complex-function transformations, such as Eq. 10-105, can be extended to produce fractal surfaces and fractal solids. Methods for generating these objects use *quaternion* representations (Appendix A) for transforming points in three-dimensional and four-dimensional space. A quaternion has four components, one real part and three imaginary parts, and can be represented as an extension of the concept of a number in the complex plane:

$$q = s + ia + jb + kc \qquad (10\text{-}110)$$

where $i^2 = j^2 = k^2 = -1$. The real part s is also referred to as the *scalar part* of the quaternion, and the imaginary terms are called the quaternion *vector part* $\mathbf{v} = (a, b, c)$.

Using the rules for quaternion multiplication and addition discussed in Appendix A, we can apply self-squaring functions and other iteration methods to generate surfaces of fractal objects instead of fractal curves. A basic procedure is to start with a position inside a fractal object and generate successive points from that position until an exterior (diverging) point is identified. The previous interior point is then retained as a surface point. Neighbors of this surface point are then tested to determine whether they are inside (converging) or outside (diverging). Any inside point that connects to an outside point is a surface point. In this way, the procedure threads its way along the fractal boundary without generating points that are too far from the surface. When four-dimensional fractals are generated, three-dimensional slices are projected onto the two-dimensional surface of the video monitor.

Procedures for generating self-squaring fractals in four-dimensional space require considerable computation time for evaluating the iteration function and for testing points. Each point on a surface can be represented as a small cube, giving the inner and outer limits of the surface. Output from such programs for the three-dimensional projections of the fractal typically contain over a million vertices for the surface cubes. Display of the fractal objects is performed by applying illumination models that determine the lighting and color for each surface cube. Hidden-surface methods are then applied so that only visible surfaces of the objects are displayed. Figures 10-101 and 10-102 show examples of self-squaring, four-dimensional fractals with projections into three-dimensions.

Self-Inverse Fractals

Various geometric inversion transformations can be used to create fractal shapes. Again, we start with an initial set of points, and we repeatedly apply nonlinear inversion operations to transform the initial points into a fractal.

As an example, we consider a two-dimensional inversion transformation with respect to a circle with radius r and center at position $\mathbf{P}_0 = (x_0, y_0)$. Any point $\mathbf{P}$ outside the circle will be inverted to a position $\mathbf{P}'$ inside the circle (Fig. 10-103) with the transformation

$$(\overline{\mathbf{P}_0\mathbf{P}})(\overline{\mathbf{P}_0\mathbf{P}'}) = r^2 \qquad (10\text{-}111)$$

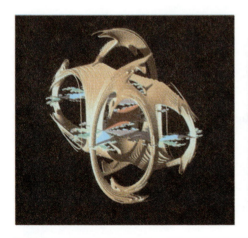 

Figure 10-101

Three-dimensional projections of four-dimensional fractals generated with the self-squaring, quaternion function $f(q) = \lambda q(1-q)$: (a) $\lambda = 1.475 + 0.9061i$, and (b) $\lambda = -0.57 + i$. *(Courtesy of Alan Norton, IBM Research.)*

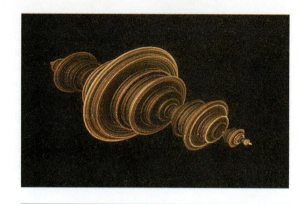

Figure 10-102
A three-dimensional surface projection of a four-dimensional object generated with the self-squaring, quaternion function $f(q) = q^2 - 1$.
(Courtesy of Alan Norton, IBM Research.)

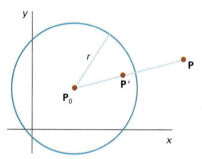

Figure 10-103
Inverting point **P** to a position **P'** inside a circle with radius r.

Reciprocally, this transformation inverts any point inside the circle to a point outside the circle. Both **P** and **P'** lie on a straight line passing through the circle center **P**$_0$.

If the coordinates of the two points are $\mathbf{P} = (x, y)$ and $\mathbf{P'} = (x', y')$, we can write Eq. 10-111 as

$$[(x - x_0)^2 + (y - y_0)^2]^{1/2}[(x' - x_0)^2 + (y' - y_0)^2]^{1/2} = r^2$$

Also, since the two points lie along a line passing through the circle center, we have $(y - y_0)/(x - x_0) = (y' - y_0)/(x' - x_0)$. Therefore, the transformed coordinate values are

$$x' = x_0 + \frac{r^2(x - x_0)}{(x - x_0)^2 + (y - y_0)^2}, \qquad y' = y_0 + \frac{r^2(y - y_0)}{(x - x_0)^2 + (y - y_0)^2} \quad (10\text{-}112)$$

Figure 10-104 illustrates the inversion of points along another circle boundary. As long as the circle to be inverted does not pass through **P**$_0$, it will transform to another circle. But if the circle circumference passes through **P**$_0$, the circle

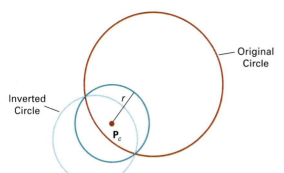

Original
Circle

Inverted
Circle

r

$\mathbf{P}_c$

Figure 10-104
Inversion of a circle with respect to
another circle.

transforms to a straight line. Conversely, points along a straight line not passing through $\mathbf{P}_0$ invert to a circle. Thus, straight lines are invariant under the inversion transformation. Also invariant under this transformation are circles that are orthogonal to the reference circle. That is, the tangents of the two circles are perpendicular at the intersection points.

   We can create various fractal shapes with this inversion transformation by starting with a set of circles and repeatedly applying the transformation using different reference circles. Similarly, we can apply circle inversion to a set of straight lines. Similar inversion methods can be developed for other objects. And, we can generalize the procedure to spheres, planes, or other shapes in three-dimensional space.

10-19

SHAPE GRAMMARS AND OTHER PROCEDURAL METHODS

A number of other procedural methods have been developed for generating object details. **Shape grammars** are sets of production rules that can be applied to an initial object to add layers of detail that are harmonious with the original shape. Transformations can be applied to alter the geometry (shape) of the object, or the transformation rules can be applied to add surface-color or surface-texture detail.

   Given a set of production rules, a shape designer can then experiment by applying different rules at each step of the transformation from a given initial object to the final structure. Figure 10-105 shows four geometric substitution rules for altering triangle shapes. The geometry transformations for these rules can be

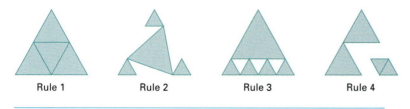

Rule 1   Rule 2   Rule 3   Rule 4

Figure 10-105
Four geometric substitution rules for subdividing and altering the shape
of an equilateral triangle.

387

written algorithmically by the system based on an input picture drawn with a production-rule editor. That is, each rule can be described graphically by showing the initial and final shapes. Implementations can then be set up in Mathematica or some other programming language with graphics capability.

An application of the geometric substitutions in Fig. 10-105 is given in Fig. 10-106, where Fig. 10-106(d) is obtained by applying the four rules in succession, starting with the initial triangle in Fig. 10-106(a). Figure 10-107 shows another shape created with triangle substitution rules.

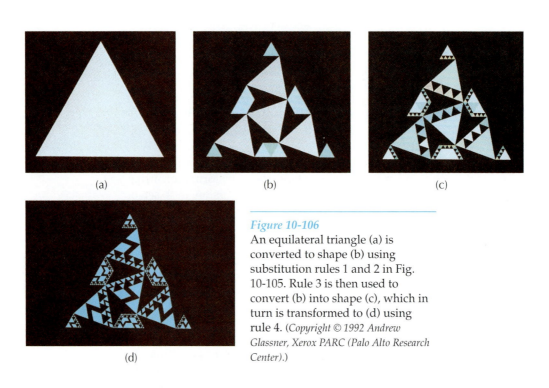

(a)   (b)   (c)

(d)

Figure 10-106
An equilateral triangle (a) is converted to shape (b) using substitution rules 1 and 2 in Fig. 10-105. Rule 3 is then used to convert (b) into shape (c), which in turn is transformed to (d) using rule 4. (*Copyright © 1992 Andrew Glassner, Xerox PARC (Palo Alto Research Center).*)

Figure 10-107
A design created with geometric substitution rules for altering triangle shapes. (*Copyright © 1992 Andrew Glassner, Xerox PARC (Palo Alto Research Center).*)

Figure 10-108
A design created with geometric substitution rules for altering prism shapes. The initial shape for this design was a representation of Rubik's Snake. (*Copyright © 1992 Andrew Glassner, Xerox PARC (Palo Alto Research Center).*)

Three-dimensional shape and surface features are transformed with similar operations. Figure 10-108 shows the results of geometric substitutions applied to polyhedra. The initial shape for the objects shown in Figure 10-109 is an icosahedron, a polyhedron with 20 faces. Geometric substitutions were applied to the plane faces of the icosahedron, and the resulting polygon vertices were projected to the surface of an enclosing sphere.

Another example of using production rules to describe the shape of objects is *L-grammars*, or *graftals*. These rules provide a method for describing plants. For instance, the topology of a tree can be described as a trunk, with some attached branches and leaves. A tree can then be modeled with rules to provide a particular connection of the branches and the leaves on the individual branches. The geometrical description is then given by placing the object structures at particular coordinate positions.

Figure 10-110 shows a scene containing various plants and trees, constructed with a commercial plant-generator package. Procedures in the software for constructing the plants are based on botanical laws.

Figure 10-109
Designs created on the surface of a sphere using triangle substitution rules applied to the plane faces of an icosahedron, followed by projections to the sphere surface. (*Copyright © 1992 Andrew Glassner, Xerox PARC (Palo Alto Research Center).*)

389

Figure 10-110
Realistic scenery generated with the TDI-AMAP software package, which can generate over 100 varieties of plants and trees using procedures based on botanical laws. (*Courtesy of Thomson Digital Image.*)

10-20

PARTICLE SYSTEMS

A method for modeling natural objects, or other irregularly shaped objects, that exhibit "fluid-like" properties is **particle systems**. This method is particularly good for describing objects that change over time by flowing, billowing, spattering, or expanding. Objects with these characteristics include clouds, smoke, fire, fireworks, waterfalls, water spray, and clumps of grass. For example, particle systems were used to model the planet explosion and expanding wall of fire due to the "genesis bomb" in the motion picture *Star Trek II—The Wrath of Khan*.

Random processes are used to generate objects within some defined region of space and to vary their parameters over time. At some random time, each object is deleted. During the lifetime of a particle, its path and surface characteristics may be color-coded and displayed.

Particle shapes can be small spheres, ellipsoids, boxes, or other shapes. The size and shape of particles may vary randomly over time. Also, other properties such as particle transparency, color, and movement all can vary randomly. In some applications, particle motion may be controlled by specified forces, such as a gravity field.

As each particle moves, its path is plotted and displayed in a particular color. For example, a fireworks pattern can be displayed by randomly generating particles within a spherical region of space and allowing them to move radially

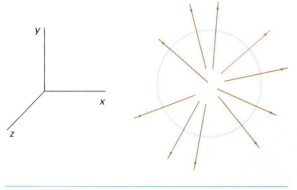

Figure 10-111
Modeling fireworks as a particle system with particles traveling radially outward from the center of the sphere.

outward, as in Fig. 10-111. The particle paths can be color-coded from red to yellow, for instance, to simulate the temperature of the exploding particles. Similarly, realistic displays of grass clumps have been modeled with "trajectory" particles (Fig. 10-112) that are shot up from the ground and fall back to earth under gravity. In this case, the particle paths can originate within a tapered cylinder, and might be color-coded from green to yellow.

Figure 10-113 illustrates a particle-system simulation of a waterfall. The water particles fall from a fixed elevation, are deflected by an obstacle, and then splash up from the ground. Different colors are used to distinguish the particle

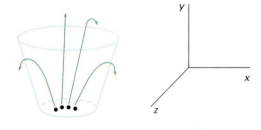

Figure 10-112
Modeling a clump of grass by firing particles upward within a tapered cylinder. The particle paths are parabolas due to the downward force of gravity.

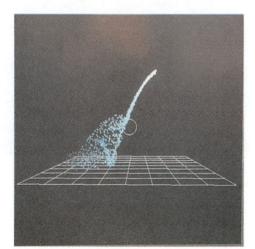

Figure 10-113
Simulation of the behavior of a waterfall hitting a stone (circle). The water particles are deflected by the stone and then splash up from the ground. (*Courtesy of M. Brooks and T. L. J. Howard, Department of Computer Science, University of Manchester.*)

391

paths at each stage. An example of an animation simulating the disintegration of an object is shown in Fig. 10-114. The object on the left disintegrates into the particle distribution on the right. A composite scene formed with a variety of representations is given in Fig. 10-115. The scene is modeled using particle-system grass, fractal mountains, and texture mapping and other surface-rendering procedures.

Figure 10-114
An object disintegrating into a cloud of particles. (*Courtesy of Autodesk, Inc.*)

Figure 10-115
A scene, entitled *Road to Point Reyes,* showing particle-system grass, fractal mountains, and texture-mapped surfaces. (*Courtesy of Pixar. Copyright © 1983 Pixar.*)

PHYSICALLY BASED MODELING

A nonrigid object, such as a rope, a piece of cloth, or a soft rubber ball, can be represented with **physically based modeling** methods that describe the behavior of the object in terms of the interaction of external and internal forces. An accurate discription of the shape of a terry cloth towel drapped over the back of a chair is obtained by considering the effect of the chair on the fabric loops in the cloth and the interaction between the cloth threads.

A common method for modeling a nonrigid object is to approximate the object with a network of point nodes with flexible connections between the nodes. One simple type of connection is a spring. Figure 10-116 shows a section of a two-dimensional spring network that could be used to approximate the behavior of a sheet of rubber. Similar spring networks can be set up in three dimensions to model a rubber ball or a block of jello. For a homogeneous object, we can use identical springs throughout the network. If we want the object to have different properties in different directions, we can use different spring properties in different directions. When external forces are applied to a spring network, the amount of stretching or compression of the individual springs depends on the value set for the *spring constant k*, also called the *force constant* for the spring.

Horizontal displacement x of a node position under the influence of a force F_x is illustrated in Fig. 10-117. If the spring is not overstretched, we can closely approximate the amount of displacement x from the equilibrium position using Hooke's law:

$$F_s = -F_x = -kx \qquad (10\text{-}113)$$

where F_s is the equal and opposite restoring force of the spring on the stretched node. This relationship holds also for horizontal compression of a spring by an amount x, and we have similar relationships for displacements and force components in the y and z directions.

If objects are completely flexible, they return to their original configuration when the external forces are removed. But if we want to model putty, or some other deformable object, we need to modify the spring characteristics so that the springs do not return to their original shape when the external forces are removed. Another set of applied forces then can deform the object in some other way.

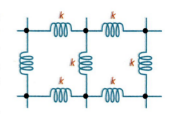

Figure 10-116
A two-dimensional spring network, constructed with identical spring constants k.

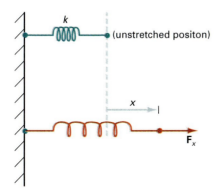

Figure 10-117
An external force F_x pulling on one end of a spring, with the other end rigidly fixed.

Instead of using springs, we can also model the connections between nodes with elastic materials, then we minimize strain-energy functions to determine object shape under the influence of external forces. This method provides a better model for cloth, and various energy functions have been devised to describe the behavior of different cloth materials.

To model a nonrigid object, we first set up the external forces acting on the object. Then we consider the propagation of the forces throughout the network representing the object. This leads to a set of simultaneous equations that we must solve to determine the displacement of the nodes throughout the network.

Figure 10-118 shows a banana peel modeled with a spring network, and the scene in Fig. 10-119 shows examples of cloth modeling using energy functions, with a texture-mapped pattern on one cloth. By adjusting the parameters in a network using energy-function calculations, different kinds of cloth can be modeled. Figure 10-120 illustrates models for cotton, wool, and polyester cotton materials draped over a table.

Physically based modeling methods are also applied in animations to more accurately describe motion paths. In the past, animations were often specified using spline paths and kinematics, where motion parameters are based only on

Figure 10-118
Modeling the flexible behavior of a banana peel with a spring network.
(*Copyright © 1992 David Laidlaw, John Snyder, Adam Woodbury, and Alan Barr, Computer Graphics Lab, California Institute of Technology.*)

Figure 10-119
Modeling the flexible behavior of cloth draped over furniture using energy-function minimization.
(*Copyright © 1992 Gene Greger and David E. Breen, Design Research Center, Rensselaer Polytechnic Institute.*)

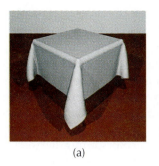
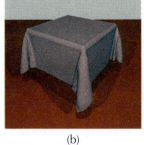
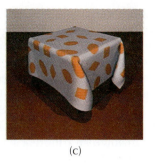

(a)   (b)   (c)

Figure 10-120
Modeling the characteristics of (a) cotton, (b) wool, and (c) polyester
cotton using energy-function minimization. (*Copyright © 1992 David E.
Breen and Donald H. House, Design Research Center, Rensselaer Polytechnic Institute.*)

position and velocity. Physically based modeling describes motion using dynamical equations, involving forces and accelerations. Animation descriptions based
on the equations of dynamics produce more realistic motions than those based on
the equations of kinematics.

10-22
VISUALIZATION OF DATA SETS

The use of graphical methods as an aid in scientific and engineering analysis is
commonly referred to as **scientific visualization**. This involves the visualization
of data sets and processes that may be difficult or impossible to analyze without
graphical methods. For example, visualization techniques are needed to deal
with the output of high-volume data sources such as supercomputers, satellite
and spacecraft scanners, radio-astronomy telescopes, and medical scanners. Millions of data points are often generated from numerical solutions of computer
simulations and from observational equipment, and it is difficult to determine
trends and relationships by simply scanning the raw data. Similarly, visualization
techniques are useful for analyzing processes that occur over a long time period
or that cannot be observed directly, such as quantum-mechanical phenomena
and special-relativity effects produced by objects traveling near the speed of
light. Scientific visualization uses methods from computer graphics, image processing, computer vision, and other areas to visually display, enhance, and manipulate information to allow better understanding of the data. Similar methods
employed by commerce, industry, and other nonscientific areas are sometimes referred to as **business visualization**.

Data sets are classified according to their spatial distribution and according
to data type. Two-dimensional data sets have values distributed over a surface,
and three-dimensional data sets have values distributed over the interior of a
cube, a sphere, or some other region of space. Data types include scalars, vectors,
tensors, and multivariate data.

Visual Representations for Scalar Fields

A scalar quantity is one that has a single value. Scalar data sets contain values
that may be distributed in time, as well as over spatial positions. Also, the data

395

values may be functions of other scalar parameters. Some examples of physical scalar quantities are energy, density, mass, temperature, pressure, charge, resistance, reflectivity, frequency, and water content.

A common method for visualizing a scalar data set is to use graphs or charts that show the distribution of data values as a function of other parameters, such as position and time. If the data are distributed over a surface, we could plot the data values as vertical bars rising up from the surface, or we can interpolate the data values to display a smooth surface. **Pseudo-color methods** are also used to distinguish different values in a scalar data set, and color-coding techniques can be combined with graph and chart methods. To color code a scalar data set, we choose a range of colors and map the range of data values to the color range. For example, blue could be assigned to the lowest scalar value, and red could be assigned to the highest value. Figure 10-121 gives an example of a color-coded surface plot. Color coding a data set can be tricky, because some color combinations can lead to misinterpretations of the data.

Contour plots are used to display *isolines* (lines of constant scalar value) for a data set distributed over a surface. The isolines are spaced at some convenient interval to show the range and variation of the data values over the region of space. A typical application is a contour plot of elevations over a ground plane. Usually, contouring methods are applied to a set of data values that is distributed over a regular grid, as in Fig. 10-122. Regular grids have equally spaced grid lines, and data values are known at the grid intersections. Numerical solutions of computer simulations are usually set up to produce data distributions on a regular grid, while observed data sets are often irregularly spaced. Contouring methods have been devised for various kinds of nonregular grids, but often nonregular data distributions are converted to regular grids. A two-dimensional contouring algorithm traces the isolines from cell to cell within the grid by checking the four corners of grid cells to determine which cell edges are crossed by a

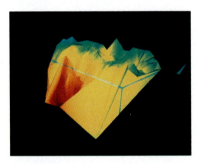

Figure 10-121
A financial surface plot showing stock-growth potential during the October 1987 stock-market crash. Red indicates high returns, and the plot shows that low-growth stocks performed better in the crash.
(*Courtesy of Eng-Kiat Koh, Information Technology Institute, Republic of Singapore.*)

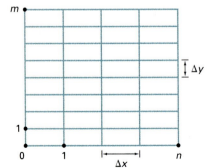

Figure 10-122
A regular, two-dimensional grid with data values at the intersection of the grid lines. The x grid lines have a constant Δx spacing, and the y grid lines have a constant Δy spacing, where the spacing in the x and y directions may not be the same.

particular isoline. The isolines are usually plotted as straight-line sections across each cell, as illustrated in Fig. 10-123. Sometimes isolines are plotted with spline curves, but spline fitting can lead to inconsistencies and misinterpretation of a data set. For example, two spline isolines could cross, or curved isoline paths might not be a true indicator of the data trends since data values are known only at the cell corners. Contouring packages can allow interactive adjustment of isolines by a researcher to correct any inconsistencies. An example of three, overlapping, color-coded contour plots in the xy plane is given in Fig. 10-124, and Fig. 10-125 shows contour lines and color coding for an irregularly shaped space.

For three-dimensional scalar data fields, we can take cross-sectional slices and display the two-dimensional data distributions over the slices. We could either color code the data values over a slice, or we could display isolines. Visualization packages typically provide a slicer routine that allows cross sections to be

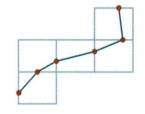

Figure 10-123
The path of an isoline across five grid cells.

Figure 10-124
Color-coded contour plots for three data sets within the same region of the xy plane. (*Courtesy of the National Center for Supercomputing Applications, University of Illinois at Urbana-Champaign.*)

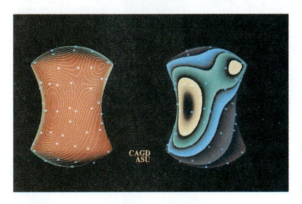

Figure 10-125
Color-coded contour plots over the surface of an apple-core-shaped region of space. (*Courtesy of Greg Nielson, Department of Computer Science and Engineering, Arizona State University.*)

397

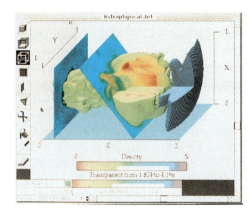

Figure 10-126
Cross-sectional slices of a three-dimensional data set. (*Courtesy of Spyglass, Inc.*)

taken at any angle. Figure 10-126 shows a display generated by a commercial slicer-dicer package.

Instead of looking at two-dimensional cross sections, we can plot one or more **isosurfaces**, which are simply three-dimensional contour plots (Fig. 10-127). When two overlapping isosurfaces are displayed, the outer surface is made transparent so that we can view the shape of both isosurfaces. Constructing an isosurface is similar to plotting isolines, except now we have three-dimensional grid cells and we need to check the values of the eight corners of a cell to locate sections of an isosurface. Figure 10-128 shows some examples of isosurface intersections with grid cells. Isosurfaces are modeled with triangle meshes, then surface-rendering algorithms are applied to display the final shape.

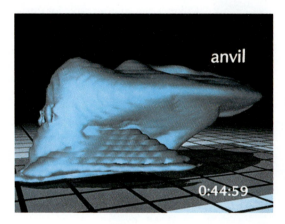

Figure 10-127
An isosurface generated from a set of water-content values obtained from a numerical model of a thunderstorm. (*Courtesy of Bob Wilhelmson, Department of Atmospheric Sciences and National Center for Supercomputing Applications, University of Illinois at Urbana Champaign.*)

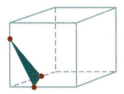 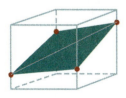 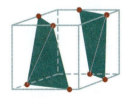 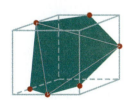

Figure 10-128
Isosurface intersections with grid cells, modeled with triangle patches.

Volume rendering, which is often somewhat like an X-ray picture, is another method for visualizing a three-dimensional data set. The interior information about a data set is projected to a display screen using the ray-casting methods introduced in Section 10-15. Along the ray path from each screen pixel (Fig. 10-129), interior data values are examined and encoded for display. Often, data values at the grid positions are averaged so that one value is stored for each voxel of the data space. How the data are encoded for display depends on the application. Seismic data, for example, is often examined to find the maximum and minimum values along each ray. The values can then be color coded to give information about the width of the interval and the minimum value. In medical applications, the data values are opacity factors in the range from 0 to 1 for the tissue and bone layers. Bone layers are completely opaque, while tissue is somewhat transparent (low opacity). Along each ray, the opacity factors are accumulated until either the total is greater than or equal to 1, or until the ray exits at the back of the three-dimensional data grid. The accumulated opacity value is then displayed as a pixel-intensity level, which can be gray scale or color. Figure 10-130 shows a volume visualization of a medical data set describing the structure of a dog heart. For this volume visualization, a color-coded plot of the distance to the maximum voxel value along each pixel ray was displayed.

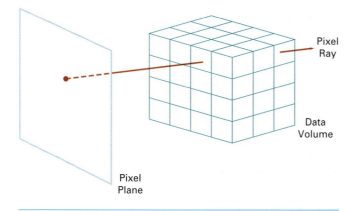

Figure 10-129
Volume visualization of a regular, Cartesian data grid using ray casting to examine interior data values.

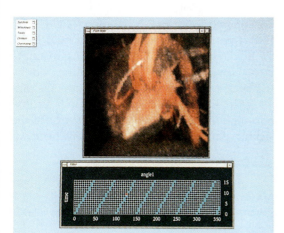

Figure 10-130
Volume visualization of a data set for a dog heart, obtained by plotting the color-coded distance to the maximum voxel value for each pixel. (*Courtesy of Patrick Moran and Clinton Potter, National Center for Supercomputing Applications, University of Illinois at Urbana-Champaign.*)

399

Visual Representations for Vector Fields

A vector quantity $\mathbf{V}$ in three-dimensional space has three scalar values (V_x, V_y, V_z), one for each coordinate direction, and a two-dimensional vector has two components (V_x, V_y). Another way to describe a vector quantity is by giving its magnitude $|\mathbf{V}|$ and its direction as a unit vector $\mathbf{u}$. As with scalars, vector quantities may be functions of position, time, and other parameters. Some examples of physical vector quantities are velocity, acceleration, force, electric fields, magnetic fields, gravitational fields, and electric current.

One way to visualize a vector field is to plot each data point as a small arrow that shows the magnitude and direction of the vector. This method is most often used with cross-sectional slices, as in Fig. 10-131, since it can be difficult to see the data trends in a three-dimensional region cluttered with overlapping arrows. Magnitudes for the vector values can be shown by varying the lengths of the arrows, or we can make all arrows the same size, but make the arrows different colors according to a selected color coding for the vector magnitudes.

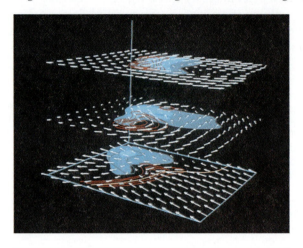

Figure 10-131

Arrow representation for a vector field over cross-sectional slices. (*Courtesy of the National Center for Supercomputing Applications, University of Illinois at Urbana-Champaign.*)

We can also represent vector values by plotting *field lines* or *streamlines*. Field lines are commonly used for electric, magnetic, and gravitational fields. The magnitude of the vector values is indicated by the spacing between field lines, and the direction is the tangent to the field, as shown in Fig. 10-132. An example of a streamline plot of a vector field is shown in Fig. 10-133. Streamlines can be displayed as wide arrows, particularly when a whirlpool, or vortex, effect is present. An example of this is given in Fig. 10-134, which displays swirling airflow patterns inside a thunderstorm. For animations of fluid flow, the behavior of the vector field can be visualized by tracking particles along the flow direction. An

lower   higher

Figure 10-132

Field-line representation for a vector data set.

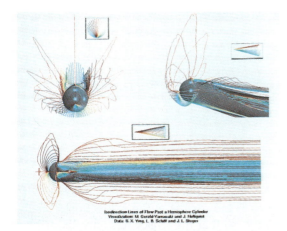

Figure 10-133
Visualizing airflow around a
cylinder with a hemispherical cap
that is tilted slightly relative to the
incoming direction of the airflow.
*(Courtesy of M. Gerald-Yamasaki, J.
Huiltquist, and Sam Uselton, NASA Ames
Research Center.)*

Figure 10-134
Twisting airflow patterns,
visualized with wide streamlines
inside a transparent isosurface plot
of a thunderstorm. *(Courtesy of Bob
Wilhelmson, Department of Atmospheric
Sciences and National Center for
Supercomputing Applications, University
of Illinois at Urbana-Champaign.)*

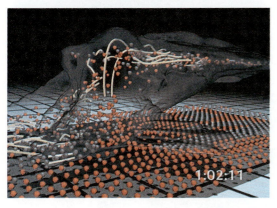

Figure 10-135
Airflow patterns, visualized with
both streamlines and particle
motion inside a transparent
isosurface plot of a thunderstorm.
Rising sphere particles are colored
orange, and falling sphere particles
are blue. *(Courtesy of Bob Wilhelmson,
Department of Atmospheric Sciences and
National Center for Supercomputing
Applications, University of Illinois at
Urbana-Champaign.)*

example of a vector-field visualization using both streamlines and particles is
shown in Fig. 10-135.

Sometimes, only the magnitudes of the vector quantities are displayed. This
is often done when multiple quantities are to be visualized at a single position, or
when the directions do not vary much in some region of space, or when vector
directions are of less interest.

Visual Representations for Tensor Fields

A tensor quantity in three-dimensional space has nine components and can be
represented with a 3 by 3 matrix. Actually, this representation is used for a *second-order tensor*, and higher-order tensors do occur in some applications, particularly general relativity. Some examples of physical, second-order tensors are

401

stress and strain in a material subjected to external forces, conductivity (or resistivity) of an electrical conductor, and the metric tensor, which gives the properties of a particular coordinate space. The stress tensor in Cartesian coordinates, for example, can be represented as

$$\begin{bmatrix} \sigma_x & \sigma_{xy} & \sigma_{xz} \\ \sigma_{yx} & \sigma_y & \sigma_{yz} \\ \sigma_{zx} & \sigma_{zy} & \sigma_z \end{bmatrix} \qquad (10\text{-}114)$$

Tensor quantities are frequently encountered in anisotropic materials, which have different properties in different directions. The x, xy, and xz elements of the conductivity tensor, for example, describe the contributions of electric field components in the x, y, and z directions to the current in the x direction. Usually, physical tensor quantities are symmetric, so that the tensor has only six distinct values. For instance, the xy and yx components of the stress tensor are the same.

Visualization schemes for representing all six components of a second-order tensor quantity are based on devising shapes that have six parameters. One graphical representation for a tensor is shown in Fig. 10-136. The three diagonal elements of the tensor are used to construct the magnitude and direction of the arrow, and the three off-diagonal terms are used to set the shape and color of the elliptical disk.

Instead of trying to visualize all six components of a tensor quantity, we can reduce the tensor to a vector or a scalar. Using a vector representation, we can simply display a vector representation for the diagonal elements of the tensor. And by applying *tensor-contraction* operations, we can obtain a scalar representation. For example, stress and strain tensors can be contracted to generate a scalar strain-energy density that can be plotted at points in a material subject to external forces (Fig. 10-137).

Visual Representations for Multivariate Data Fields

In some applications, at each grid position over some region of space, we may have multiple data values, which can be a mixture of scalar, vector, and even ten-

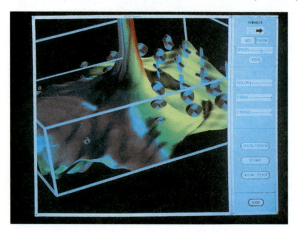

Figure 10-136
Representing stress and strain tensors with an elliptical disk and a rod over the surface of a stressed material. (*Courtesy of Bob Haber, National Center for Supercomputing Applications, University of Illinois at Urbana-Champaign.*)

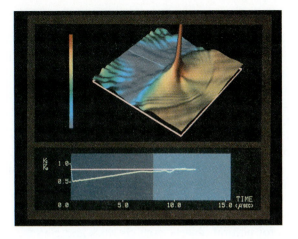

Figure 10-137
Representing stress and strain tensors with a strain-energy density plot in a visualization of crack propagation on the surface of a stressed material.
(*Courtesy of Bob Haber, National Center for Supercomputing Applications, University of Illinois at Urbana-Champaign.*)

sor values. As an example, for a fluid-flow problem, we may have fluid velocity, temperature, and density values at each three-dimensional position. Thus, we have five scalar values to display at each position, and the situation is similar to displaying a tensor field.

A method for displaying multivariate data fields is to construct graphical objects, sometimes referred to as **glyphs,** with multiple parts. Each part of a glyph represents a physical quantity. The size and color of each part can be used to display information about scalar magnitudes. To give directional information for a vector field, we can use a wedge, a cone, or some other pointing shape for the glyph part representing the vector. An example of the visualization of a multivariate data field using a glyph structure at selected grid positions is shown in Fig. 10-138.

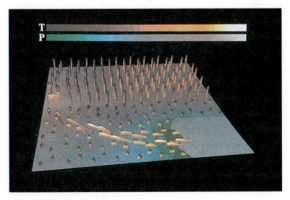

Figure 10-138
One frame from an animated visualization of a multivariate data field using glyphs. The wedge-shaped part of the glyph indicates the direction of a vector quantity at each point. (*Courtesy of the National Center for Supercomputing Applications, University of Illinois at Urbana-Champaign.*)

403

SUMMARY

Many representations have been developed for modeling the wide variety of objects that might be displayed in a graphics scene. "Standard graphics objects" are those represented with a surface mesh of polygon facets. Polygon-mesh representations are typically derived from other representations.

Surface functions, such as the quadrics, are used to describe spheres and other smooth surfaces. For design applications, we can use superquadrics, splines, or blobby objects to represent smooth surface shapes. In addition, construction techniques, such as CSG and sweep representations, are useful for designing compound object shapes that are built up from a set of simpler shapes. And interior, as well as surface, information can be stored in octree representations.

Descriptions for natural objects, such as trees and clouds, and other irregularly shaped objects can be specified with fractals, shape grammars, and particle systems. Finally, visualization techniques use graphic representations to display numerical or other types of data sets. The various types of numerical data include scalar, vector, and tensor values. Also many scientific visualizations require methods for representing multivariate data sets, that contain a combination of the various data types.

REFERENCES

A detailed discussion of superquadrics is contained in Barr (1981). For more information on blobby object modeling, see Blinn (1982). The metaball model is discussed in Nishimura (1985); and the soft-object model is discussed in Wyville, Wyville, and McPheeters (1987).

Sources of information on parametric curve and surface representations include Bezier (1972), Burt and Adelson (1983), Barsky (1983, 1984), Kochanek and Bartels (1984), Farouki and Hinds (1985), Huitric and Nahas (1985), Mortenson (1985), Farin (1988), and Rogers and Adams (1990).

Octrees and quadtrees are discussed by Doctor (1981), Yamaguchi, Kunii, and Fujimura (1984), and by Carlbom, Chakravarty, and Vanderschel (1985). Solid-modeling references include Casale and Stanton (1985) and Requicha and Rossignac (1992).

For further information on fractal representations see Mandelbrot (1977, 1982), Fournier, Fussel, and Carpenter (1982), Norton (1982), Peitgen and Richter (1986), Peitgen and Saupe (1988), Koh and Hearn (1992), and Barnsley (1993). Shape grammars are discussed in Glassner (1992), and particle systems are discussed in Reeves (1983). A discussion of physically based modeling is given in Barzel (1992).

A general introduction to visualization methods is given in Hearn and Baker (1991). Additional information on specific visualization methods can be found in Sabin (1985), Lorensen and Cline (1987), Drebin, Carpenter, and Hanrahan (1988), Sabella (1988), Upson and Keeler (1988), Frenkel (1989), Nielson, Shriver, and Rosenblum (1990), and Nielson (1993). Guidelines for visual displays of information are given in Tufte (1983, 1990).

EXERCISES

10-1. Set up geometric data tables as in Fig. 10-2 for a unit cube.

10-2. Set up geometric data tables for a unit cube using only: (a) vertex and polygon tables, and (b) a single polygon table. Compare the two methods for representing the unit cube with a representation using three data tables, and estimate storage requirements for each.

10-3. Define an efficient polygon representation for a cylinder. Justify your choice of representation.

10-4. Set up a procedure for establishing polygon tables for any input set of data points defining an object.

10-5. Devise routines for checking the data tables in Fig. 10-2 for consistency and completeness.

10-6. Write a program that calculates parameters A, B, C, and D for any set of three-dimensional plane surfaces defining an object.

10-7. Given the plane parameters A, B, C, and D for all surfaces of an object, devise an algorithm to determine whether any specified point is inside or outside the object.

10-8. How would the values for parameters A, B, C, and D in the equation of a plane surface have to be altered if the coordinate reference is changed from a right-handed system to a left-handed system?

10-9. Set up an algorithm for converting any specified sphere, ellipsoid, or cylinder to a polygon-mesh representation.

10-10. Set up an algorithm for converting a specified superellipsoid to a polygon-mesh representation.

10-11. Set up an algorithm for converting a metaball representation to a polygon-mesh representation.

10-12. Write a routine to display a two-dimensional, cardinal-spline curve, given an input set of control points in the xy plane.

10-13. Write a routine to display a two-dimensional, Kochanek-Bartels curve, given an input set of control points in the xy plane.

10-14. Determine the quadratic Bézier blending functions for three control points. Plot each function and label the maximum and minimum values.

10-15. Determine the Bézier blending functions for five control points. Plot each function and label the maximum and minimum values.

10-16. Write an efficient routine to display two-dimensional, cubic Bézier curves, given a set of four control points in the xy plane.

10-17. Write a routine to design two-dimensional, cubic Bézier curve shapes that have first-order piecewise continuity. Use an interactive technique for selecting control-point positions in the xy plane for each section of the curve.

10-18. Write a routine to design two-dimensional, cubic Bézier curve shapes that have second-order piecewise continuity. Use an interactive technique for selecting control-point positions in the xy plane for each section of the curve.

10-19. Write a routine to display a cubic Bézier curve using a subdivision method.

10-20. Determine the blending functions for uniform, periodic B-spline curves for $d = 5$.

10-21. Determine the blending functions for uniform, periodic B-spline curves for $d = 6$.

10-22. Write a program using forward differences to calculate points along a two-dimensional, uniform, periodic, cubic B-spline curve, given an input set of control points.

10-23. Write a routine to display any specified conic in the xy plane using a rational Bézier spline representation.

10-24. Write a routine to display any specified conic in the xy plane using a rational B-spline representation.

10-25. Develop an algorithm for calculating the normal vector to a Bezier surface at the point $\mathbf{P}(u, v)$.

10-26. Write a program to display any specified quadratic curve using forward differences to calculate points along the curve path.

10-27. Write a program to display any specified cubic curve using forward differences to calculate points along the curve path.

10-28. Derive expressions for calculating the forward differences for any specified quadratic curve.

10-29. Derive expressions for calculating the forward differences for any specified cubic curve.

10-30. Set up procedures for generating the description of a three-dimensional object from input parameters that define the object in terms of a translational sweep.

10-31. Develop procedures for generating the description of a three-dimensional object using input parameters that define the object in terms of a rotational sweep.

10-32. Devise an algorithm for generating solid objects as combinations of three-dimensional primitive shapes, each defined as a set of surfaces, using constructive solid-geometry methods.

10-33. Develop an algorithm for performing constructive solid-geometry modeling using a primitive set of solids defined in octree structures.

10-34. Develop an algorithm for encoding a two-dimensional scene as a quadtree representation.

10-35. Set up an algorithm for loading a quadtree representation of a scene into a frame buffer for display of the scene.

10-36. Write a routine to convert the polygon definition of a three-dimensional object into an octree representation.

10-37. Using the random, midpoint-displacement method, write a routine to create a mountain outline, starting with a horizontal line in the xy plane.

10-38. Write a routine to calculate elevations above a ground plane using the random, midpoint-displacement method.

10-39. Write a program for generating a fractal snowflake (Koch curve) for any given number of iterations.

10-40. Write a program to generate a fractal curve for a specified number of iterations using one of the generators in Fig. 10-71 or 10-72. What is the fractal dimension of your curve?

10-41. Write a program to generate fractal curves using the self-squaring function $f(z) = z^2 + \lambda$, where λ is any selected complex constant.

10-42. Write a program to generate fractal curves using the self-squaring function $f(x) = i(z^2 + 1)$, where $i = \sqrt{-1}$.

10-43. Write a routine to interactively select different color combinations for displaying the Mandelbrot set.

10-44. Write a program to interactively select any rectangular region of the Mandelbrot set and to zoom in on the selected region.

10-45. Write a routine to implement point inversion, Eq. 10-112, for any specified circle and any given point position.

10-46. Devise a set of geometric-substitution rules for altering the shape of an equilateral triangle.

10-47. Write a program to display the stages in the conversion of an equilateral triangle into another shape, given a set of geometric-substitution rules.

10-48. Write a program to model an exploding firecracker in the xy plane using a particle system.

10-49. Devise an algorithm for modeling a rectangle as a nonrigid body, using identical springs for the four sides of the rectangle.

10-50. Write a routine to visualize a two-dimensional, scalar data set using pseudo-color methods.

10-51. Write a routine to visualize a two-dimensional, scalar data set using contour lines.

10-52. Write a routine to visualize a two-dimensional, vector data set using an arrow representation for the vector values. Make all arrows the same length, but display the arrows with different colors to represent the different vector magnitudes.

C H A P T E R

11 Three-Dimensional Geometric and Modeling Transformations

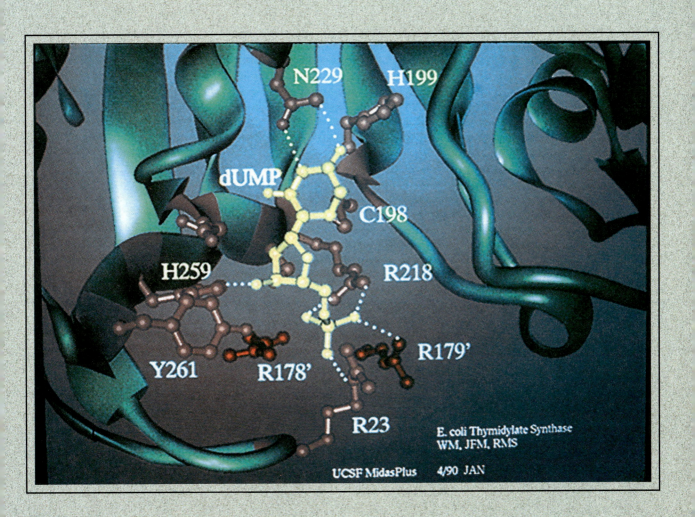

ethods for geometric transformations and object modeling in three dimensions are extended from two-dimensional methods by including considerations for the z coordinate. We now translate an object by specifying a three-dimensional translation vector, which determines how much the object is to be moved in each of the three coordinate directions. Similarly, we scale an object with three coordinate scaling factors. The extension for three-dimensional rotation is less straightforward. When we discussed two-dimensional rotations in the xy plane, we needed to consider only rotations about axes that were perpendicular to the xy plane. In three-dimensional space, we can now select any spatial orientation for the rotation axis. Most graphics packages handle three-dimensional rotation as a composite of three rotations, one for each of the three Cartesian axes. Alternatively, a user can easily set up a general rotation matrix, given the orientation of the axis and the required rotation angle. As in the two-dimensional case, we express geometric transformations in matrix form. Any sequence of transformations is then represented as a single matrix, formed by concatenating the matrices for the individual transformations in the sequence.

11-1
TRANSLATION

In a three-dimensional homogeneous coordinate representation, a point is translated (Fig. 11-1) from position $\mathbf{P} = (x, y, z)$ to position $\mathbf{P'} = (x', y', z')$ with the matrix operation

$$
\begin{bmatrix} x' \\ y' \\ z' \\ 1 \end{bmatrix} = \begin{bmatrix} 1 & 0 & 0 & t_x \\ 0 & 1 & 0 & t_y \\ 0 & 0 & 1 & t_z \\ 0 & 0 & 0 & 1 \end{bmatrix} \cdot \begin{bmatrix} x \\ y \\ z \\ 1 \end{bmatrix}
\tag{11-1}
$$

or

$$
\mathbf{P'} = \mathbf{T} \cdot \mathbf{P}
\tag{11-2}
$$

Parameters t_x, t_y, and t_z, specifying translation distances for the coordinate directions x, y, and z, are assigned any real values. The matrix representation in Eq. 11-1 is equivalent to the three equations

$$
x' = x + t_x, \qquad y' = y + t_y, \qquad z' = z + t_z
\tag{11-3}
$$

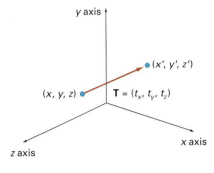

Figure 11-1
Translating a point with translation vector $\mathbf{T} = (t_x, t_y, t_z)$.

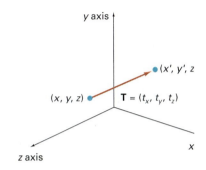

Figure 11-2
Translating an object with translation vector $\mathbf{T}$.

An object is translated in three dimensions by transforming each of the defining points of the object. For an object represented as a set of polygon surfaces, we translate each vertex of each surface (Fig. 11-2) and redraw the polygon facets in the new position.

We obtain the inverse of the translation matrix in Eq. 11-1 by negating the translation distances t_x, t_y, and t_z. This produces a translation in the opposite direction, and the product of a translation matrix and its inverse produces the identity matrix.

11-2

ROTATION

To generate a rotation transformation for an object, we must designate an axis of rotation (about which the object is to be rotated) and the amount of angular rotation. Unlike two-dimensional applications, where all transformations are carried out in the xy plane, a three-dimensional rotation can be specified around any line in space. The easiest rotation axes to handle are those that are parallel to the coordinate axes. Also, we can use combinations of coordinate-axis rotations (along with appropriate translations) to specify any general rotation.

By convention, positive rotation angles produce counterclockwise rotations about a coordinate axis, if we are looking along the positive half of the axis toward the coordinate origin (Fig. 11-3). This agrees with our earlier discussion of rotation in two dimensions, where positive rotations in the xy plane are counterclockwise about axes parallel to the z axis.

Coordinate-Axes Rotations

The two-dimensional z-**axis rotation** equations are easily extended to three dimensions:

409

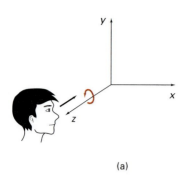

(a)

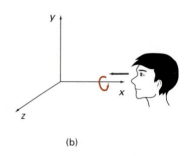

(b)

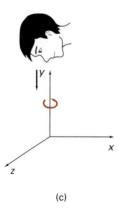

(c)

Figure 11-3
Positive rotation directions
about the coordinate axes are
counterclockwise, when looking
toward the origin from a positive
coordinate position on each axis.

$$x' = x \cos\theta - y \sin\theta$$
$$y' = x \sin\theta + y \cos\theta \qquad (11\text{-}4)$$
$$z' = z$$

Parameter θ specifies the rotation angle. In homogeneous coordinate form, the three-dimensional z-axis rotation equations are expressed as

$$
\begin{bmatrix} x' \\ y' \\ z' \\ 1 \end{bmatrix}
=
\begin{bmatrix}
\cos\theta & -\sin\theta & 0 & 0 \\
\sin\theta & \cos\theta & 0 & 0 \\
0 & 0 & 1 & 0 \\
0 & 0 & 0 & 1
\end{bmatrix}
\cdot
\begin{bmatrix} x \\ y \\ z \\ 1 \end{bmatrix}
\qquad (11\text{-}5)
$$

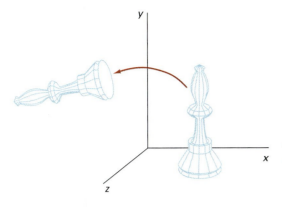

Figure 11-4
Rotation of an object about the *z* axis.

which we can write more compactly as

$$\mathbf{P}' = \mathbf{R}_z(\theta) \cdot \mathbf{P} \qquad (11\text{-}6)$$

Figure 11-4 illustrates rotation of an object about the *z* axis.

Transformation equations for rotations about the other two coordinate axes can be obtained with a cyclic permutation of the coordinate parameters *x*, *y*, and *z* in Eqs. 11-4. That is, we use the replacements

$$x \to y \to z \to x \qquad (11\text{-}7)$$

as illustrated in Fig. 11-5.

Substituting permutations 11-7 in Eqs. 11-4, we get the equations for an *x*-axis rotation:

$$
\begin{aligned}
y' &= y \cos \theta - z \sin \theta \\
z' &= y \sin \theta + z \cos \theta \\
x' &= x
\end{aligned}
\qquad (11\text{-}8)
$$

which can be written in the homogeneous coordinate form

$$
\begin{bmatrix} x' \\ y' \\ z' \\ 1 \end{bmatrix}
=
\begin{bmatrix}
1 & 0 & 0 & 0 \\
0 & \cos \theta & -\sin \theta & 0 \\
0 & \sin \theta & \cos \theta & 0 \\
0 & 0 & 0 & 1
\end{bmatrix}
\cdot
\begin{bmatrix} x \\ y \\ z \\ 1 \end{bmatrix}
\qquad (11\text{-}9)
$$

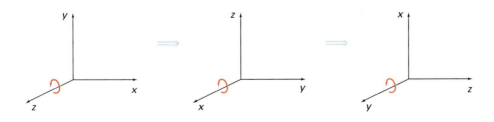

Figure 11-5
Cyclic permutation of the Cartesian-coordinate axes to produce the
three sets of coordinate-axis rotation equations.

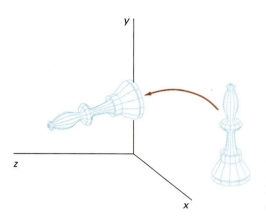

Figure 11-6
Rotation of an object about the
x axis.

or

$$\mathbf{P}' = \mathbf{R}_x(\theta) \cdot \mathbf{P} \tag{11-10}$$

Rotation of an object around the x axis is demonstrated in Fig. 11.6.

Cyclically permuting coordinates in Eqs. 11-8 give us the transformation equations for a y-**axis rotation**:

$$z' = z \cos\theta - x \sin\theta$$

$$x' = z \sin\theta + x \cos\theta \tag{11-11}$$

$$y' = y$$

The matrix representation for y-axis rotation is

$$
\begin{bmatrix} x' \\ y' \\ z' \\ 1 \end{bmatrix} =
\begin{bmatrix}
\cos\theta & 0 & \sin\theta & 0 \\
0 & 1 & 0 & 0 \\
-\sin\theta & 0 & \cos\theta & 0 \\
0 & 0 & 0 & 1
\end{bmatrix} \cdot
\begin{bmatrix} x \\ y \\ z \\ 1 \end{bmatrix} \tag{11-12}
$$

or

$$\mathbf{P}' = \mathbf{R}_y(\theta) \cdot \mathbf{P} \tag{11-13}$$

An example of y-axis rotation is shown in Fig. 11-7.

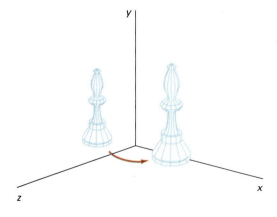

Figure 11-7
Rotation of an object about the
y axis.

An inverse rotation matrix is formed by replacing the rotation angle θ by $-\theta$. Negative values for rotation angles generate rotations in a clockwise direction, so the identity matrix is produced when any rotation matrix is multiplied by its inverse. Since only the sine function is affected by the change in sign of the rotation angle, the inverse matrix can also be obtained by interchanging rows and columns. That is, we can calculate the inverse of any rotation matrix $\mathbf{R}$ by evaluating its transpose ($\mathbf{R}^{-1} = \mathbf{R}^T$). This method for obtaining an inverse matrix holds also for any composite rotation matrix.

General Three-Dimensional Rotations

A rotation matrix for any axis that does not coincide with a coordinate axis can be set up as a composite transformation involving combinations of translations and the coordinate-axes rotations. We obtain the required composite matrix by first setting up the transformation sequence that moves the selected rotation axis onto one of the coordinate axes. Then we set up the rotation matrix about that coordinate axis for the specified rotation angle. The last step is to obtain the inverse transformation sequence that returns the rotation axis to its original position.

In the special case where an object is to be rotated about an axis that is parallel to one of the coordinate axes, we can attain the desired rotation with the following transformation sequence.

1. Translate the object so that the rotation axis coincides with the parallel coordinate axis.
2. Perform the specified rotation about that axis.
3. Translate the object so that the rotation axis is moved back to its original position.

The steps in this sequence are illustrated in Fig. 11-8. Any coordinate position $\mathbf{P}$ on the object in this figure is transformed with the sequence shown as

$$\mathbf{P}' = \mathbf{T}^{-1} \cdot \mathbf{R}_x(\theta) \cdot \mathbf{T} \cdot \mathbf{P}$$

where the composite matrix for the transformation is

$$\mathbf{R}(\theta) = \mathbf{T}^{-1} \cdot \mathbf{R}_x(\theta) \cdot \mathbf{T}$$

which is of the same form as the two-dimensional transformation sequence for rotation about an arbitrary pivot point.

When an object is to be rotated about an axis that is not parallel to one of the coordinate axes, we need to perform some additional transformations. In this case, we also need rotations to align the axis with a selected coordinate axis and to bring the axis back to its original orientation. Given the specifications for the rotation axis and the rotation angle, we can accomplish the required rotation in five steps:

1. Translate the object so that the rotation axis passes through the coordinate origin.
2. Rotate the object so that the axis of rotation coincides with one of the coordinate axes.
3. Perform the specified rotation about that coordinate axis.

413

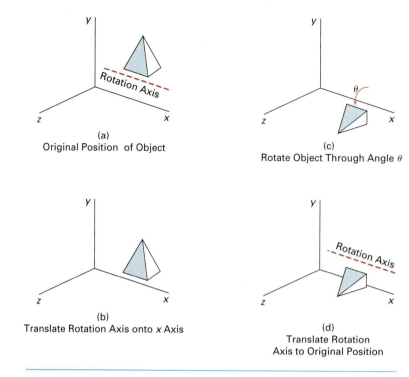

(a)
Original Position of Object

(c)
Rotate Object Through Angle θ

(b)
Translate Rotation Axis onto x Axis

(d)
Translate Rotation
Axis to Original Position

Figure 11-8

Sequence of transformations for rotating an object about an axis that is parallel to the x axis.

4. Apply inverse rotations to bring the rotation axis back to its original orientation.
5. Apply the inverse translation to bring the rotation axis back to its original position.

We can transform the rotation axis onto any of the three coordinate axes. The z axis is a reasonable choice, and the following discussion shows how to set up the transformation matrices for getting the rotation axis onto the z axis and returning the rotation axis to its original position (Fig. 11-9).

A rotation axis can be defined with two coordinate positions, as in Fig. 11-10, or with one coordinate point and direction angles (or direction cosines) between the rotation axis and two of the coordinate axes. We will assume that the rotation axis is defined by two points, as illustrated, and that the direction of rotation is to be counterclockwise when looking along the axis from P_2 to P_1. An axis vector is then defined by the two points as

$$\mathbf{V} = \mathbf{P}_2 - \mathbf{P}_1$$
$$= (x_2 - x_1, y_2 - y_1, z_2 - z_1)$$

(11-14)

A unit vector $\mathbf{u}$ is then defined along the rotation axis as

$$\mathbf{u} = \frac{\mathbf{V}}{|\mathbf{V}|} = (a, b, c)$$

(11-15)

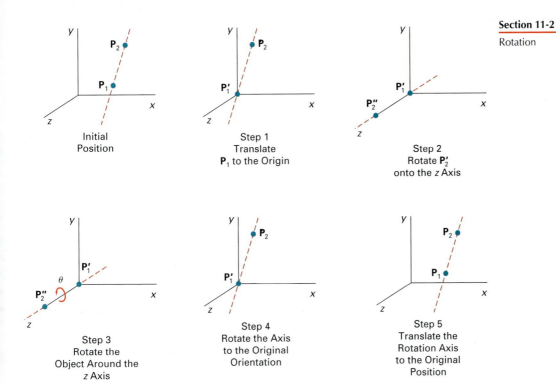

Figure 11-9
Five transformation steps for obtaining a composite matrix for rotation
about an arbitrary axis, with the rotation axis projected onto the z axis.

where the components a, b, and c of unit vector $\mathbf{u}$ are the direction cosines for the
rotation axis:

$$a = \frac{x_2 - x_1}{|\mathbf{V}|}, \qquad b = \frac{y_2 - y_1}{|\mathbf{V}|}, \qquad c = \frac{z_2 - z_1}{|\mathbf{V}|} \qquad (11\text{-}16)$$

If the rotation is to be in the opposite direction (clockwise when viewing from $\mathbf{P}_2$
to $\mathbf{P}_1$), then we would reverse axis vector $\mathbf{V}$ and unit vector $\mathbf{u}$ so that they point
from $\mathbf{P}_2$ to $\mathbf{P}_1$.

The first step in the transformation sequence for the desired rotation is to
set up the translation matrix that repositions the rotation axis so that it passes
through the coordinate origin. For the desired direction of rotation (Fig. 11-10),
we accomplish this by moving point $\mathbf{P}_1$ to the origin. (If the rotation direction had
been specified in the opposite direction, we would move $\mathbf{P}_2$ to the origin.) This
translation matrix is

$$\mathbf{T} = \begin{bmatrix} 1 & 0 & 0 & -x_1 \\ 0 & 1 & 0 & -y_1 \\ 0 & 0 & 1 & -z_1 \\ 0 & 0 & 0 & 1 \end{bmatrix} \qquad (11\text{-}17)$$

which repositions the rotation axis and the object, as shown in Fig. 11-11.

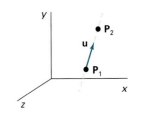

Figure 11-10
An axis of rotation (dashed
line) defined with points
$\mathbf{P}_1$ and $\mathbf{P}_2$. The direction for
the unit axis vector $\mathbf{u}$ is
determined by the specified
rotation direction.

415

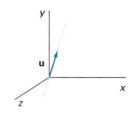

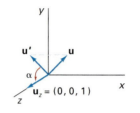

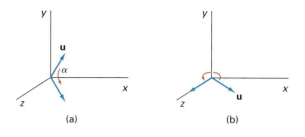

(a)   (b)

Now we need the transformations that will put the rotation axis on the z axis. We can use the coordinate-axis rotations to accomplish this alignment in two steps. There are a number of ways to perform the two steps. We will first rotate about the x axis to transform vector **u** into the xz plane. Then we swing **u** around to the z axis using a y-axis rotation. These two rotations are illustrated in Fig. 11-12 for one possible orientation of vector **u**.

Since rotation calculations involve sine and cosine functions, we can use standard vector operations (Appendix A) to obtain elements of the two rotation matrices. Dot-product operations allow us to determine the cosine terms, and vector cross products provide a means for obtaining the sine terms.

We establish the transformation matrix for rotation around the x axis by determining the values for the sine and cosine of the rotation angle necessary to get **u** into the xz plane. This rotation angle is the angle between the projection of **u** in the yz plane and the positive z axis (Fig. 11-13). If we designate the projection of **u** in the yz plane as the vector $\mathbf{u'} = (0, b, c)$, then the cosine of the rotation angle α can be determined from the dot product of **u'** and the unit vector $\mathbf{u}_z$ along the z axis:

$$\cos \alpha = \frac{\mathbf{u'} \cdot \mathbf{u}_z}{|\mathbf{u'}||\mathbf{u}_z|} = \frac{c}{d} \qquad (11\text{-}18)$$

where d is the magnitude of **u'**:

$$d = \sqrt{b^2 + c^2} \qquad (11\text{-}19)$$

Similarly, we can determine the sine of α from the cross product of **u'** and $\mathbf{u}_z$. The coordinate-independent form of this cross product is

$$\mathbf{u'} \times \mathbf{u}_z = \mathbf{u}_x |\mathbf{u'}| |\mathbf{u}_z| \sin \alpha \qquad (11\text{-}20)$$

and the Cartesian form for the cross product gives us

$$\mathbf{u'} \times \mathbf{u}_z = \mathbf{u}_x \cdot b \qquad (11\text{-}21)$$

Equating the right sides of Eqs. 11-20 and 11-21, and noting that $|\mathbf{u}_z| = 1$ and $|\mathbf{u'}| = d$, we have

$$d \sin \alpha = b$$

or

$$\sin \alpha = \frac{b}{d} \qquad (11\text{-}22)$$

Now that we have determined the values for $\cos \alpha$ and $\sin \alpha$ in terms of the components of vector $\mathbf{u}$, we can set up the matrix for rotation of $\mathbf{u}$ about the x axis:

$$\mathbf{R}_x(\alpha) = \begin{bmatrix} 1 & 0 & 0 & 0 \\ 0 & c/d & -b/d & 0 \\ 0 & b/d & c/d & 0 \\ 0 & 0 & 0 & 1 \end{bmatrix} \qquad (11\text{-}23)$$

This matrix rotates unit vector $\mathbf{u}$ about the x axis into the xz plane.

Next we need to determine the form of the transformation matrix that will swing the unit vector in the xz plane counterclockwise around the y axis onto the positive z axis. The orientation of the unit vector in the xz plane (after rotation about the x axis) is shown in Fig. 11-14. This vector, labeled $\mathbf{u}''$, has the value a for its x component, since rotation about the x axis leaves the x component unchanged. Its z component is d (the magnitude of $\mathbf{u}'$), because vector $\mathbf{u}'$ has been rotated onto the z axis. And the y component of $\mathbf{u}''$ is 0, because it now lies in the xz plane. Again, we can determine the cosine of rotation angle β from expressions for the dot product of unit vectors $\mathbf{u}''$ and $\mathbf{u}_z$:

$$\cos \beta = \frac{\mathbf{u}'' \cdot \mathbf{u}_z}{|\mathbf{u}''| \, |\mathbf{u}_z|} = d \qquad (11\text{-}24)$$

since $|\mathbf{u}_z| = |\mathbf{u}''| = 1$. Comparing the coordinate-independent form of the cross product

$$\mathbf{u}'' \times \mathbf{u}_z = \mathbf{u}_y |\mathbf{u}''| \, |\mathbf{u}_z| \sin \beta \qquad (11\text{-}25)$$

with the Cartesian form

$$\mathbf{u}'' \times \mathbf{u}_z = \mathbf{u}_y \cdot (-a) \qquad (11\text{-}26)$$

we find that

$$\sin \beta = -a \qquad (11\text{-}27)$$

Thus, the transformation matrix for rotation of $\mathbf{u}''$ about the y axis is

$$\mathbf{R}_y(\beta) = \begin{bmatrix} d & 0 & -a & 0 \\ 0 & 1 & 0 & 0 \\ a & 0 & d & 0 \\ 0 & 0 & 0 & 1 \end{bmatrix} \qquad (11\text{-}28)$$

With transformation matrices 11-17, 11-23, and 11-28, we have aligned the rotation axis with the positive z axis. The specified rotation angle θ can now be applied as a rotation about the z axis:

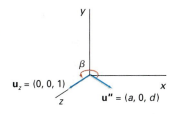

Figure 11-14
Rotation of unit vector $\mathbf{u}''$ (vector $\mathbf{u}$ after rotation into the xz plane) about the y axis. Positive rotation angle β aligns $\mathbf{u}''$ with vector $\mathbf{u}_z$.

417

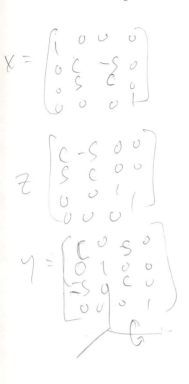

$$\mathbf{R}_z(\theta) = \begin{bmatrix} \cos\theta & -\sin\theta & 0 & 0 \\ \sin\theta & \cos\theta & 0 & 0 \\ 0 & 0 & 1 & 0 \\ 0 & 0 & 0 & 1 \end{bmatrix} \qquad (11\text{-}29)$$

To complete the required rotation about the given axis, we need to transform the rotation axis back to its original position. This is done by applying the inverse of transformations 11-17, 11-23, and 11-28. The transformation matrix for rotation about an arbitrary axis then can be expressed as the composition of these seven individual transformations:

$$\mathbf{R}(\theta) = \mathbf{T}^{-1} \cdot \mathbf{R}_x^{-1}(\alpha) \cdot \mathbf{R}_y^{-1}(\beta) \cdot \mathbf{R}_z(\theta) \cdot \mathbf{R}_y(\beta) \cdot \mathbf{R}_x(\alpha) \cdot \mathbf{T} \qquad (11\text{-}30)$$

A somewhat quicker, but perhaps less intuitive, method for obtaining the composite rotation matrix $\mathbf{R}_y(\beta) \cdot \mathbf{R}_x(\alpha)$ is to take advantage of the form of the composite matrix for any sequence of three-dimensional rotations:

$$\mathbf{R} = \begin{bmatrix} r_{11} & r_{12} & r_{13} & 0 \\ r_{21} & r_{22} & r_{23} & 0 \\ r_{31} & r_{32} & r_{33} & 0 \\ 0 & 0 & 0 & 1 \end{bmatrix} \qquad (11\text{-}31)$$

The upper left 3 by 3 submatrix of this matrix is orthogonal. This means that the rows (or the columns) of this submatrix form a set of orthogonal unit vectors that are rotated by matrix $\mathbf{R}$ onto the x, y, and z axes, respectively:

$$\mathbf{R} \cdot \begin{bmatrix} r_{11} \\ r_{12} \\ r_{13} \\ 1 \end{bmatrix} = \begin{bmatrix} 1 \\ 0 \\ 0 \\ 1 \end{bmatrix}, \quad \mathbf{R} \cdot \begin{bmatrix} r_{21} \\ r_{22} \\ r_{23} \\ 1 \end{bmatrix} = \begin{bmatrix} 0 \\ 1 \\ 0 \\ 1 \end{bmatrix}, \quad \mathbf{R} \cdot \begin{bmatrix} r_{31} \\ r_{32} \\ r_{33} \\ 1 \end{bmatrix} = \begin{bmatrix} 0 \\ 0 \\ 1 \\ 1 \end{bmatrix} \qquad (11\text{-}32)$$

Therefore, we can consider a local coordinate system defined by the rotation axis and simply form a matrix whose columns are the local unit coordinate vectors. Assuming that the rotation axis is not parallel to any coordinate axis, we can form the following local set of unit vectors (Fig. 11-15):

$$\mathbf{u}_z' = \mathbf{u}$$

$$\mathbf{u}_y' = \frac{\mathbf{u} \times \mathbf{u}_x}{|\mathbf{u} \times \mathbf{u}_x|} \qquad (11\text{-}33)$$

$$\mathbf{u}_x' = \mathbf{u}_y' \times \mathbf{u}_z'$$

If we express the elements of the local unit vectors for the rotation axis as

$$\mathbf{u}_x' = (u_{x1}', u_{x2}', u_{x3}')$$

$$\mathbf{u}_y' = (u_{y1}', u_{y2}', u_{y3}') \qquad (11\text{-}34)$$

$$\mathbf{u}_z' = (u_{z1}', u_{z2}', u_{z3}')$$

then the required composite matrix, equal to the product $\mathbf{R}_y(\beta) \cdot \mathbf{R}_x(\alpha)$, is

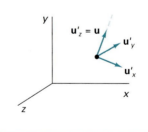

Figure 11-15
Local coordinate system for a rotation axis defined by unit vector **u**.

$$\mathbf{R} = \begin{bmatrix} u'_{x1} & u'_{x2} & u'_{x3} & 0 \\ u'_{y1} & u'_{y2} & u'_{y3} & 0 \\ u'_{z1} & u'_{z2} & u'_{z3} & 0 \\ 0 & 0 & 0 & 1 \end{bmatrix} \qquad (11\text{-}35)$$

This matrix transforms the unit vectors $\mathbf{u}'_x$, $\mathbf{u}'_y$, and $\mathbf{u}'_z$ onto the x, y, and z axes, respectively. Thus, the rotation axis is aligned with the z axis, since $\mathbf{u}'_z = \mathbf{u}$.

Rotations with Quaternions

A more efficient method for obtaining rotation about a specified axis is to use a quaternion representation for the rotation transformation. In Chapter 10, we discussed the usefulness of quaternions for generating three-dimensional fractals using self-squaring procedures. Quaternions are useful also in a number of other computer graphics procedures, including three-dimensional rotation calculations. They require less storage space than 4-by-4 matrices, and it is simpler to write quaternion procedures for transformation sequences. This is particularly important in animations that require complicated motion sequences and motion interpolations between two given positions of an object.

One way to characterize a quaternion (Appendix A) is as an ordered pair, consisting of a *scalar part* and a *vector part*:

$$q = (s, \mathbf{v})$$

We can also think of a quaternion as a higher-order complex number with one real part (the scalar part) and three complex parts (the elements of vector $\mathbf{v}$). A rotation about any axis passing through the coordinate origin is performed by first setting up a unit quaternion with the following scalar and vector parts:

$$s = \cos\frac{\theta}{2}, \qquad \mathbf{v} = \mathbf{u}\sin\frac{\theta}{2} \qquad (11\text{-}36)$$

where $\mathbf{u}$ is a unit vector along the selected rotation axis, and θ is the specified rotation angle about this axis (Fig. 11-16). Any point position $\mathbf{P}$ to be rotated by this quaternion can be represented in quaternion notation as

$$\mathbf{P} = (0, \mathbf{p})$$

with the coordinates of the point as the vector part $\mathbf{p} = (x, y, z)$. The rotation of the point is then carried out with the quaternion operation

$$\mathbf{P}' = q\mathbf{P}q^{-1} \qquad (11\text{-}37)$$

where $q^{-1} = (s, -\mathbf{v})$ is the inverse of the unit quaternion q with the scalar and vector parts given in Eqs. 11-36. This transformation produces the new quaternion with scalar part equal to 0:

$$\mathbf{P}' = (0, \mathbf{p}') \qquad (11\text{-}38)$$

and the vector part is calculated with dot and cross products as

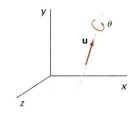

Figure 11-16
Unit quaternion parameters θ and $\mathbf{u}$ for rotation about a specified axis.

$$p' = s^2 p + v(p \cdot v) + 2s(v \times p) + v \times (v \times p) \tag{11-39}$$

Parameters s and v have the rotation values given in Eqs. 11-36. Many computer graphics systems use efficient hardware implementations of these vector calculations to perform rapid three-dimensional object rotations.

Transformation 11-37 is equivalent to rotation about an axis that passes through the coordinate origin. This is the same as the sequence of rotation transformations in Eq. 11-30 that aligns the rotation axis with the z axis, rotates about z, and then returns the rotation axis to its original position.

Using the definition for quaternion multiplication given in Appendix A, and designating the components of the vector part of q as $v = (a, b, c)$, we can evaluate the terms in Eq. 11-39 to obtain the elements for the composite rotation matrix $R_x^{-1}(\alpha) \cdot R_y^{-1}(\beta) \cdot R_z(\theta) \cdot R_y(\beta) \cdot R_x(\alpha)$ in a 3 by 3 form as

$$M_R(\theta) = \begin{bmatrix} 1 - 2b^2 - 2c^2 & 2ab - 2sc & 2ac + 2sb \\ 2ab + 2sc & 1 - 2a^2 - 2c^2 & 2bc - 2sa \\ 2ac - 2sb & 2bc + 2sa & 1 - 2a^2 - 2b^2 \end{bmatrix} \tag{11-40}$$

To obtain the complete general rotation equation 11-30, we need to include the translations that move the rotation axis to the coordinate axis and back to its original position. That is,

$$R(\theta) = T^{-1} \cdot M_R \cdot T \tag{11-41}$$

As an example, we can perform a rotation about the z axis by setting the unit quaternion parameters as

$$s = \cos\frac{\theta}{2}, \qquad v = (0, 0, 1)\sin\frac{\theta}{2}$$

where the quaternion vector elements are $a = b = 0$ and $c = \sin(\theta/2)$. Substituting these values into matrix 11-40, and using the following trigonometric identities

$$\cos^2\frac{\theta}{2} - \sin^2\frac{\theta}{2} = 1 - 2\sin^2\frac{\theta}{2} = \cos\theta, \qquad 2\cos\frac{\theta}{2}\sin\frac{\theta}{2} = \sin\theta$$

we get the 3 by 3 version of the z-axis rotation matrix $R_z(\theta)$ in transformation equation 11-5. Similarly, substituting the unit quaternion rotation values into the transformation equation 11-37 produces the rotated coordinate values in Eqs. 11-4.

11-3
SCALING

The matrix expression for the scaling transformation of a position $P = (x, y, z)$ relative to the coordinate origin can be written as

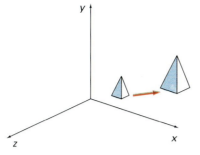

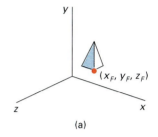

(a)

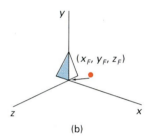

(b)

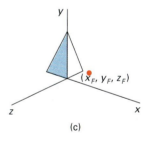

(c)

Figure 11-17
Doubling the size of an object with transformation 11-42 also moves the object farther from the origin.

$$\begin{bmatrix} x' \\ y' \\ z' \\ 1 \end{bmatrix} = \begin{bmatrix} s_x & 0 & 0 & 0 \\ 0 & s_y & 0 & 0 \\ 0 & 0 & s_z & 0 \\ 0 & 0 & 0 & 1 \end{bmatrix} \cdot \begin{bmatrix} x \\ y \\ z \\ 1 \end{bmatrix} \qquad (11\text{-}42)$$

or

$$\mathbf{P}' = \mathbf{S} \cdot \mathbf{P} \qquad (11\text{-}43)$$

where scaling parameters s_x, s_y, and s_z are assigned any positive values. Explicit expressions for the coordinate transformations for scaling relative to the origin are

$$x' = x \cdot s_x, \qquad y' = y \cdot s_y, \qquad z' = z \cdot s_z \qquad (11\text{-}44)$$

Scaling an object with transformation 11-42 changes the size of the object and repositions the object relative to the coordinate origin. Also, if the transformation parameters are not all equal, relative dimensions in the object are changed. We preserve the original shape of an object with a uniform scaling ($s_x = s_y = s_z$). The result of scaling an object uniformly with each scaling parameter set to 2 is shown in Fig. 11-17.

Scaling with respect to a selected fixed position (x_f, y_f, z_f) can be represented with the following transformation sequence:

1. Translate the fixed point to the origin.
2. Scale the object relative to the coordinate origin using Eq. 11-42.
3. Translate the fixed point back to its original position.

This sequence of transformations is demonstrated in Fig. 11-18. The matrix representation for an arbitrary fixed-point scaling can then be expressed as the concatenation of these translate-scale-translate transformations as

$$\mathbf{T}(x_f, y_f, z_f) \cdot \mathbf{S}(s_x, s_y, s_z) \cdot \mathbf{T}(-x_f, -y_f, -z_f) = \begin{bmatrix} s_x & 0 & 0 & (1 - s_x)x_f \\ 0 & s_y & 0 & (1 - s_y)y_f \\ 0 & 0 & s_z & (1 - s_z)z_f \\ 0 & 0 & 0 & 1 \end{bmatrix} \qquad (11\text{-}45)$$

We form the inverse scaling matrix for either Eq. 11-42 or Eq. 11-45 by replacing the scaling parameters s_x, s_y, and s_z with their reciprocals. The inverse ma-

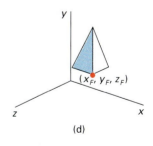

(d)

Figure 11-18
Scaling an object relative to a selected fixed point is equivalent to the sequence of transformations shown.

trix generates an opposite scaling transformation, so the concatenation of any scaling matrix and its inverse produces the identity matrix.

11-4

OTHER TRANSFORMATIONS

In addition to translation, rotation, and scaling, there are various additional transformations that are often useful in three-dimensional graphics applications. Two of these are reflection and shear.

Reflections

A three-dimensional reflection can be performed relative to a selected *reflection axis* or with respect to a selected *reflection plane*. In general, three-dimensional reflection matrices are set up similarly to those for two dimensions. Reflections relative to a given axis are equivalent to 180° rotations about that axis. Reflections with respect to a plane are equivalent to 180° rotations in four-dimensional space. When the reflection plane is a coordinate plane (either *xy*, *xz*, or *yz*), we can think of the transformation as a conversion between left-handed and right-handed systems.

An example of a reflection that converts coordinate specifications from a right-handed system to a left-handed system (or vice versa) is shown in Fig. 11-19. This transformation changes the sign of the *z* coordinates, leaving the *x*- and *y*-coordinate values unchanged. The matrix representation for this reflection of points relative to the *xy* plane is

$$RF_z = \begin{bmatrix} 1 & 0 & 0 & 0 \\ 0 & 1 & 0 & 0 \\ 0 & 0 & -1 & 0 \\ 0 & 0 & 0 & 1 \end{bmatrix} \qquad (11\text{-}46)$$

Transformation matrices for inverting *x* and *y* values are defined similarly, as reflections relative to the *yz* plane and *xz* plane, respectively. Reflections about other planes can be obtained as a combination of rotations and coordinate-plane reflections.

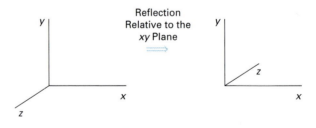

Figure 11-19
Conversion of coordinate specifications from a right-handed to a left-handed system can be carried out with the reflection transformation 11-46.

Shears

Shearing transformations can be used to modify object shapes. They are also useful in three-dimensional viewing for obtaining general projection transformations. In two dimensions, we discussed tranformations relative to the x or y axes to produce distortions in the shapes of objects. In three dimensions, we can also generate shears relative to the z axis.

As an example of three-dimensional shearing, the following transformation produces a z-axis shear:

$$ SH_z = \begin{bmatrix} 1 & 0 & a & 0 \\ 0 & 1 & b & 0 \\ 0 & 0 & 1 & 0 \\ 0 & 0 & 0 & 1 \end{bmatrix} \qquad (11\text{-}47) $$

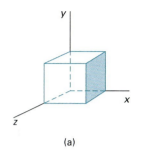

(a)

Parameters a and b can be assigned any real values. The effect of this transformation matrix is to alter x- and y-coordinate values by an amount that is proportional to the z value, while leaving the z coordinate unchanged. Boundaries of planes that are perpendicular to the z axis are thus shifted by an amount proportional to z. An example of the effect of this shearing matrix on a unit cube is shown in Fig. 11-20, for shearing values $a = b = 1$. Shearing matrices for the x axis and y axis are defined similarly.

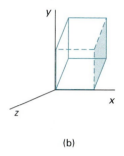

(b)

11-5
COMPOSITE TRANSFORMATIONS

Figure 11-20
A unit cube (a) is sheared
(b) by transformation matrix
11-47, with $a = b = 1$.

As with two-dimensional transformations, we form a composite three-dimensional transformation by multiplying the matrix representations for the individual operations in the transformation sequence. This concatenation is carried out from right to left, where the rightmost matrix is the first transformation to be applied to an object and the leftmost matrix is the last transformation. The following program provides an example for implementing a composite transformation. A sequence of basic, three-dimensional geometric transformations are combined to produce a single composite transformation, which is then applied to the coordinate definition of an object.

```
#include <math.h>
#include "graphics.h"

#define PI 3.14159

typedef float Matrix4x4[4][4];

Matrix4x4 theMatrix;

void matrix4x4SetIdentity (Matrix4x4 m)
{
  int r,c;

  for (r=0; r<4; r++)
    for (c=0; c<4; c++)
```

```
          m[r][c] = (r == c);
}

/* Multiplies matrix a times b, putting result in b */
void matrix4x4PreMultiply (Matrix4x4 a, Matrix4x4 b)
{
  int r,c;
  Matrix4x4 tmp;

  for (r=0; r<4; r++)
    for (c=0; c<4; c++)
      tmp[r][c] = a[r][0]*b[0][c] + a[r][1]*b[1][c] +
        a[r][2]*b[2][c] + a[r][3]*b[3][c];
  for (r=0; r<4; r++)
    for (c=0; c<4; c++)
      b[r][c] = tmp[r][c];
}

void translate3 (float tx, float ty, float tz)
{
  Matrix4x4 m;

  matrix4x4SetIdentity (m);
  m[0][3] = tx; m[1][3] = ty; m[2][3] = tz;
  matrix4x4PreMultiply (m, theMatrix);
}

void scale3 (float sx, float sy, float sz, wcPt3 center)
{
  Matrix4x4 m;

  matrix4x4SetIdentity (m);
  m[0][0] = sx;
  m[0][3] = (1 - sx) * center.x;
  m[1][1] = sy;
  m[1][3] = (1 - sy) * center.y;
  m[2][2] = sz;
  m[2][3] = (1 - sz) * center.z;
  matrix4x4PreMultiply (m, theMatrix);
}

void rotate3 (wcPt3 p1, wcPt3 p2, float radianAngle)
{
  float length = sqrt ((p2.x - p1.x) * (p2.x - p1.x) +
                       (p2.y - p1.y) * (p2.y - p1.y) +
                       (p2.z - p1.z) * (p2.z - p1.z));
  float cosA2 = cosf (radianAngle / 2.0);
  float sinA2 = sinf (radianAngle / 2.0);
  float a = sinA2 * (p2.x - p1.x) / length;
  float b = sinA2 * (p2.y - p1.y) / length;
  float c = sinA2 * (p2.z - p1.z) / length;
  Matrix4x4 m;

  translate3 (-p1.x, -p1.y, -p1.z);
  matrix4x4SetIdentity (m);
  m[0][0] = 1.0 - 2*b*b - 2*c*c;
  m[0][1] = 2*a*b - 2*cosA2*c;
  m[0][2] = 2*a*c + 2*cosA2*b;
  m[1][0] = 2*a*b + 2*cosA2*c;
  m[1][1] = 1.0 - 2*a*a - 2*c*c;
  m[1][2] = 2*b*c - 2*cosA2*a;
  m[2][0] = 2*a*c - 2*cosA2*b;
```

```
    m[2][1] = 2*b*c + 2*cosA2*a;
    m[2][2] = 1.0 - 2*a*a - 2*b*b;
    matrix4x4PreMultiply (m, theMatrix);
    translate3 (p1.x, p1.y, p1.z);
}

void transformPoints3 (int nPts, wcPt3 * pts)
{
    int k, j;
    float tmp[3];

    for (k=0; k<nPts; k++) {
        for (j=0; j<3; j++)
            tmp[j] = theMatrix[j][0] * pts[k].x + theMatrix[j][1] * pts[k].y +
                theMatrix[j][2] * pts[k].z + theMatrix[j][3];
        setWcPt3 (&pts[k], tmp[0], tmp[1], tmp[2]);
    }
}

void main (int argc, char ** argv)
{
    wcPt3 pts[5] = { 10,10,0, 100,10,0, 125,50,0, 35,50,0, 10,10,0 };
    wcPt3 p1 = { 10,10,0 }, p2 = { 10,10,10 };
    wcPt3 refPt = { 68.0,30.0,0.0 };

    long windowID = openGraphics (*argv, 200, 200);
    setBackground (WHITE);
    setColor (BLUE);
    pPolyline3 (5, pts);

    matrix4x4SetIdentity (theMatrix);
    rotate3 (p1, p2, PI/4.0);
    scale3 (0.75, 0.75, 1.0, refPt);
    translate3 (25, 40, 0);
    transformPoints3 (5, pts);
    setColor (RED);
    pPolyline3 (5, pts);

    sleep (10);
    closeGraphics (windowID);
}
```

11-6

THREE-DIMENSIONAL TRANSFORMATION FUNCTIONS

We set up matrices for modeling and other transformations with functions similar to those given in Chapter 5 for two-dimensional transformations. The major difference is that we can now specify rotations around any coordinate axis. These functions are

```
translate3 (translateVector, matrixTranslate)
rotateX (thetaX, xMatrixRotate)
rotateY (thetaY, yMatrixRotate)
rotateZ (thetaZ, zMatrixRotate)
scale3 (scaleVector, matrixScale)
```

Each of these functions produces a 4 by 4 transformation matrix that can then be used to transform coordinate positions expressed as homogeneous column vectors. Parameter `translateVector` is a pointer to the list of translation distances t_x, t_y, and t_z. Similarly, parameter `scaleVector` specifies the three scaling parameters s_x, s_y, and s_z. Rotate and scale matrices transform objects with respect to the coordinate origin.

And we can construct composite transformations with the functions

```
composeMatrix3
buildTransformationMatrix3
composeTransformationMatrix3
```

which have parameters similar to two-dimensional transformation functions for setting up composite matrices, except we can now specify three rotation angles. The order of the transformation sequence for the `buildTransformationMatrix3` and `composeTransformationMatrix3` functions is the same as in two dimensions: (1) scale, (2) rotate, and (3) translate.

Once we have specified a transformation matrix, we can apply the matrix to specified points with

```
transformPoint3 (inPoint, matrix, outPoint)
```

In addition, we can set the transformations for hierarchical constructions using structures with the function

```
setLocalTransformation3 (matrix, type)
```

where parameter `matrix` specifies the elements of a 4 by 4 transformation matrix, and parameter `type` can be assigned one of the following three values: *preconcatenate*, *postconcatenate*, or *replace*.

11-7

MODELING AND COORDINATE TRANSFORMATIONS

So far, we have discussed three-dimensional transformations as operations that move objects from one position to another within a single reference frame. There are many times, however, when we are interested in switching coordinates from one system to another. General three-dimensional viewing procedures, for example, involve an initial transformation of world-coordinate descriptions to a viewing-coordinate system. Then viewing coordinates are transformed to device coordinates. And in modeling, objects are often described in a local (modeling) coordinate reference frame, then the objects are repositioned into a world-coordinate scene. For example, tables, chairs, and other furniture, each defined in a local (modeling) coordinate system, can be placed into the description of a room, defined in another reference frame, by transforming the furniture coordinates to room coordinates. Then the room might be transformed into a larger scene, constructed in world coordinates.

An example of the use of multiple coordinate systems and hierarchical modeling with three-dimensional objects is given in Fig. 11-21. This figure illustrates simulation of tractor movement. As the tractor moves, the tractor coordinate system and front-wheel coordinate system move in the world-coordinate

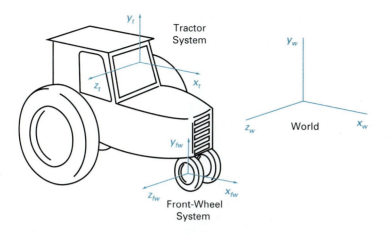

Figure 11-21
Possible coordinate systems used in simulating tractor movement.
Wheel rotations are described in the front-wheel system. Turning of
the tractor is described by a rotation of the front-wheel system in
the tractor system. Both the wheel and tractor reference frames
move in the world-coordinate system.

system. The front wheels rotate in the wheel system, and the wheel system rotates in the tractor system when the tractor turns.

Three-dimensional objects and scenes are constructed using structure (or
segment) operations similar to those discussed in Chapter 7. Modeling transformation functions can be applied to create hierarchical representation for three-dimensional objects. We can define three-dimensional object shapes in local (modeling) coordinates, then we construct a scene or a hierarchical representation with
instances of the individual objects. That is, we transform object descriptions from
modeling coordinates to world coordinates or to another system in the hierarchy.
An example of a PHIGS structure hierarchy is shown in Fig. 11-22. This display
was generated by the PHIGS Toolkit software, developed at the University of

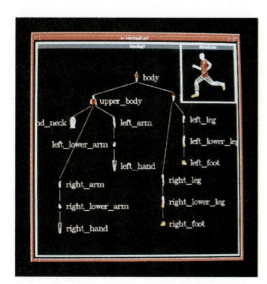

Figure 11-22
Displaying an object hierarchy
using the PHIGS Toolkit package
developed at the University of
Manchester. The displayed object
tree is itself a PHIGS structure.
(*Courtesy of T. L. J. Howard, J. G. Williams,
and W. T. Hewitt, Department of Computer
Science, University of Manchester, United
Kingdom.*)

427

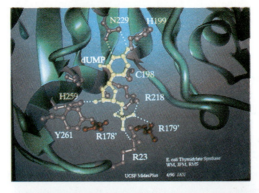

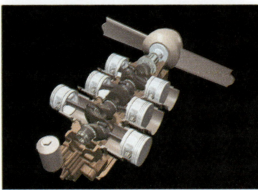

Figure 11-23
Three-dimensional modeling: (a) A
ball-and-stick representation for
key amino acid residues interacting
with the natural substrate of
Thymidylate Synthase, modeled
and rendered by Julie Newdoll,
UCSF Computer Graphics Lab. (b) A
CAD model showing individual
engine components, rendered by
Ted Malone, FTI/3D-Magic.
(Courtesy of Silicon Graphics, Inc.)

Manchester, to provide an editor, windows, menus, and other interface tools for
PHIGS applications. Figure 11-23 shows two example applications of three-
dimensional modeling.

Coordinate descriptions of objects are transferred from one system to another with the same procedures used to obtain two-dimensional coordinate
transformations. We need to set up the transformation matrix that brings the two
coordinate systems into alignment. First, we set up a translation that brings the
new coordinate origin to the position of the other coordinate origin. This is followed by a sequence of rotations that corresponding coordinate axes. If different
scales are used in the two coordinate systems, a scaling transformation may also
be necessary to compensate for the differences in coordinate intervals.

If a second coordinate system is defined with origin (x_0, y_0, z_0) and unit axis
vectors as shown in Fig. 11-24, relative to an existing Cartesian reference frame,
we first construct the translation matrix $\mathbf{T}(-x_0, -y_0, -z_0)$. Next, we can use the
unit axis vectors to form the coordinate rotation matrix

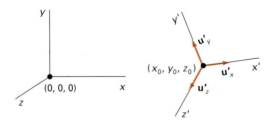

Figure 11-24
Transformation of an object
description from one coordinate
system to another.

$$\mathbf{R} = \begin{bmatrix} u'_{x1} & u'_{x2} & u'_{x3} & 0 \\ u'_{y1} & u'_{y2} & u'_{y3} & 0 \\ u'_{z1} & u'_{z2} & u'_{z3} & 0 \\ 0 & 0 & 0 & 1 \end{bmatrix} \qquad (11\text{-}48)$$

which transforms unit vectors $\mathbf{u}'_x$, $\mathbf{u}'_y$, and $\mathbf{u}'_z$ onto the x, y, and z axes, respectively. The complete coordinate-transformation sequence is then given by the composite matrix $\mathbf{R} \cdot \mathbf{T}$. This matrix correctly transforms coordinate descriptions from one Cartesian system to another even if one system is left-handed and the other is right-handed.

SUMMARY

Three-dimensional transformations useful in computer graphics applications include geometric transformations within a single coordinate system and tranformations between different coordinate systems. The basic geometric transformations are translation, rotation, and scaling. Two additional object transformations are reflections and shears. Transformations between different coordinate systems are common elements of modeling and viewing routines. In three dimensions, transformation operations are represented with 4 by 4 matrices. As in two-dimensional graphics methods, a composite transformation in three-dimensions is obtained by concatenating the matrix representations for the individual components of the overall transformation.

Representations for translation and scaling are straightforward extensions of two-dimensional transformation representations. For rotations, however, we need more general representations, since objects can be rotated about any specified axis in space. Any three-dimensional rotation can be represented as a combination of basic rotations around the x, y, and z axes. And many graphics packages provide functions for these three rotations. In general, however, it is more efficient to set up a three-dimensional rotation using either a local rotation-axis reference frame or a quaternion representation. Quaternions are particularly useful for fast generation of repeated rotations that are often required in animation sequences.

Reflections and shears in three dimensions can be carried out relative to any reference axis in space. Thus, these transformations are also more involved than the corresponding transformations in two dimensions. Transforming object descriptions from one coordinate system to another is equivalent to a transformation that brings the two reference frames into coincidence. Finally, object modeling often requires a hierarchical transformation structure that ensures that the individual components of an object move in harmony with the overall structure.

REFERENCES

For additional techniques involving matrices, modeling, and three-dimensional transformations, see Glassner (1990), Arvo (1991), and Kirk (1992). A detailed discussion of quaternion rotations is given in Shoemake (1985). Three-dimensional PHIGS and PHIGS + transformation functions are discussed in Howard et al. (1991), Gaskins (1992), and Blake (1993).

429

EXERCISES

11-1. Prove that the multiplication of three-dimensional transformation matrices for each of the following sequence of operations is commutative:
(a) Any two successive translations.
(b) Any two successive scaling operations.
(c) Any two successive rotations about any one of the coordinate axes.

11-2. Using either Eq. 11-30 or Eq. 11-41, prove that any two successive rotations about a given rotation axis is commutative.

11-3. By evaluating the terms in Eq. 11-39, derive the elements for general rotation matrix given in Eq. 11-40.

11-4. Show that rotation matrix 11-35 is equal to the composite matrix $\mathbf{R}_y(\beta) \cdot \mathbf{R}_x(\alpha)$.

11-5. Prove that the quaternion rotation matrix Eq. 11-40 reduces to the matrix representation in Eq. 11-5 when the rotation axis is the coordinate z axis.

11-6. Prove that Eq. 11-41 is equivalent to the general rotation transformation given in Eq. 11-30.

11-7. Write a procedure to implement general rotation transformations using the rotation matrix 11-35.

11-8. Write a routine to implement quaternion rotations, Eq. 11-41, for any specified axis.

11-9. Derive the transformation matrix for scaling an object by a scaling factor s in a direction defined by the direction angles α, β, and γ.

11-10. Develop an algorithm for scaling an object defined in an octree representation.

11-11. Develop a procedure for animating an object by incrementally rotating it about any specified axis. Use appropriate approximations to the trigonometric equations to speed up the calculations, and reset the object to its initial position after each complete revolution about the axis.

11-12. Devise a procedure for rotating an object that is represented in an octree structure.

11-13. Develop a routine to reflect an object about an arbitrarily selected plane.

11-14. Write a program to shear an object with respect to any of the three coordinate axes, using input values for the shearing parameters.

11-15. Develop a procedure for converting an object definition in one coordinate reference to any other coordinate system defined relative to the first system.

11-16. Develop a complete algorithm for implementing the procedures for constructive solid modeling by combining three-dimensional primitives to generate new shapes. Initially, the primitives can be combined to form subassemblies, then the subassemblies can be combined with each other and with primitive shapes to form the final assembly. Interactive input of translation and rotation parameters can be used to position the objects. Output of the algorithm is to be the sequence of operations needed to produce the final CSG object.

CHAPTER

12

Three-Dimensional Viewing

7 cameras

"eye"

In two-dimensional graphics applications, viewing operations transfer positions from the world-coordinate plane to pixel positions in the plane of the output device. Using the rectangular boundaries for the world-coordinate window and the device viewport, a two-dimensional package maps the world scene to device coordinates and clips the scene against the four boundaries of the viewport. For three-dimensional graphics applications, the situation is a bit more involved, since we now have more choices as to how views are to be generated. First of all, we can view an object from any spatial position: from the front, from above, or from the back. Or we could generate a view of what we would see if we were standing in the middle of a group of objects or inside a single object, such as a building. Additionally, three-dimensional descriptions of objects must be projected onto the flat viewing surface of the output device. And the clipping boundaries now enclose a volume of space, whose shape depends on the type of projection we select. In this chapter, we explore the general operations needed to produce views of a three-dimensional scene, and we also discuss specific viewing procedures provided in packages such as PHIGS and GL.

12-1
VIEWING PIPELINE

The steps for computer generation of a view of a three-dimensional scene are somewhat analogous to the processes involved in taking a photograph. To take a snapshot, we first need to position the camera at a particular point in space. Then we need to decide on the camera orientation (Fig. 12-1): Which way do we point the camera and how should we rotate it around the line of sight to set the up direction for the picture? Finally, when we snap the shutter, the scene is cropped to the size of the "window" (aperture) of the camera, and light from the visible sur-

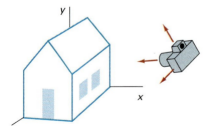

Figure 12-1
Photographing a scene involves selection of a camera position and orientation.

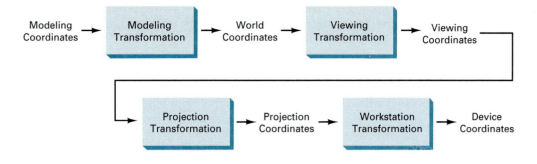

Figure 12-2
General three-dimensional transformation pipeline, from modeling coordinates to final device coordinates.

faces is projected onto the camera film. We need to keep in mind, however, that the camera analogy can be carried only so far, since we have more flexibility and many more options for generating views of a scene with a graphics package than we do with a camera.

Figure 12-2 shows the general processing steps for modeling and converting a world-coordinate description of a scene to device coordinates. Once the scene has been modeled, world-coordinate positions are converted to viewing coordinates. The viewing-coordinate system is used in graphics packages as a reference for specifying the observer viewing position and the position of the projection plane, which we can think of in analogy with the camera film plane. Next, projection operations are performed to convert the viewing-coordinate description of the scene to coordinate positions on the projection plane, which will then be mapped to the output device. Objects outside the specified viewing limits are clipped from further consideration, and the remaining objects are processed through visible-surface identification and surface-rendering procedures to produce the display within the device viewport.

12-2
VIEWING COORDINATES

Generating a view of an object in three dimensions is similar to photographing the object. We can walk around and take its picture from any angle, at various distances, and with varying camera orientations. Whatever appears in the viewfinder is projected onto the flat film surface. The type and size of the camera lens determines which parts of the scene appear in the final picture. These ideas are incorporated into three-dimensional graphics packages so that views of a scene can be generated, given the spatial position, orientation, and aperture size of the "camera".

Specifying the View Plane

We choose a particular view for a scene by first establishing the **viewing-coordinate system,** also called the **view reference coordinate system,** as shown in Fig. 12-3. A **view plane**, or **projection plane**, is then set up perpendicular to the

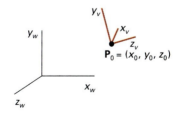

Figure 12-3
A right-handed viewing-coordinate system, with axes x_v, y_v, and z_v, relative to a world-coordinate scene.

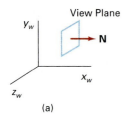

(a)

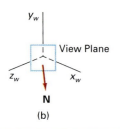

(b)

viewing z_v axis. We can think of the view plane as the film plane in a camera that has been positioned and oriented for a particular shot of the scene. World-coordinate positions in the scene are transformed to viewing coordinates, then viewing coordinates are projected onto the view plane.

To establish the viewing-coordinate reference frame, we first pick a world-coordinate position called the **view reference point**. This point is the origin of our viewing-coordinate system. The view reference point is often chosen to be close to or on the surface of some object in a scene. But we could also choose a point that is at the center of an object, or at the center of a group of objects, or somewhere out in front of the scene to be displayed. If we choose a point that is near to or on some object, we can think of this point as the position where we might want to aim a camera to take a picture of the object. Alternatively, if we choose a point that is at some distance from a scene, we could think of this as the camera position.

Next, we select the positive direction for the viewing z_v axis, and the orientation of the view plane, by specifying the **view-plane normal vector, N**. We choose a world-coordinate position, and this point establishes the direction for **N** relative either to the world origin or to the viewing-coordinate origin. Graphics packages such as GKS and PHIGS, for example, orient **N** relative to the world-coordinate origin, as shown in Fig. 12-4. The view-plane normal **N** is then the directed line segment from the world origin to the selected coordinate position. In other words, **N** is simply specified as a world-coordinate vector. Some other packages (GL from Silicon Graphics, for instance) establish the direction for **N** using the selected coordinate position as a *look-at point* relative to the view reference point (viewing-coordinate origin). Figure 12-5 illustrates this method for defining the direction of **N**, which is from the look-at point to the view reference point. Another possibility is to set up a left-handed viewing system and take **N** and the positive z_v axis from the viewing origin to the look-at point. Only the direction of **N** is needed to establish the z_v direction; the magnitude is irrelevant, because **N** will be normalized to a unit vector by the viewing calculations.

Finally, we choose the up direction for the view by specifying a vector **V**, called the **view-up vector**. This vector is used to establish the positive direction for the y_v axis. Vector **V** also can be defined as a world-coordinate vector, or in some packages, it is specified with a *twist angle* θ_t about the z_v axis, as shown in Fig. 12-6. For a general orientation of the normal vector, it can be difficult (or at least time consuming) to determine the direction for **V** that is precisely perpendicular to **N**. Therefore, viewing procedures typically adjust the user-defined orientation of vector **V**, as shown in Fig. 12-7, so that **V** is projected into a plane that is perpendicular to the normal vector. We can choose the view-up vector **V** to be in any convenient direction, as long as it is not parallel to **N**. As an example, con-

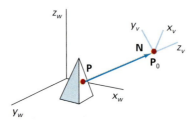

sider an interactive specification of viewing reference coordinates using PHIGS, where the view reference point is often set at the center of an object to be viewed. If we then want to view the object at the angled direction shown in Fig. 12-8, we can simply choose $\mathbf{V}$ as the world vector $(0, 1, 0)$, and this vector will be projected into the plane perpendicular to $\mathbf{N}$ to establish the y_v axis. This is much easier than trying to input a vector that is exactly perpendicular to $\mathbf{N}$.

Using vectors $\mathbf{N}$ and $\mathbf{V}$, the graphics package can compute a third vector $\mathbf{U}$, perpendicular to both $\mathbf{N}$ and $\mathbf{V}$, to define the direction for the x_v axis. Then the direction of $\mathbf{V}$ can be adjusted so that it is perpendicular to both $\mathbf{N}$ and $\mathbf{U}$ to establish the viewing y_v direction. As we will see in the next section (Transformation from World to Viewing Coordinates), these computations are conveniently carried out with unit axis vectors, which are also used to obtain the elements of the world-to-viewing-coordinate transformation matrix. The viewing system is then often described as a *uvn* system (Fig. 12-9).

Generally, graphics packages allow users to choose the position of the view plane (with some restrictions) along the z_v axis by specifying the *view-plane distance* from the viewing origin. The view plane is always parallel to the $x_v y_v$ plane, and the projection of objects to the view plane correspond to the view of the scene that will be displayed on the output device. Figure 12-10 gives examples of view-plane positioning. If we set the view-plane distance to the value 0, the $x_v y_v$ plane (or *uv* plane) of viewing coordinates becomes the view plane for the projection transformation. Occasionally, the term "*uv* plane" is used in reference to the viewing plane, no matter where it is positioned in relation to the $x_v y_v$ plane. But we will only use the term "*uv* plane" to mean the $x_v y_v$ plane, which is not necessarily the view plane.

Left-handed viewing coordinates are sometimes used in graphics packages so that the viewing direction is in the positive z_v direction. But right-handed viewing systems are more common, because they have the same orientation as the world-reference frame. This allows graphics systems to deal with only one coordinate orientation for both world and viewing references. We will follow the convention of PHIGS and GL and use a right-handed viewing system for all algorithm development.

To obtain a series of views of a scene, we can keep the view reference point fixed and change the direction of $\mathbf{N}$, as shown in Fig. 12-11. This corresponds to generating views as we move around the viewing-coordinate origin. In interac-

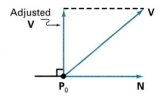

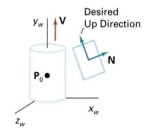

Figure 12-8
Choosing $\mathbf{V}$ along the y_w axis sets the up orientation for the view plane in the desired direction.

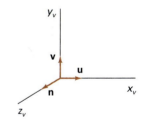

Figure 12-9
A right-handed viewing system defined with unit vectors $\mathbf{u}$, $\mathbf{v}$, and $\mathbf{n}$.

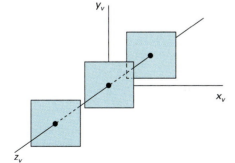

Figure 12-10
View-plane positioning along the z_v axis.

435

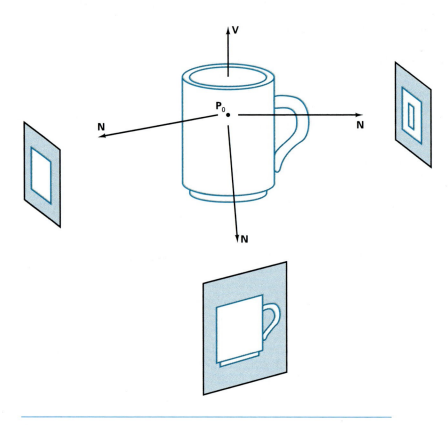

Figure 12-11
Viewing a scene from different directions with a fixed view-reference point.

tive applications, the normal vector **N** is the viewing parameter that is most often changed. By changing only the direction of **N**, we can view a scene from any direction except along the line of **V**. To obtain either of the two possible views along the line of **V**, we would need to change the direction of **V**. If we want to simulate camera motion through a scene, we can keep **N** fixed and move the view reference point around (Fig. 12-12).

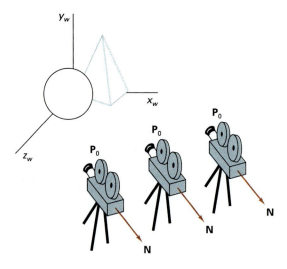

Figure 12-12
Moving around in a scene by changing the position of the view reference point.

Before object descriptions can be projected to the view plane, they must be transferred to viewing coordinates. Conversion of object descriptions from world to viewing coordinates is equivalent to a transformation that superimposes the viewing reference frame onto the world frame using the basic geometric translate-rotate operations discussed in Section 11-7. This transformation sequence is

1. Translate the view reference point to the origin of the world-coordinate system.
2. Apply rotations to align the x_v, y_v, and z_v axes with the world x_w, y_w, and z_w axes, respectively.

If the view reference point is specified at world position (x_0, y_0, z_0), this point is translated to the world origin with the matrix transformation

$$\mathbf{T} = \begin{bmatrix} 1 & 0 & 0 & -x_0 \\ 0 & 1 & 0 & -y_0 \\ 0 & 0 & 1 & -z_0 \\ 0 & 0 & 0 & 1 \end{bmatrix} \qquad (12\text{-}1)$$

The rotation sequence can require up to three coordinate-axis rotations, depending on the direction we choose for $\mathbf{N}$. In general, if $\mathbf{N}$ is not aligned with any world-coordinate axis, we can superimpose the viewing and world systems with the transformation sequence $\mathbf{R}_z \cdot \mathbf{R}_y \cdot \mathbf{R}_x$. That is, we first rotate around the world x_w axis to bring z_v into the $x_w z_w$ plane. Then, we rotate around the world y_w axis to align the z_w and z_v axes. The final rotation is about the z_w axis to align the y_w and y_v axes. Further, if the view reference system is left-handed, a reflection of one of the viewing axes (for example, the z_v axis) is also necessary. Figure 12-13 illustrates the general sequence of translate-rotate transformations. The composite transformation matrix is then applied to world-coordinate descriptions to transfer them to viewing coordinates.

Another method for generating the rotation-transformation matrix is to calculate unit *uvn* vectors and form the composite rotation matrix directly, as dis-

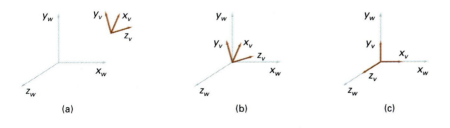

Figure 12-13
Aligning a viewing system with the world-coordinate axes using a sequence of translate-rotate transformations.

cussed in Section 11-7. Given vectors **N** and **V**, these unit vectors are calculated as

$$\mathbf{n} = \frac{\mathbf{N}}{|\mathbf{N}|} = (n_1, n_2, n_3)$$

$$\mathbf{u} = \frac{\mathbf{V} \times \mathbf{N}}{|\mathbf{V} \times \mathbf{N}|} = (u_1, u_2, u_3) \qquad (12\text{-}2)$$

$$\mathbf{v} = \mathbf{n} \times \mathbf{u} = (v_1, v_2, v_3)$$

This method also automatically adjusts the direction for **V** so that **v** is perpendicular to **n**. The composite rotation matrix for the viewing transformation is then

$$\mathbf{R} = \begin{bmatrix} u_1 & u_2 & u_3 & 0 \\ v_1 & v_2 & v_3 & 0 \\ n_1 & n_2 & n_3 & 0 \\ 0 & 0 & 0 & 1 \end{bmatrix} \qquad (12\text{-}3)$$

which transforms **u** onto the world x_w axis, **v** onto the y_w axis, and **n** onto the z_w axis. In addition, this matrix automatically performs the reflection necessary to transform a left-handed viewing system onto the right-handed world system.

The complete world-to-viewing coordinate transformation matrix is obtained as the matrix product

$$\mathbf{M}_{WC,VC} = \mathbf{R} \cdot \mathbf{T} \qquad (12\text{-}4)$$

This transformation is then applied to coordinate descriptions of objects in the scene to transfer them to the viewing reference frame.

12-3
PROJECTIONS

Once world-coordinate descriptions of the objects in a scene are converted to viewing coordinates, we can project the three-dimensional objects onto the two-dimensional view plane. There are two basic projection methods. In a **parallel projection,** coordinate positions are transformed to the view plane along parallel lines, as shown in the example of Fig. 12-14. For a **perspective projection** (Fig. 12-15), object positions are transformed to the view plane along lines that converge to a point called the **projection reference point** (or **center of projection**). The projected view of an object is determined by calculating the intersection of the projection lines with the view plane.

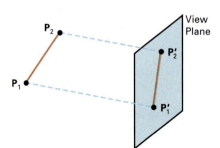

Figure 12-14
Parallel projection of an object to the view plane.

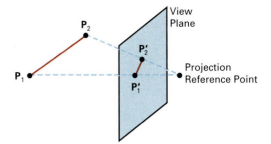

Figure 12-15
Perspective projection of an object
to the view plane.

A parallel projection preserves relative proportions of objects, and this is the method used in drafting to produce scale drawings of three-dimensional objects. Accurate views of the various sides of an object are obtained with a parallel projection, but this does not give us a realistic representation of the appearance of a three-dimensional object. A perspective projection, on the other hand, produces realistic views but does not preserve relative proportions. Projections of distant objects are smaller than the projections of objects of the same size that are closer to the projection plane (Fig. 12-16).

Parallel Projections

We can specify a parallel projection with a **projection vector** that defines the direction for the projection lines. When the projection is perpendicular to the view plane, we have an **orthographic parallel projection**. Otherwise, we have an **oblique parallel projection**. Figure 12-17 illustrates the two types of parallel projections. Some graphics packages, such as GL on Silicon Graphics workstations, do not provide for oblique projections. In this package, for example, a parallel projection is specified by simply giving the boundary edges of a rectangular parallelepiped.

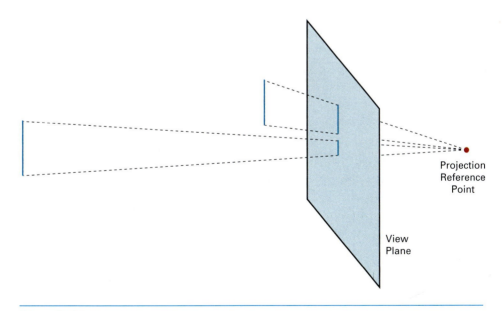

Figure 12-16
Perspective projection of equal-sized objects at different distances from the view plane.

439

Orthographic Projection
(a)

Oblique Projection
(b)

Figure 12-17
Orientation of the projection vector $\mathbf{V}_p$ to produce an orthographic projection (a) and an oblique projection (b).

Orthographic projections are most often used to produce the front, side, and top views of an object, as shown in Fig. 12-18. Front, side, and rear orthographic projections of an object are called *elevations*; and a top orthographic projection is called a *plan view*. Engineering and architectural drawings commonly employ these orthographic projections, because lengths and angles are accurately depicted and can be measured from the drawings.

We can also form orthographic projections that display more than one face of an object. Such views are called **axonometric** orthographic projections. The most commonly used axonometric projection is the **isometric** projection. We generate an isometric projection by aligning the projection plane so that it intersects each coordinate axis in which the object is defined (called the *principal axes*) at the same distance from the origin. Figure 12-19 shows an isometric projection for a

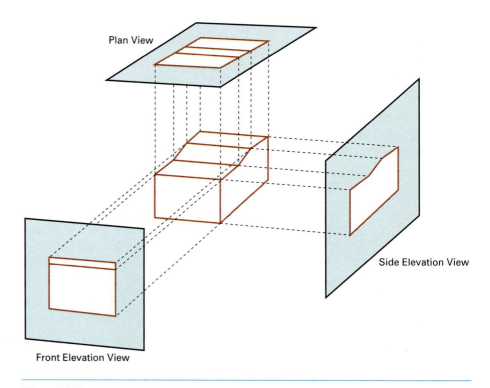

Plan View

Side Elevation View

Front Elevation View

Figure 12-18
Orthographic projections of an object, displaying plan and elevation views.

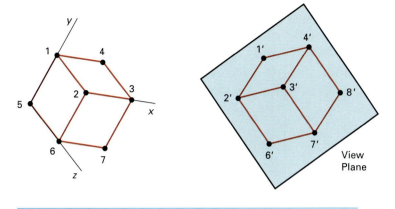

Figure 12-19
Isometric projection for a cube.

cube. The isometric projection is obtained by aligning the projection vector with the cube diagonal. There are eight positions, one in each octant, for obtaining an isometric view. All three principal axes are foreshortened equally in an isometric projection so that relative proportions are maintained. This is not the case in a general axonometric projection, where scaling factors may be different for the three principal directions.

Transformation equations for an orthographic parallel projection are straightforward. If the view plane is placed at position z_{vp} along the z_v axis (Fig. 12-20), then any point (x, y, z) in viewing coordinates is transformed to projection coordinates as

$$x_p = x, \qquad y_p = y \tag{12-5}$$

where the original z-coordinate value is preserved for the depth information needed in depth cueing and visible-surface determination procedures.

An oblique projection is obtained by projecting points along parallel lines that are not perpendicular to the projection plane. In some applications packages, an oblique projection vector is specified with two angles, α and ϕ, as shown in Fig. 12-21. Point (x, y, z) is projected to position (x_p, y_p) on the view plane. Orthographic projection coordinates on the plane are (x, y). The oblique projection line from (x, y, z) to (x_p, y_p) makes an angle α with the line on the projection plane that joins (x_p, y_p) and (x, y). This line, of length L, is at an angle ϕ with the horizontal direction in the projection plane. We can express the projection coordinates in terms of x, y, L, and ϕ as

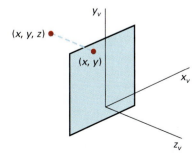

Figure 12-20
Orthographic projection of a point onto a viewing plane.

441

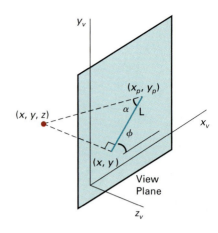

Figure 12-21
Oblique projection of coordinate
position (x, y, z) to position (x_p, y_p)
on the view plane.

$$x_p = x + L \cos \phi$$

$$y_p = y + L \sin \phi$$

(12-6)

Length L depends on the angle α and the z coordinate of the point to be projected:

$$\tan \alpha = \frac{z}{L}$$

(12-7)

Thus,

$$L = \frac{z}{\tan \alpha}$$

$$= z L_1$$

(12-8)

where L_1 is the inverse of $\tan \alpha$, which is also the value of L when $z = 1$. We can then write the oblique projection equations 12-6 as

$$x_p = x + z(L_1 \cos \phi)$$

$$y_p = y + z(L_1 \sin \phi)$$

(12-9)

The transformation matrix for producing any parallel projection onto the $x_v y_v$ plane can be written as

$$\mathbf{M}_{\text{parallel}} = \begin{bmatrix} 1 & 0 & L_1 \cos \phi & 0 \\ 0 & 1 & L_1 \sin \phi & 0 \\ 0 & 0 & 0 & 0 \\ 0 & 0 & 0 & 1 \end{bmatrix}$$

(12-10)

An orthographic projection is obtained when $L_1 = 0$ (which occurs at a projection angle α of 90°). Oblique projections are generated with nonzero values for L_1. Projection matrix 12-10 has a structure similar to that of a z-axis shear matrix. In fact, the effect of this projection matrix is to shear planes of constant z and project them onto the view plane. The x- and y-coordinate values within each plane of constant z are shifted by an amount proportional to the z value of the plane so that angles, distances, and parallel lines in the plane are projected accurately. This effect is shown in Fig. 12-22, where the back plane of the box is sheared and overlapped with the front plane in the projection to the viewing surface. An edge of the box connecting the front and back planes is projected into a line of length L_1 that makes an angle ϕ with a horizontal line in the projection plane.

Common choices for angle ϕ are 30° and 45°, which display a combination view of the front, side, and top (or front, side, and bottom) of an object. Two commonly used values for α are those for which $\tan\alpha = 1$ and $\tan\alpha = 2$. For the first case, $\alpha = 45°$ and the views obtained are called **cavalier** projections. All lines perpendicular to the projection plane are projected with no change in length. Examples of cavalier projections for a cube are given in Fig. 12-23.

When the projection angle α is chosen so that $\tan\alpha = 2$, the resulting view is called a **cabinet** projection. For this angle ($\approx 63.4°$), lines perpendicular to the viewing surface are projected at one-half their length. Cabinet projections appear more realistic than cavalier projections because of this reduction in the length of perpendiculars. Figure 12-24 shows examples of cabinet projections for a cube.

Perspective Projections

To obtain a perspective projection of a three-dimensional object, we transform points along projection lines that meet at the projection reference point. Suppose we set the projection reference point at position z_{prp} along the z_v axis, and we

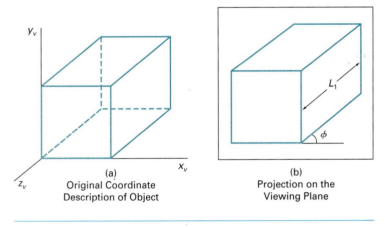

(a)
Original Coordinate
Description of Object

(b)
Projection on the
Viewing Plane

Figure 12-22
Oblique projection of a box onto the $z_v = 0$ plane.

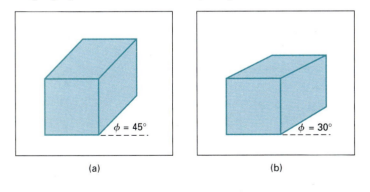

(a)   (b)

Figure 12-23
Cavalier projections of a cube onto a view plane for two values of angle ϕ.
Note: Depth of the cube is projected equal to the width and height.

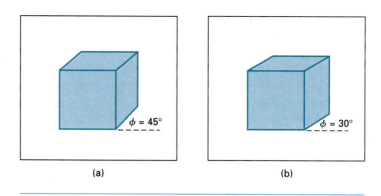

(a)   (b)

Figure 12-24
Cabinet projections of a cube onto a view plane for two values of
angle ϕ. Depth is projected as one-half that of the width and
height.

place the view plane at z_{vp}, as shown in Fig. 12-25. We can write equations describing coordinate positions along this perspective projection line in parametric form as

$$x' = x - xu$$
$$y' = y - yu \qquad (12\text{-}11)$$
$$z' = z - (z - z_{prp})u$$

Parameter u takes values from 0 to 1, and coordinate position (x', y', z') represents any point along the projection line. When $u = 0$, we are at position $\mathbf{P} = (x, y, z)$. At the other end of the line, $u = 1$ and we have the projection reference point coordinates $(0, 0, z_{prp})$. On the view plane, $z' = z_{vp}$ and we can solve the z' equation for parameter u at this position along the projection line:

$$u = \frac{z_{vp} - z}{z_{prp} - z} \qquad (12\text{-}12)$$

Substituting this value of u into the equations for x' and y', we obtain the perspective transformation equations

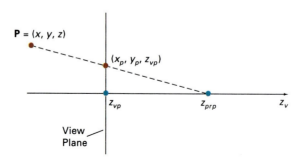

Figure 12-25
Perspective projection of a point
$\mathbf{P}$ with coordinates (x, y, z) to
position (x_p, y_p, z_{vp}) on the view
plane.

$$x_p = x\left(\frac{z_{prp} - z_{vp}}{z_{prp} - z}\right) = x\left(\frac{d_p}{z_{prp} - z}\right)$$

$$y_p = y\left(\frac{z_{prp} - z_{vp}}{z_{prp} - z}\right) = y\left(\frac{d_p}{z_{prp} - z}\right)$$

$$(12\text{-}13)$$

where $d_p = z_{prp} - z_{vp}$ is the distance of the view plane from the projection reference point.

Using a three-dimensional homogeneous-coordinate representation, we can write the perspective-projection transformation 12-13 in matrix form as

$$\begin{bmatrix} x_h \\ y_h \\ z_h \\ h \end{bmatrix} = \begin{bmatrix} 1 & 0 & 0 & 0 \\ 0 & 1 & 0 & 0 \\ 0 & 0 & -z_{vp}/d_p & z_{vp}(z_{prp}/d_p) \\ 0 & 0 & -1/d_p & z_{prp}/d_p \end{bmatrix} \cdot \begin{bmatrix} x \\ y \\ z \\ 1 \end{bmatrix}$$

$$(12\text{-}14)$$

In this representation, the homogeneous factor is

$$h = \frac{z_{prp} - z}{d_p}$$

$$(12\text{-}15)$$

and the projection coordinates on the view plane are calculated from the homogeneous coordinates as

$$x_p = x_h/h, \qquad y_p = y_h/h$$

$$(12\text{-}16)$$

where the original z-coordinate value would be retained in projection coordinates for visible-surface and other depth processing.

In general, the projection reference point does not have to be along the z_v axis. We can select any coordinate position $(x_{prp}, y_{prp}, z_{prp})$ on either side of the view plane for the projection reference point, and we discuss this generalization in the next section.

There are a number of special cases for the perspective transformation equations 12-13. If the view plane is taken to be the uv plane, then $z_{vp} = 0$ and the projection coordinates are

$$x_p = x\left(\frac{z_{prp}}{z_{prp} - z}\right) = x\left(\frac{1}{1 - z/z_{prp}}\right)$$

$$y_p = y\left(\frac{z_{prp}}{z_{prp} - z}\right) = y\left(\frac{1}{1 - z/z_{prp}}\right)$$

$$(12\text{-}17)$$

And, in some graphics packages, the projection reference point is always taken to be at the viewing-coordinate origin. In this case, $z_{prp} = 0$ and the projection coordinates on the viewing plane are

$$x_p = x\left(\frac{z_{vp}}{z}\right) = x\left(\frac{1}{z/z_{vp}}\right)$$

$$y_p = y\left(\frac{z_{vp}}{z}\right) = y\left(\frac{1}{z/z_{vp}}\right)$$

$$(12\text{-}18)$$

445

When a three-dimensional object is projected onto a view plane using perspective transformation equations, any set of parallel lines in the object that are not parallel to the plane are projected into converging lines. Parallel lines that are parallel to the view plane will be projected as parallel lines. The point at which a set of projected parallel lines appears to converge is called a **vanishing point**. Each such set of projected parallel lines will have a separate vanishing point; and in general, a scene can have any number of vanishing points, depending on how many sets of parallel lines there are in the scene.

The vanishing point for any set of lines that are parallel to one of the principal axes of an object is referred to as a **principal vanishing point**. We control the number of principal vanishing points (one, two, or three) with the orientation of the projection plane, and perspective projections are accordingly classified as one-point, two-point, or three-point projections. The number of principal vanishing points in a projection is determined by the number of principal axes intersecting the view plane. Figure 12-26 illustrates the appearance of one-point and two-point perspective projections for a cube. In Fig. 12-26(b), the view plane is aligned parallel to the *xy* object plane so that only the object *z* axis is intersected.

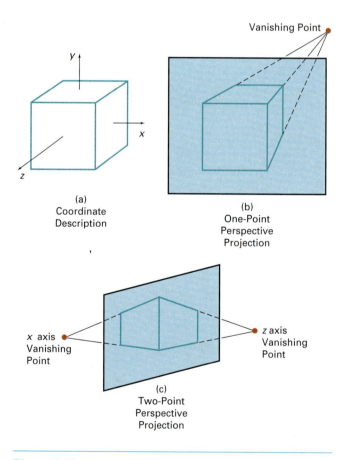

Figure 12-26

Perspective views and principal vanishing points of a cube for various orientations of the view plane relative to the principal axes of the object.

This orientation produces a one-point perspective projection with a z-axis vanishing point. For the view shown in Fig. 12-26(c), the projection plane intersects both the x and z axes but not the y axis. The resulting two-point perspective projection contains both x-axis and z-axis vanishing points.

12-4
VIEW VOLUMES AND GENERAL PROJECTION TRANSFORMATIONS

In the camera analogy, the type of lens used on the camera is one factor that determines how much of the scene is caught on film. A wide-angle lens takes in more of the scene than a regular lens. In three-dimensional viewing, a rectangular **view window,** or **projection window,** in the view plane is used to the same effect. Edges of the view window are parallel to the $x_v y_v$ axes, and the window boundary positions are specified in viewing coordinates, as shown in Fig. 12-27. The view window can be placed anywhere on the view plane.

Given the specification of the view window, we can set up a **view volume** using the window boundaries. Only those objects within the view volume will appear in the generated display on an output device; all others are clipped from the display. The size of the view volume depends on the size of the window, while the shape of the view volume depends on the type of projection to be used to generate the display. In any case, four sides of the volume are planes that pass through the edges of the window. For a parallel projection, these four sides of the view volume form an infinite parallelepiped, as in Fig. 12-28. For a perspective projection, the view volume is a pyramid with apex at the projection reference point (Fig. 12-29).

A finite view volume is obtained by limiting the extent of the volume in the z_v direction. This is done by specifying positions for one or two additional boundary planes. These z_v-boundary planes are referred to as the **front plane** and **back plane,** or the **near plane** and the **far plane,** of the viewing volume. The front and back planes are parallel to the view plane at specified positions z_{front} and z_{back}. Both planes must be on the same side of the projection reference point, and the back plane must be farther from the projection point than the front plane. Including the front and back planes produces a view volume bounded by six planes, as shown in Fig. 12-30. With an orthographic parallel projection, the six planes form a rectangular parallelepiped, while an oblique parallel projection produces an oblique parallelepiped view volume. With a perspective projection, the front and back clipping planes truncate the infinite pyramidal view volume to form a **frustum**.

Front and back clipping planes allow us to eliminate parts of the scene from the viewing operations based on depth. We can then pick out parts of a scene that we would like to view and exclude objects that are in front of or behind the part that we want to look at. Also, in a perspective projection, we can use the front clipping plane to take out large objects close to the view plane that can project into unrecognizable sections within the view window. Similarly, the back clipping plane can be used to cut out objects far from the projection reference point that can project to small blots on the output device.

Relative placement of the view plane and the front and back clipping planes depends on the type of view we want to generate and the limitations of a particular graphics package. With PHIGS, the view plane can be positioned anywhere along the z_v axis except that it cannot contain the projection reference point. And

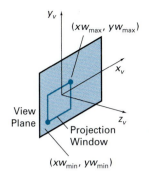

Figure 12-27
Window specification on the view plane, with minimum and maximum coordinates given in the viewing reference system.

447

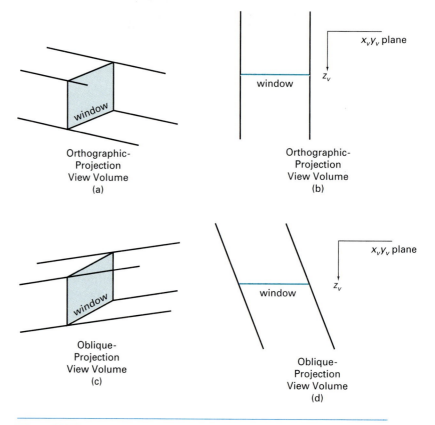

Orthographic-
Projection
View Volume
(a)

Orthographic-
Projection
View Volume
(b)

Oblique-
Projection
View Volume
(c)

Oblique-
Projection
View Volume
(d)

Figure 12-28
View volume for a parallel projection. In (a) and (b), the side and top views of the view volume for an orthographic projection are shown; and in (c) and (d), the side and top views of an oblique view volume are shown.

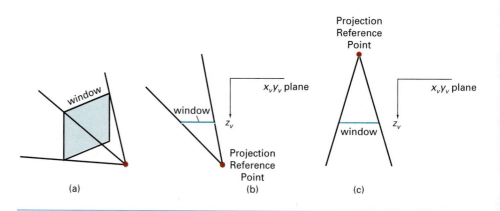

(a)

(b)

(c)

Figure 12-29
Examples of a perspective-projection view volume for various positions of the projection reference point.

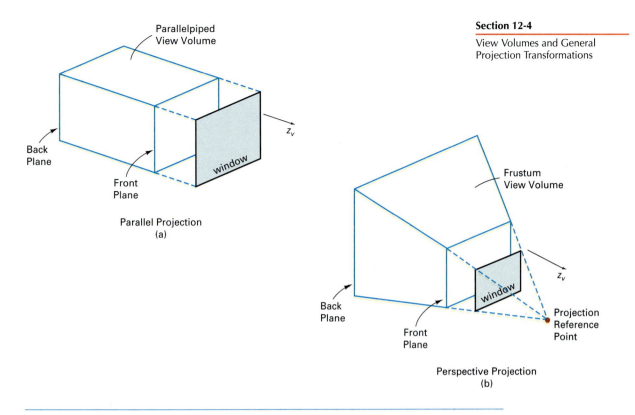

Parallelpiped
View Volume

z_v

Back
Plane

Front
Plane

window

Parallel Projection
(a)

Frustum
View Volume

z_v

Back
Plane

Front
Plane

window

Projection
Reference
Point

Perspective Projection
(b)

Figure 12-30
View volumes bounded by front and back planes, and by top, bottom, and side planes. Front
and back planes are parallel to the view plane at positions z_{front} and z_{back} along the z_v axis.

the front and back planes can be in any position relative to the view plane as long
as the projection reference point is not between the front and back planes. Figure
12-31 illustrates possible arrangements of the front and back planes in relation to
the view plane. The default view volume in PHIGS is formed as a unit cube
using a parallel projection with $z_{front} = 1$, $z_{back} = 0$, the view plane coincident with
the back plane, and the projection reference point at position (0.5, 0.5, 1.0) on the
front plane.

    Orthographic parallel projections are not affected by view-plane position-
ing, because the projection lines are perpendicular to the view plane regardless of

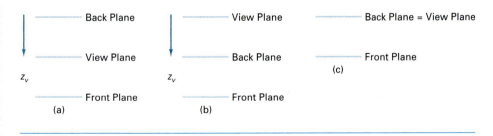

Back Plane

View Plane

z_v

Front Plane

(a)

View Plane

Back Plane

z_v

Front Plane

(b)

Back Plane = View Plane

Front Plane

(c)

Figure 12-31
Possible arrangements of the front and back clipping planes relative to the view plane.

449

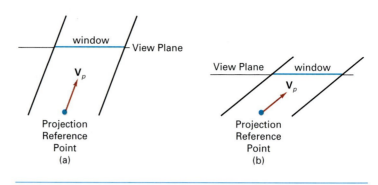

Figure 12-32
Changing the shape of the oblique-projection view volume by moving the window position, when the projection vector $\mathbf{V}_p$ is determined by the projection reference point and the window position.

its location. Oblique projections may be affected by view-plane positioning, depending on how the projection direction is to be specified. In PHIGS, the oblique projection direction is parallel to the line from the projection reference point to the center of the window. Therefore, moving the position of the view plane without moving the projection reference point changes the skewness of the sides of the view volume, as shown in Fig. 12-32. Often, the view plane is positioned at the view reference point or on the front clipping plane when generating a parallel projection.

Perspective effects depend on the positioning of the projection reference point relative to the view plane, as shown in Figure 12-33. If we place the projec-

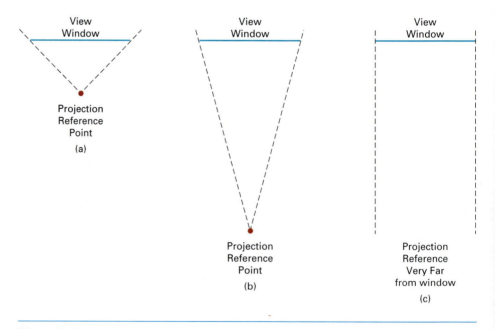

Figure 12-33
Changing perspective effects by moving the projection reference point away from the view plane.

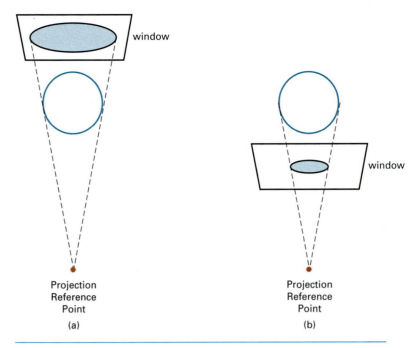

Figure 12-34
Projected object size depends on whether the view plane is positioned in
front of the object or behind it, relative to the position of the projection
reference point.

tion reference point close to the view plane, perspective effects are emphasized;
that is, closer objects will appear much larger than more distant objects of the
same size. Similarly, as we move the projection reference point farther from the
view plane, the difference in the size of near and far objects decreases. In the
limit, as we move the projection reference point infinitely far from the view
plane, a perspective projection approaches a parallel projection.

The projected size of an object in a perspective view is also affected by the
relative position of the object and the view plane (Fig. 12-34). If the view plane is
in front of the object (nearer the projection reference point), the projected size is
smaller. Conversely, object size is increased when we project onto a view plane in
back of the object.

View-plane positioning for a perspective projection also depends on
whether we want to generate a static view or an animation sequence. For a static
view of a scene, the view plane is usually placed at the viewing-coordinate origin, which is at some convenient point in the scene. Then it is easy to adjust the
size of the window to include all parts of the scene that we want to view. The
projection reference point is positioned to obtain the amount of perspective desired. In an animation sequence, we can place the projection reference point at
the viewing-coordinate origin and put the view plane in front of the scene (Fig.
12-35). This placement simulates a camera reference frame. We set the field of
view (lens angle) by adjusting the size of the window relative to the distance of
the view plane from the projection reference point. We move through the scene
by moving the viewing reference frame, and the projection reference point will
move with the view reference point.

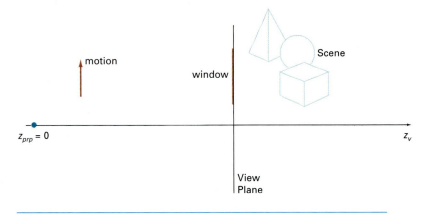

Figure 12-35
View-plane positioning to simulate a camera reference frame for an animation sequence.

General Parallel-Projection Transformations

In PHIGS, the direction of a parallel projection is specified with a projection vector from the projection reference point to the center of the view window. Figure 12-36 shows the general shape of a finite view volume for a given projection vector and projection window in the view plane. We obtain the oblique-projection transformation with a shear operation that converts the view volume in Fig. 12-36 to the regular parallelepiped shown in Fig. 12-37.

The elements of the shearing transformation needed to generate the view volume shown in Fig. 12-37 are obtained by considering the shear transformation of the projection vector. If the projection vector is specified in world coordinates, it must first be transformed to viewing coordinates using the rotation matrix discussed in Section 12-2. (The projection vector is unaffected by the translation, since it is simply a direction with no fixed position.) For graphics packages that allow specification of the projection vector in viewing coordinates, we apply the shear directly to the input elements of the projection vector.

Suppose the elements of the projection vector in viewing coordinates are

$$\mathbf{V}_p = (p_x, p_y, p_z) \tag{12-19}$$

We need to determine the elements of a shear matrix that will align the projection vector $\mathbf{V}_p$ with the view plane normal vector $\mathbf{N}$ (Fig. 12-37). This transformation can be expressed as

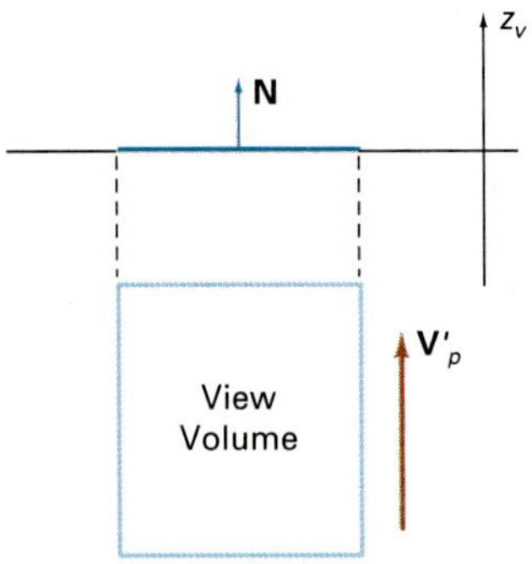

Figure 12-37
Regular parallelepiped view volume obtained by shearing the view volume in Fig. 12-36.

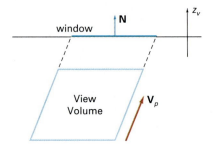

Figure 12-36
Oblique projection vector and associated view volume.

$$\mathbf{V}'_p = \mathbf{M}_{\text{parallel}} \cdot \mathbf{V}_p$$

$$= \begin{bmatrix} 0 \\ 0 \\ p_z \\ 0 \end{bmatrix} \qquad (12\text{-}20)$$

where $\mathbf{M}_{\text{parallel}}$ is equivalent to the parallel projection matrix 12-10 and represents a z-axis shear of the form

$$\mathbf{M}_{\text{parallel}} = \begin{bmatrix} 1 & 0 & a & 0 \\ 0 & 1 & b & 0 \\ 0 & 0 & 1 & 0 \\ 0 & 0 & 0 & 1 \end{bmatrix} \qquad (12\text{-}21)$$

The explicit transformation equations from 12-20 in terms of shear parameters a and b are

$$0 = p_x + ap_z$$
$$0 = p_y + bp_z \qquad (12\text{-}22)$$

so that the values for the shear parameters are

$$a = -\frac{p_x}{p_z}, \qquad b = -\frac{p_y}{p_z} \qquad (12\text{-}23)$$

Thus, we have the general parallel-projection matrix in terms of the elements of the projection vector as

$$\mathbf{M}_{\text{parallel}} = \begin{bmatrix} 1 & 0 & -p_x/p_z & 0 \\ 0 & 1 & -p_y/p_z & 0 \\ 0 & 0 & 1 & 0 \\ 0 & 0 & 0 & 1 \end{bmatrix} \qquad (12\text{-}24)$$

This matrix is then concatenated with transformation $\mathbf{R} \cdot \mathbf{T}$, from Section 12-2, to produce the transformation from world coordinates to parallel-projection coordinates. For an orthographic parallel projection, $p_x = p_y = 0$, and $\mathbf{M}_{\text{parallel}}$ is the identity matrix. From Fig. 12-38, we can relate the components of the projection vector to parameters L, α, and ϕ (Section 12-3). By similar triangles, we see that

$$\frac{L \cos \phi}{z} = -\frac{p_x}{p_z}$$
$$\frac{L \sin \phi}{z} = -\frac{p_y}{p_z} \qquad (12\text{-}25)$$

which illustrates the equivalence of the elements of transformation matrices 12-10 and 12-24. In Eqs. 12-25, z and p_z are of opposite signs, and for the positions illustrated in Fig. 12-38, $z < 0$.

453

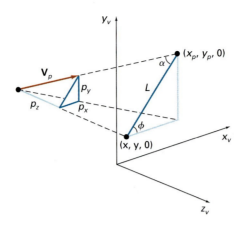

General Perspective-Projection Transformations

With the PHIGS programming standard, the projection reference point can be located at any position in the viewing system, except on the view plane or between the front and back clipping planes. Figure 12-39 shows the shape of a finite view volume for an arbitrary position of the projection reference point. We can obtain the general perspective-projection transformation with the following two operations:

1. Shear the view volume so that the centerline of the frustum is perpendicular to the view plane.
2. Scale the view volume with a scaling factor that depends on $1/z$.

The second step (scaling the view volume) is equivalent to the perspective transformation discussed in Section 12-3.

A shear operation to align a general perspective view volume with the pro-

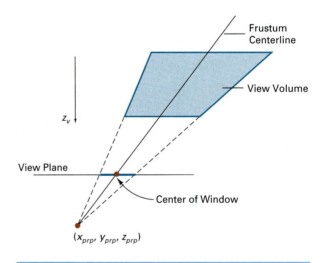

Figure 12-39
General shape for the perspective view volume with a projection reference point that is not on the z_v axis.

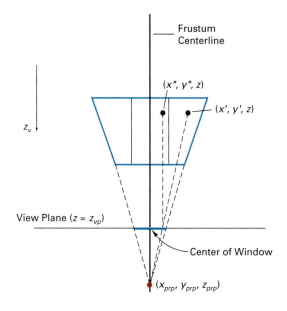

Frustum
Centerline

(x'', y'', z)

(x', y', z)

z_v

View Plane $(z = z_{vp})$

Center of Window

$(x_{prp}, y_{prp}, z_{prp})$

Figure 12-40
Shearing a general perspective view
volume to center it on the projection
window.

jection window is shown in Fig. 12-40. This transformation has the effect of shifting all positions that lie along the frustum centerline, including the window center, to a line perpendicular to the view plane. With the projection reference point at a general position $(x_{prp}, y_{prp}, z_{prp})$, the transformation involves a combination z-axis shear and a translation:

$$\mathbf{M}_{shear} = \begin{bmatrix} 1 & 0 & a & -az_{prp} \\ 0 & 1 & b & -bz_{prp} \\ 0 & 0 & 1 & 0 \\ 0 & 0 & 0 & 1 \end{bmatrix} \qquad (12\text{-}26)$$

where the shear parameters are

$$a = -\frac{x_{prp} - (xw_{min} + xw_{max})/2}{z_{prp}}$$
$$b = -\frac{y_{prp} - (yw_{min} + yw_{max})/2}{z_{prp}} \qquad (12\text{-}27)$$

Points within the view volume are transformed by this operation as

$$x' = x + a(z - z_{prp})$$
$$y' = y + b(z - z_{prp}) \qquad (12\text{-}28)$$
$$z' = z$$

When the projection reference point is on the z_v axis, $x_{prp} = y_{prp} = 0$.

Once we have converted a position (x, y, z) in the original view volume to position (x', y', z') in the sheared frustum, we then apply a scaling transformation to produce a regular parallelepiped (Fig. 12-40). The transformation for this conversion is

455

$$x'' = x'\left(\frac{z_{prp} - z_{vp}}{z_{prp} - z}\right) + x_{prp}\left(\frac{z_{vp} - z}{z_{prp} - z}\right)$$

(12-29)

$$y'' = y'\left(\frac{z_{prp} - z_{vp}}{z_{prp} - z}\right) + y_{prp}\left(\frac{z_{vp} - z}{z_{prp} - z}\right)$$

and the homogeneous matrix representation is

$$\mathbf{M}_{scale} = \begin{bmatrix} 1 & 0 & \dfrac{-x_{prp}}{z_{prp} - z_{vp}} & \dfrac{x_{prp}z_{vp}}{z_{prp} - z_{vp}} \\[2ex] 0 & 1 & \dfrac{-y_{prp}}{z_{prp} - z_{vp}} & \dfrac{y_{prp}z_{vp}}{z_{prp} - z_{vp}} \\[2ex] 0 & 0 & 1 & 0 \\[2ex] 0 & 0 & \dfrac{-1}{z_{prp} - z_{vp}} & \dfrac{z_{prp}}{z_{prp} - z_{vp}} \end{bmatrix}$$

(12-30)

Therefore, the general perspective-projection transformation can be expressed in matrix form as

$$\mathbf{M}_{perspective} = \mathbf{M}_{scale} \cdot \mathbf{M}_{shear}$$

(12-31)

The complete transformation from world coordinates to perspective-projection coordinates is obtained by right concatenating $\mathbf{M}_{perspective}$ with the composite viewing transformation $\mathbf{R} \cdot \mathbf{T}$ from Section 12-2.

12-5

CLIPPING

In this section, we first explore the general ideas involved in three-dimensional clipping by considering how clipping could be performed using the view-volume clipping planes directly. Then we discuss more efficient methods using normalized view volumes and homogeneous coordinates.

An algorithm for three-dimensional clipping identifies and saves all surface segments within the view volume for display on the output device. All parts of objects that are outside the view volume are discarded. Clipping in three dimensions can be accomplished using extensions of two-dimensional clipping methods. Instead of clipping against straight-line window boundaries, we now clip objects against the boundary planes of the view volume.

To clip a line segment against the view volume, we would need to test the relative position of the line using the view volume's boundary plane equations. By substituting the line endpoint coordinates into the plane equation of each boundary in turn, we could determine whether the endpoint is inside or outside that boundary. An endpoint (x, y, z) of a line segment is outside a boundary plane if $Ax + By + Cz + D > 0$, where A, B, C, and D are the plane parameters for that boundary. Similarly, the point is inside the boundary if $Ax + By + Cz + D < 0$. Lines with both endpoints outside a boundary plane are discarded, and those with both endpoints inside all boundary planes are saved. The intersection of a line with a boundary is found using the line equations along with the plane equation. Intersection coordinates (x_I, y_I, z_I) are values that are on the line and that satisfy the plane equation $Ax_I + By_I + Cz_I + D = 0$.

To clip a polygon surface, we can clip the individual polygon edges. First, we could test the coordinate extents against each boundary of the view volume to determine whether the object is completely inside or completely outside that boundary. If the coordinate extents of the object are inside all boundaries, we save it. If the coordinate extents are outside all boundaries, we discard it. Otherwise, we need to apply the intersection calculations. We could do this by determining the polygon edge-intersection positions with the boundary planes of the view volume, as described in the previous paragraph.

As in two-dimensional viewing, the projection operations can take place before the view-volume clipping or after clipping. All objects within the view volume map to the interior of the specified projection window. The last step is to transform the window contents to a two-dimensional viewport, which specifies the location of the display on the output device.

Clipping in two dimensions is generally performed against an upright rectangle; that is, the clip window is aligned with the x and y axes. This greatly simplifies the clipping calculations, because each window boundary is defined by one coordinate value. For example, the intersections of all lines crossing the left boundary of the window have an x coordinate equal to the left boundary.

View-volume clipping boundaries are planes whose orientations depend on the type of projection, the projection window, and the position of the projection reference point. Since the front and back clipping planes are parallel to the view plane, each has a constant z-coordinate value. The z coordinate of the intersections of lines with these planes is simply the z coordinate of the corresponding plane. But the other four sides of the view volume can have arbitrary spatial orientations. To find the intersection of a line with one of the view volume boundaries means that we must obtain the equation for the plane containing that boundary polygon. This process is simplified if we convert the view volume before clipping to a rectangular parallelepiped. In other words, we first perform the projection transformation, which converts coordinate values in the view volume to orthographic parallel coordinates, then we carry out the clipping calculations.

Clipping against a regular parallelepiped is much simpler because each surface is now perpendicular to one of the coordinate axes. As seen in Fig. 12-41, the top and bottom of the view volume are now planes of constant y, the sides are planes of constant x, and the front and back are planes of constant z. A line cutting through the top plane of the parallelepiped, for example, has an intersection point whose y-coordinate value is that of the top plane.

In the case of an orthographic parallel projection, the view volume is already a rectangular parallelepiped. As we have seen in Section 12-3, oblique-projection view volumes are converted to a rectangular parallelepiped by the shearing operation, and perspective view volumes are converted, in general, with a combination shear-scale transformation.

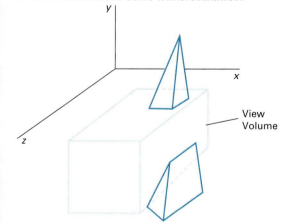

View Volume

Figure 12-41
An object intersecting a rectangular parallelepiped view volume.

457

Normalized View Volumes

Figure 12-42 shows the expanded PHIGS transformation pipeline. At the first step, a scene is constructed by transforming object descriptions from modeling coordinates to world coordinates. Next, a view mapping converts the world descriptions to viewing coordinates. At the projection stage, the viewing coordinates are transformed to projection coordinates, which effectively converts the view volume into a rectangular parallelepiped. Then, the parallelepiped is mapped into the unit cube, a **normalized view volume** called the **normalized projection coordinate** system. The mapping to normalized projection coordinates is accomplished by transforming points within the rectangular parallelepiped into a position within a specified three-dimensional viewport, which occupies part or all of the unit cube. Finally, at the workstation stage, normalized projection coordinates are converted to device coordinates for display.

The normalized view volume is a region defined by the planes

$$x = 0, \qquad x = 1, \qquad y = 0, \qquad y = 1, \qquad z = 0, \qquad z = 1 \qquad (12\text{-}32)$$

A similar transformation sequence is used in other graphics packages, with individual variations depending on the system. The GL package, for example, maps the rectangular parallelepiped into the interior of a cube with boundary planes at positions ± 1 in each coordinate direction.

There are several advantages to clipping against the unit cube instead of the original view volume or even the rectangular parallelepiped in projection coordinates. First, the normalized view volume provides a standard shape for representing any sized view volume. This separates the viewing transformations from any workstation considerations, and the unit cube then can be mapped to a workstation of any size. Second, clipping procedures are simplified and standardized with unit clipping planes or the viewport planes, and additional clipping planes can be specified within the normalized space before transforming to

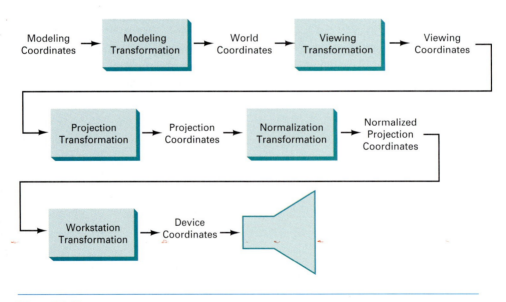

Figure 12-42
Expanded PHIGS transformation pipeline.

device coordinates. Third, depth cueing and visible-surface determination are simplified, since the z axis always points toward the viewer (the projection reference point has now been transformed to the z axis). Front faces of objects are those with normal vectors having a component along the positive z direction; and back surfaces are facing in the negative z direction.

Mapping positions within a rectangular view volume to a three-dimensional rectangular viewport is accomplished with a combination of scaling and translation, similar to the operations needed for a two-dimensional window-to-viewport mapping. We can express the three-dimensional transformation matrix for these operations in the form

$$
\begin{bmatrix}
D_x & 0 & 0 & K_x \\
0 & D_y & 0 & K_y \\
0 & 0 & D_z & K_z \\
0 & 0 & 0 & 1
\end{bmatrix}
\qquad (12\text{-}33)
$$

Factors D_x, D_y, and D_z are the ratios of the dimensions of the viewport and regular parallelepiped view volume in the x, y, and z directions (Fig. 12-43):

$$
D_x = \frac{xv_{\max} - xv_{\min}}{xw_{\max} - xw_{\min}}
$$

$$
D_y = \frac{yv_{\max} - yv_{\min}}{yw_{\max} - yw_{\min}}
$$

$$
D_z = \frac{zv_{\max} - zv_{\min}}{z_{\text{back}} - z_{\text{front}}}
$$

$$(12\text{-}34)$$

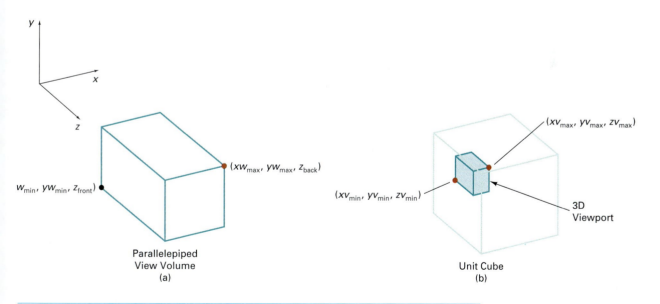

Parallelepiped
View Volume
(a)

Unit Cube
(b)

3D
Viewport

Figure 12-43
Dimensions of the view volume and three-dimensional viewport.

459

where the view-volume boundaries are established by the window limits (xw_{min}, xw_{max}, yw_{min}, yw_{max}) and the positions z_{front} and z_{back} of the front and back planes. Viewport boundaries are set with the coordinate values xv_{min}, xv_{max}, yv_{min}, yv_{max}, zv_{min}, and zv_{max}. The additive translation factors K_x, K_y, and K_z in the transformation are

$$K_x = xv_{min} - xw_{min}D_x$$
$$K_y = yv_{min} - yw_{min}D_y$$
$$K_z = zv_{min} - z_{front}D_z \qquad (12\text{-}35)$$

Viewport Clipping

Lines and polygon surfaces in a scene can be clipped against the viewport boundaries with procedures similar to those used for two dimensions, except that objects are now processed against clipping planes instead of clipping edges. Curved surfaces are processed using the defining equations for the surface boundary and locating the intersection lines with the parallelepiped planes.

The two-dimensional concept of region codes can be extended to three dimensions by considering positions in front and in back of the three-dimensional viewport, as well as positions that are left, right, below, or above the volume. For two-dimensional clipping, we used a four-digit binary region code to identify the position of a line endpoint relative to the viewport boundaries. For three-dimensional points, we need to expand the region code to six bits. Each point in the description of a scene is then assigned a six-bit region code that identifies the relative position of the point with respect to the viewport. For a line endpoint at position (x, y, z), we assign the bit positions in the region code from right to left as

$$\text{bit } 1 = 1, \qquad \text{if } x < xv_{min}\text{(left)}$$
$$\text{bit } 2 = 1, \qquad \text{if } x > xv_{max}\text{(right)}$$
$$\text{bit } 3 = 1, \qquad \text{if } y < yv_{min}\text{(below)}$$
$$\text{bit } 4 = 1, \qquad \text{if } y > yv_{max}\text{(above)}$$
$$\text{bit } 5 = 1, \qquad \text{if } z < zv_{min}\text{(front)}$$
$$\text{bit } 6 = 1, \qquad \text{if } z > zv_{max}\text{(back)}$$

For example, a region code of 101000 identifies a point as above and behind the viewport, and the region code 000000 indicates a point within the volume.

A line segment can be immediately identified as completely within the viewport if both endpoints have a region code of 000000. If either endpoint of a line segment does not have a region code of 000000, we perform the logical *and* operation on the two endpoint codes. The result of this *and* operation will be nonzero for any line segment that has both endpoints in one of the six outside regions. For example, a nonzero value will be generated if both endpoints are behind the viewport, or both endpoints are above the viewport. If we cannot identify a line segment as completely inside or completely outside the volume, we test for intersections with the bounding planes of the volume.

As in two-dimensional line clipping, we use the calculated intersection of a line with a viewport plane to determine how much of the line can be thrown away. The remaining part of the line is checked against the other planes, and we continue until either the line is totally discarded or a section is found inside the volume.

Equations for three-dimensional line segments are conveniently expressed in parametric form. The two-dimensional parametric clipping methods of Cyrus–Beck or Liang–Barsky can be extended to three-dimensional scenes. For a line segment with endpoints $\mathbf{P}_1 = (x_1, y_1, z_1)$ and $\mathbf{P}_2 = (x_2, y_2, z_2)$, we can write the parametric line equations as

$$x = x_1 + (x_2 - x_1)u, \qquad 0 \le u \le 1$$

$$y = y_1 + (y_2 - y_1)u$$

$$z = z_1 + (z_2 - z_1)u \qquad (12\text{-}36)$$

Coordinates (x, y, z) represent any point on the line between the two endpoints. At $u = 0$, we have the point $\mathbf{P}_1$, and $u = 1$ puts us at $\mathbf{P}_2$.

To find the intersection of a line with a plane of the viewport, we substitute the coordinate value for that plane into the appropriate parametric expression of Eq. 12-36 and solve for u. For instance, suppose we are testing a line against the $zv_{\min}$ plane of the viewport. Then

$$u = \frac{zv_{\min} - z_1}{z_2 - z_1} \qquad (12\text{-}37)$$

When the calculated value for u is not in the range from 0 to 1, the line segment does not intersect the plane under consideration at any point between endpoints $\mathbf{P}_1$ and $\mathbf{P}_2$ (line A in Fig. 12-44). If the calculated value for u in Eq. 12-37 is in the interval from 0 to 1, we calculate the intersection's x and y coordinates as

$$x_I = x_1 + (x_2 - x_1)\left(\frac{zv_{\min} - z_1}{z_2 - z_1} \right)$$

$$y_I = y_1 + (y_2 - y_1)\left(\frac{zv_{min} - z_1}{z_2 - z_1} \right) \qquad (12\text{-}38)$$

If either x_I or y_I is not in the range of the boundaries of the viewport, then this line intersects the front plane beyond the boundaries of the volume (line B in Fig. 12-44).

Clipping in Homogeneous Coordinates

Although we have discussed the clipping procedures in terms of three-dimensional coordinates, PHIGS and other packages actually represent coordinate positions in homogeneous coordinates. This allows the various transformations to be represented as 4 by 4 matrices, which can be concatenated for efficiency. After all viewing and other transformations are complete, the homogeneous-coordinate positions are converted back to three-dimensional points.

As each coordinate position enters the transformation pipeline, it is converted to a homogeneous-coordinate representation:

$$(x, y, z) \rightarrow (x, y, z, 1)$$

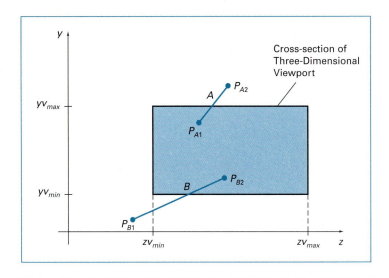

Figure 12-44
Side view of two line segments that are to be clipped against the zv_{min} plane of the viewport. For line A, Eq. 12-37 produces a value of u that is outside the range from 0 to 1. For line B, Eqs. 12-38 produce intersection coordinates that are outside the range from yv_{min} to yv_{max}.

The various transformations are applied and we obtain the final homogeneous point:

$$
\begin{bmatrix} x_h \\ y_h \\ z_h \\ h \end{bmatrix} = \begin{bmatrix} a_{11} & a_{12} & a_{13} & a_{14} \\ a_{21} & a_{22} & a_{23} & a_{24} \\ a_{31} & a_{32} & a_{33} & a_{34} \\ a_{41} & a_{42} & a_{43} & a_{44} \end{bmatrix} \cdot \begin{bmatrix} x \\ y \\ z \\ 1 \end{bmatrix} \tag{12-39}
$$

where the homogeneous parameter h may not be 1. In fact, h can have any real value. Clipping is then performed in homogeneous coordinates, and clipped homogeneous positions are converted to nonhomogeneous coordinates in three-dimensional normalized-projection coordinates:

$$
x' = \frac{x_h}{h}, \qquad y' = \frac{y_h}{h}, \qquad z' = \frac{z_h}{h} \tag{12-40}
$$

We will, of course, have a problem if the magnitude of parameter h is very small or has the value 0; but normally this will not occur, if the transformations are carried out properly. At the final stage in the transformation pipeline, the normalized point is transformed to a three-dimensional device coordinate point. The xy position is plotted on the device, and the z component is used for depth-information processing.

Setting up clipping procedures in homogeneous coordinates allows hardware viewing implementations to use a single procedure for both parallel and perspective projection transformations. Objects viewed with a parallel projection could be correctly clipped in three-dimensional normalized coordinates, provided the value $h = 1$ has not been altered by other operations. But perspective projections, in general, produce a homogeneous parameter that no longer has the value 1. Converting the sheared frustum to a rectangular parallelepiped can change the value of the homogeneous parameter. So we must clip in homogeneous coordinates to be sure that the clipping is carried out correctly. Also, rational spline representations are set up in homogeneous coordinates with arbitrary values for the homogeneous parameter, including $h < 1$. Negative values for the homogeneous parameter can also be generated in perspective projections when coordinate positions are behind the projection reference point. This can occur in applications where we might want to move inside of a building or other object to view its interior.

To determine homogeneous viewport clipping boundaries, we note that any homogeneous-coordinate position (x_h, y_h, z_h, h) is inside the viewport if it satisfies the inequalities

$$xv_{min} \leq \frac{x_h}{h} \leq xv_{max}, \qquad yv_{min} \leq \frac{y_h}{h} \leq yv_{max}, \qquad zv_{min} < \frac{z_h}{h} \leq zv_{max} \quad (12\text{-}41)$$

Thus, the homogeneous clipping limits are

$$h\,xv_{min} \leq x_h \leq h\,xv_{max}, \quad h\,yv_{min} \leq y_h \leq h\,yv_{max}, \quad h\,zv_{min} \leq z_h \leq h\,zv_{max}, \qquad \text{if } h > 0$$

$$h\,xv_{max} \leq x_h \leq h\,xv_{min}, \quad h\,yv_{max} \leq y_h \leq h\,yv_{min}, \quad h\,zv_{max} \leq z_h \leq h\,zv_{min}, \qquad \text{if } h < 0$$

$$(12\text{-}42)$$

And clipping is carried out with procedures similar to those discussed in the previous section. To avoid applying both sets of inequalities in 12-42, we can simply negate the coordinates for any point with $h < 0$ and use the clipping inequalities for $h > 0$.

12-6
HARDWARE IMPLEMENTATIONS

Most graphics processes are now implemented in hardware. Typically, the viewing, visible-surface identification, and shading algorithms are available as graphics chip sets, employing VLSI (very large-scale integration) circuitry techniques. Hardware systems are now designed to transform, clip, and project objects to the output device for either three-dimensional or two-dimensional applications.

Figure 12-45 illustrates an arrangement of components in a graphics chip set to implement the viewing operations we have discussed in this chapter. The chips are organized into a pipeline for accomplishing geometric transformations, coordinate-system transformations, projections, and clipping. Four initial chips are provided for matrix operations involving scaling, translation, rotation, and the transformations needed for converting world coordinates to projection coordinates. Each of the next six chips performs clipping against one of the viewport boundaries. Four of these chips are used in two-dimensional applications, and the other two are needed for clipping against the front and back planes of the three-dimensional viewport. The last two chips in the pipeline convert viewport coordinates to output device coordinates. Components for implementation of visible-surface identification and surface-shading algorithms can be added to this set to provide a complete three-dimensional graphics system.

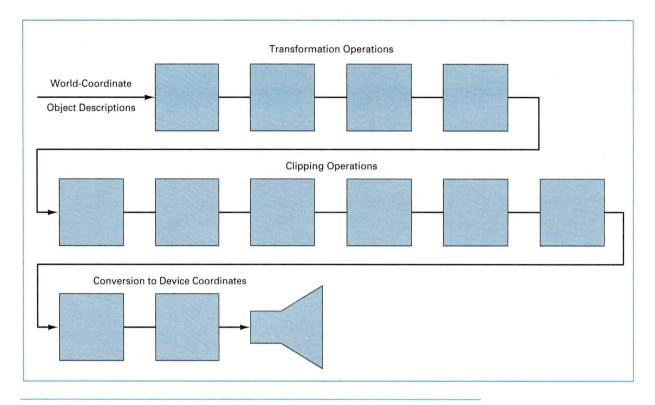

Figure 12-45
A hardware implementation of three-dimensional viewing operations using 12 chips for
the coordinate transformations and clipping operations.

Other specialized hardware implementations have been developed. These
include hardware systems for processing octree representations and for displaying three-dimensional scenes using ray-tracing algorithms (Chapter 14).

12-7
THREE-DIMENSIONAL VIEWING FUNCTIONS

Several procedures are usually provided in a three-dimensional graphics library
to enable an application program to set the parameters for viewing transformations. There are, of course, a number of different methods for structuring these
procedures. Here, we discuss the PHIGS functions for three-dimensional viewing.

With parameters specified in world coordinates, elements of the matrix for
transforming world-coordinate descriptions to the viewing reference frame are
calculated using the function

```
evaluateViewOrientationMatrix3 (x0, y0, z0, xN, yN, zN,
                                 xV, yV, zV, error, viewMatrix)
```

This function creates the `viewMatrix` from input coordinates defining the viewing system, as discussed in Section 12-2. Parameters x0, y0, and z0 specify the

464

origin (view reference point) of the viewing system. World-coordinate vector (xN, yN, zN) defines the normal to the view plane and the direction of the positive z_v viewing axis. And world-coordinate vector (xV, yV, zV) gives the elements of the view-up vector. The projection of this vector perpendicular to (xN, yN, zN) establishes the direction for the positive y_v axis of the viewing system. An integer error code is generated in parameter `error` if input values are not specified correctly. For example, an error will be generated if we set (xV, yV, zV) parallel to (xN, yN, zN).

To specify a second viewing-coordinate system, we can redefine some or all of the coordinate parameters and invoke `evaluateViewOrientationMatrix3` with a new matrix designation. In this way, we can set up any number of world-to-viewing-coordinate matrix transformations.

The matrix `projMatrix` for transforming viewing coordinates to normalized projection coordinates is created with the function

```
evaluateViewMappingMatrix3 (xwmin, xwmax, ywmin, ywmax,
         xvmin, xvmax, yvmin, yvmax, zvmin, zvmax,
            projType, xprojRef, yprojRef, zprojRef,  zview,
               zback, zfront,  error,  projMatrix)
```

Window limits on the view plane are given in viewing coordinates with parameters `xwmin`, `xwmax`, `ywmin`, and `ywmax`. Limits of the three-dimensional viewport within the unit cube are set with normalized coordinates `xvmin`, `xvmax`, `yvmin`, `yvmax`, `zvmin`, and `zvmax`. Parameter `projType` is used to choose the projection type as either *parallel* or *perspective*. Coordinate position (`xprojRef`, `yprojRef`, `zprojRef`) sets the projection reference point. This point is used as the center of projection if `projType` is set to *perspective*; otherwise, this point and the center of the view-plane window define the parallel-projection vector. The position of the view plane along the viewing z_v axis is set with parameter `zview`. Positions along the viewing z_v axis for the front and back planes of the view volume are given with parameters `zfront` and `zback`. And the `error` parameter returns an integer error code indicating erroneous input data. Any number of projection matrix transformations can be created with this function to obtain various three-dimensional views and projections.

A particular combination of viewing and projection matrices is selected on a specified workstation with

```
setViewRepresentation3 (ws, viewIndex, viewMatrix, projMatrix,
         xclipmin, xclipmax, yclipmin, yclipmax, zclipmin,
         zclipmax, clipxy, clipback, clipfront)
```

Parameter `ws` is used to select the workstation, and parameters `viewMatrix` and `projMatrix` select the combination of viewing and projection matrices to be used. The concatenation of these matrices is then placed in the workstation **view table** and referenced with an integer value assigned to parameter `viewIndex`. Limits, given in normalized projection coordinates, for clipping a scene are set with parameters `xclipmin`, `xclipmax`, `yclipmin`, `yclipmax`, `zclipmin`, and `zclipmax`. These limits can be set to any values, but they are usually set to the limits of the viewport. Values of *clip* or *noclip* are assigned to parameters `clipxy`, `clipfront`, and `clipback` to turn the clipping routines on or off for the *xy* planes or for the front or back planes of the view volume (or the defined clipping limits).

There are several times when it is convenient to bypass the clipping routines. For initial constructions of a scene, we can disable clipping so that trial placements of objects can be displayed quickly. Also, we can eliminate one or more of the clipping planes if we know that all objects are inside those planes.

Once the view tables have been set up, we select a particular view representation on each workstation with the function

```
setViewIndex (viewIndex)
```

The view index number identifies the set of viewing-transformation parameters that are to be applied to subsequently specified output primitives, for each of the active workstations.

Finally, we can use the **workstation transformation** functions to select sections of the projection window for display on different workstations. These operations are similar to those discussed for two-dimensional viewing, except now our window and viewport regions are three-dimensional regions. The window function selects a region of the unit cube, and the viewport function selects a display region for the output device. Limits, in normalized projection coordinates, for the window are set with

```
setWorkstationWindow3 (ws, xwsWindmin, xwsWindmax,
    ywsWindmin, ywsWindmax, zwsWindmin, zwsWindmax)
```

and limits, in device coordinates, for the viewport are set with

```
setWorkstationViewport3 (ws, xwsVPortmin, xwsVPortmax,
    ywsVPortmin, ywsVPortmax, zwsVPortmin, zwsVPortmax)
```

Figure 12-46 shows an example of interactive selection of viewing parameters in the PHIGS viewing pipeline, using the PHIGS Toolkit software. This software was developed at the University of Manchester to provide an interface to PHIGS with a viewing editor, windows, menus, and other interface tools.

For some applications, composite methods are used to create a display consisting of multiple views using different camera orientations. Figure 12-47 shows

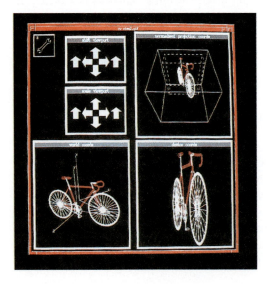

Figure 12-46
Using the PHIGS Toolkit, developed at the University of Manchester, to interactively control parameters in the viewing pipeline. *(Courtesy of T. L. J. Howard, J. G. Williams, and W. T. Hewitt, Department of Computer Science, University of Manchester, United Kingdom.)*

Figure 12-47
A wide-angle view for a virtual-reality display generated with seven sections, each from a slightly different viewing direction. (*Courtesy of the National Center for Supercomputing Applications, University of Illinois at Urbana-Champaign.*)

a wide-angle perspective display produced for a virtual-reality environment. The wide viewing angle is attained by generating seven views of the scene from the same viewing position, but with slight shifts in the viewing direction.

SUMMARY

Viewing procedures for three-dimensional scenes follow the general approach used in two-dimensional viewing. That is, we first create a world-coordinate scene from the definitions of objects in modeling coordinates. Then we set up a viewing-coordinate reference frame and transfer object descriptions from world coordinates to viewing coordinates. Finally, viewing-coordinate descriptions are transformed to device coordinates.

Unlike two-dimensional viewing, however, three-dimensional viewing requires projection routines to transform object descriptions to a viewing plane before the transformation to device coordinates. Also, three-dimensional viewing operations involve more spatial parameters. We can use the camera analogy to describe three-dimensional viewing parameters, which include camera position and orientation. A viewing-coordinate reference frame is established with a view reference point, a view-plane normal vector N, and a view-up vector V. View-plane position is then established along the viewing z axis, and object descriptions are projected to this plane. Either perspective-projection or parallel-projection methods can be used to transfer object descriptions to the view plane.

Parallel projections are either orthographic or oblique and can be specified with a projection vector. Orthographic parallel projections that display more than one face of an object are called axonometric projections. An isometric view of an object is obtained with an axonometric projection that foreshortens each principal axis by the same amount. Commonly used oblique projections are the cavalier projection and the cabinet projection. Perspective projections of objects are obtained with projection lines that meet at the projection reference point.

Objects in three-dimensional scenes are clipped against a view volume. The top, bottom, and sides of the view volume are formed with planes that are parallel to the projection lines and that pass through the view-plane window edges. Front and back planes are used to create a closed view volume. For a parallel projection, the view volume is a parallelepiped, and for a perspective projection, the view volume is a frustum. Objects are clipped in three-dimensional viewing by testing object coordinates against the bounding planes of the view volume. Clipping is generally carried out in graphics packages in homogeneous coordinates

467

after all viewing and other transformations are complete. Then, homogeneous coordinates are converted to three-dimensional Cartesian coordinates.

REFERENCES

For additional information on three-dimensional viewing and clipping operations in PHIGS and PHIGS+, see Howard et al. (1991), Gaskins (1992), and Blake (1993). Discussions of three-dimensional clipping and viewing algorithms can be found in Blinn and Newell (1978), Cyrus and Beck (1978), Riesenfeld (1981), Liang and Barsky (1984), Arvo (1991), and Blinn (1993).

EXERCISES

12-1. Write a procedure to implement the `evaluateViewOrientationMatrix3` function using Eqs. 12-2 through 12-4.

12-2. Write routines to implement the `setViewRepresentation3` and `setViewIndex` functions.

12-3. Write a procedure to transform the vertices of a polyhedron to projection coordinates using a parallel projection with a specified projection vector.

12-4. Write a procedure to obtain different parallel-projection views of a polyhedron by first applying a specified rotation.

12-5. Write a procedure to perform a one-point perspective projection of an object.

12-6. Write a procedure to perform a two-point perspective projection of an object.

12-7. Develop a routine to perform a three-point perspective projection of an object.

12-8. Write a routine to convert a perspective projection frustum to a regular parallelepiped.

12-9. Extend the Sutherland-Hodgman polygon clipping algorithm to clip three-dimensional planes against a regular parallelepiped.

12-10. Devise an algorithm to clip objects in a scene against a defined frustum. Compare the operations needed in this algorithm to those needed in an algorithm that clips against a regular parallelepiped.

12-11. Modify the two-dimensional Liang-Barsky line-clipping algorithm to clip three-dimensional lines against a specified regular parallelepiped.

12-12. Modify the two-dimensional Liang-Barsky line-clipping algorithm to clip a given polyhedron against a specified regular parallelepiped.

12-13. Set up an algorithm for clipping a polyhedron against a parallelepiped.

12-14. Write a routine to perform clipping in homogeneous coordinates.

12-15. Using any clipping procedure and orthographic parallel projections, write a program to perform a complete viewing transformation from world coordinates to device coordinates.

12-16. Using any clipping procedure, write a program to perform a complete viewing transformation from world coordinates to device coordinates for any specified parallel-projection vector.

12-17. Write a program to perform all steps in the viewing pipeline for a perspective transformation.

CHAPTER

13

Visible-Surface Detection Methods

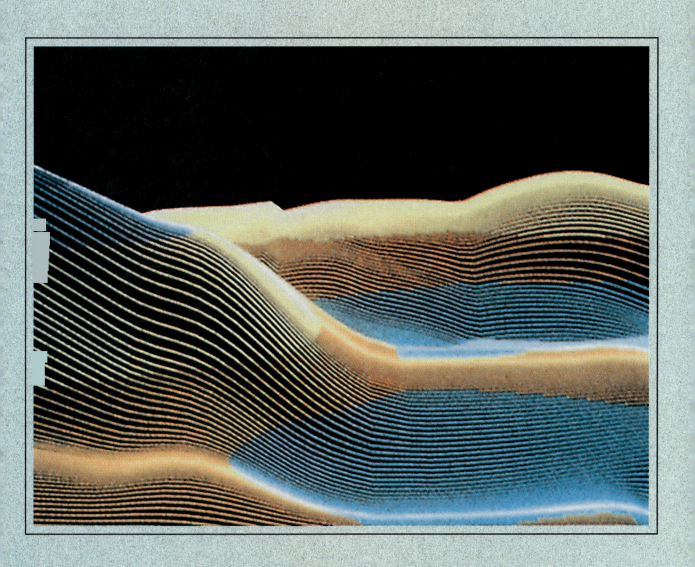

A major consideration in the generation of realistic graphics displays is identifying those parts of a scene that are visible from a chosen viewing position. There are many approaches we can take to solve this problem, and numerous algorithms have been devised for efficient identification of visible objects for different types of applications. Some methods require more memory, some involve more processing time, and some apply only to special types of objects. Deciding upon a method for a particular application can depend on such factors as the complexity of the scene, type of objects to be displayed, available equipment, and whether static or animated displays are to be generated. The various algorithms are referred to as **visible-surface detection methods.** Sometimes these methods are also referred to as **hidden-surface elimination methods,** although there can be subtle differences between identifying visible surfaces and eliminating hidden surfaces. For wireframe displays, for example, we may not want to actually eliminate the hidden surfaces, but rather to display them with dashed boundaries or in some other way to retain information about their shape. In this chapter, we explore some of the most commonly used methods for detecting visible surfaces in a three-dimensional scene.

13-1
CLASSIFICATION OF VISIBLE-SURFACE DETECTION ALGORITHMS

Visible-surface detection algorithms are broadly classified according to whether they deal with object definitions directly or with their projected images. These two approaches are called **object-space methods** and **image-space methods,** respectively. An object-space method compares objects and parts of objects to each other within the scene definition to determine which surfaces, as a whole, we should label as visible. In an image-space algorithm, visibility is decided point by point at each pixel position on the projection plane. Most visible-surface algorithms use image-space methods, although object-space methods can be used effectively to locate visible surfaces in some cases. Line-display algorithms, on the other hand, generally use object-space methods to identify visible lines in wireframe displays, but many image-space visible-surface algorithms can be adapted easily to visible-line detection.

Although there are major differences in the basic approach taken by the various visible-surface detection algorithms, most use sorting and coherence methods to improve performance. Sorting is used to facilitate depth comparisons by ordering the individual surfaces in a scene according to their distance from the view plane. Coherence methods are used to take advantage of regularities in a scene. An individual scan line can be expected to contain intervals (runs) of constant pixel intensities, and scan-line patterns often change little from one line to the next. Animation frames contain changes only in the vicinity of moving objects. And constant relationships often can be established between objects and surfaces in a scene.

13-2
BACK-FACE DETECTION

A fast and simple object-space method for identifying the **back faces** of a polyhedron is based on the "inside-outside" tests discussed in Chapter 10. A point (x, y, z) is "inside" a polygon surface with plane parameters A, B, C, and D if

$$Ax + By + Cz + D < 0 \qquad (13\text{-}1)$$

When an inside point is along the line of sight to the surface, the polygon must be a back face (we are inside that face and cannot see the front of it from our viewing position).

We can simplify this test by considering the normal vector $\mathbf{N}$ to a polygon surface, which has Cartesian components (A, B, C). In general, if $\mathbf{V}$ is a vector in the viewing direction from the eye (or "camera") position, as shown in Fig. 13-1, then this polygon is a back face if

$$\mathbf{V} \cdot \mathbf{N} > 0 \qquad (13\text{-}2)$$

Furthermore, if object descriptions have been converted to projection coordinates and our viewing direction is parallel to the viewing z_v axis, then $\mathbf{V} = (0, 0, V_z)$ and

$$\mathbf{V} \cdot \mathbf{N} = V_z C$$

so that we only need to consider the sign of C, the z component of the normal vector $\mathbf{N}$.

In a right-handed viewing system with viewing direction along the negative z_v axis (Fig. 13-2), the polygon is a back face if $C < 0$. Also, we cannot see any face whose normal has z component $C = 0$, since our viewing direction is grazing that polygon. Thus, in general, we can label any polygon as a back face if its normal vector has a z-component value:

$$C \leq 0 \qquad (13\text{-}3)$$

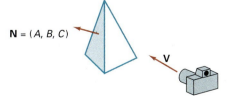

$\mathbf{N} = (A, B, C)$

V

Figure 13-1
Vector $\mathbf{V}$ in the viewing direction and a back-face normal vector $\mathbf{N}$ of a polyhedron.

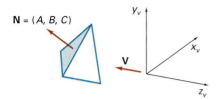

Figure 13-2

A polygon surface with plane parameter $C < 0$ in a right-handed viewing coordinate system is identified as a back face when the viewing direction is along the negative z_v axis.

Similar methods can be used in packages that employ a left-handed viewing system. In these packages, plane parameters A, B, C, and D can be calculated from polygon vertex coordinates specified in a clockwise direction (instead of the counterclockwise direction used in a right-handed system). Inequality 13-1 then remains a valid test for inside points. Also, back faces have normal vectors that point away from the viewing position and are identified by $C \geq 0$ when the viewing direction is along the positive z_v axis.

By examining parameter C for the different planes defining an object, we can immediately identify all the back faces. For a single convex polyhedron, such as the pyramid in Fig. 13-2, this test identifies all the hidden surfaces on the object, since each surface is either completely visible or completely hidden. Also, if a scene contains only nonoverlapping convex polyhedra, then again all hidden surfaces are identified with the back-face method.

For other objects, such as the concave polyhedron in Fig. 13-3, more tests need to be carried out to determine whether there are additional faces that are totally or partly obscured by other faces. And a general scene can be expected to contain overlapping objects along the line of sight. We then need to determine where the obscured objects are partially or completely hidden by other objects. In general, back-face removal can be expected to eliminate about half of the polygon surfaces in a scene from further visibility tests.

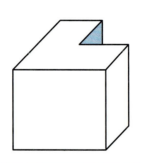

Figure 13-3
View of a concave polyhedron with one face partially hidden by other faces.

13-3

DEPTH-BUFFER METHOD

A commonly used image-space approach to detecting visible surfaces is the **depth-buffer method,** which compares surface depths at each pixel position on the projection plane. This procedure is also referred to as the z-**buffer method,** since object depth is usually measured from the view plane along the z axis of a viewing system. Each surface of a scene is processed separately, one point at a time across the surface. The method is usually applied to scenes containing only polygon surfaces, because depth values can be computed very quickly and the method is easy to implement. But the method can be applied to nonplanar surfaces.

With object descriptions converted to projection coordinates, each (x, y, z) position on a polygon surface corresponds to the orthographic projection point (x, y) on the view plane. Therefore, for each pixel position (x, y) on the view plane, object depths can be compared by comparing z values. Figure 13-4 shows three surfaces at varying distances along the orthographic projection line from position (x, y) in a view plane taken as the $x_v y_v$ plane. Surface S_1 is closest at this position, so its surface intensity value at (x, y) is saved.

We can implement the depth-buffer algorithm in normalized coordinates, so that z values range from 0 at the back clipping plane to z_{max} at the front clip-

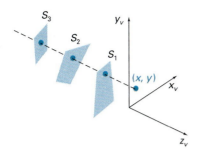

Figure 13-4
At view-plane position (x, y),
surface S_1 has the smallest depth
from the view plane and so is
visible at that position.

ping plane. The value of z_{max} can be set either to 1 (for a unit cube) or to the largest value that can be stored on the system.

As implied by the name of this method, two buffer areas are required. A depth buffer is used to store depth values for each (x, y) position as surfaces are processed, and the refresh buffer stores the intensity values for each position. Initially, all positions in the depth buffer are set to 0 (minimum depth), and the refresh buffer is initialized to the background intensity. Each surface listed in the polygon tables is then processed, one scan line at a time, calculating the depth (z value) at each (x, y) pixel position. The calculated depth is compared to the value previously stored in the depth buffer at that position. If the calculated depth is greater than the value stored in the depth buffer, the new depth value is stored, and the surface intensity at that position is determined and placed in the same xy location in the refresh buffer.

We summarize the steps of a depth-buffer algorithm as follows:

1. Initialize the depth buffer and refresh buffer so that for all buffer positions (x, y),

$$\text{depth}(x, y) = 0, \qquad \text{refresh}(x, y) = I_{backgnd}$$

2. For each position on each polygon surface, compare depth values to previously stored values in the depth buffer to determine visibility.

   - Calculate the depth z for each (x, y) position on the polygon.
   - If $z > \text{depth}(x, y)$, then set

$$\text{depth}(x, y) = z, \qquad \text{refresh}(x, y) = I_{surf}(x,y)$$

   where $I_{backgnd}$ is the value for the background intensity, and $I_{surf}(x,y)$ is the projected intensity value for the surface at pixel position (x,y). After all surfaces have been processed, the depth buffer contains depth values for the visible surfaces and the refresh buffer contains the corresponding intensity values for those surfaces.

Depth values for a surface position (x, y) are calculated from the plane equation for each surface:

$$z = \frac{-Ax - By - D}{C} \qquad (13\text{-}4)$$

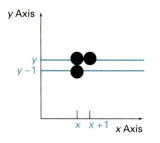

For any scan line (Fig. 13-5), adjacent horizontal positions across the line differ by 1, and a vertical y value on an adjacent scan line differs by 1. If the depth of position (x, y) has been determined to be z, then the depth z' of the next position $(x + 1, y)$ along the scan line is obtained from Eq. 13-4 as

$$z' = \frac{-A(x + 1) - By - D}{C} \tag{13-5}$$

or

$$z' = z - \frac{A}{C} \tag{13-6}$$

The ratio $-A/C$ is constant for each surface, so succeeding depth values across a scan line are obtained from preceding values with a single addition.

On each scan line, we start by calculating the depth on a left edge of the polygon that intersects that scan line (Fig. 13-6). Depth values at each successive position across the scan line are then calculated by Eq. 13-6.

We first determine the y-coordinate extents of each polygon, and process the surface from the topmost scan line to the bottom scan line, as shown in Fig. 13-6. Starting at a top vertex, we can recursively calculate x positions down a left edge of the polygon as $x' = x - 1/m$, where m is the slope of the edge (Fig. 13-7). Depth values down the edge are then obtained recursively as

$$z' = z + \frac{A/m + B}{C} \tag{13-7}$$

If we are processing down a vertical edge, the slope is infinite and the recursive calculations reduce to

$$z' = z + \frac{B}{C}$$

An alternate approach is to use a midpoint method or Bresenham-type algorithm for determining x values on left edges for each scan line. Also the method can be applied to curved surfaces by determining depth and intensity values at each surface projection point.

For polygon surfaces, the depth-buffer method is very easy to implement, and it requires no sorting of the surfaces in a scene. But it does require the availability of a second buffer in addition to the refresh buffer. A system with a resolu-

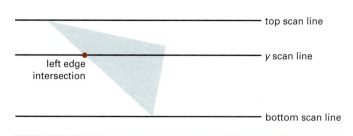

top scan line

left edge intersection

y scan line

bottom scan line

Figure 13-6
Scan lines intersecting a polygon surface.

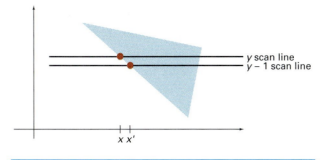

Figure 13-7

Intersection positions on successive scan lines along a left polygon edge.

tion of 1024 by 1024, for example, would require over a million positions in the depth buffer, with each position containing enough bits to represent the number of depth increments needed. One way to reduce storage requirements is to process one section of the scene at a time, using a smaller depth buffer. After each view section is processed, the buffer is reused for the next section.

13-4

A-BUFFER METHOD

An extension of the ideas in the depth-buffer method is the **A-buffer method** (at the other end of the alphabet from "z-buffer", where z represents depth). The A-buffer method represents an *antialiased, area-averaged, accumulation-buffer* method developed by Lucasfilm for implementation in the surface-rendering system called REYES (an acronym for "Renders Everything You Ever Saw").

A drawback of the depth-buffer method is that it can only find one visible surface at each pixel position. In other words, it deals only with opaque surfaces and cannot accumulate intensity values for more than one surface, as is necessary if transparent surfaces are to be displayed (Fig. 13-8). The A-buffer method expands the depth buffer so that each position in the buffer can reference a linked list of surfaces. Thus, more than one surface intensity can be taken into consideration at each pixel position, and object edges can be antialiased.

Each position in the A-buffer has two fields:

- depth field — stores a positive or negative real number
- intensity field — stores surface-intensity information or a pointer value.

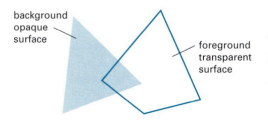

Figure 13-8

Viewing an opaque surface through a transparent surface requires multiple surface-intensity contributions for pixel positions.

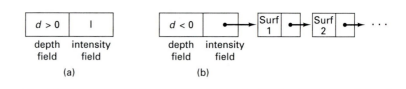

Figure 13-9

Organization of an A-buffer pixel position: (a) single-surface overlap of the corresponding pixel area, and (b) multiple-surface overlap.

If the depth field is positive, the number stored at that position is the depth of a single surface overlapping the corresponding pixel area. The intensity field then stores the RGB components of the surface color at that point and the percent of pixel coverage, as illustrated in Fig. 13-9(a).

If the depth field is negative, this indicates multiple-surface contributions to the pixel intensity. The intensity field then stores a pointer to a linked list of surface data, as in Fig. 13-9(b). Data for each surface in the linked list includes

- RGB intensity components
- opacity parameter (percent of transparency)
- depth
- percent of area coverage
- surface identifier
- other surface-rendering parameters
- pointer to next surface

The A-buffer can be constructed using methods similar to those in the depth-buffer algorithm. Scan lines are processed to determine surface overlaps of pixels across the individual scanlines. Surfaces are subdivided into a polygon mesh and clipped against the pixel boundaries. Using the opacity factors and percent of surface overlaps, we can calculate the intensity of each pixel as an average of the contributions from the overlapping surfaces.

13-5
SCAN-LINE METHOD

This image-space method for removing hidden surfaces is an extension of the scan-line algorithm for filling polygon interiors. Instead of filling just one surface, we now deal with multiple surfaces. As each scan line is processed, all polygon surfaces intersecting that line are examined to determine which are visible. Across each scan line, depth calculations are made for each overlapping surface to determine which is nearest to the view plane. When the visible surface has been determined, the intensity value for that position is entered into the refresh buffer.

We assume that tables are set up for the various surfaces, as discussed in Chapter 10, which include both an edge table and a polygon table. The edge table contains coordinate endpoints for each line in the scene, the inverse slope of each line, and pointers into the polygon table to identify the surfaces bounded by each line. The polygon table contains coefficients of the plane equation for each surface, intensity information for the surfaces, and possibly pointers into the edge table. To facilitate the search for surfaces crossing a given scan line, we can set up an active list of edges from information in the edge table. This active list will contain only edges that cross the current scan line, sorted in order of increasing x. In addition, we define a flag for each surface that is set on or off to indicate whether a position along a scan line is inside or outside of the surface. Scan lines are processed from left to right. At the leftmost boundary of a surface, the surface flag is turned on; and at the rightmost boundary, it is turned off.

Figure 13-10 illustrates the scan-line method for locating visible portions of surfaces for pixel positions along the line. The active list for scan line 1 contains information from the edge table for edges AB, BC, EH, and FG. For positions along this scan line between edges AB and BC, only the flag for surface S_1 is on. Therefore, no depth calculations are necessary, and intensity information for surface S_1 is entered from the polygon table into the refresh buffer. Similarly, between edges EH and FG, only the flag for surface S_2 is on. No other positions along scan line 1 intersect surfaces, so the intensity values in the other areas are set to the background intensity. The background intensity can be loaded throughout the buffer in an initialization routine.

For scan lines 2 and 3 in Fig. 13-10, the active edge list contains edges AD, EH, BC, and FG. Along scan line 2 from edge AD to edge EH, only the flag for surface S_1 is on. But between edges EH and BC, the flags for both surfaces are on. In this interval, depth calculations must be made using the plane coefficients for the two surfaces. For this example, the depth of surface S_1 is assumed to be less than that of S_2, so intensities for surface S_1 are loaded into the refresh buffer until boundary BC is encountered. Then the flag for surface S_1 goes off, and intensities for surface S_2 are stored until edge FG is passed.

We can take advantage of coherence along the scan lines as we pass from one scan line to the next. In Fig. 13-10, scan line 3 has the same active list of edges as scan line 2. Since no changes have occurred in line intersections, it is unnecessary again to make depth calculations between edges EH and BC. The two sur-

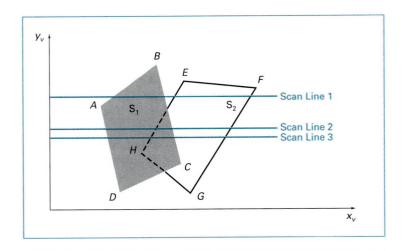

Figure 13-10
Scan lines crossing the projection of two surfaces, S_1 and S_2, in the view plane. Dashed lines indicate the boundaries of hidden surfaces.

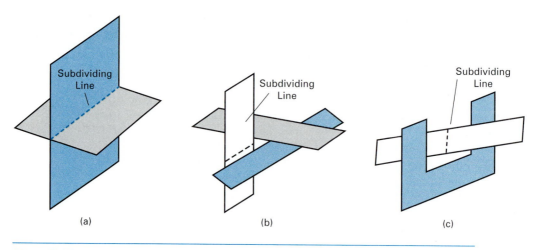

Figure 13-11
Intersecting and cyclically overlapping surfaces that alternately obscure one another.

faces must be in the same orientation as determined on scan line 2, so the intensities for surface S_1 can be entered without further calculations.

Any number of overlapping polygon surfaces can be processed with this scan-line method. Flags for the surfaces are set to indicate whether a position is inside or outside, and depth calculations are performed when surfaces overlap. When these coherence methods are used, we need to be careful to keep track of which surface section is visible on each scan line. This works only if surfaces do not cut through or otherwise cyclically overlap each other (Fig. 13-11). If any kind of cyclic overlap is present in a scene, we can divide the surfaces to eliminate the overlaps. The dashed lines in this figure indicate where planes could be subdivided to form two distinct surfaces, so that the cyclic overlaps are eliminated.

13-6
DEPTH-SORTING METHOD

Using both image-space and object-space operations, the **depth-sorting method** performs the following basic functions:

1. Surfaces are sorted in order of decreasing depth.
2. Surfaces are scan converted in order, starting with the surface of greatest depth.

Sorting operations are carried out in both image and object space, and the scan conversion of the polygon surfaces is performed in image space.

This method for solving the hidden-surface problem is often referred to as the **painter's algorithm**. In creating an oil painting, an artist first paints the background colors. Next, the most distant objects are added, then the nearer objects, and so forth. At the final step, the foreground objects are painted on the canvas over the background and other objects that have been painted on the canvas.

Each layer of paint covers up the previous layer. Using a similar technique, we first sort surfaces according to their distance from the view plane. The intensity values for the farthest surface are then entered into the refresh buffer. Taking each succeeding surface in turn (in decreasing depth order), we "paint" the surface intensities onto the frame buffer over the intensities of the previously processed surfaces.

Painting polygon surfaces onto the frame buffer according to depth is carried out in several steps. Assuming we are viewing along the $-z$ direction, surfaces are ordered on the first pass according to the smallest z value on each surface. Surface S with the greatest depth is then compared to the other surfaces in the list to determine whether there are any overlaps in depth. If no depth overlaps occur, S is scan converted. Figure 13-12 shows two surfaces that overlap in the xy plane but have no depth overlap. This process is then repeated for the next surface in the list. As long as no overlaps occur, each surface is processed in depth order until all have been scan converted. If a depth overlap is detected at any point in the list, we need to make some additional comparisons to determine whether any of the surfaces should be reordered.

We make the following tests for each surface that overlaps with S. If any one of these tests is true, no reordering is necessary for that surface. The tests are listed in order of increasing difficulty.

1. The bounding rectangles in the xy plane for the two surfaces do not overlap.
2. Surface S is completely behind the overlapping surface relative to the viewing position.
3. The overlapping surface is completely in front of S relative to the viewing position.
4. The projections of the two surfaces onto the view plane do not overlap.

We perform these tests in the order listed and proceed to the next overlapping surface as soon as we find one of the tests is true. If all the overlapping surfaces pass at least one of these tests, none of them is behind S. No reordering is then necessary and S is scan converted.

Test 1 is performed in two parts. We first check for overlap in the x direction, then we check for overlap in the y direction. If either of these directions show no overlap, the two planes cannot obscure one other. An example of two

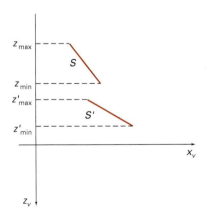

Figure 13-12
Two surfaces with no depth overlap.

479

surfaces that overlap in the z direction but not in the x direction is shown in Fig. 13-13.

We can perform tests 2 and 3 with an "inside-outside" polygon test. That is, we substitute the coordinates for all vertices of S into the plane equation for the overlapping surface and check the sign of the result. If the plane equations are set up so that the outside of the surface is toward the viewing position, then S is behind S' if all vertices of S are "inside" S' (Fig. 13-14). Similarly, S' is completely in front of S if all vertices of S are "outside" of S'. Figure 13-15 shows an overlapping surface S' that is completely in front of S, but surface S is not completely "inside" S' (test 2 is not true).

If tests 1 through 3 have all failed, we try test 4 by checking for intersections between the bounding edges of the two surfaces using line equations in the xy plane. As demonstrated in Fig. 13-16, two surfaces may or may not intersect even though their coordinate extents overlap in the x, y, and z directions.

Should all four tests fail with a particular overlapping surface S', we interchange surfaces S and S' in the sorted list. An example of two surfaces that

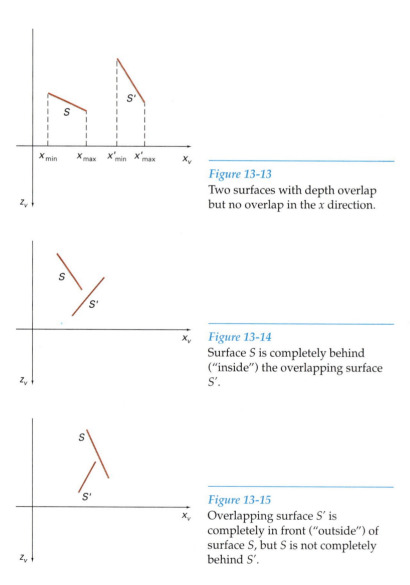

Figure 13-13
Two surfaces with depth overlap but no overlap in the x direction.

Figure 13-14
Surface S is completely behind ("inside") the overlapping surface S'.

Figure 13-15
Overlapping surface S' is completely in front ("outside") of surface S, but S is not completely behind S'.

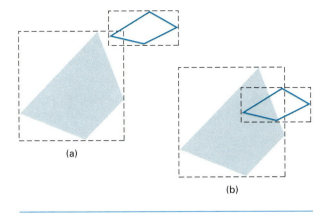

(a)

(b)

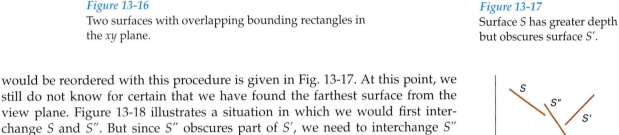

Figure 13-16
Two surfaces with overlapping bounding rectangles in the xy plane.

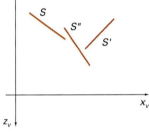

Figure 13-17
Surface S has greater depth but obscures surface S'.

would be reordered with this procedure is given in Fig. 13-17. At this point, we still do not know for certain that we have found the farthest surface from the view plane. Figure 13-18 illustrates a situation in which we would first interchange S and S''. But since S'' obscures part of S', we need to interchange S'' and S' to get the three surfaces into the correct depth order. Therefore, we need to repeat the testing process for each surface that is reordered in the list.

It is possible for the algorithm just outlined to get into an infinite loop if two or more surfaces alternately obscure each other, as in Fig. 13-11. In such situations, the algorithm would continually reshuffle the positions of the overlapping surfaces. To avoid such loops, we can flag any surface that has been reordered to a farther depth position so that it cannot be moved again. If an attempt is made to switch the surface a second time, we divide it into two parts to eliminate the cyclic overlap. The original surface is then replaced by the two new surfaces, and we continue processing as before.

Figure 13-18
Three surfaces entered into the sorted surface list in the order S, S', S'' should be reordered S', S'', S.

13-7
BSP-TREE METHOD

A **binary space-partitioning (BSP)** tree is an efficient method for determining object visibility by painting surfaces onto the screen from back to front, as in the painter's algorithm. The BSP tree is particularly useful when the view reference point changes, but the objects in a scene are at fixed positions.

Applying a BSP tree to visibility testing involves identifying surfaces that are "inside" and "outside" the partitioning plane at each step of the space subdivision, relative to the viewing direction. Figure 13-19 illustrates the basic concept in this algorithm. With plane P_1, we first partition the space into two sets of objects. One set of objects is behind, or in back of, plane P_1 relative to the viewing direction, and the other set is in front of P_1. Since one object is intersected by plane P_1, we divide that object into two separate objects, labeled A and B. Objects A and C are in front of P_1, and objects B and D are behind P_1. We next partition the space again with plane P_2 and construct the binary tree representation shown in Fig. 13-19(b). In this tree, the objects are represented as terminal nodes, with front objects as left branches and back objects as right branches.

481

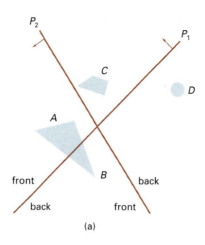

(a)

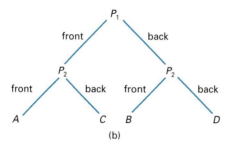

(b)

Figure 13-19
A region of space (a) is partitioned with two planes P_1 and P_2 to form the BSP tree representation in (b).

For objects described with polygon facets, we chose the partitioning planes to coincide with the polygon planes. The polygon equations are then used to identify "inside" and "outside" polygons, and the tree is constructed with one partitioning plane for each polygon face. Any polygon intersected by a partitioning plane is split into two parts. When the BSP tree is complete, we process the tree by selecting the surfaces for display in the order back to front, so that foreground objects are painted over the background objects. Fast hardware implementations for constructing and processing BSP trees are used in some systems.

13-8

AREA-SUBDIVISION METHOD

This technique for hidden-surface removal is essentially an image-space method, but object-space operations can be used to accomplish depth ordering of surfaces. The **area-subdivision method** takes advantage of area coherence in a scene by locating those view areas that represent part of a single surface. We apply this method by successively dividing the total viewing area into smaller and smaller rectangles until each small area is the projection of part of a single visible surface or no surface at all.

To implement this method, we need to establish tests that can quickly identify the area as part of a single surface or tell us that the area is too complex to analyze easily. Starting with the total view, we apply the tests to determine whether we should subdivide the total area into smaller rectangles. If the tests indicate that the view is sufficiently complex, we subdivide it. Next, we apply the tests to each of the smaller areas, subdividing these if the tests indicate that visibility of a single surface is still uncertain. We continue this process until the subdivisions are easily analyzed as belonging to a single surface or until they are reduced to the size of a single pixel. An easy way to do this is to successively divide the area into four equal parts at each step, as shown in Fig. 13-20. This approach is similar to that used in constructing a quadtree. A viewing area with a resolution of 1024 by 1024 could be subdivided ten times in this way before a subarea is reduced to a point.

Tests to determine the visibility of a single surface within a specified area are made by comparing surfaces to the boundary of the area. There are four possible relationships that a surface can have with a specified area boundary. We can describe these relative surface characteristics in the following way (Fig. 13-21):

Surrounding surface—One that completely encloses the area.
Overlapping surface—One that is partly inside and partly outside the area.
Inside surface—One that is completely inside the area.
Outside surface—One that is completely outside the area.

The tests for determining surface visibility within an area can be stated in terms of these four classifications. No further subdivisions of a specified area are needed if one of the following conditions is true:

1. All surfaces are outside surfaces with respect to the area.
2. Only one inside, overlapping, or surrounding surface is in the area.
3. A surrounding surface obscures all other surfaces within the area boundaries.

Test 1 can be carried out by checking the bounding rectangles of all surfaces against the area boundaries. Test 2 can also use the bounding rectangles in the xy plane to identify an inside surface. For other types of surfaces, the bounding rectangles can be used as an initial check. If a single bounding rectangle intersects the area in some way, additional checks are used to determine whether the surface is surrounding, overlapping, or outside. Once a single inside, overlapping, or surrounding surface has been identified, its pixel intensities are transferred to the appropriate area within the frame buffer.

One method for implementing test 3 is to order surfaces according to their minimum depth from the view plane. For each surrounding surface, we then compute the maximum depth within the area under consideration. If the maxi-

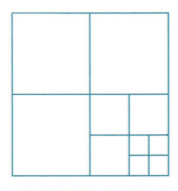

Figure 13-20
Dividing a square area into equal-sized quadrants at each step.

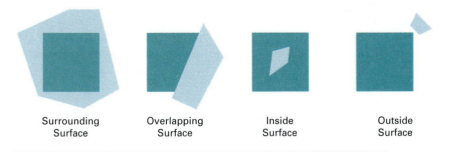

| Surrounding Surface | Overlapping Surface | Inside Surface | Outside Surface |

Figure 13-21
Possible relationships between polygon surfaces and a rectangular area.

483

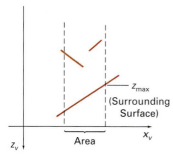

Figure 13-22
Within a specified area, a surrounding surface with a maximum depth of z_{max} obscures all surfaces that have a minimum depth beyond z_{max}.

mum depth of one of these surrounding surfaces is closer to the view plane than the minimum depth of all other surfaces within the area, test 3 is satisfied. Figure 13-22 shows an example of the conditions for this method.

Another method for carrying out test 3 that does not require depth sorting is to use plane equations to calculate depth values at the four vertices of the area for all surrounding, overlapping, and inside surfaces. If the calculated depths for one of the surrounding surfaces is less than the calculated depths for all other surfaces, test 3 is true. Then the area can be filled with the intensity values of the surrounding surface.

For some situations, both methods of implementing test 3 will fail to identify correctly a surrounding surface that obscures all the other surfaces. Further testing could be carried out to identify the single surface that covers the area, but it is faster to subdivide the area than to continue with more complex testing. Once outside and surrounding surfaces have been identified for an area, they will remain outside and surrounding surfaces for all subdivisions of the area. Furthermore, some inside and overlapping surfaces can be expected to be eliminated as the subdivision process continues, so that the areas become easier to analyze. In the limiting case, when a subdivision the size of a pixel is produced, we simply calculate the depth of each relevant surface at that point and transfer the intensity of the nearest surface to the frame buffer.

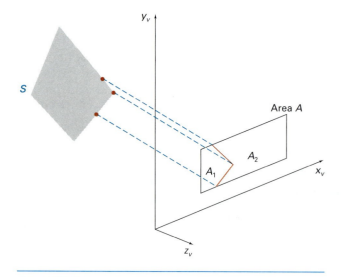

Figure 13-23
Area A is subdivided into A_1 and A_2 using the boundary of surface S on the view plane.

As a variation on the basic subdivision process, we could subdivide areas along surface boundaries instead of dividing them in half. If the surfaces have been sorted according to minimum depth, we can use the surface with the smallest depth value to subdivide a given area. Figure 13-23 illustrates this method for subdividing areas. The projection of the boundary of surface S is used to partition the original area into the subdivisions A_1 and A_2. Surface S is then a surrounding surface for A_1 and visibility tests 2 and 3 can be applied to determine whether further subdividing is necessary. In general, fewer subdivisions are required using this approach, but more processing is needed to subdivide areas and to analyze the relation of surfaces to the subdivision boundaries.

13-9
OCTREE METHODS

When an octree representation is used for the viewing volume, hidden-surface elimination is accomplished by projecting octree nodes onto the viewing surface in a front-to-back order. In Fig. 13-24, the front face of a region of space (the side toward the viewer) is formed with octants 0, 1, 2, and 3. Surfaces in the front of these octants are visible to the viewer. Any surfaces toward the rear of the front octants or in the back octants (4, 5, 6, and 7) may be hidden by the front surfaces.

Back surfaces are eliminated, for the viewing direction given in Fig. 13-24, by processing data elements in the octree nodes in the order 0, 1, 2, 3, 4, 5, 6, 7. This results in a depth-first traversal of the octree, so that nodes representing octants 0, 1, 2, and 3 for the entire region are visited before the nodes representing octants 4, 5, 6, and 7. Similarly, the nodes for the front four suboctants of octant 0 are visited before the nodes for the four back suboctants. The traversal of the octree continues in this order for each octant subdivision.

When a color value is encountered in an octree node, the pixel area in the frame buffer corresponding to this node is assigned that color value only if no values have previously been stored in this area. In this way, only the front colors are loaded into the buffer. Nothing is loaded if an area is void. Any node that is found to be completely obscured is eliminated from further processing, so that its subtrees are not accessed.

Different views of objects represented as octrees can be obtained by applying transformations to the octree representation that reorient the object according

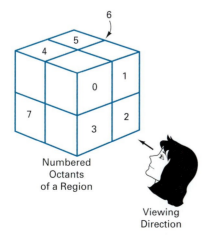

Numbered
Octants
of a Region

Viewing
Direction

Figure 13-24
Objects in octants 0, 1, 2, and 3 obscure objects in the back octants (4, 5, 6, 7) when the viewing direction is as shown.

485

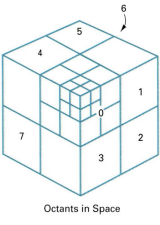

Octants in Space

to the view selected. We assume that the octree representation is always set up so that octants 0, 1, 2, and 3 of a region form the front face, as in Fig. 13-24.

A method for displaying an octree is first to map the octree onto a quadtree of visible areas by traversing octree nodes from front to back in a recursive procedure. Then the quadtree representation for the visible surfaces is loaded into the frame buffer. Figure 13-25 depicts the octants in a region of space and the corresponding quadrants on the view plane. Contributions to quadrant 0 come from octants 0 and 4. Color values in quadrant 1 are obtained from surfaces in octants 1 and 5, and values in each of the other two quadrants are generated from the pair of octants aligned with each of these quadrants.

Recursive processing of octree nodes is demonstrated in the following procedure, which accepts an octree description and creates the quadtree representation for visible surfaces in the region. In most cases, both a front and a back octant must be considered in determining the correct color values for a quadrant. But if the front octant is homogeneously filled with some color, we do not process the back octant. For heterogeneous regions, the procedure is recursively called, passing as new arguments the child of the heterogeneous octant and a newly created quadtree node. If the front is empty, the rear octant is processed. Otherwise, two recursive calls are made, one for the rear octant and one for the front octant.

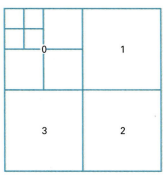

Quadrants for
the View Plane

Figure 13-25
Octant divisions for a region of space and the corresponding quadrant plane.

```
typedef enum { SOLID, MIXED } Status;

#define EMPTY -1

typedef struct tOctree {
  int id;
  Status status;
  union {
    int color;
    struct tOctree * children[8];
  } data;
} Octree;

typedef struct tQuadtree {
  int id;
  Status status;
  union {
    int color;
    struct tQuadtree * children[4];
  } data;
} Quadtree;

int nQuadtree = 0;

void octreeToQuadtree (Octree * oTree, Quadtree * qTree)
{
  Octree * front, * back;
  Quadtree * newQuadtree;
  int i, j;

  if (oTree->status == SOLID) {
    qTree->status = SOLID;
    qTree->data.color = oTree->data.color;
    return;
  }
  qTree->status = MIXED;
  /* Fill in each quad of the quadtree */
  for (i=0; i<4; i++) {
    front = oTree->data.children[i];
```

```
    back = oTree->data.children[i+4];
    newQuadtree = (Quadtree *) malloc (sizeof (Quadtree));
    newQuadtree->id = nQuadtree++;
    newQuadtree->status = SOLID;
    qTree->data.children[i] = newQuadtree;

    if (front->status == SOLID)
      if (front->data.color != EMPTY)
        qTree->data.children[i]->data.color = front->data.color;
      else
        if (back->status == SOLID)
          if (back->data.color != EMPTY)
            qTree->data.children[i]->data.color = back->data.color;
          else
            qTree->data.children[i]->data.color = EMPTY;
        else { /* back node is mixed */
          newQuadtree->status = MIXED;
          octreeToQuadtree (back, newQuadtree);
        }
    else { /* front node is mixed */
      newQuadtree->status = MIXED;
      octreeToQuadtree (back, newQuadtree);
      octreeToQuadtree (front, newQuadtree);
    }
  }
}
```

13-10
RAY-CASTING METHOD

If we consider the line of sight from a pixel position on the view plane through a scene, as in Fig. 13-26, we can determine which objects in the scene (if any) intersect this line. After calculating all ray–surface intersections, we identify the visible surface as the one whose intersection point is closest to the pixel. This visibility-detection scheme uses *ray-casting procedures* that were introduced in Section 10-15. Ray casting, as a visibility-detection tool, is based on geometric optics methods, which trace the paths of light rays. Since there are an infinite number of light rays in a scene and we are interested only in those rays that pass through

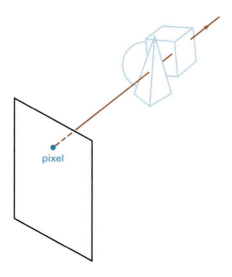

pixel

Figure 13-26
A ray along the line of sight from a pixel position through a scene.

487

pixel positions, we can trace the light-ray paths backward from the pixels through the scene. The ray-casting approach is an effective visibility-detection method for scenes with curved surfaces, particularly spheres.

We can think of ray casting as a variation on the depth-buffer method (Section 13-3). In the depth-buffer algorithm, we process surfaces one at a time and calculate depth values for all projection points over the surface. The calculated surface depths are then compared to previously stored depths to determine visible surfaces at each pixel. In ray-casting, we process pixels one at a time and calculate depths for all surfaces along the projection path to that pixel.

Ray casting is a special case of *ray-tracing algorithms* (Section 14-6) that trace multiple ray paths to pick up global reflection and refraction contributions from multiple objects in a scene. With ray casting, we only follow a ray out from each pixel to the nearest object. Efficient ray–surface intersection calculations have been developed for common objects, particularly spheres, and we discuss these intersection methods in detail in Chapter 14.

13-11
CURVED SURFACES

Effective methods for determining visibility for objects with curved surfaces include ray-casting and octree methods. With ray casting, we calculate ray–surface intersections and locate the smallest intersection distance along the pixel ray. With octrees, once the representation has been established from the input definition of the objects, all visible surfaces are identified with the same processing procedures. No special considerations need be given to different kinds of curved surfaces.

We can also approximate a curved surface as a set of plane, polygon surfaces. In the list of surfaces, we then replace each curved surface with a polygon mesh and use one of the other hidden-surface methods previously discussed. With some objects, such as spheres, it can be more efficient as well as more accurate to use ray casting and the curved-surface equation.

Curved-Surface Representations

We can represent a surface with an implicit equation of the form $f(x, y, z) = 0$ or with a parametric representation (Appendix A). Spline surfaces, for instance, are normally described with parametric equations. In some cases, it is useful to obtain an explicit surface equation, as, for example, a height function over an xy ground plane:

$$z = f(x, y)$$

Many objects of interest, such as spheres, ellipsoids, cylinders, and cones, have quadratic representations. These surfaces are commonly used to model molecular structures, roller bearings, rings, and shafts.

Scan-line and ray-casting algorithms often involve numerical approximation techniques to solve the surface equation at the intersection point with a scan line or with a pixel ray. Various techniques, including parallel calculations and fast hardware implementations, have been developed for solving the curved-surface equations for commonly used objects.

Surface Contour Plots

For many applications in mathematics, physical sciences, engineering and other fields, it is useful to display a surface function with a set of contour lines that show the surface shape. The surface may be described with an equation or with data tables, such as topographic data on elevations or population density. With an explicit functional representation, we can plot the visible-surface contour lines and eliminate those contour sections that are hidden by the visible parts of the surface.

To obtain an xy plot of a functional surface, we write the surface representation in the form

$$y = f(x, z) \qquad (13-8)$$

A curve in the xy plane can then be plotted for values of z within some selected range, using a specified interval Δz. Starting with the largest value of z, we plot the curves from "front" to "back" and eliminate hidden sections. We draw the curve sections on the screen by mapping an xy range for the function into an xy pixel screen range. Then, unit steps are taken in x and the corresponding y value for each x value is determined from Eq. 13-8 for a given value of z.

One way to identify the visible curve sections on the surface is to maintain a list of y_{min} and y_{max} values previously calculated for the pixel x coordinates on the screen. As we step from one pixel x position to the next, we check the calculated y value against the stored range, y_{min} and y_{max}, for the next pixel. If $y_{min} \leq y \leq y_{max}$, that point on the surface is not visible and we do not plot it. But if the calculated y value is outside the stored y bounds for that pixel, the point is visible. We then plot the point and reset the bounds for that pixel. Similar procedures can be used to project the contour plot onto the xz or the yz plane. Figure 13-27 shows an example of a surface contour plot with color-coded contour lines.

Similar methods can be used with a discrete set of data points by determining isosurface lines. For example, if we have a discrete set of z values for an n_x by n_y grid of xy values, we can determine the path of a line of constant z over the surface using the contour methods discussed in Section 10-21. Each selected contour line can then be projected onto a view plane and displayed with straight-line

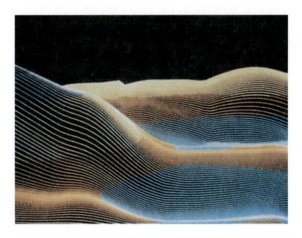

Figure 13-27
A color-coded surface contour plot. (*Courtesy of Los Alamos National Laboratory.*)

segments. Again, lines can be drawn on the display device in a front-to-back depth order, and we eliminate contour sections that pass behind previously drawn (visible) contour lines.

13-12
WIREFRAME METHODS

When only the outline of an object is to be displayed, visibility tests are applied to surface edges. Visible edge sections are displayed, and hidden edge sections can either be eliminated or displayed differently from the visible edges. For example, hidden edges could be drawn as dashed lines, or we could use depth cueing to decrease the intensity of the lines as a linear function of distance from the view plane. Procedures for determining visibility of object edges are referred to as **wireframe-visibility methods.** They are also called **visible-line detection methods** or **hidden-line detection methods.** Special wireframe-visibility procedures have been developed, but some of the visible-surface methods discussed in preceding sections can also be used to test for edge visibility.

A direct approach to identifying the visible lines in a scene is to compare each line to each surface. The process involved here is similar to clipping lines against arbitrary window shapes, except that we now want to determine which sections of the lines are hidden by surfaces. For each line, depth values are compared to the surfaces to determine which line sections are not visible. We can use coherence methods to identify hidden line segments without actually testing each coordinate position. If both line intersections with the projection of a surface boundary have greater depth than the surface at those points, the line segment between the intersections is completely hidden, as in Fig. 13-28(a). This is the usual situation in a scene, but it is also possible to have lines and surfaces intersecting each other. When a line has greater depth at one boundary intersection and less depth than the surface at the other boundary intersection, the line must penetrate the surface interior, as in Fig. 13-28(b). In this case, we calculate the intersection point of the line with the surface using the plane equation and display only the visible sections.

Some visible-surface methods are readily adapted to wireframe visibility testing. Using a back-face method, we could identify all the back surfaces of an object and display only the boundaries for the visible surfaces. With depth sorting, surfaces can be painted into the refresh buffer so that surface interiors are in the background color, while boundaries are in the foreground color. By processing the surfaces from back to front, hidden lines are erased by the nearer surfaces. An area-subdivision method can be adapted to hidden-line removal by displaying only the boundaries of visible surfaces. Scan-line methods can be used to display visible lines by setting points along the scan line that coincide with boundaries of visible surfaces. Any visible-surface method that uses scan conversion can be modified to an edge-visibility detection method in a similar way.

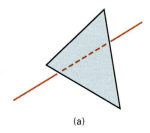

(a)

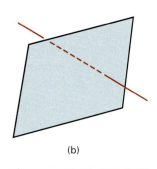

(b)

Figure 13-28
Hidden-line sections (dashed) for a line that (a) passes behind a surface and (b) penetrates a surface.

13-13
VISIBILITY-DETECTION FUNCTIONS

Often, three-dimensional graphics packages accommodate several visible-surface detection procedures, particularly the back-face and depth-buffer methods. A particular function can then be invoked with the procedure name, such as `back-Face` or `depthBuffer`.

In general programming standards, such as GKS and PHIGS, visibility methods are implementation-dependent. A table of available methods is listed at each installation, and a particular visibility-detection method is selected with the hidden-line-hidden-surface-removal (HLHSR) function:

```
setHLHSRidentifier (visibilityFunctionIndex)
```

Parameter visibilityFunctionIndex is assigned an integer code to identify the visibility method that is to be applied to subsequently specified output primitives.

SUMMARY

Here, we give a summary of the visibility-detection methods discussed in this chapter and a comparison of their effectiveness. Back-face detection is fast and effective as an initial screening to eliminate many polygons from further visibility tests. For a single convex polyhedron, back-face detection eliminates all hidden surfaces, but in general, back-face detection cannot completely identify all hidden surfaces. Other, more involved, visibility-detection schemes will correctly produce a list of visible surfaces.

A fast and simple technique for identifying visible surfaces is the depth-buffer (or z-buffer) method. This procedure requires two buffers, one for the pixel intensities and one for the depth of the visible surface for each pixel in the view plane. Fast incremental methods are used to scan each surface in a scene to calculate surface depths. As each surface is processed, the two buffers are updated. An improvement on the depth-buffer approach is the A-buffer, which provides additional information for displaying antialiased and transparent surfaces. Other visible-surface detection schemes include the scan-line method, the depth-sorting method (painter's algorithm), the BSP-tree method, area subdivision, octree methods, and ray casting.

Visibility-detection methods are also used in displaying three-dimensional line drawings. With curved surfaces, we can display contour plots. For wireframe displays of polyhedrons, we search for the various edge sections of the surfaces in a scene that are visible from the view plane.

The effectiveness of a visible-surface detection method depends on the characteristics of a particular application. If the surfaces in a scene are spread out in the z direction so that there is very little depth overlap, a depth-sorting or BSP-tree method is often the best choice. For scenes with surfaces fairly well separated horizontally, a scan-line or area-subdivision method can be used efficiently to locate visible surfaces.

As a general rule, the depth-sorting or BSP-tree method is a highly effective approach for scenes with only a few surfaces. This is because these scenes usually have few surfaces that overlap in depth. The scan-line method also performs well when a scene contains a small number of surfaces. Either the scan-line, depth-sorting, or BSP-tree method can be used effectively for scenes with up to several thousand polygon surfaces. With scenes that contain more than a few thousand surfaces, the depth-buffer method or octree approach performs best. The depth-buffer method has a nearly constant processing time, independent of the number of surfaces in a scene. This is because the size of the surface areas decreases as the number of surfaces in the scene increases. Therefore, the depth-buffer method exhibits relatively low performance with simple scenes and relatively high perfor-

491

mance with complex scenes. BSP trees are useful when multiple views are to be generated using different view reference points.

When octree representations are used in a system, the hidden-surface elimination process is fast and simple. Only integer additions and subtractions are used in the process, and there is no need to perform sorting or intersection calculations. Another advantage of octrees is that they store more than surfaces. The entire solid region of an object is available for display, which makes the octree representation useful for obtaining cross-sectional slices of solids.

If a scene contains curved-surface representations, we use octree or ray-casting methods to identify visible parts of the scene. Ray-casting methods are an integral part of ray-tracing algorithms, which allow scenes to be displayed with global-illumination effects.

It is possible to combine and implement the different visible-surface detection methods in various ways. In addition, visibility-detection algorithms are often implemented in hardware, and special systems utilizing parallel processing are employed to increase the efficiency of these methods. Special hardware systems are used when processing speed is an especially important consideration, as in the generation of animated views for flight simulators.

REFERENCES

Additional sources of information on visibility algorithms include Elber and Cohen (1990), Franklin and Kankanhalli (1990), Glassner (1990), Naylor, Amanatides, and Thibault (1990), and Segal (1990).

EXERCISES

13-1. Develop a procedure, based on a back-face detection technique, for identifying all the visible faces of a convex polyhedron that has different-colored surfaces. Assume that the object is defined in a right-handed viewing system with the *xy*-plane as the viewing surface.

13-2. Implement a back-face detection procedure using an orthographic parallel projection to view visible faces of a convex polyhedron. Assume that all parts of the object are in front of the view plane, and provide a mapping onto a screen viewport for display.

13-3. Implement a back-face detection procedure using a perspective projection to view visible faces of a convex polyhedron. Assume that all parts of the object are in front of the view plane, and provide a mapping onto a screen viewport for display.

13-4. Write a program to produce an animation of a convex polyhedron. The object is to be rotated incrementally about an axis that passes through the object and is parallel to the view plane. Assume that the object lies completely in front of the view plane. Use an orthographic parallel projection to map the views successively onto the view plane.

13-5. Implement the depth-buffer method to display the visible surfaces of a given polyhedron. How can the storage requirements for the depth buffer be determined from the definition of the objects to be displayed?

13-6. Implement the depth-buffer method to display the visible surfaces in a scene containing any number of polyhedrons. Set up efficient methods for storing and processing the various objects in the scene.

13-7. Implement the A-buffer algorithm to display a scene containing both opaque and transparent surfaces. As an optional feature, your algorithm may be extended to include antialiasing.

13-8. Develop a program to implement the scan-line algorithm for displaying the visible surfaces of a given polyhedron. Use polygon and edge tables to store the definition of the object, and use coherence techniques to evaluate points along and between scan lines.

13-9. Write a program to implement the scan-line algorithm for a scene containing several polyhedrons. Use polygon and edge tables to store the definition of the object, and use coherence techniques to evaluate points along and between scan lines.

13-10. Set up a program to display the visible surfaces of a convex polyhedron using the painter's algorithm. That is, surfaces are to be sorted on depth and painted on the screen from back to front.

13-11. Write a program that uses the depth-sorting method to display the visible surfaces of any given object with plane faces.

13-12. Develop a depth-sorting program to display the visible surfaces in a scene containing several polyhedrons.

13-13. Write a program to display the visible surfaces of a convex polyhedron using the BSP-tree method.

13-14. Give examples of situations where the two methods discussed for test 3 in the area-subdivision algorithm will fail to identify correctly a surrounding surface that obscures all other surfaces.

13-15. Develop an algorithm that would test a given plane surface against a rectangular area to decide whether it is a surrounding, overlapping, inside, or outside surface.

13-16. Develop an algorithm for generating a quadtree representation for the visible surfaces of an object by applying the area-subdivision tests to determine the values of the quadtree elements.

13-17. Set up an algorithm to load a given quadtree representation of an object into a frame buffer for display.

13-18. Write a program on your system to display an octree representation for an object so that hidden-surfaces are removed.

13-19. Devise an algorithm for viewing a single sphere using the ray-casting method.

13-20. Discuss how antialiasing methods can be incorporated into the various hidden-surface elimination algorithms.

13-21. Write a routine to produce a surface contour plot for a given surface function $f(x, y)$.

13-22. Develop an algorithm for detecting visible line sections in a scene by comparing each line in the scene to each surface.

13-23. Discuss how wireframe displays might be generated with the various visible-surface detection methods discussed in this chapter.

13-24. Set up a procedure for generating a wireframe display of a polyhedron with the hidden edges of the object drawn with dashed lines.

CHAPTER

14

Illumination Models and Surface-Rendering Methods

494

R ealistic displays of a scene are obtained by generating perspective projections of objects and by applying natural lighting effects to the visible surfaces. An **illumination model,** also called a **lighting model** and sometimes referred to as a **shading model,** is used to calculate the intensity of light that we should see at a given point on the surface of an object. A **surface-rendering algorithm** uses the intensity calculations from an illumination model to determine the light intensity for all projected pixel positions for the various surfaces in a scene. Surface rendering can be performed by applying the illumination model to every visible surface point, or the rendering can be accomplished by interpolating intensities across the surfaces from a small set of illumination-model calculations. Scan-line, image-space algorithms typically use interpolation schemes, while ray-tracing algorithms invoke the illumination model at each pixel position. Sometimes, surface-rendering procedures are termed *surface-shading methods*. To avoid confusion, we will refer to the model for calculating light intensity at a single surface point as an *illumination model* or a *lighting model,* and we will use the term *surface rendering* to mean a procedure for applying a lighting model to obtain pixel intensities for all the projected surface positions in a scene.

Photorealism in computer graphics involves two elements: accurate graphical representations of objects and good physical descriptions of the lighting effects in a scene. Lighting effects include light reflections, transparency, surface texture, and shadows.

Modeling the colors and lighting effects that we see on an object is a complex process, involving principles of both physics and psychology. Fundamentally, lighting effects are described with models that consider the interaction of electromagnetic energy with object surfaces. Once light reaches our eyes, it triggers perception processes that determine what we actually "see" in a scene. Physical illumination models involve a number of factors, such as object type, object position relative to light sources and other objects, and the light-source conditions that we set for a scene. Objects can be constructed of opaque materials, or they can be more or less transparent. In addition, they can have shiny or dull surfaces, and they can have a variety of surface-texture patterns. Light sources, of varying shapes, colors, and positions, can be used to provide the illumination effects for a scene. Given the parameters for the optical properties of surfaces, the relative positions of the surfaces in a scene, the color and positions of the light sources, and the position and orientation of the viewing plane, illumination models calculate the intensity projected from a particular surface point in a specified viewing direction.

Illumination models in computer graphics are often loosely derived from the physical laws that describe surface light intensities. To minimize intensity calculations, most packages use empirical models based on simplified photometric calculations. More accurate models, such as the radiosity algorithm, calculate light intensities by considering the propagation of radiant energy between the surfaces and light sources in a scene. In the following sections, we first take a look at the basic illumination models often used in graphics packages; then we discuss more accurate, but more time-consuming, methods for calculating surface intensities. And we explore the various surface-rendering algorithms for applying the lighting models to obtain the appropriate shading over visible surfaces in a scene.

14-1
LIGHT SOURCES

When we view an opaque nonluminous object, we see reflected light from the surfaces of the object. The total reflected light is the sum of the contributions from **light sources** and other reflecting surfaces in the scene (Fig. 14-1). Thus, a surface that is not directly exposed to a light source may still be visible if nearby objects are illuminated. Sometimes, light sources are referred to as *light-emitting sources*; and reflecting surfaces, such as the walls of a room, are termed *light-reflecting sources*. We will use the term *light source* to mean an object that is emitting radiant energy, such as a light bulb or the sun.

A luminous object, in general, can be both a light source and a light reflector. For example, a plastic globe with a light bulb inside both emits and reflects light from the surface of the globe. Emitted light from the globe may then illuminate other objects in the vicinity.

The simplest model for a light emitter is a **point source**. Rays from the source then follow radially diverging paths from the source position, as shown in Fig. 14-2. This light-source model is a reasonable approximation for sources whose dimensions are small compared to the size of objects in the scene. Sources, such as the sun, that are sufficiently far from the scene can be accurately modeled as point sources. A nearby source, such as the long fluorescent light in Fig. 14-3, is more accurately modeled as a **distributed light source**. In this case, the illumination effects cannot be approximated realistically with a point source, because the area of the source is not small compared to the surfaces in the scene. An accurate model for the distributed source is one that considers the accumulated illumination effects of the points over the surface of the source.

When light is incident on an opaque surface, part of it is reflected and part is absorbed. The amount of incident light reflected by a surface depends on the type of material. Shiny materials reflect more of the incident light, and dull surfaces absorb more of the incident light. Similarly, for an illuminated transparent

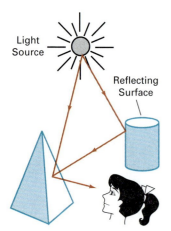

Figure 14-1
Light viewed from an opaque nonluminous surface is in general a combination of reflected light from a light source and reflections of light reflections from other surfaces.

Figure 14-2
Diverging ray paths from a point light source.

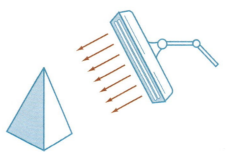

Figure 14-3
An object illuminated with a distributed light source.

surface, some of the incident light will be reflected and some will be transmitted through the material.

Surfaces that are rough, or grainy, tend to scatter the reflected light in all directions. This scattered light is called **diffuse reflection**. A very rough matte surface produces primarily diffuse reflections, so that the surface appears equally bright from all viewing directions. Figure 14-4 illustrates diffuse light scattering from a surface. What we call the color of an object is the color of the diffuse reflection of the incident light. A blue object illuminated by a white light source, for example, reflects the blue component of the white light and totally absorbs all other components. If the blue object is viewed under a red light, it appears black since all of the incident light is absorbed.

In addition to diffuse reflection, light sources create highlights, or bright spots, called **specular reflection**. This highlighting effect is more pronounced on shiny surfaces than on dull surfaces. An illustration of specular reflection is shown in Fig. 14-5.

14-2

BASIC ILLUMINATION MODELS

Here we discuss simplified methods for calculating light intensities. The empirical models described in this section provide simple and fast methods for calculating surface intensity at a given point, and they produce reasonably good results for most scenes. Lighting calculations are based on the optical properties of surfaces, the background lighting conditions, and the light-source specifications. Optical parameters are used to set surface properties, such as glossy, matte, opaque, and transparent. This controls the amount of reflection and absorption of incident light. All light sources are considered to be point sources, specified with a coordinate position and an intensity value (color).

Ambient Light

A surface that is not exposed directly to a light source still will be visible if nearby objects are illuminated. In our basic illumination model, we can set a general level of brightness for a scene. This is a simple way to model the combination of light reflections from various surfaces to produce a uniform illumination called the **ambient light,** or **background light**. Ambient light has no spatial or directional characteristics. The amount of ambient light incident on each object is a constant for all surfaces and over all directions.

We can set the level for the ambient light in a scene with parameter I_a, and each surface is then illuminated with this constant value. The resulting reflected light is a constant for each surface, independent of the viewing direction and the spatial orientation of the surface. But the intensity of the reflected light for each surface depends on the optical properties of the surface; that is, how much of the incident energy is to be reflected and how much absorbed.

Diffuse Reflection

Ambient-light reflection is an approximation of global diffuse lighting effects. Diffuse reflections are constant over each surface in a scene, independent of the viewing direction. The fractional amount of the incident light that is diffusely re-

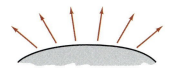

Figure 14-4
Diffuse reflections from a surface.

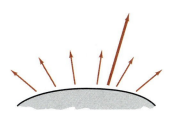

Figure 14-5
Specular reflection superimposed on diffuse reflection vectors.

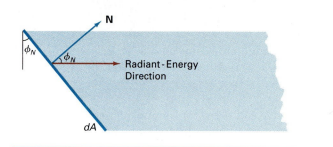

Figure 14-6
Radiant energy from a surface area dA in direction ϕ_N relative
to the surface normal direction.

flected can be set for each surface with parameter k_d, the **diffuse-reflection coefficient,** or **diffuse reflectivity**. Parameter k_d is assigned a constant value in the interval 0 to 1, according to the reflecting properties we want the surface to have. If
we want a highly reflective surface, we set the value of k_d near 1. This produces a
bright surface with the intensity of the reflected light near that of the incident
light. To simulate a surface that absorbs most of the incident light, we set the reflectivity to a value near 0. Actually, parameter k_d is a function of surface color,
but for the time being we will assume k_d is a constant.

If a surface is exposed only to ambient light, we can express the intensity of
the diffuse reflection at any point on the surface as

$$I_{\text{ambdiff}} = k_d I_a \tag{14-1}$$

Since ambient light produces a flat uninteresting shading for each surface (Fig.
14-19(b)), scenes are rarely rendered with ambient light alone. At least one light
source is included in a scene, often as a point source at the viewing position.

We can model the diffuse reflections of illumination from a point source in a
similar way. That is, we assume that the diffuse reflections from the surface are
scattered with equal intensity in all directions, independent of the viewing direction. Such surfaces are sometimes referred to as *ideal diffuse reflectors*. They are
also called *Lambertian reflectors,* since radiated light energy from any point on the
surface is governed by *Lambert's cosine law*. This law states that the radiant energy
from any small surface area dA in any direction ϕ_N relative to the surface normal
is proportional to $\cos\phi_N$ (Fig. 14-6). The light intensity, though, depends on the
radiant energy per projected area perpendicular to direction ϕ_N, which is dA
$\cos\phi_N$. Thus, for Lambertian reflection, the intensity of light is the same over all
viewing directions. We discuss photometry concepts and terms, such as radiant
energy, in greater detail in Section 14-7.

Even though there is equal light scattering in all directions from a perfect
diffuse reflector, the brightness of the surface does depend on the orientation of
the surface relative to the light source. A surface that is oriented perpendicular to
the direction of the incident light appears brighter than if the surface were tilted
at an oblique angle to the direction of the incoming light. This is easily seen by
holding a white sheet of paper or smooth cardboard parallel to a nearby window
and slowly rotating the sheet away from the window direction. As the angle between the surface normal and the incoming light direction increases, less of the
incident light falls on the surface, as shown in Fig. 14-7. This figure shows a beam
of light rays incident on two equal-area plane surface patches with different spatial orientations relative to the incident light direction from a distant source (par-

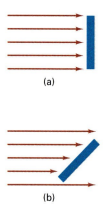

Figure 14-7
A surface perpendicular to
the direction of the incident
light (a) is more illuminated
than an equal-sized surface at
an oblique angle (b) to the
incoming light direction.

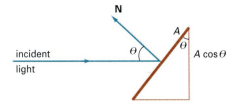

Figure 14-8
An illuminated area projected perpendicular to the path of the incoming light rays.

allel incoming rays). If we denote the **angle of incidence** between the incoming light direction and the surface normal as θ (Fig. 14-8), then the projected area of a surface patch perpendicular to the light direction is proportional to $\cos\theta$. Thus, the amount of illumination (or the "number of incident light rays" cutting across the projected surface patch) depends on $\cos\theta$. If the incoming light from the source is perpendicular to the surface at a particular point, that point is fully illuminated. As the angle of illumination moves away from the surface normal, the brightness of the point drops off. If I_l is the intensity of the point light source, then the diffuse reflection equation for a point on the surface can be written as

$$I_{l,\text{diff}} = k_d I_l \cos\theta \qquad (14\text{-}2)$$

A surface is illuminated by a point source only if the angle of incidence is in the range $0°$ to $90°$ ($\cos\theta$ is in the interval from 0 to 1). When $\cos\theta$ is negative, the light source is "behind" the surface.

If $\mathbf{N}$ is the unit normal vector to a surface and $\mathbf{L}$ is the unit direction vector to the point light source from a position on the surface (Fig. 14-9), then $\cos\theta = \mathbf{N} \cdot \mathbf{L}$ and the diffuse reflection equation for single point-source illumination is

$$I_{l,\text{diff}} = k_d I_l (\mathbf{N} \cdot \mathbf{L}) \qquad (14\text{-}3)$$

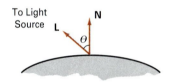

Figure 14-9
Angle of incidence θ between the unit light-source direction vector $\mathbf{L}$ and the unit surface normal $\mathbf{N}$.

Reflections for point-source illumination are calculated in world coordinates or viewing coordinates before shearing and perspective transformations are applied. These transformations may transform the orientation of normal vectors so that they are no longer perpendicular to the surfaces they represent. Transformation procedures for maintaining the proper orientation of surface normals are discussed in Chapter 11.

Figure 14-10 illustrates the application of Eq. 14-3 to positions over the surface of a sphere, using various values of parameter k_d between 0 and 1. Each projected pixel position for the surface was assigned an intensity as calculated by the diffuse reflection equation for a point light source. The renderings in this figure illustrate single point-source lighting with no other lighting effects. This is what we might expect to see if we shined a small light on the object in a completely darkened room. For general scenes, however, we expect some background lighting effects in addition to the illumination effects produced by a direct light source.

We can combine the ambient and point-source intensity calculations to obtain an expression for the total diffuse reflection. In addition, many graphics packages introduce an **ambient-reflection coefficient** k_a to modify the ambient-light intensity I_a for each surface. This simply provides us with an additional parameter to adjust the light conditions in a scene. Using parameter k_a, we can write the total diffuse reflection equation as

$$I_{\text{diff}} = k_a I_a + k_d I_l (\mathbf{N} \cdot \mathbf{L}) \qquad (14\text{-}4)$$

499

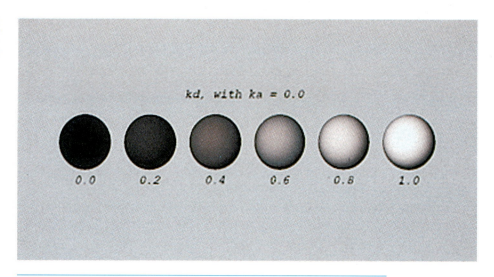

Figure 14-10
Diffuse reflections from a spherical surface illuminated by a point light
source for values of the diffuse reflectivity coefficient in the interval
$0 \le k_d \le 1$.

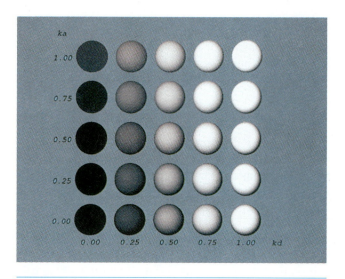

Figure 14-11
Diffuse reflections from a spherical surface illuminated with
ambient light and a single point source for values of k_a and
k_d in the interval (0, 1).

where both k_a and k_d depend on surface material properties and are assigned values in the range from 0 to 1. Figure 14-11 shows a sphere displayed with surface
intensitities calculated from Eq. 14-4 for values of parameters k_a and k_d between 0
and 1.

Specular Reflection and the Phong Model

When we look at an illuminated shiny surface, such as polished metal, an apple,
or a person's forehead, we see a highlight, or bright spot, at certain viewing di-

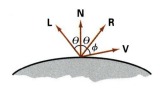

rections. This phenomenon, called *specular reflection*, is the result of total, or near total, reflection of the incident light in a concentrated region around the **specular-reflection angle**. Figure 14-12 shows the specular reflection direction at a point on the illuminated surface. The specular-reflection angle equals the angle of the incident light, with the two angles measured on opposite sides of the unit normal surface vector **N**. In this figure, we use **R** to represent the unit vector in the direction of ideal specular reflection; **L** to represent the unit vector directed toward the point light source; and **V** as the unit vector pointing to the viewer from the surface position. Angle ϕ is the viewing angle relative to the specular-reflection direction **R**. For an ideal reflector (perfect mirror), incident light is reflected only in the specular-reflection direction. In this case, we would only see reflected light when vectors **V** and **R** coincide ($\phi = 0$).

Figure 14-12
Specular-reflection angle equals angle of incidence θ.

    Objects other than ideal reflectors exhibit specular reflections over a finite range of viewing positions around vector **R**. Shiny surfaces have a narrow specular-reflection range, and dull surfaces have a wider reflection range. An empirical model for calculating the specular-reflection range, developed by Phong Bui Tuong and called the **Phong specular-reflection model,** or simply the **Phong model,** sets the intensity of specular reflection proportional to $\cos^{n_s}\phi$. Angle ϕ can be assigned values in the range $0°$ to $90°$, so that $\cos\phi$ varies from 0 to 1. The value assigned to *specular-reflection parameter* n_s is determined by the type of surface that we want to display. A very shiny surface is modeled with a large value for n_s (say, 100 or more), and smaller values (down to 1) are used for duller surfaces. For a perfect reflector, n_s is infinite. For a rough surface, such as chalk or cinderblock, n_s would be assigned a value near 1. Figures 14-13 and 14-14 show the effect of n_s on the angular range for which we can expect to see specular reflections.

    The intensity of specular reflection depends on the material properties of the surface and the angle of incidence, as well as other factors such as the polarization and color of the incident light. We can approximately model monochromatic specular intensity variations using a **specular-reflection coefficient,** $W(\theta)$, for each surface. Figure 14-15 shows the general variation of $W(\theta)$ over the range $\theta = 0°$ to $\theta = 90°$ for a few materials. In general, $W(\theta)$ tends to increase as the angle of incidence increases. At $\theta = 90°$, $W(\theta) = 1$ and all of the incident light is reflected. The variation of specular intensity with angle of incidence is described by *Fresnel's Laws of Reflection*. Using the spectral-reflection function $W(\theta)$, we can write the Phong specular-reflection model as

$$I_{spec} = W(\theta)I_l \cos^{n_s} \phi \qquad (14\text{-}5)$$

where I_l is the intensity of the light source, and ϕ is the viewing angle relative to the specular-reflection direction **R**.

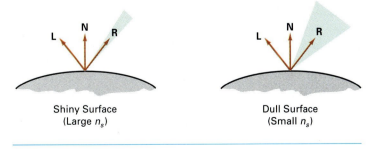

Shiny Surface
(Large n_s)

Dull Surface
(Small n_s)

Figure 14-13
Modeling specular reflections (shaded area) with parameter n_s.

501

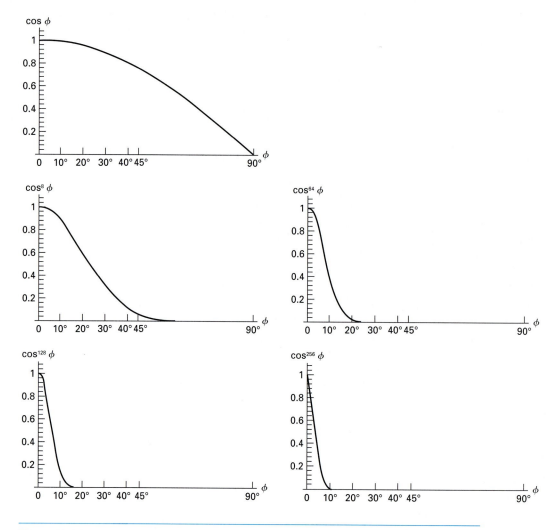

Figure 14-14
Plots of $\cos^{n_s}\phi$ for several values of specular parameter n_s.

As seen in Fig. 14-15, transparent materials, such as glass, only exhibit appreciable specular reflections as θ approaches 90°. At $\theta = 0°$, about 4 percent of the incident light on a glass surface is reflected. And for most of the range of θ, the reflected intensity is less than 10 percent of the incident intensity. But for many opaque materials, specular reflection is nearly constant for all incidence angles. In this case, we can reasonably model the reflected light effects by replacing $W(\theta)$ with a constant specular-reflection coefficient k_s. We then simply set k_s equal to some value in the range 0 to 1 for each surface.

Since **V** and **R** are unit vectors in the viewing and specular-reflection directions, we can calculate the value of $\cos\phi$ with the dot product $\mathbf{V} \cdot \mathbf{R}$. Assuming the specular-reflection coefficient is a constant, we can determine the intensity of the specular reflection at a surface point with the calculation

$$I_{\text{spec}} = k_s I_l (\mathbf{V} \cdot \mathbf{R})^{n_s}$$

(14-6)

502

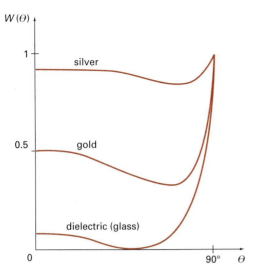

Figure 14-15
Approximate variation of the specular-reflection coefficient as a function of angle of incidence for different materials.

Vector **R** in this expression can be calculated in terms of vectors **L** and **N**. As seen in Fig. 14-16, the projection of **L** onto the direction of the normal vector is obtained with the dot product **N** · **L**. Therefore, from the diagram, we have

$$\mathbf{R} + \mathbf{L} = (2\mathbf{N} \cdot \mathbf{L})\mathbf{N}$$

and the specular-reflection vector is obtained as

$$\mathbf{R} = (2\mathbf{N} \cdot \mathbf{L})\mathbf{N} - \mathbf{L} \qquad (14\text{-}7)$$

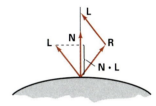

Figure 14-16
Calculation of vector **R** by considering projections onto the direction of the normal vector **N**.

Figure 14-17 illustrates specular reflections for various values of k_s and n_s on a sphere illuminated with a single point light source.

A somewhat simplified Phong model is obtained by using the *halfway vector* **H** between **L** and **V** to calculate the range of specular reflections. If we replace **V** · **R** in the Phong model with the dot product **N** · **H**, this simply replaces the empirical $\cos \phi$ calculation with the empirical $\cos \alpha$ calculation (Fig. 14-18). The halfway vector is obtained as

$$\mathbf{H} = \frac{\mathbf{L} + \mathbf{V}}{|\mathbf{L} + \mathbf{V}|} \qquad (14\text{-}8)$$

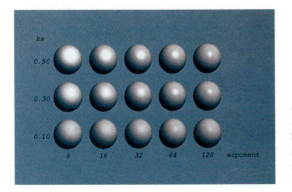

Figure 14-17
Specular reflections from a spherical surface for varying specular parameter values and a single light source.

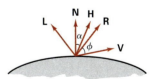

Figure 14-18
Halfway vector **H** along the bisector of the angle between **L** and **V**.

If both the viewer and the light source are sufficiently far from the surface, both **V** and **L** are constant over the surface, and thus **H** is also constant for all surface points. For nonplanar surfaces, $\mathbf{N} \cdot \mathbf{H}$ then requires less computation than $\mathbf{V} \cdot \mathbf{R}$ since the calculation of **R** at each surface point involves the variable vector **N**.

For given light-source and viewer positions, vector **H** is the orientation direction for the surface that would produce maximum specular reflection in the viewing direction. For this reason, **H** is sometimes referred to as the surface orientation direction for maximum highlights. Also, if vector **V** is coplanar with vectors **L** and **R** (and thus **N**), angle α has the value $\phi/2$. When **V**, **L**, and **N** are not coplanar, $\alpha > \phi/2$, depending on the spatial relationship of the three vectors.

Combined Diffuse and Specular Reflections with Multiple Light Sources

For a single point light source, we can model the combined diffuse and specular reflections from a point on an illuminated surface as

$$
\begin{aligned}
I &= I_{\text{diff}} + I_{\text{spec}} \\
&= k_a I_a + k_d I_l (\mathbf{N} \cdot \mathbf{L}) + k_s I_l (\mathbf{N} \cdot \mathbf{H})^{n_s}
\end{aligned}
\tag{14-9}
$$

Figure 14-19 illustrates surface lighting effects produced by the various terms in Eq. 14-9. If we place more than one point source in a scene, we obtain the light reflection at any surface point by summing the contributions from the individual sources:

$$
I = k_a I_a + \sum_{i=1}^{n} I_{li} [k_d (\mathbf{N} \cdot \mathbf{L}_i) + k_s (\mathbf{N} \cdot \mathbf{H}_i)^{n_s}]
\tag{14-10}
$$

To ensure that any pixel intensity does not exceed the maximum allowable value, we can apply some type of normalization procedure. A simple approach is to set a maximum magnitude for each term in the intensity equation. If any calculated term exceeds the maximum, we simply set it to the maximum value. Another way to compensate for intensity overflow is to normalize the individual terms by dividing each by the magnitude of the largest term. A more complicated procedure is first to calculate all pixel intensities for the scene, then the calculated intensities are scaled onto the allowable intensity range.

Warn Model

So far we have considered only point light sources. The **Warn model** provides a method for simulating studio lighting effects by controlling light intensity in different directions.

Light sources are modeled as points on a reflecting surface, using the Phong model for the surface points. Then the intensity in different directions is controlled by selecting values for the Phong exponent. In addition, light controls, such as "barn doors" and spotlighting, used by studio photographers can be simulated in the Warn model. *Flaps* are used to control the amount of light emitted by a source in various directions. Two flaps are provided for each of the *x*, *y*, and *z* directions. *Spotlights* are used to control the amount of light emitted within a cone with apex at a point-source position. The Warn model is implemented in

(a) (b)

(c) (d)

Figure 14-19

A wireframe scene (a) is displayed only with ambient lighting in (b), and the surface of
each object is assigned a different color. Using ambient light and diffuse reflections due to
a single source with $k_s = 0$ for all surfaces, we obtain the lighting effects shown in (c).
Using ambient light and both diffuse and specular reflections due to a single light source,
we obtain the lighting effects shown in (d).

PHIGS+, and Fig. 14-20 illustrates lighting effects that can be produced with this
model.

Intensity Attenuation

As radiant energy from a point light source travels through space, its amplitude
is attenuated by the factor $1/d^2$, where d is the distance that the light has traveled.
This means that a surface close to the light source (small d) receives a higher incident intensity from the source than a distant surface (large d). Therefore, to produce realistic lighting effects, our illumination model should take this intensity
attenuation into account. Otherwise, we are illuminating all surfaces with the
same intensity, no matter how far they might be from the light source. If two parallel surfaces with the same optical parameters overlap, they would be indistin-
guishable from each other. The two surfaces would be displayed as one surface.

505

Figure 14-20
Studio lighting effects produced with the Warn model, using
five light sources to illuminate a Chevrolet Camaro. (*Courtesy of
David R. Warn, General Motors Research Laboratories.*)

Our simple point-source illumination model, however, does not always
produce realistic pictures, if we use the factor $1/d^2$ to attenuate intensities. The
factor $1/d^2$ produces too much intensity variations when d is small, and it produces very little variation when d is large. This is because real scenes are usually
not illuminated with point light sources, and our illumination model is too simple to accurately describe real lighting effects.

Graphics packages have compensated for these problems by using inverse
linear or quadratic functions of d to attenuate intensities. For example, a general
inverse quadratic **attenuation function** can be set up as

$$f(d) = \frac{1}{a_0 + a_1 d + a_2 d^2}$$
(14-11)

A user can then fiddle with the coefficients a_0, a_1, and a_2 to obtain a variety of
lighting effects for a scene. The value of the constant term a_0 can be adjusted to
prevent $f(d)$ from becoming too large when d is very small. Also, the values for
the coefficients in the attenuation function, and the optical surface parameters for
a scene, can be adjusted to prevent calculations of reflected intensities from ex-
ceeding the maximum allowable value. This is an effective method for limiting
intensity values when a single light source is used to illuminate a scene. For multiple light-source illumination, the methods described in the preceding section
are more effective for limiting the intensity range.

With a given set of attenuation coefficients, we can limit the magnitude of
the attenuation function to 1 with the calculation

$$f(d) = \min\left(1, \frac{1}{a_0 + a_1 d + a_2 d^2}\right)$$
(14-12)

Using this function, we can then write our basic illumination model as

$$I = k_a I_a + \sum_{i=1}^{n} f(d_i) I_{li} [k_d (\mathbf{N} \cdot \mathbf{L}_i) + k_s (\mathbf{N} \cdot \mathbf{H}_i)^{n_s}]$$
(14-13)

where d_i is the distance light has traveled from light source i.

Figure 14-21
Light reflections from the surface of
a black nylon cushion, modeled as
woven cloth patterns and rendered
using Monte Carlo ray-tracing
methods. (*Courtesy of Stephen H. Westin,
Program of Computer Graphics, Cornell
University.*)

Color Considerations

Most graphics displays of realistic scenes are in color. But the illumination model
we have described so far considers only monochromatic lighting effects. To incorporate color, we need to write the intensity equation as a function of the color
properties of the light sources and object surfaces.

For an RGB description, each color in a scene is expressed in terms of red,
green, and blue components. We then specify the RGB components of light-
source intensities and surface colors, and the illumination model calculates the
RGB components of the reflected light. One way to set surface colors is by specifying the reflectivity coefficients as three-element vectors. The diffuse reflection-
coefficient vector, for example, would then have RGB components (k_{dR}, k_{dG}, k_{dB}). If
we want an object to have a blue surface, we select a nonzero value in the range
from 0 to 1 for the blue reflectivity component, k_{dB}, while the red and green reflectivity components are set to zero $(k_{dR} = k_{dG} = 0)$. Any nonzero red or green components in the incident light are absorbed, and only the blue component is reflected. The intensity calculation for this example reduces to the single expression

$$I_B = k_{aB}I_{aB} + \sum_{i=1}^{n} f_i(d)I_{lBi}[k_{dB}(\mathbf{N} \cdot \mathbf{L}_i) + k_{sB}(\mathbf{N} \cdot \mathbf{H}_i)^{n_s}] \qquad (14\text{-}14)$$

Surfaces typically are illuminated with white light sources, and in general we can
set surface color so that the reflected light has nonzero values for all three RGB
components. Calculated intensity levels for each color component can be used to
adjust the corresponding electron gun in an RGB monitor.

In his original specular-reflection model, Phong set parameter k_s to a constant value independent of the surface color. This produces specular reflections
that are the same color as the incident light (usually white), which gives the surface a plastic appearance. For a nonplastic material, the color of the specular reflection is a function of the surface properties and may be different from both the
color of the incident light and the color of the diffuse reflections. We can approximate specular effects on such surfaces by making the specular-reflection coefficient color-dependent, as in Eq. 14-14. Figure 14-21 illustrates color reflections
from a matte surface, and Figs. 14-22 and 14-23 show color reflections from metal

Figure 14-22
Light reflections from a teapot with
reflectance parameters set to
simulate brushed aluminum
surfaces and rendered using Monte
Carlo ray-tracing methods. (*Courtesy
of Stephen H. Westin, Program of Computer
Graphics, Cornell University.*)

507

surfaces. Light reflections from object surfaces due to multiple colored light
sources is shown in Fig. 14-24.

Another method for setting surface color is to specify the components of
diffuse and specular color vectors for each surface, while retaining the reflectivity
coefficients as single-valued constants. For an RGB color representation, for in-
stance, the components of these two surface-color vectors can be denoted as (S_{dR}, S_{dG}, S_{dB}) and (S_{sR}, S_{sG}, S_{sB}). The blue component of the reflected light is then calculated as

$$I_B = k_a S_{dB} I_{aB} + \sum_{i=1}^{n} f_i(d)\, I_{lBi}[k_d S_{dB}(\mathbf{N} \cdot \mathbf{L}_i) + k_s S_{sB}(\mathbf{N} \cdot \mathbf{H}_i)^{ns}] \qquad (14\text{-}15)$$

This approach provides somewhat greater flexibility, since surface-color parameters can be set independently from the reflectivity values.

Other color representations besides RGB can be used to describe colors in a
scene. And sometimes it is convenient to use a color model with more than three
components for a color specification. We discuss color models in detail in the
next chapter. For now, we can simply represent any component of a color specification with its spectral wavelength λ. Intensity calculations can then be expressed as

$$I_\lambda = k_a S_{d\lambda} I_{a\lambda} + \sum_{i=1}^{n} f_i(d) I_{l\lambda i}[k_d S_{d\lambda}(\mathbf{N} \cdot \mathbf{L}_i) + k_s S_{s\lambda}(\mathbf{N} \cdot \mathbf{H}_i)^{ns}] \qquad (14\text{-}16)$$

Transparency

A transparent surface, in general, produces both reflected and transmitted light.
The relative contribution of the transmitted light depends on the degree of trans-

parency of the surface and whether any light sources or illuminated surfaces are behind the transparent surface. Figure 14-25 illustrates the intensity contributions to the surface lighting for a transparent object.

When a transparent surface is to be modeled, the intensity equations must be modified to include contributions from light passing through the surface. In most cases, the transmitted light is generated from reflecting objects in back of the surface, as in Fig. 14-26. Reflected light from these objects passes through the transparent surface and contributes to the total surface intensity.

Both diffuse and specular transmission can take place at the surfaces of a transparent object. Diffuse effects are important when a partially transparent surface, such as frosted glass, is to be modeled. Light passing through such materials is scattered so that a blurred image of background objects is obtained. Diffuse refractions can be generated by decreasing the intensity of the refracted light and spreading intensity contributions at each point on the refracting surface onto a finite area. These manipulations are time-comsuming, and most lighting models employ only specular effects.

Realistic transparency effects are modeled by considering light refraction. When light is incident upon a transparent surface, part of it is reflected and part is **refracted** (Fig. 14-27). Because the speed of light is different in different materials, the path of the refracted light is different from that of the incident light. The direction of the refracted light, specified by the **angle of refraction,** is a function of the **index of refraction** of each material and the direction of the incident light. Index of refraction for a material is defined as the ratio of the speed of light in a vacuum to the speed of light in the material. Angle of refraction θ_r is calculated from the angle of incidence θ_i, the index of refraction η_i of the "incident" material (usually air), and the index of refraction η_r of the refracting material according to Snell's law:

$$\sin \theta_r = \frac{\eta_i}{\eta_r} \sin \theta_i \qquad (14\text{-}17)$$

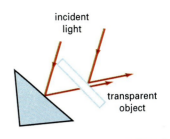

Figure 14-26
A ray-traced view of a transparent glass surface, showing both light transmission from objects behind the glass and light reflection from the glass surface.
(*Courtesy of Eric Haines, 3D/EYE Inc.*)

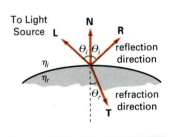

Figure 14-27
Reflection direction **R** and refraction direction **T** for a ray of light incident upon a surface with index of refraction η_r.

509

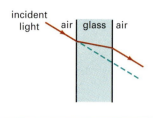

Figure 14-28

Refraction of light through a glass object. The emerging refracted ray travels along a path that is parallel to the incident light path (dashed line).

Actually, the index of refraction of a material is a function of the wavelength of the incident light, so that the different color components of a light ray will be refracted at different angles. For most applications, we can use an average index of refraction for the different materials that are modeled in a scene. The index of refraction of air is approximately 1, and that of crown glass is about 1.5. Using these values in Eq. 14-17 with an angle of incidence of 30° yields an angle of refraction of about 19°. Figure 14-28 illustrates the changes in the path direction for a light ray refracted through a glass object. The overall effect of the refraction is to shift the incident light to a parallel path. Since the calculations of the trigonometric functions in Eq. 14-17 are time-consuming, refraction effects could be modeled by simply shifting the path of the incident light a small amount.

From Snell's law and the diagram in Fig. 14-27, we can obtain the unit transmission vector **T** in the refraction direction θ_r as

$$\mathbf{T} = \left(\frac{\eta_i}{\eta_r} \cos \theta_i - \cos \theta_r \right) \mathbf{N} - \frac{\eta_i}{\eta_r} \mathbf{L} \qquad (14\text{-}18)$$

where **N** is the unit surface normal, and **L** is the unit vector in the direction of the light source. Transmission vector **T** can be used to locate intersections of the refraction path with objects behind the transparent surface. Including refraction effects in a scene can produce highly realistic displays, but the determination of refraction paths and object intersections requires considerable computation. Most scan-line image-space methods model light transmission with approximations that reduce processing time. We return to the topic of refraction in our discussion of ray-tracing algorithms (Section 14-6).

A simpler procedure for modeling transparent objects is to ignore the path shifts altogether. In effect, this approach assumes there is no change in the index of refraction from one material to another, so that the angle of refraction is always the same as the angle of incidence. This method speeds up the calculation of intensities and can produce reasonable transparency effects for thin polygon surfaces.

We can combine the transmitted intensity I_{trans} through a surface from a background object with the reflected intensity I_{refl} from the transparent surface (Fig. 14-29) using a **transparency coefficient** k_t. We assign parameter k_t a value between 0 and 1 to specify how much of the background light is to be transmitted. Total surface intensity is then calculated as

$$I = (1 - k_t)I_{\text{refl}} + k_t I_{\text{trans}} \qquad (14\text{-}19)$$

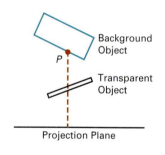

Background Object

P

Transparent Object

Projection Plane

Figure 14-29

The intensity of a background object at point **P** can be combined with the reflected intensity off the surface of a transparent object along a perpendicular projection line (dashed).

The term $(1 - k_t)$ is the **opacity factor**.

For highly transparent objects, we assign k_t a value near 1. Nearly opaque objects transmit very little light from background objects, and we can set k_t to a value near 0 for these materials (opacity near 1). It is also possible to allow k_t to be a function of position over the surface, so that different parts of an object can transmit more or less background intensity according to the values assigned to k_t.

Transparency effects are often implemented with modified depth-buffer (z-buffer) algorithms. A simple way to do this is to process opaque objects first to determine depths for the visible opaque surfaces. Then, the depth positions of the transparent objects are compared to the values previously stored in the depth buffer. If any transparent surface is visible, its reflected intensity is calculated and combined with the opaque-surface intensity previously stored in the frame buffer. This method can be modified to produce more accurate displays by using additional storage for the depth and other parameters of the transparent

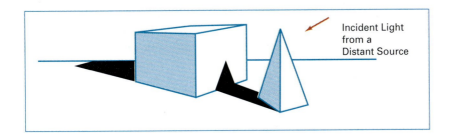

Figure 14-30
Objects modeled with shadow regions.

surfaces. This allows depth values for the transparent surfaces to be compared to each other, as well as to the depth values of the opaque surfaces. Visible transparent surfaces are then rendered by combining their surface intensities with those of the visible and opaque surfaces behind them.

Accurate displays of transparency and antialiasing can be obtained with the *A*-buffer algorithm. For each pixel position, surface patches for all overlapping surfaces are saved and sorted in depth order. Then, intensities for the transparent and opaque surface patches that overlap in depth are combined in the proper visibility order to produce the final averaged intensity for the pixel, as discussed in Chapter 13.

A depth-sorting visibility algorithm can be modified to handle transparency by first sorting surfaces in depth order, then determining whether any visible surface is transparent. If we find a visible transparent surface, its reflected surface intensity is combined with the surface intensity of objects behind it to obtain the pixel intensity at each projected surface point.

Shadows

Hidden-surface methods can be used to locate areas where light sources produce shadows. By applying a hidden-surface method with a light source at the view position, we can determine which surface sections cannot be "seen" from the light source. These are the shadow areas. Once we have determined the shadow areas for all light sources, the shadows could be treated as surface patterns and stored in pattern arrays. Figure 14-30 illustrates the generation of shading patterns for two objects on a table and a distant light source. All shadow areas in this figure are surfaces that are not visible from the position of the light source. The scene in Fig. 14-26 shows shadow effects produced by multiple light sources.

Shadow patterns generated by a hidden-surface method are valid for any selected viewing position, as long as the light-source positions are not changed. Surfaces that are visible from the view position are shaded according to the lighting model, which can be combined with texture patterns. We can display shadow areas with ambient-light intensity only, or we can combine the ambient light with specified surface textures.

14-3

DISPLAYING LIGHT INTENSITIES

Values of intensity calculated by an illumination model must be converted to one of the allowable intensity levels for the particular graphics system in use. Some

511

systems are capable of displaying several intensity levels, while others are capable of only two levels for each pixel (on or off). In the first case, we convert intensities from the lighting model into one of the available levels for storage in the frame buffer. For bilevel systems, we can convert intensities into halftone patterns, as discussed in the next section.

Assigning Intensity Levels

We first consider how grayscale values on a video monitor can be distributed over the range between 0 and 1 so that the distribution corresponds to our perception of equal intensity intervals. We perceive relative light intensities the same way that we perceive relative sound intensities: on a logarithmic scale. This means that if the ratio of two intensities is the same as the ratio of two other intensities, we perceive the difference between each pair of intensities to be the same. As an example, we perceive the difference between intensities 0.20 and 0.22 to be the same as the difference between 0.80 and 0.88. Therefore, to display $n + 1$ successive intensity levels with equal perceived brightness, the intensity levels on the monitor should be spaced so that the ratio of successive intensities is constant:

$$\frac{I_1}{I_0} = \frac{I_2}{I_1} = \cdots = \frac{I_n}{I_{n-1}} = r \qquad (14\text{-}20)$$

Here, we denote the lowest level that can be displayed on the monitor as I_0 and the highest as I_n. Any intermediate intensity can then be expressed in terms of I_0 as

$$I_k = r^k I_0 \qquad (14\text{-}21)$$

We can calculate the value of r, given the values of I_0 and n for a particular system, by substituting $k = n$ in the preceding expression. Since $I_n = 1$, we have

$$r = \left(\frac{1}{I_0}\right)^{1/n} \qquad (14\text{-}22)$$

Thus, the calculation for I_k in Eq. 14-21 can be rewritten as

$$I_k = I_0^{(n-k)/n} \qquad (14\text{-}23)$$

As an example, if $I_0 = 1/8$ for a system with $n = 3$, we have $r = 2$, and the four intensity values are $1/8, 1/4, 1/2$, and 1.

The lowest intensity value I_0 depends on the characteristics of the monitor and is typically in the range from 0.005 to around 0.025. As we saw in Chapter 2, a "black" region displayed on a monitor will always have some intensity value above 0 due to reflected light from the screen phosphors. For a black-and-white monitor with 8 bits per pixel ($n = 255$) and $I_0 = 0.01$, the ratio of successive intensities is approximately $r = 1.0182$. The approximate values for the 256 intensities on this system are 0.0100, 0.0102, 0.0104, 0.0106, 0.0107, 0.0109, . . . , 0.9821, and 1.0000.

With a color system, we set up intensity levels for each component of the color model. Using the RGB model, for example, we can relate the blue component of intensity at level k to the lowest attainable blue value as in Eq. 14-21:

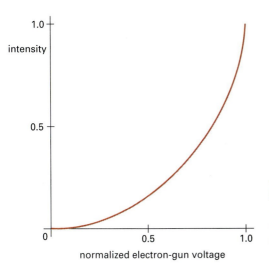

normalized electron-gun voltage

Figure 14-31
A typical monitor response curve,
showing the displayed screen
intensity as a function of
normalized electron-gun voltage.

$$I_{Bk} = r_B^k I_{B0} \qquad (14\text{-}24)$$

where

$$r_B = \left(\frac{1}{I_{B0}}\right)^{1/n} \qquad (14\text{-}25)$$

and n is the number of intensity levels. Similar expressions hold for the other
color components.

Gamma Correction and Video Lookup Tables

Another problem associated with the display of calculated intensities is the nonlinearity of display devices. Illumination models produce a linear range of intensities. The RGB color (0.25, 0.25, 0.25) obtained from a lighting model represents
one-half the intensity of the color (0.5, 0.5, 0.5). Usually, these calculated intensities are then stored in an image file as integer values, with one byte for each of
the three RGB components. This intensity file is also linear, so that a pixel with
the value (64, 64, 64) has one-half the intensity of a pixel with the value (128, 128,
128). A video monitor, however, is a nonlinear device. If we set the voltages for
the electron gun proportional to the linear pixel values, the displayed intensities
will be shifted according to the **monitor response curve** shown in Fig. 14-31.

To correct for monitor nonlinearities, graphics systems use a **video lookup
table** that adjusts the linear pixel values. The monitor response curve is described
by the exponential function

$$I = aV^{\gamma} \qquad (14\text{-}26)$$

Parameter I is the displayed intensity, and parameter V is the input voltage. Values for parameters a and γ depend on the characteristics of the monitor used in
the graphics system. Thus, if we want to display a particular intensity value I, the
correct voltage value to produce this intensity is

$$V = \left(\frac{I}{a}\right)^{1/\gamma} \qquad (14\text{-}27)$$

513

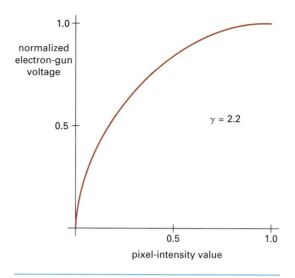

Figure 14-32
A video lookup correction curve for mapping pixel intensities to electron-gun voltages using gamma correction with $\gamma = 2.2$. Values for both pixel intensity and monitor voltages are normalized on the interval 0 to 1.

This calculation is referred to as **gamma correction** of intensity. Monitor gamma values are typically between 2.0 and 3.0. The National Television System Committee (NTSC) signal standard is $\gamma = 2.2$. Figure 14-32 shows a gamma-correction curve using the NTSC gamma value. Equation 14-27 is used to set up the video lookup table that converts integer pixel values in the image file to values that control the electron-gun voltages.

We can combine gamma correction with logarithmic intensity mapping to produce a lookup table that contains both conversions. If I is an input intensity value from an illumination model, we first locate the nearest intensity I_k from a table of values created with Eq. 14-20 or Eq. 14-23. Alternatively, we could determine the level number for this intensity value with the calculation

$$k = \text{round}\left(\log_r \frac{I}{I_0}\right) \qquad (14\text{-}28)$$

then we compute the intensity value at this level using Eq. 14-23. Once we have the intensity value I_k, we can calculate the electron-gun voltage:

$$V_k = \left(\frac{I_k}{a}\right)^{1/\gamma} \qquad (14\text{-}29)$$

Values V_k can then be placed in the lookup tables, and values for k would be stored in the frame-buffer pixel positions. If a particular system has no lookup table, computed values for V_k can be stored directly in the frame buffer. The combined conversion to a logarithmic intensity scale followed by calculation of the V_k using Eq.14-29 is also sometimes referred to as gamma correction.

514

Figure 14-33
A continuous-tone photograph (a) printed with (b) two intensity levels,
(c) four intensity levels, and (d) eight intensity levels.

If the video amplifiers of a monitor are designed to convert the linear input pixel values to electron-gun voltages, we cannot combine the two intensity-conversion processes. In this case, gamma correction is built into the hardware, and the logarithmic values I_k must be precomputed and stored in the frame buffer (or the color table).

Displaying Continuous-Tone Images

High-quality computer graphics systems generally provide 256 intensity levels for each color component, but acceptable displays can be obtained for many applications with fewer levels. A four-level system provides minimum shading capability for continuous-tone images, while photorealistic images can be generated on systems that are capable of from 32 to 256 intensity levels per pixel.

Figure 14-33 shows a continuous-tone photograph displayed with various intensity levels. When a small number of intensity levels are used to reproduce a continuous-tone image, the borders between the different intensity regions (called *contours*) are clearly visible. In the two-level reproduction, the features of the photograph are just barely identifiable. Using four intensity levels, we begin to identify the original shading patterns, but the contouring effects are glaring. With eight intensity levels, contouring effects are still obvious, but we begin to have a better indication of the original shading. At 16 or more intensity levels, contouring effects diminish and the reproductions are very close to the original. Reproductions of continuous-tone images using more than 32 intensity levels show only very subtle differences from the original.

515

HALFTONE PATTERNS AND DITHERING TECHNIQUES

When an output device has a limited intensity range, we can create an apparent increase in the number of available intensities by incorporating multiple pixel positions into the display of each intensity value. When we view a small region consisting of several pixel positions, our eyes tend to integrate or average the fine detail into an overall intensity. Bilevel monitors and printers, in particular, can take advantage of this visual effect to produce pictures that appear to be displayed with multiple intensity values.

Continuous-tone photographs are reproduced for publication in newspapers, magazines, and books with a printing process called **halftoning,** and the reproduced pictures are called **halftones**. For a black-and-white photograph, each intensity area is reproduced as a series of black circles on a white background. The diameter of each circle is proportional to the darkness required for that intensity region. Darker regions are printed with larger circles, and lighter regions are printed with smaller circles (more white area). Figure 14-34 shows an enlarged section of a gray-scale halftone reproduction. Color halftones are printed using dots of various sizes and colors, as shown in Fig. 14-35. Book and magazine halftones are printed on high-quality paper using approximately 60 to 80 circles of varying diameter per centimeter. Newspapers use lower-quality paper and lower resolution (about 25 to 30 dots per centimeter).

Halftone Approximations

In computer graphics, halftone reproductions are approximated using rectangular pixel regions, called *halftone patterns* or *pixel patterns*. The number of intensity

Figure 14-34
An enlarged section of a photograph reproduced with a halftoning method, showing how tones are represented with varying size dots.

(a)

(b)

(c)

Figure 14-35
Color halftone dot patterns. The top half of the clock in the color halftone (a) is enlarged by a factor of 10 in (b) and by a factor of 50 in (c).

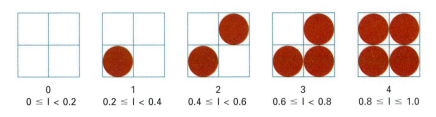

0	1	2	3	4
$0 \le I < 0.2$	$0.2 \le I < 0.4$	$0.4 \le I < 0.6$	$0.6 \le I < 0.8$	$0.8 \le I \le 1.0$

Figure 14-36

A 2 by 2 pixel grid used to display five intensity levels on a bilevel system. The intensity values that would be mapped to each grid are listed below each pixel pattern.

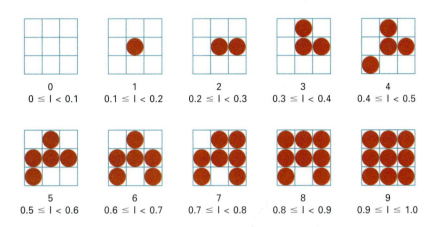

0	1	2	3	4
$0 \le I < 0.1$	$0.1 \le I < 0.2$	$0.2 \le I < 0.3$	$0.3 \le I < 0.4$	$0.4 \le I < 0.5$

5	6	7	8	9
$0.5 \le I < 0.6$	$0.6 \le I < 0.7$	$0.7 \le I < 0.8$	$0.8 \le I < 0.9$	$0.9 \le I \le 1.0$

Figure 14-37

A 3 by 3 pixel grid can be used to display 10 intensities on a bilevel system. The intensity values that would be mapped to each grid are listed below each pixel pattern.

levels that we can display with this method depends on how many pixels we include in the rectangular grids and how many levels a system can display. With n by n pixels for each grid on a bilevel system, we can represent $n^2 + 1$ intensity levels. Figure 14-36 shows one way to set up pixel patterns to represent five intensity levels that could be used with a bilevel system. In pattern 0, all pixels are turned off; in pattern 1, one pixel is turned on; and in pattern 4, all four pixels are turned on. An intensity value I in a scene is mapped to a particular pattern according to the range listed below each grid shown in the figure. Pattern 0 is used for $0 \le I < 0.2$, pattern 1 for $0.2 \le I < 0.4$, and pattern 4 is used for $0.8 \le I \le 1.0$.

With 3 by 3 pixel grids on a bilevel system, we can display 10 intensity levels. One way to set up the 10 pixel patterns for these levels is shown in Fig. 14-37. Pixel positions are chosen at each level so that the patterns approximate the increasing circle sizes used in halftone reproductions. That is, the "on" pixel positions are near the center of the grid for lower intensity levels and expand outward as the intensity level increases.

For any pixel-grid size, we can represent the pixel patterns for the various possible intensities with a "mask" of pixel position numbers. As an example, the following mask can be used to generate the nine 3 by 3 grid patterns for intensity levels above 0 shown in Fig. 14-37.

$$\begin{bmatrix} 8 & 3 & 7 \\ 5 & 1 & 2 \\ 4 & 9 & 6 \end{bmatrix} \qquad (14\text{-}30)$$

To display a particular intensity with level number k, we turn on each pixel whose position number is less than or equal to k.

Although the use of n by n pixel patterns increases the number of intensities that can be displayed, they reduce the resolution of the displayed picture by a factor of $1/n$ along each of the x and y axes. A 512 by 512 screen area, for instance, is reduced to an area containing 256 by 256 intensity points with 2 by 2 grid patterns. And with 3 by 3 patterns, we would reduce the 512 by 512 area to 128 intensity positions along each side.

Another problem with pixel grids is that subgrid patterns become apparent as the grid size increases. The grid size that can be used without distorting the intensity variations depends on the size of a displayed pixel. Therefore, for systems with lower resolution (fewer pixels per centimeter), we must be satisfied with fewer intensity levels. On the other hand, high-quality displays require at least 64 intensity levels. This means that we need 8 by 8 pixel grids. And to achieve a resolution equivalent to that of halftones in books and magazines, we must display 60 dots per centimeter. Thus, we need to be able to display $60 \times 8 = 480$ dots per centimeter. Some devices, for example high-quality film recorders, are able to display this resolution.

Pixel-grid patterns for halftone approximations must also be constructed to minimize contouring and other visual effects not present in the original scene. Contouring can be minimized by evolving each successive grid pattern from the previous pattern. That is, we form the pattern at level k by adding an "on" position to the grid pattern at level $k - 1$. Thus, if a pixel position is on for one grid level, it is on for all higher levels (Figs. 14-36 and 14-37). We can minimize the introduction of other visual effects by avoiding symmetrical patterns. With a 3 by 3 pixel grid, for instance, the third intensity level above zero would be better represented by the pattern in Fig. 14-38(a) than by any of the symmetrical arrangements in Fig. 14-38(b). The symmetrical patterns in this figure would produce vertical, horizontal, or diagonal streaks in any large area shaded with intensity level 3. For hard-copy output on devices such as film recorders and some printers, isolated pixels are not effectly reproduced. Therefore, a grid pattern with a single "on" pixel or one with isolated "on" pixels, as in Fig. 14-39, should be avoided.

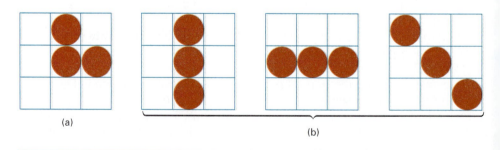

(a)

(b)

Figure 14-38

For a 3 by 3 pixel grid, pattern (a) is to be preferred to the patterns in (b) for representing the third intensity level above 0.

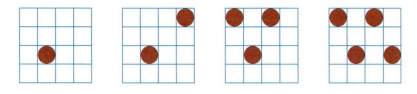

Figure 14-39
Halftone grid patterns with isolated pixels that cannot be effectively reproduced on some hard-copy devices.

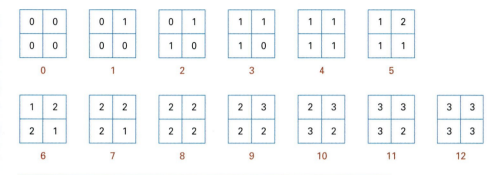

Figure 14-40

Intensity levels 0 through 12 obtained with halftone approximations using 2 by 2 pixel grids on a four-level system.

Halftone approximations also can be used to increase the number of intensity options on systems that are capable of displaying more than two intensities per pixel. For example, on a system that can display four intensity levels per pixel, we can use 2 by 2 pixel grids to extend the available intensity levels from 4 to 13. In Fig. 14-36, the four grid patterns above zero now represent several levels each, since each pixel position can display three intensity values above zero. Figure 14-40 shows one way to assign the pixel intensities to obtain the 13 distinct levels. Intensity levels for individual pixels are labeled 0 through 3, and the overall levels for the system are labeled 0 through 12.

Similarly, we can use pixel-grid patterns to increase the number of intensities that can be displayed on a color system. As an example, suppose we have a three-bit per pixel RGB system. This gives one bit per color gun in the monitor, providing eight colors (including black and white). Using 2 by 2 pixel-grid patterns, we now have 12 phosphor dots that can be used to represent a particular color value, as shown in Fig. 14-41. Each of the three RGB colors has four phosphor dots in the pattern, which allows five possible settings per color. This gives us a total of 125 different color combinations.

Figure 14-41
An RGB 2 by 2 pixel-grid pattern.

Dithering Techniques

The term **dithering** is used in various contexts. Primarily, it refers to techniques for approximating halftones without reducing resolution, as pixel-grid patterns do. But the term is also applied to halftone-approximation methods using pixel grids, and sometimes it is used to refer to color halftone approximations only.

Random values added to pixel intensities to break up contours are often referred to as *dither noise*. Various algorithms have been used to generate the ran-

519

dom distributions. The effect is to add noise over an entire picture, which tends to soften intensity boundaries.

Ordered-dither methods generate intensity variations with a one-to-one mapping of points in a scene to the display pixels. To obtain n^2 intensity levels, we set up an n by n dither matrix D_n, whose elements are distinct positive integers in the range 0 to $n^2 - 1$. For example, we can generate four intensity levels with

$$D_2 = \begin{bmatrix} 3 & 1 \\ 0 & 2 \end{bmatrix} \qquad (14\text{-}31)$$

and we can generate nine intensity levels with

$$D_3 = \begin{bmatrix} 7 & 2 & 6 \\ 4 & 0 & 1 \\ 3 & 8 & 5 \end{bmatrix} \qquad (14\text{-}32)$$

The matrix elements for D_2 and D_3 are in the same order as the pixel mask for setting up 2 by 2 and 3 by 3 pixel grids, respectively. For a bilevel system, we then determine display intensity values by comparing input intensities to the matrix elements. Each input intensity is first scaled to the range $0 \leq I \leq n^2$. If the intensity I is to be applied to screen position (x, y), we calculate row and column numbers for the dither matrix as

$$i = (x \bmod n) + 1, \qquad j = (y \bmod n) + 1 \qquad (14\text{-}33)$$

If $I > D_n(i,j)$, we turn on the pixel at position (x, y). Otherwise, the pixel is not turned on.

Elements of the dither matrix are assigned in accordance with the guidelines discussed for pixel grids. That is, we want to minimize added visual effect in a displayed scene. Order dither produces constant-intensity areas identical to those generated with pixel-grid patterns when the values of the matrix elements correspond to the grid mask. Variations from the pixel-grid displays occur at boundaries of the intensity levels.

Typically, the number of intensity levels is taken to be a multiple of 2. Higher-order dither matrices are then obtained from lower-order matrices with the recurrence relation:

$$D_n = \begin{bmatrix} 4D_{n/2} + D_2(1,1)U_{n/2} & 4D_{n/2} + D_2(1,2)U_{n/2} \\ 4D_{n/2} + D_2(2,1)U_{n/2} & 4D_{n/2} + D_2(2,2)U_{n/2} \end{bmatrix} \qquad (14\text{-}34)$$

assuming $n \geq 4$. Parameter $U_{n/2}$ is the "unity" matrix (all elements are 1). As an example, if D_2 is specified as in Eq. 14-31, then recurrence relation 14-34 yields

$$D_4 = \begin{bmatrix} 15 & 7 & 13 & 5 \\ 3 & 11 & 1 & 9 \\ 12 & 4 & 14 & 6 \\ 0 & 8 & 2 & 10 \end{bmatrix} \qquad (14\text{-}35)$$

Another method for mapping a picture with m by n points to a display area with m by n pixels is *error diffusion*. Here, the error between an input intensity value and the displayed pixel intensity level at a given position is dispersed, or diffused, to pixel positions to the right and below the current pixel position. Starting with a matrix **M** of intensity values obtained by scanning a photograph, we want to construct an array I of pixel intensity values for an area of the screen. We do this by first scanning across the rows of **M**, from left to right, top to bottom, and determining the nearest available pixel-intensity level for each element of **M**. Then the error between the value stored in matrix **M** and the displayed intensity level at each pixel position is distributed to neighboring elements in **M**, using the following simplified algorithm:

```
for (i=0; i<m; i++)
    for (j=0; j<n; j++) {
        /* Determine the available intensity level I_k */
        /* that is closest to the value M_{i,j}. */
        I_{i,j} := I_k;
        err := M_{i,j} - I_{i,j};
        M_{i,j+1} := M_{i,j+1} + α · err;
        M_{i+1,j-1} := M_{i+1,j-1} + β · err;
        M_{i+1,j} := M_{i+1,j} + γ · err;
        M_{i+1,j+1} := M_{i+1,j+1} + δ · err;
    }
```

Once the elements of matrix **I** have been assigned intensity-level values, we then map the matrix to some area of a display device, such as a printer or video monitor. Of course, we cannot disperse the error past the last matrix column ($j = n$) or below the last matrix row ($i = m$). For a bilevel system, the available intensity levels are 0 and 1. Parameters for distributing the error can be chosen to satisfy the following relationship

$$\alpha + \beta + \gamma + \delta \leq 1 \qquad (14\text{-}36)$$

One choice for the error-diffusion parameters that produces fairly good results is $(\alpha, \beta, \gamma, \delta) = (7/16, 3/16, 5/16, 1/16)$. Figure 14-42 illustrates the error distribution using these parameter values. Error diffusion sometimes produces "ghosts" in a picture by repeating, or echoing, certain parts of the picture, particularly with facial features such as hairlines and nose outlines. Ghosting can be re-

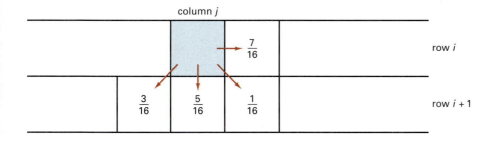

Figure 14-42
Fraction of intensity error that can be distributed to neighboring pixel positions using an error-diffusion scheme.

521

34	48	40	32	29	15	23	31
42	58	56	53	21	5	7	10
50	62	61	45	13	1	2	18
38	46	54	37	25	17	9	26
28	14	22	30	35	49	41	33
20	4	6	11	43	59	57	52
12	0	3	19	51	63	60	44
24	16	8	27	39	47	55	36

Figure 14-43
One possible distribution scheme for dividing the intensity array into 64 dot-diffusion classes, numbered from 0 through 63.

duced by choosing values for the error-diffusion parameters that sum to a value less than 1 and by rescaling the matrix values after the dispersion of errors. One way to rescale is to multiply all elements of **M** by 0.8 and then add 0.1. Another method for improving picture quality is to alternate the scanning of matrix rows from right to left and left to right.

A variation on the error-diffusion method is *dot diffusion*. In this method, the m by n array of intensity values is divided into 64 classes numbered from 0 to 63, as shown in Fig. 14-43. The error between a matrix value and the displayed intensity is then distributed only to those neighboring matrix elements that have a larger class number. Distribution of the 64 class numbers is based on minimizing the number of elements that are completely surrounded by elements with a lower class number, since this would tend to direct all errors of the surrounding elements to that one position.

14-5
POLYGON-RENDERING METHODS

In this section, we consider the application of an illumination model to the rendering of standard graphics objects: those formed with polygon surfaces. The objects are usually polygon-mesh approximations of curved-surface objects, but they may also be polyhedra that are not curved-surface approximations. Scanline algorithms typically apply a lighting model to obtain polygon surface rendering in one of two ways. Each polygon can be rendered with a single intensity, or the intensity can be obtained at each point of the surface using an interpolation scheme.

Constant-Intensity Shading

A fast and simple method for rendering an object with polygon surfaces is **constant-intensity shading,** also called **flat shading**. In this method, a single intensity is calculated for each polygon. All points over the surface of the polygon are then displayed with the same intensity value. Constant shading can be useful for quickly displaying the general appearance of a curved surface, as in Fig. 14-47.

In general, flat shading of polygon facets provides an accurate rendering for an object if all of the following assumptions are valid:

- The object is a polyhedron and is not an approximation of an object with a curved surface.

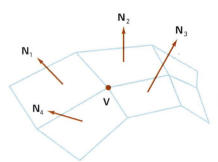

Figure 14-44
The normal vector at vertex **V** is calculated as the average of the surface normals for each polygon sharing that vertex.

- All light sources illuminating the object are sufficiently far from the surface so that $\mathbf{N} \cdot \mathbf{L}$ and the attenuation function are constant over the surface.
- The viewing position is sufficiently far from the surface so that $\mathbf{V} \cdot \mathbf{R}$ is constant over the surface.

Even if all of these conditions are not true, we can still reasonably approximate surface-lighting effects using small polygon facets with flat shading and calculate the intensity for each facet, say, at the center of the polygon.

Gouraud Shading

This **intensity-interpolation** scheme, developed by Gouraud and generally referred to as **Gouraud shading,** renders a polygon surface by linearly interpolating intensity values across the surface. Intensity values for each polygon are matched with the values of adjacent polygons along the common edges, thus eliminating the intensity discontinuities that can occur in flat shading.

Each polygon surface is rendered with Gouraud shading by performing the following calculations:

- Determine the average unit normal vector at each polygon vertex.
- Apply an illumination model to each vertex to calculate the vertex intensity.
- Linearly interpolate the vertex intensities over the surface of the polygon.

At each polygon vertex, we obtain a normal vector by averaging the surface normals of all polygons sharing that vertex, as illustrated in Fig. 14-44. Thus, for any vertex position **V,** we obtain the unit vertex normal with the calculation

$$\mathbf{N}_V = \frac{\displaystyle\sum_{k=1}^{n} \mathbf{N}_k}{\left| \displaystyle\sum_{k=1}^{n} \mathbf{N}_k \right|} \tag{14-37}$$

Once we have the vertex normals, we can determine the intensity at the vertices from a lighting model.

Figure 14-45 demonstrates the next step: interpolating intensities along the polygon edges. For each scan line, the intensity at the intersection of the scan line with a polygon edge is linearly interpolated from the intensities at the edge endpoints. For the example in Fig. 14-45, the polygon edge with endpoint vertices at positions 1 and 2 is intersected by the scan line at point 4. A fast method for obtaining the intensity at point 4 is to interpolate between intensities I_1 and I_2 using only the vertical displacement of the scan line:

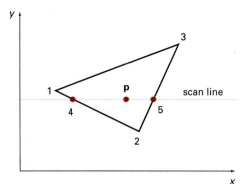

Figure 14-45
For Gouraud shading, the intensity at point 4 is linearly interpolated from the intensities at vertices 1 and 2. The intensity at point 5 is linearly interpolated from intensities at vertices 2 and 3. An interior point **p** is then assigned an intensity value that is linearly interpolated from intensities at positions 4 and 5.

$$I_4 = \frac{y_4 - y_2}{y_1 - y_2}I_1 + \frac{y_1 - y_4}{y_1 - y_2}I_2 \qquad (14\text{-}38)$$

Similarly, intensity at the right intersection of this scan line (point 5) is interpolated from intensity values at vertices 2 and 3. Once these bounding intensities are established for a scan line, an interior point (such as point **p** in Fig. 14-45) is interpolated from the bounding intensities at points 4 and 5 as

$$I_p = \frac{x_5 - x_p}{x_5 - x_4}I_4 + \frac{x_p - x_4}{x_5 - x_4}I_5 \qquad (14\text{-}39)$$

Incremental calculations are used to obtain successive edge intensity values between scan lines and to obtain successive intensities along a scan line. As shown in Fig. 14-46, if the intensity at edge position (x, y) is interpolated as

$$I = \frac{y - y_2}{y_1 - y_2}I_1 + \frac{y_1 - y}{y_1 - y_2}I_2 \qquad (14\text{-}40)$$

then we can obtain the intensity along this edge for the next scan line, $y - 1$, as

$$I' = I + \frac{I_2 - I_1}{y_1 - y_2} \qquad (14\text{-}41)$$

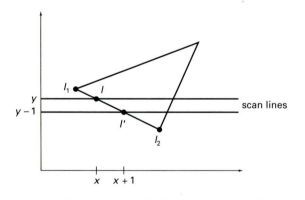

Figure 14-46
Incremental interpolation of intensity values along a polygon edge for successive scan lines.

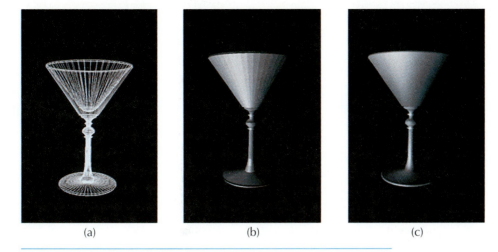

(a)	(b)	(c)

Figure 14-47
A polygon mesh approximation of an object (a) is rendered with flat
shading (b) and with Gouraud shading (c).

Similar calculations are used to obtain intensities at successive horizontal pixel
positions along each scan line.

When surfaces are to be rendered in color, the intensity of each color component is calculated at the vertices. Gouraud shading can be combined with a
hidden-surface algorithm to fill in the visible polygons along each scan line. An
example of an object shaded with the Gouraud method appears in Fig. 14-47.

Gouraud shading removes the intensity discontinuities associated with the
constant-shading model, but it has some other deficiencies. Highlights on the
surface are sometimes displayed with anomalous shapes, and the linear intensity
interpolation can cause bright or dark intensity streaks, called Mach bands, to appear on the surface. These effects can be reduced by dividing the surface into a
greater number of polygon faces or by using other methods, such as Phong shading, that require more calculations.

Phong Shading

A more accurate method for rendering a polygon surface is to interpolate normal
vectors, and then apply the illumination model to each surface point. This
method, developed by Phong Bui Tuong, is called **Phong shading,** or **normal-
vector interpolation shading**. It displays more realistic highlights on a surface
and greatly reduces the Mach-band effect.

A polygon surface is rendered using Phong shading by carrying out the following steps:

- Determine the average unit normal vector at each polygon vertex.
- Linearly interpolate the vertex normals over the surface of the polygon.
- Apply an illumination model along each scan line to calculate projected
  pixel intensities for the surface points.

Interpolation of surface normals along a polygon edge between two vertices
is illustrated in Fig. 14-48. The normal vector **N** for the scan-line intersection
point along the edge between vertices 1 and 2 can be obtained by vertically interpolating between edge endpoint normals:

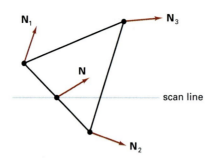

Figure 14-48
Interpolation of surface normals
along a polygon edge.

$$\mathbf{N} = \frac{y - y_2}{y_1 - y_2}\mathbf{N}_1 + \frac{y_1 - y}{y_1 - y_2}\mathbf{N}_2 \qquad (14\text{-}42)$$

Incremental methods are used to evaluate normals between scan lines and along each individual scan line. At each pixel position along a scan line, the illumination model is applied to determine the surface intensity at that point.

Intensity calculations using an approximated normal vector at each point along the scan line produce more accurate results than the direct interpolation of intensities, as in Gouraud shading. The trade-off, however, is that Phong shading requires considerably more calculations.

Fast Phong Shading

Surface rendering with Phong shading can be speeded up by using approximations in the illumination-model calculations of normal vectors. **Fast Phong shading** approximates the intensity calculations using a Taylor-series expansion and triangular surface patches.

Since Phong shading interpolates normal vectors from vertex normals, we can express the surface normal $\mathbf{N}$ at any point (x, y) over a triangle as

$$\mathbf{N} = \mathbf{A}x + \mathbf{B}y + \mathbf{C} \qquad (14\text{-}43)$$

where vectors $\mathbf{A}$, $\mathbf{B}$, and $\mathbf{C}$ are determined from the three vertex equations:

$$\mathbf{N}_k = \mathbf{A}x_k + \mathbf{B}y_k + \mathbf{C}, \qquad k = 1, 2, 3 \qquad (14\text{-}44)$$

with (x_k, y_k) denoting a vertex position.

Omitting the reflectivity and attenuation parameters, we can write the calculation for light-source diffuse reflection from a surface point (x, y) as

$$
\begin{aligned}
I_{\text{diff}}(x, y) &= \frac{\mathbf{L} \cdot \mathbf{N}}{|\mathbf{L}|\,|\mathbf{N}|} \\[2mm]
&= \frac{\mathbf{L} \cdot (\mathbf{A}x + \mathbf{B}y + \mathbf{C})}{|\mathbf{L}|\,|\mathbf{A}x + \mathbf{B}y + \mathbf{C}|} \\[2mm]
&= \frac{(\mathbf{L} \cdot \mathbf{A})x + (\mathbf{L} \cdot \mathbf{B})y + \mathbf{L} \cdot \mathbf{C}}{|\mathbf{L}|\,|\mathbf{A}x + \mathbf{B}y + \mathbf{C}|}
\end{aligned}
\qquad (14\text{-}45)
$$

We can rewrite this expression in the form

$$I_{\text{diff}}(x, y) = \frac{ax + by + c}{(dx^2 + exy + fy^2 + gx + hy + i)^{1/2}} \qquad (14\text{-}46)$$

where parameters such as a, b, c, and d are used to represent the various dot products. For example,

$$a = \frac{\mathbf{L} \cdot \mathbf{A}}{|\mathbf{L}|} \qquad (14\text{-}47)$$

Finally, we can express the denominator in Eq. 14-46 as a Taylor-series expansion and retain terms up to second degree in x and y. This yields

$$I_{\text{diff}}(x, y) = T_5 x^2 + T_4 xy + T_3 y^2 + T_2 x + T_1 y + T_0 \qquad (14\text{-}48)$$

where each T_k is a function of parameters a, b, c, and so forth.

Using forward differences, we can evaluate Eq. 14-48 with only two additions for each pixel position (x, y) once the initial forward-difference parameters have been evaluated. Although fast Phong shading reduces the Phong-shading calculations, it still takes approximately twice as long to render a surface with fast Phong shading as it does with Gouraud shading. Normal Phong shading using forward differences takes about six to seven times longer than Gouraud shading.

Fast Phong shading for diffuse reflection can be extended to include specular reflections. Calculations similar to those for diffuse reflections are used to evaluate specular terms such as $(\mathbf{N} \cdot \mathbf{H})^{n_s}$ in the basic illumination model. In addition, we can generalize the algorithm to include polygons other than triangles and finite viewing positions.

14-6
RAY-TRACING METHODS

In Section 10-15, we introduced the notion of *ray casting,* where a ray is sent out from each pixel position to locate surface intersections for object modeling using constructive solid geometry methods. We also discussed the use of ray casting as a method for determining visible surfaces in a scene (Section 13-10). **Ray tracing** is an extension of this basic idea. Instead of merely looking for the visible surface for each pixel, we continue to bounce the ray around the scene, as illustrated in Fig. 14-49, collecting intensity contributions. This provides a simple and powerful rendering technique for obtaining global reflection and transmission effects. The basic ray-tracing algorithm also provides for visible-surface detection, shadow effects, transparency, and multiple light-source illumination. Many extensions to the basic algorithm have been developed to produce photorealistic displays. Ray-traced displays can be highly realistic, particularly for shiny objects, but they require considerable computation time to generate. An example of the global reflection and transmission effects possible with ray tracing is shown in Fig. 14-50.

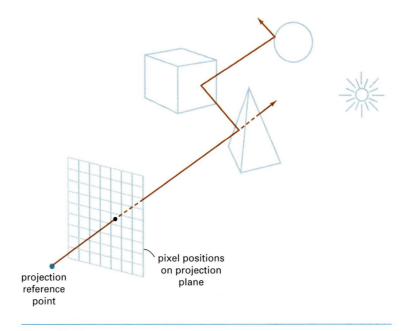

projection
reference
point

pixel positions
on projection
plane

Figure 14-49
Tracing a ray from the projection reference point through a pixel
position with multiple reflections and transmissions.

Basic Ray-Tracing Algorithm

We first set up a coordinate system with the pixel positions designated in the xy
plane. The scene description is given in this reference frame (Fig. 14-51). From the
center of projection, we then determine a ray path that passes through the center
of each screen-pixel position. Illumination effects accumulated along this ray
path are then assigned to the pixel. This rendering approach is based on the principles of geometric optics. Light rays from the surfaces in a scene emanate in all
directions, and some will pass through the pixel positions in the projection plane.
Since there are an infinite number of ray paths, we determine the contributions to
a particular pixel by tracing a light path backward from the pixel to the scene. We
first consider the basic ray-tracing algorithm with one ray per pixel, which is
equivalent to viewing the scene through a pinhole camera.

Figure 14-50
A ray-traced scene, showing global
reflection and transmission
illumination effects from object
surfaces. (*Courtesy of Evans &
Sutherland.*)

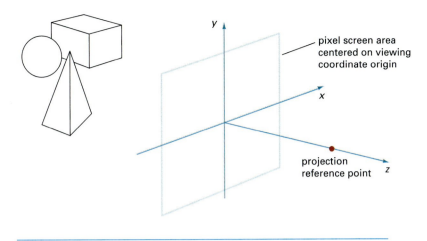

pixel screen area
centered on viewing
coordinate origin

projection
reference point

Figure 14-51
Ray-tracing coordinate-reference frame.

For each pixel ray, we test each surface in the scene to determine if it is intersected by the ray. If a surface is intersected, we calculate the distance from the pixel to the surface-intersection point. The smallest calculated intersection distance identifies the visible surface for that pixel. We then reflect the ray off the visible surface along a specular path (angle of reflection equals angle of incidence). If the surface is transparent, we also send a ray through the surface in the refraction direction. Reflection and refraction rays are referred to as *secondary rays*.

This procedure is repeated for each secondary ray: Objects are tested for intersection, and the nearest surface along a secondary ray path is used to recursively produce the next generation of reflection and refraction paths. As the rays from a pixel ricochet through the scene, each successively intersected surface is added to a binary *ray-tracing tree*, as shown in Fig. 14-52. We use left branches in the tree to represent reflection paths, and right branches represent transmission paths. Maximum depth of the ray-tracing trees can be set as a user option, or it can be determined by the amount of storage available. A path in the tree is then terminated if it reaches the preset maximum or if the ray strikes a light source.

The intensity assigned to a pixel is then determined by accumulating the intensity contributions, starting at the bottom (terminal nodes) of its ray-tracing tree. Surface intensity from each node in the tree is attenuated by the distance from the "parent" surface (next node up the tree) and added to the intensity of the parent surface. Pixel intensity is then the sum of the attenuated intensities at the root node of the ray tree. If no surfaces are intersected by a pixel ray, the ray-tracing tree is empty and the pixel is assigned the intensity value of the background. If a pixel ray intersects a nonreflecting light source, the pixel can be assigned the intensity of the source, although light sources are usually placed beyond the path of the initial rays.

Figure 14-53 shows a surface intersected by a ray and the unit vectors needed for the reflected light-intensity calculations. Unit vector **u** is in the direction of the ray path, **N** is the unit surface normal, **R** is the unit reflection vector, **L** is the unit vector pointing to the light source, and **H** is the unit vector halfway between **V** (opposite to **u**) and **L**. The path along **L** is referred to as the **shadow ray**. If any object intersects the shadow ray between the surface and the point light

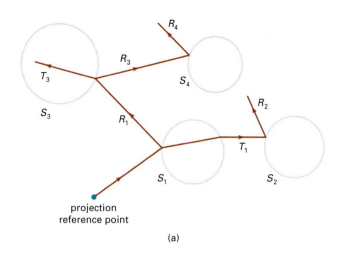

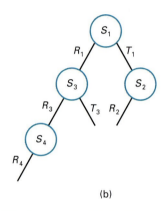

Figure 14-52
(a) Reflection and refraction ray paths through a scene for a
screen pixel. (b) Binary ray-tracing tree for the paths shown
in (a).

source, the surface is in shadow with respect to that source. Ambient light at the
surface is calculated as $k_a I_a$; diffuse reflection due to the source is proportional to
$k_d(\mathbf{N} \cdot \mathbf{L})$; and the specular-reflection component is proportional to $k_s(\mathbf{H} \cdot \mathbf{N})^{n_s}$. As
discussed in Section 14-2, the specular-reflection direction for the secondary ray
path $\mathbf{R}$ depends on the surface normal and the incoming ray direction:

$$\mathbf{R} = \mathbf{u} - (2\mathbf{u} \cdot \mathbf{N})\mathbf{N} \qquad (14\text{-}49)$$

For a transparent surface, we also need to obtain intensity contributions
from light transmitted through the material. We can locate the source of this contribution by tracing a secondary ray along the transmission direction $\mathbf{T}$, as shown
in Fig. 14-54. The unit transmission vector can be obtained from vectors $\mathbf{u}$ and $\mathbf{N}$
as

$$\mathbf{T} = \frac{\eta_i}{\eta_r}\mathbf{u} - (\cos \theta_r - \frac{\eta_i}{\eta_r}\cos \theta_i)\mathbf{N} \qquad (14\text{-}50)$$

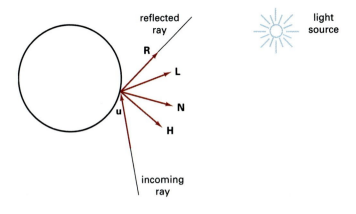

Figure 14-53
Unit vectors at the surface of an object intersected by an
incoming ray along direction **u**.

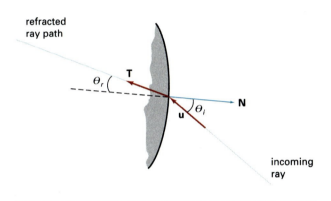

Figure 14-54
Refracted ray path **T** through a transparent material.

Parameters η_i and η_r are the indices of refraction in the incident material and the
refracting material, respectively. Angle of refraction θ_r can be calculated from
Snell's law:

$$\cos \theta_r = \sqrt{1 - \left(\frac{\eta_i}{\eta_r}\right)^2 (1 - \cos^2 \theta_i)} \qquad (14\text{-}51)$$

Ray-Surface Intersection Calculations

A ray can be described with an initial position $\mathbf{P}_0$ and unit direction vector **u**, as
illustrated in Fig. 14-55. The coordinates of any point **P** along the ray at a distance
s from $\mathbf{P}_0$ is computed from the **ray equation**:

$$\mathbf{P} = \mathbf{P}_0 + s\mathbf{u} \qquad (14\text{-}52)$$

Initailly, $\mathbf{P}_0$ can be set to the position of the pixel on the projection plane, or it
could be chosen to be the projection reference point. Unit vector **u** is initially ob-

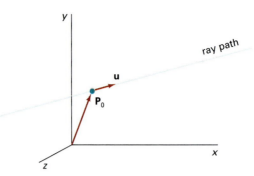

Figure 14-55
Describing a ray with an initial-
position vector $\mathbf{P}_0$ and unit direction
vector $\mathbf{u}$.

tained from the position of the pixel through which the ray passes and the projection reference point:

$$\mathbf{u} = \frac{\mathbf{P}_{\text{pix}} - \mathbf{P}_{\text{prp}}}{\left|\mathbf{P}_{\text{pix}} - \mathbf{P}_{\text{prp}}\right|} \qquad (14\text{-}53)$$

At each intersected surface, vectors $\mathbf{P}_0$ and $\mathbf{u}$ are updated for the secondary rays
at the ray-surface intersection point. For the secondary rays, reflection direction
for $\mathbf{u}$ is $\mathbf{R}$ and the transmission direction is $\mathbf{T}$. To locate surface intersections, we
simultaneously solve the ray equation and the surface equation for the individ-
ual objects in the scene.

The simplest objects to ray trace are spheres. If we have a sphere of radius r
and center position $\mathbf{P}_c$ (Fig. 14-56), then any point $\mathbf{P}$ on the surface must satisfy
the sphere equation:

$$\left|\mathbf{P} - \mathbf{P}_c\right|^2 - r^2 = 0 \qquad (14\text{-}54)$$

Substituting the ray equation 14-52, we have

$$\left|\mathbf{P}_0 + s\mathbf{u} - \mathbf{P}_c\right|^2 - r^2 = 0 \qquad (14\text{-}55)$$

If we let $\Delta\mathbf{P} = \mathbf{P}_c - \mathbf{P}_0$ and expand the dot product, we obtain the quadratic equation

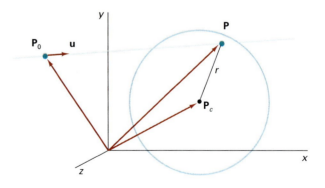

Figure 14-56
A ray intersecting a sphere with radius r centered on
position $\mathbf{P}_c$.

Figure 14-57
A "sphereflake" rendered with ray tracing using 7381 spheres and 3 light sources. (*Courtesy of Eric Haines, 3D/EYE Inc.*)

$$s^2 - 2(\mathbf{u} \cdot \Delta\mathbf{P})s + (|\Delta\mathbf{P}|^2 - r^2) = 0 \qquad (14\text{-}56)$$

whose solution is

$$s = \mathbf{u} \cdot \Delta\mathbf{P} \pm \sqrt{(\mathbf{u} \cdot \Delta\mathbf{P})^2 - |\Delta\mathbf{P}|^2 + r^2} \qquad (14\text{-}57)$$

If the discriminant is negative, the ray does not intersect the sphere. Otherwise, the surface-intersection coordinates are obtained from the ray equation 14-52 using the smaller of the two values from Eq. 14-57.

For small spheres that are far from the initial ray position, Eq. 14-57 is susceptible to roundoff errors. That is, if

$$r^2 << |\Delta\mathbf{P}|^2$$

we could lose the r^2 term in the precision error of $|\Delta\mathbf{P}|^2$. We can avoid this for most cases by rearranging the calculation for distance s as

$$s = \mathbf{u} \cdot \Delta\mathbf{P} \pm \sqrt{r^2 - |\Delta\mathbf{P} - (\mathbf{u} \cdot \Delta\mathbf{P})\mathbf{u}|^2} \qquad (14\text{-}58)$$

Figure 14-57 shows a snowflake pattern of shiny spheres rendered with ray tracing to display global surface reflections.

Polyhedra require more processing than spheres to locate surface intersections. For that reason, it is often better to do an initial intersection test on a bounding volume. For example, Fig. 14-58 shows a polyhedron bounded by a sphere. If a ray does not intersect the sphere, we do not need to do any further testing on the polyhedron. But if the ray does intersect the sphere, we first locate "front" faces with the test

$$\mathbf{u} \cdot \mathbf{N} < 0 \qquad (14\text{-}59)$$

where $\mathbf{N}$ is a surface normal. For each face of the polyhedron that satisifies inequality 14-59, we solve the plane equation

$$\mathbf{N} \cdot \mathbf{P} = -D \qquad (14\text{-}60)$$

for surface position $\mathbf{P}$ that also satisfies the ray equation 14-52. Here, $\mathbf{N} = (A, B, C)$

533

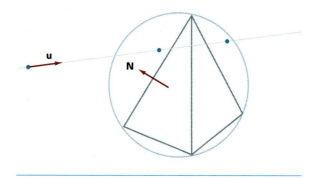

Figure 14-58
Polyhedron enclosed by a bounding sphere.

and D is the fourth plane parameter. Position $\mathbf{P}$ is both on the plane and on the ray path if

$$\mathbf{N} \cdot (\mathbf{P}_0 + s\mathbf{u}) = -D \qquad (14\text{-}61)$$

And the distance from the initial ray position to the plane is

$$s = -\frac{D + \mathbf{N} \cdot \mathbf{P}_0}{\mathbf{N} \cdot \mathbf{u}} \qquad (14\text{-}62)$$

This gives us a position on the infinite plane that contains the polygon face, but this position may not be inside the polygon boundaries (Fig. 14-59). So we need to perform an "inside-outside" test (Chapter 3) to determine whether the ray intersected this face of the polyhedron. We perform this test for each face satisfying inequality 14-59. The smallest distance s to an inside point identifies the intersected face of the polyhedron. If no intersection positions from Eq. 14-62 are inside points, the ray does not intersect the object.

Similar procedures are used to calculate ray-surface intersection positions for other objects, such as quadric or spline surfaces. We combine the ray equation with the surface definition and solve for parameter s. In many cases, numerical root-finding methods and incremental calculations are used to locate intersection

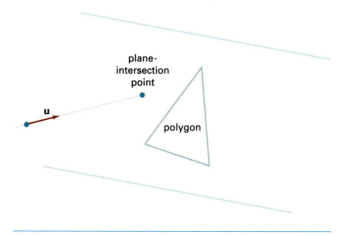

plane-
intersection
point

u

polygon

Figure 14-59
Ray intersection with the plane of a polygon.

Figure 14-60
A ray-traced scene showing global reflection of surface-texture patterns. (*Courtesy of Sun Microsystems.*)

points over a surface. Figure 14-60 shows a ray-traced scene containing multiple objects and texture patterns.

Reducing Object-Intersection Calculations

Ray-surface intersection calculations can account for as much as 95 percent of the processing time in a ray tracer. For a scene with many objects, most of the processing time for each ray is spent checking objects that are not visible along the ray path. Therefore, several methods have been developed for reducing the processing time spent on these intersection calculations.

One method for reducing the intersection calculations is to enclose groups of adjacent objects within a bounding volume, such as a sphere or a box (Fig. 14-61). We can then test for ray intersections with the bounding volume. If the ray does not intersect the bounding object, we can eliminate the intersection tests with the enclosed surfaces. This approach can be extended to include a hierarchy of bounding volumes. That is, we enclose several bounding volumes within a larger volume and carry out the intersection tests hierarchically. First, we test the outer bounding volume; then, if necessary, we test the smaller inner bounding volumes; and so on.

Space-Subdivision Methods

Another way to reduce intersection calculations, is to use *space-subdivision methods*. We can enclose a scene within a cube, then we successively subdivide the cube until each subregion (cell) contains no more than a preset maximum number of surfaces. For example, we could require that each cell contain no more than one surface. If parallel- and vector-processing capabilities are available, the maximum number of surfaces per cell can be determined by the size of the vector

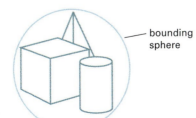

bounding sphere

Figure 14-61
A group of objects enclosed within a bounding sphere.

535

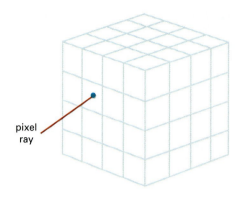

Figure 14-62
Ray intersection with a cube
enclosing all objects in a scene.

registers and the number of processors. Space subdivision of the cube can be stored in an octree or in a binary-partition tree. In addition, we can perform a *uniform subdivision* by dividing the cube into eight equal-size octants at each step, or we can perform an *adaptive subdivision* and subdivide only those regions of the cube containing objects.

We then trace rays through the individual cells of the cube, performing intersection tests only within those cells containing surfaces. The first object surface intersected by a ray is the visible surface for that ray. There is a trade-off between the cell size and the number of surfaces per cell. If we set the maximum number of surfaces per cell too low, cell size can become so small that much of the savings in reduced intersection tests goes into cell-traversal processing.

Figure 14-62 illustrates the intersection of a pixel ray with the front face of the cube enclosing a scene. Once we calculate the intersection point on the front face of the cube, we determine the initial cell intersection by checking the intersection coordinates against the cell boundary positions. We then need to process the ray through the cells by determining the entry and exit points (Fig. 14-63) for each cell traversed by the ray until we intersect an object surface or exit the cube enclosing the scene.

Given a ray direction **u** and a ray entry position $\mathbf{P}_{in}$ for a cell, the potential exit faces are those for which

$$\mathbf{u} \cdot \mathbf{N}_k > 0 \qquad (14\text{-}63)$$

If the normal vectors for the cell faces in Fig. 14-63 are aligned with the coordinates axes, then

$$N_k = \begin{cases} (\pm 1, 0, 0) \\ (0, \pm 1, 0) \\ (0, 0, \pm 1) \end{cases}$$

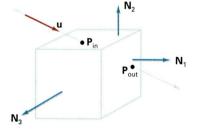

Figure 14-63
Ray traversal through a subregion
(cell) of a cube enclosing a scene.

and we only need to check the sign of each component of **u** to determine the three candidate exit planes. The exit position on each candidate plane is obtained from the ray equation:

$$\mathbf{P}_{\text{out},k} = \mathbf{P}_{\text{in}} + s_k \mathbf{u} \qquad (14\text{-}64)$$

where s_k is the distance along the ray from $\mathbf{P}_{\text{in}}$ to $\mathbf{P}_{\text{out},k}$. Substituting the ray equation into the plane equation for each cell face:

$$\mathbf{N}_k \cdot \mathbf{P}_{\text{out},k} = -D \qquad (14\text{-}65)$$

we can solve for the ray distance to each candidate exit face as

$$s_k = \frac{-D - \mathbf{N}_k \cdot \mathbf{P}_{\text{in}}}{\mathbf{N}_k \cdot \mathbf{u}} \qquad (14\text{-}66)$$

and then select smallest s_k. This calculation can be simplified if the normal vectors $\mathbf{N}_k$ are aligned with the coordinate axes. For example, if a candidate normal vector is $(1, 0, 0)$, then for that plane we have

$$s_k = \frac{x_k - x_0}{u_x} \qquad (14\text{-}67)$$

where $\mathbf{u} = (u_x, u_y, u_z)$, and x_k is the value of the right boundary face for the cell.

Various modifications can be made to the cell-traversal procedures to speed up the processing. One possibility is to take a trial exit plane k as the one perpendicular to the direction of the largest component of **u**. The sector on the trial plane (Fig. 14-64) containing $\mathbf{P}_{\text{out},k}$ determines the true exit plane. If the intersection point $\mathbf{P}_{\text{out},k}$ is in sector 0, the trial plane is the true exit plane and we are done. If the intersection point is sector 1, the true exit plane is the top plane and we simply need to calculate the exit point on the top boundary of the cell. Similarly, sector 3 identifies the bottom plane as the true exit plane; and sectors 4 and 2 identify the true exit plane as the left and right cell planes, respectively. When the trial exit point falls in sector 5, 6, 7, or 8, we need to carry out two additional intersection calculations to identify the true exit plane. Implementation of these methods on parallel vector machines provides further improvements in performance.

The scene in Fig. 14-65 was ray traced using space-subdivision methods. Without space subdivision, the ray-tracing calculations took 10 times longer. Eliminating the polygons also speeded up the processing. For a scene containing 2048 spheres and no polygons, the same algorithm executed 46 times faster than the basic ray tracer.

Figure 14-66 illustrates another ray-traced scene using spatial subdivision and parallel-processing methods. This image of Rodin's Thinker was ray traced with over 1.5 million rays in 24 seconds.

The scene shown in Fig. 14-67 was rendered with a *light-buffer technique*, a form of spatial partitioning. Here, a cube is centered on each point light source, and each side of the cube is partitioned with a grid of squares. A sorted list of objects that are visible to the light through each square is then maintained by the ray tracer to speed up processing of shadow rays. To determine surface-illumination effects, the square for each shadow ray is computed and the shadow ray is then processed against the list of objects for that square.

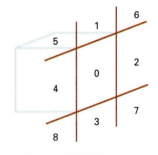

Figure 14-64
Sectors of the trial exit plane.

537

Intersection tests in ray-tracing programs can also be reduced with directional subdivision procedures, by considering sectors that contain a bundle of rays. Within each sector, we can sort surfaces in depth order, as in Fig. 14-68. Each ray then only needs to test objects within the sector that contains that ray.

Antialiased Ray Tracing

Two basic techniques for antialiasing in ray-tracing algorithms are *supersampling* and *adaptive sampling*. Sampling in ray tracing is an extension of the sampling methods we discussed in Chapter 4. In supersampling and adaptive sampling,

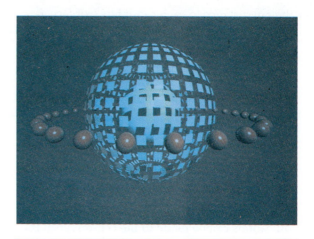

Figure 14-65
A parallel ray-traced scene containing 37 spheres and 720 polygon surfaces. The ray-tracing algorithm used 9 rays per pixel and a tree depth of 5. Spatial subdivision methods processed the scene 10 times faster than the basic ray-tracing algorithm on an Alliant FX/8. (*Courtesy of Lee-Hian Quek, Information Technology Institute, Republic of Singapore.*)

Figure 14-66
This ray-traced scene took 24 seconds to render on a Kendall Square Research KSR1 parallel computer with 32 processors. Rodin's Thinker was modeled with 3036 primitives. Two light sources and one primary ray per pixel were used to obtain the global illumination effects from the 1,675,776 rays processed. (*Courtesy of M. J. Keates and R. J. Hubbold, Department of Computer Science, University of Manchester.*)

(a)

(b)

Figure 14-67
A room scene illuminated with 5 light sources (a) was rendered using the ray-tracing light-buffer technique to process shadow rays. A closeup (b) of part of the room shown in (a) illustrates the global illumination effects. The room is modeled with 1298 polygons, 4 spheres, 76 cylinders, and 35 quadrics. Rendering time was 246 minutes on a VAX 11/780, compared to 602 minutes without using light buffers. (*Courtesy of Eric Haines and Donald P. Greenberg, Program of Computer Graphics, Cornell University.*)

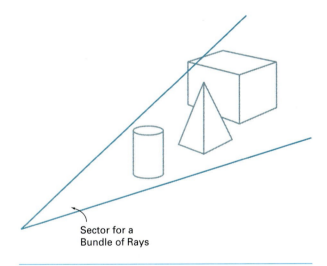
Sector for a
Bundle of Rays

Figure 14-68
Directional subdivision of space. All rays in this sector only need to test the surfaces within the sector in depth order.

the pixel is treated as a finite square area instead of a single point. Supersampling uses multiple, evenly spaced rays (samples) over each pixel area. Adaptive sampling uses unevenly spaced rays in some regions of the pixel area. For example, more rays can be used near object edges to obtain a better estimate of the pixel intensities. Another method for sampling is to randomly distribute the rays over the pixel area. We discuss this approach in the next section. When multiple rays

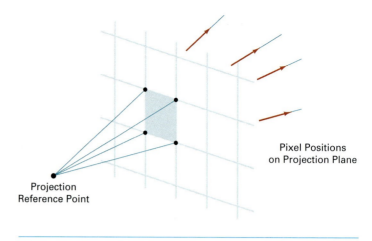

Figure 14-69
Supersampling with four rays per pixel, one at each pixel corner.

per pixel are used, the intensities of the pixel rays are averaged to produce the overall pixel intensity.

Figure 14-69 illustrates a simple supersampling procedure. Here, one ray is generated through each corner of the pixel. If the intensities for the four rays are not approximately equal, or if some small object lies between the four rays, we divide the pixel area into subpixels and repeat the process. As an example, the pixel in Fig. 14-70 is divided into nine subpixels using 16 rays, one at each subpixel corner. Adaptive sampling is then used to further subdivide those subpixels that do not have nearly equal-intensity rays or that subtend some small object. This subdivision process can be continued until each subpixel has approximately equal-intensity rays or an upper bound, say, 256, has been reached for the number of rays per pixel.

The cover picture for this book was rendered with adaptive-subdivision ray tracing, using Rayshade version 3 on a Macintosh II. An extended light source was used to provide realistic soft shadows. Nearly 26 million primary rays were generated, with 33.5 million shadow rays and 67.3 million reflection rays. Wood grain and marble surface patterns were generated using solid texturing methods with a noise function. Total rendering time with the extended light source was 213 hours. Each image of the stereo pair shown in Fig. 2-20 was generated in 45 hours using a point light source.

Instead of passing rays through pixel corners, we can generate rays through subpixel centers, as in Fig. 14-71. With this approach, we can weight the rays according to one of the sampling schemes discussed in Chapter 4.

Another method for antialiasing displayed scenes is to treat a pixel ray as a cone, as shown in Fig. 14-72. Only one ray is generated per pixel, but the ray now has a finite cross section. To determine the percent of pixel-area coverage with objects, we calculate the intersection of the pixel cone with the object surface. For a sphere, this requires finding the intersection of two circles. For a polyhedron, we must find the intersection of a circle with a polygon.

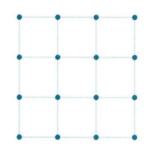

Figure 14-70
Subdividing a pixel into nine subpixels with one ray at each subpixel corner.

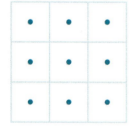

Figure 14-71
Ray positions centered on subpixel areas.

Distributed Ray Tracing

This is a stochastic sampling method that randomly distributes rays according to the various parameters in an illumination model. Illumination parameters in-

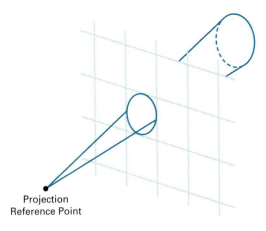

Projection
Reference Point

Figure 14-72
A pixel ray cone.

clude pixel area, reflection and refraction directions, camera lens area, and time. Aliasing effects are thus replaced with low-level "noise", which improves picture quality and allows more accurate modeling of surface gloss and translucency, finite camera apertures, finite light sources, and motion-blur displays of moving objects. **Distributed ray tracing** (also referred to as *distribution ray tracing*) essentially provides a Monte Carlo evaluation of the multiple integrals that occur in an accurate description of surface lighting.

Pixel sampling is accomplished by randomly distributing a number of rays over the pixel surface. Choosing ray positions completely at random, however, can result in the rays clustering together in a small region of the pixel area, and leaving other parts of the pixel unsampled. A better approximation of the light distribution over a pixel area is obtained by using a technique called *jittering* on a regular subpixel grid. This is usually done by initially dividing the pixel area (a unit square) into the 16 subareas shown in Fig. 14-73 and generating a random *jitter position* in each subarea. The random ray positions are obtained by jittering the center coordinates of each subarea by small amounts, δ_x and δ_y, where both δ_x and δ_y are assigned values in the interval $(-0.5, 0.5)$. We then choose the ray position in a cell with center coordinates (x, y) as the jitter position $(x + \delta_x, y + \delta_y)$.

Integer codes 1 through 16 are randomly assigned to each of the 16 rays, and a table lookup is used to obtain values for the other parameters (reflection angle, time, etc.), as explained in the following discussion. Each subpixel ray is then processed through the scene to determine the intensity contribution for that ray. The 16 ray intensities are then averaged to produce the overall pixel intensity. If the subpixel intensities vary too much, the pixel is further subdivided.

To model camera-lens effects, we set a lens of assigned focal length f in front of the projection plane and distribute the subpixel rays over the lens area. Assuming we have 16 rays per pixel, we can subdivide the lens area into 16 zones. Each ray is then sent to the zone corresponding to its assigned code. The ray position within the zone is set to a jittered position from the zone center. Then the ray is projected into the scene from the jittered zone position through the focal point of the lens. We locate the focal point for a ray at a distance f from the lens along the line from the center of the subpixel through the lens center, as shown in Fig. 14-74. Objects near the focal plane are projected as sharp images. Objects in front or in back of the focal plane are blurred. To obtain better displays of out-of-focus objects, we increase the number of subpixel rays.

Ray reflections at surface-intersection points are distributed about the specular reflection direction **R** according to the assigned ray codes (Fig. 14-75). The

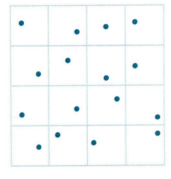

Figure 14-73
Pixel sampling using 16 subpixel areas and a jittered ray position from the center coordinates for each subarea.

541

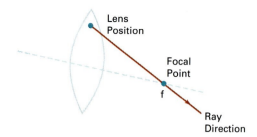

Figure 14-74
Distributing subpixel rays over a
camera lens of focal length f.

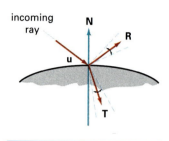

Figure 14-75
Distributing subpixel rays
about the reflection direction
R and the transmission
direction **T**.

maximum spread about **R** is divided into 16 angular zones, and each ray is reflected in a jittered position from the zone center corresponding to its integer
code. We can use the Phong model, $\cos^{ns}\phi$, to determine the maximum reflection
spread. If the material is transparent, refracted rays are distributed about the
transmission direction **T** in a similar manner.

Extended light sources are handled by distributing a number of shadow
rays over the area of the light source, as demonstrated in Fig. 14-76. The light
source is divided into zones, and shadow rays are assigned jitter directions to the
various zones. Additionally, zones can be weighted according to the intensity of
the light source within that zone and the size of the projected zone area onto the
object surface. More shadow rays are then sent to zones with higher weights. If
some shadow rays are blocked by opaque objects between the surface and the
light source, a penumbra is generated at that surface point. Figure 14-77 illustrates the regions for the umbra and penumbra on a surface partially shielded
from a light source.

We create motion blur by distributing rays over time. A total frame time
and the frame-time subdivisions are determined according to the motion dynamics required for the scene. Time intervals are labeled with integer codes, and each
ray is assigned to a jittered time within the interval corresponding to the ray
code. Objects are then moved to their positions at that time, and the ray is traced

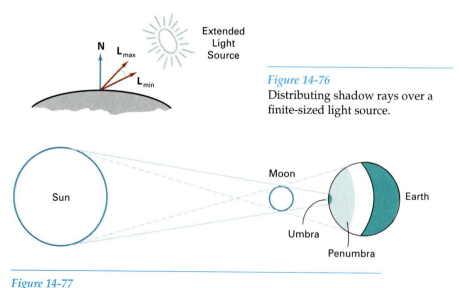

Figure 14-76
Distributing shadow rays over a
finite-sized light source.

Figure 14-77
Umbra and penumbra regions created by a solar eclipse on the surface
of the earth.

Figure 14-78
A scene, entitled *1984*, rendered with distributed ray tracing,
illustrating motion-blur and penumbra effects. (*Courtesy of Pixar. © 1984
Pixar. All rights reserved.*)

through the scene. Additional rays are used for highly blurred objects. To reduce
calculations, we can use bounding boxes or spheres for initial ray-intersection
tests. That is, we move the bounding object according to the motion requirements
and test for intersection. If the ray does not intersect the bounding object, we do
not need to process the individual surfaces within the bounding volume. Figure
14-78 shows a scene displayed with motion blur. This image was rendered using
distributed ray tracing with 4096 by 3550 pixels and 16 rays per pixel. In addition
to the motion-blurred reflections, the shadows are displayed with penumbra
areas resulting from the extended light sources around the room that are illuminating the pool table.

Additional examples of objects rendered with distributed ray-tracing methods are given in Figs. 14-79 and 14-80. Figure 14-81 illustrates focusing, refraction, and antialiasing effects with distributed ray tracing.

Figure 14-79
A brushed aluminum wheel
showing reflectance and shadow
effects generated with distributed
ray-tracing techniques. (*Courtesy of
Stephen H. Westin, Program of Computer
Graphics, Cornell University.*)

543

Figure 14-80
A room scene rendered with
distributed ray-tracing methods.
(*Courtesy of John Snyder, Jed Lengyel,
Devendra Kalra, and Al Barr, Computer
Graphics Lab, California Institute of
Technology. Copyright © 1988 Caltech.*)

Figure 14-81
A scene showing the focusing,
antialiasing, and illumination
effects possible with a combination
of ray-tracing and radiosity
methods. Realistic physical models
of light illumination were used to
generate the refraction effects,
including the caustic in the shadow
of the glass. (*Courtesy of Peter Shirley,
Department of Computer Science, Indiana
University.*)

14-7
RADIOSITY LIGHTING MODEL

We can accurately model diffuse reflections from a surface by considering the radiant energy transfers between surfaces, subject to conservation of energy laws. This method for describing diffuse reflections is generally referred to as the **radiosity model**.

Basic Radiosity Model

In this method, we need to consider the radiant-energy interactions between all surfaces in a scene. We do this by determining the differential amount of radiant energy dB leaving each surface point in the scene and summing the energy contributions over all surfaces to obtain the amount of energy transfer between surfaces. With reference to Fig. 14-82, dB is the visible radiant energy emanating from the surface point in the direction given by angles θ and ϕ within differential solid angle $d\omega$ per unit time per unit surface area. Thus, dB has units of *joules/(second · meter²)*, or *watts/meter²*.

Intensity I, or *luminance*, of the diffuse radiation in direction (θ, ϕ) is the radiant energy per unit time per unit projected area per unit solid angle with units *watts/(meter² · steradians)*:

$$I = \frac{dB}{d\omega \cos \phi}$$

(*14-68*)

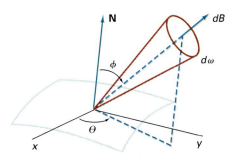

Figure 14-82
Visible radiant energy emitted from a surface point in direction (θ, ϕ) within solid angle $d\omega$.

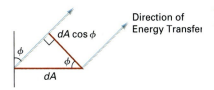

Figure 14-83
For a unit surface element, the projected area perpendicular to the direction of energy transfer is equal to $\cos\phi$.

Assuming the surface is an ideal diffuse reflector, we can set intensity I to a constant for all viewing directions. Thus, $dB/d\omega$ is proportional to the projected surface area (Fig. 14-83). To obtain the total rate of energy radiation from the surface point, we need to sum the radiation for all directions. That is, we want the total energy emanating from a hemisphere centered on the surface point, as in Fig. 14-84:

$$B = \int_{\text{hemi}} dB \qquad (14\text{-}69)$$

For a perfect diffuse reflector, I is a constant, so we can express radiant energy B as

$$B = I \int_{\text{hemi}} \cos\phi \, d\omega \qquad (14\text{-}70)$$

Also, the differential element of solid angle $d\omega$ can be expressed as (Appendix A)

$$d\omega = \frac{dS}{r^2} = \sin\phi \, d\phi \, d\theta$$

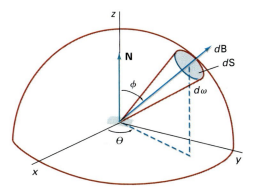

Figure 14-84
Total radiant energy from a surface point is the sum of the contributions in all directions over a hemisphere centered on the surface point.

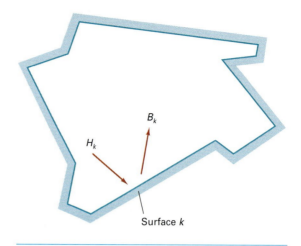

Figure 14-85
An enclosure of surfaces for the radiosity model.

so that

$$B = I \int_0^{2\pi} \int_0^{\pi/2} \cos\phi \sin\phi \, d\phi \, d\theta \qquad (14\text{-}71)$$
$$= I\pi$$

A model for the light reflections from the various surfaces is formed by setting up an "enclosure" of surfaces (Fig. 14-85). Each surface in the enclosure is either a reflector, an emitter (light source), or a combination reflector-emitter. We designate radiosity parameter B_k as the total rate of energy leaving surface k per unit area. Incident-energy parameter H_k is the sum of the energy contributions from all surfaces in the enclosure arriving at surface k per unit time per unit area. That is,

$$H_k = \sum_j B_j F_{jk} \qquad (14\text{-}72)$$

where parameter F_{jk} is the *form factor* for surfaces j and k. Form factor F_{jk} is the fractional amount of radiant energy from surface j that reaches surface k.

For a scene with n surfaces in the enclosure, the radiant energy from surface k is described with the **radiosity equation**:

$$B_k = E_k + \rho_k H_k$$
$$= E_k + \rho_k \sum_{j=1}^n B_j F_{jk} \qquad (14\text{-}73)$$

If surface k is not a light source, $E_k = 0$. Otherwise, E_k is the rate of energy emitted from surface k per unit area ($watts/meter^2$). Parameter ρ_k is the reflectivity factor for surface k (percent of incident light that is reflected in all directions). This reflectivity factor is related to the diffuse reflection coefficient used in empirical illumination models. Plane and convex surfaces cannot "see" themselves, so that no self-incidence takes place and the form factor F_{kk} for these surfaces is 0.

To obtain the illumination effects over the various surfaces in the enclosure, we need to solve the simultaneous radiosity equations for the n surfaces given the array values for E_k, ρ_k, and F_{jk}. That is, we must solve

$$(1 - \rho_k F_{kk})B_k - \rho_k \sum_{j \neq k} B_j F_{jk} = E_k, \qquad k = 1, 2, 3, \ldots, n \qquad (14\text{-}74)$$

or

$$\begin{bmatrix} 1 - \rho_1 F_{11} & -\rho_1 F_{12} & \cdots & -\rho_1 F_{1n} \\ -\rho_2 F_{21} & 1 - \rho_2 F_{22} & \cdots & -\rho_2 F_{2n} \\ \vdots & \vdots & & \vdots \\ -\rho_n F_{n1} & -\rho_2 F_{n2} & \cdots & 1 - \rho_n F_{nn} \end{bmatrix} \cdot \begin{bmatrix} B_1 \\ B_2 \\ \vdots \\ B_n \end{bmatrix} = \begin{bmatrix} E_1 \\ E_2 \\ \vdots \\ E_n \end{bmatrix} \qquad (14\text{-}75)$$

We then convert to intensity values I_k by dividing the radiosity values B_k by π. For color scenes, we can calculate the individual RGB components of the radiosity (B_{kR}, B_{kG}, B_{kB}) from the color components of ρ_k and E_k.

Before we can solve Eq. 14-74, we need to determine the values for form factors F_{jk}. We do this by considering the energy transfer from surface j to surface k (Fig. 14-86). The rate of radiant energy falling on a small surface element dA_k from area element dA_j is

$$dB_j \, dA_j = (I_j \cos \phi_j \, d\omega) dA_j \qquad (14\text{-}76)$$

But solid angle $d\omega$ can be written in terms of the projection of area element dA_k perpendicular to the direction dB_j:

$$d\omega = \frac{dA}{r^2} = \frac{\cos \phi_k dA_k}{r^2} \qquad (14\text{-}77)$$

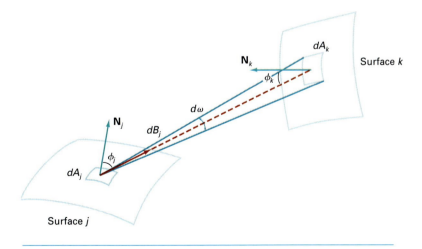

Figure 14-86
Rate of energy transfer dB_j from a surface element with area dA_j to surface element dA_k.

so we can express Eq. 14-76 as

$$dB_j \, dA_j = \frac{I_j \cos \phi_j \, \cos \phi_k \, dA_j \, dA_k}{r^2} \qquad (14\text{-}78)$$

The form factor between the two surfaces is the percent of energy emanating from area dA_j that is incident on dA_k:

$$F_{dA_j, dA_k} = \frac{\text{energy incident on } dA_k}{\text{total energy leaving } dA_j} \qquad (14\text{-}79)$$

$$= \frac{I_j \cos \phi_j \, \cos \phi_k \, dA_j \, dA_k}{r^2} \cdot \frac{1}{B_j \, dA_j}$$

Also $B_j = \pi I_j$, so that

$$F_{dA_j, dA_k} = \frac{\cos \phi_j \, \cos \phi_k \, dA_k}{\pi r^2} \qquad (14\text{-}80)$$

The fraction of emitted energy from area dA_j incident on the entire surface k is then

$$F_{dA_j, A_k} = \int_{\text{surf}_j} \frac{\cos \phi_j \, \cos \phi_k}{\pi r^2} dA_k \qquad (14\text{-}81)$$

where A_k is the area of surface k. We now can define the form factor between the two surfaces as the area average of the previous expression:

$$F_{jk} = \frac{1}{A_j} \int_{\text{surf}_j} \int_{\text{surf}_k} \frac{\cos \phi_j \, \cos \phi_k}{\pi r^2} dA_k \, dA_j \qquad (14\text{-}82)$$

Integrals 14-82 are evaluated using numerical integration techniques and stipulating the following conditions:

- $\sum_{k=1}^{n} F_{jk} = 1$, for all k (conservation of energy)
- $A_j F_{jk} = A_k F_{kj}$ (uniform light reflection)
- $F_{jj} = 0$, for all j (assuming only plane or convex surface patches)

Each surface in the scene can be subdivided into many small polygons, and the smaller the polygon areas, the more realistic the display appears. We can speed up the calculation of the form factors by using a hemicube to approximate the hemisphere. This replaces the spherical surface with a set of linear (plane) surfaces. Once the form factors are evaluated, we can solve the simultaneous linear equations 14-74 using, say, Gaussian elimination or LU decomposition methods (Appendix A). Alternatively, we can start with approximate values for the B_j and solve the set of linear equations iteratively using the Gauss–Seidel method. At each iteration, we calculate an estimate of the radiosity for surface patch k using the previously obtained radiosity values in the radiosity equation:

$$B_k = E_k + \rho_k \sum_{j=1}^{n} B_j F_{jk}$$

We can then display the scene at each step, and an improved surface rendering is viewed at each iteration until there is little change in the calculated radiosity values.

Progressive Refinement Radiosity Method

Although the radiosity method produces highly realistic surface renderings, there are tremendous storage requirements, and considerable processing time is needed to calculate the form factors. Using *progressive refinement*, we can restructure the iterative radiosity algorithm to speed up the calculations and reduce storage requirements at each iteration.

From the radiosity equation, the radiosity contribution between two surface patches is calculated as

$$B_k \text{ due to } B_j = \rho_k B_j F_{jk} \qquad (14\text{-}83)$$

Reciprocally,

$$B_j \text{ due to } B_k = \rho_j B_k F_{kj}, \qquad \text{for all } j \qquad (14\text{-}84)$$

which we can rewrite as

$$B_j \text{ due to } B_k = \rho_j B_k F_{jk} \frac{A_j}{A_k}, \qquad \text{for all } j \qquad (14\text{-}85)$$

This relationship is the basis for the progressive refinement approach to the radiosity calculations. Using a single surface patch k, we can calculate all form factors F_{jk} and "shoot" light from that patch to all other surfaces in the environment. Thus, we need only to compute and store one hemicube and the associated form factors at a time. We then discard these values and choose another patch for the next iteration. At each step, we display the approximation to the rendering of the scene.

Initially, we set $B_k = E_k$ for all surface patches. We then select the patch with the highest radiosity value, which will be the brightest light emitter, and calculate the next approximation to the radiosity for all other patches. This process is repeated at each step, so that light sources are chosen first in order of highest radiant energy, and then other patches are selected based on the amount of light received from the light sources. The steps in a simple progressive refinement approach are given in the following algorithm.

549

Figure 14-87
Nave of Chartres Cathedral
rendered with a progressive-
refinement radiosity model by John
Wallace and John Lin, using the
Hewlett-Packard Starbase Radiosity
and Ray Tracing software. Radiosity
form factors were computed with
ray-tracing methods. (*Courtesy of Eric
Haines, 3D/EYE Inc. © 1989, Hewlett-
Packard Co.*)

```
for each patch k
/* set up hemicube, calculate form factors Fjk*/

for each patch j {
        Δrad := ρjBkFjkAj/Ak;
        ΔBj := ΔBj + Δrad;
        Bj := Bj + Δrad;
}

ΔBk = 0;
```

At each step, the surface patch with the highest value for $\Delta B_k A_k$ is selected as the shooting patch, since radiosity is a measure of radiant energy per unit area. And we choose the initial values as $\Delta B_k = B_k = E_k$ for all surface patches. This progressive refinement algorithm approximates the actual propagation of light through a scene.

Displaying the rendered surfaces at each step produces a sequence of views that proceeds from a dark scene to a fully illuminated one. After the first step, the only surfaces illuminated are the light sources and those nonemitting patches that are visible to the chosen emitter. To produce more useful initial views of the scene, we can set an ambient light level so that all patches have some illumination. At each stage of the iteration, we then reduce the ambient light according to the amount of radiant energy shot into the scene.

Figure 14-87 shows a scene rendered with the progressive-refinement radiosity model. Radiosity renderings of scenes with various lighting conditions are illustrated in Figs. 14-88 to 14-90. Ray-tracing methods are often combined with the radiosity model to produce highly realistic diffuse and specular surface shadings, as in Fig. 14-81.

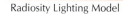

Figure 14-88
Image of a constructivist museum rendered with a progressive-refinement radiosity method.
(Courtesy of Shenchang Eric Chen, Stuart I. Feldman, and Julie Dorsey, Program of Computer Graphics, Cornell University. © 1988, Cornell University, Program of Computer Graphics.)

Figure 14-89
Simulation of the stair tower of the Engineering Theory Center Building at Cornell University rendered with a progressive-refinement radiosity method.
(Courtesy of Keith Howie and Ben Trumbore, Program of Computer Graphics, Cornell University. © 1990, Cornell University, Program of Computer Graphics.)

(a)   (b)

Figure 14-90
Simulation of two lighting schemes for the Parisian garret from the Metropolitan Opera's production of *La Boheme*: (a) day view and (b) night view. *(Courtesy of Julie Dorsey and Mark Shepard, Program of Computer Graphics, Cornell University. © 1991, Cornell University, Program of Computer Graphics.)*

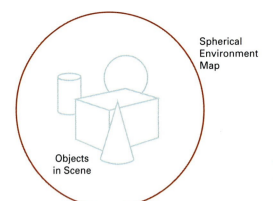

Spherical
Environment
Map

Objects
in Scene

Figure 14-91
A spherical enclosing universe
containing the environment map.

14-8
ENVIRONMENT MAPPING

An alternate procedure for modeling global reflections is to define an array of intensity values that describes the environment around a single object or a set of objects. Instead of interobject ray tracing or radiosity calculations to pick up the global specular and diffuse illumination effects, we simply map the *environment array* onto an object in relationship to the viewing direction. This procedure is referred to as **environment mapping,** also called **reflection mapping** although transparency effects could also be modeled with the environment map. Environment mapping is sometimes referred to as the "poor person's ray-tracing" method, since it is a fast approximation of the more accurate global-illumination rendering techniques we discussed in the previous two sections.

The environment map is defined over the surface of an enclosing universe. Information in the environment map includes intensity values for light sources, the sky, and other background objects. Figure 14-91 shows the enclosing universe as a sphere, but a cube or a cylinder is often used as the enclosing universe.

To render the surface of an object, we project pixel areas onto the surface and then reflect the projected pixel area onto the environment map to pick up the surface-shading attributes for each pixel. If the object is transparent, we can also refract the projected pixel area to the environment map. The environment-mapping process for reflection of a projected pixel area is illustrated in Fig. 14-92. Pixel intensity is determined by averaging the intensity values within the intersected region of the environment map.

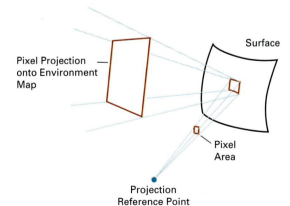

Pixel Projection
onto Environment
Map

Surface

Pixel
Area

Projection
Reference Point

Figure 14-92
Projecting a pixel area to a surface,
then reflecting the area to the
environment map.

552

ADDING SURFACE DETAIL

So far we have discussed rendering techniques for displaying smooth surfaces, typically polygons or splines. However, most objects do not have smooth, even surfaces. We need surface texture to model accurately such objects as brick walls, gravel roads, and shag carpets. In addition, some surfaces contain patterns that must be taken into account in the rendering procedures. The surface of a vase could contain a painted design; a water glass might have the family crest engraved into the surface; a tennis court contains markings for the alleys, service areas, and base line; and a four-lane highway has dividing lines and other markings, such as oil spills and tire skids. Figure 14-93 illustrates objects displayed with various surface detail.

Modeling Surface Detail with Polygons

A simple method for adding surface detail is to model structure and patterns with polygon facets. For large-scale detail, polygon modeling can give good results. Some examples of such large-scale detail are squares on a checkerboard, dividing lines on a highway, tile patterns on a linoleum floor, floral designs in a smooth low-pile rug, panels in a door, and lettering on the side of a panel truck. Also, we could model an irregular surface with small, randomly oriented polygon facets, provided the facets were not too small.

(a)

(b)

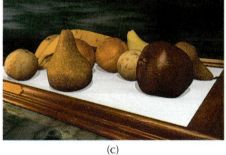

(c)

(d)

Figure 14-93
Scenes illustrating computer graphics generation of surface detail.
((a) © 1992 Deborah R. Fowler, Przemyslaw Prusinkiewicz, and Johannes Battjes;
(b) © 1992 Deborah R. Fowler, Hans Meinhardt, and Przemyslaw Prusinkiewicz,
University of Calgary; (c) and (d) Courtesy of SOFTIMAGE, Inc.)

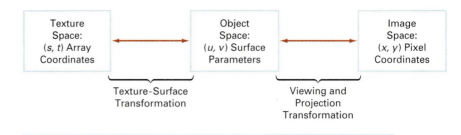

Figure 14-94
Coordinate reference systems for texture space, object space, and image
space.

Surface-pattern polygons are generally overlaid on a larger surface polygon
and are processed with the parent surface. Only the parent polygon is processed
by the visible-surface algorithms, but the illumination parameters for the surface-
detail polygons take precedence over the parent polygon. When intricate or fine
surface detail is to be modeled, polygon methods are not practical. For example,
it would be difficult to accurately model the surface structure of a raisin with
polygon facets.

Texture Mapping

A common method for adding surface detail is to map texture patterns onto the
surfaces of objects. The texture pattern may either be defined in a rectangular
array or as a procedure that modifies surface intensity values. This approach is
referred to as **texture mapping** or **pattern mapping**.

Usually, the texture pattern is defined with a rectangular grid of intensity
values in a *texture space* referenced with (s, t) coordinate values, as shown in Fig.
14-94. Surface positions in the scene are referenced with uv object-space coordinates, and pixel positions on the projection plane are referenced in xy Cartesian
coordinates. Texture mapping can be accomplished in one of two ways. Either we
can map the texture pattern to object surfaces, then to the projection plane; or we
can map pixel areas onto object surfaces, then to texture space. Mapping a texture
pattern to pixel coordinates is sometimes called *texture scanning*, while the mapping from pixel coordinates to texture space is referred to as *pixel-order scanning*
or *inverse scanning* or *image-order scanning*.

To simplify calculations, the mapping from texture space to object space is
often specified with parametric linear functions

$$u = f_u(s,t) = a_u s + b_u t + c_u$$
$$v = f_v(s,t) = a_v s + b_v t + c_v$$

(14-86)

The object-to-image space mapping is accomplished with the concatenation of
the viewing and projection transformations. A disadvantage of mapping from
texture space to pixel space is that a selected texture patch usually does not
match up with the pixel boundaries, thus requiring calculation of the fractional
area of pixel coverage. Therefore, mapping from pixel space to texture space (Fig.
14-95) is the most commonly used texture-mapping method. This avoids pixel-
subdivision calculations, and allows antialiasing (filtering) procedures to be eas-

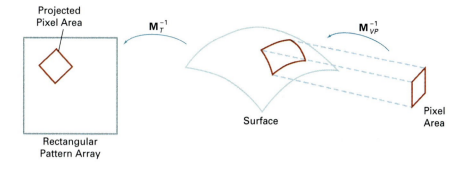

Rectangular
Pattern Array

Projected
Pixel Area

$\mathbf{M}_T^{-1}$

Surface

$\mathbf{M}_{VP}^{-1}$

Pixel
Area

Figure 14-95
Texture mapping by projecting pixel areas to texture space.

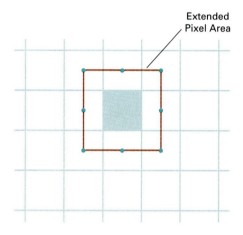

Extended
Pixel Area

Figure 14-96
Extended area for a pixel that
includes centers of adjacent pixels.

ily applied. An effective antialiasing procedure is to project a slightly larger pixel area that includes the centers of neighboring pixels, as shown in Fig. 14-96, and applying a pyramid function to weight the intensity values in the texture pattern. But the mapping from image space to texture space does require calculation of the inverse viewing-projection transformation $\mathbf{M}_{VP}^{-1}$ and the inverse texture-map transformation $\mathbf{M}_T^{-1}$. In the following example, we illustrate this approach by mapping a defined pattern onto a cylindrical surface.

Example 14-1 Texture Mapping

To illustrate the steps in texture mapping, we consider the transfer of the pattern shown in Fig. 14-97 to a cylindrical surface. The surface parameters are

$$u = \theta, \qquad v = z$$

with

$$0 \le \theta \le \pi/2, \qquad 0 \le z \le 1$$

555

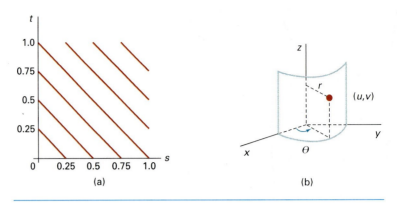

Figure 14-97
Mapping a texture pattern defined on a unit square (a) to a cylindrical
surface (b).

And the parametric representation for the surface in the Cartesian reference
frame is

$$x = r\cos u, \qquad y = r\sin u, \qquad z = v$$

We can map the array pattern to the surface with the following linear transformation, which maps the pattern origin to the lower left corner of the surface.

$$u = s\pi/2, \qquad v = t$$

Next, we select a viewing position and perform the inverse viewing transformation from pixel coordinates to the Cartesian reference for the cylindrical surface.
Cartesian coordinates are then mapped to the surface parameters with the transformation

$$u = \tan^{-1}(y/x), \qquad v = z$$

and projected pixel positions are mapped to texture space with the inverse transformation

$$s = 2u/\pi, \qquad t = v$$

Intensity values in the pattern array covered by each projected pixel area are then
averaged to obtain the pixel intensity.

Procedural Texturing Methods

Another method for adding surface texture is to use procedural definitions of the
color variations that are to be applied to the objects in a scene. This approach
avoids the transformation calculations involved in transferring two-dimensional
texture patterns to object surfaces.

When values are assigned throughout a region of three-dimensional space,
the object color variations are referred to as **solid textures**. Values from *texture*

Figure 14-98
A scene with surface characteristics generated using solid-texture methods. (*Courtesy of Peter Shirley, Computer Science Department, Indiana University.*)

space are transferred to object surfaces using procedural methods, since it is usually impossible to store texture values for all points throughout a region of space. Other procedural methods can be used to set up texture values over two-dimensional surfaces. Solid texturing allows cross-sectional views of three-dimensional objects, such as bricks, to be rendered with the same texturing as the outside surfaces.

As examples of procedural texturing, wood grains or marble patterns can be created using harmonic functions (sine curves) defined in three-dimensional space. Random variations in the wood or marble texturing can be attained by superimposing a noise function on the harmonic variations. Figure 14-98 shows a scene displayed using solid textures to obtain wood-grain and other surface patterns. The scene in Fig. 14-99 was rendered using procedural descriptions of materials such as stone masonry, polished gold, and banana leaves.

Figure 14-99
A scene rendered with VG Shaders and modeled with RenderMan using polygonal facets for the gem faces, quadric surfaces, and bicubic patches. In addition to surface texturing, procedural methods were used to create the steamy jungle atmosphere and the forest canopy dappled lighting effect. (*Courtesy of the VALIS Group. Reprinted from Graphics Gems III, edited by David Kirk. Copyright © 1992, Academic Press, Inc.*)

Bump Mapping

Although texture mapping can be used to add fine surface detail, it is not a good method for modeling the surface roughness that appears on objects such as oranges, strawberries, and raisins. The illumination detail in the texture pattern usually does not correspond to the illumination direction in the scene. A better method for creating surface bumpiness is to apply a perturbation function to the surface normal and then use the perturbed normal in the illumination-model calculations. This techniques is called **bump mapping**.

If $\mathbf{P}(u, v)$ represents a position on a parametric surface, we can obtain the surface normal at that point with the calculation

$$\mathbf{N} = \mathbf{P}_u \times \mathbf{P}_v \tag{14-87}$$

where $\mathbf{P}_u$ and $\mathbf{P}_v$ are the partial derivatives of $\mathbf{P}$ with respect to parameters u and v. To obtain a perturbed normal, we modify the surface-position vector by adding a small perturbation function, called a *bump function*:

$$\mathbf{P}'(u, v) = \mathbf{P}(u, v) + b(u, v)\mathbf{n} \tag{14-88}$$

This adds bumps to the surface in the direction of the unit surface normal $\mathbf{n} = \mathbf{N}/|\mathbf{N}|$. The perturbed surface normal is then obtained as

$$\mathbf{N}' = \mathbf{P}'_u \times \mathbf{P}'_v \tag{14-89}$$

We calculate the partial derivative with respect to u of the perturbed position vector as

$$\mathbf{P}'_u = \frac{\partial}{\partial u}(\mathbf{P} + b\mathbf{n})$$
$$= \mathbf{P}_u + b_u\mathbf{n} + b\mathbf{n}_u \tag{14-90}$$

Assuming the bump function b is small, we can neglect the last term and write:

$$\mathbf{P}'_u \approx \mathbf{P}_u + b_u\mathbf{n} \tag{14-91}$$

Similarly,

$$\mathbf{P}'_v \approx \mathbf{P}_v + b_v\mathbf{n} \tag{14-92}$$

And the perturbed surface normal is

$$\mathbf{N}' = \mathbf{P}_u \times \mathbf{P}_v + b_v(\mathbf{P}_u \times \mathbf{n}) + b_u(\mathbf{n} \times \mathbf{P}_v) + b_u b_v(\mathbf{n} \times \mathbf{n})$$

But $\mathbf{n} \times \mathbf{n} = 0$, so that

$$\mathbf{N}' = \mathbf{N} + b_v(\mathbf{P}_u \times \mathbf{n}) + b_u(\mathbf{n} \times \mathbf{P}_v) \tag{14-93}$$

The final step is to normalize $\mathbf{N}'$ for use in the illumination-model calculations.

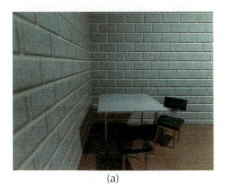
(a)

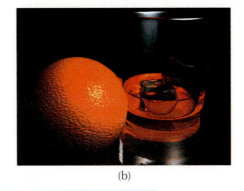
(b)

Figure 14-100

Surface roughness characteristics rendered with bump mapping.

(Courtesy of (a) Peter Shirley, Computer Science Department, Indiana University and (b) SOFTIMAGE, Inc.)

Figure 14-101

The stained-glass knight from the motion picture *Young Sherlock Holmes*. A combination of bump mapping, environment mapping, and texture mapping was used to render the armor surface. (*Courtesy of Industrial Light & Magic. Copyright © 1985 Paramount Pictures/Amblin.*)

There are several ways in which we can specify the bump function $b(u, v)$. We can actually define an analytic expression, but bump values are usually obtained with table lookups. With a bump table, values for b can be obtained quickly with linear interpolation and incremental calculations. Partial derivatives b_u and b_v are approximated with finite differences. The bump table can be set up with random patterns, regular grid patterns, or character shapes. Random patterns are useful for modeling irregular surfaces, such as a raisin, while a repeating pattern could be used to model the surface of an orange, for example. To antialiase, we subdivide pixel areas and average the computed subpixel intensities.

Figure 14-100 shows examples of surfaces rendered with bump mapping. An example of combined surface-rendering methods is given in Fig. 14-101. The armor for the stained-glass knight in the film *Young Sherlock Holmes* was rendered with a combination of bump mapping, environment mapping, and texture mapping. An environment map of the surroundings was combined with a bump map to produce background illumination reflections and surface roughness. Then additional color and surface illumination, bumps, spots of dirt, and stains for the seams and rivets were added to produce the overall effect shown in Fig. 14-101.

Frame Mapping

This technique is an extension of bump mapping. In **frame mapping,** we perturb both the surface normal **N** and a local coordinate system (Fig. 14-102) attached to

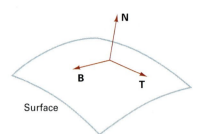

Figure 14-102
A local coordinate system at a
surface point.

N. The local coordinates are defined with a surface-tangent vector **T** and a binormal vector $\mathbf{B} = \mathbf{T} \times \mathbf{N}$.

Frame mapping is used to model anisotropic surfaces. We orient **T** along the "grain" of the surface and apply directional perturbations, in addition to bump perturbations in the direction of **N**. In this way, we can model wood-grain patterns, cross-thread patterns in cloth, and streaks in marble or similar materials. Both bump and directional perturbations can be obtained with table lookups.

SUMMARY

In general, an object is illuminated with radiant energy from light-emitting sources and from the reflective surfaces of other objects in the scene. Light sources can be modeled as point sources or as distributed (extended) sources. Objects can be either opaque or transparent. And lighting effects can be described in terms of diffuse and specular components for both reflections and refractions.

An empirical, point light-source, illumination model can be used to describe diffuse reflections with Lambert's cosine law and to describe specular reflections with the Phong model. General background (ambient) lighting can be modeled with a fixed intensity level and a coefficient of reflection for each surface. In this basic model, we can approximate transparency effects by combining surface intensities using a transparency coefficient. Accurate geometric modeling of light paths through transparent materials is obtained by calculating refraction angles using Snell's law. Color is incorporated into the model by assigning a triple of RGB values to intensities and surface reflection coefficients. We can also extend the basic model to incorporate distributed light sources, studio lighting effects, and intensity attenuation.

Intensity values calculated with an illumination model must be mapped to the intensity levels available on the display system in use. A logarithmic intensity scale is used to provide a set of intensity levels with equal perceived brightness. In addition, gamma correction is applied to intensity values to correct for the nonlinearity of diaplay devices. With bilevel monitors, we can use halftone patterns and dithering techniques to simulate a range of intensity values. Halftone approximations can also be used to increase the number of intensity options on systems that are capable of displaying more than two intensities per pixel. Ordered-dither, error-diffusion, and dot-diffusion methods are used to simulate a range of intensities when the number of points to be plotted in a scene is equal to the number of pixels on the display device.

Surface rendering can be accomplished by applying a basic illumination model to the objects in a scene. We apply an illumination model using either constant-intensity shading, Gouraud shading, or Phong shading. Constant shading is accurate for polyhedrons or for curved-surface polygon meshes when the viewing and light-source positions are far from the objects in a scene. Gouraud shading approximates light reflections from curved surfaces by calculating intensity values at polygon vertices and interpolating these intensity values across the polygon facets. A more accurate, but slower, surface-rendering procedure is Phong shading, which interpolates the average normal vectors for polygon vertices over the polygon facets. Then, surface intensities are calculated using the interpolated normal vectors. Fast Phong shading can be used to speed up the calculations using Taylor series approximations.

Ray tracing provides an accurate method for obtaining global, specular reflection and transmission effects. Pixel rays are traced through a scene, bouncing from object to object while accumulating intensity contributions. A ray-tracing tree is constructed for each pixel, and intensity values are combined from the terminal nodes of the tree back up to the root. Object-intersection calculations in ray tracing can be reduced with space-subdivision methods that test for ray-object intersections only within subregions of the total space. Distributed (or distribution) ray tracing traces multiple rays per pixel and distributes the rays randomly over the various ray parameters, such as direction and time. This provides an accurate method for modeling surface gloss and translucency, finite camera apertures, distributed light sources, shadow effects, and motion blur.

Radiosity methods provide accurate modeling of diffuse-reflection effects by calculating radiant energy transfer between the various surface patches in a scene. Progressive refinement is used to speed up the radiosity calculations by considering energy transfer from one surface patch at a time. Highly photorealistic scenes are generated using a combination of ray tracing and radiosity.

A fast method for approximating global illumination effects is environment mapping. An environment array is used to store background intensity information for a scene. This array is then mapped to the objects in a scene based on the specified viewing direction.

Surface detail can be added to objects using polygon facets, texture mapping, bump mapping, or frame mapping. Small polygon facets can be overlaid on larger surfaces to provide various kinds of designs. Alternatively, texture patterns can be defined in a two-dimensional array and mapped to object surfaces. Bump mapping is a means for modeling surface irregularities by applying a bump function to perturb surface normals. Frame mapping is an extension of bump mapping that allows for horizontal surface variations, as well as vertical variations.

REFERENCES

A general discussion of energy propagation, transfer equations, rendering processes, and our perception of light and color is given in Glassner (1994). Algorithms for various surface-rendering techniques are presented in Glassner (1990), Arvo (1991), and Kirk (1992). For further discussion of ordered dither, error diffusion, and dot diffusion see Knuth (1987). Additional information on ray-tracing methods can be found in Quek and Hearn (1988), Glassner (1989), Shirley (1990), and Koh and Hearn (1992). Radiosity methods are discussed in Goral et al. (1984), Cohen and Greenberg (1985), Cohen et al. (1988), Wallace, Elmquist, and Haines (1989), Chen et al. (1991), Dorsey, Sillion, and Greenberg (1991), He et al. (1992), Sillion et al. (1991), Schoeneman et al. (1993), and Lischinski, Tampieri, and Greenberg (1993).

EXERCISES

14.1 Write a routine to implement Eq. 14-4 of the basic illumination model using a single point light source and constant surface shading for the faces of a specified polyhedron. The object description is to be given as a set of polygon tables, including surface normals for each of the polygon faces. Additional input parameters include the ambient intensity, light-source intensity, and the surface reflection coefficients. All coordinate information can be specified directly in the viewing reference frame.

14-2. Modify the routine in Exercise 14-1 to render a polygon surface mesh using Gouraud shading.

14-3. Modify the routine in Exercise 14-1 to render a polygon surface mesh using Phong shading.

14-4. Write a routine to implement Eq. 14-9 of the basic illumination model using a single point light source and Gouraud surface shading for the faces of a specified polygon mesh. The object description is to be given as a set of polygon tables, including surface normals for each of the polygon faces. Additional input includes values for the ambient intensity, light-source intensity, surface reflection coefficients, and the specular-reflection parameter. All coordinate information can be specified directly in the viewing reference frame.

14-5. Modify the routine in Exercise 14-4 to render the polygon surfaces using Phong shading.

14-6. Modify the routine in Exercise 14-4 to include a linear intensity attenuation function.

14-7. Modify the routine in Exercise 14-4 to render the polygon surfaces using Phong shading and a linear intensity attenuation function.

14-8. Modify the routine in Exercise 14-4 to implement Eq. 14-13 with any specified number of polyhedrons and light sources in the scene.

14-9. Modify the routine in Exercise 14-4 to implement Eq. 14-14 with any specified number of polyhedrons and light sources in the scene.

14-10. Modify the routine in Exercise 14-4 to implement Eq. 14-15 with any specified number of polyhedrons and light sources in the scene.

14-11. Modify the routine in Exercise 14-4 to implement Eqs. 14-15 and 14-19 with any specified number of light sources and polyhedrons (either opaque or transparent) in the scene.

14-12. Discuss the differences you might expect to see in the appearance of specular reflections modeled with $(\mathbf{N} \cdot \mathbf{H})^{n_s}$ compared to specular reflections modeled with $(\mathbf{V} \cdot \mathbf{R})^{n_s}$.

14-13. Verify that $2\alpha = \phi$ in Fig. 14-18 when all vectors are coplanar, but that in general, $2\alpha \neq \phi$.

14-14. Discuss how the different visible-surface detection methods can be combined with an intensity model for displaying a set of polyhedrons with opaque surfaces.

14-15. Discuss how the various visible-surface detection methods can be modified to process transparent objects. Are there any visible-surface detection methods that cannot handle transparent surfaces?

14-16. Set up an algorithm, based on one of the visible-surface detection methods, that will identify shadow areas in a scene illuminated by a distant point source.

14-17. How many intensity levels can be displayed with halftone approximations using n by n pixel grids where each pixel can be displayed with m different intensities?

14-18. How many different color combinations can be generated using halftone approximations on a two-level RGB system with a 3 by 3 pixel grid?

14-19. Write a routine to display a given set of surface-intensity variations using halftone approximations with 3 by 3 pixel grids and two intensity levels (0 and 1) per pixel.

14-20. Write a routine to generate ordered-dither matrices using the recurrence relation in Eq. 14-34.

14-21. Write a procedure to display a given array of intensity values using the ordered-dither method.

14-22. Write a procedure to implement the error-diffusion algorithm for a given m by n array of intensity values.

14-23. Write a program to implement the basic ray-tracing algorithm for a scene containing a single sphere hovering over a checkerboard ground square. The scene is to be illuminated with a single point light source at the viewing position.

14-24. Write a program to implement the basic ray-tracing algorithm for a scene containing any specified arrangement of spheres and polygon surfaces illuminated by a given set of point light sources.

14-25. Write a program to implement the basic ray-tracing algorithm using space-subdivision methods for any specified arrangement of spheres and polygon surfaces illuminated by a given set of point light sources.

14-26. Write a program to implement the following features of distributed ray tracing: pixel sampling with 16 jittered rays per pixel, distributed reflection directions, distributed refraction directions, and extended light sources.

14-27. Set up an algorithm for modeling the motion blur of a moving object using distributed ray tracing.

14-28. Implement the basic radiosity algorithm for rendering the inside surfaces of a cube when one inside face of the cube is a light source.

14-29. Devise an algorithm for implementing the progressive refinement radiosity method.

14-30. Write a routine to transform an environment map to the surface of a sphere.

14-31. Write a program to implement texture mapping for (a) spherical surfaces and (b) polyhedrons.

14-32. Given a spherical surface, write a bump-mapping procedure to generate the bumpy surface of an orange.

14-33. Write a bump-mapping routine to produce surface-normal variations for any specified bump function.

CHAPTER

15 Color Models and Color Applications

Our discussions of color up to this point have concentrated on the mechanisms for generating color displays with combinations of red, green, and blue light. This model is helpful in understanding how color is represented on a video monitor, but several other color models are useful as well in graphics applications. Some models are used to describe color output on printers and plotters, and other models provide a more intuitive color-parameter interface for the user.

A **color model** is a method for explaining the properties or behavior of color within some particular context. No single color model can explain all aspects of color, so we make use of different models to help describe the different perceived characteristics of color.

15-1
PROPERTIES OF LIGHT

What we perceive as "light", or different colors, is a narrow frequency band within the electromagnetic spectrum. A few of the other frequency bands within this spectrum are called radio waves, microwaves, infrared waves, and X-rays. Figure 15-1 shows the approximate frequency ranges for some of the electromagnetic bands.

Each frequency value within the visible band corresponds to a distinct color. At the low-frequency end is a red color (4.3×10^{14} hertz), and the highest frequency we can see is a violet color (7.5×10^{14} hertz). Spectral colors range from the reds through orange and yellow at the low-frequency end to greens, blues, and violet at the high end.

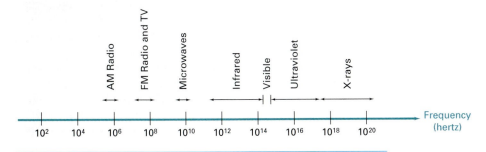

Figure 15-1
Electromagnetic spectrum.

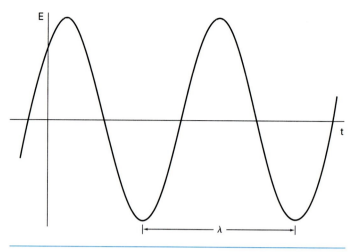

Figure 15-2
Time variations for one electric frequency component of a plane-polarized electromagnetic wave.

Since light is an electromagnetic wave, we can describe the various colors in terms of either the frequency f or the wavelength λ of the wave. In Fig. 15-2, we illustrate the oscillations present in a monochromatic electromagnetic wave, polarized so that the electric oscillations are in one plane. The wavelength and frequency of the monochromatic wave are inversely proportional to each other, with the proportionality constant as the speed of light c:

$$c = \lambda f \qquad (15\text{-}1)$$

Frequency is constant for all materials, but the speed of light and the wavelength are material-dependent. In a vacuum, $c = 3 \times 10^{10}$ cm/sec. Light wavelengths are very small, so length units for designating spectral colors are usually either angstroms ($1\text{Å} = 10^{-8}$ cm) or nanometers (1 nm $= 10^{-7}$ cm). An equivalent term for nanometer is millimicron. Light at the red end of the spectrum has a wavelength of approximately 700 nanometers (nm), and the wavelength of the violet light at the other end of the spectrum is about 400 nm. Since wavelength units are somewhat more convenient to deal with than frequency units, spectral colors are typically specified in terms of wavelength.

A light source such as the sun or a light bulb emits all frequencies within the visible range to produce white light. When white light is incident upon an object, some frequencies are reflected and some are absorbed by the object. The combination of frequencies present in the reflected light determines what we perceive as the color of the object. If low frequencies are predominant in the reflected light, the object is described as red. In this case, we say the perceived light has a **dominant frequency** (or **dominant wavelength**) at the red end of the spectrum. The dominant frequency is also called the **hue**, or simply the **color**, of the light.

Other properties besides frequency are needed to describe the various characteristics of light. When we view a source of light, our eyes respond to the color (or dominant frequency) and two other basic sensations. One of these we call the **brightness**, which is the perceived intensity of the light. Intensity is the radiant energy emitted per unit time, per unit solid angle, and per unit projected area of the source. Radiant energy is related to the **luminance** of the source. The second

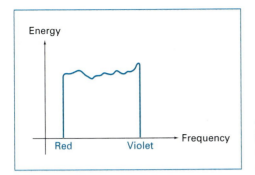

Figure 15-3
Energy distribution of a white-light source.

perceived characteristic is the **purity**, or **saturation**, of the light. Purity describes how washed out or how "pure" the color of the light appears. Pastels and pale colors are described as less pure. These three characteristics, dominant frequency, brightness, and purity, are commonly used to describe the different properties we perceive in a source of light. The term **chromaticity** is used to refer collectively to the two properties describing color characteristics: purity and dominant frequency.

Energy emitted by a white-light source has a distribution over the visible frequencies as shown in Fig. 15-3. Each frequency component within the range from red to violet contributes more or less equally to the total energy, and the color of the source is described as white. When a dominant frequency is present, the energy distribution for the source takes a form such as that in Fig. 15-4. We would now describe the light as having the color corresponding to the dominant frequency. The energy density of the dominant light component is labeled as E_D in this figure, and the contributions from the other frequencies produce white light of energy density E_W. We can calculate the brightness of the source as the area under the curve, which gives the total energy density emitted. Purity depends on the difference between E_D and E_W. The larger the energy E_D of the dominant frequency compared to the white-light component E_W, the more pure the light. We have a purity of 100 percent when $E_W = 0$ and a purity of 0 percent when $E_W = E_D$.

When we view light that has been formed by a combination of two or more sources, we see a resultant light with characteristics determined by the original sources. Two different-color light sources with suitably chosen intensities can be used to produce a range of other colors. If the two color sources combine to pro-

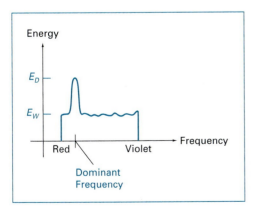

Figure 15-4
Energy distribution of a light source with a dominant frequency near the red end of the frequency range.

567

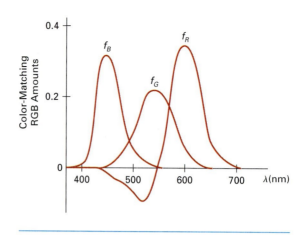

Figure 15-5
Amounts of RGB primaries needed to display
spectral colors.

duce white light, they are referred to as **complementary colors**. Examples of
complementary color pairs are red and cyan, green and magenta, and blue and
yellow. With a judicious choice of two or more starting colors, we can form a
wide range of other colors. Typically, color models that are used to describe combinations of light in terms of dominant frequency (hue) use three colors to obtain
a reasonably wide range of colors, called the **color gamut** for that model. The two
or three colors used to produce other colors in such a color model are referred to
as **primary colors**.

   No finite set of real primary colors can be combined to produce all possible
visible colors. Nevertheless, three primaries are sufficient for most purposes, and
colors not in the color gamut for a specified set of primaries can still be described
by extended methods. If a certain color cannot be produced by combining the
three primaries, we can mix one or two of the primaries with that color to obtain
a match with the combination of remaining primaries. In this extended sense, a
set of primary colors can be considered to describe all colors. Figure 15-5 shows
the amounts of red, green, and blue needed to produce any spectral color. The
curves plotted in Fig. 15-5, called *color-matching functions*, were obtained by averaging the judgments of a large number of observers. Colors in the vicinity of 500
nm can only be matched by "subtracting" an amount of red light from a combination of blue and green lights. This means that a color around 500 nm is described only by combining that color with an amount of red light to produce the
blue–green combination specified in the diagram. Thus, an RGB color monitor
cannot display colors in the neighborhood of 500 nm.

15-2

STANDARD PRIMARIES AND THE CHROMATICITY DIAGRAM

Since no finite set of color light sources can be combined to display all possible
colors, three standard primaries were defined in 1931 by the International Commission on Illumination, referred to as the CIE (Commission Internationale de
l'Éclairage). The three standard primaries are imaginary colors. They are defined
mathematically with positive color-matching functions (Fig. 15-6) that specify the

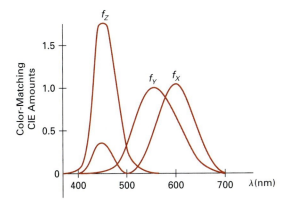

Figure 15-6
Amounts of CIE primaries needed
to display spectral colors.

amount of each primary needed to describe any spectral color. This provides an international standard definition for all colors, and the CIE primaries eliminate negative-value color matching and other problems associated with selecting a set of real primaries.

XYZ Color Model

The set of CIE primaries is generally referred to as the XYZ, or ($\mathbf{X}$, $\mathbf{Y}$, $\mathbf{Z}$), color model, where $\mathbf{X}$, $\mathbf{Y}$, and $\mathbf{Z}$ represent vectors in a three-dimensional, additive color space. Any color C_λ is then expressed as

$$C_\lambda = X\mathbf{X} + Y\mathbf{Y} + Z\mathbf{Z} \qquad (15\text{-}2)$$

where X, Y, and Z designate the amounts of the standard primaries needed to match C_λ.

In discussing color properties, it is convenient to normalize the amounts in Eq. 15-2 against luminance ($X + Y + Z$). Normalized amounts are thus calculated as

$$x = \frac{X}{X + Y + Z}, \qquad y = \frac{Y}{X + Y + Z}, \qquad z = \frac{Z}{X + Y + Z} \qquad (15\text{-}3)$$

with $x + y + z = 1$. Thus, any color can be represented with just the x and y amounts. Since we have normalized against luminance, parameters x and y are called the *chromaticity values* because they depend only on hue and purity. Also, if we specify colors only with x and y values, we cannot obtain the amounts X, Y, and Z. Therefore, a complete description of a color is typically given with the three values x, y, and Y. The remaining CIE amounts are then calculated as

$$X = \frac{x}{y}Y, \qquad Z = \frac{z}{y}Y \qquad (15\text{-}4)$$

where $z = 1 - x - y$. Using chromaticity coordinates (x, y), we can represent all colors on a two-dimensional diagram.

CIE Chromaticity Diagram

When we plot the normalized amounts x and y for colors in the visible spectrum, we obtain the tongue-shaped curve shown in Fig. 15-7. This curve is called the **CIE chromaticity diagram**. Points along the curve are the "pure" colors in the

569

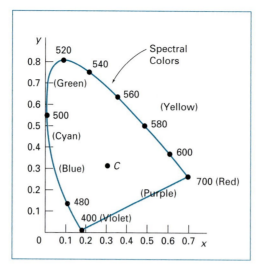

Figure 15-7
CIE chromaticity diagram. Spectral
color positions along the curve are
labeled in wavelength units (nm).

electromagnetic spectrum, labeled according to wavelength in nanometers from
the red end to the violet end of the spectrum. The line joining the red and violet
spectral points, called the *purple line*, is not part of the spectrum. Interior points
represent all possible visible color combinations. Point C in the diagram corresponds to the white-light position. Actually, this point is plotted for a white-light
source known as **illuminant C**, which is used as a standard approximation for
"average" daylight.

Luminance values are not available in the chromaticity diagram because of
normalization. Colors with different luminance but the same chromaticity map to
the same point. The chromaticity diagram is useful for the following:

- Comparing color gamuts for different sets of primaries.
- Identifying complementary colors.
- Determining dominant wavelength and purity of a given color.

Color gamuts are represented on the chromaticity diagram as straight line
segments or as polygons. All colors along the line joining points C_1 and C_2 in Fig.
15-8 can be obtained by mixing appropriate amounts of the colors C_1 and C_2. If a
greater proportion of C_1 is used, the resultant color is closer to C_1 than to C_2. The
color gamut for three points, such as C_3, C_4, and C_5 in Fig. 15-8, is a triangle with
vertices at the three color positions. Three primaries can only generate colors inside or on the bounding edges of the triangle. Thus, the chromaticity diagram
helps us understand why no set of three primaries can be additively combined to
generate all colors, since no triangle within the diagram can encompass all colors.
Color gamuts for video monitors and hard-copy devices are conveniently compared on the chromaticity diagram.

Since the color gamut for two points is a straight line, complementary colors must be represented on the chromaticity diagram as two points situated on
opposite sides of C and connected with a straight line. When we mix proper
amounts of the two colors C_1 and C_2 in Fig. 15-9, we can obtain white light.

We can also use the interpretation of color gamut for two primaries to determine the dominant wavelength of a color. For color point C_1 in Fig. 15-10, we
can draw a straight line from C through C_1 to intersect the spectral curve at point

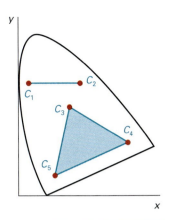

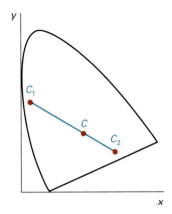

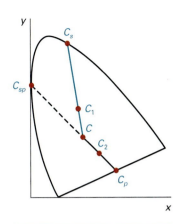

Figure 15-8
Color gamuts defined on the chromaticity diagram for a two-color and a three-color system of primaries.

Figure 15-9
Representing complementary colors on the chromaticity diagram.

Figure 15-10
Determining dominant wavelength and purity with the chromaticity diagram.

C_s. Color C_1 can then be represented as a combination of white light C and the spectral color C_s. Thus, the dominant wavelength of C_1 is C_s. This method for determining dominant wavelength will not work for color points that are between C and the purple line. Drawing a line from C through point C_2 in Fig. 15-10 takes us to point C_p on the purple line, which is not in the visible spectrum. Point C_2 is referred to as a *nonspectral* color, and its dominant wavelength is taken as the compliment of C_p that lies on the spectral curve (point C_{sp}). Nonspectral colors are in the purple–magenta range and have spectral distributions with subtractive dominant wavelengths. They are generated by subtracting the spectral dominant wavelength (such as C_{sp}) from white light.

For any color point, such as C_1 in Fig. 15-10, we determine the purity as the relative distance of C_1 from C along the straight line joining C to C_s. If d_{c1} denotes the distance from C to C_1 and d_{cs} is the distance from C to C_s, we can calculate purity as the ratio d_{c1}/d_{cs}. Color C_1 in this figure is about 25 percent pure, since it is situated at about one-fourth the total distance from C to C_s. At position C_s, the color point would be 100 percent pure.

15-3

INTUITIVE COLOR CONCEPTS

An artist creates a color painting by mixing color pigments with white and black pigments to form the various shades, tints, and tones in the scene. Starting with the pigment for a "pure color" (or "pure hue"), the artist adds a black pigment to produce different **shades** of that color. The more black pigment, the darker the shade. Similarly, different **tints** of the color are obtained by adding a white pigment to the original color, making it lighter as more white is added. **Tones** of the color are produced by adding both black and white pigments.

To many, these color concepts are more intuitive than describing a color as a set of three numbers that give the relative proportions of the primary colors. It is generally much easier to think of making a color lighter by adding white and making a color darker by adding black. Therefore, graphics packages providing color palettes to a user often employ two or more color models. One model provides an intuitive color interface for the user, and others describe the color components for the output devices.

15-4
RGB COLOR MODEL

Based on the *tristimulus theory* of vision, our eyes perceive color through the stimulation of three visual pigments in the cones of the retina. These visual pigments have a peak sensitivity at wavelengths of about 630 nm (red), 530 nm (green), and 450 nm (blue). By comparing intensities in a light source, we perceive the color of the light. This theory of vision is the basis for displaying color output on a video monitor using the three color primaries, red, green, and blue, referred to as the RGB color model.

We can represent this model with the unit cube defined on R, G, and B axes, as shown in Fig. 15-11. The origin represents black, and the vertex with coordinates (1, 1, 1) is white. Vertices of the cube on the axes represent the primary colors, and the remaining vertices represent the complementary color for each of the primary colors.

As with the XYZ color system, the RGB color scheme is an additive model. Intensities of the primary colors are added to produce other colors. Each color point within the bounds of the cube can be represented as the triple (R, G, B), where values for R, G, and B are assigned in the range from 0 to 1. Thus, a color C_λ is expressed in RGB components as

$$C_\lambda = R\mathbf{R} + G\mathbf{G} + B\mathbf{B} \qquad (15\text{-}5)$$

The magenta vertex is obtained by adding red and blue to produce the triple (1, 0, 1), and white at (1, 1, 1) is the sum of the red, green, and blue vertices. Shades of gray are represented along the main diagonal of the cube from the origin (black) to the white vertex. Each point along this diagonal has an equal contribution from each primary color, so that a gray shade halfway between black and

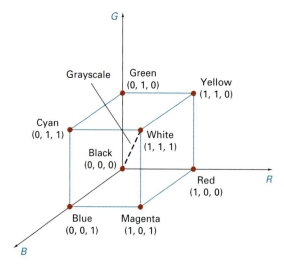

Figure 15-11

The RGB color model, defining colors with an additive process within the unit cube.

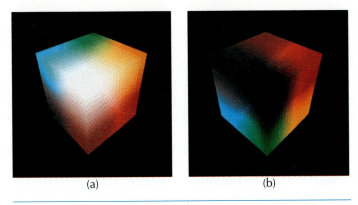

(a)   (b)

Figure 15-12

Two views of the RGB color cube: (a) along the grayscale
diagonal from white to black and (b) along the grayscale diagonal
from black to white.

TABLE 15-1

RGB (*X, Y*) CHROMACITY COORDINATES

	NTSC Standard	*CIE Model*	*Approx. Color Monitor Values*
R	(0.670,0.330)	(0.735, 0.265)	(0.628, 0.346)
G	(0.210, 0.710)	(0.274, 0.717)	(0.268, 0.588)
B	(0.140, 0.080)	(0.167, 0.009)	(0.150, 0.070)

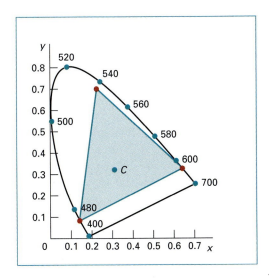

Figure 15-13

RGB color gamut.

white is represented as (0.5, 0.5, 0.5). The color graduations along the front and
top planes of the RGB cube are illustrated in Fig. 15-12.

Chromaticity coordinates for an NTSC standard RGB phosphor are listed in
Table 15-1. Also listed are the RGB chromaticity coordinates for the CIE RGB
color model and the approximate values used for phosphors in color monitors.
Figure 15-13 shows the color gamut for the NTSC standard RGB primaries.

15-5

YIQ COLOR MODEL

Whereas an RGB monitor requires separate signals for the red, green, and blue components of an image, a television monitor uses a single composite signal. The National Television System Committee (NTSC) color model for forming the composite video signal is the YIQ model, which is based on concepts in the CIE XYZ model.

In the YIQ color model, parameter Y is the same as in the XYZ model. Luminance (brightness) information is contained in the Y parameter, while chromaticity information (hue and purity) is incorporated into the I and Q parameters. A combination of red, green, and blue intensities are chosen for the Y parameter to yield the standard luminosity curve. Since Y contains the luminance information, black-and-white television monitors use only the Y signal. The largest bandwidth in the NTSC video signal (about 4 MHz) is assigned to the Y information. Parameter I contains orange–cyan hue information that provides the flesh-tone shading, and occupies a bandwidth of approximately 1.5 MHz. Parameter Q carries green–magenta hue information in a bandwidth of about 0.6 MHz.

An RGB signal can be converted to a television signal using an NTSC encoder, which converts RGB values to YIQ values, then modulates and superimposes the I and Q information on the Y signal. The conversion from RGB values to YIQ values is accomplished with the transformation

$$\begin{bmatrix} Y \\ I \\ Q \end{bmatrix} = \begin{bmatrix} 0.299 & 0.587 & 0.144 \\ 0.596 & -0.275 & -0.321 \\ 0.212 & -0.528 & 0.311 \end{bmatrix} \cdot \begin{bmatrix} R \\ G \\ B \end{bmatrix} \qquad (15\text{-}6)$$

This transformation is based on the NTSC standard RGB phosphor, whose chromaticity coordinates were given in the preceding section. The larger proportions of red and green assigned to parameter Y indicate the relative importance of these hues in determining brightness, compared to blue.

An NTSC video signal can be converted to an RGB signal using an NTSC decoder, which separates the video signal into the YIQ components, then converts to RGB values. We convert from YIQ space to RGB space with the inverse matrix transformation from Eq. 15-6:

$$\begin{bmatrix} R \\ G \\ B \end{bmatrix} = \begin{bmatrix} 1.000 & 0.956 & 0.620 \\ 1.000 & -0.272 & -0.647 \\ 1.000 & -1.108 & 1.705 \end{bmatrix} \cdot \begin{bmatrix} Y \\ I \\ Q \end{bmatrix} \qquad (15\text{-}7)$$

15-6

CMY COLOR MODEL

A color model defined with the primary colors cyan, magenta, and yellow (CMY) is useful for describing color output to hard-copy devices. Unlike video monitors, which produce a color pattern by combining light from the screen phosphors, hard-copy devices such as plotters produce a color picture by coating a paper with color pigments. We see the colors by reflected light, a subtractive process.

As we have noted, cyan can be formed by adding green and blue light. Therefore, when white light is reflected from cyan-colored ink, the reflected light must have no red component. That is, red light is absorbed, or subtracted, by the ink. Similarly, magenta ink subtracts the green component from incident light, and yellow subtracts the blue component. A unit cube representation for the CMY model is illustrated in Fig. 15-14.

In the CMY model, point (1, 1, 1) represents black, because all components of the incident light are subtracted. The origin represents white light. Equal amounts of each of the primary colors produce grays, along the main diagonal of the cube. A combination of cyan and magenta ink produces blue light, because the red and green components of the incident light are absorbed. Other color combinations are obtained by a similar subtractive process.

The printing process often used with the CMY model generates a color point with a collection of four ink dots, somewhat as an RGB monitor uses a collection of three phosphor dots. One dot is used for each of the primary colors (cyan, magenta, and yellow), and one dot is black. A black dot is included because the combination of cyan, magenta, and yellow inks typically produce dark gray instead of black. Some plotters produce different color combinations by spraying the ink for the three primary colors over each other and allowing them to mix before they dry.

We can express the conversion from an RGB representation to a CMY representation with the matrix transformation

$$\begin{bmatrix} C \\ M \\ Y \end{bmatrix} = \begin{bmatrix} 1 \\ 1 \\ 1 \end{bmatrix} - \begin{bmatrix} R \\ G \\ B \end{bmatrix} \qquad (15\text{-}8)$$

where the white is represented in the RGB system as the unit column vector. Similarly, we convert from a CMY color representation to an RGB representation with the matrix transformation

$$\begin{bmatrix} R \\ G \\ B \end{bmatrix} = \begin{bmatrix} 1 \\ 1 \\ 1 \end{bmatrix} - \begin{bmatrix} C \\ M \\ Y \end{bmatrix} \qquad (15\text{-}9)$$

where black is represented in the CMY system as the unit column vector.

15-7
HSV COLOR MODEL

Instead of a set of color primaries, the HSV model uses color descriptions that have a more intuitive appeal to a user. To give a color specification, a user selects a spectral color and the amounts of white and black that are to be added to obtain different shades, tints, and tones. Color parameters in this model are *hue* (H), *saturation* (S), and *value* (V).

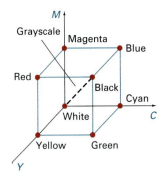

Figure 15-14
The CMY color model, defining colors with a subtractive process inside a unit cube.

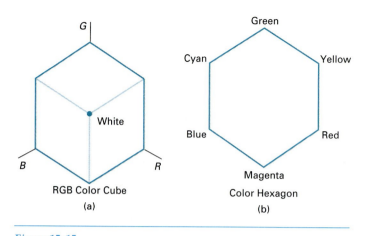

Figure 15-15
When the RGB color cube (a) is viewed along the diagonal from
white to black, the color-cube outline is a hexagon (b).

The three-dimensional representation of the HSV model is derived from the
RGB cube. If we imagine viewing the cube along the diagonal from the white
vertex to the origin (black), we see an outline of the cube that has the hexagon
shape shown in Fig. 15-15. The boundary of the hexagon represents the various
hues, and it is used as the top of the HSV hexcone (Fig. 15-16). In the hexcone,
saturation is measured along a horizontal axis, and value is along a vertical axis
through the center of the hexcone.

Hue is represented as an angle about the vertical axis, ranging from 0° at
red through 360°. Vertices of the hexagon are separated by 60° intervals. Yellow is
at 60°, green at 120°, and cyan opposite red at $H = 180°$. Complementary colors
are 180° apart.

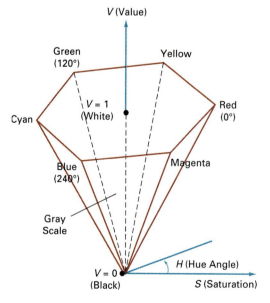

Figure 15-16
The HSV hexcone.

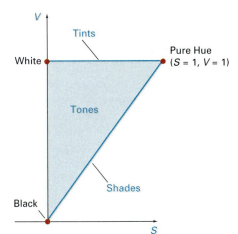

Figure 15-17

Cross section of the HSV hexcone, showing regions for shades, tints, and tones.

Saturation S varies from 0 to 1. It is represented in this model as the ratio of the purity of a selected hue to its maximum purity at $S = 1$. A selected hue is said to be one-quarter pure at the value $S = 0.25$. At $S = 0$, we have the gray scale.

Value V varies from 0 at the apex of the hexcone to 1 at the top. The apex represents black. At the top of the hexcone, colors have their maximum intensity. When $V = 1$ and $S = 1$, we have the "pure" hues. White is the point at $V = 1$ and $S = 0$.

This is a more intuitive model for most users. Starting with a selection for a pure hue, which specifies the hue angle H and sets $V = S = 1$, we describe the color we want in terms of adding either white or black to the pure hue. Adding black decreases the setting for V while S is held constant. To get a dark blue, V could be set to 0.4 with $S = 1$ and $H = 240°$. Similarly, when white is to be added to the hue selected, parameter S is decreased while keeping V constant. A light blue could be designated with $S = 0.3$ while $V = 1$ and $H = 240°$. By adding some black and some white, we decrease both V and S. An interface for this model typically presents the HSV parameter choices in a color palette.

Color concepts associated with the terms shades, tints, and tones are represented in a cross-sectional plane of the HSV hexcone (Fig. 15-17). Adding black to a pure hue decreases V down the side of the hexcone. Thus, various shades are represented with values $S = 1$ and $0 \leq V \leq 1$. Adding white to a pure tone produces different tints across the top plane of the hexcone, where parameter values are $V = 1$ and $0 \leq S \leq 1$. Various tones are specified by adding both black and white, producing color points within the triangular cross-sectional area of the hexcone.

The human eye can distinguish about 128 different hues and about 130 different tints (saturation levels). For each of these, a number of shades (value settings) can be detected, depending on the hue selected. About 23 shades are discernible with yellow colors, and about 16 different shades can be seen at the blue end of the spectrum. This means that we can distinguish about $128 \times 130 \times 23 = 82{,}720$ different colors. For most graphics applications, 128 hues, 8 saturation levels, and 15 value settings are sufficient. With this range of parameters in the HSV color model, 16,384 colors would be available to a user, and the system would need 14 bits of color storage per pixel. Color lookup tables could be used to reduce the storage requirements per pixel and to increase the number of available colors.

15-8

CONVERSION BETWEEN HSV AND RGB MODELS

If HSV color parameters are made available to a user of a graphics package, these parameters are transformed to the RGB settings needed for the color monitor. To determine the operations needed in this transformation, we first consider how the HSV hexcone can be derived from the RGB cube. The diagonal of this cube from black (the origin) to white corresponds to the V axis of the hexcone. Also, each subcube of the RGB cube corresponds to a hexagonal cross-sectional area of the hexcone. At any cross section, all sides of the hexagon and all radial lines from the V axis to any vertex have the value V. For any set of RGB values, V is equal to the maximum value in this set. The HSV point corresponding to the set of RGB values lies on the hexagonal cross section at value V. Parameter S is then determined as the relative distance of this point from the V axis. Parameter H is determined by calculating the relative position of the point within each sextant of the hexagon. An algorithm for mapping any set of RGB values into the corresponding HSV values is given in the following procedure:

```c
#include <math.h>

/* Input:   h, s, v in range [0..1]
   Outputs: r, g, b in range [0..1] */
void hsvToRgb(float h, float s, float v, float * r, float * g, float * b)
{
  int i;
  float aa, bb, cc, f;

  if (s == 0) /* Grayscale */
    *r = *g = *b = v;
  else {
    if (h == 1.0) h = 0;
    h *= 6.0;
    i = ffloor (h);
    f = h - i;
    aa = v * (1 - s);
    bb = v * (1 - (s * f));
    cc = v * (1 - (s * (1 - f)));
    switch (i) {
    case 0: *r = v;  *g = cc; *b = aa; break;
    case 1: *r = bb; *g = v;  *b = aa; break;
    case 2: *r = aa; *g = v;  *b = cc; break;
    case 3: *r = aa; *g = bb; *b = v;  break;
    case 4: *r = cc; *g = aa; *b = v;  break;
    case 5: *r = v;  *g = aa; *b = bb; break;
    }
  }
}
```

We obtain the transformation from HSV parameters to RGB parameters by determining the inverse of the equations in rgbToHsv procedure. These inverse operations are carried out for each sextant of the hexcone. The resulting transformation equations are summarized in the following algorithm:

```c
#include <math.h>

#define MIN(a,b) (a<b?a:b)
#define MAX(a,b) (a>b?a:b)
```

```
#define NO_HUE    -1

/* Input:   r, g, b in range [0..1]
   Outputs: h, s, v in range [0..1]
*/
void rgbToHsv (float r, float g, float b, float * h, float * s, float * v)
{
  float max = MAX (r, MAX (g, b)), min = MIN (r, MIN (g, b));
  float delta = max - min;

  *v = max;
  if (max != 0.0)
    *s = delta / max;
  else
    *s = 0.0;
  if (*s == 0.0) *h = NO_HUE;
  else {
    if (r == max)
      *h = (g - b) / delta;
    else if (g == max)
      *h = 2 + (b - r) / delta;
    else if (b == max)
      *h = 4 + (r - g) / delta;
    *h *= 60.0;
    if (*h < 0) *h += 360.0;
    *h /= 360.0;
  }
}
```

15-9
HLS COLOR MODEL

Another model based on intuitive color parameters is the HLS system used by Tektronix. This model has the double-cone representation shown in Fig. 15-18. The three color parameters in this model are called *hue* (*H*), *lightness* (*L*), and *saturation* (*S*).

Hue has the same meaning as in the HSV model. It specifies an angle about the vertical axis that locates a chosen hue. In this model, $H = 0°$ corresponds to blue. The remaining colors are specified around the perimeter of the cone in the same order as in the HSV model. Magenta is at 60°, red is at 120°, and cyan is located at $H = 180°$. Again, complementary colors are 180° apart on the double cone.

The vertical axis in this model is called lightness, L. At $L = 0$, we have black, and white is at $L = 1$. Gray scale is along the L axis, and the "pure hues" lie on the $L = 0.5$ plane.

Saturation parameter S again specifies relative purity of a color. This parameter varies from 0 to 1, and pure hues are those for which $S = 1$ and $L = 0.5$. As S decreases, the hues are said to be less pure. At $S = 0$, we have the gray scale.

As in the HSV model, the HLS system allows a user to think in terms of making a selected hue darker or lighter. A hue is selected with hue angle H, and the desired shade, tint, or tone is obtained by adjusting L and S. Colors are made lighter by increasing L and made darker by decreasing L. When S is decreased, the colors move toward gray.

579

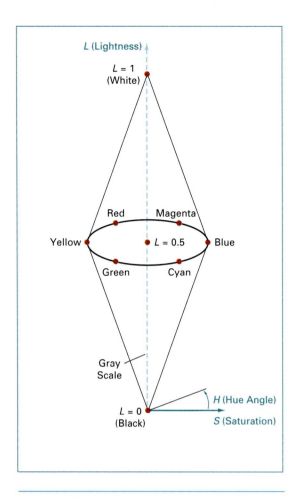

Figure 15-18
The HLS double cone.

15-10
COLOR SELECTION AND APPLICATIONS

A graphics package can provide color capabilities in a way that aids us in making color selections. Various combinations of colors can be selected using sliders and color wheels, and the system can also be designed to aid in the selection of harmonizing colors. In addition, the designer of a package can follow some basic color rules when designing the color displays that are to be presented to a user.

One method for obtaining a set of coordinating colors is to generate the set from some subspace of a color model. If colors are selected at regular intervals along any straight line within the RGB or CMY cube, for example, we can expect to obtain a set of well-matched colors. Randomly selected hues can be expected to produce harsh and clashing color combinations. Another consideration in the selection of color combinations is that different colors are perceived at different depths. This occurs because our eyes focus on colors according to their frequency. Blues, in particular, tend to recede. Displaying a blue pattern next to a red pattern can cause eye fatigue, because we continually need to refocus when our attention is switched from one area to the other. This problem can be reduced by separating these colors or by using colors from one-half or less of the color hexagon in the HSV model. With this technique, a display contains either blues and greens or reds and yellows.

As a general rule, the use of a smaller number of colors produces a more pleasing display than a large number of colors, and tints and shades blend better than pure hues. For a background, gray or the complement of one of the foreground colors is usually best.

SUMMARY

In this chapter, we have discussed the basic properties of light and the concept of a color model. Visible light can be characterized as a narrow frequency distribution within the electromagnetic spectrum. Light sources are described in terms of their dominant frequency (or hue), luminance (or brightness), and purity (or saturation). Complementary color sources are those that combine to produce white light.

One method for defining a color model is to specify a set of two or more primary colors that are combined to produce various other colors. Common color models defined with three primary colors are the RGB and CMY models. Video monitor displays use the RGB model, while hardcopy devices produce color output using the CMY model. Other color models, based on specification of luminance and purity values, include the YIQ, HSV, and HLS color models. Intuitive color models, such as the HSV and HLS models, allow colors to be specified by selecting a value for hue and the amounts of white and black to be added to the selected hue.

Since no model specified with a finite set of color parameters is capable of describing all possible colors, a set of three hypothetical colors, called the CIE primaries, has been adopted as the standard for defining all color combinations. The set of CIE primaries is commonly referred to as the XYZ color model. Plotting normalized values for the X and Y standards produces the CIE chromaticity diagram, which gives a representation for any color in terms of hue and purity. We can use this diagram to compare color gamuts for different color models, to identify complementary colors, and to determine dominant frequency and purity for a given color.

An important consideration in the generation of a color display is the selection of harmonious color combinations. We can do this by following a few simple rules. Coordinating colors usually can be selected from within a small subspace of a color model. Also, we should avoid displaying adjacent colors that differ widely in dominant frequency. And we should limit displays to a small number of color combinations formed with tints and shades, rather than with pure hues.

REFERENCES

A comprehensive discussion of the science of color is given in Wyszecki and Stiles (1982). Color models and color display techniques are discussed in Durrett (1987), Hall (1989), and Travis (1991). Algorithms for various color applications are presented in Glassner (1990), Arvo (1991), and Kirk (1992). For additional information on the human visual system and our perception of light and color, see Glassner (1994).

EXERCISES

15.1. Derive expressions for converting RGB color parameters to HSV values.

15.2. Derive expressions for converting HSV color values to RGB values.

15-3. Write an interactive procedure that allows selection of HSV color parameters from a displayed menu, then the HSV values are to be converted to RGB values for storage in a frame buffer.

15-4. Derive expressions for converting RGB color values to HLS color parameters.

15-5. Derive expressions for converting HLS color values to RGB values.

15-6. Write a program that allows interactive selection of HLS values from a color menu then converts these values to corresponding RGB values.

15-7. Write a program that will produce a set of colors that are linearly interpolated between any two specified positions in RGB space.

15-8. Write an interactive routine for selecting color values from within a specified subspace of RGB space.

15-9. Write a program that will produce a set of colors that are linearly interpolated between any two specified positions in HSV space.

15-10. Write a program that will produce a set of colors that are linearly interpolated between any two specified positions in HLS space.

15-11. Display two RGB color grids, side by side on a video monitor. Fill one grid with a set of randomly selected RGB colors, and fill the other grid with a set of colors that are selected from a small RGB subspace. Experiment with different random selections and different RGB subspaces and compare the two color grids.

15-12. Display the two color grids in Exercise 15-11 using color selections from either the HSV or the HLS color space.

CHAPTER

16

Computer Animation

Some typical applications of computer-generated animation are entertainment (motion pictures and cartoons), advertising, scientific and engineering studies, and training and education. Although we tend to think of animation as implying object motions, the term **computer animation** generally refers to any time sequence of visual changes in a scene. In addition to changing object position with translations or rotations, a computer-generated animation could display time variations in object size, color, transparency, or surface texture. Advertising animations often transition one object shape into another: for example, transforming a can of motor oil into an automobile engine. Computer animations can also be generated by changing camera parameters, such as position, orientation, and focal length. And we can produce computer animations by changing lighting effects or other parameters and procedures associated with illumination and rendering.

Many applications of computer animation require realistic displays. An accurate representation of the shape of a thunderstorm or other natural phenomena described with a numerical model is important for evaluating the reliability of the model Also, simulators for training aircraft pilots and heavy-equipment operators must produce reasonably accurate representations of the environment. Entertainment and advertising applications, on the other hand, are sometimes more interested in visual effects. Thus, scenes may be displayed with exaggerated shapes and unrealistic motions and transformations. There are many entertainment and advertising applications that do require accurate representations for computer-generated scenes. And in some scientific and engineering studies, realism is not a goal. For example, physical quantities are often displayed with pseudo-colors or abstract shapes that change over time to help the researcher understand the nature of the physical process.

16-1
DESIGN OF ANIMATION SEQUENCES

In general, an animation sequence is designed with the following steps:

- Storyboard layout
- Object definitions
- Key-frame specifications
- Generation of in-between frames

This standard approach for animated cartoons is applied to other animation applications as well, although there are many special applications that do not follow this sequence. Real-time computer animations produced by flight simulators, for instance, display motion sequences in response to settings on the aircraft controls. And visualization applications are generated by the solutions of the numerical models. For *frame-by-frame animation*, each frame of the scene is separately generated and stored. Later, the frames can be recorded on film or they can be consecutively displayed in "real-time playback" mode.

The *storyboard* is an outline of the action. It defines the motion sequence as a set of basic events that are to take place. Depending on the type of animation to be produced, the storyboard could consist of a set of rough sketches or it could be a list of the basic ideas for the motion.

An *object definition* is given for each participant in the action. Objects can be defined in terms of basic shapes, such as polygons or splines. In addition, the associated movements for each object are specified along with the shape.

A *key frame* is a detailed drawing of the scene at a certain time in the animation sequence. Within each key frame, each object is positioned according to the time for that frame. Some key frames are chosen at extreme positions in the action; others are spaced so that the time interval between key frames is not too great. More key frames are specified for intricate motions than for simple, slowly varing motions.

In-betweens are the intermediate frames between the key frames. The number of in-betweens needed is determined by the media to be used to display the animation. Film requires 24 frames per second, and graphics terminals are refreshed at the rate of 30 to 60 frames per second. Typically, time intervals for the motion are set up so that there are from three to five in-betweens for each pair of key frames. Depending on the speed specified for the motion, some key frames can be duplicated. For a 1-minute film sequence with no duplication, we would need 1440 frames. With five in-betweens for each pair of key frames, we would need 288 key frames. If the motion is not too complicated, we could space the key frames a little farther apart.

There are several other tasks that may be required, depending on the application. They include motion verification, editing, and production and synchronization of a soundtrack. Many of the functions needed to produce general animations are now computer-generated. Figures 16-1 and 16-2 show examples of computer-generated frames for animation sequences.

Figure 16-1
One frame from the award-winning computer-animated short film *Luxo Jr*. The film was designed using a key-frame animation system and cartoon animation techniques to provide lifelike actions of the lamps. Final images were rendered with multiple light sources and procedural texturing techniques. (*Courtesy of Pixar. © 1986 Pixar.*)

Figure 16-2
One frame from the short film *Tin Toy*, the first computer-animated film to win an Oscar. Designed using a key-frame animation system, the film also required extensive facial expression modeling. Final images were rendered using procedural shading, self-shadowing techniques, motion blur, and texture mapping. (*Courtesy of Pixar. © 1988 Pixar.*)

16-2
GENERAL COMPUTER-ANIMATION FUNCTIONS

Some steps in the development of an animation sequence are well-suited to computer solution. These include object manipulations and rendering, camera motions, and the generation of in-betweens. Animation packages, such as Wavefront, for example, provide special functions for designing the animation and processing individual objects.

One function available in animation packages is provided to store and manage the object database. Object shapes and associated parameters are stored and updated in the database. Other object functions include those for motion generation and those for object rendering. Motions can be generated according to specified constraints using two-dimensional or three-dimensional transformations. Standard functions can then be applied to identify visible surfaces and apply the rendering algorithms.

Another typical function simulates camera movements. Standard motions are zooming, panning, and tilting. Finally, given the specification for the key frames, the in-betweens can be automatically generated.

16-3
RASTER ANIMATIONS

On raster systems, we can generate real-time animation in limited applications using *raster operations*. As we have seen in Section 5-8, a simple method for translation in the xy plane is to transfer a rectangluar block of pixel values from one location to another. Two-dimensional rotations in multiples of 90° are also simple to perform, although we can rotate rectangular blocks of pixels through arbitrary angles using antialiasing procedures. To rotate a block of pixels, we need to determine the percent of area coverage for those pixels that overlap the rotated block. Sequences of raster operations can be executed to produce real-time animation of either two-dimensional or three-dimensional objects, as long as we restrict the animation to motions in the projection plane. Then no viewing or visible-surface algorithms need be invoked.

We can also animate objects along two-dimensional motion paths using the *color-table transformations*. Here we predefine the object at successive positions along the motion path, and set the successive blocks of pixel values to color-table

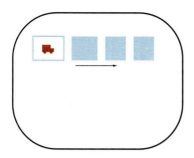

Figure 16-3
Real-time raster color-table
animation.

entries. We set the pixels at the first position of the object to "on" values, and we set the pixels at the other object positions to the background color. The animation is then accomplished by changing the color-table values so that the object is "on" at successively positions along the animation path as the preceding position is set to the background intensity (Fig. 16-3).

16-4
COMPUTER-ANIMATION LANGUAGES

Design and control of animation sequences are handled with a set of animation routines. A general-purpose language, such as C, Lisp, Pascal, or FORTRAN, is often used to program the animation functions, but several specialized animation languages have been developed. Animation functions include a graphics editor, a key-frame generator, an in-between generator, and standard graphics routines. The graphics editor allows us to design and modify object shapes, using spline surfaces, constructive solid-geometry methods, or other representation schemes.

A typical task in an animation specification is *scene description*. This includes the positioning of objects and light sources, defining the photometric parameters (light-source intensities and surface-illumination properties), and setting the camera parameters (position, orientation, and lens characteristics). Another standard function is *action specification*. This involves the layout of motion paths for the objects and camera. And we need the usual graphics routines: viewing and perspective transformations, geometric transformations to generate object movements as a function of accelerations or kinematic path specifications, visible-surface identification, and the surface-rendering operations.

Key-frame systems are specialized animation languages designed simply to generate the in-betweens from the user-specified key frames. Usually, each object in the scene is defined as a set of rigid bodies connected at the joints and with a limited number of degrees of freedom. As an example, the single-arm robot in Fig. 16-4 has six degrees of freedom, which are called arm sweep, shoulder swivel, elbow extension, pitch, yaw, and roll. We can extend the number of degrees of freedom for this robot arm to nine by allowing three-dimensional translations for the base (Fig. 16-5). If we also allow base rotations, the robot arm can have a total of 12 degrees of freedom. The human body, in comparison, has over 200 degrees of freedom.

Parameterized systems allow object-motion characteristics to be specified as part of the object definitions. The adjustable parameters control such object characteristics as degrees of freedom, motion limitations, and allowable shape changes.

587

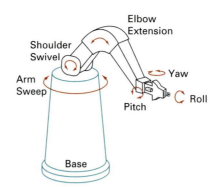

Elbow
Extension

Shoulder
Swivel

Arm
Sweep

Yaw

Pitch   Roll

Base

Figure 16-4
Degrees of freedom for a stationary, single-arm robot.

Scripting systems allow object specifications and animation sequences to be defined with a user-input *script*. From the script, a library of various objects and motions can be constructed.

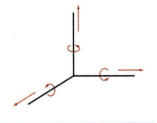

Figure 16-5
Translational and rotational degrees of freedom for the base of the robot arm.

16-5
KEY-FRAME SYSTEMS

We generate each set of in-betweens from the specification of two (or more) key frames. Motion paths can be given with a *kinematic description* as a set of spline curves, or the motions can be *physically based* by specifying the forces acting on the objects to be animated.

For complex scenes, we can separate the frames into individual components or objects called *cels* (celluloid transparencies), an acronym from cartoon animation. Given the animation paths, we can interpolate the positions of individual objects between any two times.

With complex object transformations, the shapes of objects may change over time. Examples are clothes, facial features, magnified detail, evolving shapes, exploding or disintegrating objects, and transforming one object into another object. If all surfaces are described with polygon meshes, then the number of edges per polygon can change from one frame to the next. Thus, the total number of line segments can be different in different frames.

Morphing

Transformation of object shapes from one form to another is called **morphing**, which is a shortened form of metamorphosis. Morphing methods can be applied to any motion or transition involving a change in shape.

Given two key frames for an object transformation, we first adjust the object specification in one of the frames so that the number of polygon edges (or the number of vertices) is the same for the two frames. This preprocessing step is illustrated in Fig. 16-6. A straight-line segment in key frame k is transformed into two line segments in key frame $k + 1$. Since key frame $k + 1$ has an extra vertex, we add a vertex between vertices 1 and 2 in key frame k to balance the number of vertices (and edges) in the two key frames. Using linear interpolation to generate the in-betweens, we transition the added vertex in key frame k into vertex 3' along the straight-line path shown in Fig. 16-7. An example of a triangle linearly expanding into a quadrilateral is given in Fig. 16-8. Figures 16-9 and 16-10 show examples of morphing in television advertising.

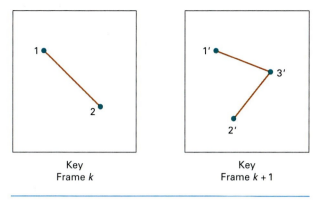

Figure 16-6
An edge with vertex positions 1 and 2 in key frame k
evolves into two connected edges in key frame $k + 1$.

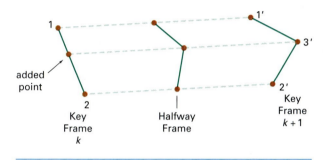

Figure 16-7
Linear interpolation for transforming a line segment in
key frame k into two connected line segments in key
frame $k + 1$.

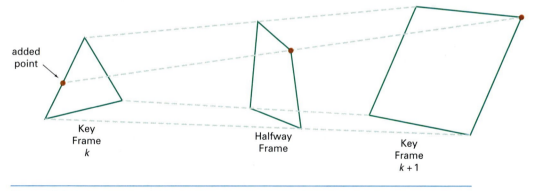

Figure 16-8
Linear interpolation for transforming a triangle into a quadrilateral.

We can state general preprocessing rules for equalizing key frames in terms
of either the number of edges or the number of vertices to be added to a key
frame. Suppose we equalize the edge count, and parameters L_k and L_{k+1} denote
the number of line segments in two consecutive frames. We then define

$$L_{max} = \max(L_k, L_{k+1}), \qquad L_{min} = \min(L_k, L_{k+1}) \qquad (16\text{-}1)$$

589

and

$$N_e = L_{\max} \bmod L_{\min}$$

$$N_s = \text{int}\left(\frac{L_{\max}}{L_{\min}}\right)$$

(16-2)

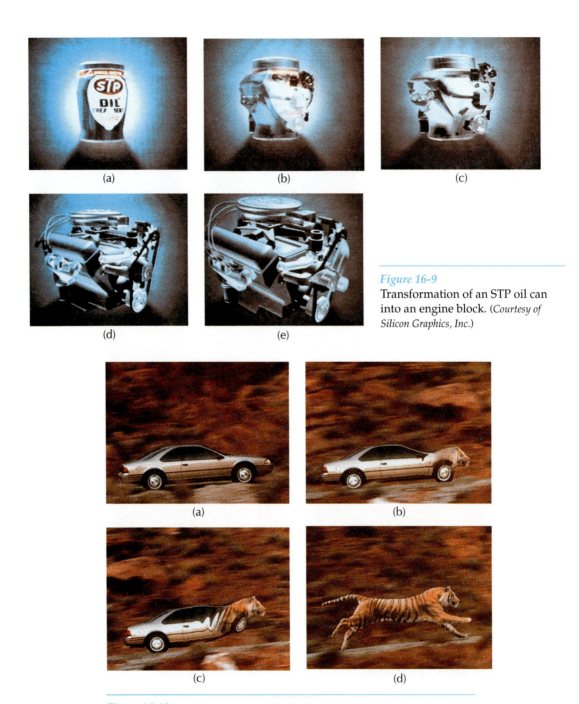

Figure 16-9
Transformation of an STP oil can into an engine block. (*Courtesy of Silicon Graphics, Inc.*)

Figure 16-10
Transformation of a moving automobile into a running tiger. (*Courtesy of Exxon Company USA and Pacific Data Images.*)

Then the preprocessing is accomplished by

1. dividing N_e edges of *keyframe*$_{min}$ into $N_s + 1$ sections
2. dividing the remaining lines of *keyframe*$_{min}$ into N_s sections

As an example, if $L_k = 15$ and $L_{k+1} = 11$, we would divide 4 lines of *keyframe*$_{k+1}$ into 2 sections each. The remaining lines of *keyframe*$_{k+1}$ are left intact.

If we equalize the vertex count, we can use parameters V_k and V_{k+1} to denote the number of vertices in the two consecutive frames. In this case, we define

$$V_{max} = \max(V_k, V_{k+1}), \qquad V_{min} = \min(V_k, V_{k+1}) \qquad (16\text{-}3)$$

and

$$N_{ls} = (V_{max} - 1) \bmod (V_{min} - 1)$$

$$N_p = \text{int}\left(\frac{V_{max} - 1}{V_{min} - 1}\right) \qquad (16\text{-}4)$$

Preprocessing using vertex count is performed by

1. adding N_p points to N_{ls} line sections of *keyframe*$_{min}$
2. adding $N_p - 1$ points to the remaining edges of *keyframe*$_{min}$

For the triangle-to-quadrilateral example, $V_k = 3$ and $V_{k+1} = 4$. Both N_{ls} and N_p are 1, so we would add one point to one edge of *keyframe*$_k$. No points would be added to the remaining lines of *keyframe*$_{k+1}$.

Simulating Accelerations

Curve-fitting techniques are often used to specify the animation paths between key frames. Given the vertex positions at the key frames, we can fit the positions with linear or nonlinear paths. Figure 16-11 illustrates a nonlinear fit of key-frame positions. This determines the trajectories for the in-betweens. To simulate accelerations, we can adjust the time spacing for the in-betweens.

For constant speed (zero acceleration), we use equal-interval time spacing for the in-betweens. Suppose we want n in-betweens for key frames at times t_1 and t_2 (Fig. 16-12). The time interval between key frames is then divided into $n + 1$ subintervals, yielding an in-between spacing of

$$\Delta t = \frac{t_2 - t_1}{n + 1} \qquad (16\text{-}5)$$

We can calculate the time for any in-between as

$$tB_j = t_1 + j\,\Delta t, \qquad j = 1, 2, \ldots, n \qquad (16\text{-}6)$$

and determine the values for coordinate positions, color, and other physical parameters.

Nonzero accelerations are used to produce realistic displays of speed changes, particularly at the beginning and end of a motion sequence. We can model the start-up and slow-down portions of an animation path with spline or

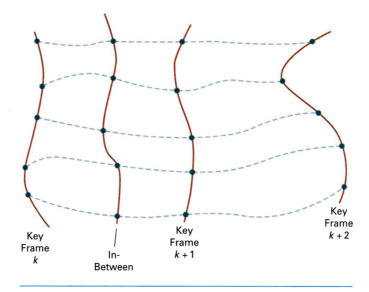

Key
Frame
k

In-
Between

Key
Frame
k + 1

Key
Frame
k + 2

Figure 16-11
Fitting key-frame vertex positions with nonlinear splines.

trignometric functions. Parabolic and cubic time functions have been applied to acceleration modeling, but trignometric functions are more commonly used in animation packages.

To model increasing speed (positive acceleration), we want the time spacing between frames to increase so that greater changes in position occur as the object moves faster. We can obtain an increasing interval size with the function

$$1 - \cos\theta, \qquad 0 < \theta < \pi/2$$

For n in-betweens, the time for the jth in-between would then be calculated as

$$tB_j = t_1 + \Delta t\left[1 - \cos\frac{j\pi}{2(n+1)}\right], \qquad j = 1, 2, \ldots, n \qquad (16\text{-}7)$$

where Δt is the time difference between the two key frames. Figure 16-13 gives a plot of the trigonometric acceleration function and the in-between spacing for $n = 5$.

We can model decreasing speed (deceleration) with $\sin\theta$ in the range $0 < \theta < \pi/2$. The time position of an in-between is now defined as

$$tB_j = t_1 + \Delta t \sin\frac{j\pi}{2(n+1)}, \qquad j = 1, 2, \ldots, n \qquad (16\text{-}8)$$

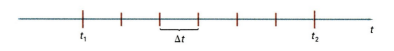

t_1

Δt

t_2

t

Figure 16-12
In-between positions for motion at constant speed.

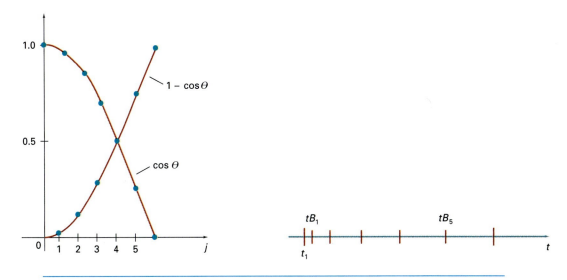

Figure 16-13
A trigonometric acceleration function and the corresponding in-between spacing for $n = 5$ and $\theta = j\pi/12$ in Eq. 16-7, producing increased coordinate changes as the object moves through each time interval.

A plot of this function and the decreasing size of the time intervals is shown in Fig. 16-14 for five in-betweens.

Often, motions contain both speed-ups and slow-downs. We can model a combination of increasing–decreasing speed by first increasing the in-between time spacing, then we decrease this spacing. A function to accomplish these time changes is

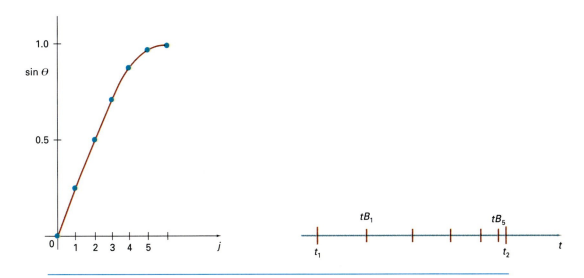

Figure 16-14
A trigonometric deceleration function and the corresponding in-between spacing for $n = 5$ and $\theta = j\pi/12$ in Eq. 16-8, producing decreased coordinate changes as the object moves through each time interval.

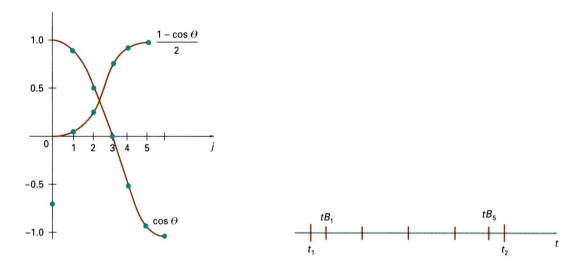

Figure 16-15

A trigonometric accelerate–decelerate function and the corresponding in-between spacing for $n = 5$ in Eq. 16-9.

$$\frac{1}{2}(1 - \cos\theta), \qquad 0 < \theta < \pi/2$$

The time for the jth in-between is now calculated as

$$tB_j = t_1 + \Delta t\left\{\frac{1 - \cos[j\pi/(n + 1)]}{2}\right\}, \qquad j = 1, 2, \ldots, n \qquad (16\text{-}9)$$

with Δt denoting the time difference for the two key frames. Time intervals for the moving object first increase, then the time intervals decrease, as shown in Fig. 16-15.

Processing the in-betweens is simplified by initially modeling "skeleton" (wireframe) objects. This allows interactive adjustment of motion sequences. After the animation sequence is completely defined, objects can be fully rendered.

16-6

MOTION SPECIFICATIONS

There are several ways in which the motions of objects can be specified in an animation system. We can define motions in very explicit terms, or we can use more abstract or more general approaches.

Direct Motion Specification

The most straightforward method for defining a motion sequence is *direct specification* of the motion parameters. Here, we explicitly give the rotation angles and translation vectors. Then the geometric transformation matrices are applied to transform coordinate positions. Alternatively, we could use an approximating

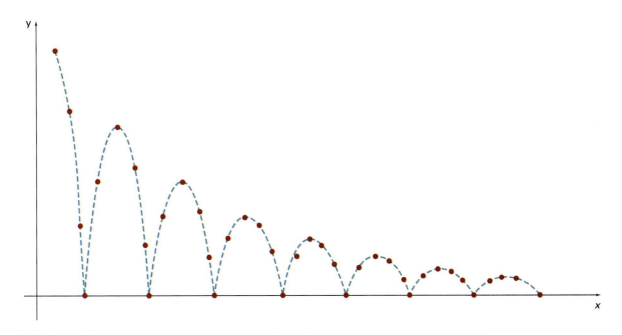

Figure 16-16
Approximating the motion of a bouncing ball with a damped *sine* function (Eq. 16-10).

equation to specify certain kinds of motions. We can approximate the path of a bouncing ball, for instance, with a damped, rectified, *sine* curve (Fig. 16-16):

$$y(x) = A \left| \sin(\omega x + \theta_0) \right| e^{-kx} \qquad (16\text{-}10)$$

where A is the initial amplitude, ω is the angular frequence, θ_0 is the phase angle, and k is the damping constant. These methods can be used for simple user-programmed animation sequences.

Goal-Directed Systems

At the opposite extreme, we can specify the motions that are to take place in general terms that abstractly describe the actions. These systems are referred to as *goal directed* because they determine specific motion parameters given the goals of the animation. For example, we could specify that we want an object to "walk" or to "run" to a particular destination. Or we could state that we want an object to "pick up" some other specified object. The input directives are then interpreted in terms of component motions that will accomplish the selected task. Human motions, for instance, can be defined as a hierarchical structure of submotions for the torso, limbs, and so forth.

Kinematics and Dynamics

We can also construct animation sequences using *kinematic* or *dynamic* descriptions. With a kinematic description, we specify the animation by giving motion parameters (position, velocity, and acceleration) without reference to the forces that cause the motion. For constant velocity (zero acceleration), we designate the motions of rigid bodies in a scene by giving an initial position and velocity vector

595

for each object. As an example, if a velocity is specified as (3, 0, −4) km/sec, then this vector gives the direction for the straight-line motion path and the speed (magnitude of velocity) is 5 km/sec. If we also specify accelerations (rate of change of velocity), we can generate speed-ups, slow-downs, and curved motion paths. Kinematic specification of a motion can also be given by simply describing the motion path. This is often done using spline curves.

An alternate approach is to use *inverse kinematics*. Here, we specify the initial and final positions of objects at specified times and the motion parameters are computed by the system. For example, assuming zero accelerations, we can determine the constant velocity that will accomplish the movement of an object from the initial position to the final position. This method is often used with complex objects by giving the positions and orientations of an end node of an object, such as a hand or a foot. The system then determines the motion parameters of other nodes to accomplish the desired motion.

Dynamic descriptions on the other hand, require the specification of the forces that produce the velocities and accelerations. Descriptions of object behavior under the influence of forces are generally referred to as a *physically based modeling* (Chapter 10). Examples of forces affecting object motion include electromagnetic, gravitational, friction, and other mechanical forces.

Object motions are obtained from the force equations describing physical laws, such as Newton's laws of motion for gravitational and friction processes, Euler or Navier–Stokes equations describing fluid flow, and Maxwell's equations for electromagnetic forces. For example, the general form of Newton's second law for a particle of mass m is

$$\mathbf{F} = \frac{d}{dt}(m\mathbf{v}) \qquad (16\text{-}11)$$

with $\mathbf{F}$ as the force vector, and $\mathbf{v}$ as the velocity vector. If mass is constant, we solve the equation $\mathbf{F} = m\mathbf{a}$, where $\mathbf{a}$ is the acceleration vector. Otherwise, mass is a function of time, as in relativistic motions or the motions of space vehicles that consume measurable amounts of fuel per unit time. We can also use *inverse dynamics* to obtain the forces, given the initial and final positions of objects and the type of motion.

Applications of physically based modeling include complex rigid-body systems and such nonrigid systems as cloth and plastic materials. Typically, numerical methods are used to obtain the motion parameters incrementally from the dynamical equations using initial conditions or boundary values.

SUMMARY

A computer-animation sequence can be set up by specifying the storyboard, the object definitions, and the key frames. The storyboard is an outline of the action, and the key frames define the details of the object motions for selected positions in the animation. Once the key frames have been established, a sequence of in-betweens can be generated to construct a smooth motion from one key frame to the next. A computer animation can involve motion specifications for the objects in a scene as well as motion paths for a camera that moves through the scene. Computer-animation systems include key-frame systems, parameterized systems, and scripting systems. For motion in two-dimensions, we can use the raster-animation techniques discussed in Chapter 5.

For some applications, key frames are used to define the steps in a morphing sequence that changes one object shape into another. Other in-between methods include generation of variable time intervals to simulate accelerations and decelerations in the motion.

Motion specifications can be given in terms of translation and rotation parameters, or motions can be described with equations or with kinematic or dynamic parameters. Kinematic motion descriptions specify positions, velocities, and accelerations. Dynamic motion descriptions are given in terms of the forces acting on the objects in a scene.

REFERENCES

For additional information on computer animation systems and techniques, see Magnenat-Thalmann and Thalmann (1985), Barzel (1992), and Watt and Watt (1992). Algorithms for animation applications are presented in Glassner (1990), Arvo (1991), Kirk (1992), Gascuel (1993), Ngo and Marks (1993), van de Panne and Fiume (1993), and in Snyder et al. (1993). Morphing techniques are discussed in Beier and Neely (1992), Hughes (1992), Kent, Carlson, and Parent (1992), and in Sederberg and Greenwood (1992). A discussion of animation techniques in PHIGS is given in Gaskins (1992).

EXERCISES

16-1. Design a storyboard layout and accompanying key frames for an animation of a single polyhedron.

16-2. Write a program to generate the in-betweens for the key frames specified in Exercise 16-1 using linear interpolation.

16-3. Expand the animation sequence in Exercise 16-1 to include two or more moving objects.

16-4. Write a program to generate the in-betweens for the key frames in Exercise 16-3 using linear interpolation.

16-5. Write a morphing program to transform a sphere into a specified polyhedron.

16-6. Set up an animation specification involving accelerations and implement Eq. 16-7.

16-7. Set up an animation specification involving both accelerations and decelerations and implement the in-between spacing calculations given in Eqs. 16-7 and 16-8.

16-8. Set up an animation specification implementing the acceleration-deceleration calculations of Eq. 16-9.

16-9. Write a program to simulate the linear, two-dimensional motion of a filled circle inside a given rectangular area. The circle is to be given an initial velocity, and the circle is to rebound from the walls with the angle of reflection equal to the angle of incidence.

16-10. Convert the program of Exercise 16-9 into a ball and paddle game by replacing one side of the rectangle with a short line segment that can be moved back and forth to intercept the circle path. The game is over when the circle escapes from the interior of the rectangle. Initial input parameters include circle position, direction, and speed. The game score can include the number of times the circle is intercepted by the paddle.

16-11. Expand the program of Exercise 16-9 to simulate the three-dimensional motion of a sphere moving inside a parallelepiped. Interactive viewing parameters can be set to view the motion from different directions.

16-12. Write a program to implement the simulation of a bouncing ball using Eq. 16-10.

16-13. Write a program to implement the motion of a bouncing ball using a downward

597

gravitational force and a ground-plane friction force. Initially, the ball is to be projected into space with a given velocity vector.

16-14. Write a program to implement the two-player pillbox game. The game can be implemented on a flat plane with fixed pillbox positions, or random terrain features and pillbox placements can be generated at the start of the game.

16-15. Write a program to implement dynamic motion specifications. Specify a scene with two or more objects, initial motion parameters, and specified forces. Then generate the animation from the solution of the force equations. (For example, the objects could be the earth, moon, and sun with attractive gravitational forces that are proportional to mass and inversely proportional to distance squared.)

APPENDIX

Mathematics for Computer Graphics

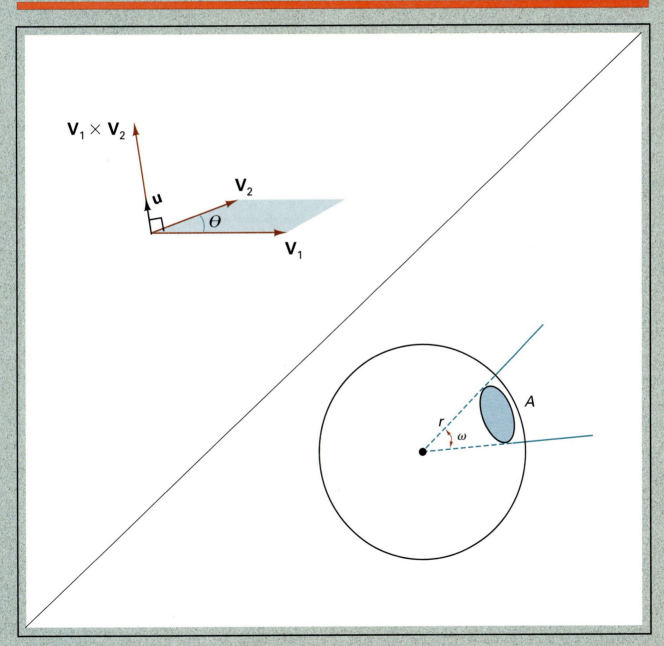

C omputer graphics algorithms make use of many mathematical concepts and techniques. Here, we provide a brief reference for the topics from analytic geometry, linear algebra, vector analysis, tensor analysis, complex numbers, numerical analysis, and other areas that are referred to in the graphics algorithms discussed throughout this book.

A-1
COORDINATE REFERENCE FRAMES

Graphics packages typically require that coordinate parameters be specified with respect to Cartesian reference frames. But in many applications, non-Cartesian coordinate systems are useful. Spherical, cylindrical, or other symmetries often can be exploited to simplify expressions involving object descriptions or manipulations. Unless a specialized graphics system is available, however, we must first convert any non-Cartesian descriptions to Cartesian coordinates. In this section, we first review standard Cartesian coordinate systems, then we consider a few common non-Cartesian systems.

Two-Dimensional Cartesian Reference Frames

Figure A-1 shows two possible orientations for a Cartesian screen reference system. The standard coordinate orientation shown in Fig. A-1(a), with the coordinate origin in the lower-left corner of the screen, is a commonly used reference

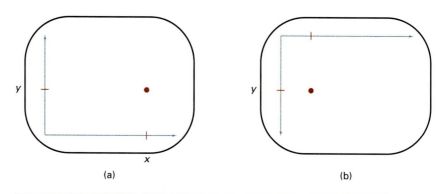

(a)   (b)

Figure A-1
Screen Cartesian reference systems: (a) coordinate origin at the lower-left screen corner and (b) coordinate origin in the upper-left corner.

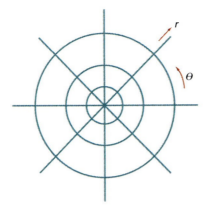

Figure A-2
A polar coordinate reference frame, formed with concentric circles and radial lines.

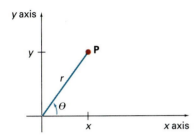

Figure A-3
Relationship between polar and Cartesian coordinates.

frame. Some systems, particularly personal computers, orient the Cartesian reference frame as in Fig. A-1(b), with the origin at the upper left corner. In addition, it is possible in some graphics packages to select a position, such as the center of the screen, for the coordinate origin.

Polar Coordinates in the *xy* Plane

A frequently used non-Cartesian system is a polar-coordinate reference frame (Fig. A-2), where a coordinate position is specified with a radial distance r from the coordinate origin, and an angular displacement θ from the horizontal. Positive angular displacements are counterclockwise, and negative angular displacements are clockwise. Angle θ can be measured in degrees, with one complete counterclockwise revolution about the origin as 360°. The relation between Cartesian and polar coordinates is shown in Fig. A-3. Considering the right triangle in Fig. A-4, and using the definition of the trigonometric functions, we transform from polar coordinates to Cartesian coordinates with the expressions

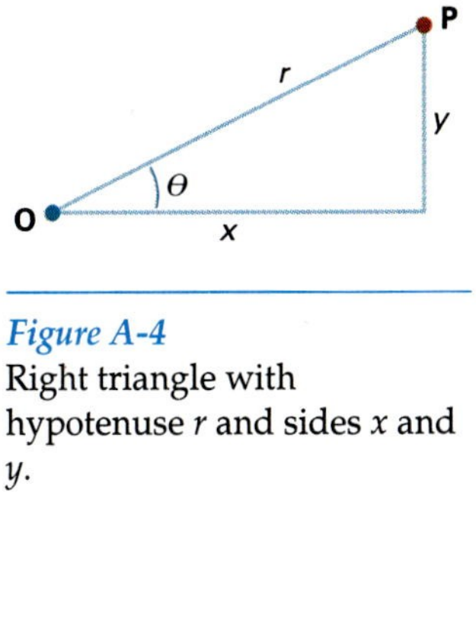

Figure A-4
Right triangle with hypotenuse r and sides x and y.

$$x = r\cos\theta, \qquad y = r\sin\theta \qquad (A\text{-}1)$$

The inverse transformation from Cartesian to polar coordinates is

$$r = \sqrt{x^2 + y^2}, \qquad \theta = \tan^{-1}\left(\frac{y}{x}\right) \qquad (A\text{-}2)$$

Other conics, besides circles, can be used to specify coordinate positions. For example, using concentric ellipses instead of circles, we can give coordinate positions in elliptical coordinates. Similarly, other types of symmetries can be exploited with hyperbolic or parabolic plane coordinates.

601

Angular values can be specified in degrees or they can be given in dimensionless units (radians). Figure A-5 shows two intersecting lines in a plane and a circle centered on the intersection point **P**. The value of angle θ in radians is then given by

$$\theta = \frac{s}{r} \qquad (A\text{-}3)$$

where s is the length of the circular arc subtending θ, and r is the radius of the circle. Total angular distance around point **P** is the length of the circle perimeter ($2\pi r$) divided by r, or 2π radians.

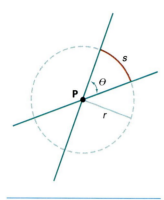

Figure A-5
An angle θ subtended by a circular arc of length s and radius r.

Three-Dimensional Cartesian Reference Frames

Figure A-6(a) shows the conventional orientation for the coordinate axes in a three-dimensional Cartesian reference system. This is called a right-handed system because the right-hand thumb points in the positive z direction when we imagine grasping the z axis with the fingers curling from the positive x axis to the positive y axis (through 90°), as illustrated in Fig. A-6(b). Most computer graphics packages require object descriptions and manipulations to be specified in right-handed Cartesian coordinates. For discussions throughout this book (including the appendix), we assume that all Cartesian reference frames are right-handed.

Another possible arrangement of Cartesian axes is the left-handed system shown in Fig. A-7. For this system, the left-hand thumb points in the positive z direction when we imagine grasping the z axis so that the fingers of the left hand curl from the positive x axis to the positive y axis through 90°. This orientation of axes is sometimes convenient for describing depth of objects relative to a display screen. If screen locations are described in the xy plane of a left-handed system with the coordinate origin in the lower-left screen corner, positive z values indicate positions behind the screen, as in Fig. A-7(a). Larger values along the positive z axis are then interpreted as being farther from the viewer.

Three-Dimensional Curvilinear Coordinate Systems

Any non-Cartesian reference frame is referred to as a **curvilinear coordinate system**. The choice of coordinate system for a particular graphics application depends on a number of factors, such as symmetry, ease of computation, and visu-

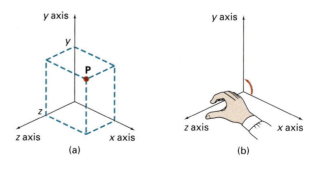

Figure A-6
Coordinate representation of a point **P** at position (x, y, z) in a right-handed Cartesian reference system.

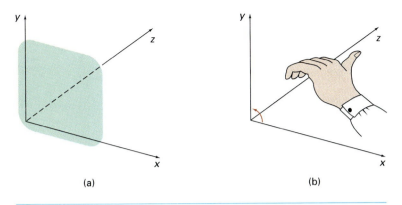

(a)   (b)

Figure A-7
Left-handed Cartesian coordinate system superimposed on the surface
of a video monitor.

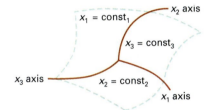

Figure A-8
A general curvilinear coordinate
reference frame.

alization advantages. Figure A-8 shows a general curvilinear coordinate reference
frame formed with three *coordinate surfaces*, where each surface has one coordinate
held constant. For instance, the x_1x_2 surface is defined with x_3 held constant.
Coordinate axes in any reference frame are the intersection curves of the coordinate
surfaces. If the coordinate surfaces intersect at right angles, we have an **orthogonal
curvilinear coordinate system**. Nonorthogonal reference frames are
useful for specialized spaces, such as visualizations of motions governed by the
laws of general relativity, but in general, they are used less frequently in graphics
applications than orthogonal systems.

A *cylindrical-coordinate* specification of a spatial position is shown in Fig. A-
9 in relation to a Cartesian reference frame. The surface of constant ρ is a vertical

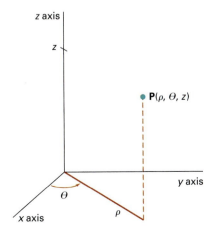

Figure A-9
Cylindrical coordinates: ρ, θ, z.

603

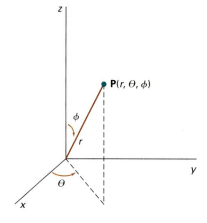

$P(r, \Theta, \phi)$

ϕ

r

θ

Figure A-10
Spherical coordinates: r, θ, ϕ.

cylinder; the surface of constant θ is a vertical plane containing the z axis; and the surface of constant z is a horizontal plane parallel to the Cartesian xy plane. We transform from a cylindrical coordinate specification to a Cartesian reference frame with the calculations

$$x = \rho\cos\theta, \qquad y = \rho\sin\theta, \qquad z = z \qquad (A\text{-}4)$$

Figure A-10 shows a *spherical-coordinate* specification of a spatial position in reference to a Cartesian reference frame. Spherical coordinates are sometimes referred to as *polar coordinates in space*. The surface of constant r is a sphere; the surface of constant θ is a vertical plane containing the z axis (same θ surface as in cylindrical coordinates); and the surface of constant ϕ is a cone with apex at the coordinate origin. If $\phi < 90°$, the cone is above the xy plane. If $\phi > 90°$, the cone is below the xy plane. We transfrom from a spherical-coordinate specification to a Cartesian reference frame with the calculations

$$x = r\cos\theta\sin\phi, \qquad y = r\sin\theta\sin\phi, \qquad z = r\cos\phi \qquad (A\text{-}5)$$

Solid Angle

We define a solid angle in analogy with that for a two-dimensional angle θ between two intersecting lines (Eq. A-3). Instead of a circle, we consider any sphere with center position **P**. The solid angle ω within a cone-shaped region with apex at **P** is defined as

$$\omega = \frac{A}{r^2} \qquad (A\text{-}6)$$

where A is the area of the spherical surface intersected by the cone (Fig. A-11), and r is the radius of the sphere.

Also, in analogy with two-dimensional polar coordinates, the dimensionless unit for solid angles is called the **steradian**. The total solid angle about a point is the total area of the spherical surface ($4\pi r^2$) divided by r^2, or 4π steradians.

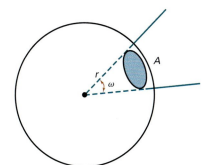

Figure A-11

A solid angle ω subtended by a
spherical surface patch of area A
with radius r.

A-2
POINTS AND VECTORS

There is a fundamental difference between the concept of a point and that of a
vector. A point is a position specified with coordinate values in some reference
frame, so that the distance from the origin depends on the choice of refer–
ence frame. Figure A-12 illustrates coordinate specification in two reference
frames. In frame A, point coordinates are given by the values of the ordered pair
(x, y). In frame B, the same point has coordinates $(0, 0)$ and the distance to the origin of frame B is 0.

A vector, on the other hand, is defined as the difference between two point
positions. Thus, for a two-dimensional vector (Fig. A-13), we have

$$\mathbf{V} = \mathbf{P}_2 - \mathbf{P}_1$$
$$= (x_2 - x_1, y_2 - y_1) \qquad (A\text{-}7)$$
$$= (V_x, V_y)$$

where the Cartesian *components* (or Cartesian *elements*) V_x and V_y are the projections of $\mathbf{V}$ onto the x and y axes. Given two point positions, we can obtain vector
components in the same way for any coordinate reference frame.

We can describe a vector as a *directed line segment* that has two fundamental
properties: magnitude and direction. For the two-dimensional vector in Fig. A-
13, we calculate vector magnitude using the Pythagorean theorem:

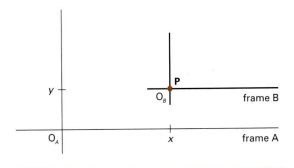

Figure A-12

Position of point $\mathbf{P}$ with respect to two different
Cartesian reference frames.

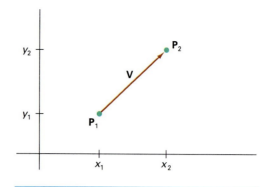

Figure A-13
Vector **V** in the xy plane of a Cartesian reference frame.

$$|\mathbf{V}| = \sqrt{V_x^2 + V_y^2} \qquad (A\text{-}8)$$

The direction for this two-dimensional vector can be given in terms of the angular displacement from the x axis as

$$\alpha = \tan^{-1}\left(\frac{V_y}{V_x}\right) \qquad (A\text{-}9)$$

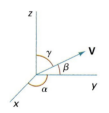

Figure A-14
Direction angles α, β, and γ.

A vector has the same properties (magnitude and direction) no matter where we position the vector within a single coordinate system. And the vector magnitude is independent of the coordinate representation. Of course, if we change the coordinate representation, the values for the vector components change.

For a three-dimensional Cartesian space, we calculate the vector magnitude as

$$|\mathbf{V}| = \sqrt{V_x^2 + V_y^2 + V_z^2} \qquad (A\text{-}10)$$

Vector direction is given with the *direction angles*, α, β, and γ, that the vector makes with each of the coordinate axes (Fig. A-14). Direction angles are the positive angles that the vector makes with each of the positive coordinate axes. We calculate these angles as

$$\cos\alpha = \frac{V_x}{|\mathbf{V}|}, \qquad \cos\beta = \frac{V_y}{|\mathbf{V}|}, \qquad \cos\gamma = \frac{V_z}{|\mathbf{V}|} \qquad (A\text{-}11)$$

The values $\cos\alpha$, $\cos\beta$, and $\cos\gamma$ are called the *direction cosines* of the vector. Actually, we only need to specify two of the direction cosines to give the direction of **V**, since

$$\cos^2\alpha + \cos^2\beta + \cos^2\gamma = 1 \qquad (A\text{-}12)$$

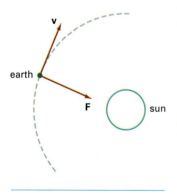

Figure A-15
A gravitational force vector **F** and a velocity vector **v**.

Vectors are used to represent any quantities that have the properties of magnitude and direction. Two common examples are force and velocity (Fig. A-15). A force can be thought of as a push or a pull of a certain amount in a par-

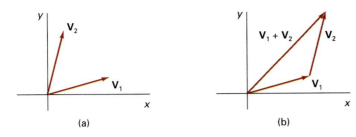

(a)

(b)

Figure A-16

Two vectors (a) can be added geometrically by positioning the two vectors end to end (b) and drawing the resultant vector from the start of the first vector to the tip of the second vector.

ticular direction. A velocity vector specifies how fast (*speed*) an object is moving in a certain direction.

Vector Addition and Scalar Multiplication

By definition, the sum of two vectors is obtained by adding corresponding components:

$$\mathbf{V}_1 + \mathbf{V}_2 = (V_{1x} + V_{2x}, V_{1y} + V_{2y}, V_{1z} + V_{2z}) \qquad (A\text{-}13)$$

Vector addition is illustrated geometrically in Fig. A-16. We obtain the vector sum by placing the start position of one vector at the tip of the other vector and drawing the summation vector as in Fig. A-16.

Addition of vectors and scalars is undefined, since a scalar always has only one numerical value while a vector has n numerical components in an n-dimensional space. Scalar multiplication of a three-dimensional vector is defined as

$$a\mathbf{V} = (aV_x, aV_y, aV_z) \qquad (A\text{-}14)$$

For example, if the scalar parameter a has the value 2, each component of $\mathbf{V}$ is doubled.

We can also multiply two vectors, but there are two possible ways to do this. The multiplication can be carried out so that either we obtain another vector or we obtain a scalar quantity.

Scalar Product of Two Vectors

Vector multiplication for producing a scalar is defined as

$$\mathbf{V}_1 \cdot \mathbf{V}_2 = |\mathbf{V}_1| \, |\mathbf{V}_2| \cos\theta, \qquad 0 \le \theta \le \pi \qquad (A\text{-}15)$$

where θ is the angle between the two vectors (Fig. A-17). This product is called the **scalar product** (or **dot product**) of two vectors. It is also referred to as the *inner product*, particularly in discussing scalar products in tensor analysis. Equation A-15 is valid in any coordinate representation and can be interpreted as the product of parallel components of the two vectors.

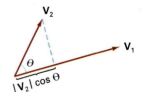

Figure A-17
The dot product of two vectors is obtained by multiplying parallel components.

607

In addition to the coordinate-independent form of the scalar product, we can express this product in specific coordinate representations. For a Cartesian reference frame, the scalar product is calculated as

$$\mathbf{V}_1 \cdot \mathbf{V}_2 = V_{1x}V_{2x} + V_{1y}V_{2y} + V_{1z}V_{2z} \qquad\qquad (A\text{-}16)$$

The dot product of a vector with itself is simply another statement of the Pythagorean theorem. Also, the scalar product of two vectors is zero if and only if the two vectors are perpendicular (**orthogonal**). Dot products are commutative

$$\mathbf{V}_1 \cdot \mathbf{V}_2 = \mathbf{V}_2 \cdot \mathbf{V}_1 \qquad\qquad (A\text{-}17)$$

because this operation produces a scalar, and dot products are distributive with respect to vector addition

$$\mathbf{V}_1 \cdot (\mathbf{V}_2 + \mathbf{V}_3) = \mathbf{V}_1 \cdot \mathbf{V}_2 + \mathbf{V}_1 \cdot \mathbf{V}_3 \qquad\qquad (A\text{-}18)$$

Vector Product of Two Vectors

Multiplication of two vectors to produce another vector is defined as

$$\mathbf{V}_1 \times \mathbf{V}_2 = \mathbf{u}\,|\mathbf{V}_1|\,|\mathbf{V}_2|\sin\theta, \qquad 0 \le \theta \le \pi \qquad\qquad (A\text{-}19)$$

where $\mathbf{u}$ is a unit vector (magnitude 1) that is perpendicular to both $\mathbf{V}_1$ and $\mathbf{V}_2$ (Fig. A-18). The direction for $\mathbf{u}$ is determined by the *right-hand rule*: We grasp an axis that is perpendicular to the plane of $\mathbf{V}_1$ and $\mathbf{V}_2$ so that the fingers of the right hand curl from $\mathbf{V}_1$ to $\mathbf{V}_2$. Our right thumb then points in the direction of $\mathbf{u}$. This product is called the **vector product** (or **cross product**) of two vectors, and Equation A-19 is valid in any coordinate representation. The cross product of two vectors is a vector that is perpendicular to the plane of the two vectors and with magnitude equal to the area of the parallelogram formed by the two vectors.

We can also express the cross product in terms of vector components in a specific reference frame. In a Cartesian coordinate system, we calculate the components of the cross product as

$$\mathbf{V}_1 \times \mathbf{V}_2 = (V_{1y}V_{2z} - V_{1z}V_{2y},\ V_{1z}V_{2x} - V_{1x}V_{2z},\ V_{1x}V_{2y} - V_{1y}V_{2x}) \qquad (A\text{-}20)$$

If we let $\mathbf{u}_x$, $\mathbf{u}_y$, and $\mathbf{u}_z$ represent unit vectors (magnitude 1) along the x, y, and z axes, we can write the cross product in terms of Cartesian components using determinant notation:

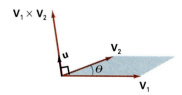

$V_1 \times V_2$

Figure A-18

The cross product of two vectors is a vector in a direction perpendicular to the two original vectors and with a magnitude equal to the area of the shaded parallelogram.

$$\mathbf{V}_1 \times \mathbf{V}_2 = \begin{vmatrix} \mathbf{u}_x & \mathbf{u}_y & \mathbf{u}_z \\ V_{1x} & V_{1y} & V_{1z} \\ V_{2x} & V_{2y} & V_{2z} \end{vmatrix} \qquad (A\text{-}21)$$

The cross product of any two parallel vectors is zero. Therefore, the cross product of a vector with itself is zero. Also, the cross product is not commutative; it is anticommutative:

$$\mathbf{V}_1 \times \mathbf{V}_2 = -(\mathbf{V}_2 \times \mathbf{V}_1) \qquad (A\text{-}22)$$

And the cross product is not associative:

$$\mathbf{V}_1 \times (\mathbf{V}_2 \times \mathbf{V}_3) \neq (\mathbf{V}_1 \times \mathbf{V}_2) \times \mathbf{V}_3 \qquad (A\text{-}23)$$

But the cross product is distributive with respect to vector addition; that is,

$$\mathbf{V}_1 \times (\mathbf{V}_2 + \mathbf{V}_3) = (\mathbf{V}_1 \times \mathbf{V}_2) + (\mathbf{V}_1 \times \mathbf{V}_3) \qquad (A\text{-}24)$$

A-3
BASIS VECTORS AND THE METRIC TENSOR

We can specify the coordinate axes in any reference frame with a set of vectors, one for each axis (Fig. A-19). Each coordinate-axis vector gives the direction of that axis at any point along the axis. These vectors form a linearly independent set of vectors. That is, the axis vectors cannot be written as linear combinations of each other. Also, any other vector in that space can be written as a linear combination of the axis vectors, and the set of axis vectors is called a **basis** (or **a set of base vectors**) for the space. In general, the space is referred to as a *vector space* and the basis contains the minimum number of vectors to represent any other vector in the space as a linear combination of the base vectors.

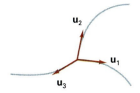

Figure A-19
Curvilinear coordinate-axis vectors.

Orthonormal Basis

Often, vectors in a basis are normalized so that each vector has a magnitude of 1. In this case, the set of unit vectors is called a **normal basis**. Also, for Cartesian reference frames and other commonly used coordinate systems, the coordinate axes are mutually perpendicular, and the set of base vectors is referred to as an **orthogonal basis**. If, in addition, the base vectors are all unit vectors, we have an **orthonormal basis** that satisfies the following conditions:

$$\mathbf{u}_k \cdot \mathbf{u}_k = 1, \qquad \text{for all } k$$
$$\mathbf{u}_j \cdot \mathbf{u}_k = 0, \qquad \text{for all } j \neq k \qquad (A\text{-}25)$$

Most commonly used reference frames are orthogonal, but nonorthogonal coordinate reference frames are useful in some applications including relativity theory and visualization of certain data sets.

For a two-dimensional Cartesian system, the orthonormal basis is

609

$$\mathbf{u}_x = (1, 0), \qquad \mathbf{u}_y = (0, 1) \tag{A-26}$$

And the orthonormal basis for a three-dimensional Cartesian reference frame is

$$\mathbf{u}_x = (1, 0, 0), \qquad \mathbf{u}_y = (0, 1, 0), \qquad \mathbf{u}_z = (0, 0, 1) \tag{A-27}$$

Metric Tensor

Tensors are generalizations of the notion of a vector. Specifically, a **tensor** is a quantity having a number of components, depending on the tensor rank and the dimension of the space, that satisfy certain transformation properties when converted from one coordinate representation to another. For orthogonal systems, the transformation properties are straightforward. Formally, a vector is a tensor of rank one, and a scalar is a tensor of rank zero. Another way to view this classification is to note that the components of a vector are specified with one subscript, while a scalar always has a single value and, hence, no subscripts. A tensor of rank two thus has two subscripts, and in three-dimensional space, a tensor of rank two has nine components (three values for each subscript).

For any general (curvilinear) coordinate system, the elements (or coefficients) of the **metric tensor** for that space are defined as

$$g_{jk} = \mathbf{u}_j \cdot \mathbf{u}_k \tag{A-28}$$

Thus, the metric tensor is of rank two and it is symmetric: $g_{jk} = g_{kj}$. Metric tensors have several useful properties. The elements of a metric tensor can be used to determine (1) distance between two points in that space, (2) transformation equations for conversion to another space, and (3) components of various differential vector operators (such as gradient, divergence, and curl) within that space.

In an orthogonal space:

$$g_{jk} = 0, \qquad \text{for } j \neq k \tag{A-29}$$

And in a Cartesian coordinate system (assuming unit base vectors):

$$g_{jk} = \begin{cases} 1, & \text{if } j = k \\ 0, & \text{otherwise} \end{cases} \tag{A-30}$$

The unit base vectors in polar coordinates can be expressed in terms of Cartesian base vectors as

$$\mathbf{u}_r = \mathbf{u}_x \cos\theta + \mathbf{u}_y \sin\theta, \qquad \mathbf{u}_\theta = -\mathbf{u}_x r \sin\theta + \mathbf{u}_y r \cos\theta \tag{A-31}$$

Substituting these expressions into Eq. A-28, we obtain the elements of the metric tensor, which can be written in the matrix form:

$$\mathbf{g} = \begin{bmatrix} 1 & 0 \\ 0 & r^2 \end{bmatrix} \tag{A-32}$$

For a cylindrical coordinate reference frame, the base vectors are

$$\mathbf{u}_\rho = \mathbf{u}_x \cos\theta + \mathbf{u}_y \sin\theta, \qquad \mathbf{u}_\theta = -\mathbf{u}_x \rho \sin\theta + \mathbf{u}_y \rho \cos\theta, \qquad \mathbf{u}_z \tag{A-33}$$

And the matrix representation for the metric tensor in cylindrical coordinates is

$$\mathbf{g} = \begin{bmatrix} 1 & 0 & 0 \\ 0 & \rho & 0 \\ 0 & 0 & 1 \end{bmatrix} \qquad (A\text{-}34)$$

We can write the base vectors in spherical coordinates as

$$\mathbf{u}_r = \mathbf{u}_x \cos\theta \sin\phi + \mathbf{u}_y \sin\theta \sin\phi + \mathbf{u}_z \cos\phi$$

$$\mathbf{u}_\theta = -\mathbf{u}_x r \sin\theta \sin\phi + \mathbf{u}_y r \cos\theta \sin\phi$$

$$\mathbf{u}_\phi = \mathbf{u}_x r \cos\theta \cos\phi + \mathbf{u}_y r \sin\theta \cos\phi - \mathbf{u}_z r \sin\phi \qquad (A\text{-}35)$$

Then the matrix representation for the metric tensor in spherical coordinates is

$$\mathbf{g} = \begin{bmatrix} 1 & 0 & 0 \\ 0 & r^2 \sin^2\phi & 0 \\ 0 & 0 & r^2 \end{bmatrix} \qquad (A\text{-}36)$$

A-4

MATRICES

A matrix is a rectangular array of quantities (numbers, functions, or numerical expressions), called the elements of the matrix. Some examples of matrices are

$$\begin{bmatrix} 3.60 & -0.01 & 2.00 \\ -5.46 & 0.00 & 1.63 \end{bmatrix}, \quad \begin{bmatrix} e^x & x \\ e^{2x} & x^2 \end{bmatrix}, \quad [a_1\ a_2\ a_3], \quad \begin{bmatrix} x \\ y \\ z \end{bmatrix} \qquad (A\text{-}37)$$

We identify matrices according to the number of rows and number of columns. For these examples, the matrices in left-to-right order are 2 by 3, 2 by 2, 1 by 3, and 3 by 1. When the number of rows is the same as the number of columns, as in the second example, the matrix is called a *square matrix*.

In general, we can write an m by n matrix as

$$\mathbf{A} = \begin{bmatrix} a_{11} & a_{12} & \cdots & a_{1n} \\ a_{21} & a_{22} & \cdots & a_{2n} \\ \vdots & \vdots & & \vdots \\ a_{m1} & a_{m2} & \cdots & a_{mn} \end{bmatrix} \qquad (A\text{-}38)$$

where the a_{jk} represent the elements of matrix $\mathbf{A}$. The first subscript of any element gives the row number, and the second subscript gives the column number.

A matrix with a single row or a single column represents a vector. Thus, the last two matrix examples in A-37 are, respectively, a *row vector* and a *column vector*. In general, a matrix can be viewed as a collection of row vectors or as a collection of column vectors.

When various operations are expressed in matrix form, the standard mathematical convention is to represent a vector with a column matrix. Following this convention, we write the matrix representation for a three-dimensional vector in

Cartesian coordinates as

$$\mathbf{V} = \begin{bmatrix} V_x \\ V_y \\ V_z \end{bmatrix} \qquad (A\text{-}39)$$

We will use this matrix representation for both points and vectors, but we must keep in mind the distinction between them. It is often convenient to consider a point as a vector with start position at the coordinate origin within a single coordinate reference frame, but points do not have the properties of vectors that remain invariant when switching from one coordinate system to another. Also, in general, we cannot apply vector operations, such as vector addition, dot product, and cross product, to points.

Scalar Multiplication and Matrix Addition

To multiply a matrix $\mathbf{A}$ by a scalar value s, we multiply each element a_{jk} by the scalar. As an example, if

$$\mathbf{A} = \begin{bmatrix} 1 & 2 & 3 \\ 4 & 5 & 6 \end{bmatrix}$$

then

$$3\mathbf{A} = \begin{bmatrix} 3 & 6 & 9 \\ 12 & 15 & 18 \end{bmatrix}$$

Matrix addition is defined only for matrices that have the same number of rows m and the same number of columns n. For any two m by n matrices, the sum is obtained by adding corresponding elements. For example,

$$\begin{bmatrix} 1 & 2 & 3 \\ 4 & 5 & 6 \end{bmatrix} + \begin{bmatrix} 0 & 1.5 & 0.2 \\ -6 & 1.1 & -10 \end{bmatrix} = \begin{bmatrix} 1 & 3.5 & 3.2 \\ -2 & 6.1 & -4 \end{bmatrix}$$

Matrix Multiplication

The product of two matrices is defined as a generalization of the vector dot product. We can multiply an m by n matrix $\mathbf{A}$ by a p by q matrix $\mathbf{B}$ to form the matrix product $\mathbf{AB}$, providing that the number of columns in $\mathbf{A}$ is equal to the number of rows in $\mathbf{B}$ (i.e., $n = p$). We then obtain the product matrix by forming sums of the products of the elements in the row vectors of $\mathbf{A}$ with the corresponding elements in the column vectors of $\mathbf{B}$. Thus, for the following product

$$\mathbf{C} = \mathbf{A}\mathbf{B} \qquad (A\text{-}40)$$

we obtain an m by q matrix $\mathbf{C}$ whose elements are calculated as

$$c_{ij} = \sum_{k=1}^{n} a_{ik} b_{kj} \qquad (A\text{-}41)$$

In the following example, a 3 by 2 matrix is postmultiplied by a 2 by 2 matrix to produce a 3 by 2 product matrix:

$$\begin{bmatrix} 0 & -1 \\ 5 & 7 \\ -2 & 8 \end{bmatrix} \begin{bmatrix} 1 & 2 \\ 3 & 4 \end{bmatrix} = \begin{bmatrix} 0 \cdot 1 + (-1) \cdot 3 & 0 \cdot 2 + (-1) \cdot 4 \\ 5 \cdot 1 + 7 \cdot 3 & 5 \cdot 2 + 7 \cdot 4 \\ -2 \cdot 1 + 8 \cdot 3 & -2 \cdot 2 + 8 \cdot 4 \end{bmatrix} = \begin{bmatrix} -3 & -4 \\ 26 & 38 \\ 22 & 28 \end{bmatrix}$$

Vector multiplication in matrix notation produces the same result as the dot product, providing the first vector is expressed as a row vector and the second vector is expressed as a column vector:

$$[1\ 2\ 3] \begin{bmatrix} 4 \\ 5 \\ 6 \end{bmatrix} = [32]$$

This vector product results in a matrix with a single element (a 1-by-1 matrix). If we multiply the vectors in reverse order, we obtain a 3 by 3 matrix:

$$\begin{bmatrix} 4 \\ 5 \\ 6 \end{bmatrix} [1\ 2\ 3] = \begin{bmatrix} 4 & 8 & 12 \\ 5 & 10 & 15 \\ 6 & 12 & 18 \end{bmatrix}$$

As the previous two vector products illustrate, matrix multiplication, in general, is not commutative. That is,

$$\mathbf{AB} \neq \mathbf{BA} \tag{A-42}$$

But matrix multiplication is distributive with respect to matrix addition:

$$\mathbf{A(B + C) = AB + AC} \tag{A-43}$$

Matrix Transpose

The **transpose** A^T of a matrix is obtained by interchanging rows and columns. For example,

$$\begin{bmatrix} 1 & 2 & 3 \\ 4 & 5 & 6 \end{bmatrix}^T = \begin{bmatrix} 1 & 4 \\ 2 & 5 \\ 3 & 6 \end{bmatrix}, \qquad [a\ b\ c]^T = \begin{bmatrix} a \\ b \\ c \end{bmatrix} \tag{A-44}$$

For a matrix product, the transpose is

$$(\mathbf{AB})^T = \mathbf{B}^T \mathbf{A}^T \tag{A-45}$$

Determinant of a Matrix

For a square matrix, we can combine the matrix elements to produce a single number called the **determinant**. Determinants are defined recursively. For a 2 by 2 matrix, the **second-order determinant** is defined to be

$$\begin{vmatrix} a_{11} & a_{12} \\ a_{21} & a_{22} \end{vmatrix} = a_{11}a_{22} - a_{12}a_{21} \tag{A-46}$$

613

We then calculate higher-order determinants in terms of lower-order determinants. To calculate the determinants of order 3 or greater, we can select any column k of an n by n matrix and compute the determinant as

$$\det \mathbf{A} = \sum_{j=1}^{n} (-1)^{j+k} a_{jk} \det \mathbf{A}_{jk} \qquad (A\text{-}47)$$

where $\det \mathbf{A}_{jk}$ is the $(n-1)$ by $(n-1)$ determinant of the submatrix obtained from $\mathbf{A}$ by deleting the jth row and the kth column. Alternatively, we can select any row j and calculate the determinant as

$$\det \mathbf{A} = \sum_{k=1}^{n} (-1)^{j+k} a_{jk} \det \mathbf{A}_{jk} \qquad (A\text{-}48)$$

Calculating determinants for large matrices ($n > 4$, say) can be done more efficiently using numerical methods. One way to compute a determinant is to decompose the matrix into two factors: $\mathbf{A} = \mathbf{LU}$, where all elements of matrix $\mathbf{L}$ that are above the diagonal are zero, and all elements of matrix $\mathbf{U}$ that are below the diagonal are zero. We then compute the product of the diagonals for both $\mathbf{L}$ and $\mathbf{U}$, and we obtain $\det \mathbf{A}$ by multiplying these two products together. This method is based on the following property of determinants:

$$\det(\mathbf{AB}) = (\det \mathbf{A})(\det \mathbf{B}) \qquad (A\text{-}49)$$

Another method for calculating determinants is based on Gaussian elimination procedures (Section A-9).

Matrix Inverse

With square matrices, we can obtain an *inverse matrix* if and only if the determinant of the matrix is nonzero. If an inverse exists, the matrix is said to be a **nonsingular matrix**. Otherwise, the matrix is called a **singular matrix**. For most practical applications, where a matrix represents a physical operation, we can expect the inverse to exist.

The inverse of an n by n square matrix $\mathbf{A}$ is denoted as $\mathbf{A}^{-1}$ and

$$\mathbf{A}\mathbf{A}^{-1} = \mathbf{A}^{-1}\mathbf{A} = \mathbf{I} \qquad (A\text{-}50)$$

where $\mathbf{I}$ is the identiy matrix. All diagonal elements of $\mathbf{I}$ have the value 1, and all other (off diagonal) elements are zero.

Elements for the inverse matrix $\mathbf{A}^{-1}$ can be calculated from the elements of $\mathbf{A}$ as

$$a_{jk}^{-1} = \frac{(-1)^{j+k} \det \mathbf{A}_{kj}}{\det \mathbf{A}} \qquad (A\text{-}51)$$

where a_{jk}^{-1} is the element in the jth row and kth column of $\mathbf{A}^{-1}$, and $\mathbf{A}_{kj}$ is the $(n-1)$ by $(n-1)$ submatrix obtained by deleting the kth row and jth column of matrix $\mathbf{A}$. Again, numerical methods can be used to evaluate the determinant and the elements of the inverse matrix for large values of n.

By definition, a **complex number** z is an ordered pair of real numbers:

$$z = (x, y) \qquad (A\text{-}52)$$

where x is called the **real part** of z, and y is called the **imaginary part** of z. Real and imaginary parts of a complex number are designated as

$$x = \text{Re}(z), \qquad y = \text{Im}(z) \qquad (A\text{-}53)$$

Geometrically, a complex number is represented in the *complex plane*, as in Fig. A-20.

Complex numbers arise from solutions of equations such as

$$x^2 + 1 = 0, \qquad x^2 - 2x + 5 = 0$$

which have no real-number solutions. Thus, complex numbers and complex arithmetic are set up as extensions of real numbers that provide solutions to such equations.

Addition, subtraction, and scalar multiplication of complex numbers are carried out using the same rules as for two-dimensional vectors. Multiplication of complex numbers is defined as

$$(x_1, y_1)(x_2, y_2) = (x_1 x_2 - y_1 y_2, x_1 y_2 + x_2 y_1) \qquad (A\text{-}54)$$

This definition for complex numbers gives the same result as for real-number multiplication when the imaginary parts are zero:

$$(x_1, 0)(x_2, 0) = (x_1 x_2, 0)$$

Thus, we can write a real number in complex form as

$$x = (x, 0)$$

Similarly, a *pure imaginary number* has a real part equal to 0: $(0, y)$.

The complex number $(0, 1)$ is called the *imaginary unit*, and it is denoted by

$$i = (0, 1) \qquad (A\text{-}55)$$

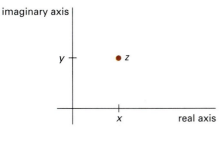

Figure A-20
Position of a point z in the complex plane.

Electrical engineers often use the symbol j for the imaginary unit, because the symbol i is used to represent electrical current. From the rule for complex multiplication, we have

$$i^2 = (0, 1)(0, 1) = (-1, 0)$$

Therefore, i^2 is the real number -1, and

$$i = \sqrt{-1} \qquad (A\text{-}56)$$

Using the rule for complex multiplication, we can write any pure imaginary number in the form

$$iy = (0, 1)(0, y) = (0, y)$$

Also, by the addition rule, we can write any complex number as the sum

$$z = (x, 0) + (0, y)$$

Therefore, another representation for a complex number is

$$z = x + iy \qquad (A\text{-}57)$$

which is the usual form used in practical applications.

Another concept associated with a complex number is the *complex conjugate*:

$$\bar{z} = x - iy \qquad (A\text{-}58)$$

Modulus, or *absolute value*, of a complex number is defined to be

$$|z| = z\bar{z} = \sqrt{x^2 + y^2} \qquad (A\text{-}59)$$

which gives the length of the "vector" representing the complex number (i.e., the distance from the origin of the complex plane to point z). Real and imaginary parts for the division of two complex numbers is obtained as

$$
\begin{aligned}
\frac{z_1}{z_2} &= \frac{z_1\bar{z_2}}{z_2\bar{z_2}} \\
&= \frac{(x_1, y_1)(x_2, -y_2)}{x_2^2 + y_2^2}, \\
&= \left(\frac{x_1 x_2 + y_1 y_2}{x_2^2 + y_2^2}, \frac{x_2 y_1 - x_1 y_2}{x_2^2 + y_2^2} \right)
\end{aligned}
\qquad (A\text{-}60)
$$

A particularly useful representation for complex numbers is to express the real and imaginary parts in terms of polar coordinates (Fig. A-21):

$$z = r(\cos\theta + i\sin\theta) \qquad (A\text{-}61)$$

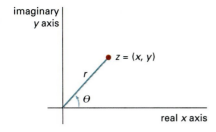

Figure A-21
Polar coordinate position of a
complex number z.

We can also write the polar form of z as

$$z = re^{i\theta} \qquad (A\text{-}62)$$

where e is the base of the natural logarithms ($e = 2.718281828 \ldots$), and

$$e^{i\theta} = \cos\theta + i\sin\theta \qquad (A\text{-}63)$$

which is *Euler's formula*. Complex multiplications and divisions are easily obtained as

$$z_1 z_2 = r_1 r_2 e^{i(\theta_1 + \theta_2)}, \qquad \frac{z_1}{z_2} = r_1 r_2 e^{i(\theta_1 - \theta_2)}$$

And the nth roots of a complex number are calculated as

$$\sqrt[n]{z} = \sqrt[n]{r}\left[\cos\left(\frac{\theta + 2k\pi}{n}\right) + i\sin\left(\frac{\theta + 2k\pi}{n}\right)\right], \qquad k = 0, 1, 2, \ldots, n - 1 \quad (A\text{-}64)$$

The n roots lie on a circle of radius $\sqrt[n]{r}$ with center at the origin of the complex plane and form the vertices of a regular polygon with n sides.

A-6
QUATERNIONS

Complex number concepts are extended to higher dimensions with **quaternions**, which are numbers with one real part and three imaginary parts, written as

$$q = s + ia + jb + kc \qquad (A\text{-}65)$$

where the coefficients a, b, and c in the imaginary terms are real numbers, and parameter s is a real number called the *scalar part*. Parameters i, j, k are defined with the properties

$$i^2 = j^2 = k^2 = -1, \qquad ij = -ji = k \qquad (A\text{-}66)$$

From these properties, it follows that

$$jk = -kj = i, \qquad ki = -ik = j \qquad (A\text{-}67)$$

617

Scalar multiplication is defined in analogy with the corresponding operations for vectors and complex numbers. That is, each of the four components of the quaternion is multiplied by the scalar value. Similarly, quaternion addition is defined as

$$q_1 + q_2 = (s_1 + s_2) + i(a_1 + a_2) + j(b_1 + b_2) + k(c_1 + c_2) \qquad (A\text{-}68)$$

Multiplication of two quaternions is carried out using the operations in Eqs. A-66 and A-67.

An ordered-pair notation for a quaternion is also formed in analogy with complex-number notation:

$$q = (s, \mathbf{v}) \qquad (A\text{-}69)$$

where $\mathbf{v}$ is the vector (a, b, c). In this notation, quaternion addition is expressed as

$$q_1 + q_2 = (s_1 + s_2, \mathbf{v}_1 + \mathbf{v}_2) \qquad (A\text{-}70)$$

Quaternion multiplication can then be expressed in terms of vector dot and cross products as

$$q_1 q_2 = (s_1 s_2 - \mathbf{v}_1 \cdot \mathbf{v}_2, s_1 \mathbf{v}_2 + s_2 \mathbf{v}_1 + \mathbf{v}_1 \times \mathbf{v}_2) \qquad (A\text{-}71)$$

As an extension of complex operations, the magnitude squared of a quaternion is defined using the vector dot product as

$$|q|^2 = s^2 + \mathbf{v} \cdot \mathbf{v} \qquad (A\text{-}72)$$

And the inverse of a quaternion is

$$q^{-1} = \frac{1}{|q|^2}(s, -\mathbf{v}) \qquad (A\text{-}73)$$

so that

$$q q^{-1} = q^{-1} q = (1, 0)$$

A-7
NONPARAMETRIC REPRESENTATIONS

When we write object descriptions directly in terms of the coordinates of the reference frame in use, the respresentation is called **nonparametric**. For example, we can represent a surface with either of the following Cartesian functions:

$$f(x, y, z) = 0, \qquad \text{or} \qquad z = f(x, y) \qquad (A\text{-}74)$$

The first form in A-74 gives an *implicit* expression for the surface, and the second form gives an *explicit* representation, with x and y as the independent variables, and with z as the dependent variable.

Similarly, we can represent a three-dimensional curved line in nonparametric form as the intersection of two surface functions, or we could represent the curve with the pair of functions

$$y = f(x), \qquad z = g(x) \qquad\qquad (A\text{-}75)$$

where coordinate x is selected as the independent variable. Values for the dependent variables y and z are then determined from Eqs. A-75 as we step through values for x from one line endpoint to the other endpoint.

Nonparametric representations are useful in describing objects within a given reference frame, but they have some disadvantages when used in graphics algorithms. If we want a smooth plot, we must change the independent variable whenever the first derivative (slope) of either $f(x)$ or $g(x)$ becomes greater than 1. This means that we must continually check values of the derivatives, which may become infinite at some points. Also, Eqs. A-75 provide an awkward format for representing multiple-valued functions. For instance, the implicit equation of a circle centered on the origin in the xy plane is

$$x^2 + y^2 = r^2$$

and the explicit expression for y is the multivalued function

$$y = \pm\sqrt{r^2 - x^2}$$

In general, a more convenient representation for object descriptions in graphics algorithms is in terms of parametric equations.

A-8
PARAMETRIC REPRESENTATIONS

Euclidean curves are one-dimensional objects, and positions along the path of a three-dimensional curve can be described with a single parameter u. That is, we can express each of the three Cartesian coordinates in terms of parameter u, and any point on the curve can then be represented with the following vector point function (relative to a particular Cartesian reference frame):

$$\mathbf{P}(u) = (x(u), y(u), z(u)) \qquad\qquad (A\text{-}76)$$

Often, the coordinate equations can be set up so that parameter u is defined over the unit interval from 0 to 1. For example, a circle in the xy plane with center at the coordinate origin could be defined in parametric form as

$$x(u) = r\cos(2\pi u), \qquad y(u) = r\sin(2\pi u), \qquad z(u) = 0, \qquad 0 \le u \le 1 \quad (A\text{-}77)$$

Other parametric forms are also possible for describing circles and circular arcs.

Curved (or plane) Euclidean surfaces are two-dimensional objects, and positions on a surface can be described with two parameters u and v. A coordinate position on the surface is then represented with the parametric vector function

$$\mathbf{P}(u, v) = (x(u, v), y(u, v), z(u, v)) \qquad\qquad (A\text{-}78)$$

619

where the Cartesian coordinate values for x, y, and z are expressed as functions of parameters u and v. As with curves, it is often possible to arrange the parametric descriptions so that parameters u and v are defined over the range from 0 to 1. A spherical surface with center at the coordinate origin, for example, can be described with the equations

$$x(u,v) = r \sin(\pi u) \cos(2\pi v)$$
$$y(u,v) = r \sin(\pi u) \sin(2\pi v)$$
$$z(u,v) = r \cos(\pi u) \qquad (A\text{-}79)$$

where r is the radius of the sphere. Parameter u describes lines of constant latitude over the surface, and parameter v describes lines of constant longitude. By keeping one of these parameters fixed while varying the other over a subinterval of the range from 0 to 1, we could plot latitude and longitude lines for any spherical section (Fig. A-22).

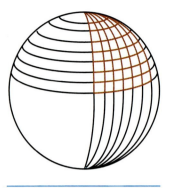

Figure A-22
Section of a spherical surface described by lines of constant u and lines of constant v in Eqs. A-79.

A-9
NUMERICAL METHODS

In computer graphics algorithms, it is often necessary to solve sets of linear equations, nonlinear equations, integral equations, and other functional forms. Also, to visualize a discrete set of data points, it may be useful to display a continuous curve or surface function that approximates the points of the data set. In this section, we briefly summarize some common algorithms for solving various numerical problems.

Solving Sets of Linear Equations

For variables x_k, $k = 1, 2, \ldots , n$, we can write a system of n linear equations as

$$a_{11}x_1 + a_{12}x_2 + \cdots + a_{1n}x_n = b_1$$
$$a_{21}x_1 + a_{22}x_2 + \cdots + a_{2n}x_n = b_2$$
$$\vdots \qquad\qquad\qquad\qquad \vdots$$
$$a_{n1}x_1 + a_{n2}x_2 + \cdots + a_{nn}x_n = b_n \qquad (A\text{-}80)$$

where the values for parameters a_{jk} and b_j are known. This set of equations can be expressed in the matrix form:

$$\mathbf{A}\mathbf{X} = \mathbf{B} \qquad (A\text{-}81)$$

with $\mathbf{A}$ as an n by n square matrix whose elements are the coefficients a_{jk}, $\mathbf{X}$ as the column matrix of x_j values, and $\mathbf{B}$ as the column matrix of b_j values. The solution for the set of simultaneous linear equation can be expressed in matrix form as

$$\mathbf{X} = \mathbf{A}^{-1}\mathbf{B} \qquad (A\text{-}82)$$

which depends on the inverse of the coefficient matrix $\mathbf{A}$. Thus the system of equations can be solved if and only if $\mathbf{A}$ is a nonsingular matrix; that is, its determinant is nonzero.

One method for solving the set of equations is *Cramer's Rule*:

$$x_k = \frac{\det \mathbf{A}_k}{\det \mathbf{A}} \qquad (A\text{-}83)$$

where $\mathbf{A}_k$ is the matrix $\mathbf{A}$ with the kth column replaced with the elements of $\mathbf{B}$. This method is adequate for problems with a few variables. For more than three or four variables, the method is extremely inefficient due to the large number of multiplications needed to evaluate each determinant. Evaluation of a single n by n determinant requires more that $n!$ multiplications.

We can solve the system of equations more efficiently using variations of *Gaussian elimination*. The basic ideas in Gaussian elimination can be illustrated with the following set of two simultaneous equations

$$\begin{aligned} x_1 + 2x_2 &= -4 \\ 3x_1 + 4x_2 &= 1 \end{aligned} \qquad (A\text{-}84)$$

To solve this set of equations, we can multiply the first equation by -3, then we add the two equations to eliminate the x_1 term, yielding the equation

$$-2x_2 = 13$$

which has the solution $x_2 = -13/2$. This value can then be substituted into either of the original equations to obtain the solution for x_1, which is 9. Efficient algorithms have been devised to carry out the elimination and back-substitution steps.

Gaussian elimination is sometimes susceptible to high roundoff errors, and it may not be possible to obtain an accurate solution. In those cases, we may be able to obtain a solution using the *Gauss–Seidel method*. We start with an initial "guess" for the values of variables x_k, then we repeatedly calculate successive approximations until the difference between successive values is "small." At each iteration, we calculate the approximate values for the variables as

$$x_1 = \frac{b_1 - a_{12}x_2 - a_{13}x_3 - \cdots - a_{1n}x_n}{a_{11}}$$

$$x_2 = \frac{b_2 - a_{11}x_1 - a_{12}x_2 - \cdots - a_{1n}x_n}{a_{12}} \qquad (A\text{-}85)$$

$$\vdots$$

If we can rearrange matrix $\mathbf{A}$ so that each diagonal element has a magnitude greater than the sum of the magnitudes of the other elements across that row, than the Gauss–Seidel method is guaranteed to converge to a solution.

Finding Roots of Nonlinear Equations

A root of a function $f(x)$ is a value for x that satisfies the equation $f(x) = 0$. One of the most popular methods for finding roots of nonlinear equations is the *Newton–Raphson algorithm*. This algorithm is an iterative procedure that approximates a function $f(x)$ with a straight line at each step of the iteration, as shown in Fig. A-23. We start with an initial "guess" x_0 for the value of the root, then we calcu-

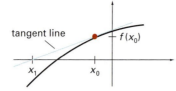

late the next approximation to the root as x_1 by determining where the tangent line from x_0 crosses the x axis. At x_0, the slope (first derivative) of the curve is

$$\frac{df}{dx} = \frac{f(x_0)}{x_0 - x_1} \qquad (A\text{-}86)$$

Thus, the next approximation to the root is

$$x_1 = x_0 - \frac{f(x_0)}{f'(x_0)} \qquad (A\text{-}87)$$

We repeat this procedure at each calculated approximation until the difference between successive approximations is "small enough".

If the Newton–Raphson algorithm converges to a root, it will converge faster than any other root-finding method. But it may not always converge. For example, the method fails if the derivative $f'(x)$ is 0 at some point in the iteration. Also, depending on the oscillations of the curve, successive approximation may diverge from the position of a root. The Newton–Raphson algorithm can be applied to a function of a complex variable, $f(z)$, and to sets of simultaneous nonlinear functions, real or complex.

Another method, slower but guaranteed to converge, is the *bisection method*. Here we need to first determine an x interval that contains a root, then we apply a binary search procedure to close in on the root. We first look at the midpoint of the interval to determine whether the root is in the lower or upper half of the interval. This procedure is repeated for each successive subinterval until the difference between successive midpoint positions is smaller than some preset value. A speedup can be attained by interpolating successive x positions instead of halving each subinterval (*false-position method*).

Evaluating Integrals

Integration is a summation process. For a function of a single variable x, the integral of $f(x)$ is the area "under" the curve, as illustrated in Fig. A-24.

An integral of $f(x)$ can be numerically approximated with the following summation

$$\int_b^a f(x)\,dx \approx \sum_{k=1}^{n} f_k(x)\,\Delta x_k \qquad (A\text{-}88)$$

where $f_k(x)$ is an approximation to $f(x)$ over the interval Δx_k. For example, we can approximate the curve with a constant value in each subinterval and add the areas of the resulting rectangles (Fig. A-25). The smaller the subdivisions for the interval from a to b, the better the approximation (up to a point). Actually, if

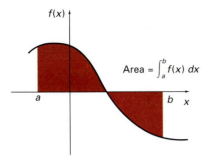

$$\text{Area} = \int_a^b f(x)\, dx$$

Figure A-24
The integral of $f(x)$ is equal to the amount of area between the function and the x axis over the interval from a to b.

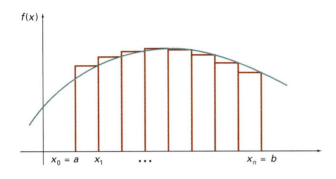

Figure A-25
Approximating an integral as the sum of the areas of small rectangles.

the intervals get too small, the values of successive rectangular areas can get lost in the roundoff error.

Polynomial approximations for the function in each subinterval generally give better results than the rectangle approach. Using a linear approximation, we obtain subareas that are trapezoids, and the approximation method is then referred to as the *trapezoid rule*. If we use a quadratic polynomial (parabola) to approximate the function in each subinterval, the method is called *Simpson's rule* and the integral approximation is

$$\int_a^b f(x)\, dx \approx \frac{\Delta x}{3}\left[f(a) + f(b) + 4\sum_{\substack{k=1 \\ \text{odd}}}^{n-1} f(x_k) + 2\sum_{\substack{k=2 \\ \text{even}}}^{n-2} f(x_k) \right] \qquad (A\text{-}89)$$

where the interval from a to b is divided into n equal-width intervals:

$$\Delta x = \frac{b-a}{n} \qquad (A\text{-}90)$$

where n is a multiple of 2, and with

$$x_0 = a, \qquad x_k = x_{k-1} + \Delta x, \qquad k = 1, 2, \ldots, n$$

For functions with high-frequency oscillations (Fig. A-26), the approximation methods previously discussed may not give accurate results. Also, multiple integrals (involving several integration variables) are difficult to solve with Simp-

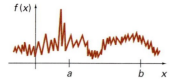

son's rule or the other approximation methods. In these cases, we can apply *Monte Carlo* integration techniques. The term Monte Carlo is applied to any method that uses random numbers to solve deterministic problems.

We apply a Monte Carlo method to evaluate the integral of a function such as the one shown in Fig. A-26 by generating n random positions in a rectangular area that contains $f(x)$ over the interval from a to b (Fig. A-27). An approximation for the integral is then calculated as

$$\int_a^b f(x)\,dx \approx h(b-a)\frac{n_{count}}{n} \qquad (A\text{-}91)$$

where parameter n_{count} is the count of the number of random points that are between $f(x)$ and the x axis. A random position (x, y) in the rectangular region is computed by first generating two random numbers, r_1 and r_2, and then carrying out the calculations

$$h = y_{max} - y_{min}, \qquad x = a + r_1(b-a), \qquad y = y_{min} + r_2 h \qquad (A\text{-}92)$$

Similar methods can be applied to multiple integrals.

Random numbers r_1 and r_2 are uniformly distributed over the interval (0, 1). We can obtain random numbers from a random-number function in a high-level language, or from a statistical package, or we can use the following algorithm, called the *linear congruential generator*:

$$i_k = a\,i_{k-1} + c(\mathrm{mod}\,m), \qquad k = 1, 2, 3, \ldots$$
$$r_k = \frac{i_k}{m} \qquad (A\text{-}93)$$

where parameters a, c, m, and i_0 are integers, and i_0 is a starting value called the *seed*. Parameter m is chosen to be as large as possible on a particular machine, with values for a and c chosen to make the string of random numbers as long as possible before a value is repeated. For example, on a machine with 32-bit integer representations, we can set $m = 2^{32}$, $a = 1664525$, and $c = 1013904223$.

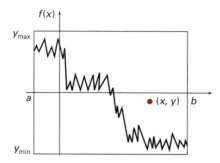

624

Fitting Curves to Data Sets

A standard method for fitting a function (linear or nonlinear) to a set of data points is the *least-squares algorithm*. For a two-dimensional set of data points (x_k, y_k), $k = 1, 2, \ldots$, we first select a functional form $f(x)$, which could be a straight-line function, a polynomial function, or some other curve shape. We then determine the differences (deviations) between $f(x)$ and the y_k values at each x_k and compute the sum of deviations squared:

$$E = \sum_{k=1}^{n} [y_k - f(x_k)]^2 \qquad (A\text{-}94)$$

Parameters in the function $f(x)$ are determined by minimizing the expression for E. For example, for the linear function

$$f(x) = a_0 + a_1 x$$

parameters a_0 and a_1 are assigned values that minimize E. We determine the values for a_0 and a_1 by solving the two simultaneous linear equations that result from the minimization requirements. That is, E will be minimum if the partial derivative with respect to a_0 is 0 and the partial derivative with respect to a_1 is 0:

$$\frac{\partial E}{\partial a_0} = 0, \qquad \frac{\partial E}{\partial a_1} = 0$$

Similar calculations are carried out for other functions. For the polynomial

$$f(x) = a_0 + a_1 x + a_2 x^2 + \cdots + a_n x^n$$

we need to solve a set of n linear equations to determine values for parameters a_k. And we can also apply least-squares fitting to functions of several variables $f(x_1, x_2, \ldots, x_m)$ that can be linear or nonlinear in each of the variables.

Bibliography

AKELEY, K. AND T. JERMOLUK (1988). "High-Performance Polygon Rendering", in proceedings of SIGGRAPH '88, *Computer Graphics*, 22(4), pp. 239–246.

AKELEY, K. (1993). "RealityEngine Graphics", in proceedings of SIGGRAPH '93, *Computer Graphics Proceedings*, pp. 109–116.

AMANATIDES, J. (1984). "Ray Tracing with Cones", in proceedings of SIGGRAPH '84, *Computer Graphics*, 18(3), pp. 129–135.

AMBURN, P., E. GRANT AND T. WHITTED (1986). "Managing Geometric Complexity with Enhanced Procedural Models", in proceedings of SIGGRAPH '86, *Computer Graphics*, 20(4), pp. 189–196.

ANJYO, K., Y. USAMI AND T. KURIHARA (1992). "A Simple Method for Extracting the Natural Beauty of Hair", in proceedings of SIGGRAPH '92, *Computer Graphics*, 26(2), pp. 111–120.

APPLE COMPUTER, INC. (1985). *Inside Macintosh*, Volume I, Addison-Wesley, Reading, MA.

APPLE COMPUTER, INC. (1987). *Human Interface Guidelines: The Apple Desktop Interface*, Addison-Wesley, Reading, MA.

ARVO, J. AND D. KIRK (1987). "Fast Ray Tracing by Ray Classification", in proceedings of SIGGRAPH '87, *Computer Graphics*, 21(4), pp. 55–64.

ARVO, J. AND D. KIRK (1990). "Particle Transport and Image Synthesis", in proceedings of SIGGRAPH '90, *Computer Graphics*, 24(4), pp. 63–66.

ARVO, J., ED. (1991). *Graphics Gems II*, Academic Press, Inc., San Diego, CA.

ATHERTON, P. R. (1983). "A Scan-Line Hidden Surface Removal Procedure for Constructive Solid Geometry", in proceedings of SIGGRAPH '83, *Computer Graphics*, 17(3), pp. 73–82.

BARAFF, D. (1989). "Analytical Methods for Dynamic Simulation of Non-Penetrating Rigid Bodies", in proceedings of SIGGRAPH '89, *Computer Graphics*, 23(3), pp. 223–232.

BARAFF, D. AND A. WITKIN (1992). "Dynamic Simulation of Non-Penetrating Flexible Bodies", in proceedings of SIGGRAPH '92, *Computer Graphics*, 26(2), pp. 303–308.

BARKANS, A. C. (1990). "High-Speed, High-Quality, Antialised Vector Generation", in proceedings of SIGGRAPH '90, *Computer Graphics*, 24(4), pp. 319–326.

BARNSLEY, M. F., A. JACQUIN, F. MALASSENT, ET AL. (1988). "Harnessing Chaos for Image Synthesis", in proceedings of SIGGRAPH '88, *Computer Graphics*, 22(4), pp. 131–140.

BARNSLEY, M. (1993). *Fractals Everywhere*, Second Edition, Academic Press, Inc., San Diego, CA.

BARR, A. H. (1981). "Superquadrics and Angle-Preserving Transformations", *IEEE Computer Graphics and Applications*, 1(1), pp. 11–23.

BARR, A. H. (1986). "Ray Tracing Deformed Surfaces", in proceedings of SIGGRAPH '86, *Computer Graphics*, 20(4), pp. 287–296.

BARSKY, B. A. AND J. C. BEATTY (1983). "Local Control of Bias and Tension in Beta-Splines", *ACM Transactions on Graphics*, 2(2), pp. 109–134.

BARSKY, B. A. (1984). "A Discription and Evaluation of Various 3-D Models", *IEEE Computer Graphics and Applications*, 4(1), pp. 38–52.

BARZEL, R. AND A. H. BARR (1988). "A Modeling System Based on Dynamic Constraints", in proceedings of SIGGRAPH '88, *Computer Graphics*, 22(4), pp. 179–188.

BARZEL, R. (1992). *Physically-Based Modeling for Computer Graphics*, Academic Press, Inc., San Diego, CA.

BAUM, D. R., S. MANN, K. P. SMITH, ET AL. (1991). "Making Radiosity Usable: Automatic Preprocessing and Meshing Techniques for the Generation of Accurate Radiosity Solutions", in proceedings of SIGGRAPH '91, *Computer Graphics*, 25(4), pp. 51–61.

BECKER, S. C., W. A. BARRETT, AND D. R. OLSEN JR. (1991). "Interactive Measurement of Three-Dimensional Objects Using a Depth Buffer and Linear Probe", *ACM Transactions on Graphics*, 10(2), pp. 201–207.

BECKER, B. G. AND N. L. MAX (1993). "Smooth Transitions between Bump-Rendering Algorithms", in proceedings of SIGGRAPH '93, *Computer Graphics Proceedings*, pp. 183–190.

BEIER, T. AND S. NEELY (1992). "Feature-Based Image Metamorphosis", in proceedings of SIGGRAPH '92, *Computer Graphics*, 26(2), pp. 35–42.

BERGMAN, L., H. FUCHS, E. GRANT, ET AL. (1986). "Image Rendering by Adaptive Refinement", in proceedings of SIGGRAPH '86, *Computer Graphics*, 20(4), pp. 29–38.

BERGMAN, L. D., J. S. RICHARDSON, D. C. RICHARDSON, ET AL. (1993). "VIEW—an Eploratory Molecular Visualization System with User-Definable Interaction Sequences", in proceedings of SIGGRAPH '93, *Computer Graphics Proceedings*, pp. 117–126.

BÉZIER, P. (1972). *Numerical Control: Mathematics and Applications*, translated by A. R. Forrest and A. F. Pankhurst, John Wiley & Sons, London.

BIER, E. A., S. A. MACKAY, D. A. STEWART, ET AL. (1986). "Snap-Dragging", in proceedings of SIGGRAPH '86, *Computer Graphics*, 20(4), pp. 241–248.

BIER, E. A., M. C. STONE, K. PIER, ET AL. (1993). "Toolglass and Magic Lenses: The See-Through Interface", in proceedings of SIGGRAPH '93, *Computer Graphics Proceedings*, pp. 73–80.

BISHOP, G. AND D. M. WIEMER (1986). "Fast Phong Shading", in proceedings of SIGGRAPH '86, *Computer Graphics*, 20(4), pp. 103–106.

BLAKE, J. W. (1993). *PHIGS and PHIGS Plus*, Academic Press, London.

BLESER, T. (1988). "TAE Plus Styleguide User Interface Description", NASA Goddard Space Flight Center, Greenbelt, MD.

BLINN, J. F. AND M. E. NEWELL (1976). "Texture and Reflection in Computer-Generated Images", CACM, 19(10), pp. 542–547.

BLINN, J. F. (1977). "Models of Light Reflection for Computer-Synthesized Pictures", Computer Graphics, 11(2), pp. 192–198.

BLINN, J. F. AND M. E. NEWELL (1978). "Clipping Using Homogeneous Coordinates", Computer Graphics, 12(3), pp. 245–251.

BLINN, J. F. (1978). "Simulation of Wrinkled Surfaces", Computer Graphics, 12(3), pp. 286–292.

BLINN, J. F. (1982). "A Generalization of Algebraic Surface Drawing", *ACM Transactions on Graphics*, 1(3), pp. 235–256.

BLINN, J. F. (1982). "Light Reflection Functions for Simulation of Clouds and Dusty Surfaces", in proceedings of SIGGRAPH '82, *Computer Graphics*, 16(3), pp. 21–29.

BLINN, J. F. (1993). "A Trip Down the Graphics Pipeline: The Homogeneous Perspective Transform", *IEEE Computer Graphics and Applications*, 13(3), pp. 75–80.

BLOOMENTHAL, J. (1985). "Modeling the Mighty Maple", in proceedings of SIGGRAPH '85, *Computer Graphics*, 19(3), pp. 305–312.

BONO, P. R., J. L. ENCARNACAO, F. R. A. HOPGOOD, ET AL. (1982). "GKS: The First Graphics Standard", *IEEE Computer Graphics and Applications*, 2(5), pp. 9–23.

BOOTH, K. S., M. P. BRYDEN, W. B. COWAN, ET AL. (1987). "On the Parameters of Human Visual Performance: An Investigation of the Benefits of Antialiasing", *IEEE Computer Graphics and Applications*, 7(9), pp. 34–41.

BRESENHAM, J. E. (1965). "Algorithm for Computer Control of A Digital Plotter", IBM Systems Journal, 4(1), pp. 25–30.

BRESENHAM, J. E. (1977). "A Linear Algorithm for Incremental Digital Display of Circular Arcs", CACM, 20(2), pp. 100–106.

BROOKS, F. P., JR. (1986). "Walkthrough: A Dynamic Graphics System for Simulating Virtual Buildings", Interactive 3D 1986.

BROOKS, F. P., JR. (1988). "Grasping Reality Through Illusion: Interactive Graphics Serving Science", CHI '88, pp. 1–11.

BROOKS, J., P. FREDERICK, M. OUH-YOUNG, J. J. BATTER, ET AL. (1990). "Project GROPE - Haptic Display for Scientific Visualization", in proceedings of SIGGRAPH '90, *Computer Graphics*, 24(4), 24(4), pp. 177–185.

BROWN, M. H. AND R. SEDGEWICK (1984). "A System for Algorithm Animation", in proceedings of SIGGRAPH '84, *Computer Graphics*, 18(3), pp. 177–186.

BROWN, J. R. AND S. CUNNINGHAM (1989). *Programming the User Interface*, John Wiley & Sons, New York.

BRUDERLIN, A. AND T. W. CALVERT (1989). "Goal-Directed, Dynamic Animation of Human Walking", in proceedings of SIGGRAPH '89, *Computer Graphics*, 23(3), pp. 233–242.

BRUNET, P. AND I. NAVAZO (1990). "Solid Representation and Operation Using Extended Octrees", *ACM Transactions on Graphics*, 9(2), pp. 170–197.

BRYSON, S. AND C. LEVIT (1992). "The Virtual Wind Tunnel", *IEEE Computer Graphics and Applications*, 12(4), pp. 25–34.

BURT, P. J. AND E. H. ADELSON (1983). "A Multiresolution Spline with Application to Image Mosaics", ACM Transactions on Graphics, 2(4), pp. 217–236.

BUXTON, W., M. R. LAMB, D. SHERMAN, ET AL. (1983). "Towards a Comprehensive User Interface Management System", in proceedings of SIGGRAPH '83, *Computer Graphics*, 17(3), pp. 35–42.

BUXTON, W., R. HILL, AND P. ROWLEY (1985). "Issues and Techniques in Touch-Sensitive Tablet Input", in proceedings of SIGGRAPH '85, *Computer Graphics*, 19(3), pp. 215–224.

CALVERT, T., A. BRUDERLIN, J. DILL, ET AL. (1993). "Desktop Animation of Multiple Human Figures", *IEEE Computer Graphics and Applications*, 13(3), pp. 18–26.

CAMBELL, G., T. A. DEFANTI, J. FREDERIKSEN, ET AL. (1986). "Two Bit/Pixel Full-Color Encoding", in proceedings of SIGGRAPH '86, *Computer Graphics*, 20(4), pp. 215–224.

CAMPBELL, III., A. T. AND D. S. FUSSELL (1990). "Adaptive Mesh Generation for Global Diffuse Illumination", in proceedings of SIGGRAPH '90, *Computer Graphics*, 24(4), pp. 155–164.

CARD, S. K., J. D. MACKINLAY, AND G. G. ROBERTSON (1991). "The Information Visualizer, an Information Workspace", CHI '91, pp. 181–188.

CARIGNAN, M., Y. YANG, N. M. THALMANN, ET AL. (1992). "Dressing Animated Synthetic Actors with Complex Deformable Clothes", in proceedings of SIGGRAPH '92, *Computer Graphics*, 26(2), pp. 99–104.

CARLBOM, I., I. CHAKRAVARTY, AND D. VANDERSCHEL (1985). "A Hierarchical Data Structure for Representing the Spatial Decomposition of 3-D Objects", *IEEE Computer Graphics and Applications*, 5(4), pp. 24–31.

CARPENTER, L. (1984). "The A-Buffer: An Antialiased Hidden-Surface Method", in proceedings of SIGGRAPH '84, *Computer Graphics*, 18(3), pp. 103–108.

CARROLL, J. M. AND C. CARRITHERS (1984). "Training Wheels in a User Interface", CACM, 27(8), pp. 800–806.

CASALE M. S. AND E. L. STANTON (1985). "An Overview of Analytic Solid Modeling", *IEEE Computer Graphics and Applications*, 5(2), pp. 45–56.

CATMULL, E. (1975). "Computer Display of Curved Surfaces", in proceedings of the IEEE Conference on Computer Graphics, *Pattern Recognition and Data Structures*. Also in Freeman (1980), PP. 309–315.

CATMULL, E. (1984). "An Analytic Visible Surface Algorithm for Independent Pixel Processing", in proceedings of SIGGRAPH '84, *Computer Graphics*, 18(3), pp. 109–115.

CHAZELLE, B. AND J. INCERPI (1984). "Triangulation and Shape Complexity", *ACM Transactions on Graphics*, 3(2), pp. 135–152.

CHEN, M., S. J. MOUNTFORD, AND A. SELLEN (1988). "A Study in Interactive 3D Rotation Using 2D Control Devices", in proceedings of SIGGRAPH '88, *Computer Graphics*, 22(4), pp. 121–130.

CHEN, S. E., H. E. RUSHMEIER, G. MILLER, ET AL. (1991). "A Progressive Multi-Pass Method for Global Illumination", in proceedings of SIGGRAPH '91, *Computer Graphics*, 25(4), pp. 165–174.

CHIN, N. AND S. FEINER (1989). "Near Real-Time Shadow Generation Using BSP Trees", in proceedings of SIGGRAPH '89, *Computer Graphics*, 23(3), pp. 99–106.

CHUANG, R. AND G. ENTIS (1983). "3—D Shaded Computer Animation—Step by Step", *IEEE Computer Graphics and Applications*, 3(3), pp. 18–25.

CHUNG, J. C., ET AL. (1989). "Exploring Virtual Worlds with Head-Mounted Visual Displays", *Proceedings of SPIE Meeting on Non-Holographic True 3-Dimensional Display Technologies*, 1083, January 1989, pp. 15–20.

CLARK, J. H. (1982). "The Geometry Engine: A VLSI Geometry System for Graphics", in proceedings of SIGGRAPH '82, *Computer Graphics*, 16(3), pp. 127–133.

COHEN, M. F. AND D. P. GREENBERG (1985). "The Hemi-Cube: A Radiosity Solution for Complex Environments", in proceedings of SIGGRAPH '85, *Computer Graphics*, 19(3), pp. 31–40.

COHEN, M. F., S. E. CHEN, J. R. WALLACE, ET AL. (1988). "A Progressive Refinement Approach to Fast Radiosity Image Generation", in proceedings of SIGGRAPH '88, *Computer Graphics*, 22(4), pp. 75–84.

COHEN, M. F. AND J. R. WALLACE (1993). *Radiosity and Realistic Image Synthesis*, Academic Press, Boston, MA.

COOK, R. L. AND K. E. TORRANCE (1982). "A Reflectance Model for Computer Graphics", *ACM Transactions on Graphics*, 1(1), pp. 7–24.

COOK, R. L., T. PORTER, AND L. CARPENTER (1984). "Distributed Ray Tracing", in proceedings of SIGGRAPH '84, *Computer Graphics*, 18(3), pp. 137–145.

COOK, R. L. (1984). "Shade Trees", in proceedings of SIGGRAPH '84, *Computer Graphics*, 18(3), pp. 223–231.

COOK, R. L. (1986). "Stochastic Sampling in Computer Graphics", *ACM Transactions on Graphics*, 6(1), pp. 51–72.

COOK, R. L., L. CARPENTER, AND E. CATMULL (1987). "The Reyes Image Rendering Architecture", in proceedings of SIGGRAPH '87, *Computer Graphics*, 21(4), pp. 95–102.

COQUILLART, S. AND P. JANCENE (1991). "Animated Free-Form Deformation: An Interactive Animation Technique", in proceedings of SIGGRAPH '91, *Computer Graphics*, 25(4), pp. 23–26.

CROW, F. C. (1977). "The Aliasing Problem in Computer-Synthesized Shaded Images", CACM, 20(11), pp. 799–805.

CROW, F. C. (1977). "Shadow Algorithms for Computer Graphics", in proceedings of SIGGRAPH '77, *Computer Graphics*, 11(2), pp. 242–248.

CROW, F. C. (1978). "The Use of Grayscale for Improved Raster Display of Vectors and Characters", in proceedings of SIGGRAPH '78, *Computer Graphics*, 12(3), pp. 1–5.

CROW, F. C. (1981). "A Comparison of Antialiasing Techniques", *IEEE Computer Graphics and Applications*, 1(1), pp. 40–49.

CROW, F. C. (1982). "A More Flexible Image Generation Environment", in proceedings of SIGGRAPH '82, *Computer Graphics*, 16(3), pp. 9–18.

CRUZ-NEIRA, C., D. J. SANDIN, AND T. A. DEFANTI (1993). "Surround-Screen Projection-Based Virtual Reality: The Design and Implementation of the CAVE", in proceedings of SIGGRAPH '93, *Computer Graphics Proceedings*, pp. 135–142.

CUNNINGHAM, S., N. K. CRAIGHILL, M. W. FONG, ET AL., ED. (1992). *Computer Graphics Using Object-Oriented Programming*, John Wiley & Sons, New York.

CUTLER, E., D. GILLY, AND T. O'REILLY, ED. (1992). *The X Window System in a Nutshell*, Second Edition, O'Reilly & Assoc., Inc., Sebastopol, CA.

CYRUS, M. AND J. BECK (1978). "Generalized Two- and Three-Dimensional Clipping", Computers and Graphics, 3(1), pp. 23–28.

DAY, A. M. (1990). "The Implementation of an Algorithm to Find the Convex Hull of a Set of Three-Dimensional Points", *ACM Transactions on Graphics*, 9(1), pp. 105–132.

DE REFFYE, P., C. EDELIN, J. FRANCON, ET AL. (1988). "Plant Models Faithful to Botanical Structure and Development", in proceedings of SIGGRAPH '88, *Computer Graphics*, 22(4), pp. 151–158.

DEERING, M. (1992). "High Resolution Virtual Reality", in proceedings of SIGGRAPH '92, *Computer Graphics*, 26(2), pp. 195–202.

DEERING, M. F. AND S. R. NELSON (1993). "Leo: A System for Cost-Effective 3D Shaded Graphics", in proceedings of SIGGRAPH '93, *Computer Graphics Proceedings*, pp. 101–108.

DEMKO, S., L. HODGES, AND B. NAYLOR (1985). "Construction of Fractal Objects with Iterated Function Systems", in proceedings of SIGGRAPH '85, *Computer Graphics*, 19(3), pp. 271–278.

DEPP, S. W. AND W. E. HOWARD (1993). "Flat-Panel Displays", Scientific American, 266(3), pp. 90–97.

DEROSE, T. D. (1988). "Geometric Continuity, Shape Parameters, and Geometric Constructions for Catmull-Rom Splines", *ACM Transactions on Graphics*, 7(1), pp. 1–41.

DIGITAL EQUIPMENT CORP. (1989). "Digital Equipment Corporation XUI Style Guide", Maynard, MA.

DIPPE, M. AND J. SWENSEN (1984). "An Adaptive Subdivision Algorithm and Parallel Architecture for Realistic Image Synthesis", in proceedings of SIGGRAPH '84, *Computer Graphics*, 18(3), pp. 149–158.

DOBKIN, D., L. GUIBAS, J. HERSHBERGER, ET AL. (1988). "An Efficient Algorithm for Finding the CSG Representation of a Simple Polygon", in proceedings of SIGGRAPH '88, *Computer Graphics*, 22(4), pp. 31–40.

DOCTOR, L. J. AND J. G. TORBERG (1981). "Display Techniques for Octree-Encoded Objects", *IEEE Computer Graphics and Applications*, 1(3), pp. 29–38.

DORSEY, J. O., F. X. SILLION, AND D. P. GREENBERG (1991). "Design and Simulation of Opera Lighting and Projection Effects", in proceedings of SIGGRAPH '91, *Computer Graphics*, 25(4), pp. 41–50.

DREBIN, R. A., L. CARPENTER, AND P. HANRAHAN (1988). "Volume Rendering", in proceedings of SIGGRAPH '88, *Computer Graphics*, 22(4), pp. 65–74.

DUFF, T. (1985). "Compositing 3D Rendered Images", in proceedings of SIGGRAPH '85, *Computer Graphics*, 19(3), pp. 41–44.

DURRETT, H. J., ED. (1987). *Color and the Computer*, Academic Press, Boston.

DUVANENKO, V. (1990). "Improved Line Segment Clipping", Dr. Dobb's Journal, July 1990.

DYER, S. AND S. WHITMAN (1987). "A Vectorized Scan-Line Z-Buffer Rendering Algorithm", *IEEE Computer Graphics and Applications*, 7(7), pp. 34–45.

DYER, S. (1990). "A Dataflow Toolkit for Visualization", *IEEE Computer Graphics and Applications*, 10(4), pp. 60–69.

EARNSHAW, R. A., ED. (1985). *Fundamental Algorithms for Computer Graphics*, Springer-Verlag, Berlin.

EDELSBRUNNER, H. (1987). *Algorithms in Computational Geometry*, Springer-Verlag, Berlin.

EDELSBRUNNER, H. AND E. P. MUCKE (1990). "Simulation of Simplicity: A Technique to Cope with Degenerate Cases in Geometric Algorithms", *ACM Transactions on Graphics*, 9(1), pp. 66–104.

ELBER, G. AND E. COHEN (1990). "Hidden Curve Removal for Free Form Surfaces", in proceedings of SIGGRAPH '90, *Computer Graphics*, 24(4), pp. 95–104.

ENDERLE, G., K. KANSY, AND G. PFAFF (1984). *Computer Graphics Programming: GKS—The Graphics Standard*, Springer-Verlag, Berlin.

FARIN, G. (1988). *Curves and Surfaces for Computer Aided Geometric Design*, Academic Press, Boston, MA.

FAROUKI, R. T. AND J. K. HINDS (1985). "A Hierarchy of Geometric Forms", *IEEE Computer Graphics and Applications*, 5(5), pp. 51–78.

FEDER, J. (1988). *Fractals*, Plenum Press, New York.

FEINER, S., S. NAGY, AND A. VAN DAM (1982). "An Experimental System for Creating and Presenting Interactive Graphical Documents", *ACM Transactions on Graphics*, 1(1), pp. 59–77.

FERWERDA, J. A. AND D. P. GREENBERG (1988). "A Psychophysical Approach to Assessing the Quality of Antialiased Images", *IEEE Computer Graphics and Applications*, 8(5), pp. 85–95.

FISHKIN, K. P. AND B. A. BARSKY (1984). "A Family of New Algorithms for Soft Filling", in proceedings of SIGGRAPH '84, *Computer Graphics*, 18(3), pp. 235–244.

FIUME, E. L. (1989). *The Mathematical Structure of Raster Graphics*, Academic Press, Boston.

FOLEY, J. D., V. L. WALLACE, AND P. CHAN (1984). "The Human Factors of Computer Graphics Interaction Techniques", *IEEE Computer Graphics and Applications*, 4(11), pp. 13–48.

FOLEY, J. D. (1987). "Interfaces for Advanced Computing", Scientific American, 257(4), pp. 126–135.

FOLEY, J. D., A. VAN DAM, S. K. FEINER, ET AL. (1990). *Computer Graphics: Principles and Practice*, Addison-Wesley, Reading, MA.

FOURNIER, A., D. FUSSEL, AND L. CARPENTER (1982). "Computer Rendering of Stochastic Models", CACM, 25(6), pp. 371–384.

FOURNIER, A. AND D. Y. MONTUNO (1984). "Triangulating Simple Polygons and Equivalent Problems", *ACM Transactions on Graphics*, 3(2), pp. 153–174.

FOURNIER, A. AND W. T. REEVES (1986). "A Simple Model of Ocean Waves", in proceedings of SIGGRAPH '86, *Computer Graphics*, 20(4), pp. 75–84.

FOURNIER, A. AND D. FUSSELL (1988). "On the Power of the Frame Buffer", *ACM Transactions on Graphics*, 7(2), pp. 103–128.

FOURNIER, A. AND E. FIUME (1988). "Constant-Time Filtering with Space-Variant Kernels", in proceedings of SIGGRAPH '88, *Computer Graphics*, 22(4), pp. 229–238.

FOWLER, D. R., H. MEINHARDT, AND P. PRUSINKIEWICZ (1992). "Modeling Seashells", in proceedings of SIGGRAPH '92, *Computer Graphics*, 26(2), pp. 379–387.

FOX, D. AND M. WAITE (1984). *Computer Animation Primer*, McGraw-Hill, New York.

FRANCIS, G. K. (1987). *A Topological Picturebook*, Springer-Verlag, New York.

629

FRANKLIN, W. R. AND M. S. KANKANHALLI (1990). "Parallel Object-Space Hidden Surface Removal", in proceedings of SIGGRAPH '90, *Computer Graphics*, 24(4), pp. 87–94.

FREEMAN, H. ED. (1980). *Tutorial and Selected readings in Interactive Computer Graphics*, IEEE Computer Society Press, Silver Springs, MD.

FRENKEL, K. A. (1989). "Volume Rendering", CACM, 32(4), pp. 426–435.

FRIEDER, G., D. GORDON, AND R. A. REYNOLD (1985). "Back-to-Front Display of Voxel-Based Objects", *IEEE Computer Graphics and Applications*, 5(1), pp. 52–60.

FRIEDHOFF, R. M. AND W. BENZON (1989). *The Second Computer Revolution: Visualization*, Harry N. Abrams, Inc., New York.

FUCHS, H., S. M. PIZER, E. R. HEINZ, S. H. BLOOMBER, L. TSAI, AND D. C. STRICKLAND (1982). "Design of and Image Editing with a Space-Filling Three-Dimensional Display Based on a Standard Raster Graphics System", *Proceedings of SPIE*, 367, August 1982, pp. 117–127.

FUCHS, H., J. POULTON, J. EYLES, ET AL. (1989). "Pixel-Planes 5: A Heterogeneous Multiprocessor Graphics System Using Processor-Enhanced Memories", in proceedings of SIGGRAPH '89, *Computer Graphics*, 23(3), pp. 79–88.

FUJIMOTO, A. AND K. IWATA (1983). "Jag-Free Images on Raster Displays", *IEEE Computer Graphics and Applications*, 3(9), pp. 26–34.

FUNKHOUSER, T. A. AND C. H. SEQUIN (1993). "Adaptive Display Algorithms for Interactive Frame Rates During Visualization Complex Virtual Environments", in proceedings of SIGGRAPH '93, *Computer Graphics Proceedings*, pp. 247–254.

GALYEAN, T. A. AND J. F. HUGHES (1991). "Sculpting: An Interactive Volumetric Modeling Technique", in proceedings of SIGGRAPH '91, *Computer Graphics*, 25(4), pp. 267–274.

GARDNER, G. Y. (1985). "Visual Simulation of Clouds", in proceedings of SIGGRAPH '85, *Computer Graphics*, 19(3), pp. 297–304.

GASCUEL, M.-P. (1993). "An Implicit Formulation for Precise Contact Modeling between Flexible Solids", in proceedings of SIGGRAPH '93, *Computer Graphics*, pp. 313–320.

GASKINS, T. (1992). *PHIGS Programming Manual*, O'Reilly & Associates, Sebastopol, CA.

GHARACHORLOO, N., S. GUPTA, R. F. SPROULL, ET AL. (1989). "A Characterization of Ten Rasterization Algorithms", in proceedings of SIGGRAPH '89, *Computer Graphics*, 23(3), pp. 355–368.

GIRARD, M. (1987). "Interactive Design of 3D Computer-Animated Legged Animal Motion", *IEEE Computer Graphics and Applications*, 7(6), pp. 39–51.

GLASSNER, A. S. (1984). "Space Subdivision for Fast Ray Tracing", *IEEE Computer Graphics and Applications*, 4(10), pp. 15–22.

GLASSNER, A. S. (1986). "Adaptive Precision in Texture Mapping", in proceedings of SIGGRAPH '86, *Computer Graphics*, 20(4), pp. 297–306.

GLASSNER, A. S. (1988). "Spacetime Ray Tracing for Animation", *IEEE Computer Graphics and Applications*, 8(2), pp. 60–70.

GLASSNER, A. S., ED. (1989). *An Introduction to Ray Tracing*, Academic Press, San Diego, CA.

GLASSNER, A. S., ED. (1990). *Graphics Gems*, Academic Press, San Diego, CA.

GLASSNER, A. S. (1992). "Geometric Substitution: A Tutorial", *IEEE Computer Graphics and Applications*, 12(1), pp. 22–36.

GLASSNER, A. S. (1994). *Principles of Digital Image Synthesis*, Morgan-Kaufmann, Inc., New York.

GLEICHER, M. AND A. WITKIN (1992). "Through-the-Lens Camera Control", in proceedings of SIGGRAPH '92, *Computer Graphics*, 26(2), pp. 331–340.

GOLDSMITH, J. AND J. SALMON (1987). "Automatic Creation of Object Hierarchies for Ray Tracing", *IEEE Computer Graphics and Applications*, 7(5), pp. 14–20.

GONZALEZ, R. C. AND P. WINTZ (1987). *Digital Image Processing*, Addison-Wesley, Reading, MA.

GOOD, D. M., J. A. WHITESIDE, D. R. WIXON, AND S. J. JONES (1984). "Building A User-Derived Interface", CACM, 27(10), pp. 1032–1042.

GOODMAN, T. AND R. SPENCE (1978). "The Effect of System Response Time on Interactive Computer-Aided Problem Solving", in proceedings of SIGGRAPH '78, *Computer Graphics*, 12(3), pp. 100–104.

GORAL, C. M., K. E. TORRANCE, D. P. GREENBERG, ET AL. (1984). "Modeling the Interaction of Light Between Diffuse Surfaces", in proceedings of SIGGRAPH '84, *Computer Graphics*, 18(3), pp. 213–222.

GORDON, D. AND S. CHEN (1991). "Front-to-Back Display of BSP Trees", *IEEE Computer Graphics and Applications*, 11(5), pp. 79–85.

GORTLER, S. J., P. SCHRODER, M. F. COHEN, ET AL. (1993). "Wavelet Radiosity", in proceedings of SIGGRAPH '93, *Computer Graphics Proceedings*, pp. 221–230.

GREEN, M. (1985). "The University of Alberta User Interface Management System", in proceedings of SIGGRAPH '85, *Computer Graphics*, 19(3), pp. 205–214.

GREENE, N., M. KASS, AND G. MILLER (1993). "Hierarchical Z-Buffer Visibility", in proceedings of SIGGRAPH '93, *Computer Graphics Proceedings*, pp. 231–238.

HAEBERLI, P. AND K. AKELEY (1990). "The Accumulation Buffer: Hardware Support for High-Quality Rendering", in proceedings of SIGGRAPH '90, *Computer Graphics*, 24(4), pp. 309–318.

HAHN, J. K. (1988). "Realistic Animation of Rigid Bodies", in proceedings of SIGGRAPH '88, *Computer Graphics*, 22(4), pp. 299–308.

HALL, R. A. AND D. P. GREENBERG (1983). "A Testbed for Realistic Image Synthesis", *IEEE Computer Graphics and Applications*, 3(8), pp. 10–20.

HALL, R. (1989). *Illumination and Color in Computer Generated Imagery*, Springer-Verlag, New York.

HANRAHAN, P. (1982). "Creating Volume Models from Edge-Vertex Graphs", in proceedings of SIGGRAPH '82, *Computer Graphics*, 16(3), pp. 77–84.

HANRAHAN, P. AND J. LAWSON (1990). "A Language for Shading and Lighting Calculations", in proceedings of SIGGRAPH '90, *Computer Graphics*, 24(4), pp. 289–298.

HART, J. C., D. J. SANDIN, AND L. H. KAUFFMAN (1989). "Ray Tracing Deterministic 3D Fractals", in proceedings of SIGGRAPH '89, *Computer Graphics*, 23(3), pp. 289–296.

HART, J. C. AND T. A. DeFANTI (1991). "Efficient Antialiased Rendering of 3—D Linear Fractals", in proceedings of SIGGRAPH '91, *Computer Graphics*, 25(4), pp. 91–100.

HE, X. D., P. O. HEYNEN, R. L. PHILLIPS, ET AL. (1992). "A Fast and Accurate Light Reflection Model", in proceedings of SIGGRAPH '92, *Computer Graphics*, 26(2), pp. 253–254.

HEARN, D. AND P. BAKER (1991). "Scientific Visualization: An Introduction", *Eurographics '91 Technical Report Series*, Tutorial Lecture 6.

HECKBERT, P. (1982). "Color Image Quantization for Frame Buffer Display", in proceedings of SIGGRAPH '82, *Computer Graphics*, 16(3), pp. 297–307.

HECKBERT, P. AND P. HANRAHAN (1984). "Beam Tracing Polygonal Objects", in proceedings of SIGGRAPH '84, *Computer Graphics*, 18(3), pp. 119–127.

HOPGOOD, F. R. A., D. A. DUCE, J. R. GALLOP, ET AL. (1983). *Introduction to the Graphical Kernel System (GKS)*, Academic Press, London.

HOPGOOD, F. R. A. AND D. A. DUCE (1991). *A Primer for PHIGS*, John Wiley & Sons, Chichester, England.

HOPPE, H., T. DeROSE, T. McDONALD, ET AL. (1993). "Mesh Optimization", in proceedings of SIGGRAPH '93, *Computer Graphics Proceedings*, pp. 19–26.

HOWARD, T. L. J., W. T. HEWITT, R. J. HUBBOLD, ET AL. (1991). *A Practical Introduction to PHIGS and PHIGS Plus*, Addison-Wesley, Wokingham, England.

HUGHES, J. F. (1992). "Scheduled Fourier Volume Morphing", in proceedings of SIGGRAPH '92, *Computer Graphics*, 26(2), pp. 43–46.

HUITRIC, H. AND M. NAHAS (1985). "B-Spline Surfaces: A Tool for Computer Painting", *IEEE Computer Graphics and Applications*, 5(3), pp. 39–47.

IKEDO, T. (1984). "High-Speed Techniques for a 3-D Color Graphics Terminal", *IEEE Computer Graphics and Applications*, 4(5), pp. 46–58.

IMMEL, D. S., M. F. COHEN, AND D. P. GREENBERG (1986). "A Radiosity Method for Non-Diffuse Environments", in proceedings of SIGGRAPH '86, *Computer Graphics*, 20(4), pp. 133–142.

ISAACS, P. M. AND M. F. COHEN (1987). "Controlling Dynamic Simulation with Kinematic Constraints, Behavior Functions, and Inverse Dynamics", in proceedings of SIGGRAPH '87, *Computer Graphics*, 21(4), pp. 215–224.

JARVIS, J. F., C. N. JUDICE, AND W. H. NINKE (1976). "A Survey of Techniques for the Image Display of Continuous Tone Pictures on Bilevel Displays", *Computer Graphics and Image Processing*, 5(1), pp. 13–40.

JOHNSON, S. A. (1982). "Clinical Varifocal Mirror Display System at the University of Utah", *Proceedings of SPIE*, 367, August 1982, pp. 145–148.

KAJIYA, J. T. (1983). "New Techniques for Ray Tracing Procedurally Defined Objects", *ACM Transactions on Graphics*, 2(3), pp. 161–181.

KAJIYA, J. T. (1986). "The Rendering Equation", in proceedings of SIGGRAPH '86, *Computer Graphics*, 20(4), pp. 143–150.

KAJIYA, J. T. AND T. L. KAY (1989). "Rendering Fur with Three-Dimensional Textures", in proceedings of SIGGRAPH '89, *Computer Graphics*, 23(3), pp. 271–280.

KAPPEL, M. R. (1985). "An Ellipse-Drawing Algorithm for Faster Displays", in *Fundamental Algorithms for Computer Graphics*, Springer-Verlag, Berlin, pp. 257–280.

KARASICK, M., D. LIEBER, AND L. R. NACKMAN (1991). "Efficient Delaunay Triangulation Using Rational Arithmetic", *ACM Transactions on Graphics*, 10(1), pp. 71–91.

KASS, M. (1992). "CONDOR: Constraint-Based Dataflow", in proceedings of SIGGRAPH '92, *Computer Graphics*, 26(2), pp. 321–330.

KASSON, J. M. AND W. PLOUFFE (1992). "An Analysis of Selected Computer Interchange Color Spaces", *ACM Transactions on Graphics*, 11(4), pp. 373–405.

KAUFMAN, A. (1987). "Efficient Algorithms for 3D Scan-Conversion of Parametric Curves, Surfaces, and Volumes", in proceedings of SIGGRAPH '87, *Computer Graphics*, 21(4), pp. 171–179.

KAWAGUCHI, Y. (1982). "A Morphological Study of the Form of Nature", in proceedings of SIGGRAPH '82, *Computer Graphics*, 16(3), pp. 223–232.

KAY, T. L. AND J. T. KAJIYA (1986). "Ray Tracing Complex Scenes", in proceedings of SIGGRAPH '86, *Computer Graphics*, 20(4), pp. 269–278.

KAY, D. C. AND J. R. LEVINE (1992). *Graphics File Formats*, Windcrest/McGraw-Hill, New York.

KELLEY, A. D., M. C. MALIN, AND G. M. NIELSON (1988). "Terrain Simulation using a Model of Stream Erosion", in proceedings of SIGGRAPH '88, *Computer Graphics*, 22(4), pp. 263–268.

KENT, J. R., W. E. CARLSON, AND R. E. PARENT (1992). "Shape Transformation for Polyhedral Objects", in proceedings of SIGGRAPH '92, *Computer Graphics*, 26(2), pp. 47–54.

KIRK, D. AND J. ARVO (1991). "Unbiased Sampling Techniques for Image Synthesis", in proceedings of SIGGRAPH '91, *Computer Graphics*, 25(4), pp. 153–156.

KIRK, D., ED. (1992). *Graphics Gems III*, Academic Press, San Diego, CA.

KNUTH, D. E. (1987). "Digital Halftones by Dot Diffusion", *ACM Transactions on Graphics*, 6(4), pp. 245–273.

KOCHANEK, D. H. U. AND R. H. BARTELS (1984). "Interpolating Splines with Local Tension, Continuity, and Bias Control", in proceedings of SIGGRAPH '84, *Computer Graphics*, 18(3), pp. 33–41.

KOH, E.-K. AND D. HEARN (1992). "Fast Generation and Surface Structuring Methods for Terrain and Other Natural Phenomena", in proceedings of Eurographs '92 *Computer Graphics Forum*, 11(3), pp. C-169–180.

KORIEN, J. U. AND N. I. BADLER (1982). "Techniques for Generating the Goal-Directed Motion of Articulated Structures", *IEEE Computer Graphics and Applications*, 2(9), pp. 71–81.

KORIEN, J. U. AND N. I. BADLER (1983). "Temporal antialiasing in Computer-Generated Animation", in proceedings of SIGGRAPH '83, *Computer Graphics*, 17(3), pp. 377–388.

LASSETER, J. (1987). "Principles of Traditional Animation Applied to 3D Computer Animation", in proceedings of SIGGRAPH '87, *Computer Graphics*, 21(4), pp. 35–44.

LAUR, D. AND P. HANRAHAN (1991). "Hierarchical Splatting: A Progressive Refinement Algorithm for Volume Rendering", in proceedings of SIGGRAPH '91, *Computer Graphics*, 25(4), pp. 285–288.

LAUREL, B. (1990). *The Art of Human-Computer Interface Design*, Addision-Wesley, Reading, MA.

LEE, M. E., R. A. REDNER, AND S. P. USELTON (1985). "Statisically Optimized Sampling for Distributed Ray Tracing", in proceedings of SIGGRAPH '85, *Computer Graphics*, 19(3), pp. 61–68.

LEVINTHAL, A. AND T. PORTER (1984). "CHAP — A SIMD Graphics Processor", in proceedings of SIGGRAPH '84, *Computer Graphics*, 18(3), pp. 77–82.

LEVOY, M. (1988). "Display of Surfaces from Volume Data", *IEEE Computer Graphics and Applications*, 8(3), pp. 29–37.

LEVOY, M. (1990). "A Hybrid Ray Tracer for Rendering Polygon and Volume Data", *IEEE Computer Graphics and Applications*, 10(2), pp. 33–40.

LEWIS, J.-P. (1989). "Algorithms for Solid Noise Synthesis", in proceedings of SIGGRAPH '89, *Computer Graphics*, 23(3), pp. 263–270.

LIANG, Y.-D. AND B. A. BARSKY (1983). "An Analysis and Algorithm for Polygon Clipping." CACM, 26(11), pp. 868–877.

LIANG, Y.-D. AND B. A. BARSKY (1984). "A New Concept and Method for Line Clipping", *ACM Transactions on Graphics*, 3(1), pp. 1–22.

LIEN, S.-L., M. SHANTZ, AND V. PRATT (1987). "Adaptive Forward Differencing for Rendering Curves and Surfaces", in proceedings of SIGGRAPH '87, *Computer Graphics*, 21(4), pp. 111–118.

LINDLEY, C. A. (1992). *Practical Ray Tracing in C*, John Wiley & Sons, New York.

LISCHINSKI, D., F. TAMPIERI, AND D. P. GREENBERG (1993). "Combining Hierarchical Radiosity and Discontinuity Meshing", in proceedings of SIGGRAPH '93, *Computer Graphics*, pp. 199–208.

LITWINOWICZ, P. C. (1991). "Inkwell: A 2 1/2–D Animation System", in proceedings of SIGGRAPH '91, *Computer Graphics*, 25(4), pp. 113–122.

LODDING, K. N. (1983). "Iconic Interfacing", *IEEE Computer Graphics and Applications*, 3(2), pp. 11–20.

LOKE, T.-S., D. TAN, H.-S. SEAH, ET AL. (1992). "Rendering Fireworks Displays", *IEEE Computer Graphics and Applications*, 12(3), pp. 33–43.

LOOMIS, J., H. POIZNER, U. BELLUGI, ET AL. (1983). "Computer Graphic Modeling of American Sign Language", in proceedings of SIGGRAPH '83, *Computer Graphics*, 17(3), pp. 105–114.

LORENSON, W. E. AND H. CLINE (1987). "Marching Cubes: A High-Resolution 3D Surface Construction Algorithm", in proceedings of SIGGRAPH '87, *Computer Graphics*, 21(4), pp. 163–169.

MACKINLAY, J. D., S. K. CARD, AND G. G. ROBERTSON (1990). "Rapid Controlled Movement Through a Virtual 3D Workspace", SIGGRAPH 90, pp. 171–176.

MACKINLAY, J. D., G. G. ROBERTSON, AND S. K. CARD (1991). "The Perspective Wall: Detail and Context Smoothly Integrated", CHI '91, pp. 173–179.

MAGNENAT-THALMANN, N. AND D. THALMANN (1985). *Computer Animation: Theory and Practice*, Springer-Verlag, Tokyo.

MAGNENAT-THALMANN, N. AND D. THALMANN (1987). *Image Synthesis*, Springer-Verlag, Tokyo.

MAGNENAT-THALMANN, N. AND D. THALMANN (1991). "Complex Models for Animating Synthetic Actors", *IEEE Computer Graphics and Applications*, 11(5), pp. 32–45.

MANDELBROT, B. B. (1977). *Fractals: Form, Chance, and Dimension*, Freeman Press, San Francisco.

MANDELBROT, B. B. (1982). *The Fractal Geometry of Nature*, Freeman Press, New York.

MANTYLA, M. (1988). *An Introduction to Solid Modeling*, Computer Science Press, Rockville, MD.

MAX, N. L. AND D. M. LERNER (1985). "A Two-and-a-Half-D Motion Blur Algorithm", in proceedings of SIGGRAPH '85, *Computer Graphics*, 19(3), pp. 85–94.

MAX, N. L. (1986). "Atmospheric Illumination and Shadows", in proceedings of SIGGRAPH '86, *Computer Graphics*, 20(4), pp. 117–124.

MAX, N. L. (1990). "Cone-Spheres", in proceedings of SIGGRAPH '90, *Computer Graphics*, 24(4), pp. 59–62.

METAXAS, D. AND D. TERZOPOULOS (1992). "Dynamic Deformation of Solid Primitives with Constraints", in proceedings of SIGGRAPH '92, *Computer Graphics*, 26(2), pp. 309–312.

MEYER, G. W., H. E. RUSHMEIER, M. F. COHEN, ET AL. (1986). "An Experimental Evaluation of Computer Graphics Imagery", *ACM Transactions on Graphics*, 6(1), pp. 30–50.

MEYER, G. W. AND D. P. GREENBERG (1988). "Color-Defective Vision and Computer Graphics Displays", *IEEE Computer Graphics and Applications*, 8(5), pp. 28–40.

MEYERS, D., S. SKINNER, AND K. SLOAN (1992). "Surfaces from Contours", *ACM Transactions on Graphics*, 11(3), pp. 228–258.

MILLER, G. S. P. (1988). "The Motion Dynamics of Snakes and Worms", in proceedings of SIGGRAPH '88, *Computer Graphics*, 22(4), pp. 169–178.

MILLER, J. V., D. E. BREEN, W. E. LORENSON, ET AL. (1991). "Geometrically Deformed Models: A Method for Extracting Closed Geometric Models from Volume Data", in proceedings of SIGGRAPH '91, *Computer Graphics*, 25(4), pp. 217–226.

MITCHELL, D. P. (1991). "Spectrally Optimal Sampling for Distribution Ray Tracing", in proceedings of SIGGRAPH '91, *Computer Graphics*, 25(4), pp. 157–165.

MITCHELL, D. P. AND P. HANRAHAN (1992). "Illumination from Curved Reflectors", in proceedings of SIGGRAPH '92, *Computer Graphics*, 26(2), pp. 283–291.

MIYATA, K. (1990). "A Method of Generating Stone Wall Patterns", in proceedings of SIGGRAPH '90, *Computer Graphics*, 24(4), pp. 387–394.

MOLNAR, S., J. EYLES, AND J. POULTON (1992). "PixelFlow: High-Speed Rendering Using Image Composition", in proceedings of SIGGRAPH '92, *Computer Graphics*, 26(2), pp. 231–240.

MOON, F. C. (1992). *Chaotic and Fractal Dynamics*, John Wiley & Sons, New York.

MOORE, M. AND J. WILHELMS (1988). "Collision Detection and Response for Computer Animation", in proceedings of SIGGRAPH '88, *Computer Graphics*, 22(4), pp. 289–298.

MORTENSON, M. E. (1985). *Geometric Modeling*, John Wiley & Sons, New York.

MURAKI, S. (1991). "Volumetric Shape Description of Range Data Using the `Blobby Model' ", in proceedings of SIGGRAPH '91, *Computer Graphics*, 25(4), pp. 227–235.

MUSGRAVE, F. K., C. E. KOLB, AND R. S. MACE (1989). "The Synthesis and Rendering of Eroded Fractal Terrains", in proceedings of SIGGRAPH '89, *Computer Graphics*, 23(3), pp. 41–50.

MYERS, B. A. AND W. BUXTON (1986). "Creating High-Interactive and Graphical User Interfaces by Demonstration", in proceedings of SIGGRAPH '86, *Computer Graphics*, 20(4), pp. 249–258.

NAYLOR, B., J. AMANATIDES, AND W. THIBAULT (1990). "Merging BSP Trees Yields Polyhedral Set Operations", in proceedings of SIGGRAPH '90, *Computer Graphics*, 24(4), pp. 115–124.

NEWMAN, W. H. (1968). "A System for Interactive Graphical Programming", *SJCC, Thompson Books*, Washington, D. C., pp. 47–54.

NEWMAN, W. H. AND R. F. SPROULL (1979). *Principles of Interactive Computer Graphics*, McGraw-Hill, New York.

NGO, J. T. AND J. MARKS (1993). "Spacetime Constraints Revisited", in proceedings of SIGGRAPH '93, *Computer Graphics*, pp. 343–350.

NICHOLL, T. M., D. T. LEE, AND R. A. NICHOLL (1987). "An Efficient New Algorithm for 2D Line Clipping: Its Development and Analysis", in proceedings of SIGGRAPH '87, *Computer Graphics*, 21(4), pp. 253–262.

NIELSON, G. M., B. SHRIVER, AND L. ROSENBLUM, ED. (1990). *Visualization in Scientific Computing*, IEEE Computer Society Press, Los Alamitos, CA.

NIELSON, G. M. (1993). "Scattered Data Modeling", *IEEE Computer Graphics and Applications*, 13(1), pp. 60–70.

NISHIMURA, H. (1985). "Object Modeling by Distribution Function and a Method of Image Generation", Journal Electronics Comm. Conf. '85, J68(4), pp. 718–725.

NISHITA, T. AND E. NAKAMAE (1986). "Continuous-Tone Representation of Three-Dimensional Objects Illuminated by Sky Light", in proceedings of SIGGRAPH '86, *Computer Graphics*, 20(4), pp. 125–132.

NISHITA, T., T. SIRAI, K. TADAMURA, ET AL. (1993). "Display of the Earth Taking into Account Atmospheric Scattering", in proceedings of SIGGRAPH '93, *Computer Graphics Proceedings*, pp. 175–182.

NORTON, A. (1982). "Generation and Display of Geometric Fractals in 3–D", in proceedings of SIGGRAPH '82, *Computer Graphics*, 16(3), pp. 61–67.

NSF INVITATIONAL WORKSHOP (1992). "Research Directions in Virtual Environments", Computer Graphics, 26(3), pp. 153–177.

OKABE, H., H. IMAOKA, T. TOMIHA, ET AL. (1992). "Three-Dimensional Apparel CAD System", in proceedings of SIGGRAPH '92, *Computer Graphics*, 26(2), pp. 105–110.

OPENGL ARCHITECTURE REVIEW BOARD (1993). *OpenGL Programming Guide*, Addision-Wesley, Reading, MA.

OPPENHEIMER, P. E. (1986). "Real-Time Design and Animation of Fractal Plants and Trees", in proceedings of SIGGRAPH '86, *Computer Graphics*, 20(4), pp. 55–64.

OSF/MOTIF (1989). *OSF/Motif Style Guide*, Open Software Foundation, Prentice-Hall, Englewood Cliffs, NJ.

PAINTER, J. AND K. SLOAN (1989). "Antialiased Ray Tracing by Adaptive Progressive Refinement", in proceedings of SIGGRAPH '89, *Computer Graphics*, 23(3), pp. 281–288.

PANG, A. T. (1990). "Line-Drawing Algorithms for Parallel Machines", *IEEE Computer Graphics and Applications*, 10(5), pp. 54–59.

PAVLIDIS, T. (1982). *Algorithms For Graphics and Image Processing*, Computer Science Press, Rockville, MD.

PAVLIDIS, T. (1983). "Curve Fitting with Conic Splines", *ACM Transactions on Graphics*, 2(1), pp. 1–31.

PEACHEY, D. R. (1986). "Modeling Waves and Surf", in proceedings of SIGGRAPH '86, *Computer Graphics*, 20(4), pp. 65–74.

PEITGEN, H.-O. AND P. H. RICHTER (1986). *The Beauty of Fractals*, Springer-Verlag, Berlin.

PEITGEN, H.-O. AND D. SAUPE, ED. (1988). *The Science of Fractal Images*, Springer-Verlag, Berlin.

PENTLAND, A. AND J. WILLIAMS (1989). "Good Vibrations: Modal Dynamics for Graphics and Animation", in proceedings of SIGGRAPH '89, *Computer Graphics*, 23(3), pp. 215–222.

PERLIN, K. AND E. M. HOFFERT (1989). "Hypertexture", in proceedings of SIGGRAPH '89, *Computer Graphics*, 23(3), pp. 253–262.

PHILLIPS, R. L. (1977). "A Query Language for a Network Data Base with Graphical Entities", in proceedings of SIGGRAPH '77, *Computer Graphics*, 11(2), pp. 179–185.

PHONG, B. T. (1975). "Illumination for Computer-Generated Images", CACM, 18(6), pp. 311–317.

PINEDA, J. (1988). "A Parallel Algorithm for Polygon Rasterization", in proceedings of SIGGRAPH '88, *Computer Graphics*, 22(4), pp. 17–20.

PTTEWAY, M. L. V. AND D. J. WATKINSON (1980). "Bresenham's Algorithm with Gray Scale", CACM, 23(11), pp. 625–626.

PLATT, J. C. AND A. H. BARR (1988). "Constraint Methods for Flexible Models", in proceedings of SIGGRAPH '88, *Computer Graphics*, 22(4), pp. 279–288.

PORTER, T. AND T. DUFF (1984). "Compositing Digital Images", in proceedings of SIGGRAPH '84, *Computer Graphics*, 18(3), pp. 253–259.

POTMESIL, M. AND I. CHAKRAVARTY (1982). "Synthetic Image Generation with a Lens and Aperture Camera Model", *ACM Transactions on Graphics*, 1(2), pp. 85–108.

POTMESIL, M. AND I. CHAKRAVARTY (1983). "Modeling Motion Blur in Computer-Generated Images", in proceedings of SIGGRAPH '83, *Computer Graphics*, 17(3), pp. 389–399.

POTMESIL, M. AND E. M. HOFFERT (1987). "FRAMES: Software Tools for Modeling, Rendering and Animation of 3D Scenes", in proceedings of SIGGRAPH '87, *Computer Graphics*, 21(4), pp. 85–93.

POTMESIL, M. AND E. M. HOFFERT (1989). "The Pixel Machine: A Parallel Image Computer", in proceedings of SIGGRAPH '89, *Computer Graphics*, 23(3), pp. 69–78.

PRATT, W. K. (1). *Digital Image Processing*, John Wiley & Sons, New York.

PREPARATA, F. P. AND M. I. SHAMOS (1985). *Computational Geometry*, Springer-Verlag, New York.

PRESS, W. H., S. A. TEUKOLSKY, W. T. VETTERLING, ET AL. (1992). *Numerical Recipes in C*, Cambridge University Press, Cambridge, England.

PRUSINKIEWICZ, P., M. S. HAMMEL, AND E. MJOLSNESS (1993). "Animation of Plant Development", in proceedings of SIGGRAPH '93, *Computer Graphics Proceedings*, pp. 351–360.

PRUYN, P. W. AND D. P. GREENBERG (1993). "Exploring 3D Computer Graphics in Cockpit Avionics", *IEEE Computer Graphics and Applications*, 13(3), pp. 28–35.

QUEK, L.-H. AND D. HEARN (1988). "Efficient Space-Subdivision Methods in Ray-Tracing Algorithms", University of Illinois, Department of Computer Science Report UIUCDCS-R-88-1468.

RAIBERT, M. H. AND J. K. HODGINS (1991). "Animation of Dynamic Legged Locomotion", in proceedings of SIGGRAPH '91, *Computer Graphics*, 25(4), pp. 349–358.

REEVES, W. T. (1983). "Particle Systems: A Technique for Modeling a Class of Fuzzy Objects", *ACM Transactions on Graphics*, 2(2), pp. 91–108.

REEVES, W. T. (1983). "Particle Systems—A Technique for Modeling a Class of Fuzzy Objects", in proceedings of SIGGRAPH '83, *Computer Graphics*, 17(3), pp. 359–376.

REEVES, W. T. AND R. BLAU (1985). "Approximate and Probabilistic Algorithms for Shading and Rendering Structured Particle Systems", in proceedings of SIGGRAPH '85, *Computer Graphics*, 19(3), pp. 313–321.

REEVES, W. T., D. H. SALESIN, AND R. L. COOK (1987). "Rendering Antialiased Shadows with Depth Maps", in proceedings of SIGGRAPH '87, *Computer Graphics*, 21(4), pp. 283–291.

REQUICHA, A. A. G. AND J. R. ROSSIGNAC (1992). "Solid Modeling and Beyond", *IEEE Computer Graphics and Applications*, 12(5), pp. 31–44.

REYNOLDS, C. W. (1982). "Computer Animation with Scripts and Actors", in proceedings of SIGGRAPH '82, *Computer Graphics*, 16(3), pp. 289–296.

REYNOLDS, C. W. (1987). "Flocks, Herds, and Schools: A Distributed Behavioral Model", in proceedings of SIGGRAPH '87, *Computer Graphics*, 21(4), pp. 25–34.

RIESENFELD, R. F. (1981). "Homogeneous Coordinates and Projective Planes in Computer Graphics", *IEEE Computer Graphics and Applications*, 1(1), pp. 50–55.

ROBERTSON, P. K. (1988). "Visualizing Color Gamuts: A User Interface for the Effective Use of Perceptual Color Spaces in Data Displays", *IEEE Computer Graphics and Applications*, 8(5), pp. 50–64.

ROBERTSON, G. G., J. D. MACKINLAY AND S. K. CARD (1991). "Cone Trees: Animated 3D Visualizations of Hierarchical Information", CHI '91, pp. 189–194.

ROGERS, D. F. AND R. A. EARNSHAW, ED. (1987). *Techniques for Computer Graphics*, Springer-Verlag, New York.

ROGERS, D. F. AND J. A. ADAMS (1990). *Mathematical Elements for Computer Graphics*, McGraw-Hill, New York.

ROSENTHAL, D. S. H., ET AL. (1982). "The Detailed Semantics of Graphics Input Devices", in proceedings of SIGGRAPH '82, *Computer Graphics*, 16(3), pp. 33–38.

RUBINE, D. (1991). "Specifying Gestures by Example", in proceedings of SIGGRAPH '91, *Computer Graphics*, 25(4), pp. 329–337.

RUSHMEIER, H. AND K. TORRANCE (1987). "The Zonal Method for Calculating Light Intensities in the Presence of a Participating Medium", in proceedings of SIGGRAPH '87, *Computer Graphics*, 21(4), pp. 293–302.

RUSHMEIER, H. E. AND K. E. TORRANCE (1990). "Extending the Radiosity Method to Include Specularly Reflecting and Translucent Materials", *ACM Transactions on Graphics*, 9(1), pp. 1–27.

SABELLA, P. (1988). "A Rendering Algorithm for Visualizing 3D Scalar Fields", in proceedings of SIGGRAPH '88, *Computer Graphics*, 22(4), pp. 51–58.

SABIN, M. A. (1985). "Contouring: The State of the Art", in *Fundamental Algorithms for Computer Graphics*, R. A. Earnshaw, ed, Springer-Verlag, Berlin, pp. 411–482.

SALESIN, D. AND R. BARZEL (1993). "Adjustable Tools: An Object-Oriented Interaction Metaphor", *ACM Transactions on Graphics*, 12(1), pp. 103–107.

SAMET, H. AND R. E. WEBBER (1985). "Sorting a Collection of Polygons using Quadtrees", *ACM Transactions on Graphics*, 4(3), pp. 182–222.

SAMET, H. AND M. TAMMINEN (1985). "Bintrees, CSG Trees, and Time", in proceedings of SIGGRAPH '85, *Computer Graphics*, 19(3), pp. 121–130.

SAMET, H. AND R. E. WEBBER (1988). "Hierarchical Data Structures and Algorithms for Computer Graphics: Part 1", *IEEE Computer Graphics and Applications*, 8(4), pp. 59–75.

SAMET, H. AND R. E. WEBBER (1988). "Hierarchical Data Structures and Algorithms for Computer Graphics: Part 2", *IEEE Computer Graphics and Applications*, 8(3), pp. 48–68.

SCHEIFLER, R. W. AND J. GETTYS (1986). "The X Window System", *ACM Transactions on Graphics*, 5(2), pp. 79–109.

SCHOENEMAN, C., J. DORSEY, B. SMITS, ET AL. (1993). "Global Illumination", in proceedings of SIGGRAPH '93, *Computer Graphics Proceedings*, pp. 143–146.

SCHRODER, P. AND P. HANRAHAN (1993). "On the Form Factor Between Two Polygons", in proceedings of SIGGRAPH '93, *Computer Graphics Proceedings*, pp. 163–164.

SCHWARTZ, M. W., W. B. COWAN, AND J. C. BEATTY (1987). "An Experimental Comparison of RGB, YIQ, LAB, HSV, and Opponent Color Models", *ACM Transactions on Graphics*, 6(2), pp. 123–158.

SEDERBERG, T. W. AND E. GREENWOOD (1992). "A Physically Based Approached to 2-D Shape Bending", in proceedings of SIGGRAPH '92, *Computer Graphics*, 26(2), pp. 25–34.

SEDERBERG, T. W., P. GAO, G. WANG, ET AL. (1993). "2D Shape Blending: An Intrinsic Solution to the Vertex Path Problem", in proceedings of SIGGRAPH '93, *Computer Graphics Proceedings*, pp. 15–18.

SEGAL, M. (1990). "Using Tolerances to Guarantee Valid Polyhedral Modeling Results", in proceedings of SIGGRAPH '90, *Computer Graphics*, 24(4), pp. 105–114.

SEGAL, M., C. KOROBKIN, R. VAN WIDENFELT, ET AL. (1992). "Fast Shadows and Lighting Effects Using Texture Mapping", in proceedings of SIGGRAPH '92, *Computer Graphics*, 26(2), pp. 249–252.

SEQUIN, C. H. AND E. K. SMYRL (1989). "Parameterized Ray-Tracing", in proceedings of SIGGRAPH '89, *Computer Graphics*, 23(3), pp. 307–314.

SHERR, S. (1993). *Electronic Displays*, John Wiley & Sons, New York.

SHILLING, A. AND W. STRASSER (1993). "EXACT: Algorithm and Hardware Architecture for an Improved A-Buffer", in proceedings of SIGGRAPH '93, *Computer Graphics Proceedings*, pp. 85–92.

SHIRLEY, P. (1990). "A Ray Tracing Method for Illumination Calculation in Diffuse-Specular Scenes", Graphics Interface '90, pp. 205–212.

SHNEIDERMAN, B. (1986). *Designing the User Interface*, Addison-Wesley, Reading, MA.

SHOEMAKE, K. (1985). "Animating Rotation with Quaternion Curves", in proceedings of SIGGRAPH '85, *Computer Graphics*, 19(3), pp. 245–254.

SIBERT, J. L., W. D. HURLEY, AND T. W. BLESER (1986). "An Object-Oriented User Interface Management System", in proceedings of SIGGRAPH '86, *Computer Graphics*, 20(4), pp. 259–268.

SILLION, F. X. AND C. PUECH (1989). "A General Two-Pass Method Integrating Specular and Diffuse Reflection", in proceedings of SIGGRAPH '89, *Computer Graphics*, 23(3), pp. 335–344.

SILLION, F. X., J. R. ARVO, S. H. WESTIN, ET AL. (1991). "A Global Illumination Solution for General Reflectance Distributions", in proceedings of SIGGRAPH '91, *Computer Graphics*, 25(4), pp. 187–196.

SIMS, K. (1990). "Particle Animation and Rendering Using Data Parallel Computation", in proceedings of SIGGRAPH '90, *Computer Graphics*, 24(4), pp. 405–413.

SIMS, K. (1991). "Artificial Evolution for Computer Graphics", in proceedings of SIGGRAPH '91, *Computer Graphics*, 25(4), pp. 319–328.

SINGH, B., J. C. BEATTY, K. S. BOOTH, ET AL. (1983). "A Graphics Editor for Benesh Movement Notation", in proceedings of SIGGRAPH '83, *Computer Graphics*, 17(3), pp. 51–62.

SMITH, A. R. (1978). "Color Gamut Transform Pairs", Computer Graphics, 12(3), pp. 12–19.

SMITH, A. R. (1979). "Tint Fill", Computer Graphics, 13(2), pp. 276–283.

SMITH, A. R. (1984). "Plants, Fractals, and Formal Languages", in proceedings of SIGGRAPH '84, *Computer Graphics*, 18(3), pp. 1–10.

SMITH, R. B. (1987). "Experiences with the Alternate Reality Kit: An Example of the Tension Between Literalism and Magic", *IEEE Computer Graphics and Applications*, 7(9), pp. 42–50.

SMITH, A. R. (1987). "Planar 2–Pass Texture Mapping and Warping", in proceedings of SIGGRAPH '87, *Computer Graphics*, 21(4), pp. 263–272.

SMITS, B. E., J. R. ARVO, AND D. H. SALESIN (1992). "An Importance-Driven Radiosity Algorithm", in proceedings of SIGGRAPH '92, *Computer Graphics*, 26(2), pp. 273–282.

SNYDER, J. M. AND J. T. KAJIYA (1992). "Generative Modeling: A Symbolic System for Geometric Modeling", in proceedings of SIGGRAPH '92, *Computer Graphics*, 26(2), pp. 369–378.

SNYDER, J. M., A. R. WOODBURY, K. FLEISCHER, ET AL. (1993). "Interval Method for Multi-Point Collisions between Time-Dependent Curved Surfaces", in proceedings of SIGGRAPH '93, *Computer Graphics*, pp. 321–334.

SPROULL, R. F. AND I. E. SUTHERLAND (1968). "A Clipping Divider", AFIPS Fall Joint Computer Conference.

STAM, J. AND E. FIUME (1993). "Turbulent Wind Fields for Gaseous Phenomena", in proceedings of SIGGRAPH '93, *Computer Graphics Proceedings*, pp. 369–376.

STETTNER, A. AND D. P. GREENBERG (1989). "Computer Graphics Visualization for Acoustic Simulation", in proceedings of SIGGRAPH '89, *Computer Graphics*, 23(3), pp. 195–206.

STRASSMANN, S. (1986). "Hairy Brushes", in proceedings of SIGGRAPH '86, *Computer Graphics*, 20(4), pp. 225–232.

STRAUSS, P. S. AND R. CAREY (1992). "An Object-Oriented 3D Graphics Toolkit", in proceedings of SIGGRAPH '92, *Computer Graphics*, 26(2), pp. 341–349.

SUNG, H. C. K., G. ROGERS, AND W. J. KUBITZ (1990). "A Critical Evaluation of PEX", *IEEE Computer Graphics and Applications*, 10(6), pp. 65–75.

SUTHERLAND, I. E. (1963). "Sketchpad: A Man-Machine Graphical Communication System", AFIPS Spring Joint Computer Conference, 23 pp. 329–346.

SUTHERLAND, I. E., R. F. SPROULL, AND R. SCHUMACKER (1974). "A Characterization of Ten Hidden Surface Algorithms", ACM Computing Surveys, 6(1), pp. 1–55.

SUTHERLAND, I. E. AND G. W. HODGMAN (1974). "Reentrant Polygon Clipping", CACM, 17(1), pp. 32–42.

SWEZEY, R. W. AND E. G. DAVIS (1983). "A Case Study of Human Factors Guidelines in Computer Graphics", *IEEE Computer Graphics and Applications*, 3(8), pp. 21–30.

TAKALA, T. AND J. HAHN (1992). "Sound Rendering", in proceedings of SIGGRAPH '92, *Computer Graphics*, 26(2), pp. 211–220.

TANNAS, J., LAWRENCE E., ED. (1985). *Flat-Panel Displays and CRTs*, Van Nostrand Reinhold Company, New York.

TELLER, S. AND P. HANRAHAN (1993). "Global Visibility Algorithms for Illumination Computations", in proceedings of SIGGRAPH '93, *Computer Graphics Proceedings*, pp. 239–246.

TERZOPOULOS, D., J. PLATT, A. H. BARR, ET AL. (1987). "Elastically Deformable Models", in proceedings of SIGGRAPH '87, *Computer Graphics*, 21(4), pp. 205–214.

THALMANN, D., ED. (1990). *Scientific Visualization and Graphics Simulation*, John Wiley & Sons, Chichester, England.

THIBAULT, W. C. AND B. F. NAYLOR (1987). "Set Operations on Polyhedra using Binary Space Partitioning Trees", in proceedings of SIGGRAPH '87, *Computer Graphics*, 21(4), pp. 153–162.

TORBERG, J. G. (1987). "A Parallel Processor Architecture for Graphics Arithmetic Operations", in proceedings of SIGGRAPH '87, *Computer Graphics*, 21(4), pp. 197–204.

TORRANCE, K. E. AND E. M. SPARROW (1967). "Theory for Off-Specular Reflection from Roughened Surfaces", *J. Optical Society of America*, 57(9), pp. 1105–1114.

TRAVIS, D. (1991). *Effective Color Displays*, Academic Press, London.

TUFTE, E. R. (1983). *The Visual Display of Quantitative Information*, Graphics Press, Cheshire, CN.

TUFTE, E. R. (1990). *Envisioning Information*, Graphics Press, Cheshire, CN.

TURKOWSKI, K. (1982). "Antialiasing Through the Use of Coordinate Transformations", ACM Transactions on Graphics, 1(3), pp. 215–234.

UPSON, C. AND M. KEELER (1988). "VBUFFER: Visible Volume Rendering", in proceedings of SIGGRAPH '88, *Computer Graphics*, 22(4), pp. 59–64.

UPSON, C., T. FAULHABER JR., D. KAMINS, ET AL. (1989). "The Application Visualization System: A Computational Environment for Scientific Visualization", *IEEE Computer Graphics and Applications*, 9(4), pp. 30–42.

UPSTILL, S. (1990). *The RenderMan Companion*, Addison-Wesley, Reading, MA.

VAN DE PANNE, M. AND E. FIUME (1993). "Sensor-Actuator Networks", in proceedings of SIGGRAPH '93, *Computer Graphics Proceedings*, pp. 335–342.

VAN WIJK, J. J. (1991). "Spot Noise-Texture Synthesis for Data Visualization", in proceedings of SIGGRAPH '91, *Computer Graphics*, 25(4), pp. 309–318.

VEENSTRA, J. AND N. AHUJA (1988). "Line Drawings of Octree-Represented Objects", *ACM Transactions on Graphics*, 7(1), pp. 61–75.

VELHO, L. AND J. D. M. GOMES (1991). "Digital Halftoning with Space-Filling Curves", in proceedings of SIGGRAPH '91, *Computer Graphics*, 25(4), pp. 81–90.

VON HERZEN, B., A. H. BARR, AND H. R. ZATZ (1990). "Geometric Collisions for Time-Dependent Parametric Surfaces", in proceedings of SIGGRAPH '90, *Computer Graphics*, 24(4), pp. 39–48.

WALLACE, V. L. (1976). "The Semantics of Graphic Input Devices", in proceedings of SIGGRAPH '76, *Computer Graphics*, 10(1), pp. 61–65.

WALLACE, J. R., K. A. ELMQUIST, AND E. A. HAINES (1989). "A Ray-Tracing Algorithm for Progressive Radiosity", in proceedings of SIGGRAPH '89, *Computer Graphics*, 23(3), pp. 315–324.

WANGER, L. R., J. A. FERWERDA, AND D. P. GREENBERG (1992). "Perceiving Spatial Relationships in Computer-Generated Images", *IEEE Computer Graphics and Applications*, 12(3), pp. 44–58.

WARE, C. (1988). "Color Sequences for Univariate Maps: Theory, Experiments, and Principles", *IEEE Computer Graphics and Applications*, 8(5), pp. 41–49.

WARN, D. R. (1983). "Lighting Controls for Synthetic Images", in proceedings of SIGGRAPH '83, *Computer Graphics*, 17(3), pp. 13–21.

WARNOCK, J. AND D. K. WYATT (1982). "A Device-Independent Graphics Imaging Model for Use with Raster Devices", in proceedings of SIGGRAPH '82, *Computer Graphics*, 16(3), pp. 313–319.

WATT, A. (1989). *Fundamentals of Three-Dimensional Computer Graphics*, Addison-Wesley, Wokingham, England.

WATT, M. (1990). "Light-Water Interaction Using Backward Beam Tracing", in proceedings of SIGGRAPH '90, *Computer Graphics*, 24(4), pp. 377–386.

WATT, A. AND M. WATT (1992). *Advanced Animation and Rendering Techniques*, Addison-Wesley, Wokingham, England.

WEGHORST, H., G. HOOPER, AND D. P. GREENBERG (1984). "Improved Computational Methods for Ray Tracing", *ACM Transactions on Graphics*, 3(1), pp. 52–69.

WEIL, J. (1986). "The Synthesis of Cloth Objects", in proceedings of SIGGRAPH '86, *Computer Graphics*, 20(4), pp. 49–54.

WEILER, K. AND P. ATHERTON (1977). "Hidden-Surface Removal Using Polygon Area Sorting", in proceedings of SIGGRAPH '77, *Computer Graphics*, 11(2), pp. 214–222.

WEILER, K. (1980). "Polygon Comparison Using a Graph Representation", in proceedings of SIGGRAPH '80, *Computer Graphics*, 14(3), pp. 10–18.

WESTIN, S. H., J. R. ARVO, AND K. E. TORRANCE (1992). "Predicting Reflectance Functions from Complex Surfaces", in proceedings of SIGGRAPH '92, *Computer Graphics*, 26(2), pp. 255–264.

WESTOVER, L. (1990). "Footprint Evaluation for Volume Rendering", in proceedings of SIGGRAPH '90, *Computer Graphics*, 24(4), pp. 367–376.

WHITTED, T. (1980). "An Improved Illumination Model for Shaded Display", CACM, 23(6), pp. 343–349.

WHITTED, T. AND D. M. WEIMER (1982). "A Software Testbed for the Development of 3D Raster Graphics Systems", *ACM Transactions on Graphics*, 1(1), pp. 43–58.

WHITTED, T. (1983). "Antialiased Line Drawing Using Brush Extrusion", in proceedings of SIGGRAPH '83, *Computer Graphics*, 17(3), pp. 151–156.

WILHELMS, J. (1987). "Toward Automatic Motion Control", *IEEE Computer Graphics and Applications*, 7(4), pp. 11–22.

WILHELMS, J. AND A. V. GELDER (1991). "A Coherent Projection Approach for Direct Volume Rendering", in proceedings of SIGGRAPH '91, *Computer Graphics*, 25(4), pp. 275–284.

WILHELMS, J. AND A. van GELDER (1992). "Octrees for Faster Isosurface Generation", *ACM Transactions on Graphics*, 11(3), pp. 201–227.

WILLIAMS, L. (1990). "Performance-Driven Facial Animation", in proceedings of SIGGRAPH '90, *Computer Graphics*, 24(4), pp. 235–242.

WILLIAMS, P. L. (1992). "Visibility Ordering Meshed Polyhedra", *ACM Transactions on Graphics*, 11(2), pp. 103–126.

WITKIN, A. AND W. WELCH (1990). "Fast Animation and Control of Nonrigid Structures", in proceedings of SIGGRAPH '90, *Computer Graphics*, 24(4), pp. 243–252.

WITKIN, A. AND M. KASS (1991). "Reaction-Diffusion Textures", in proceedings of SIGGRAPH '91, *Computer Graphics*, 25(4), pp. 299–308.

WOLFRAM, S. (1991). *Mathematica*, Addison-Wesley, Reading, MA.

WOO, A., P. POULIN, AND A. FOURNIER (1990). "A Survey of Shadow Algorithms", *IEEE Computer Graphics and Applications*, 10(6), pp. 13–32.

WRIGHT, W. E. (1990). "Parallelization of Bresenham's Line and Circle Algorithms", *IEEE Computer Graphics and Applications*, 10(5), pp. 60–67.

WU, X. (1991). "An Efficient Antialiasing Technique", in proceedings of SIGGRAPH '91, *Computer Graphics*, 25(4), pp. 143–152.

WYSZECKI, G. AND W. S. STILES (1982). *Color Science*, John Wiley & Sons, New York.

WYVILL, G., B. WYVILL, AND C. McPHEETERS (1987). "Solid Texturing of Soft Objects", *IEEE Computer Graphics and Applications*, 7(12), pp. 20–26.

YAEGER, L., C. UPSON, AND R. MYERS (1986). "Combining Physical and Visual Simulation: Creation of the Planet Jupiter for the Film "2010"", in proceedings of SIGGRAPH '86, *Computer Graphics*, 20(4), pp. 85–94.

YAGEL, R., D. COHEN, AND A. KAUFMAN (1992). "Discrete Ray Tracing", *IEEE Computer Graphics and Applications*, 12(5), pp. 19–28.

YAMAGUCHI, K., T. L. KUNII, AND FUJIMURA (1984). "Octree-Related Data Structures and Algorithms", *IEEE Computer Graphics and Applications*, 4(1), pp. 53–59.

YOUNG, D. A. (1990). *The X Window System - Programming and Applications with Xt, OSF/Motif Edition*, Prentice-Hall, Englewood Cliffs, NJ.

ZELEZNICK, R. C., D. B. CONNER, M. M. WLOKA, ET AL. (1991). "An Object-Oriented Framework for the Integration of Interactive Animation Techniques", in proceedings of SIGGRAPH '91, *Computer Graphics*, 25(4), pp. 105–112.

ZELTZER, D. (1982). "Motor Control Techniques for Figure Animation", *IEEE Computer Graphics and Applications*, 2(9), pp. 53–60.

ZHANG, Y. AND R. E. WEBBER (1993). "Space Diffusion: An Improved Parallel Halftoning Technique Using Space-Filling Curves", in proceedings of SIGGRAPH '93, *Computer Graphics Proceedings*, pp. 305–312.

Subject Index

644

Function Index

651